A DICTIONARY ENGLISH PRONUNCIATION WITH AMERICAN VARIANTS

A DICTIONARY ENGLISH PRONUNCIATION WITH AMERICAN VARIANTS

H.E.PALMER J. VICTOR MARTIN
FG BLANDFORD

GYAN

Published by

GYAN

Gyan Publishing House
5, Ansari Road
Daryaganj, New Delhi-110002
Phone: 011-47034999, 9811692060
E-mail: books@gyanbooks.com

Distribution Network
gyanbooks.com
India, USA, Canada, UK, Australia

ISBN: 978-93-7097-346-6 (PB)

First Published, 1927

2nd Impression 2025

Printed at: Gyan Press, Delhi.

A DICTIONARY ENGLISH PRONUNCIATION WITH AMERICAN VARIANTS

Author: H.E.PALMER J. VICTOR MARTIN FG BLANDFORD

A DICTIONARY OF ENGLISH PRONUNCIATION WITH AMERICAN VARIANTS

(In Phonetic Transcription)

BY

H. E. PALMER

Linguistic Adviser to the Japanese Ministry of Education

J. VICTOR MARTIN

Aoyama Gakuin

AND

F. G. BLANDFORD, M.A.

Corpus Christi College, Cambridge

D. APPLETON AND COMPANY
NEW YORK MCMXXVII

PREFACE

WHILE I lived in Europe I took it for granted that there was such a thing as American pronunciation; I took it equally for granted that educated Americans used and respected American pronunciation just in the same way as educated English people use and respect English pronunciation or that educated Scots use and respect Scottish pronunciation. On this matter, no question arose in my mind; it seemed in the natural order of things that it should be so. My English friends (phoneticians and others) held the same view. Some of my phonetician friends even expressed the view that to advocate the adoption of British pronunciation in the United States would be in point of impertinence about equal to advocating the adoption of the British flag in the United States.

Coming to Japan four years ago, and thereby coming into very close contact with the not inconsiderable American population here, I discovered certain disconcerting facts concerning this matter of pronunciation. I would be engaged in conversation with an English-speaking person, and eventually enquire from what part of England he hailed.

The Stranger: Oh, I'm American.

Myself: Really? Naturalized?

The Stranger: Oh no, native born. A hundred per cent American.

Myself [*too astonished to be tactful*]: But, but, you . . . well . . . you pronounce English just as if you were English!

The Stranger [*too annoyed to be gentle*]: Well, hang it all, man, I hope you don't suppose that all Americans are backwoodsmen or raw country hayseeds comparable to the yokels of Sussex or Yorkshire!

That sort of conversation, repeated in modified form with other Americans, made me realize that the people who grow red and angry at the mention or the assumption of American pronunciation are the Americans themselves. Not all, of course, but still, a good many.

I receive publications and pamphlets from America, ay, and letters too, all assuring me that there is no such thing as Standard American Pronunciation, or, worse, that what many call "American Pronunciation" is synonymous with "Amurrican Pronunciation," in other terms, the "Uneducated Pronunciation of America" or "Cockney American." I am assured that there is only one pronunciation that is ever worth mentioning or thinking about, and that is neither British nor American nor Scottish nor Slocum-in-the-Hole pronunciation, but simply "Good Pronunciation," the same for America as for the British Isles and Empire.

Then comes Professor Wyld, who states (backing up his statements with incontrovertible evidence) that what many have termed "Southern English" or "British English" has a name but no local habitation, and the name is "Received Standard," the same for England (South or North) as for America (East, Canada, West or Southern States).

Nevertheless, I have taken the initiative in proposing that column in this dictionary entitled "American Variants," that is to say: Pronunciations found in America which differ from the pronunciation of those American and British friends of mine who use the Received Pronunciation.

My above-mentioned American friends and correspondents are protesting against this column, which they consider to be a pillory rather than a pedestal.

But let us look at the other side. For every one of my American friends, acquaintances or correspondents who uses the Received Pronunciation, I know about ten who do not. Some of them even allude to the Received Pronunciation as a local dialect confined to London and its environs. Then I have before me the works of Professor Krapp and the book of Professor Kenyon, evidences of scholarly research. On both sides a place is claimed for the pronunciation which is that of the vast majority of educated Americans. Then we have the evidence afforded by Hempl's dictionary, and a host of other witnesses testifying not only to the existence of

American pronunciation, but to its eligibility to be considered as American Standard Pronunciation.

Not to mention the evidence of Professor Mencken who, going beyond the bounds of American Pronunciation, claims the rights of the American Language.

And so with the help of one of my American colleagues, who with me has verified most of the statements made by American phoneticians, I have ventured to make one of the chief features of this dictionary the column entitled "American Variants."

HAROLD E. PALMER.

TOKYO,
May, 1926.

CONTENTS

INTRODUCTORY

The Object of this Dictionary

THE object of this dictionary is threefold:

(1) To provide phoneticians, students of phonetics, and foreign students of English with a dictionary using the "narrower" system of English phonetic notation.

> By "narrower system of English phonetic notation" is meant any system that makes use of the symbols [ɪ], [ɛ], [ɒ], [ʊ], [ɜ]. For some years past the tendency to use the narrower system has been increasing. The *Maître Phonétique*, the organ of the International Phonetic Association, makes an exclusive use of it, as does also the supplement *Textes pour nos élèves*. School textbooks using this notation have made their appearance, and their number is growing. What has been lacking, however, is a dictionary to serve as a key to the narrower notation and to the way of using it. The first object of the present dictionary is to provide such a key.

(2) To provide an English pronouncing dictionary that will include not only the more important variants in that sort of English pronunciation which may be called "Received," but also the more important variants used by educated Americans whose standard of pronunciation is other than Received.

> Whether such a thing exists as Standard American Pronunciation we are prepared neither to affirm nor to deny. It may, however, be affirmed that the vast majority of Americans and Canadians use a pronunciation which varies considerably from that pronunciation called by Jones in the latest edition of his dictionary "Received Pronunciation" (identical with the P.S.P. of earlier editions) and by Wyld "Received Standard Pronunciation." In this dictionary we have attempted to record that variety of American pronunciation that seems most characteristic of educated speakers.

(3) To provide foreign students of English and their teachers (including those who are engaged in composing textbooks for them) with a vocabulary selected in such a way as to include essential and to exclude non-essential words.

On the principle of "All beginnings are difficult," the first few thousand English words are more difficult for the foreign student than the many thousands that he may learn subsequently. The foreign student, bewildered at the extent and variety of our English vocabulary, rarely knows which words are of importance and which are without importance for his purpose. Our selection may be considered as a collection of "Words worth Learning"; it constitutes a vocabulary of "Plain English," excluding alike the trivial on one hand, and the decorative on the other. The vocabulary therefore has been deliberately restricted, so that many comparatively frequent words will not be found in it. (See pp. xxi-xxviii, "Choice of Words.")

Utility of this Book

This book may prove of general utility to those who wish to ascertain the most usual pronunciations in England and America of some 9000 of the most useful English words and their inflected forms.

It may help an English or American student better to realize what sounds he uses when he speaks. This knowledge will be particularly useful to him when he is learning the pronunciation of foreign languages, or if he should be called upon to teach his own pronunciation of English.

By comparing the forms given in the two columns, the British student of pronunciation will better be enabled to familiarize himself with the forms characteristic of the speech of (probably) the majority of educated Americans; the user of Received Pronunciation (be he British or American) will better be enabled to realize the differences between his dialect and a dialect which is not his; and the American student whose pronunciation is not Received will be better enabled to realize what Received Pronunciation is, and to what extent Received Pronunciation is a class dialect rather than a Regional Pronunciation of speakers living in London and the South of England.

The foreign student of English will realize the important fact, fundamental to all linguistic study, that great variations of pronunciation exist and are likely to be expected.

Foreign students whose circumstances are likely to bring them into contact with America rather than with England will find it to their advantage to realize the nature of what has probably been represented to them as American pronunciation, and to familiarize themselves with it.

Lastly, the facts recorded in this dictionary will furnish evidence to those who wish to see realised certain reforms of existing pronunciations on either side of the Atlantic.

Pronunciation

In the present dictionary two distinct types of pronunciation are given, each in its respective column.

The one is headed *Received Pronunciation* (which term we may abbreviate to R.P.), and the other *American Variants* (which term we may abbreviate to A.V.).

A casual observer, glancing at these two columns, is likely to assume that the first stands for that local pronunciation characteristic of the southern counties of England, and that the second is that local pronunciation characteristic of certain parts of the United States. Or his assumption may take a more concise and more generalized form; the first is British and the second is American. Or, moved by linguistic prejudice, the casual observer may (according to the direction of his bias) stigmatize the first as "cockney" or the second as "Amurrican."

But his assumptions are ill-founded.

In the South of England, as in the North, as in Scotland, Ireland or America, there are regional pronunciations, but these Southern English Regional pronunciations (including cockney) have no closer connection with R.P. than have certain regional pronunciations of the United States or Canada.

If it required a Jones[1] to describe and set forth the nature of what he called Received Pronunciation, it required a Wyld[2] to show us conclusively, what ought to have been self-evident, that this pronunciation (called by him Received Standard Pronunciation) is not one of the regional pronunciations at all, but a special sort of class dialect that is independent of locality.

The casual observer may be excused if he shares the illusion so widely prevalent, viz. that all educated people pronounce alike. If it were true that all educated people pronounced alike, there would certainly be no need for a dictionary showing variant pronunciations, American or other.

Whether the existence of a Standard American pronunciation is a myth or not is a matter which hardly concerns those who have collaborated in writing the A.V. column. We note, however, that when we do hear protests against the types of pronunciation figuring in this column, the protests almost invariably come from American users of R.P.

Although the comparison of these two columns may indirectly throw some light on certain divergencies between British and American usages, the two columns are not intended to set forth and to contrast British and American pronunciations.

A user of R.P. is by no means necessarily an inhabitant of the British Isles, nor of England in particular, still less perhaps of London, a city in which probably the majority of natives consider R.P. only slightly less humorous than the rawest of American dialectal pronunciations.

The column headed *Received Pronunciation* is intended to show one way (or more than one way) in which words are pronounced by *those speakers who are the least influenced by Regional Dialects* (such as Cockney, Devonshire, Yorkshire, Edinburgh, Belfast, New England, New York, Toronto, Middle West, Southern States, or other). In this column is

[1] *An English Pronouncing Dictionary* (Dent), Professor D. Jones, University College, London.

[2] *A History of Modern Colloquial English* (Fisher Unwin), Professor H. C. Wyld, Merton College, Oxford.

included a number of those variants which are commonly heard among the same class of speakers.

The column headed *American Variants* (as the heading implies) is not intended to represent any given standard of pronunciation. Its object is to provide a place for noting variants which are rarely heard beyond the limits of the United States and Canada.

A given native hundred-per-cent American or Canadian may or may not use R.P. Similarly, a given native hundred-per-cent Englishman or Scot may or may not use R.P. But rare are the cases, if any, of an Englishman or Scot using habitually the pronunciations shown in the A.V. column.

We trust some day to see a similar dictionary (or a new edition of this one) providing a third column for *Scottish Variants*, and then probably some of us will be astonished to find how much more these will occasionally differ from R.P. than do the American Variants. Among other examples we might see:

	R.P.	A.V.	Sc.V.
first	fɜˑst	fɜəst	fərst
harmonious	hɑ′mounɪəs	hɑə′mounɪəs	hər′monjəs
where	*h*wɛə	hwɛə	ʍeˑr, ʍɛˑr
thither	′ðɪðə	′ðɪðə	′θɪθər, ′ðɪðər

Those who have had little occasion to reflect upon the problems involved in composing a pronouncing dictionary may imagine the work to be one of elementary simplicity. "It is quite a simple matter: you write down in the most appropriate system of notation the pronunciation that seems to be in the greatest conformity with correct usage." Even the far more difficult and delicate duty of distinguishing between variants which are American and variants which are not may give the impression of being one involving no considerations beyond that of accurate observation.

"Take a typical American, hear him pronounce each word, and whenever his pronunciation differs from the typical pronunciation of the user of Received Pronunciation, write down his pronunciation in the column reserved for American Variants."

Such empirical methods as these, however, will not suffice. Moreover, there are in the above two pieces of well-meant advice three or four examples of question-begging. We have to ask ourselves, "What *is* the most appropriate system of notation" (especially for a pronouncing dictionary that includes more than one dialect)?

And we have to determine in some way or other the meaning of the term "good usage," avoiding on the one hand the trivial and slovenly, and on the other the pedantic and affected.

Then again what is a "typical American"? It is only a little less difficult than finding a "typical Briton."

From the point of view of certain Americans, the procedure might be reversed, as "Take a typical Briton; hear him pronounce each word, and whenever his pronunciation makes you laugh, write down his pronunciation in the column reserved for Briticisms."

But the finest example of question-begging is represented by the term "user of Received Pronunciation," for until we have defined the term Received Pronunciation (and, not content with defining it, come to realize what it stands for), we shall be no nearer the solution of our problems.

Empiricism, an excellent thing in its way, is insufficient for the solving of the two main problems involved in the composing of a dictionary such as this.

The first problem is "What is Received Pronunciation"?

The second problem is: "In our phonetic notations, are we to use one symbol for every sound or one symbol for every phone"? The second problem we shall consider in its right place. The first problem cannot well be discussed without reference to Wyld, who is the originator of the term Received Standard Dialect, and apparently the discoverer of the abstraction for which the term stands.

"Dialect"

In popular usage, the term "dialect" is generally taken to mean: variety of a language other than the standard type, such as local *patois*. In this sense, the term "dialect" is used as the antithesis of "standard" or "classical," and implies a certain amount of reproach or disdain. Among philologists, however, the term "dialect" is used in the sense of: *any* variety of a given language, including its most standard or classical variety. Thus Wyld speaks of Regional Dialects, of the Received Standard Dialects and of Modified Standard Dialects. In the same sense, we may use such terms as the "American Dialect" of English, or the "Court Dialect of fourteenth century English," or the "Academic Dialect" of French, etc., etc.

"Dialect" and "Pronunciation"

Any dialect is marked off from any other dialect by three criteria: Pronunciation, Grammar and Vocabulary. So far as English is concerned, the factor of pronunciation is the most important. Wyld says, in this connection:

"A great deal has been said about different types of dialect, and it is well to be quite clear as to the nature of the distinctions which separate these. It will be convenient to deal with these under the three main heads of Pronunciation, Accidence, or Grammatical forms, and Vocabulary."

"Perhaps the most important characteristic of dialect is its pronunciation. At the present time, it is certainly this feature which chiefly distinguishes Received Standard from the different kinds of Modified Standard, especially when the latter, as so often happens, is spoken by persons who are more or less highly educated. Such people will hardly differ in their grammar from Received Standard, and as regards Vocabulary, except in a limited number of familiar colloquialisms and slang which certainly do vary from class to class, it may be said that, on the whole, persons of the same kind or degree of instruction possess approximately the same range of words."

When, therefore, we speak of the Received Standard Dialect, or of the Regional Dialects, or of the Modified Standard Dialects, the compilers of this pronouncing dictionary are concerned solely with the pronunciation aspect of these dialects. What Jones calls Received Pronunciation is hardly anything other than the pronunciation aspect of Wyld's "Received Standard Dialect."

The Wyld Theory of Dialect

Henry Cecil Wyld, Merton Professor of English Language and Literature at Oxford, in his various books and articles,[1] has set forth the only theory of English dialect which (in its broad lines at any rate) affords a simple and reasonable explanation of linguistic facts as we find them. From one point of view, however, Wyld errs on the side of over-conscientiousness in his scholarly research. Although his theory fits the linguistic facts of English in England and America, he makes no statement that he cannot prove, and we therefore find in his works no reference to the place of Received Standard in America, nor indeed any reference whatever to America (either the United States or Canada). The theory explains the facts of dialects other than those of English. It seems of equal application notably to languages so widely differing as French and Japanese.

The limited space afforded by the introductory pages of a dictionary such as this renders it impossible to set forth the theory in the actual words of Professor Wyld, but the following (partly quoted, partly abridged, partly interpreted freely) may give a sufficiently clear idea of the theory in question. The remarks added between parentheses are our own, and may not represent Wyld's opinion.

Regional Dialects.

Written English is fixed and uniform. On the other hand, we find almost endless variety in the spoken language. It is apparent that two or three different types of spoken English differ very much from each other in almost every respect. Their sounds are different, so too, in many respects are the grammatical forms, and there are differences in the names of quite common objects.

[1] Notably: *The Historical Study of the Mother Tongue* (Murray); *The Place of the Mother Tongue in National Education* (Murray); *The Growth of English* (Murray); *A History of Modern Colloquial English* (Fisher Unwin).

As a rule, when we speak of English dialects we mean varieties of English which are associated with particular geographical areas or countries. Many of these types are distinguished, according to the popular view, chiefly by possessing a more or less strange pronunciation and certain elements in their vocabulary which are not current in every part of the country, and especially not among the more educated portion of the community. Speech varieties of this kind confined to particular areas, we may call Regional Dialects.

Received Standard.

By the side of these, there are numerous other types of English which are not characteristic of any special geographical area, but rather of social divisions or sections of the population, in other terms they are types of English which are tinged neither with the Northern nor Midland, nor Southern (Wyld might have added: nor Eastern, Middle-West, or Southern States) peculiarities of speech, which give no indication, in fact, of where the speaker comes from—the form of English which is generally known simply as *Good English, Well-bred English, Upper-class English*, and it is sometimes, too vaguely, referred to as *Standard English.* Received Standard is spoken, within certain social boundaries, with an extraordinary degree of uniformity all over the country (we might add: and the English-speaking world). It is not any more the English of London, as it is sometimes mistakenly maintained, than it is of York (we might add: *New* York), or Exeter, or Cirencester or Oxford, or Chester, or Leicester (we might add: Harvard, or Chicago, or New Orleans, or San Francisco). In each and all of these places, and in many others throughout the length and breadth of England (we might replace "England" by "the English-speaking world"), Received Standard is spoken among the same kind of people, and it is spoken everywhere, allowing for individual idiosyncrasies, to all intents and purposes, in precisely the same way.

It has been suggested that perhaps the main factor in this singular degree of uniformity is the custom of sending youths from certain social strata to the great public schools. (But this does not account for the uniformity of Received Standard pronunciation among those Americans who use it.) If we were to say that Received English at the present day is Public School English, we should not be far wrong.

Since this form of English is not now confined to any one province, but is spoken by people of corresponding education and cultivation all over the country, we say that it is no longer *Regional Dialect*, but the dialect of a class, using the word in a very wide sense. (Or, to be precise, in Great Britain by the *majority* of people of corresponding education and cultivation, and, considering a wider geographical field, by a certain number of people of corresponding education and cultivation, in the United States and Canada.)

Modified Standard.

By the side of Received Standard there exist innumerable varieties, all more or less resembling Received Standard, but differing from it in all sorts of subtle ways. These varieties are certainly not Regional Dialects, and, just as certainly, they are not Received Standard. Until recently it has been usual to regard them as being practically identical with Received Standard, and to group them together with it under the general title of Standard English or Educated English. This old classification was very inadequate, since it ignored the existence of more than one Class Dialect, and included under a single title many varieties which differ as much from what we now call Received Standard as this does from the Regional Dialects.

It is now proposed to call these variants *Modified Standard.* This additional term is a great gain to clear thinking. These forms of Modified Standard may, in some cases, differ but slightly from Received Standard, so that they are felt merely as eccentricities by speakers of the latter; in others they differ very considerably, and in several ways, from this type, and are regarded as vulgarisms. It is a grave error to assume that what are known as "educated" persons, meaning thereby highly trained, instructed and learned persons, invariably speak Received Standard. Naturally, such speakers do not make "mistakes" in grammar, they may have a high and keen perception of the right uses of words, but with all this they may, and often do, use a type of pronunciation which is quite alien to Received Standard, either in isolated words or in whole groups. These deviations from the habits of Received Standard may be shown just as readily in over-careful pronunciation (as when *t* is pronounced in *often*) as in too careless a pronunciation (as when buttered toast is pronounced *butter toce*). Again the deviation from Received Standard may be in another direction. There may be simply a difference of sound, as when *clerk* is made to rhyme with *shirk*.

Different social grades have different standards of what is becoming in speech, as they have in dress or manners. Thus, for example, where some habitually use *'em*, *ain't*, *broke* (past participle), *shillin*, others would regard such usage with disapproval.

Wyld then goes on to show that one type of London speech of the fourteenth century is the ancestor not only of Literary English, but also of our present-day Received Standard.

In concluding these observations and quotations having reference to dialects and pronunciation types, we may say in the spirit that inspired the Jones dictionary: to those who believe that a universal standard of English pronunciation is necessary must be left the task of deciding what is to be approved and what is to be condemned. This book will provide them with certain materials which will serve as data for their invidious task.

How the facts were ascertained

Thanks to the painstaking work accomplished over ten years ago by Jones during the preparation of his dictionary, the bulk of the materials used in the present dictionary were already to hand when the compilers started their work. With very few exceptions, we have accepted the facts as stated by Jones, and divergencies from his treatment are rare. But, for more than one reason, the facts afforded by the Jones dictionary were too voluminous and too detailed to be incorporated in their entirety into the present work.

In the first place, the greater the choice of variant pronunciations, the greater the *embarras du choix* on the part of those for whom this dictionary is primarily designed. We have to reduce to the minimum the number of variant pronunciations both on the side of the R.P. and of the A.V. columns. Moreover, our attempt to show the characteristic divergencies between R.P. usage and the usage of Americans who do not use R.P. has necessitated certain adjustments in both columns. Without such adjustments the divergencies would seem to be either greater or less than is really the case.

The evidence afforded by the phonetic transcription in Cassell's French-English and English-French Dictionary has been of value in many cases in which the choice between one or more variants presented difficulty. In certain cases the pronunciation of the English compilers, and the evidence offered by their own observations, have been used to determine doubtful points.

The tendency has been to level under one form variants of little importance or significance.

To ascertain the facts concerning the American variants, we have consulted the works of three American phoneticians: Hempl,[1] Krapp,[2] and Kenyon,[3] and brought them to concordance through the first-hand and second-hand evidence provided by Mr. J. V. Martin, whose pronunciation is characteristic of the educated American whose standard is other than the more or less special pronunciations of the Southern States and the Atlantic seaboard.

[1] *International French-English and English-French Dictionary*, Editorial critic of English Pronunciations: George Hempl, Professor of English Philology and General Linguistics in the University of Michigan, President of the American Dialect Society, and recently President of the American Philological Association, and President of the Modern Language Association of America.

[2] *Pronunciation of Standard English in America*, George Philip Krapp, Professor of English in Columbia University. *First Lessons in Speech Improvement*, Birmingham and Krapp.

[3] *American Pronunciation*, John Samuel Kenyon, Ph.D., Professor of the English Language in Hiram College.

Apparent Inconsistencies

With regard to apparent inconsistencies, we cannot do better than quote from the introduction to the Jones dictionary:

"A word may be said here on the 'inconsistency fallacy' because some critics of books on phonetics (particularly foreign critics) are always on the look-out for what they are pleased to call inconsistencies. Such critics have not fully realized the important fact that in linguistic matters consistency (so-called) means inaccuracy."

"In the best type of book on phonetics, viz. that which aims at recording accurately, there may be errors of observation, but there can be no such thing as inconsistency. The word 'inconsistency' presupposes the existence of rules or principles. The accurate record is not concerned with rules; it furnishes materials from which rules may be deduced, and if the material is complete or nearly so, the principles deduced therefrom will probably be correct."

Choice of Words

The object of the compilers has not been to present a exhaustive vocabulary, but, on the contrary, to furnish that sort of vocabulary which is likely to be of the greatest utility to those for whose use it is primarily designed. (See "The Object of this Dictionary.")

The selecting of the words was no simple task; to decide whether a given word should be included or excluded entailed the deep consideration of such questions as those of frequency, utility, proportion, style, and grammar. It was necessary to choose the words systematically, and in accordance with a more or less definite plan.

For reasons into which we cannot enter here, the principle of *relative frequency of occurrence* would not have proved adequate, otherwise we might have been content to use the various word-lists so painstakingly compiled, notably by American educationists.

The choice was determined largely by considerations set forth in the following pages.

Words may, of course, be classified in various ways. They may be classified grammatically, each category being a given part of speech. Again, nouns may be grouped under such headings as singular, plural, uncountable, common, proper, etc., and verbs may be classified under such headings as infinitive, present-tense, preterite, participles, transitive, intransitive, regular, irregular, etc. Words may be classified on a basis of etymology as when in English we distinguish words of Germanic, Latin, French, Greek, etc., origin.

But, in addition to such bases of classification, there is one which is concerned neither with grammar nor with etymology, but with what we may call (for want of a better term) *style, or tone colour*. The words *precious* and *valuable* are synonymous (so far as any two words may be synonymous), they are both adjectives, but they are distinguished by a something to which it is not easy to give a name. While awaiting the development of the science of Semantics[1] we must content ourselves with calling it "a difference of style" or "a difference of tone colour."

The word *precious* has an emotional content not suggested by the dry and matter-of-fact word *valuable*. Similarly, *to plunder* is of a different style-category (or has a tone colour different) from that of *to rob*, and *plight* from that of *predicament*.

Some words, then, convey not only a *concept*, but also the *emotion* felt by the user of such words. We may call them *words with emotional colour*, or *dramatic words*. Under the letter P we may note the following examples:

paltry	perish	plunder
pamper	pestilential	poesy
pander	piteous	precious
pang	plague	preposterous
peal	plead	prowess
perfidy	plenteous	puny
perilous		

Such words as these are used only when the speaker or

[1] Consult such works as *La Sémantique* (Bréal), *Significs and Language* (Welby), *The Meaning of Meaning* (Ogden and Richards), *Word Magic* (Ogden), etc., etc.

writer is actually moved with some sort of emotion (e.g. admiration, detestation, scorn, tenderness, protest, fear, etc.).

Closely allied to these are words which, without implying definite emotion on the part of the user, convey or suggest ideas in which there is some special "tone colour," words which are descriptive, even vividly so, evoking picturesque or striking images, of movements, of behaviour, or of appearance. Such words (which we may term *words of descriptive colour*) are part of the vocabulary of the "painter in words." Under the letter P, we may note the following examples:

peep	pettish	prank
peer	portly	prattle
peevish	pounce	prowl
pelt	prance	puffy
pert		

These "words of descriptive colour" lead almost insensibly into the group of onomatopœic words, in fact, onomatopœic words might be included as a subdivision of the group. The chief examples under P are:

patter	plash	pop
ping	plop	prickle
pish	pom	purr
pit-a-pat		

To these might be added such doubtful "words" as *pooh*, *pshaw* and *phew*.

These "words of descriptive colour" lead in their turn towards or into a style-category that might be called *trivial words*. They are "coloured" with the tints of jocularity or familiarity suggestive of the colloquial style as used among intimate friends. Under P, we find the following examples:

pal	phiz	poser (problem)
pants (noun)	phossy	pram
papa	piccanniny	preachify
pasty	pickaback	prig
peckish	piffle	pub
pelf	piggy	pup
pep	piggish	puss
peppery	podgy	pussy
pesky		

It will be seen that some of these are frankly slang words, others vulgar, others childish, etc.

Returning to the *words of emotional colour*, we note that these are words that are most frequently met with in the elevated styles of oratory and poetry. But there is another class of words which, for a different reason, produce the same or a very similar emotional effect. These are the archaic, obsolete and obsolescent words. Just as a ruin or an ancient building may have a greater appeal to the artist than a modern structure, so do most of our dead and dying words convey an impression of charm, of glamour and picturesqueness. Let us call these: *words of antique colour*. Out of a list of some forty words occurring under the letter P, we may note the following most typical examples:

panoply	philtre	pottage
paynim	pipkin	pottle
peradventure	plaguy	prepense
perchance	plaudit	prithee
perforce	pother	

Many words of this class are obsolete or obsolescent, for the simple reason that the objects, customs, etc., for which they stand are no longer extant. *Drawbridge* is a dying word, not by reason of anything inherent in the word itself, but to the fact that drawbridges themselves have become obsolete.

In a different category from any of these are words which are suggestive of dignity of diction; pompous words, sententious words; words which, when used too freely or in an inappropriate context, betray the pedant or the prig. Dignity in such cases lapses into pretentiousness, and the dignified into the stilted. So well is this recognized, unconscious though such recognition may be, that a certain type of humour consists in the facetious use of these words, which we may call *words of dignified colour*.

Among these, choosing once again our examples from words under P, we find

pabulum	potation	progeny
palpability	prandial	prognosticate
peregrinate	prefatorial	propinquity
pertain	prestidigitation	protuberance
peruse	predilection	proximity
pluvial	procrastinate	pusillanimity
ponderosity	profundity	

Another category, which may be divided into sub-categories, we may call *words of foreign classical and exotic colour.* Among those of French origin, we find

panache	personnel	penchant
persiflage	prestige	piquancy

among those of Latin origin:

peccavi	pomatum	paterfamilias
penates	proviso	

among those originating in America (including Spanish-American and American-Indian):

palaver	palmetto	powwow
parakeet	pampas	pueblo
papoose		

with which we may include

paleface and pathfinder

among those from the East:

pariah	pundit	punkah
pasha		

Returning to the vocabulary of pomposity, the *words of dignified colour,* we may here remark that there are two categories of words which are often unjustly confused with these, viz.

Technical words (including the terminology of science and special subjects), and *precise words.* (Or, continuing to use the term "colour" in designating the various categories, we may speak of these respectively as *words of technical colour* and *words tinted with the colour of precision.*)

Among the 120 or so *technical* words figuring under the letter P in an ordinary dictionary, we find such typical examples as:

phanerogam	pisciculture	pragmatism
pleonastic	plesiosaurus	phosphite
parthenogenesis	polonaise	patentee
pawl	piscina	polyandrous
parabola		

These technical words are, after all, nothing other than words of extreme precision as used by technicians whose business it is to call by their names things which are relatively unknown to the majority of users of languages.

Under the letter P, we find about the same number of words which cannot be assigned to any particular branch of science or to any particular technical subject, but which are none the less words of *precision*, words which express certain ideas more concisely and more aptly than their more popular synonyms (when such exist). Among these are:

palliative	phase	proficiency
penetration	postulate	provisional
permeate	prejudicial	provocative
perspicacity	procedure	pugnacity

Then comes a category coloured by the tint of *artificiality*. words which are obvious inventions. Among these:

pantechnicon	palmistry	pianola
phonography	philately	plasticine
pantograph		

Now all the words in all the categories that we have been considering have this much in common: that, in addition to expressing some concept, they suggest in various ways the mood, attitude, point of view, and even the character of the user, or the conditions in which the word is used. For diverse reasons each of these words may be said to be a word with some sort of "tone colour."

All the other words that make up the sum of the English vocabulary may, in contrast, be called *colourless words*. If we call a cat a *cat* we are using a word without colour, the word *cat* suggests a cat and nothing more. If we call a cat a *puss*, a *pussy* or a *pussy-cat*, we are using words that suggest the child's attitude towards the cat; if we call a cat a *domestic feline quadruped* we are using terms that suggest the point of view of the scientist, the humourist or the pedant.

In the ordinary dictionary, wherein all words are duly set forth in alphabetical order, the "colourless" words seem to be in a poor minority. On the other hand, on any printed page of connected text, or in the speech of an orator or of a conversationalist, we shall probably find that it is made up of from 90 per cent. to 100 per cent. of "colourless" words.

One of the purposes of the present dictionary is to present a selection of words which shows the truer proportion. Having in mind the needs of foreign students of English we have given the benefit to "colourless" words, and have included all those which, in our judgment, stand for those concepts which in ordinary circumstances are the most necessary for readers and for speakers.

Among these "colourless" words we find notably "form-words," such as prepositions, connectives, personal pronouns and determinatives, and such "full-words" as the names of common objects, together with the commonest abstract nouns, verbs, adjectives, and adverbs. Common "colourless" words had the first right of admission in our select and restricted vocabulary.

Among the words with "colour," the first place was given to *words tinted with the colour of precision*, the words that figure with such profusion in such works as encyclopædias, articles in reviews, leading and special articles in newspapers, in other terms: in the language of those who furnish information with the minimum of emotion.

Other words of "colour" received less attention, and of these relatively smaller proportions were chosen.

A bushel basket can contain nothing more than a bushel of whatever we choose to put in it, and a dictionary intentionally limited to some 9,000 words cannot contain more than 9,000 of the words we consider necessary to insert in it[1]. In accordance with the claims of proportion, we have admitted a certain percentage of words of every category. The categories which have the fewest representatives are those of the onomatopœic words, words of antique colouring, words with foreign, exotic and artificial colourings, words with pompous colourings, words with technical colourings, and words associated with the tone-colour of the emotional and subjective.

A certain number of proper nouns have been included. These are for the most part the commonest christian names

[1] Actually this dictionary contains 9,645 words in heavy type.

and the best-known or the oldest-known geographical names. In the case of these and of other words, the compilers will welcome expressions of opinion concerning the desirability of including in a future edition those which, intentionally or unintentionally, have been omitted in the present edition.

"Plain English" is an attractive term and an inspiring ideal, but a term which, from its very nature, must be and remain indefinite and provokingly vague. But those who have selected the present vocabulary have endeavoured to bring together a representative collection of words which may be considered as a vocabulary of Plain English, the sort of English which constitutes from 95 per cent. to 100 per cent. of the great majority of English as used in connected speech or texts.

PHONETIC SYMBOLS

Phones

In the system of notation and transcription used in this dictionary, English (R.P. or A.V.) has been considered as consisting of so many independent integral units of pronunciation called "phones." A *sound*, as such, may constitute a *phone*, but more often a *phone* consists of a group of interchangeable sounds.

Thus [f] is both a *sound* and an English *phone*; [k] represents an English *phone*, which is in reality a group of sounds varying between the initial sound of *key* and the initial sound of *cool*, and [l] is a *phone* varying between the *l* of *leap* and the *l* of *fool*.

[eɩ], [oʊ], [aɩ], [aʊ], [ɔɩ], and other units are successions of sounds, but each of these successions constitutes for practical purposes one integral unit of English pronunciation, and each is therefore considered as an independent phone. The theory of the phone may or may not be considered as difficult or abstract, but the effect of the theory is towards a simplification of the problems of phonetic transcription.

The Notation

The notation used is that of the International Phonetic Association. The more precise form of notation has been adopted; a form which is in its essence identical with that used in the *Maître Phonétique*, the organ of the Association. In the interest of a greater latitude and facility, the symbol [ɩ] has been added. The device of "bigraphs" (i.e. the fusion of two adjacent letter-shapes in one symbol), e.g. [eɩ], [aɩ], [ɛə], [tʃ], has been adopted as tending to a better grasping of the nature of English phones (i.e. phonetic units).

Received Pronunciation Column

The symbols (with their values) used in the column headed "Received Pronunciation" are those figuring in the following list.

Vowels.

(*a*) Five "free" vowels, i.e. more or less static vowels occurring in any position; initially, medially or finally, and in any sort of syllable, stressed or unstressed. In stressable syllables they take the length-mark [ˑ].

1. [i] *see* [siˑ], *me* [miˑ], [mi].
2. [ɑ] *France* [frɑˑns], *are* [ɑˑ], [ɑ], *artistic* [ɑ'tɪstɪk].
3. [ɔ] *chalk* [tʃɔˑk], *blackboard* ['blækbɔd], *although* [ɔl'ðoʊ].
4. [u] *too* [tuˑ], *you* [juˑ], [ju], *value* ['vælju].
5. [ɜ] *bird* [bɜˑd], *her* [hɜˑ], [hɜ], *suburb* ['sʌbɜb].

(*b*) Six "checked" vowels, i.e. static vowels occurring, in stressed syllables, only before a consonant that checks their duration. They generally do occur in stressed positions, but not always. [æ] alone may be lengthened and that only in certain words.

6. [ɪ] *live* [lɪv], *mislay* [mɪs'leɪ].
7. [ɛ] *desk* [dɛsk], *parallel* ['pærəlɛl].
8. [æ] *map* [mæp], *bad* [bæd], *enthusiasm* [ɪn'θjuˑzɪæzm̩].
9. [ʌ] *front* [frʌnt], *product* ['prɒdʌkt].
10. [ɒ] *box* [bɒks], *voluminous* [vɒ'ljuˑmɪnəs].
11. [ʊ] *book* [bʊk], *painful* ['peɪnfʊl].

(*c*) Five kinetic free vowels, or diphthongs, occurring in any position and in stressed or unstressed syllables.

12. [eɪ] *name* [neɪm], *estimate* (verb) ['ɛstɪmeɪt].
13. [oʊ] *no* [noʊ], *omit* [oʊ'mɪt].

In unstressed syllables the two above phones tend towards [e] and [o]. The tendency seems more marked in typical American than in R.P.

14. [aɪ] *my* [maɪ], *idea* [aɪ'dɪə].
15. [aʊ] *house* [haʊs], *outside* [aʊt'saɪd].

The first element of the above two phones varies between cardinal [a] and cardinal [ɑ] both in R.P. and typical American usage.

16. [ɔɪ] *boy* [bɔɪ], *royal* [rɔɪəl].

(*d*) Two "obscure" vowels, occurring only in unstressed positions, often (in rapid fluent speech) weakened to a point at which one can hardly be distinguished from the other, or (in slow and careful speech) strengthened to points at which they are almost indistinguishable respectively from [ʌ] or [ɪ] (or from other vowels).

17. [ə] *America* [əˈmɛrɪkə], *better* [ˈbɛtə], *understand* [ʌndəˈstænd], *magazine* [mægəˈziˑn].

In slow and careful speech, [ə] tends towards [ʌ], [ɔ], [oʊ], [u], or [ɛə]. See R.P. Variants.

18. [ɩ] *city* [ˈsɪtɩ], *eleven* [ɩˈlɛvn̩], *majesty* [ˈmæʤɪstɩ], *houses* [ˈhaʊzɩz], *goodness* [ˈgʊdnɩs], *useless* [ˈjuˑslɩs], *obvious* [ˈɒbvɩəs], *magistrate* [ˈmæʤɪstrɩt]], *adequate* [ˈædɩkwɩt].

In slow and careful speech, [ɩ] tends towards [ɪ], [ɛ], [eɩ], [i], or [ə].

(*e*) Four "murmur diphthongs," so-called as they end in the murmur-glide of [ə].

19. [ɪə] *here* [hɪə], *pier* [pɪə].
20. [ɛə] *chair* [ʧɛə], *prayer* [prɛə].
21. [ɔə] *door* [dɔə], *war* [wɔə].
22. [ʊə] *poor* [pʊə], *cure* [kjʊə].

Some speakers invariably replace [ɔə] by [ɔ].

CONSONANTS.

23. [p] *piece* [piˑs], *map* [mæp].
24. [b] *box* [bɒks], *rub* [rʌb].
25. [t] *too* [tuˑ], *not* [nɒt].
26. [d] *desk* [dɛsk], *send* [sɛnd].
27. [k] *come* [kʌm], *book* [bʊk].
28. [g] *go* [goʊ], *dog* [dɒg].
29. [m] *my* [maɪ], *gum* [gʌm].
30. [n] *no* [noʊ], *man* [mæn].
31. [ŋ] *wing* [wɪŋ].
32. [l] *look* [lʊk], *small* [smɔˑl].

When not followed by a vowel [l] is usually pronounced as "dark-*l*," for which the phonetic symbol is [ɫ].

33. [f] *four* [fɔə], *if* [ɪf].
34. [v] *very* [vɛrɩ], *five* [faɪv].
35. [θ] *thing* [θɪŋ], *earth* [ɜˑθ].
36. [ð] *that* [ðæt], *with* [wɪð].
37. [s] *see* [siˑ], *piece* [piˑs].
38. [z] *zone* [zoʊn], *nose* [noʊz].
39. [ʃ] *shoe* [ʃuˑ], *brush* [brʌʃ].
40. [ʒ] *measure* [ˈmɛʒə].
41. [r] *red* [rɛd].
42. [h] *hot* [hɒt].
43. [ʧ] *chalk* [ʧɔˑk], *which* [*h*wɪʧ].
44. [ʤ] *June* [ʤuˑn], *large* [lɑˑʤ].
45. [j] *yes* [jɛs].
46. [w] *wash* [wɒʃ].

In the pronunciation of many speakers [hw] counts as an independent phone, as an integral unit of the English phonetic system. In the R.P. column this is shown throughout as [*h*w].

Miscellaneous Signs.

[ˈ] The stress mark. This shows that the stress may fall on the syllable that it precedes. The use of two stress marks in one word shows that the stress may fall on one syllable or the other, in accordance with the rules governing sentence-stress. Thus, the entry [ˈfɪfˈtiˑn] indicates that the word may be stressed as [fɪfˈtiˑn] as in [aɪ sɔˑ fɪfˈtiˑn], or as [ˈfɪftin], as in [aɪ sɔˑ ˈfɪftin ˈpiˑpl̩ ðɛə].

[ˑ] The length mark. This shows that the vowel to which it is attached is long. The length mark is used only in syllables that are susceptible of being stressed.

Italics. A phonetic symbol printed in italics indicates that the sound for which it stands is often omitted, especially in fluent speech. (See "Received Pronunciation Variants," Categories 1 to 5.)

[(r] This indicates that when the word is followed without a break or pause by a word beginning with a vowel, the sound [r] is added. Thus the entry [ˈbɛtə(r] means, for example, that *This one is better* is pronounced [ðɪs wʌn z ˈbɛtə], but that *This is a better example* is pronounced [ðɪs ɪz ə bɛtər ɪgˈzɑˑmpl̩].

[ˌ] The syllabic mark. Placed under [l], [n] or (rarely) [m], it indicates that the consonant has the value of a syllable, suggestive of a preceding [ə] or [ɪ].

American Variants Column

The symbols (with their values) used in the column headed "American Variants" are essentially the same as those figuring in the preceding list.

In transcribing certain American variants six additional symbols are required:

[a] This symbol designates any sound between the two extremes of [ɑ] and [æ]. Thus the entry [paˑs] means that

the word is pronounced variously as [pɑ·s], [pæ·s], or in some manner intermediate between these two extremes.

[o̞] This symbol is used notably before [ɚ] to represent the vowel of *soar* [so̞ɚ]. Compare this with [souɚ], which represents the pronunciation of *sower* (one who sows). It is also used in those cases in which the [ɚ], by reason of a following vowel, becomes [r], thus *soaring*, *story*, *pouring*, etc., are transcribed [ˈso̞·rɪŋ], [ˈsto̞·rɪ], [ˈpo̞·rɪŋ], etc.

[ɚ] stands for the "retroflex" variety of [ə]. Similarly [ɛɚ] and [ɔɚ] are used for the "retroflex" varieties of [ɛə] and [ɔə].

For further details on these and other points, see the general explanation of "American Variants."

Received Pronunciation Variants

To record all the possible variant pronunciations of the Received Standard dialect of English is a task lying outside the scope of the present dictionary. Those who wish for further or more detailed information on the subject would do well to consult Jones' *An English Pronouncing Dictionary*. For more than one reason, however, we have thought it desirable to provide in many cases one or more variant pronunciations. In the first place, the recording of variants affords a more liberal or broader interpretation of pronunciation values. In the second place, it often happens that two variant pronunciations seem to be equally common, and the invidious task of selecting the one and rejecting the other is one that we do not feel justified in undertaking.

Another important reason for providing Received Pronunciation variants is the presence of the column headed *American Variants*. It frequently happens that a pronunciation typical of American speech is at the same time not unknown as a Received Pronunciation variant; to omit the Received variant in such cases would convey an exaggerated or erroneous impression concerning the kind or degree of divergencies between Received and typical American usage. Thus the first vowel of the word *either* is generally [i·] according to typical American usage; to give in the R.P. column [naɪðə(r] and [ni·ðə] in the A.V. column would imply that the word *neither* pronounced with [i·] is an Americanism, whereas this pronunciation is common both to R.P. and to typical American, although rarer in R.P.

A certain number of variant entries are in the nature of isolated cases. Possibly *nephew* is the only word in which [v] and [f] are variants. Possibly *primer* is the only word in which [ɪ] and [aɪ] are interchangeable. But the great majority of the variants recorded fall into categories, most of which are easily recognized.

Variant pronunciations are shown:

(*a*) By italicizing a symbol with the convention that the sound for which the symbol stands may be or need not be pronounced. Thus the entry [ˈkʌmf*ə*təbl̩] means [ˈkʌmfətəbl̩] or [ˈkʌmftəbl̩].

(*b*) By re-spelling the word. The first of two or more forms indicates that it is the one which seems the most prevalent. Thus

neither ˈnaɪðə
ˈni·ðə

indicates that the word has two pronunciation-values, and that [ˈnaɪðə] seems more prevalent than [ni·ðə].

(*c*) In one case we have used the device of placing a dagger (†) before certain words. This dagger serves as a reference to note 30, p. xxxv. concerning a certain category of variation.

The following is a list of the more important categories:—

1.	Omission of [ə]	ˈkʌmf*ə*təbl̩
2.	Omission of [ɪ]	ˈpju·p*ɪ*l
3.	Omission of [j]	rɛvəˈl*j*u·ʃən
4.	Omission of [h]	*h*wɒt
5.	Omission of various consonants	ˈlæn*d*lɔd, lɛŋ*k*θ, prɒm*p*t
6.	[jə] for [ɪə] and vice versa	pri·vjəs, pri·vɪəs
7.	[j] for [ɪ] and vice versa	pɪˈænoʊ, ˈpjænoʊ
8.	[ɪə] for [i·ə] and vice versa	ri·əl, rɪəl
9.	[i] for [ɪ] and vice versa	riˈpleɪs, rɪˈpleɪs
12.	[ə] for [ɛ] and vice versa	ˈpærəlɛl, ˈpærələl

13. [eɪ] for [ɪ] and vice versa 'mædʒɪstrɪt, 'mædʒɪstreɪt
10. [ə] for [ɪ] and vice versa 'pɒlɪsɪ, 'pɒləsɪ
11. [ɛ] for [ɪ] and vice versa lɪ'geɪʃən, lɛ'geɪʃən
14. [eɪ] for [ə] and vice versa kə'mju·nɪkətɪv, kə'mju·nɪkeɪtɪv
15. [i·] for [ɛ] and vice versa 'pri·mətjuə, 'prɛmətjuə
16. [ɜ] for [ə] and vice versa pə'sweɪd, pɜ'sweɪd
17. [æ] for [ə] and vice versa və'lɪdɪtɪ, væ'lɪdɪtɪ
18. [æ] for [ɑ] and vice versa trɑns'leɪt, træns'leɪt
19. [æ] for [æ·] and vice versa 'bæ·dlɪ, 'bædlɪ
20. [ə] for [ɑ] and vice versa pɑ'tɪʃən, pə'tɪʃən
21. [æ] for [eɪ] and vice versa 'peɪtn̩t, 'pætn̩t
22. [ʌ] for [ə] and vice versa ən'lɛs, ʌn'lɛs
23. [ɒ] for [ɔ] and vice versa lɔst, lɒst
24. [ə] for [ɔ] and vice versa 'mɛlbən, 'mɛlbɔn
25. [ə] for [ɒ] and vice versa vɒl'ju·mɪnəs, və'lju·mɪnəs
26. [ɔ·] for [ɔə] and vice versa mɔən, mɔ·n (*mourn*)
27. [ɑ·] for [ɔ·] and vice versa lɔ·ntʃ, lɑ·ntʃ
28. [ə] for [oʊ] and vice versa oʊ'beɪ, ə'beɪ
29. [ɒ] for [oʊ] and vice versa 'proʊgrɛs, 'prɒgrɛs
30. [oʊ], [ɔ], [ɒ], or sounds intermediate between them for [ə], marked by [†ə], thus [†ə'rɪdʒɪneɪt] may stand for [ə'rɪdʒɪneɪt], [oʊ'rɪdʒɪneɪt], [ɔ'rɪdʒɪneɪt], or [ɒ'rɪdʒɪneɪt].
31. [ɔ] for [oʊ] and vice versa 'poʊɪtrɪ, 'pɔɪtrɪ
32. [ɔə] for [uə] and vice versa puə, pɔə (*poor*)
33. [ʊ] for [u·] and vice versa 'bru·ərɪ, 'brʊərɪ
34. [ə] for [ʊə] and vice versa 'ju·ʒʊəl, 'ju·ʒəl
35. [ə] for [ʊ] and vice versa 'lɔ·fʊlɪ, 'lɔ·fəlɪ
36. [ɪ] for [aɪ] and vice versa maɪ'nɒrɪtɪ, mɪ'nɒrɪtɪ
37. Miscellaneous Vowel Variants such as leɪə, lɛə (*layer*)
38. Voiced for Voiceless Consonants and vice versa træn'sɪʒən, træn'zɪʃən
39. Miscellaneous Consonant Variants such as 'pʌnktjueɪt, 'pʌnktʃueɪt
40. Stress Variants with or without vowel variation 'rɛprɪmɑnd, rɛprɪ'mɑ·nd
rɪ'mɒnstreɪt, 'rɛmɔnstreɪt
41. Strong and Weak Forms of the "Weakenable Words" indicated in the text by the *s.f.* (= strong form) and *w.f.* (= weak form). æt *s.f.*, ət *w.f.*

R.P. Variants not noted in the Dictionary

(Many of these are also common to A.V.)

Among these are the following:

1. [i] tends towards, and is often replaced by, a diphthong consisting of [ɪ] followed by [i].
2. [u] tends towards, and is often replaced by, a diphthong consisting of [ʊ] followed by [u].
3. [iə] tends towards, and is often replaced by, [ɪ] followed by [ə] in one syllable.
4. [uə] tends towards, and is often replaced by, [ʊ] followed by [ə] in one syllable.
6. [ɑ] varies between cardinal [ɑ] and a point about half-way between cardinal [ɑ] and cardinal [a].
7. [ɔ] is subject to slight variations, more especially in the matter of the amount of lip-rounding.
8. [ʊ] is subject to the same sort of variations in the matter of the amount of lip-rounding.
9. [ɜ] varies to some extent.
10. [ə] varies noticeably according to its position in the word and in the sentence. In final position, it is often replaced by [ʌ]. Three different values may be heard in the words *China, cathedral*; in the latter word, the second [ə] has a lower and more retracted position than the first [ə].
11. [eɪ] tends towards, and is often replaced by, [ɛɪ] or [ɛe], and sometimes by a sound practically indistinguishable from [e].
12. [oʊ] varies considerably, generally in the direction of being advanced towards the mixed position, also to some extent by partial unrounding of the first element; with some the diphthong approaches [ɔʊ], especially when followed by a "dark" [l]. Others again tend to make it [o], especially in unstressed syllables.
13. [aɪ] varies slightly both in the direction of [æɪ] and in the direction of [ɑɪ].
14. [aʊ] varies between [aʊ] (with cardinal [a] and [ɑʊ] (almost with cardinal [ɑ]).
15. [ɪə] when final tends towards and is often replaced by [ɪʌ].
16. [ɛə] tends towards, and is often replaced by [æə. When final, it tends towards and is often replaced by [ɛʌ] or [æʌ].
17. [ɔə] when final tends to have a rather open variety of [ə].
18. [ʊə] when final tends to have a rather open variety of [ə].

For more detailed information concerning the above variants see Jones' *An English Pronouncing Dictionary*, pages xxii–xxiii, on which the foregoing summary of variants is based.

American Variants

In the column headed "American Variants" figure variant pronunciations other than those given in the "Received Pronunciation" column. We have called these "American Variants" because these particular variants are never (or only exceptionally) heard except from Americans and Canadians. *The inclusion of any of these variants does not by any means imply that all speakers in America use the form indicated*; it implies merely that a large number of educated Americans (including Canadians) use or tend to use instead of the Received Pronunciation, the pronunciation indicated, or one closely approximating to it.

The variants indicated in this column may be classified under the following 12 headings:

VARIANT 1. [ɑ] for [ɒ].

A large number of speakers replace or tend to replace the R P. [ɒ] by a vowel more or less approximating to [ɑ]. Thus *hot, box, stop,* etc., which are pronounced [hɒt], [bɒks], [stɒp], etc., in R.P., appear in the A.V. column as [hɑt], [bɑks], [stɑp], etc.

This, however, does not apply to all words with R.P. [ɒ]. *Long, wrong, dog,* etc., remain [lɒŋ], [rɒŋ], [dɒg], or, with certain speakers, tend rather towards [ɔ] or [ɔ·], [lɔŋ], [rɔŋ], [dɔg].

VARIANT 2. [a·] for [ɑ·].

In certain important categories of words most American speakers replace the R.P. [ɑ·] by more advanced varieties of the phone, these ranging between [ɑ·] and [æ·]. Such varieties are indicated by the symbol [a·],

Thus *half, brass, ask, nasty*, etc., are transcribed with the symbol [a·], indicating that the vowel varies between [ɑ·] and [æ].

	R.P.		A.V.
half	hɑ·f	ha·f	= hɑ·f, ha·f, hæ·f, *etc.*
brass	brɑ·s	bra·s	= brɑ·s, bra·s, bræ·s, *etc.*
ask	ɑ·sk	a·sk	= ɑ·sk, a·sk, æ·sk, *etc.*
nasty	nɑ·stɩ	na·stɩ	= nɑ·stɩ, na·stɩ, næ·stɩ, *etc.*

The most general value given to this phone in America is probably that of "cardinal" [a].

VARIANT 3. [ɚ] for [ə].

In "most parts of New England, New York City and vicinity, the South-East and large parts of the South of the United States" (Kenyon), speakers conform to the Received usage of the [ə], thus *better, actor*, etc., are pronounced ['bɛtə], ['æktə], etc.

In the other regions, most American speakers replace or tend to replace [ə] by [ɚ] in all cases where the letter *r* figures in the traditional spelling.[1] This [ɚ] is a "retroflex" [ə], i.e. a variety of [ə] which is produced while the tip of the tongue is raised and slightly curled back. Krapp represents it by the symbol [ɹ], and describes it as "a voiced sound, but the friction accompanying the vocal element is so slight that one might hesitate to group it with the fricatives, or with the consonants at all. . . . In pronouncing this sound, the point of the tongue is not tilted as high as in [r], but if it were permitted to touch the roof of the mouth, which it does not do, it would strike the region just back of the upper teeth and in front of the place where the concavity of the roof begins."

It should be mentioned here that the form of the symbol [ɚ] was designed by Krapp to represent the sound of the first element of the *ir* of *bird* (which he represents as [bɚɹd]).

Considering, however, that the *ir* of *bird* may be more aptly represented by [ɜɚ], and that the symbol [ɹ] is specified by the International Phonetic Association to be the "narrow"

[1] And at least in one case (*colonel*) where *r* does not figure.

representation of the true "fricative" *r* (as in *red, rich, try,* etc.), we have taken the liberty of using Krapp's symbol [ə] to represent the "retroflex" variety of [ə], for which Krapp uses the symbol [ɹ].

Examples :

	R.P.	A.V.
better	'bɛtə	'bɛtə
actor	'æktə	'æktə
collar	'kɒlə	'kɑlə
honour	'ɒnə	'ɑnə
measure	'mɛʒə	'mɛʒə

Notes concerning [ər].

When, however, R.P. [ə] is followed immediately by [r] (either in the same or in the next word), the [ə] remains and does not become [ə]. Thus:

	R.P.	A.V.
remember	rɪ'mɛmbə	rɪ'mɛmbə
remembering	rɪ'mɛmbərɪŋ	(same as R.P.)
after	'ɑˑftə	'aˑftə
after all	ɑˑftər 'ɔˑl	aˑftər 'ɔˑl

Variant 4. [ɑə] for [ɑˑ].

In a certain important category of words spelt with *ar* (occasionally, however, *ear*, *uar*, and, in one case, *er*), most American speakers give to this letter *r* the value of [ə] (see Variant 3). This does not apply, however, to the majority of speakers in "most parts of New England, New York City and vicinity, the South-East and a large part of the South of the United States" (Kenyon), in which regions either [ɑˑ] remains [ɑˑ] or is replaced by [ɑə] (see "Variants Omitted").

Examples :

	R.P.	A.V.
far	fɑˑ	fɑə
farm	fɑˑm	fɑəm
heart	hɑˑt	hɑət
guard	gɑˑd	gɑəd
artist	ɑˑtɪst	ɑətɪst
artistic	ɑ'tɪstɪk	ɑə'tɪstɪk
sergeant	'sɑˑdʒənt	sɑədʒənt

Note concerning [ɑˑr].

When, however, [ɑˑ] is followed immediately by [r], either in the same word or in the next word, [ɑˑ] generally remains [ɑˑ], and does not become [ɑə]. Thus:

	R.P.	A.V.
far	fɑˑ	fɑə
far away	fɑˑr əˈweɪ	(same as R.P.)
bar	bɑˑ	bɑə
barring	ˈbɑˑrɪŋ	(same as R.P.)

VARIANT 5. [ɜə] for [ɜˑ].

With the exception of speakers in "most parts of New England, New York City, and vicinity, the South-East, and a large part of the South of the United States" (Kenyon), most speakers in America replace or tend to replace Received Standard [ɜ] by a variant which we represent by the symbol [ɜə].

According to Kenyon, in such words as *her, stir, fur, hers, stirred*, etc., the *r*-sound is not made before or after the vowel, but is the vowel itself, and he represents it by the symbol [ɝ]. Krapp, however, implies that there is a vocalic element (which he represents by [ə]) followed by an *r*-element (which he represents by [ɹ]).

Examples :

	R.P.	A.V.
bird	bɜˑd	bɜəd
hurt	hɜˑt	hɜət
girl	gɜˑl	gɜəl
convert	kənˈvɜˑt	kənˈvɜət

Note concerning [ɜˑr].

When, however, [ɜə] is followed immediately by [r], either in the same word or in the next word, the [ɜ] is lengthened and the [ə] is omitted. Thus:

	R.P.	A.V.
stir	stɜˑ	stɜə
stirring	ˈstɜˑrɪŋ	(same as R.P.)
stir away	stɜˑr əˈweɪ	(same as R.P.)
fur	fɜˑ	fɜə
furry	ˈfɜˑrɪ	(same as R.P.)

VARIANT 6. [ɛɚ] for [ɛə].

With the exception of speakers in "most parts of New England, New York City and vicinity, the South-East, and a large part of the South of the United States" (Kenyon), the majority of speakers in America replace or tend to replace Received Pronunciation [ɛə] by a variant which we represent by the symbol [ɛɚ].

The variation consists in replacing the vowel [ə] by the retroflex variety [ɚ]. See Variant 3.

Examples :

	R.P.	A.V.
care	kɛə	kɛɚ
dare	dɛə	dɛɚ
fair	fɛə	fɛɚ
wear	wɛə	wɛɚ

Note concerning [ɛər].

When, however, [ɛə] is followed immediately by [r], the variant is generally [ɛˑr]. Thus:

	R.P.	A.V.
fair	fɛə	fɛɚ
fairy	'fɛərɪ	'fɛˑrɪ
wear	wɛə	wɛɚ
wearing	'wɛərɪŋ	'wɛˑrɪŋ

See Variant 12.

VARIANT 7. [ɔɚ] for [ɔˑ] and [ɔə].

In a certain important category of the words containing in R.P. the vowel [ɔˑ], or its R.P. variant [ɔə], the majority of speakers in America replace or tend to replace this phone by a variant which we represent by the symbol [ɔɚ]. This variant, however, is not commonly used by speakers in "most parts of New England, New York City and vicinity, the South-East, and a large part of the South of the United States" (Kenyon).

The variation consists in adding the retroflex vowel [ɚ] or in using it in place of [ə].

See Variant 3.

Examples :

	R.P.	A.V.
corn	kɔ·n	kɔən
fork	fɔ·k	fɔək
war	wɔ·, wɔə	wɔə
Norway	ˈnɔ·weɪ	ˈnɔəweɪ

Note concerning [ɔ·r] and [ɔər].

When, however, [ɔ·] is followed immediately by [r], instead of [ɔər] we generally hear [ɔ·r]. Thus:

	R.P.	A.V.
nor	nɔ·	nɔə
nor I	nɔ·r aɪ	(same as R.P.)
for	fɔ·	fɔə
for it	fɔ·r ɪt	(same as R.P.)
adore	əˈdɔə	əˈdɔə
adoring	əˈdɔərɪŋ	əˈdɔ·rɪŋ

See Variant 12.

VARIANT 8. [oə] for [ɔə], [ɔ·].

In an important category of the words containing in Received Standard the vowel [ɔə] (in most cases with [ɔ·] as a variant), the majority of speakers in America replace or tend to replace this [ɔə] by a variant which we represent by the symbol [oə]. In the pronunciation of speakers in "most parts of New England, New York City and vicinity, the South-East and a large part of the South of the United States" (Kenyon) this particular variant is commonly replaced by [oə].

See "Variants Omitted."

The main variation consists in replacing [ɔ] by [o]. The secondary variation consists in replacing [ə] by the retroflex variety [ə].

Examples :

	R.P.	A.V.
force	fɔəs, fɔ·s	foəs
mourn	mɔən, mɔ·n	moən
store	stɔə, stɔ·	stoə
four	fɔə, fɔ·	foə

Note concerning [ɔər].

When, however, [ɔə] is followed immediately by [r], instead of [oər], we generally hear [o·r]. Thus:

	R.P.	A.V.
store	stɔə	stoə
story	'stɔ·rɩ	'sto·rɩ
pour	pɔə	poə
pouring	'pɔərɩŋ	'po·rɩŋ

See Variant 12.

VARIANT 9. [ɜr] for [ʌr].

In most cases in which R.P. has [ʌr], a large number of speakers in America use [ɜr].

Examples :

	R.P.	A.V.
hurry	'hʌrɩ	'hɜrɩ
hurried	'hʌrɩd	'hɜrɩd
worry	'wʌrɩ	'wɜrɩ
thorough	'θʌrə	'θɜrə

(But *borough* apparently remains ['bʌroʊ].)

VARIANT 10. [ɛrɩ] for [ərɩ].

The ending *-ary* or *-ery* is generally pronounced in R.P. as [ərɩ]. The majority of speakers in America pronounce it as [ɛrɩ].

Examples :

	R.P.	A.V.
customary	'kʌstəmərɩ	'kʌstəmɛrɩ
dictionary	'dɩkʃənərɩ	'dɩkʃənɛrɩ
ordinary	'ɔ·dɩnərɩ	'ɔ·dɩnɛrɩ
stationary	'steɩʃənərɩ	'steɩʃənɛrɩ

VARIANT 11. [orɩ] for [ərɩ].

The ending *-ory* is generally pronounced in R.P. as [ərɩ]. The majority of speakers in America pronounce it as [orɩ].

Examples :

	R.P.	A.V.
category	'kætɩgərɩ	'kætɩgorɩ
oratory	'ɒrətərɩ	'ɑrətorɩ
preparatory	prɩ'pærətərɩ	prɩ'pærətorɩ
territory	'tɛrɩtərɩ	'tɛrɩtorɩ

Variant 12. Omission of [ə].

Under the heading "Variant 3" we have noted that R.P. [ə] may have as an A.V. [ɚ], or that it may undergo no change. In the following cases, however, R.P. [ə] is represented neither by [ɚ] nor by [ə] but by an omission of the vowel (with or without lengthening of the preceding vowel):

R.P. [ɪər], [ʊər], [ɛər], [ɔər], [aɪər], and [aʊər].

See notes to Variants 3, 6, 7, and 8.

Examples :

	R.P.	A.V.
fearing	ˈfɪərɪŋ	ˈfɪˑrɪŋ
fear it	ˈfɪər ɪt	ˈfɪˑr ɪt
touring	ˈtʊərɪŋ	ˈtʊˑrɪŋ
tour and . . .	ˈtʊər ənd . . .	ˈtʊˑr ənd . . .
during	ˈdjʊərɪŋ	ˈdjʊˑrɪŋ
Europe	ˈjʊərəp	ˈjʊˑrəp
caring	ˈkɛərɪŋ	ˈkɛˑrɪŋ
Mary	ˈmɛərɪ	ˈmɛˑrɪ
fairy	ˈfɛərɪ	ˈfɛˑrɪ

	R.P.	A.V.
wearing	ˈwɛərɪŋ	ˈwɛˑrɪŋ
wear it	ˈwɛər ɪt	ˈwɛˑr ɪt
warring	ˈwɔərɪŋ	ˈwɔˑrɪŋ
war of	ˈwɔər əv	ˈwɔˑr əv
soaring	ˈsɔˑrɪŋ	ˈsoˑrɪŋ
story	ˈstɔˑrɪ	ˈstoˑrɪ
pour out	pɔˑr ˈaʊt	poˑr ˈaʊt

In all the above cases the preceding vowel is lengthened as a compensation for the omission of [ə].

	R.P.	A.V.
firing	ˈfaɪərɪŋ	ˈfaɪrɪŋ
fire away	faɪər əˈweɪ	faɪr əˈweɪ
environment	ɪnˈvaɪərənmənt	ɪnˈvaɪrənmənt
overpowering	oʊvəˈpaʊərɪŋ	oʊvəˈpaʊrɪŋ

Miscellaneous Variants

In addition to the 12 groups of variants noted above, there will be found a number of smaller groups, and of individual words in which variations from R.P. may be noted. Among these are, for instance, the well-known variants:

	R.P.	A.V.
clerk	klɑˑk	klɜək
mayor	mɛə	meɪə
schedule	′ʃɛdjul	′skɛdjul
lieutenant	lɛf′tɛnənt	lu′tɛnənt

American Variants not noted in the Dictionary

In addition to the American Variants indicated in this dictionary, American pronunciation is or may be marked by other and minor variants. Most of these may be covered by conventions, the chief of which are indicated below.

(1) [ɯˑ] for [uˑ] and [ɯ] for [ʊ]. Some speakers articulate [uˑ] and [ʊ] with little lip-rounding, and the tongue in an advanced position so that they approximate to the sound represented in phonetic notation by [ɯ].

(2) [eˑ] or [e] for [eɪ]. Many speakers replace the kinetic (or diphthongal) vowel [eɪ] by vowels tending towards the static [e]. This is especially the case in unstressed syllables. But in very few cases is the [e] so markedly static as the [e] of certain Scottish pronunciations. Thus *take* may be heard as [teˑk], and *allocate* as [′æləket].

(3) [oˑ] or [o] for [oʊ]. Many speakers replace the kinetic (or diphthongal) vowel [oʊ] by vowels tending towards the static [oˑ]. This is especially the case in unstressed syllables. But in very few cases is the [o] so markedly static as the [o] of certain Scottish pronunciations. Thus *home* may be heard as [hoˑm], and *obey* as [o′beɪ].

(4) In general, the vowel represented by [ɛ] tends to be articulated in a more open position than in R.P.

(5) [eə] for [ɛə]. Some speakers tend to replace [ɛə] by [eə]. Thus *care* may be heard as [keə], and, as a consequence, the distinction between *fairy* and *ferry* may be heard as [′feˑrɪ] and [′fɛrɪ].

(6) [ɹ] for [ɚ]. Some speakers use in place of the retroflex vowel [ɚ] sounds more closely approximating to a consonant *r*, thus *better* may be heard as [′bɛtər].

(7) [ə] for [ɪ]. The tendency to use in certain categories of words [ə] for [ɪ] is more marked among users of the A.V. pronunciation than among users of R.P. Thus:

['kærɪz] (*carries*) tends to ['kærəz]
['kærɪd] (*carried*) tends to ['kærəd]
['juˑslɪs] (*useless*) tends to ['juˑsləs]
['gʊdnɪs] (*goodness*) tends to ['gʊdnəs].

It is difficult to say to what extent this is the result of speakers (possibly aiming at a "careful" pronunciation) tending to make their pronunciation conform to the conventional spelling.

These seven categories of non-recorded variants seem fairly usual, and are not considered by Americans to represent any particular local or undesirable dialect. As much cannot be said for the seven following categories. Most educated Americans would probably consider them as undesirable pronunciations and would never deliberately set out to teach them to foreign students of English.

(8) [ɔ] for [ɒ]. Some speakers tend to replace in certain words [ɒ] by [ɔ]. Thus *on, long,* etc., may be pronounced by such speakers as [ɔn], [lɔŋ], etc.

(9) [æʊ] for [aʊ]. Certain speakers in the States adjoining the Atlantic seaboard tend to replace [a] by [æ] as the first element of the diphthong. Thus [haʊs] (*house*) may be heard as [hæʊs]. The tendency is not unknown in England.

(10) [uˑ] for [juˑ]. Some speakers habitually make this substitution in a very large number of words. Thus [njuˑ] *new* may be heard as [nuˑ].

(11) [œy] for [ɜˑ]. The vowel [œy] seems identical in acoustic effect with the Dutch *ui* in *huis*, and is distinct from the [ɔɪ] of the admittedly vulgar variety of New York dialect.

[œy] is used by a large number of educated speakers in the Southern States, and [bɜəd] (*bird*) is heard as [bœyd].

(12) *Flapped t.* Many speakers replace plosive [t] by a "flapped" variety, giving the effect of an *r*. Thus *thirty, forty,* may give the impression of *thirry, forry.*

(13) *Flapped n.* When *n* is followed by *t*, many speakers

tend to combine the *n* and the *t* in a sound known as "flapped-*n*." Thus, *twenty*, *wanted*, give the impression of *twenny*, *wannid*.

(14) *Nasal Vowels*. In certain of the Eastern States, especially in New England, many speakers tend to nasalize the vowels.

We may take the opportunity to note here an interesting fact concerning certain phenomena of "weakening." It is assumed by users of R.P. that in typical American pronunciation, weakening is more prevalent than in R.P., and they will point to such occasional weak forms as [gə] *go*, [kəm] *come*, or *too* [tə], as in [gə ˈhoum] *go home*, [kəm ˈhiə] *come here*, [tə ˈbæˑd] *too bad*. Similarly users of typical American assume the same thing of R.P. pointing to such occasional weak forms as [noubədɩ] *nobody* or [n̩ɩθɪŋ] *anything*. As a matter of fact, honours seem to be about evenly divided in this respect. "Mr. Martin of Birmingham" will be pronounced in R.P. as [mɪstə ˈmɑˑtɪn əv ˈbɜˑmɪŋəm], with the *i* of Martin pronounced very distinctly and the *ham* of *Birmingham* reduced to [əm]. The user of the pronunciation represented in the A.V. column, on the contrary, will pronounce [mɪstə ˈmɑətn̩ əv ˈbəˑmɪŋhæm], with the *i* of Martin omitted, but with the *ham* of *Birmingham* given its full value.

NOTE BY THE AMERICAN COLLABORATOR

THE foregoing introduction has dealt with the main purpose or purposes of this book. It remains only for a brief word to be added concerning the matter of variants.

The scope and size of the present book admit of only a minimum of variants. These have been selected with great care. All available trustworthy authorities[1] have been consulted. Unfortunately (or is it fortunately?) there is no *commonly accepted* Received Standard American English pronunciation and therefore no final authority on the subject can be cited. Scholars who have attempted to deal with the subject often do not agree, and in consequence the compiler of such a book as this is compelled to sum up the pros and cons and record his findings. If a tie occurs, his personal opinion must then be exercised and added to one side or the other. Happily in the present work this has not been frequently the case. Indeed, only a few such instances have occurred. Nevertheless, the undersigned holds himself responsible for the variants recorded, and while realizing the impossibility of avoiding some mistakes, and while further realizing the utter hopelessness of meeting the approval of all his fellow American teachers and American phoneticians, he hopes that his errors may be few and that his critics will be charitable.

It will of course be understood by users of this book that the omissions in the third column merely indicate that Received Pronunciation is most commonly used for those words in America as well as in England.

As this part of the dictionary is pioneer work it may serve either as a guide to some abler person to do a more perfect and completer work, or as a warning of what is good not to do.

JAMES VICTOR MARTIN.

AOYAMA GAKUIN, TOKYO,
July 1, 1926.

[1] Particular mention may be made of Krapp, Kenyon and Hempl.

FURTHER NOTE

THIS third preface is at once an apology and a minority report. The apology is for any textual errors and misprints that may have been overlooked in preparing the MS. for the press and in marking the proofs. For such errors my colleagues are in no way to blame.

For the plan and general conception of the book I can claim no credit and in certain details of treatment,—notably, the selection of words and the inclusion or rejection of variant pronunciations,—I have very rarely modified the original draft even when I may have felt some modification to be desirable.

I am in entire agreement with my colleagues on the important question of the value of differentiating [ɪ] and [ɩ]. In the present work we have rigidly observed the rule of keeping [ɪ] in stressed syllables only; but I think it safe to say that when much work of observation and reclassification has been done, which lack of time prevents for the purpose of this dictionary, a further very important distinction will be established, namely, certain categories of *unstressed* syllables in which [ɪ] alone can occur and cannot be replaced by any "obscure" vowel.

I hope to be able before long to offer the results of such observation to those who may be interested.

F. G. BLANDFORD.

CAMBRIDGE,
Sept. 1926.

A

Traditional Spelling	Received Pronunciation	American Variants
A	eɪ	
A's	eɪz	
a	eɪ *s.f.*, ə *w.f.*	
aback	ə'bæk	
abandon	ə'bændən	
abandons	ə'bændənz	
abandoned	ə'bændənd	
abandoning	ə'bændənɪŋ	
abate	ə'beɪt	
abates	ə'beɪts	
abated	ə'beɪtɪd	
abating	ə'beɪtɪŋ	
abbey	'æbɪ	
abbeys	'æbɪz	
abbreviate	ə'bri·vɪeɪt	
abbreviates	ə'bri·vɪeɪts	
abbreviated	ə'bri·vɪeɪtɪd	
abbreviating	ə'bri·vɪeɪtɪŋ	
abbreviation	əbrivɪ'eɪʃən	
abbreviations	əbrivɪ'eɪʃənz	
abdicate	'æbdɪkeɪt	
abdicates	'æbdɪkeɪts	
abdicated	'æbdɪkeɪtɪd	
abdicating	'æbdɪkeɪtɪŋ	
abdication	æbdɪ'keɪʃən	
abdications	æbdɪ'keɪʃənz	
abdomen	æb'doʊmən	
abdomens	æb'doʊmənz	
abdominal	æb'dɒmɪnl̩	æb'dɑmɪnl̩
abduct	əb'dʌkt	
abducts	əb'dʌkts	
abducted	əb'dʌktɪd	
abducting	əb'dʌktɪŋ	
abduction	əb'dʌkʃən	
abductions	əb'dʌkʃənz	
abhor	əb'hɔ·(r	əb'hɔə
abhors	əb'hɔ·z	əb'hɔəz
abhorred	əb'hɔ·d	əb'hɔəd
abhorring	əb'hɔ·rɪŋ	
abhorrence	əb'hɒrəns	əb'hɑrəns
abhorrent	əb'hɒrənt	əb'hɑrənt
ability	ə'bɪlɪtɪ	
abilities	ə'bɪlɪtɪz	

Traditional Spelling	Received Pronunciation	American Variants
able	ˈeɪbl̩	
abler	ˈeɪblə(r	eɪblə
ablest	ˈeɪblɪst	
ably	ˈeɪblɪ	
abnormal	æbˈnɔˑməl	æbˈnɔəməl
abnormally	æbˈnɔˑməlɪ	æbˈnɔəməlɪ
aboard	əˈbɔˑd	əˈbɔəd
abolish	əˈbɒlɪʃ	əˈbɑlɪʃ
abolishes	əˈbɒlɪʃɪz	əˈbɑlɪʃɪz
abolished	əˈbɒlɪʃt	əˈbɑlɪʃt
abolishing	əˈbɒlɪʃɪŋ	əˈbɑlɪʃɪŋ
abolition	æbəˈlɪʃən	
abominable	əˈbɒmɪnəbl̩	əˈbɑmɪnəbl̩
abominably	əˈbɒmɪnəblɪ	əˈbɑmɪnəblɪ
abound	əˈbaʊnd	
abounds	əˈbaʊndz	
abounded	əˈbaʊndɪd	
abounding	əˈbaʊndɪŋ	
about	əˈbaʊt	
above	əˈbʌv	
abreast	əˈbrɛst	
abridge	əˈbrɪʤ	
abridges	əˈbrɪʤɪz	
abridged	əˈbrɪʤd	
abridging	əˈbrɪʤɪŋ	
abroad	əˈbrɔˑd	
abrupt	əˈbrʌpt	
abruptly	əˈbrʌptlɪ	
abruptness	əˈbrʌptnɪs	
abscond	əbˈskɒnd	əbˈskɑnd
absconds	əbˈskɒndz	əbˈskɑndz
absconded	əbˈskɒndɪd	əbˈskɑndɪd
absconding	əbˈskɒndɪŋ	əbˈskɑndɪŋ
absence	ˈæbsn̩s	
absences	ˈæbsn̩sɪz	
absent, *adj.*	ˈæbsn̩t	
absent	əbˈsɛnt	
absents	əbˈsɛnts	
absented	əbˈsɛntɪd	
absenting	əbˈsɛntɪŋ	
absent-minded	ˈæbsn̩tˈmaɪndɪd	
absolute	ˈæbsəlut	
absolutely	ˈæbsəlutlɪ	
absolve	əbˈzɒlv	əbˈsɑlv
absolves	əbˈzɒlvz	əbˈsɑlvz
absolved	əbˈzɒlvd	əbˈsɑlvd
absolving	əbˈzɒlvɪŋ	əbˈsɑlvɪŋ

Traditional Spelling	Received Pronunciation	American Variants
absorb	əb'sɔ·b	əb'sɔəb
absorbs	əb'sɔ·bz	əb'sɔəbz
absorbed	əb'sɔ·bd	əb'sɔəbd
absorbing	əb'sɔ·bɪŋ	əb'sɔəbɪŋ
abstain	əb'steɪn	
abstains	əb'steɪnz	
abstained	əb'steɪnd	
abstaining	əb'steɪnɪŋ	
abstainer	əb'steɪnə(r	əb'steɪnə
abstainers	əb'steɪnəz	əb'steɪnəz
abstemious	əb'sti·mɪəs	
abstention	əb'stɛnʃən	
abstentions	əb'stɛnʃənz	
abstinence	'æbstɪnəns	
abstinent	'æbstɪnənt	
abstract, *noun, adj.*	'æbstrækt	
absurd	əb'sɜ·d	əb'sɜəd
absurdly	əb'sɜ·dlɪ	əb'sɜədlɪ
absurdity	əb'sɜ·dɪtɪ	əb'sɜədɪtɪ
absurdities	əb'sɜ·dɪtɪz	əb'sɜədɪtɪz
abundance	ə'bʌndəns	
abundant	ə'bʌndənt	
abundantly	ə'bʌndəntlɪ	
abuse, *noun*	ə'bju·s	
abuses	ə'bju·sɪz	
abuse, *verb*	ə'bju·z	
abuses	ə'bju·zɪz	
abused	ə'bju·zd	
abusing	ə'bju·zɪŋ	
abusive	ə'bju·sɪv	
academic	ækə'dɛmɪk	
academy	ə'kædəmɪ	
academies	ə'kædəmɪz	
accede	ək'si·d	
accedes	ək'si·dz	
acceded	ək'si·dɪd	
acceding	ək'si·dɪŋ	
accent, *noun*	'æksənt	
accents	'æksənts	
accent, *verb*	ək'sɛnt	
accents	ək'sɛnts	
accented	ək'sɛntɪd	
accenting	ək'sɛntɪŋ	
accentuate	ək'sɛntjueɪt	
accentuates	ək'sɛntjueɪts	
accentuated	ək'sɛntjueɪtɪd	
accentuating	ək'sɛntjueɪtɪŋ	

Traditional Spelling	Received Pronunciation	American Variants
accentuation	əksɛntjuˈeɪʃən	
accentuations	əksɛntjuˈeɪʃənz	
accept	əkˈsɛpt	
accepts	əkˈsɛpts	
accepted	əkˈsɛptɪd	
accepting	əkˈsɛptɪŋ	
acceptable	əkˈsɛptəbl̩	
acceptably	əkˈsɛptəblɪ	
acceptance	ˈsɛptəns	
acceptances	əkˈsɛptənsɪz	
acceptation	æksɛpˈteɪʃən	
acceptations	æksɛpˈteɪʃənz	
access	ˈæksɛs	
accessible	əkˈsɛsɪbl̩, əkˈsɛsəbl̩	
accession	əkˈsɛʃən	
accident	ˈæksɪdənt	
accidents	ˈæksɪdənts	
accidental	æksɪˈdɛntl̩	
accidentally	æksɪˈdɛntəlɪ	
acclimatize	əˈklaɪmətaɪz	
acclimatizes	əˈklaɪmətaɪzɪz	
acclimatized	əˈklaɪmətaɪzd	
acclimatizing	əˈklaɪmətaɪzɪŋ	
accommodate	əˈkɒmədeɪt	əˈkɑmədeɪt
accommodates	əˈkɒmədeɪts	əˈkɑmədeɪts
accommodated	əˈkɒmədeɪtɪd	əˈkɑmədeɪtɪd
accommodating	əˈkɒmədeɪtɪŋ	əˈkɑmədeɪtɪŋ
accommodation	əkɒməˈdeɪʃən	əkɑməˈdeɪʃən
accommodations	əkɒməˈdeɪʃənz	əkɑməˈdeɪʃənz
accompaniment	əˈkʌmpənɪmənt	
accompaniments	əˈkʌmpənɪmənts	
accompanist	əˈkʌmpənɪst	
accompanists	əˈkʌmpənɪsts	
accompany	əˈkʌmpənɪ	
accompanies	əˈkʌmpənɪz	
accompanied	əˈkʌmpənɪd	
accompanying	əˈkʌmpənɪɪŋ	
accomplice	əˈkɒmplɪs	əˈkɑmplɪs
accomplices	əˈkɒmplɪsɪz	əˈkɑmplɪsɪz
accomplish	əˈkɒmplɪʃ	əˈkɑmplɪʃ
accomplishes	əˈkɒmplɪʃɪz	əˈkɑmplɪʃɪz
accomplished	əˈkɒmplɪʃt	əˈkɑmplɪʃt
accomplishing	əˈkɒmplɪʃɪŋ	əˈkɑmplɪʃɪŋ
accomplishment	əˈkɒmplɪʃmənt	əˈkɑmplɪʃmənt
accomplishments	əˈkɒmplɪʃmənts	əˈkɑmplɪʃmənts
accord	əˈkɔˑd	əˈkɔəd
accords	əˈkɔˑdz	əˈkɔədz

Traditional Spelling	Received Pronunciation	American Variants
accorded	ə'kɔ·dɪd	ə'kɔədɪd
according	ə'kɔ·dɪŋ	ə'kɔədɪŋ
accordance	ə'kɔ·dəns	ə'kɔədəns
accordingly	ə'kɔ·dɪŋlɪ	ə'kɔədɪŋlɪ
account	ə'kaʊnt	
accounts	ə'kaʊnts	
accounted	ə'kaʊntɪd	
accounting	ə'kaʊntɪŋ	
accountable	ə'kaʊntəbl̩	
accountant	ə'kaʊntənt	
accountants	ə'kaʊntənts	
accumulate	ə'kju·mjʊleɪt	
accumulates	ə'kju·mjʊleɪts	
accumulated	ə'kju·mjʊleɪtɪd	
accumulating	ə'kju·mjʊleɪtɪŋ	
accumulative	ə'kju·mjʊleɪtɪv	
accumulation	əkjumjʊ'leɪʃən	
accumulations	əkjumjʊ'leɪʃənz	
accuracy	'ækjʊrəsɪ	
accurate	'ækjʊrɪt	
accurately	'ækjʊrɪtlɪ	
accusation	ækjʊ'zeɪʃən	
accusations	ækjʊ'zeɪʃənz	
accuse	ə'kju·z	
accuses	ə'kju·zɪz	
accused	ə'kju·zd	
accusing	ə'kju·zɪŋ	
accustom	ə'kʌstəm	
accustoms	ə'kʌstəmz	
accustomed	ə'kʌstəmd	
accustoming	ə'kʌstəmɪŋ	
ace	'eɪs	
aces	'eɪsɪz	
acetylene	ə'sɛtɪlin	
ache	'eɪk	
aches	'eɪks	
ached	'eɪkt	
aching	'eɪkɪŋ	
achieve	ə'tʃi·v	
achieves	ə'tʃi·vz	
achieved	ə'tʃi·vd	
achieving	ə'tʃi·vɪŋ	
achievement	ə'tʃi·vmənt	
achievements	ə'tʃi·vmənts	
acid	'æsɪd	
acids	'æsɪdz	
acidity	ə'sɪdɪtɪ	

Traditional Spelling	Received Pronunciation	American Variants
acknowledge	ək'nɒlɪʤ	ək'nɑlɪʤ
acknowledges	ək'nɒlɪʤɪz	ək'nɑlɪʤɪz
acknowledged	ək'nɒlɪʤd	ək'nɑlɪʤd
acknowledging	ək'nɒlɪʤɪŋ	ək'nɑlɪʤɪŋ
acknowledgment	ək'nɒlɪʤmənt	ək'nɑlɪʤmənt
acknowledgments	ək'nɒlɪʤmənts	ək'nɑlɪʤmənts
acorn	'eɪkɔ·n	'eɪkɔən
acorns	'eɪkɔ·nz	'eɪkɔənz
acoustic	ə'kaʊstɪk, ə'ku·stɪk	
acoustically	ə'kaʊstɪkəlɪ, ə'ku·stɪkəlɪ	
acoustics	ə'kaʊstɪks, ə'ku·stɪks	
acquaint	ə'kweɪnt	
acquaints	ə'kweɪnts	
acquainted	ə'kweɪntɪd	
acquainting	ə'kweɪntɪŋ	
acquaintance	ə'kweɪntəns	
acquaintances	ə'kweɪntənsɪz	
acquaintanceship	ə'kweɪntənsʃɪp	
acquaintanceships	ə'kweɪntənsʃɪps	
acquiesce	ækwɪ'ɛs	
acquiesces	ækwɪ'ɛsɪz	
acquiesced	ækwɪ'ɛst	
acquiescing	ækwɪ'ɛsɪŋ	
acquire	ə'kwaɪə(r	ə'kwaɪə
acquires	ə'kwaɪəz	ə'kwaɪəz
acquired	ə'kwaɪəd	ə'kwaɪəd
acquiring	ə'kwaɪərɪŋ	ə'kwaɪrɪŋ
acquirement	ə'kwaɪəmənt	ə'kwaɪəmənt
acquirements	ə'kwaɪəmənts	ə'kwaɪəmənts
acquisition	ækwɪ'zɪʃən	
acquisitions	ækwɪ'zɪʃənz	
acquit	ə'kwɪt	
acquits	ə'kwɪts	
acquitted	ə'kwɪtɪd	
acquitting	ə'kwɪtɪŋ	
acre	'eɪkə(r	eɪkə
acres	'eɪkəz	'eɪkəz
acrimonious	ækrɪ'moʊnjəs	
acrimoniously	ækrɪ'moʊnjəslɪ	
acrobat	'ækrəbæt	
acrobats	'ækrəbæts	
acrobatic	ækrə'bætɪk	
across	ə'krɔs, ə'krɒs	
acrostic	ə'krɒstɪk	
acrostics	ə'krɒstɪks	
act	'ækt	

Traditional Spelling	Received Pronunciation	American Variants
acts	ˈækts	
acted	ˈæktɪd	
acting	ˈæktɪŋ	
action	ˈækʃən	
actions	ˈækʃənz	
active	ˈæktɪv	
activity	ækˈtɪvɪtɪ	
activities	ækˈtɪvɪtɪz	
actively	ˈæktɪvlɪ	
actor	ˈæktə(r	ˈæktə
actors	ˈæktəz	ˈæktəz
actress	ˈæktrɪs	
actresses	ˈæktrɪsɪz	
actual	ˈæktjʊəl	
actually	ˈæktjʊəlɪ	
actuality	æktjʊˈælɪtɪ	
actualities	æktjʊˈælɪtɪz	
actuary	ˈæktjʊərɪ	ˈæktjʊɛrɪ
actuaries	ˈæktjʊərɪz	ˈæktjʊɛrɪz
acute	əˈkjuˑt	
acuter	əˈkjuˑtə(r	əˈkjuˑtə
acutest	əˈkjuˑtɪst	
acutely	əˈkjuˑtlɪ	
acuteness	əˈkjuˑtnɪs	
A.D.	ˈeɪˈdiˑ(ˈænoʊˈdɒmɪnaɪ)	
adapt	əˈdæpt	
adapts	əˈdæpts	
adapted	əˈdæptɪd	
adapting	əˈdæptɪŋ	
adaptability	ədæptəˈbɪlɪtɪ	
adaptable	əˈdæptəbl̩	
adaptation	ædæpˈteɪʃən	
adaptations	ædæpˈteɪʃənz	
add	ˈæd	
adds	ˈædz	
added	ˈædɪd	
adding	ˈædɪŋ	
addition	əˈdɪʃən	
additions	əˈdɪʃənz	
additional	əˈdɪʃənəl	
address	əˈdrɛs	
addresses	əˈdrɛsɪz	
addressed	əˈdrɛst	
addressing	əˈdrɛsɪŋ	
adept, ***noun***	ˈædɛpt, əˈdɛpt	
adepts	ˈædɛpts, əˈdɛpts	
adept, ***adj.***	əˈdɛpt, æˈdɛpt	

Traditional Spelling	Received Pronunciation	American Variants
adequacy	ˈædɪkwəsɪ	
adequate	ˈædɪkwɪt	
adequately	ˈædɪkwɪtlɪ	
adhere	ədˈhɪə(r	ədˈhɪə
adheres	ədˈhɪəz	ədˈhɪəz
adhered	ədˈhɪəd	ədˈhɪəd
adhering	ədˈhɪərɪŋ	ədˈhɪˑrɪŋ
adherer	ədˈhɪərə(r	ədˈhɪˑrə
adherers	ədˈhɪərəz	ədˈhɪˑrəz
adherence	ədˈhɪərəns	ədˈhɪˑrəns
adherent	ədˈhɪərənt	ədˈhɪˑrənt
adherents	ədˈhɪərənts	ədˈhɪˑrənts
adhesion	ədˈhiˑʒən	
adhesions	ədˈhiˑʒənz	
adjectival	ædʒɪkˈtaɪvəl	
adjectivally	ædʒɪkˈtaɪvəlɪ	
adjective	ˈædʒɪktɪv	
adjectives	ˈædʒɪktɪvz	
adjoin	əˈdʒɔɪn	
adjoins	əˈdʒɔɪnz	
adjoined	əˈdʒɔɪnd	
adjoining	əˈdʒɔɪnɪŋ	
adjourn	əˈdʒɜˑn	əˈdʒɜən
adjourns	əˈdʒɜˑnz	əˈdʒɜənz
adjourned	əˈdʒɜˑnd	əˈdʒɜənd
adjourning	əˈdʒɜˑnɪŋ	əˈdʒɜənɪŋ
adjournment	əˈdʒɜˑnmənt	əˈdʒɜənmənt
adjournments	əˈdʒɜˑnmənts	əˈdʒɜənmənts
adjunct	ˈædʒʌŋkt	
adjuncts	ˈædʒʌŋkts	
adjust	əˈdʒʌst	
adjusts	əˈdʒʌsts	
adjusted	əˈdʒʌstɪd	
adjusting	əˈdʒʌstɪŋ	
adjustment	əˈdʒʌstmənt	
adjustments	əˈdʒʌstmənts	
adjutant	ˈædʒutənt	
adjutants	ˈædʒutənts	
administer	ədˈmɪnɪstə(r	ədˈmɪnɪstə
administers	ədˈmɪnɪstəz	ədˈmɪnɪstəz
administered	ədˈmɪnɪstəd	ədˈmɪnɪstəd
administering	ədˈmɪnɪstərɪŋ	
administration	ədmɪnɪsˈtreɪʃən	
administrations	ədmɪnɪsˈtreɪʃənz	
administrative	ədˈmɪnɪstrətɪv	ədˈmɪnɪstreɪtɪv
administrator	ədˈmɪnɪstreɪtə	
admirable	ˈædmərəbl̩	

Traditional Spelling	Received Pronunciation	American Variants
admirably	'ædmərəbl̩ɪ	
admiral	'ædmərəl	
admirals	'ædmərəlz	
admiralty	'ædmərəltɪ	
admiration	ædmə'reɪʃən	
admire	əd'maɪə(r	əd'maɪə
admires	əd'maɪəz	əd'maɪəz
admired	əd'maɪəd	əd'maɪəd
admiring	əd'maɪərɪŋ	əd'maɪrɪŋ
admiringly	əd'maɪərɪŋlɪ	əd'maɪrɪŋlɪ
admissible	əd'mɪsɪbl̩	
admission	əd'mɪʃən	
admissions	əd'mɪʃənz	
admit	əd'mɪt	
admits	əd'mɪts	
admitted	əd'mɪtɪd	
admitting	əd'mɪtɪŋ	
admittedly	əd'mɪtɪdlɪ	
admittance	əd'mɪtəns	
admittances	əd'mɪtənsɪz	
ado	ə'duˑ	
adolescence	ædə'lɛsəns	
adolescent	ædə'lɛsənt	
adopt	ə'dɒpt	ə'dɑpt
adopts	ə'dɒpts	ə'dɑpts
adopted	ə'dɒptɪd	ə'dɑptɪd
adopting	ə'dɒptɪŋ	ə'dɑptɪŋ
adoption	ə'dɒpʃən	ə'dɑpʃən
adoptions	ə'dɒpʃənz	ə'dɑpʃənz
adorable	ə'dɔˑrəbl̩	
adorably	ə'dɔˑrəbl̩ɪ	
adoration	ædə'reɪʃən	
adorations	ædə'reɪʃənz	
adore	ə'dɔə(r	ə'dɔə
adores	ə'dɔəz	ə'dɔəz
adored	ə'dɔəd	ə'dɔəd
adoring	ə'dɔərɪŋ	ə'dɔˑrɪŋ
adorer	ə'dɔərə(r	ə'dɔˑrə
adorers	ə'dɔərəz	ə'dɔˑrəz
adorn	ə'dɔˑn	ə'dɔən
adorns	ə'dɔˑnz	ə'dɔənz
adorned	ə'dɔˑnd	ə'dɔənd
adorning	ə'dɔˑnɪŋ	ə'dɔənɪŋ
adornment	ə'dɔˑnmənt	ə'dɔənmənt
adornments	ə'dɔˑnmənts	ə'dɔənmənts
adrift	ə'drɪft	
adult	ə'dʌlt	

Traditional Spelling	Received Pronunciation	American Variants
adults	ə'dʌlts	
adulterate	ə'dʌltəreɪt	
adulterates	ə'dʌltəreɪts	
adulterated	ə'dʌltəreɪtɪd	
adultering	ə'dʌltəreɪtɪŋ	
adulteration	ədʌltə'reɪʃən	
adulterations	ədʌltə'reɪʃənz	
advance	əd'vɑːns	əd'vaːns
advances	əd'vɑːnsɪz	əd'vaːnsɪz
advanced	əd'vɑːnst	əd'vanst
advancing	əd'vɑːnsɪŋ	əd'vansɪŋ
advantage	əd'vɑːntɪʤ	əd'vantɪʤ
advantages	əd'vɑːntɪʤɪz	əd'vantɪʤiz
advantageous	ædvən'teɪʤəs	
advantageously	ædvən'teɪʤəslɪ	
adventure	əd'vɛntʃə(r	əd'vɛntʃə
adventures	əd'vɛntʃəz	əd'vɛntʃəz
adventurous	əd'vɛntʃərəs	
adverb	'ædvɜb	'ædvɜəb
adverbs	'ædvɜbz	'ædvɜəbz
adverbial	əd'vɜːbɪəl	əd'vɜəbɪəl
adverbially	əd'vɜːbɪəlɪ	əd'vɜəbɪəlɪ
adverse	'ædvɜs	'ædvɜəs
adversely	'æd'vɜːslɪ	'æd'vɜəslɪ
advertise	'ædvətaɪz	'ædvətaɪz
advertises	'ædvətaɪzɪz	'ædvətaɪzɪz
advertised	'ædvətaɪzd	'ædvətaɪzd
advertising	'ædvətaɪzɪŋ	'ædvətaɪziŋ
advertisement	əd'vɜːtɪsmənt	'ædvətaɪzmənt
advertisements	əd'vɜːtɪsmənts	'ædvətaɪzmənts
advice	əd'vaɪs	
advices	əd'vaɪsɪz	
advisability	ədvaɪzə'bɪlɪtɪ	
advisable	əd'vaɪzəbl̩	
advise	əd'vaɪz	
advises	əd'vaɪzɪz	
advised	əd'vaɪzd	
advising	əd'vaɪzɪŋ	
adviser	əd'vaɪzə(r	əd'vaɪzə
advisers	əd'vaɪzəz	əd'vaɪzəz
advisory	əd'vaɪzərɪ	
advocate	'ædvəkeɪt	
advocates	'ædvəkeɪts	
advocated	'ædvəkeɪtɪd	
advocating	'ædvəkeɪtɪŋ	
aerial	'ɛərɪəl	eɪ'iːrɪəl
aerially	'ɛərɪəlɪ	eɪ'iːrɪəlɪ

Traditional Spelling	Received Pronunciation	American Variants
aeronaut	′ɛərənɔt	
aeronauts	′ɛərənɔts	
aeronautic	ɛərə′nɔˑtɪk	
aeronautical	ɛərə′nɔˑtɪkəl	
aeronautics	ɛərə′nɔˑtɪks	
aeroplane	′ɛərəpleɪn	
aeroplanes	′ɛərəpleɪnz	
aesthetic	ɛs′θɛtɪk, is′θɛtɪk	
aesthetically	ɛs′θɛtɪkəlɪ, is′θɛtɪkəlɪ	
affable	′æfəbl̩	
affair	ə′fɛə(r	ə′fɛə
affairs	ə′fɛəz	ə′fɛəz
affect	ə′fɛkt	
affects	ə′fɛkts	
affected	ə′fɛktɪd	
affecting	ə′fɛktɪŋ	
affectation	æfɛk′teɪʃən	
affectations	æfɛk′teɪʃənz	
affection	ə′fɛkʃən	
affections	ə′fɛkʃənz	
affectionate	ə′fɛkʃənɪt	
affectionately	ə′fɛkʃənɪtlɪ	
affiliate	ə′fɪlɪeɪt	
affiliates	ə′fɪlɪeɪts	
affiliated	ə′fɪlɪeɪtɪd	
affiliating	ə′fɪlɪeɪtɪŋ	
affinity	ə′fɪnɪtɪ	
affinities	ə′fɪnɪtɪz	
affirm	ə′fɜˑm	ə′fɜəm
affirms	ə′fɜˑmz	ə′fɜəmz
affirmed	ə′fɜˑmd	ə′fɜəmd
affirming	ə′fɜˑmɪŋ	ə′fɜəmɪŋ
affirmation	æfə′meɪʃən	æfə′meɪʃən
affirmations	æfə′meɪʃənz	æfə′meɪʃənz
affirmative	ə′fɜˑmətiv	ə′fɜəmətiv
affirmatively	ə′fɜˑmətivlɪ	ə′fɜəmətivlɪ
afflict	ə′flɪkt	
afflicts	ə′flɪkts	
afflicted	ə′flɪktɪd	
afflicting	ə′flɪktɪŋ	
affliction	ə′flɪkʃən	
afflictions	ə′flɪkʃənz	
afford	ə′fɔˑd	ə′foəd
affords	ə′fɔˑdz	ə′foədz
afforded	ə′fɔˑdɪd	ə′foədɪd
affording	ə′fɔˑdɪŋ	ə′foədɪŋ
afraid	ə′freɪd	

Traditional Spelling	Received Pronunciation	American Variants
afresh	ə'frɛʃ	
Africa	'æfrɪkə	
African	'æfrɪkən	
Africans	'æfrɪkənz	
after	'ɑˑftə(r	'aˑftə
afternoon	ɑftə'nuˑn	aftə'nuˑn
afternoons	ɑftə'nuˑnz	aftə'nuˑnz
afterthought	'ɑˑftəθɔt	'aˑftəθɔt
afterwards	'ɑˑftəwədz	'aˑftəwədz
again	ə'geɪn, ə'gɛn	
against	ə'geɪnst, ə'gɛnst	
age	'eɪʤ	
ages	'eɪʤɪz	
aged, *adj.*	'eɪʤɪd	
agency	'eɪʤənsɪ	
agencies	'eɪʤənsɪz	
agent	'eɪʤənt	
agents	'eɪʤənts	
aggravate	'ægrəveɪt	
aggravates	'ægrəveɪts	
aggravated	'ægrəveɪtɪd	
aggravating	'ægrəveɪtɪŋ	
aggressive	ə'grɛsɪv	
aggressively	ə'grɛsɪvlɪ	
agile	'æʤaɪl	'æʤɪl
agility	ə'ʤɪlɪtɪ	
agitate	'æʤɪteɪt	
agitates	'æʤɪteɪts	
agitated	'æʤɪteɪtɪd	
agitating	'æʤɪteɪtɪŋ	
agitator	'æʤɪteɪtə(r	'æʤɪteɪtə
agitators	'æʤɪteɪtəz	'æʤɪteɪtəz
agitation	æʤɪ'teɪʃən	
agitations	æʤɪ'teɪʃənz	
agnostic	æg'nɒstɪk, əg'nɒstɪk	æg'nɑstɪk
agnostics	æg'nɒstɪks, əg'nɒstɪks	æg'nɑstɪks
ago	ə'goʊ	
agony	'ægənɪ	
agonies	'ægənɪz	
agree	ə'griˑ	
agrees	ə'griˑz	
agreed	ə'griˑd	
agreeing	ə'griˑɪŋ	
agreeable	ə'grɪəbl̩, ə'griˑəbl̩	
agreeably	ə'grɪəblɪ. ə'griˑəblɪ	
agreement	ə'griˑmənt	

Traditional Spelling	Received Pronunciation	American Variants
agreements	əˈgri·mənts	
agricultural	ægrɪˈkʌltʃərəl	
agriculture	ˈægrɪkʌltʃə(r	ˈægrɪkʌltʃə
aground	əˈgraʊnd	
ague	ˈeɪgju	
ah	ˈɑ·	
aha	ɑˈhɑ·	
ahead	əˈhɛd	
ahem	ˈm, ˈhm	
aid	ˈeɪd	
aids	ˈeɪdz	
aided	ˈeɪdɪd	
aiding	ˈeɪdɪŋ	
aim	eɪm	
aims	ˈeɪmz	
aimed	ˈeɪmd	
aiming	ˈeɪmɪŋ	
ain't	ˈeɪnt	
air	ɛə(r	ɛə
airs	ˈɛəz	ɛəz
aired	ˈɛəd	ɛəd
airing	ˈɛərɪŋ	ɛ·rɪŋ
airship	ˈɛəʃɪp	ˈɛəʃɪp
airships	ˈɛəʃɪps	ˈɛəʃɪps
aisle	aɪl	
aisles	ˈaɪlz	
aitch, H	eɪtʃ	
aitches, H's	ˈeɪtʃɪz	
alarm	əˈlɑ·m	əˈlɑəm
alarms	əˈlɑ·mz	əˈlɑəmz
alarmed	əˈlɑ·md	əˈlɑəmd
alarming	əˈlɑ·mɪŋ	əˈlɑəmɪŋ
alarmingly	əˈlɑ·mɪŋlɪ	əˈlɑəmɪŋlɪ
alas	əˈlæs, əˈlɑ·s	
Albert	ˈælbət	ˈælbət
album	ˈælbəm	
albums	ˈælbəmz	
alcohol	ˈælkəhɒl	
alcoholic	ælkəˈhɒlɪk	
alert	əˈlɜ·t	əˈlɜət
Alexander	ˈælɪgˈzændə(r ˈælɪgˈzɑ·ndə(r	ælɪgˈza·ndə
Alfred	ˈælfrɪd	
algebra	ˈældʒɪbrə	
algebraic	ældʒɪˈbreɪɪk	
algebraically	ældʒɪˈbreɪɪkəlɪ	
Algeria	ælˈdʒɪərɪə	ælˈdʒɪ·rɪə
alien	ˈeɪlɪən, ˈeɪljən	

Traditional Spelling	Received Pronunciation	American Variants
aliens	ˈeɪlɪənz,ˈeɪljənz	
alight	əˈlaɪt	
alights	əˈlaɪts	
alighted	əˈlaɪtɪd	
alighting	əˈlaɪtɪŋ	
alike	əˈlaɪk	
alive	əˈlaɪv	
alkali	ˈælkəlaɪ	
alkalies	ˈælkəlaɪz	
all	ˈɔːl	
allay	əˈleɪ	
allays	əˈleɪz	
allayed	əˈleɪd	
allaying	əˈleɪɪŋ	
allegation	ælɪˈgeɪʃən	
allegations	ælɪˈgeɪʃənz	
allege	əˈlɛʤ	
alleges	əˈlɛʤɪz	
alleged	əˈlɛʤd	
alleging	əˈlɛʤɪŋ	
allegiance	əˈliːʤəns	
allegory	ˈælɪgərɪ	ˈælɪgɔrɪ
allegories	ˈælɪgərɪz	ˈælɪgɔrɪz
alleviate	əˈliːvɪeɪt	
alleviates	əˈliːvɪeɪts	
alleviated	əˈliːvɪeɪtɪd	
alleviating	əˈliːvɪeɪtɪŋ	
alley	ˈælɪ	
alleys	ˈælɪz	
alliance	əˈlaɪəns	
alliances	əˈlaɪənsɪz	
alliterate	əˈlɪtəreɪt	
alliterates	əˈlɪtəreɪts	
alliterated	əˈlɪtəreɪtɪd	
alliterating	əˈlɪtəreɪtɪŋ	
alliteration	əlɪtəˈreɪʃən	
alliterations	əlɪtəˈreɪʃənz	
allocate	†ˈæləkeɪt	
allocates	†ˈæləkeɪts	
allocated	†ˈæləkeɪtɪd	
allocating	†ˈæləkeɪtɪŋ	
allocation	†æləˈkeɪʃən	
allocations	†æləˈkeɪʃənz	
allot	əˈlɒt	əˈlɑt
allots	əˈlɒts	əˈlɑts
allotted	əˈlɒtɪd	əˈlɑtɪd

† See Note 30, p. xxxv. in Introduction.

Traditional Spelling	Received Pronunciation	American Variants
allotting	ə'lɒtɪŋ	ə'lɑtɪŋ
allotment	ə'lɒtmənt	ə'lɑtmənt
allotments	ə'lɒtmənts	ə'lɑtmənts
allow	ə'laʊ	
allows	ə'laʊz	
allowed	ə'laʊd	
allowing	ə'laʊɪŋ	
allowance	ə'laʊəns	
allowances	ə'laʊənsɪz	
all right	'ɔl'raɪt	
allude	ə'lju·d	
alludes	ə'lju·dz	
alluded	ə'lju·dɪd	
alluding	ə'lju·dɪŋ	
allure	ə'ljʊə(r	ə'ljʊə
allures	ə'ljʊəz	ə'ljʊəz
allured	ə'ljʊəd	ə'ljʊəd
alluring	ə'ljʊərɪŋ	ə'ljʊ·rɪŋ
alluringly	ə'ljʊərɪŋlɪ	
allusion	ə'lju·ʒən	
allusions	ə'lju·ʒənz	
ally, *noun*	'ælaɪ	
allies	'ælaɪz	
ally, *verb*	ə'laɪ	
allies	ə'laɪz	
allied	ə'laɪd	
allying	ə'laɪɪŋ	
almanac	'ɔ·lmənæk	
almanacs	'ɔ·lmənæks	
almighty	ɔl'maɪtɪ	
almond	'ɑ·mənd	'a·mənd
almonds	'ɑ·məndz	'a·məndz
almost	'ɔ·lmoʊst	
alms	ɑ·mz	
alone	ə'loʊn	
along	ə'lɒŋ	
alongside	əlɒŋ'saɪd	
aloof	ə'lu·f	
aloofness	ə'lu·fnɪs	
aloud	ə'laʊd	
alpaca	æl'pækə	
alphabet	'ælfəbɪt	'ælfəbɛt
alphabets	'ælfəbɪts	'ælfəbɛts
alphabetic	ælfə'bɛtɪk	
alphabetical	ælfə'bɛtɪkəl	
alphabetically	ælfə'bɛtɪkəli	
already	'ɔl'rɛdɪ	

Traditional Spelling	Received Pronunciation	American Variants
also	ˈɔˑlsoʊ	
altar	ˈɔˑltə(r, ˈɒltə(r	ˈɔˑltə
altars	ˈɔˑltəz, ˈɒltəz	ˈɔˑltəz
alter	ˈɔˑltə(r, ˈɒltə(r	ˈɔˑltə
alters	ˈɔˑltəz,ˈɒltə(z	ˈɔˑltəz
altered	ˈɔˑltəd,ˈɒltəd	ˈɔˑltəd
altering	ˈɔˑltərɪŋ, ˈɒltərɪŋ	
alteration	ɔltəˈreɪʃən, ɒltəˈreɪʃən	
alterations	ɔltəˈreɪʃənz, ɒltəˈreɪʃənz	
altercation	ɔltəˈkeɪʃən, ɒltəˈkeɪʃən	
altercations	ɔltəˈkeɪʃənz, ɒltəˈkeɪʃənz	
alternate, *adj.*	ɔlˈtɜˑnɪt	ɔlˈtɜənɪt
alternately	ɔlˈtɜˑnɪtlɪ	ɔlˈtɜənɪtlɪ
alternate, *verb*	ˈɔˑltɜneɪt	ˈɔˑltɜəneɪt
alternates	ˈɔˑltɜneɪts	ˈɔˑltɜəneɪts
alternated	ˈɔˑltɜneɪtɪd	ˈɔˑltɜəneɪtɪd
alternating	ˈɔˑltɜneɪtɪŋ	ˈɔˑltɜəneɪtɪŋ
alternation	ɔltɜˈneɪʃən	ɔltɜəˈneɪʃən
alternations	ɔltɜˈneɪʃənz	ɔltɜəˈneɪʃənz
alternative	ɔlˈtɜˑnətɪv	ɔlˈtɜənətɪv
alternatives	ɔlˈtɜˑnətivz	ɔlˈtɜənətɪvz
alternatively	ɔlˈtɜˑnətɪvlɪ	ɔlˈtɜənətivlɪ
although	ɔlˈðoʊ	
altho (*Amer.*)		
altogether	ɔltəˈgɛðə(r	ɔltəˈgɛðə
altruism	ˈæltrʊɪzm̩	
altruist	ˈæltrʊɪst	
altruists	ˈæltrʊɪsts	
altruistic	æltrʊˈɪstɪk	
altruistically	æltrʊˈɪstɪkəlɪ	
alum	ˈæləm	
aluminium	æljʊˈmɪnjəm, æljʊˈmɪnɪəm	
aluminum (*used only*	*in America*)	əˈljuˑmɪnəm
alveolar	ˈælvɪələ(r, ælvɪˈoʊlə(r	ælvɪˈoʊlə
alveolars	ˈælvɪələz, ælvɪˈoʊləz	ælvɪˈoʊləz
alveole	ˈælvɪoʊl	
alveoles	ˈælvɪoʊlz	
always	ˈɔˑlwɪz, ˈɔˑlwəz, ˈɔˑlweɪz	
a.m.	ˈeɪ ˈɛm	
AM *from* be	æm *s.f.*	
	əm, m, *w.fs.*	
amalgamate	əˈmælgəmeɪt	

Traditional Spelling	Received Pronunciation	American Variants
amalgamates	əˈmælgəmeɪts	
amalgamated	əˈmælgəmeɪtɪd	
amalgamating	əˈmælgəmeɪtɪŋ	
amalgamation	əmælgəˈmeɪʃən	
amalgamations	əmælgəˈmeɪʃənz	
amass	əˈmæs	
amasses	əˈmæsɪz	
amassed	əˈmæst	
amassing	əˈmæsɪŋ	
amateur	ˈæmətjʊə(r, ˈæməˈtɜː(r	ˈæmətʃə, ˈæmətjʊə, ˈæməˈtɜə
amateurs	ˈæmətjʊəz, ˈæməˈtɜːz	ˈæmətʃəz, ˈæmətjʊə ˈæməˈtɜəz
amateurish	ˈæməˈtjʊərɪʃ ˈæməˈtɜːrɪʃ	æməˈtjʊːrɪʃ
amaze	əˈmeɪz	
amazes	əˈmeɪzɪz	
amazed	əˈmeɪzd	
amazing	əˈmeɪzɪŋ	
amazingly	əˈmeɪzɪŋlɪ	
ambassador	æmˈbæsədə(r	æmˈbæsədə
ambassadors	æmˈbæsədəz	æmˈbæsədəz
ambiguity	æmbɪˈgjuɪtɪ	
ambiguities	æmbɪˈgjuɪtɪz	
ambiguous	æmˈbɪgjʊəs	
ambiguously	æmˈbɪgjʊəslɪ	
ambition	æmˈbɪʃən	
ambitions	ˈæmˈbɪʃənz	
ambitious	æmˈbɪʃəs	
ambitiously	æmˈbɪʃəslɪ	
ambulance	ˈæmbjʊləns	
ambulances	ˈæmbjʊlənsɪz	
amend	əˈmend	
amends	əˈmendz	
amended	əˈmendɪd	
amending	əˈmendɪŋ	
amendment	əˈmendmənt	
amendments	əˈmendmənts	
America	əˈmerɪkə	
American	əˈmerɪkən	
Americans	əˈmerɪkənz	
americanism	əˈmerɪkənɪzṃ	
americanisms	əˈmerɪkənɪzṃz	
americanize	əˈmerɪkənaɪz	
americanizes	əˈmerɪkənaɪzɪz	
americanized	əˈmerɪkənaɪzd	
americanizing	əˈmerɪkənaɪzɪŋ	

Traditional Spelling	Received Pronunciation	American Variants
amiable	ˈeɪmjəbl̩, ˈeɪmɪəbl̩	
amiably	ˈeɪmjəblɪ, ˈeɪmɪəblɪ	
amicable	ˈæmɪkəbl̩	
amicably	ˈæmɪkəblɪ	
among	əˈmʌŋ	
amongst	əˈmʌŋst	
amorous	ˈæmərəs	
amorously	ˈæmərəslɪ	
amount	əˈmaʊnt	
amounts	əˈmaʊnts	
amounted	əˈmaʊntɪd	
amounting	əˈmaʊntɪŋ	
ample	ˈæmpl̩	
ampler	ˈæmplə(r	ˈæmplə
amplest	ˈæmplɪst	
amply	ˈæmplɪ	
amplification	æmplɪfɪˈkeɪʃən	
amplifications	æmplɪfɪˈkeɪʃənz	
amplify	ˈæmplɪfaɪ	
amplifies	ˈæmplɪfaɪz	
amplified	ˈæmplɪfaɪd	
amplifying	ˈæmplɪfaɪɪŋ	
amputate	ˈæmpjʊteɪt	
amputates	ˈæmpjʊteɪts	
amputated	ˈæmpjʊteɪtɪd	
amputating	ˈæmpjʊteɪtɪŋ	
amputation	æmpjʊˈteɪʃən	
amputations	æmpjʊˈteɪʃənz	
Amsterdam	ˈæmstəˈdæm	ˈæmstədæm
amuse	əˈmjuˑz	
amuses	əˈmjuˑzɪz	
amused	əˈmjuˑzd	
amusing	əˈmjuˑzɪŋ	
amusingly	əˈmjuˑzɪŋlɪ	
amusement	əˈmjuˑzmənt	
amusements	əˈmjuˑzmənts	
an	æn *s.f.*, ən *w.f.*	
anachronism	əˈnækrənɪzm̩	
anachronisms	əˈnækrənɪzm̩z	
anæmic	əˈniˑmɪk	
anæsthetics	ænɪsˈθɛtɪks	
analogous	əˈnæləgəs	
analogously	əˈnæləgəslɪ	
analogy	əˈnæləʤɪ	
analogies	əˈnæləʤɪz	
analyse	ˈænəlaɪz	
analyses	ˈænəlaɪzɪz	

Traditional Spelling	Received Pronunciation	American Variants
analysed	ˈænəlaɪzd	
analysing	ˈænəlaɪzɪŋ	
analysis	əˈnæləsɪs	
analyses	əˈnæləsiz	
analyst	ˈænəlɪst	
analysts	ˈænəlɪsts	
anarchist	ˈænəkɪst, ˈænɑkɪst	ˈænəkɪst, ˈænɑəkɪst
anarchists	ˈænəkɪst, ˈænɑkɪsts	ˈænəkɪsts, ˈænɑəkɪsts
anarchy	ˈænəkɪ, ˈænɑkɪ	ˈænəkɪ, ˈænɑəkɪ
anatomy	əˈnætəmɪ	
ancestor	ˈænsɪstə(r, ˈænsɛstə(r	ˈænsɛstə
ancestors	ˈænsɪstəz, ˈænsɛstəz	ˈænsɛstəz
ancestral	ænsɛstrəl	
ancestry	ˈænsɪstrɪ, ˈænsɛstrɪ	
anchor	ˈæŋkə(r	ˈæŋkə
anchors	ˈæŋkəz	ˈæŋkəz
anchored	ˈæŋkəd	ˈæŋkəd
anchoring	ˈæŋkərɪŋ	
ancient	ˈeɪnʃənt	
anciently	ˈeɪnʃəntlɪ	
and	ˈænd *s.f.*, ənd *w.f.*	
Andrew	ˈændru	
anecdote	ˈænɪkdoʊt	
anecdotes	ˈænɪkdoʊts	
aneroid	ˈænərɔɪd	
aneroids	ˈænərɔɪdz	
angel	ˈeɪnʤəl	
angels	ˈeɪnʤəlz	
anger	ˈæŋgə(r	ˈæŋgə
angle	ˈæŋgḷ	
angles	ˈæŋgḷz	
anglicism	ˈæŋglɪsɪzṃ	
anglicisms	ˈæŋglɪsɪzṃz	
anglicize	ˈæŋglɪsaɪz	
anglicizes	ˈæŋglɪsaɪzɪz	
anglicized	ˈæŋglɪsaɪzd	
anglicizing	ˈæŋglɪsaɪzɪŋ	
Anglo-, *prefix*	ˈæŋgloʊ	
angry	ˈæŋgrɪ	
angrier	ˈæŋgrɪə(r	ˈæŋgrɪə
angriest	ˈæŋgrɪɪst	
angrily	ˈæŋgrɪlɪ	
anguish	ˈæŋgwɪʃ	
angular	ˈæŋgjʊlə(r	ˈæŋgjʊlə

Traditional Spelling	Received Pronunciation	American Variants
aniline	ˈænɪlɪn, ˈænɪlaɪn	
animal	ˈænɪməl	
animals	ˈænɪməlz	
animate	ˈænɪmeɪt	
animates	ˈænɪmeɪts	
animated	ˈænɪmeɪtɪd	
animating	ˈænɪmeɪtɪŋ	
animation	ænɪˈmeɪʃən	
animosity	ænɪˈmɒsɪtɪ	ænɪˈmɑsɪtɪ
animosities	ænɪˈmɒsɪtɪz	ænɪˈmɑsɪtɪz
ankle	ˈæŋkl̩	
ankles	ˈæŋkl̩z	
Ann(e)	ˈæn	
annals	ˈænəlz	
annex, *verb*	əˈnɛks	
annexes	əˈnɛksɪz	
annexed	əˈnɛkst	
annexing	əˈnɛksɪŋ	
annex, *noun*	ˈænɛks	
annexes	ˈænɛksɪz	
annexation	ænɛkˈseɪʃən	
annexations	ænɛkˈseɪʃənz	
annihilate	əˈnaɪəleɪt əˈnaɪɪleɪt	
annihilates	əˈnaɪəleɪts əˈnaɪɪleɪts	
annihilated	əˈnaɪəleɪtɪd əˈnaɪɪleɪtɪd	
annihilating	əˈnaɪəleɪtɪŋ əˈnaɪɪleɪtɪŋ	
annihilation	ənaɪəˈleɪʃən ənaɪɪˈleɪʃən	
annihilations	ənaɪəˈleɪʃənz ənaɪɪˈleɪʃənz	
anniversary	ænɪˈvɜːsəri	ænɪˈvɝsərɪ
anniversaries	ænɪˈvɜːsərɪz	ænɪˈvɝsərɪz
announce	əˈnaʊns	
announces	əˈnaʊnsɪz	
announced	əˈnaʊnst	
announcing	əˈnaʊnsɪŋ	
announcement	əˈnaʊnsmənt	
announcements	əˈnaʊnsmənts	
annoy	əˈnɔɪ	
annoys	əˈnɔɪz	
annoyed	əˈnɔɪd	
annoying	əˈnɔɪɪŋ	
annoyance	əˈnɔɪəns	

Traditional Spelling	Received Pronunciation	American Variants
annoyances	ə'nɔɪənsɪz	
annual	'ænjʊəl	
annually	'ænjʊəlɪ	
anomalous	ə'nɒmələs	ə'nɑmələs
anomaly	ə'nɒməlɪ	ə'nɑməlɪ
anomalies	ə'nɒməlɪz	ə'nɑməlɪz
anonymous	ə'nɒnɪməs	ə'nɑnəməs
anonymously	ə'nɒnɪməslɪ	ə'nɑnəməslɪ
another	ə'nʌðə(r	ə'nʌðə
answer	'ɑˑnsə(r	'aˑnsə
answers	'ɑˑnsəz	'aˑnsəz
answered	'ɑˑnsəd	'aˑnsəd
answering	'ɑˑnsərɪŋ	'aˑnsərɪŋ
answerable	'ɑˑnsərəbl̩	'aˑnsərəbl̩
ant	'ænt	
ants	'ænts	
a'n't, *am not*	'ɑˑnt	(*apparently not used in America*)
antagonism	æn'tægənɪzm̩	
antagonisms	æn'tægənɪzm̩z	
antagonist	æn'tægənɪst	
antagonists	æn'tægənɪsts	
antagonistic	æntægə'nɪstɪk	
antagonize	æn'tægənaɪz	
antagonizes	æn'tægənaɪzɪz	
antagonized	æn'tægənaɪzd	
antagonizing	æn'tægənaɪzɪŋ	
antecedent	æntɪ'siˑdənt	
antecedents	æntɪ'siˑdənts	
antelope	'æntɪloup	
antelopes	'æntɪloups	
anterior	æn'tɪərɪə(r	æn'tɪˑrɪə
anthracite	'ænθrəsaɪt	
anti-, *prefix*	'æntɪ	
antics	'æntɪks	
anticipate	æn'tɪsɪpeɪt	
anticipates	æn'tɪsɪpeɪts	
anticipated	æn'tɪsɪpeɪtɪd	
anticipating	æn'tɪsɪpeɪtɪŋ	
anticipation	æntɪsɪ'peɪʃən	
anticipations	æntɪsɪ'peɪʃənz	
antidote	'æntɪdout	
antidotes	'æntɪdouts	
antipathy	æn'tɪpəθɪ	
antipathies	æn'tɪpəθɪz	
antipodes	æn'tɪpədiz	
antiquarian	æntɪ'kwɛərɪən	æntɪ'kwɛˑrɪən

Traditional Spelling	Received Pronunciation	American Variants
antiquarians	æntɪ'kwɛərɪənz	æntɪ'kwɛ·rɪənz
antiquated	'æntɪkweɪtɪd	
antique	æn'ti·k	
antiques	æn'ti·ks	
antiquity	æn'tɪkwɪtɪ	
antiquities	æn'tɪkwɪtɪz	
antiseptic	æntɪ'sɛptɪk	
antiseptics	æntɪ'sɛptɪks	
anxiety	æŋ'zaɪətɪ	
anxieties	æŋ'zaɪətɪz	
anxious	'æŋ*k*ʃəs	
anxiously	'æŋ*k*ʃəslɪ	
any	'ɛnɪ *s.f.*, n̩ɪ *w.f.*	
anybody	'ɛnɪbɒdɪ, 'ɛnɪbədɪ	'ɛnɪbɑdɪ
anyhow	'ɛnɪhaʊ	
anything	'ɛnɪθɪŋ	
anywhere	'ɛnɪ*h*wɛə(r	'ɛnɪhwɛə
anyway	'ɛnɪweɪ	
apart	ə'pɑ·t	ə'pɑət
apartment	ə'pɑ·tmənt	ə'pɑətmənt
apartments	ə'pɑ·tmənts	ə'pɑətmənts
ape	'eɪp	
apes	'eɪps	
apiece	ə'pi·s	
apologetic	əpɒlə'dʒɛtɪk	əpɑlə'dʒɛtɪk
apologetically	əpɒlə'dʒɛtɪkəlɪ	əpɑlə'dʒɛtikəlɪ
apologize	ə'pɒlədʒaɪz	ə'pɑlədʒaɪz
apologizes	ə'pɒlədʒaɪzɪz	ə'pɑlədʒaɪzɪz
apologized	ə'pɒlədʒaɪzd	ə'pɑlədʒaɪzd
apologizing	ə'pɒlədʒaɪzɪŋ	ə'pɑlədʒaɪzɪŋ
apology	ə'pɒlədʒɪ	ə'pɑlədʒɪ
apologies	ə'pɒlədʒɪz	ə'pɑlədʒɪz
apostle	ə'pɒsl̩	ə'pɑsl̩
apostles	ə'pɒsl̩z	ə'pɑsl̩z
apostrophe	ə'pɒstrəfɪ	ə'pɑstrəfɪ
apostrophes	ə'pɒstrəfɪz	ə'pɑstrəfɪz
appal	ə'pɔ·l	
appals	ə'pɔ·lz	
appalled	ə'pɔ·ld	
appalling	ə'pɔ·lɪŋ	
appallingly	ə'pɔ·lɪŋlɪ	
apparatus	æpə'reɪtəs	
apparent	ə'pærənt	
apparently	ə'pærəntlɪ	
appeal	ə'pi·l	
appeals	ə'pi·lz	
appealed	ə'pi·ld	

Traditional Spelling	Received Pronunciation	American Variants
appealing	əˈpiˑlɪŋ	
appear	əˈpɪə(r	əˈpɪə
appears	əˈpɪəz	əˈpɪəz
appeared	əˈpɪəd	əˈpɪəd
appearing	əˈpɪərɪŋ	
appearance	əˈpɪərəns	əˈpɪˑrəns
appearances	əˈpɪərənsɪz	əˈpɪˑrənsɪz
append	əˈpɛnd	
appends	əˈpɛndz	
appended	əˈpɛndɪd	
appending	əˈpɛndɪŋ	
appendicitis	əpɛndɪˈsaɪtɪs	
appendix	əˈpɛndɪks	
appendixes	əˈpɛndɪksɪz	
appendices	əˈpɛndɪsiz	
appetite	ˈæpɪtaɪt	
appetites	ˈæpɪtaɪts	
appetize	ˈæpɪtaɪz	
appetizing	ˈæpɪtaɪzɪŋ	
applaud	əˈplɔˑd	
applauds	əˈplɔˑdz	
applauded	əˈplɔˑdɪd	
applauding	əˈplɔˑdɪŋ	
applause	əˈplɔˑz	
apple	ˈæpl̩	
apples	ˈæpl̩z	
appliance	əˈplaɪəns	
appliances	əˈplaɪənsɪz	
applicable	ˈæplɪkəbl̩	
applicant	ˈæplɪkənt	
applicants	ˈæplɪkənts	
application	æplɪˈkeɪʃən	
applications	æplɪˈkeɪʃənz	
apply	əˈplaɪ	
applies	əˈplaɪz	
applied	əˈplaɪd	
applying	əˈplaɪɪŋ	
appoint	əˈpɔɪnt	
appoints	əˈpɔɪnts	
appointed	əˈpɔɪntɪd	
appointing	əˈpɔɪntɪŋ	
appointment	əˈpɔɪntmənt	
appointments	əˈpɔɪntmənts	
appreciable	əˈpriˑʃɪəbl̩	
appreciably	əˈpriˑʃɪəbl̩i	
appreciate	əˈpriˑʃɪeɪt	
appreciates	əˈpriˑʃɪeɪts	

Traditional Spelling	Received Pronunciation	American Variants
appreciated	ə'pri·ʃɪeɪtɪd	
appreciating	ə'pri·ʃɪeɪtɪŋ	
appreciation	əpriʃɪ'eɪʃən	
appreciations	əpriʃɪ'eɪʃənz	
appreciative	ə'pri·ʃɪətɪv	ə'pri·ʃɪeɪtɪv
apprentice	ə'prɛntɪs	
apprentices	ə'prɛntɪsɪz	
approach	ə'proʊtʃ	
approaches	ə'proʊtʃɪz	
approached	ə'proʊtʃt	
approaching	ə'proʊtʃɪŋ	
approbation	æprə'beɪʃən æproʊ'beɪʃən	
appropriate, *adj.*	ə'proʊprɪɪt	
appropriate, *verb*	ə'proʊprɪeɪt	
appropriates	ə'proʊprɪeɪts	
appropriated	ə'proʊprɪeɪtɪd	
appropriating	ə'proʊprɪeɪtɪŋ	
approval	ə'pru·vəl	
approve	ə'pru·v	
approves	ə'pru·vz	
approved	ə'pru·vd	
approving	ə'pru·vɪŋ	
approvingly	ə'pru·vɪŋlɪ	
approximate, *adj.*	ə'prɒksɪmɪt	ə'prɑksɪmɪt
approximate, *verb*	ə'prɒksɪmeɪt	ə'prɑksɪmeɪt
approximately	ə'prɒksɪmɪtlɪ	ə'prɑksɪmɪtlɪ
approximation	əprɒksɪ'meɪʃən	əprɑksɪ'meɪʃən
approximations	əprɒksɪ'meɪʃənz	əprɑksɪ'meɪʃənz
April	'eɪprəl, 'eɪprɪl	
apron	'eɪprən	
aprons	'eɪprənz	
apt	'æpt	
aptly	'æptlɪ	
aptitude	'æptɪtjud	
aptitudes	'æptɪtjudz	
Arab	'ærəb	
Arabs	'ærəbz	
Arabia	ə'reɪbɪə	
Arabic	'ærəbɪk	
arbitrary	'ɑ·bɪtrərɪ	'ɑəbɪtrɛrɪ
arbitrarily	'ɑ·bɪtrərɪlɪ	'ɑəbɪtrɛrɪlɪ
arbitrate	'ɑ·bɪtreɪt	ɑəbɪtreɪt
arbitrates	'ɑ·bɪtreɪts	ɑəbɪtreɪts
arbitrated	'ɑ·bɪtreɪtɪd	ɑəbɪtreɪtɪd
arbitrating	'ɑ·bɪtreɪtɪŋ	ɑəbɪtreɪtɪŋ
arbitration	ɑ·bɪ'treɪʃən	ɑəbɪ'treɪʃən

Traditional Spelling	Received Pronunciation	American Variants
arbitrations	ɑ·bɪˈtreɪʃənz	ɑəbɪˈtreɪʃənz
arc	ɑ·k	ɑək
arcs	ɑ·ks	ɑəks
arcade	ɑˈkeɪd	ɑəˈkeɪd
arcades	ɑˈkeɪdz	ɑəˈkeɪdz
arch	ɑ·tʃ	ɑətʃ
arches	ˈɑ·tʃɪz	ɑətʃɪz
arch-, *prefix*	ɑ·tʃ	ɑətʃ
archæological	ɑ·kɪəˈlɒdʒɪkəl	ɑəkɪəˈlɑdʒɪkl̩
archæology	ɑ·kɪˈɒlədʒɪ	ɑəkɪˈɑlədʒɪ
archaic	ɑ·keɪɪk	ɑəˈkeɪɪk
archaism	ɑ·keɪɪzm̩	ˈɑəkeɪɪzm̩
archaisms	ˈɑ·keɪɪzm̩z	ɑəkeɪɪzm̩z
archbishop	ɑ·tʃbɪʃəp	ɑətʃˈbɪʃəp
archbishops	ɑ·tʃˈbɪʃəps	ɑətʃˈbɪʃəps
archer	ˈɑ·tʃə(r	ɑətʃə
archers	ˈɑ·tʃəz	ˈɑətʃəz
archery	ˈɑ·tʃərɪ	ˈɑətʃərɪ
architect	ˈɑ·kɪtɛkt	ɑəkɪtɛkt
architects	ˈɑ·kɪtɛkts	ˈɑəkɪtɛkts
architectural	ɑ·kɪˈtɛktʃərəl	ɑəkɪˈtɛktʃərəl
architecture	ˈɑ·kɪtɛktʃə	ɑəkɪtɛktʃə
archway	ˈɑ·tʃweɪ	ˈɑətʃweɪ
archways	ˈɑ·tʃweɪz	ˈɑətʃweɪz
arctic	ˈɑ·ktɪk	ˈɑəktɪk
arduous	ˈɑ·djʊəs	ˈɑədjʊəs
ARE	ɑ·(r *s.f.*, ə(r *w.f.*	ɑə *s.f.*, ə *w.f.*
AREN'T	ɑ·nt	ɑənt
area	ˈɛərɪə	ˈɛ·rɪə
areas	ˈɛərɪəz	ˈɛ·rɪəz
Argentina	ɑdʒənˈti·nə	ɑədʒənˈti·nə
Argentine	ˈɑ·dʒəntaɪn	ˈɑədʒəntaɪn
argue	ˈɑ·gju	ˈɑəgju
argues	ˈɑ·gjuz	ˈɑəgjuz
argued	ˈɑ·gjud	ˈɑəgjud
arguing	ˈɑ·gjʊɪŋ	ˈɑəgjʊɪŋ
argument	ˈɑ·gjʊmənt	ˈɑəgjʊmənt
arguments	ˈɑ·gjʊmənts	ˈɑəgjʊmənts
argumentative	ɑgjʊˈmɛntətɪv	ɑəgjʊˈmɛntətɪv
aristocracy	ærɪˈstɒkrəsɪ	ærɪˈstɑkrəsɪ
aristocracies	ærɪˈstɒkrəsɪz	ærɪˈstɑkrəsɪz
aristocrat	ˈærɪstəkræt	
aristocrats	ˈærɪstəkræts	
aristocratic	ærɪstəˈkrætɪk	
arithmetic	əˈrɪθmətɪk	
arithmetrical	ærɪθˈmɛtɪkəl	
arithmetically	ærɪθmɛtɪkəlɪ	

Traditional Spelling	Received Pronunciation	American Variants
arithmetician	ərɪθmə'tɪʃən ærɪθmə'tɪʃən	
arithmeticians	ərɪθmə'tɪʃənz ærɪθmə'tɪʃənz	
ark	ɑ·k	ɑək
arks	ɑ·ks	ɑəks
arm	ɑ·m	ɑəm
arms	ɑ·mz	ɑəmz
armed	ɑ·md	ɑəmd
arming	'ɑ·mɪŋ	ɑəmɪŋ
armament	'ɑ·məmənt	ɑəməmənt
armaments	'ɑ·məmənts	'ɑəməmənts
armchair	ɑ·m'tʃɛə(r, 'ɑ·mtʃɛə(r	ɑəm'tʃɛə
armchairs	ɑ·m'tʃɛəz, 'ɑ·mtʃɛəz	ɑəm'tʃɛəz
armful	'ɑ·mful	'ɑəmful
armfuls	'ɑ·mfulz	'ɑəmfulz
armistice	'ɑ·mɪstɪs	'ɑəmɪstɪs
armistices	'ɑ·mɪstɪsɪz	'ɑəmɪstɪsɪz
armour	'ɑ·mə(r	'ɑəmə
army	'ɑ· mɪ	'ɑəmɪ
armies	'ɑ·mɪz	'ɑəmɪz
army-corps	'ɑ·mɪkɔ·(r, 'ɑ·mɪkɔə(r	'ɑəmɪkoə
around	ə'raʊnd	
arouse	ə'raʊz	
arouses	ə'raʊzɪz	
aroused	ə'raʊzd	
arousing	ə'raʊzɪŋ	
arrange	ə'reɪndʒ	
arranges	ə'reɪndʒɪz	
arranged	ə'reɪndʒd	
arranging	ə'reɪndʒɪŋ	
arrangement	ə'reɪndʒmənt	
arrangements	ə'reɪndʒmənts	
arrest	ə'rɛst	
arrests	ə'rɛsts	
arrested	ə'rɛstɪd	
arresting	ə'rɛstɪŋ	
arrive	ə'raɪv	
arrives	ə'raɪvz	
arrived	ə'raɪvd	
arriving	ə'raɪvɪŋ	
arrival	ə'raɪvəl	
arrivals	ə'raɪvəlz	
arrogant	†'ærəgənt	
arrogantly	†'ærəgəntlɪ	
arrow	'ærou	

† See Note **30**, p. xxxv. in Introduction

Traditional Spelling	Received Pronunciation	American Variants
arrows	ˈærouz	
arsenal	ˈɑˑsɪnəl	ˈɑəsɪnəl
arsenals	ˈɑˑsɪnəlz	ˈɑəsɪnəlz
art	ɑˑt	ɑət
arts	ɑˑts	ɑəts
artery	ˈɑˑtərɪ	ˈɑətərɪ
arteries	ˈɑˑtərɪz	ˈɑətərɪz
artful	ˈɑˑtful	ˈɑətfl̩
artfully	ˈɑˑtfəlɪ, ˈɑˑtfulɪ	ˈɑətfəlɪ, ˈɑətfulɪ
Arthur	ɑˑθə(r	ˈɑəθə
article	ˈɑˑtɪkl̩	ˈɑətɪkl̩
articles	ˈɑˑtɪkl̩z	ˈɑətɪkl̩z
articulate, *adj.*	ɑˑˈtɪkjulɪt	ɑəˈtɪkjulɪt
articulate	ɑˑˈtɪkjuleɪt	ɑəˈtɪkjuleɪt
articulates	ɑˑˈtɪkjuleɪts	ɑəˈtɪkjuleɪts
articulated	ɑˑˈtɪkjuleɪtɪd	ɑəˈtɪkjuleɪtɪd
articulating	ɑˑˈtɪkjuleɪtɪŋ	ɑəˈtɪkjuleɪtɪŋ
articulation	ɑˑtɪkjuˈleɪʃən	ɑətɪkjuˈleɪʃən
articulations	ɑˑtɪkjuˈleɪʃənz	ɑətɪkjuˈleɪʃənz
artificial	ɑˑtɪˈfɪʃəl	ɑətɪˈfɪʃəl
artificially	ɑˑtɪˈfɪʃəlɪ	ɑətɪˈfɪʃəlɪ
artificiality	ɑˑtɪfɪʃɪˈælɪtɪ	ɑətɪfɪʃɪˈælɪtɪ
artillery	ɑˑˈtɪləri	ɑəˈtɪlərɪ
artist	ˈɑˑtɪst	ˈɑətɪst
artists	ˈɑˑtɪsts	ˈɑətɪsts
artistic	ɑˑˈtɪstɪk	ɑəˈtɪstɪk
artistically	ɑˑˈtɪstɪkəlɪ	ɑəˈtɪstɪkəlɪ
as	æz *s.f.*, əz *w.f.*	
ascent	əˈsent	
ascents	əˈsents	
ascertain	æsəˈteɪn	
ascertains	æsəˈteɪnz	
ascertained	æsəˈteɪnd	
ascertaining	æsəˈteɪnɪŋ	
ash	æʃ	
ashes	ˈæʃɪz	
ashamed	əˈʃeɪmd	
ashore	əˈʃɔə(r	əˈʃoə
Asia	ˈeɪʃə	
Asiatic	eɪʃɪˈætɪk	
Asiatics	eɪʃɪˈætɪks	
aside	əˈsaɪd	
ask	ɑˑsk	aˑsk
asks	ɑˑsks	aˑsks
asked	ɑˑs*k*t	aˑs*k*t
asking	ˈɑˑskɪŋ	ˈaˑskɪŋ
asleep	əˈsliˑp	

Traditional Spelling	Received Pronunciation	American Variants
asparagus	əs'pærəgəs	
aspect	'æspɛkt	
aspects	'æspɛkts	
aspirate, *noun*	'æspərɪt	
aspirates	'æspərɪts	
aspirate, *verb*	'æspəreɪt	
aspirates	'æspəreɪts	
aspirated	'æspəreɪtɪd	
aspirating	'æspəreɪtɪŋ	
ass	'æs	
asses	'æsɪz	
assassin	ə'sæsɪn	
assassins	ə'sæsɪnz	
assassinate	ə'sæsɪneɪt	
assassinates	ə'sæsɪneɪts	
assassinated	ə'sæsineɪtɪd	
assassinating	ə'sæsɪneɪtɪŋ	
assassination	əsæsɪ'neɪʃən	
assassinations	əsæsɪ'neɪʃənz	
assault	ə'sɔlt, ə'sɒlt	
assaults	ə'sɔlts, ə'sɒlts	
assaulted	ə'sɔltɪd, ə'sɒltɪd	
assaulting	ə'sɔltɪŋ, ə'sɒltɪŋ	
assemble	ə'sɛmbl̩	
assembles	ə'sɛmbl̩z	
assembled	ə'sɛmbl̩d	
assembling	ə'sɛmblɪŋ	
assent	ə'sɛnt	
assents	ə'sɛnts	
assented	ə'sɛntɪd	
assenting	ə'sɛntɪŋ	
assert	ə'sɜ·t	ə'sɜət
asserts	ə'sɜ·ts	ə'sɜəts
asserted	ə'sɜ·tɪd	ə'sɜətɪd
asserting	ə'sɜ·tɪŋ	ə'sɜətɪŋ
assertion	ə'sɜ·ʃən	ə'sɜəʃən
assertions	ə'sɜ·ʃənz	ə'sɜəʃənz
assets	'æsɛts	
assimilate	ə'sɪmɪleɪt	
assimilates	ə'sɪmɪleɪts	
assimilated	ə'sɪmɪleɪtɪd	
assimilating	ə'sɪmɪleɪtɪŋ	
assimilation	əsɪmɪ'leɪʃən	
assimilations	əsɪmɪ'leɪʃənz	
assist	ə'sɪst	
assists	ə'sɪsts	
assisted	ə'sɪstɪd	

Traditional Spelling	Received Pronunciation	American Variants
assisting	ə'sɪstɪŋ	
assistance	ə'sɪstəns	
assistances	ə'sɪstənsɪz	
assistant	ə'sɪstənt	
assistants	ə'sɪstənts	
associate, *noun*	ə'souʃɪt	
associates	ə'souʃɪts	
associate, *verb*	ə'souʃɪeɪt	
associates	ə'souʃɪeɪts	
associated	ə'souʃɪeɪtɪd	
associating	ə'souʃɪeɪtɪŋ	
association	əsouʃɪ'eɪʃən	
	əsousɪ'eɪʃən	
associations	əsouʃɪ'eɪʃənz	
	əsousɪ'eɪʃənz	
assort	ə'sɔ·t	ə'sɔət
assorts	ə'sɔ·ts	ə'sɔəts
assorted	ə'sɔ·tɪd	ə'sɔətɪd
assorting	ə'sɔ·tɪŋ	ə'sɔətɪŋ
assortment	ə'sɔ·tmənt	ə'sɔətmənt
assortments	ə'sɔ·tmənts	ə'sɔətmənts
assume	ə'sju·m	
assumes	ə'sju·mz	
assumed	ə'sju·md	
assuming	ə'sju·mɪŋ	
assumption	ə'sʌmpʃən	
assumptions	ə'sʌmpʃənz	
assure	ə'ʃʊə	
assures	ə'ʃʊəz	ə'ʃʊɔz
assured	ə'ʃʊəd	ə'ʃʊəd
assuring	ə'ʃʊərɪŋ	ə'ʃʊ·rɪŋ
assurance	ə'ʃʊərəns	ə'ʃʊ·rəns
assurances	ə'ʃʊərənsɪz	ə'ʃʊ·rənsɪz
asterisk	'æstərɪsk	
asterisks	'æstərɪsks	
asthma	'æsmə	'æzmə
astonish	ə'stɒnɪʃ	ə'stɑnɪʃ
astonishes	ə'stɒnɪʃɪz	ə'stɑnɪʃɪz
astonished	ə'stɒnɪʃt	ə'stɑnɪʃt
astonishing	ə'stɒnɪʃɪŋ	ə'stɑnɪʃɪŋ
astonishingly	ə'stɒnɪʃɪŋlɪ	ə'stɑnɪʃɪŋlɪ
astonishment	ə'stɒnɪʃmənt	ə'stɑnɪʃmənt
astound	ə'staʊnd	
astounds	ə'staʊndz	
astounded	ə'staʊndɪd	
astounding	ə'staʊndɪŋ	
astray	ə'streɪ	

Traditional Spelling	Received Pronunciation	American Variants
astrology	ə'strɒlədʒɪ	ə'strɑlədʒɪ
astronomer	ə'strɒnəmə(r	ə'strɑnəmə
astronomers	ə'strɒnəməz	ə'strɑnəməz
astronomical	æstrə'nɒmɪkəl	æstrə'nɑmɪkəl
astronomy	ə'strɒnəmɪ	ə'strɑnəmɪ
at	æt *s.f.*, ət *w.f.*	
ATE, *from* eat	'ɛt	eɪt
atheist	'eɪθɪɪst	
atheists	'eɪθɪɪsts	
Athens	'æθɪnz	
athlete	'æθlit	
athletes	'æθlits	
athletic	æθ'lɛtɪk	
atlas	'ætləs	
atlases	'ætləsɪz	
atmosphere	'ætməsfɪə(r	'ætməsfɪə
atmospheres	'ætməsfɪəz	'ætməsfɪəz
atom	'ætəm	
atoms	'ætəmz	
atrocious	ə'troʊʃəs	
atrociously	ə'troʊʃəslɪ	
atrocity	ə'trɒsɪtɪ	ə'trɑsɪtɪ
atrocities	ə'trɒsɪtɪz	ə'trɑsɪtɪz
attach	ə'tætʃ	
attaches	ə'tætʃɪz	
attached	ə'tætʃt	
attaching	ə'tætʃɪŋ	
attachment	ə'tætʃmənt	
attachments	ə'tætʃmənts	
attack	ə'tæk	
attacks	ə'tæks	
attacked	ə'tækt	
attacking	ə'tækɪŋ	
attain	ə'teɪn	
attains	ə'teɪnz	
attained	ə'teɪnd	
attaining	ə'teɪnɪŋ	
attainment	ə'teɪnmənt	
attainments	ə'teɪnmənts	
attempt	ə'tɛm*p*t	
attempts	ə'tɛm*p*ts	
attempted	ə'tɛm*p*tɪd	
attempting	ə'tɛm*p*tɪŋ	
attend	ə'tɛnd	
attends	ə'tɛndz	
attended	ə'tɛndɪd	
attending	ə'tɛndɪŋ	

Traditional Spelling	Received Pronunciation	American Variants
attendance	ə'tɛndəns	
attendances	ɔ'tɛndənsɪz	
attendant	ə'tɛndənt	
attendants	ɔ'tɛndənts	
attention	ə'tɛnʃən	
attentions	ɔ'tɛnʃənz	
attentive	ə'tɛntɪv	
attentively	ɔ'tɛntɪvlɪ	
attitude	'ætɪtjud	
attitudes	'ætɪtjudz	
attract	ə'trækt	
attracts	ə'trækts	
attracted	ə'træktɪd	
attracting	ə'træktɪŋ	
attraction	ə'trækʃən	
attractions	ɔ'trækʃənz	
attractive	ə'træktɪv	
attractively	ɔ'træktɪvlɪ	
attribute	'ætrɪbjut	
attributes	'ætrɪbjuts	
attribute	ə'trɪbjut	
attributes	ɔ'trɪbjuts	
attributed	ə'trɪbjutɪd	
attributing	ə'trɪbjutɪŋ	
auction	'ɔːkʃən	
auctions	'ɔːkʃənz	
auctioneer	ɔkʃə'nɪə(r	ɔkʃə'nɪə
auctioneers	ɔkʃə'nɪəz	ɔkʃə'nɪəz
audacious	ɔ'deɪʃəs	
audaciously	ɔ'deɪʃəslɪ	
audacity	ɔ'dæsɪtɪ	
audible	'ɔːdɪbl̩	
audience	'ɔːdjəns, 'ɔːdɪəns	
audiences	'ɔːdjənsɪz, 'ɔːdɪənsɪz	
audition	ɔ'dɪʃən	
auditorium	ɔdɪ'tɔːrɪəm	ɔdɪ'toːrɪəm
auditoriums	ɔdɪ'tɔːrɪəmz	ɔdɪ'toːrɪəmz
August	'ɔːgəst	
aunt	ɑːnt	aːnt
aunts	ɑːnts	aːnts
auspices	'ɔːspɪsɪz	
Australia	ɔs'treɪljə	
Australian	ɔs'treɪljən	
Australians	ɔs'treɪljənz	
Austria	'ɔːstrɪə, 'ɒstrɪə	
Austrian	'ɔːtrɪən, 'ɒstrɪən	
Austrians	'ɔːstrɪənz, 'ɒstrɪənz	

Traditional Spelling	Received Pronunciation	American Variants
authentic	ɔ'θɛntɪk	
author	'ɔ·θə(r	'ɔ·θə
authors	'ɔ·θəz	'ɔ·θəz
authoress	'ɔ·θərɪs	
authoresses	'ɔ·θərɪsɪz	
authority	ə'θɒrɪtɪ, ɔ'θɒrɪtɪ	ə'θɑrɪtɪ, ɔ'θɑrɪtɪ
authorities	ə'θɒrɪtɪz, ɔ'θɒrɪtɪz	ə'θɑrɪtɪz, ɔ'θɑrɪtɪz
authorization	ɔθəraɪ'zeɪʃən	
authorizations	ɔθəraɪ'zeɪʃənz	
authorize	'ɔ·θəraɪz	
authorizes	'ɔ·θəraɪzɪz	
authorized	'ɔ·θəraɪzd	
authorizing	'ɔ·θəraɪzɪŋ	
autocrat	'ɔ·təkræt	
autocrats	'ɔ·təkræts	
autocratic	ɔtə'krætɪk	
autograph	'ɔ·təgræf, 'ɔ·təgrɑf	
autographs	'ɔ·təgræfs, 'ɔ·təgrɑfs	
automatic	ɔtə'mætɪk	
automobile	ɔtə'moubɪl	ɔtəmou'bi·l
automobiles	ɔtə'moubɪlz	ɔtəmou'bi·lz
autumn	'ɔ·təm	
auxiliary	ɔg'zɪljərɪ, ɔk'zɪljərɪ	
auxiliaries	ɔg'zɪljərɪz, ɔk'zɪljərɪz	
avail	ə'veɪl	
avails	ə'veɪlz	
availed	ə'veɪld	
availing	ə'veɪlɪŋ	
available	ə'veɪləbḷ	
avalanche	'ævəlɑ·nʃ	'ævəla·nʃ
avalanches	'ævəlɑ·nʃɪz	'ævəla·nʃɪz
avarice	'ævərɪs	
avaricious	ævə'rɪʃəs	
avenge	ə'vɛnʤ	
avenges	ə'vɛnʤɪz	
avenged	ə'vɛnʤd	
avenging	ə'vɛnʤɪŋ	
avenger	ə'vɛnʤə(r	ə'vɛnʤə
avengers	ə'vɛnʤəz	ə'vɛnʤəz
avenue	'ævɪnju	
avenues	'ævɪnjuz	
averse	ə'vɜ·s	ə'vɝs
aversion	ə'vɜ·ʃən	ə'vɝʃən
aversions	ə'vɜ·ʃənz	ə'vɝʃənz
avert	ə'vɜ·t	ə'vɝt
averts	ə'vɜ·ts	ə'vɝts

Traditional Spelling	Received Pronunciation	American Variants
averted	əˈvɜˑtɪd	əˈvɜətɪd
averting	əˈvɜˑtɪŋ	əˈvɜətɪŋ
aviation	eɪvɪˈeɪʃən	
aviator	ˈeɪvɪeɪtə(r	ˈeɪvɪeɪtə
aviators	ˈeɪvɪeɪtəz	ˈeɪvɪeɪtəz
avoid	əˈvɔɪd	
avoids	əˈvɔɪdz	
avoided	əˈvɔɪdɪd	
avoiding	əˈvɔɪdɪŋ	
await	əˈweɪt	
awaits	əˈweɪts	
awaited	əˈweɪtɪd	
awaiting	əˈweɪtɪŋ	
awake	əˈweɪk	
awakes	əˈweɪks	
awaking	əˈweɪkɪŋ	
awaken	əˈweɪkən	
awakens	əˈweɪkənz	
awakened	əˈweɪkənd	
awakening	əˈweɪkənɪŋ	
aware	əˈwɛə	əˈwɛə
away	əˈweɪ	
awful	ˈɔˑfl̩, ɔˑful	
awfully	ˈɔˑfəlɪ, ˈɔˑfulɪ	
awkward	ˈɔˑkwəd	ˈɔˑkwəd
awkwardly	ˈɔˑkwədlɪ	ˈɔˑkwədlɪ
awkwardness	ˈɔˑkwədnɪs	ˈɔˑkwədnɪs
awoke	əˈwoʊk	
axe (*Amer.* **ax**)	æks	
axes	ˈæksɪz	

B

B	biˑ	
B's	biˑz	
baby	ˈbeɪbɪ	
babies	ˈbeɪbɪz	
bachelor	ˈbætʃələ(r	bætʃələ
bachelors	ˈbætʃələz	ˈbætʃələz
back	bæk	
backs	bæks	
background	ˈbækgraʊnd	
backgrounds	ˈbækgraʊndz	
bacon	ˈbeɪkən	
bad	bæd	
badge	bædʒ	

Traditional Spelling	Received Pronunciation	American Variants
badges	ˈbæʤɪz	
badly	ˈbædlɪ	
baffling	ˈbæflɪŋ	
bag	bæg	
bags	bægz	
baggage	ˈbægɪʤ	
bait	beɪt	
bake	beɪk	
bakes	beɪks	
baked	beɪkt	
baking	ˈbeɪkɪŋ	
baker	ˈbeɪkə(r	beɪkə
bakers	ˈbeɪkəz	beɪkəz
balance	ˈbæləns	
balances	ˈbælənsɪz	
balanced	ˈbælənst	
balancing	ˈbælənsɪŋ	
bald	bɔˑld	
bale	beɪl	
bales	beɪlz	
baled	beɪld	
baling	ˈbeɪlɪŋ	
ball	bɔˑl	
balls	bɔˑlz	
balloon	bəˈluˑn	
balloons	bəˈluˑnz	
Baltic	ˈbɔltɪk, ˈbɒltɪk	
bamboo	bæmˈbuˑ	
bamboos	bæmˈbuˑz	
banana	bəˈnɑˑnə	bəˈnaˑnə
bananas	bəˈnɑˑnəz	bəˈnaˑnəz
band	bænd	
bands	bændz	
bandage	ˈbændɪʤ	
bandages	ˈbændɪʤɪz	
bandaged	ˈbændɪʤd	
bandaging	ˈbændɪʤɪŋ	
bandmaster	ˈbæn*d*mɑstə(r	ˈbæn*d*mastə
bandmasters	ˈbæn*d*mɑstəz	ˈbæn*d*mastəz
bandstand	ˈbæn*d*stænd	
bandstands	ˈbæn*d*stændz	
bang	bæŋ	
bangs	bæŋz	
banged	bæŋd	
banging	ˈbæŋɪŋ	
banish	ˈbænɪʃ	
banishes	ˈbænɪʃɪz	

Traditional Spelling	Received Pronunciation	American Variants
banished	ˈbænɪʃt	
banishing	ˈbænɪʃɪŋ	
banishment	ˈbænɪʃmənt	
banishments	ˈbænɪʃmənts	
bank	bæŋk	
banks	bæŋks	
banker	ˈbæŋkə(r	bæŋkə
bankers	ˈbæŋkəz	ˈbæŋkəz
bank-note	ˈbæŋknoʊt	
bank-notes	ˈbæŋknoʊts	
bankrupt	ˈbæŋkrʌpt ˈbæŋkrəpt	
bankrupts	ˈbæŋkrʌpts ˈbæŋkrəpts	
baptism	ˈbæptɪzm̩	
baptisms	ˈbæptɪzm̩z	
baptist	ˈbæptɪst	
baptists	ˈbæptɪsts	
baptize	bæpˈtaɪz	
baptizes	bæpˈtaɪzɪz	
baptized	bæpˈtaɪzd	
baptizing	bæpˈtaɪzɪŋ	
bar	bɑˑ(r	bɑə
bars	bɑˑz	bɑəz
barred	bɑˑd	bɑəd
barring	bɑˑrɪŋ	
barbarian	bɑˈbɛərɪən	bɑəˈbɛˑrɪən
barbarians	bɑˈbɛərɪənz	bɑəˈbɛˑrɪənz
barbarous	ˈbɑˑbɚrəs	ˈbɑəbɚrəs
barbarously	ˈbɑˑbɚrəslɪ	ˈbɑəbɚrəslɪ
barber	ˈbɑˑbə(r	ˈbɑəbə
barbers	ˈbɑˑbəz	ˈbɑəbəz
Barcelona	ˈbɑsɪˈloʊnə	ˈbɑəsɪˈloʊnə
bare	bɛə(r	bɛə
bareness	ˈbɛənɪs	ˈbɛənɪs
bargain	ˈbɑˑgɪn	ˈbɑəgɪn
bargains	ˈbɑˑgɪnz	ˈbɑəgɪnz
bargained	ˈbɑˑgɪnd	ˈbɑəgɪnd
bargaining	ˈbɑˑgɪnɪŋ	ˈbɑəgɪnɪŋ
barge	bɑˑʤ	bɑəʤ
barges	ˈbɑˑʤɪz	ˈbɑəʤɪz
bark	bɑˑk	bɑək
barks	bɑˑks	bɑəks
barked	bɑˑkt	bɑəkt
barking	ˈbɑˑkɪŋ	ˈbɑəkɪŋ
barley	ˈbɑˑlɪ	ˈbɑəlɪ
barn	bɑˑn	bɑən

Traditional Spelling	Received Pronunciation	American Variants
barns	bɑ·nz	bɑənz
barometer	bəˈrɒmɪtə(r	bəˈrɑmɪtə
barometers	bəˈrɒmɪtəz	bəˈrɑmɪtəz
baron	ˈbærən	
barons	ˈbærənz	
barrack	ˈbærək	
barracks	ˈbærəks	
barrel	ˈbærəl	
barrels	ˈbærəlz	
barren	ˈbærən	
barrier	ˈbærɪə(r	ˈbærɪə
barriers	ˈbærɪəz	ˈbærɪəz
barrister	ˈbærɪstə(r	ˈbærɪstə
barristers	ˈbærɪstəz	ˈbærɪstəz
base	beɪs	
bases	ˈbeɪsɪz	
based	beɪst	
basing	ˈbeɪsɪŋ	
baser	ˈbeɪsə(r	beɪsə
basest	ˈbeɪsɪst	
basely	ˈbeɪslɪ	
baseness	ˈbeɪsnɪs	
bashful	ˈbæʃful	
bashfully	ˈbæʃfəlɪ, ˈbæʃfulɪ	
bashfulness	ˈbæʃfəlnɪs, ˈbæʃfulnɪs	
basic	ˈbeɪsɪk	
basin	ˈbeɪsn̩	
basins	ˈbeɪsn̩z	
basis	ˈbeɪsɪs	
bases	ˈbeɪsiz	
basket	ˈbɑ·skɪt	ˈba·skɪt
baskets	ˈbɑ·skɪts	ˈba·skɪts
basketful	ˈbɑ·skɪtful	ˈba·skɪtful
basketfuls	ˈbɑ·skɪtfulz	ˈba·skɪtfulz
bass (*in music*)	beɪs	
bat	bæt	
bats	bæts	
batch	bætʃ	
batches	bætʃɪz	
bath, *noun*	bɑ·θ	ba·θ
baths, *noun*	bɑðz	ba·ðz
bath, *verb*	bɑ·θ	ba·θ
baths	bɑ·θs	ba·θs
bathed	bɑ·θt	ba·θt
bathing	ˈbɑ·θɪŋ	ˈba·θɪŋ
bathe	beɪð	
bathes	beɪðz	

Traditional Spelling	Received Pronunciation	American Variants
bathed	beɪðd	
bathing	'beɪðɪŋ	
bathroom	'bɑˑθrum, 'bɑˑθrʊm	'baˑθrum
bathrooms	'bɑˑθrumz	'baˑθrumz
	'bɑˑθrʊmz	
battalion	bə'tæljən	
battalions	bə'tæljənz	
battle	'bætl̩	
battles	'bætl̩z	
Bavaria	bə'vɛərɪə	bə'vɛˑrɪə
Bavarian	bə'vɛərɪən	bə'vɛˑrɪən
Bavarians	bə'vɛərɪənz	bə'vɛˑrɪənz
bazaar	bə'zɑˑ(r	bə'zɑə
bazaars	bə'zɑˑz	bə'zɑəz
be	biˑ *s.f.*, bi, bɪ *w.fs.*	
being	'biˑɪŋ	
been	biˑn, bɪn, *s.fs.*	(*usually* bɪn)
	bɪn *w.f.*	
am	æm *s.f.*, əm, m *w.fs.*	
is	ɪz *s.f.*, z, s *w.fs.*	
are	ɑˑ(r *s.f.*, ə(r *w.f.*	ɑə *s.f.*, ə *w.f.*
was	wɒz *s.f.*, wəz *w.f.*	wɑz *s.f.*, wəz *w.f.*
were	wɜˑ(r wɛə(r, *s.fs.*,	wɜə *s.f.*, wə *w.f.*
	wə(r *w.f.*	
beach	biˑtʃ	
beaches	'biˑtʃɪz	
bead	biˑd	
beads	biˑdz	
beak	biˑk	
beaks	biˑks	
beam	biˑm	
beams	biˑmz	
bean	biˑn	
beans	biˑnz	
bear	bɛə(r	bɛə
bears	bɛəz	bɛəz
bore	bɔə(r	boə
borne	bɔˑn, bɔən	boən
bearing	'bɛərɪŋ	bɛˑrɪŋ
bearer	'bɛərə(r	'bɛˑrə
bearers	'bɛərəz	'bɛˑrəz
beard	bɪəd	bɪəd
beards	bɪədz	bɪədz
bearded	'bɪədɪd	'bɪədɪd
beast	biˑst	
beasts	biˑsts	
beastly	'biˑstlɪ	

Traditional Spelling	Received Pronunciation	American Variants
beat	biˑt	
beats	biˑts	
beaten	biˑtn̩	
beating	biˑtɪŋ	
beautiful	ˈbjuˑtɪfʊl	
beautifully	ˈbjuˑtɪfəlɪ	
beauty	ˈbjuˑtɪ	
beauties	ˈbjuˑtɪz	
BECAME *from* become	bɪˈkeɪm	
because	bɪˈkɒz, bɪˈkɔz	
beckon	ˈbɛkən	
beckons	ˈbɛkənz	
beckoned	ˈbɛkənd	
beckoning	ˈbɛkənɪŋ	
become	bɪˈkʌm	
becomes	bɪˈkʌmz	
became	bɪˈkeɪm	
becoming, ***adj.***	bɪˈkʌmɪŋ	
bed	bɛd	
beds	bɛdz	
bedroom	ˈbɛdrum, ˈbɛdrʊm	
bedrooms	bɛdrumz, ˈbɛdrʊmz	
bee	biˑ	
bees	biˑz	
beef	biˑf	
beefsteak	ˈbiˑfˈsteɪk	
beefsteaks	ˈbiˑfˈsteɪks	
BEEN *from* be	biˑn, bɪn	(*usually* bɪn)
beer	bɪə(r	bɪə
beetle	ˈbiˑtl̩	
beetles	ˈbiˑtl̩z	
before	bɪˈfɔə(r	bɪˈfoə
beforehand	bɪˈfɔəhænd	bɪˈfoəhænd
beg	bɛg	
begs	bɛgz	
begged	bɛgd	
begging	ˈbɛgɪŋ	
BEGAN *from* begin	bɪˈgæn	
beggar	ˈbɛgə(r	bɛgə
beggars	ˈbɛgəz	ˈbɛgəz
begin	bɪˈgɪn	
begins	bɪˈgɪnz	
began	bɪˈgæn	
begun	bɪˈgʌn	
beginning, ***noun***	bɪˈgɪnɪŋ	
behalf	bɪˈhɑˑf	bɪˈhaˑf
behave	bɪˈheɪv	

Traditional Spelling	Received Pronunciation	American Variants
behaves	bɪ'heɪvz	
behaved	bɪ'heɪvd	
behaving	bɪ'heɪvɪŋ	
behavior (*Amer.*)		
behaviors (*Amer.*)		
behaviour	bɪ'heɪvjə(r	bɪ'heɪvjə
behaviours	bɪ'heɪvjəz	bɪ'heɪvjəz
behind	bɪ'haɪnd	
behindhand	bɪ'haɪndhænd	
being, *noun*	'bi·ɪŋ	
beings	'bi·ɪŋz	
BEING *from* be	'bi·ɪŋ	
Belgian	'bɛlʤən	
Belgians	'bɛlʤənz	
Belgium	'bɛlʤəm	
Belgrade	bɛl'greɪd	
belief	bɪ'li·f	
beliefs	bɪ'li·fs	
believe	bɪ'li·v	
believes	bɪ'li·vz	
believed	bɪ'li·vd	
believing	bɪ'li·vɪŋ	
believer	bɪ'li·və(r	bɪ'li·və
believers	bɪ'li·vəz	bɪ'li·vəz
bell	bɛl	
bells	bɛlz	
bellows	'bɛloʊz	
belly	'bɛlɪ	
bellies	'bɛlɪz	
belong	bɪ'lɒŋ	
belongs	bɪ'lɒŋz	
belonged	bɪ'lɒŋd	
belonging	bɪ'lɒŋɪŋ	
below	bɪ'loʊ	
belt	bɛlt	
belts	bɛlts	
bench	bɛntʃ	
benches	bɛntʃɪz	
bend	bɛnd	
bends	bɛndz	
bent	bɛnt	
bending	bɛndɪŋ	
beneath	bɪ'ni·θ	
benefactor	'bɛnɪfæktə(r	bɛnɪ'fæktə
benefactors	'bɛnɪfæktəz	bɛnɪ'fæktəz
beneficial	bɛnɪ'fɪʃəl	
benefit	'bɛnɪfɪt	

Traditional Spelling	Received Pronunciation	American Variants
benefits	ˈbenɪfɪts	
benefited	ˈbenɪfɪtɪd	
benefiting	ˈbenɪfɪtɪŋ	
benevolence	bɪˈnɛvələns	
benevolent	bɪˈnɛvələnt	
benevolently	bɪˈnɛvələntlɪ	
Bengal	beŋˈgɔˑl, benˈgɔˑl	
BENT *from* bend	bent	
Berlin	ˈbɜˑˈlɪn	ˈbɜəˈlɪn
berry	ˈberɪ	
berries	ˈberɪz	
berth	bɜˑθ	bɜəθ
berths	bɜˑθs, bɜˑðz	bɜəθs
beside	bɪˈsaɪd	
besides	bɪˈsaɪdz	
best	best	
bet	bet	
bets	bets	
betted	ˈbetɪd	
betting	ˈbetɪŋ	
betray	bɪˈtreɪ	
betrays	bɪˈtreɪz	
betrayed	bɪˈtreɪd	
betraying	bɪˈtreɪɪŋ	
better	ˈbetə(r	betə
betterment	ˈbetəmənt	ˈbetəmənt
between	bɪˈtwiˑn, bəˈtwiˑn	
bewilder	bɪˈwɪldə(r	bɪˈwɪldə
bewilders	bɪˈwɪldəz	bɪˈwɪldəz
bewildered	bɪˈwɪldəd	bɪˈwɪldəd
bewildering	bɪˈwɪldərɪŋ	bɪˈwɪldərɪŋ
beyond	bɪˈjɒnd	bɪˈjɑnd
Bible	ˈbaɪbl̩	
Bibles	ˈbaɪbl̩z	
biblical	ˈbɪblɪkl̩	
bicycle	ˈbaɪsɪkl̩	
bicycles	ˈbaɪsɪkl̩z	
bid	bɪd	
bids	bɪdz	
bidding	ˈbɪdɪŋ	
big	bɪg	
bigger	ˈbɪgə(r	ˈbɪgə
biggest	ˈbɪgɪst	
bill	bɪl	
bills	bɪlz	
billiard	ˈbɪljəd	ˈbɪljəd
billiards	ˈbɪljədz	ˈbɪljədz

Traditional Spelling	Received Pronunciation	American Variants
bind	baɪnd	
binds	baɪndz	
bound	baʊnd	
binding	ˈbaɪndɪŋ	
biography	baɪˈɒgrəfɪ	baɪˈɑgrəfɪ
biographies	baɪˈɒgrəfɪz	baɪˈɑgrəfɪz
biology	baɪɒlədʒɪ	baɪˈɑlədʒɪ
birch	bɜˑtʃ	bɜətʃ
birches	bɜˑtʃɪz	bɜətʃɪz
bird	bɜˑd	bɜəd
birds	bɜˑdz	bɜədz
Birmingham	ˈbɜˑmɪŋəm	ˈbɜəmɪŋhæm
birth	bɜˑθ	bɜəθ
births	bɜˑθs	bɜəθs
birthday	ˈbɜˑθdeɪ	ˈbɜəθdeɪ
birthdays	ˈbɜˑθdeɪz	ˈbɜəθdeɪz
birthplace	ˈbɜˑθpleɪs	ˈbɜəθpleɪs
birthplaces	ˈbɜˑθpleɪsɪz	ˈbɜəθpleɪsɪz
biscuit	ˈbɪskɪt	
biscuits	ˈbɪskɪts	
bisect	baɪˈsɛkt	
bisects	baɪˈsɛkts	
bisected	baɪˈsɛktɪd	
bisecting	baɪsɛktɪŋ	
bishop	ˈbɪʃəp	
bishops	ˈbɪʃəps	
bit	bɪt	
bits	bɪts	
bite	baɪt	
bites	baɪts	
bit	bɪt	
bitten	bɪtn̩	
biting	ˈbaɪtɪŋ	
bitter	ˈbɪtə(r	ˈbɪtə
bitterer	ˈbɪtərə(r	ˈbɪtərə
bitterest	ˈbɪtərɪst	ˈbɪtrɪst
bitterly	ˈbɪtəlɪ	ˈbɪtəlɪ
bitterness	ˈbɪtənɪs	ˈbɪtənɪs, bɪtənəs
black	blæk	
blacker	ˈblækə(r	ˈblækə
blackest	ˈblækɪst	
blackish	ˈblækɪʃ	
blackness	ˈblæknɪs	
blackbird	ˈblækbɜd	ˈblækbɜəd
blackbirds	ˈblækbɜdz	ˈblækbɜədz
blackboard	ˈblækbɔˑd	ˈblækboəd
blackboards	ˈblækbɔˑdz	ˈblækboədz

Traditional Spelling	Received Pronunciation	American Variants
blacken	ˈblækən	
blackens	ˈblækənz	
blackened	ˈblækənd	
blackening	ˈblækənɪŋ	
blacksmith	ˈblæksmɪθ	
blacksmiths	ˈblæksmɪθs	
blade	bleɪd	
blades	bleɪdz	
blame	bleɪm	
blames	bleɪmz	
blamed	bleɪmd	
blaming	bleɪmɪŋ	
blameless	ˈbleɪmlɪs	
blank	blæŋk	
blanks	blæŋks	
blanker	ˈblæŋkə(r	ˈblæŋkə
blankest	ˈblæŋkɪst	
blankly	ˈblæŋklɪ	
blanket	ˈblæŋkɪt	
blankets	ˈblæŋkɪts	
bleed	bliˑd	
bleeds	bliˑdz	
bled	blɛd	
bleeding	ˈbliˑdɪŋ	
bless	blɛs	
blesses	ˈblɛsɪz	
blessed	blɛst	
blessing	ˈblɛsɪŋ	
blessings	ˈblɛsɪŋz	
blessed, *adj.*	ˈblɛsɪd	
BLEW *from* blow	bluˑ	
blind	blaɪnd	
blinder	ˈblaɪndə(r	blaɪndə
blindest	ˈblaɪndɪst	
blinds	ˈblaɪndz	
blinded	ˈblaɪndɪd	
blinding	ˈblaɪndɪŋ	
blindfold	ˈblaɪn*d*fould	
blindfolds	ˈblaɪn*d*fouldz	
blindfolded	ˈblaɪn*d*fouldɪd	
blindfolding	ˈblaɪn*d*fouldɪŋ	
blindly	ˈblaɪndlɪ	
blindness	ˈblaɪndnɪs	
blister	ˈblɪstə(r	ˈblɪstə
blisters	ˈblɪstəz	ˈblɪstəz
block	blɒk	blɑk
blocks	blɒks	blɑks

Traditional Spelling	Received Pronunciation	American Variants
blocked	blɒkt	blɑkt
blocking	'blɒkɪŋ	'blɑkɪŋ
blockade	blɒ'keɪd	blɑ'keɪd
blockades	blɒ'keɪdz	blɑ'keɪdz
blockaded	blɒ'keɪdɪd	blɑ'keɪdɪd
blockading	blɒ'keɪdɪŋ	blɑ'keɪdɪŋ
blood	blʌd	
bloom	blu·m	
blooms	blu·mz	
bloomed	blu·md	
blooming	blu·mɪŋ	
blossom	'blɒsəm	'blɑsəm
blossoms	'blɒsəmz	'blɑsəmz
blossomed	'blɒsəmd	'blɑsəmd
blossoming	'blɒsəmɪŋ	'blɑsəmɪŋ
blot	blɒt	blɑt
blots	blɒts	blɑts
blotted	'blɒtɪd	'blɑtɪd
blotting	'blɒtɪŋ	'blɑtɪŋ
blotter	'blɒtə(r	'blɑtə
blotters	'blɒtəz	'blɑtəz
blotting-paper	'blɒtɪŋpeɪpə(r	'blɑtɪŋpeɪpə
blouse	blaʊz	
blouses	'blaʊzɪz	
blow	bloʊ	
blows	bloʊz	
blew	blu·	
blown	bloʊn	
blowing	'bloʊɪŋ	
blue	blu·	
blues	blu·z	
blueness	'blu·nɪs	
bluish	'blu·ɪʃ	
blunder	'blʌndə(r	'blʌndə
blunders	'blʌndəz	'blʌndəz
blundered	'blʌndəd	'blʌndəd
blundering	'blʌndərɪŋ	
blunderer	'blʌndərə(r	'blʌndərə
blunderers	'blʌndərəz	'blʌndərəz
blunt	blʌnt	
blunter	'blʌntə(r	'blʌntə
bluntest	'blʌntɪst	
blunts	blʌnts	
blunted	'blʌntɪd	
blunting	'blʌntɪŋ	
bluntly	'blʌntlɪ	
bluntness	'blʌntnɪs	

Traditional Spelling	Received Pronunciation	American Variants
blush	blʌʃ	
blushes	ˈblʌʃɪz	
blushed	blʌʃt	
blushing	ˈblʌʃɪŋ	
boa	bɔə, ˈboʊə	boə
boas	bɔəz, ˈboʊəz	boəz
boar	bɔə(r	boə
boars	bɔəz	boəz
board	bɔˑd, bɔəd	boəd
boards	bɔˑdz, bɔədz	boədz
boarded	ˈbɔˑdɪd, bɔədɪd	ˈboədɪd
boarding	ˈbɔˑdɪŋ, bɔədɪŋ	ˈboədɪŋ
boarder	ˈbɔˑdə(r, ˈbɔədə(r	ˈboədə
boarders	ˈbɔˑdəz, ˈbɔədəz	ˈboədəz
boarding-house	ˈbɔˑdɪŋhaʊs ˈbɔədɪŋhaʊs	ˈboədɪŋhaʊs
boarding-houses	ˈbɔˑdɪŋhaʊzɪz ˈbɔədɪŋhaʊzɪz	ˈboədɪŋhaʊzɪz
boarding-school	ˈbɔˑdɪŋskuˑl ˈbɔədɪŋskuˑlz	ˈboədɪŋskuˑl
boarding-schools	ˈbɔˑdɪŋskuˑlz ˈbɔədɪŋskuˑlz	ˈboədɪŋskuˑlz
boast	boʊst	
boasts	boʊsts	
boasted	ˈboʊstɪd	
boasting	ˈboʊstɪŋ	
boaster	ˈboʊstə(r	ˈboʊstə
boasters	ˈboʊstəz	ˈboʊstəz
boastful	ˈboʊstfʊl	
boastfully	ˈboʊstfəlɪ, ˈboʊstfʊlɪ	
boat	boʊt	
boats	boʊts	
boating	ˈboʊtɪŋ	
boatman	ˈboʊtmən	
boatmen	ˈboʊtmən	
bodily	ˈbɒdɪlɪ	ˈbɑdɪlɪ
body	ˈbɒdɪ	ˈbɑdɪ
bodies	ˈbɒdɪz	ˈbɑdɪz
Bohemia	boʊˈhiˑmjə, boʊˈhiˑmɪə	
Bohemian	boʊˈhiˑmjən boʊˈhiˑmɪən	
Bohemians	boʊˈhiˑmjənz boʊˈhiˑmɪənz	
boil	bɔɪl	
boils	bɔɪlz	
boiled	bɔɪld	

Traditional Spelling	Received Pronunciation	American Variants
boiling	'bɔɪlɪŋ	
boiler	'bɔɪlə(r	'bɔɪlə
boilers	'bɔɪləz	'bɔɪləz
boisterous	'bɔɪstərəs	
bold	bould	
bolder	'bouldə(r	'bouldə
boldest	'bouldɪst	
boldly	'bouldlɪ	
boldness	'bouldnɪs	
Bolivia	†bə'lɪvɪə	
Bolivian	†bə'lɪvɪən	
Bolivians	†bə'lɪvɪənz	
bolster	'boulstə(r	'boulstə
bolsters	'boulstəz	'boulstəz
bolt	boult	
bolts	boults	
bolted	'boultɪd	
bolting	'boultɪŋ	
bomb	bɒm	bɒm, bʌm
bombs	bɒmz	bɒmz, bʌmz
bombard	bɒm'bɑ·d	bɒm'bɑəd
bombards	bɒm'bɑ·dz	bɒm'bɑədz
bombarded	bɒm'bɑ·dɪd	bɒm'bɑədɪd
bombarding	bɒm'bɑ·dɪŋ	bɒm'bɑədɪŋ
bombardment	bɒm'bɑ·dmənt	bɒm'bɑədmənt
bombardments	bɒm'bɑ·dmənts	bɒm'bɑədmənts
Bombay	'bɒm'beɪ	'bɑm'beɪ
bond	bɒnd	bɑnd
bonds	bɒndz	bɑndz
bone	boun	
bones	bounz	
bonfire	'bɒnfaɪə(r	'bɑnfaɪə
bonfires	'bɒnfaɪəz	'bɑnfaɪəz
bonnet	'bɒnɪt	'bɑnɪt
bonnets	'bɒnɪts	'bɑnɪts
book	buk	
books	buks	
booked	bukt	
booking	'bukɪŋ	
bookbinder	'bukbaɪndə(r	'bukbaɪndə
bookbinders	'bukbaɪndəz	'bukbaɪndəz
bookbinding	'bukbaɪndɪŋ	
bookcase	'bukkeɪs	
bookcases	'bukkeɪsɪz	
book-keeper	'bukki·pə(r	'bukki·pə

† See Note 30, p. xxxv. in Introduction.

Traditional Spelling	Received Pronunciation	American Variants
book-keepers	ˈbʊkkiˑpəz	ˈbʊkkiˑpəz
book-keeping	ˈbʊkkiˑpɪŋ	
book-seller	ˈbʊksɛlə(r	ˈbʊksɛlə
book-sellers	ˈbʊksɛləz	ˈbʊksɛləz
book-shelf	ˈbʊkʃɛlf	
book-shelves	ˈbʊkʃɛlvz	
book-shop	ˈbʊkʃɒp	ˈbʊkʃɑp
book-shops	ˈbʊkʃɒps	ˈbʊkʃɑps
book-stall	ˈbʊkstɔˑl	
book-stalls	ˈbʊkstɔˑlz	
boot	buˑt	
boots	buˑts	
border	ˈbɔˑdə(r	ˈbɔədə
borders	ˈbɔˑdəz	ˈbɔədəz
bordered	ˈbɔˑdəd	ˈbɔədəd
bordering	ˈbɔˑdᵊrɪŋ	ˈbɔədᵊrɪŋ
bore	bɔˑ(r, bɔə(r	boə
bores	bɔˑz, bɔəz	boəz
bored	bɔˑd, bɔəd	boəd
boring	ˈbɔˑrɪŋ, bɔərɪŋ	ˈboˑrɪŋ
BORN *from* bear, *bring forth*	bɔˑn	bɔən
BORNE *from* bear, *carry*	bɔˑn, bɔən	boən
borough	ˈbʌrə	ˈbʌroʊ
boroughs	ˈbʌrəz	ˈbʌroʊz
borrow	ˈbɒroʊ	ˈbɑroʊ
borrows	ˈbɒroʊz	ˈbɑroʊz
borrowed	ˈbɒroʊd	ˈbɑroʊd
borrowing	ˈbɒroʊɪŋ	ˈbɑroʊɪŋ
Boston	ˈbɒstᵊn	ˈbɑstᵊn
botanical	bəˈtænɪkᵊl	
botanist	ˈbɒtənɪst	ˈbɑtənɪst
botanists	ˈbɒtənɪsts	ˈbɑtənɪsts
botany	ˈbɒtənɪ	ˈbɑtənɪ
both	boʊθ	
bother	ˈbɒðə(r	ˈbɑðə
bothers	ˈbɒðəz	ˈbɑðəz
bothered	ˈbɒðəd	ˈbɑðəd
bothering	ˈbɒðərɪŋ	ˈbɑðərɪŋ
bottle	ˈbɒtl̩	ˈbɑtl̩
bottles	ˈbɒtl̩z	ˈbɑtl̩z
bottled	ˈbɒtl̩d	ˈbɑtl̩d
bottling	ˈbɒtlɪŋ, ˈbɒtl̩ɪŋ	ˈbɑtlɪŋ, ˈbɑtl̩ɪŋ
bottom	ˈbɒtəm	ˈbɑtəm
bottoms	ˈbɒtəmz	ˈbɑtəmz
bough	baʊ	

Traditional Spelling	Received Pronunciation	American Variants
boughs	baʊz	
BOUGHT *from* buy	bɔˑt	
bounce	baʊns	
bounces	ˈbaʊnsɪz	
bounced	baʊnst	
bouncing	ˈbaʊnsɪŋ	
bound	baʊnd	
bounds	baʊndz	
BOUND *from* bind	baʊnd	
boundary	ˈbaʊndərɪ	
boundaries	ˈbaʊndərɪz	
bow, *for shooting, etc., knot*	boʊ	
bows	boʊz	
bow, *bend*	baʊ	
bows	baʊz	
bowed	baʊd	
bowing	baʊɪŋ	
bowl	boʊl	
bowls	boʊlz	
bowled	boʊld	
bowling	ˈboʊlɪŋ	
box	bɒks	bɑks
boxes	ˈbɒksɪz	ˈbɑksɪz
boxed	bɒkst	bɑkst
boxing	ˈbɒksɪŋ	ˈbɑksɪŋ
boxer	ˈbɒksə(r	ˈbɑksə
boxers	ˈbɒksəz	ˈbɑksəz
boy	bɔɪ	
boys	bɔɪz	
boyhood	ˈbɔɪhʊd	
boyish	ˈbɔɪɪʃ	
brace	breɪs	
braces	ˈbreɪsɪz	
bracelet	ˈbreɪslɪt	
bracelets	ˈbreɪslɪts	
bracket	ˈbrækɪt	
brackets	ˈbrækɪts	
brag	bræg	
brags	brægz	
bragged	brægd	
bragging	ˈbrægɪŋ	
braid	breɪd	
brain	breɪn	
brains	breɪnz	
brake	breɪk	
brakes	breɪks	

Traditional Spelling	Received Pronunciation	American Variants
branch	brɑˑntʃ	braˑntʃ
branches	ˈbrɑˑntʃɪz	ˈbraˑntʃɪz
branched	brɑˑntʃt	braˑntʃt
branching	ˈbrɑˑntʃɪŋ	ˈbraˑntʃɪŋ
brand	brænd	
brands	brændz	
brandy	ˈbrændɪ	
brass	brɑˑs	braˑs
brave	breɪv	
braver	ˈbreɪvə(r	ˈbreɪvə
bravest	ˈbreɪvɪst	
bravely	ˈbreɪvlɪ	
bravery	ˈbreɪvərɪ	
Brazil	brəˈzɪl, brɪˈzɪl	
Brazilian	brəˈzɪljən, brɪˈzɪljən	
Brazilians	brəˈzɪljənz	
	brɪˈzɪljənz	
bread	brɛd	
breadth	brɛdθ	
break	breɪk	
breaks	breɪks	
broke	broʊk	
broken	ˈbroʊkən	
breaking	ˈbreɪkɪŋ	
breakable	ˈbreɪkəbl̩	
breakfast	ˈbrɛkfəst	
breakfasts	ˈbrɛkfəsts	
breakfasted	ˈbrɛkfəstɪd	
breakfasting	ˈbrɛkfəstɪŋ	
breast	brɛst	
breasts	brɛsts	
breath	brɛθ	
breaths	brɛθs	
breathe	briˑð	
breathes	briˑðz	
breathed	briˑðd	
breathing	ˈbriˑðɪŋ	
breathless	ˈbrɛθlɪs	
breathlessly	ˈbrɛθlɪslɪ	
breed	briˑd	
breeds	briˑdz	
bred	brɛd	
breeding	briˑdɪŋ	
breeze	briˑz	
breezes	briˑzɪz	
brevity	ˈbrɛvɪtɪ	
brew	bruˑ	

Traditional Spelling	Received Pronunciation	American Variants
brews	bru·z	
brewed	bru·d	
brewing	ˈbru·ɪŋ	
brewer	ˈbru·ə(r	ˈbru·ə
brewers	ˈbru·əz	ˈbru·əz
brewery	ˈbru·ərɪ, ˈbrʊərɪ	
breweries	ˈbru·ərɪz, ˈbrʊərɪz	
bribe	braɪb	
bribes	braɪbz	
bribed	braɪbd	
bribing	ˈbraɪbɪŋ	
brick	brɪk	
bricks	brɪks	
bricklayer	ˈbrɪkleɪə(r	ˈbrɪkleɪə
bricklayers	ˈbrɪkleɪəz	ˈbrɪkleɪəz
bride	braɪd	
brides	braɪdz	
bridegroom	ˈbraɪdgrum ˈbraɪdgrʊm	
bridegrooms	ˈbraɪdgrumz ˈbraɪdgrʊmz	
bridge	brɪʤ	
bridges	brɪʤɪz	
brief	bri·f	
briefer	ˈbri·fə(r	ˈbri·fə
briefest	ˈbri·fɪst	
briefly	ˈbri·flɪ	
brigand	ˈbrɪgənd	
brigands	ˈbrɪgəndz	
bright	braɪt	
brighter	ˈbraɪtə(r	ˈbraɪtə
brightest	ˈbraɪtɪst	
brightly	ˈbraɪtlɪ	
brightness	ˈbraɪtnɪs	
brilliance	ˈbrɪljəns	
brilliant	ˈbrɪljənt	
brilliantly	ˈbrɪljəntlɪ	
brim	brɪm	
brims	brɪmz	
bring	brɪŋ	
brings	brɪŋz	
brought	brɔ·t	
bringing	ˈbrɪŋɪŋ	
brink	brɪŋk	
brinks	brɪŋks	
brisk	brɪsk	
briskly	ˈbrɪsklɪ	

Traditional Spelling	Received Pronunciation	American Variants
Britain	ˈbrɪtən	
British	ˈbrɪtɪʃ	
brittle	ˈbrɪtl̩	
brittler	ˈbrɪtl̩ə(r	ˈbrɪtlə
brittlest	ˈbrɪtl̩ɪst	
broad	brɔˑd	
broader	ˈbrɔˑdə(r	ˈbrɔˑdə
broadest	ˈbrɔˑdɪst	
broadly	ˈbrɔˑdlɪ	
broadcast	ˈbrɔˑdkɑst	ˈbrɔˑdkast
broadcasts	ˈbrɔˑdkɑsts	ˈbrɔˑdkasts
broadcasting	ˈbrɔˑdkɑstɪŋ	ˈbrɔˑdkastɪŋ
broaden	ˈbrɔˑdn̩	
broadens	ˈbrɔˑdn̩z	
broadened	ˈbrɔˑdn̩d	
broadening	ˈbrɔˑdn̩ɪŋ	
BROKE *from* break	broʊk	
bronchitis	brɒnˈkaɪtɪs brɒŋˈkaɪtɪs	brɑnˈkaɪtɪs
bronze	brɒnz	brɑnz
bronzes	ˈbrɒnzɪz	ˈbrɑnzɪz
brooch	broʊʧ	
brooches	ˈbroʊʧɪz	
brook	brʊk	
brooks	brʊks	
broom	bruˑm, brʊm	
brooms	bruˑmz, brʊmz	
broth	brɔθ, brɒθ	
broths	brɔθs, brɔðz	
brother	ˈbrʌðə(r	ˈbrʌðə
brothers	ˈbrʌðəz	ˈbrʌðəz
brotherhood	ˈbrʌðəhʊd	ˈbrʌðəhʊd
brotherhoods	ˈbrʌðəhʊdz	ˈbrʌðəhʊdz
brother-in-law	ˈbrʌðərɪnlɔ	
brothers-in-law	ˈbrʌðəzɪnlɔ	ˈbrʌðəzɪnlɔ
brotherly	ˈbrʌðəlɪ	ˈbrʌðəlɪ
BROUGHT *from* bring	brɔˑt	
brown	braʊn	
browner	ˈbraʊnə(r	ˈbraʊnə
brownest	ˈbraʊnɪst	
bruise	bruˑz	
bruises	ˈbruˑzɪz	
bruised	bruˑzd	
bruising	ˈbruˑzɪŋ	
brush	brʌʃ	
brushes	ˈbrʌʃɪz	
brushed	brʌʃt	
brushing	ˈbrʌʃɪŋ	

Traditional Spelling	Received Pronunciation	American Variants
Brussels	'brʌsl̩z	
brutal	'bru·tl̩	
brutally	'bru·təlɪ	
brutality	bru·'tælɪtɪ	
brutalities	bru·'tælɪtɪz	
brute	bru·t	
brutes	bru·ts	
bubble	'bʌbl̩	
bubbles	'bʌbl̩z	
bucket	'bʌkɪt	
buckets	'bʌkɪts	
bucketful	'bʌkɪtful	
bucketfuls	'bʌkɪtfulz	
buckle	'bʌkl̩	
buckles	'bʌkl̩z	
buckled	'bʌkl̩d	
buckling	'bʌklɪŋ, 'bʌkl̩ɪŋ	
bud	bʌd	
buds	bʌdz	
budded	'bʌdɪd	
budding	'bʌdɪŋ	
budget	'bʌʤɪt	
budgets	'bʌʤɪts	
bug	bʌg	
bugs	bʌgz	
bugle	'bju·gl̩	
bugles	'bju·gl̩z	
bugler	'bju·glə(r	'bju·glə
buglers	'bju·gləz	'bju·gləz
build	bɪld	
builds	bɪldz	
built	bɪlt	
building	'bɪldɪŋ	
builder	'bɪldə(r	'bɪldə
builders	'bɪldəz	'bɪldəz
bulb	bʌlb	
bulbs	bʌlbz	
bulge	bʌlʤ	
bulges	'bʌlʤɪz	
bulged	bʌlʤd	
bulging	'bʌlʤɪŋ	
bulky	'bʌlkɪ	
bulkier	'bʌlkɪə(r	'bʌlkɪə
bulkiest	'bʌlkɪɪst	
bull	bul	
bulls	bulz	
bull-dog	'buldɒg	

Traditional Spelling	Received Pronunciation	American Variants
bull-dogs	'buldɒgz	
bullet	'bulɪt	
bullets	'bulɪts	
bulletin	'bulɪtɪn	'bulɪtn̩
bulletins	'bulɪtɪnz	'bulɪtn̩z
bully	'bulɪ	
bullies	'bulɪz	
bullied	'bulɪd	
bullying	'bulɪɪŋ	
bump	bʌmp	
bumps	bʌmps	
bumped	bʌmpt	
bumping	'bʌmpɪŋ	
bun	bʌn	
buns	bʌnz	
bunch	bʌntʃ	
bunches	'bʌntʃɪz	
bundle	'bʌndl̩	
bundles	'bʌndl̩z	
bungalow	'bʌŋgəlou	
bungalows	'bʌŋgəlouz	
buoy	bɔɪ	
buoys	bɔɪz	
burden	'bɜ·dn̩	'bɜədn̩
burdens	'bɜ·dn̩z	'bɜədn̩z
burdened	'bɜ·dn̩d	'bɜədn̩d
burdening	'bɜ·dn̩ɪŋ	'bɜədn̩ɪŋ
bureau	bjuə'rou, 'bjuərou	'bjurou
bureaus	bjuə'rouz 'bjuərouz	'bjurouz
burglar	'bɜ·glə(r	'bɜəglə
burglars	'bɜ·gləz	'bɜəgləz
burglary	'bɜ·glərɪ	'bɜəglərɪ
burglaries	'bɜ·glərɪz	'bɜəglərɪz
burial	'berɪəl	
burials	'berɪəlz	
burn	bɜ·n	bɜən
burns	bɜ·nz	bɜənz
burned	bɜ·nt	bɜənt
burnt	bɜ·nt	bɜənt
burning	'bɜ·nɪŋ	'bɜənɪŋ
burner	'bɜ·nə(r	'bɜənə
burners	'bɜ·nəz	'bɜənəz
burst	bɜ·st	bɜəst
bursts	bɜ·sts	bɜəsts
bursting	'bɜ·stɪŋ	'bɜəstɪŋ
bury	'berɪ	

Traditional Spelling	Received Pronunciation	American Variants
buries	ˈbɛrɪz	
buried	ˈbɛrɪd	
burying	ˈbɛrɪɪŋ	
bus	bʌs	
buses	bʌsɪz	
bush	bʊʃ	
bushes	bʊʃɪz	
bushel	ˈbʊʃəl	
bushels	ˈbʊʃəlz	
business	ˈbɪznɪs, ˈbɪzn̩ɪs	
businesses	ˈbɪznɪsɪz	
bustle	ˈbʌsl̩	
bustles	ˈbʌsl̩z	
bustled	ˈbʌsl̩d	
bustling	ˈbʌsl̩ɪŋ, ˈbʌslɪŋ	
busy	ˈbɪzɪ	
busier	ˈbɪzɪə(r	ˈbɪzɪə
busiest	ˈbɪzɪɪst	
busily	ˈbɪzɪlɪ	
but	bʌt *s.f.*, bət *w.f.*	
butcher	ˈbʊtʃə(r	ˈbʊtʃə
butchers	ˈbʊtʃəz	ˈbʊtʃəz
butler	ˈbʌtlə(r	ˈbʌtlə
butlers	ˈbʌtləz	ˈbʌtləz
butterfly	ˈbʌtəflaɪ	
butterflies	ˈbʌtəflaɪz	
button	ˈbʌtn̩	
buttons	ˈbʌtn̩z	
buttoned	ˈbʌtn̩d	
buttoning	ˈbʌtn̩ɪŋ	
buy	baɪ	
buys	baɪz	
bought	bɔˑt	
buying	baɪɪŋ	
buyer	ˈbaɪə(r	ˈbaɪə
buyers	ˈbaɪəz	ˈbaɪəz
by	baɪ, *normal form*	
	bɪ, bə, *weak forms*	
by-and-by	ˈbaɪənd*ˈ*baɪ	
by-product	ˈbaɪprɒdəkt	ˈbaɪprɑdəkt
	ˈbaɪprɒdʌkt	
by-products	ˈbaɪprɒdəkts	ˈbaɪprɑdəkts
	ˈbaɪprɒdʌkts	
by-road	ˈbaɪroʊd	
by-roads	ˈbaɪroʊdz	
by-the-by(e)	ˈbaɪðəˈbaɪ	

C

Traditional Spelling	Received Pronunciation	American Variants
C	siˑ	
C's	siˑz	
cab	kæb	
cabs	kæbz	
cabbage	ˈkæbɪʤ	
cabbages	ˈkæbɪʤɪz	
cabin	ˈkæbɪn	
cabins	ˈkæbɪnz	
cabinet	ˈkæbɪnɪt	ˈkæbɪnət
cabinets	ˈkæbɪnɪts	ˈkæbɪnəts
cable	ˈkeɪbl̩	
cables	ˈkeɪbl̩z	
cabled	ˈkeɪbl̩d	
cabling	ˈkeɪblɪŋ, ˈkeɪbl̩ɪŋ	
cafe	ˈkæfeɪ, ˈkæfɪ	kæˈfeɪ
cafes	ˈkæfeɪz, ˈkæfɪz	kæˈfeɪz
cage	keɪʤ	
cages	ˈkeɪʤɪz	
caged	keɪʤd	
caging	ˈkeɪʤɪŋ	
Cairo	ˈkaɪərou	ˈkaɪrou
cake	keɪk	
cakes	keɪks	
calamity	kəˈlæmɪtɪ	
calamities	kəˈlæmɪtɪz	
calculable	ˈkælkjuləbl̩	
calculate	ˈkælkjuleɪt	
	ˈkælkjəleɪt	
calculates	ˈkælkjuleɪts	
	ˈkælkjəleɪts	
calculated	ˈkælkjuleɪtɪd	
	ˈkælkjəleɪtɪd	
calculating	ˈkælkjuleɪtɪŋ	
	ˈkælkjəleɪtɪŋ	
calculation	kælkjuˈleɪʃən	
	kælkjəˈleɪʃən	
calculations	kælkjuˈleɪʃənz	
	kælkjəˈleɪʃənz	
Calcutta	kælˈkʌtə	
calendar	ˈkælɪndə(r	ˈkælɪndə
calendars	ˈkælɪndəz	ˈkælɪndəz
calf	kɑˑf	kaˑf
calves	kɑˑvz	kaˑvz
calm	kɑˑm	
calmer	ˈkɑˑmə(r	ˈkɑˑmə

Traditional Spelling	Received Pronunciation	American Variants
calmest	'kɑ·mɪst	
calms	kɑ·mz	
calmed	kɑ·md	
calming	'kɑ·mɪŋ	
calmly	'kɑ·mlɪ	
calmness	'kɑ·mnɪs	
CAME (*from* come)	keɪm	
camel	'kæməl	
camels	'kæməlz	
camera	'kæmərə	
cameras	'kæmərəz	
camp	kæmp	
camps	kæmps	
camped	kæmpt	
camping	'kæmpɪŋ	
campaign	kæm'peɪn	
campaigns	kæm'peɪnz	
can, *noun*	kæn	
cans	kænz	
can, *verb*	kæn *s.f.*, kən *w.f.*	
could	kʊd *s.f.*, kəd *w.f.*	
Canada	'kænədə	
Canadian	kə'neɪdɪən, kə'neɪdjən	
Canadians	kə'neɪdɪənz, kə'neɪdjənz	
canal	kə'næl	
canals	kə'nælz	
canary	kə'nɛərɪ	
canaries	kə'nɛərɪz	
cancel	'kænsəl	
cancels	'kænsəlz	
cancelled	'kænsəld	
cancelling	'kænsəlɪŋ	
cancer	'kænsə(r	'kænsə
cancers	'kænsəz	'kænsəz
candid	'kændɪd	
candidly	'kændɪdlɪ	
candidate	'kændɪdɪt, 'kændɪdeɪt	
candidates	'kændɪdɪts 'kændɪdeɪts	
candle	'kændḷ	
candles	'kændḷz	
candle-stick	'kændḷstɪk	
candle-sticks	'kændḷstɪks	
candor (*Amer.*)		
candour	'kændə(r	'kændə
candy	'kændɪ	

Traditional Spelling	Received Pronunciation	American Variants
cane	keɪn	
canes	keɪnz	
cannibal	ˈkænɪbəl	
cannibals	ˈkænɪbəlz	
cannon	ˈkænən	
cannons	ˈkænənz	
cannot	ˈkænɒt	ˈkænɑt
	(*contracted* kɑˑnt)	(*contr.* kaˑnt, kænt
canoe	kəˈnuˑ	
canoes	kəˈnuˑz	
canon	ˈkænjən	
canons	ˈkænjɔnz	
can't	kɑˑnt	kaˑnt, kænt
Canton	ˈkænˈtɒn	
canvas	ˈkænvəs	
canvases	kænvəsɪz	
cap	kæp	
caps	kæps	
capability	keɪpəˈbɪlɪtɪ	
capabilities	keɪpəˈbɪlɪtɪz	
capable	ˈkeɪpɔbl̩	
capably	ˈkeɪpəblɪ	
capacious	kəˈpeɪʃəs	
capacity	kəˈpæsɪtɪ	
capacities	kəˈpæsɪtɪz	
cape	keɪp	
capes	keɪps	
Capetown	ˈkeɪpˈtaʊn	
capital	ˈkæpɪtl̩	
capitals	ˈkæpɪtl̩z	
capitalism	ˈkæpɪtəlɪzm̩	
capitalist	ˈkæpɪtəlɪst	
capitalists	ˈkæpɪtəlɪsts	
capricious	kəˈprɪʃəs	
capsize	kæpˈsaɪz	
capsizes	kæpˈsaɪzɪz	
capsized	kæpˈsaɪzd	
capsizing	kæpˈsaɪzɪŋ	
captain	ˈkæptɪn	
captains	ˈkæptɪnz	
captive	ˈkæptɪv	
captives	ˈkæptɪvz	
captivity	kæpˈtɪvɪtɪ	
capture	ˈkæptʃə(r	ˈkæptʃɚ
captures	ˈkæptʃəz	ˈkæptʃɚz
captured	ˈkæptʃəd	ˈkæptʃɚd
capturing	ˈkæptʃərɪŋ	

Traditional Spelling	Received Pronunciation	American Variants
car	kɑ·(r	kɑə
cars	kɑ·z	kɑəz
caravan	ˈkærəˈvæn	
caravans	ˈkærəˈvænz	
carbon	ˈkɑ·bən	ˈkɑəbən
carbons	ˈkɑ·bənz	ˈkɑəbənz
card	kɑ·d	kɑəd
cards	kɑ·dz	kɑədz
card-board	ˈkɑ·dbɔ·d	ˈkɑədboəd
cardinal	ˈkɑ·dɪnl̩	ˈkɑədɪnl̩
care	kɛə(r	kɛə
cares	kɛəz	kɛəz
cared	kɛəd	kɛəd
caring	ˈkɛərɪŋ	ˈkɛ·rɪŋ
career	kəˈrɪə(r	kəˈrɪə
careers	kəˈrɪəz	kəˈrɪəz
careful	ˈkɛəfʊl	ˈkɛəfʊl
carefully	ˈkɛəfəlɪ, ˈkɛəfʊlɪ	ˈkɛəfəlɪ, kɛəfʊlɪ
careless	ˈkɛəlɪs	ˈkɛəlɪs
carelessly	ˈkɛəlɪslɪ	ˈkɛəlɪslɪ
carelessness	ˈkɛəlɪsnɪs	ˈkɛəlɪsnɪs
caretaker	ˈkɛəteɪkə(r	ˈkɛəteɪkə
caretakers	ˈkɛəteɪkəz	ˈkɛəteɪkəz
cargo	ˈkɑ·goʊ	ˈkɑəgo
cargoes	ˈkɑ·goʊz	ˈkɑəgoz
caricature	ˈkærɪkəˈtjʊə(r	ˈkærɪkəˈtjʊə
caricatures	ˈkærɪkəˈtjʊəz	ˈkærɪkəˈtjʊəz
caricatured	ˈkærɪkəˈtjʊəd	ˈkærɪkəˈtjʊəd
caricaturing	ˈkærɪkəˈtjʊərɪŋ	ˈkærɪkəˈtjʊ·rɪŋ
carnation	kɑˈneɪʃən	kɑəˈneɪʃən
carnations	kɑˈneɪʃənz	kɑəˈneɪʃənz
carnival	ˈkɑ·nɪvəl	ˈkɑənɪvəl
carnivals	ˈkɑ·nɪvəlz	ˈkɑənɪvəlz
carp	kɑ·p	kɑəp
carps	kɑ·ps	kɑəps
carpenter	ˈkɑ·pəntə(r ˈkɑ·pɪntə(r	ˈkɑəpəntə
carpenters	ˈkɑ·pəntəz ˈkɑ·pɪntəz	ˈkɑəpəntəz
carpentering	ˈkɑ·pəntərɪŋ ˈkɑ·pɪntərɪŋ	ˈkɑəpəntərɪŋ
carpet	ˈkɑ·pɪt	ˈkɑəpɪt
carpets	ˈkɑ·pɪts	ˈkɑəpɪts
carriage	ˈkærɪʤ	
carriages	ˈkærɪʤɪz	
carrot	ˈkærət	
carrots	ˈkærəts	

Traditional Spelling	Received Pronunciation	American Variants
carry	'kærɪ	
carries	'kærɪz	
carried	'kærɪd	
carrying	'kærɪɪŋ	
carrier	'kærɪə(r	'kærɪə
carriers	'kærɪəz	'kærɪəz
cart	kɑ·t	kɑət
carts	kɑ·ts	kɑəts
carted	'kɑ·tɪd	'kɑətɪd
carting	kɑ·tɪŋ	'kɑətɪŋ
carter	'kɑ·tə(r	'kɑətə
carters	'kɑ·təz	'kɑətəz
carve	kɑ·v	kɑəv
carves	kɑ·vz	kɑəvz
carved	kɑ·vd	kɑəvd
carving	'kɑ·vɪŋ	'kɑəvɪŋ
case	keɪs	
cases	'keɪsɪz	
cash	kæʃ	
cashes	'kæʃɪz	
cashed	kæʃt	
cashing	'kæʃɪŋ	
cashier	kæ'ʃɪə(r	kæ'ʃɪə
cashiers	kæ'ʃɪəz	kæ'ʃɪəz
cask	kɑ·sk	ka·sk
casks	kɑ·sks	ka·sks
cast	kɑ·st	ka·st
casts	kɑ·sts	ka·sts
casting	'kɑ·stɪŋ	'ka·stɪŋ
castle	'kɑ·sl̩	'ka·sl̩, 'kæsl̩
castles	'kɑ·sl̩z	'ka·sl̩z, 'kæsl̩z
casual	'kæʒ*j*ʊəl	
casually	'kæʒ*j*ʊəlɪ	
cat	kæt	
cats	kæts	
catalog (*Amer.*)		
catalogue	'kætəlɒg	'kætəlɑg
catalogs (*Amer.*)		
catalogues	'kætəlɒgz	'kætəlɑgz
catastrophe	kə'tæstrəfɪ	
catastrophes	kə'tæstrəfɪz	
catch	kætʃ	
catches	'kætʃɪz	
caught	kɔ·t	
catching	'kætʃɪŋ	
categoric	kætɪ'gɒrɪk	
categorical	kætɪ'gɒrɪkəl	

Traditional Spelling	Received Pronunciation	American Variants
categorically	kætɪ'gɒrɪkəli	
category	'kætɪgərɪ	'kætɪgorɪ
categories	'kætɪgərɪz	'kætɪgorɪz
cathedral	kə'θi·drəl	
cathedrals	kə'θi·drəlz	
Catholic	'kæθəlɪk	
Catholics	'kæθəlɪks	
catholicism	kə'θɒlɪsɪzm̩	kə'θɑlɪsɪzm̩
cattle	'kætl̩	
CAUGHT *from* catch	kɔ·t	
cause	kɔ·z	
causes	'kɔ·zɪz	
caused	kɔ·zd	
causing	'kɔ·zɪŋ	
caution	'kɔ·ʃən	
cautious	'kɔ·ʃəs	
cautiously	'kɔ·ʃəslɪ	
cavalry	'kævəlrɪ	
cave	keɪv	
caves	keɪvz	
cavern	'kævən, 'kævɜn	'kævən
caverns	'kævənz, 'kævɜnz	'kævənz
cavity	'kævɪtɪ	
cavities	'kævɪtɪz	
cease	si·s	
ceases	'si·sɪz	
ceased	si·st	
ceasing	'si·sɪŋ	
ceiling	'si·lɪŋ	
ceilings	'si·lɪŋz	
celebrate	'sɛlɪbreɪt	
celebrates	'sɛlɪbreɪts	
celebrated	'sɛlɪbreɪtɪd	
celebrating	'sɛlɪbreɪtɪŋ	
celebration	sɛlɪ'breɪʃən	
celebrations	sɛlɪ'breɪʃənz	
cell	sɛl	
cells	sɛlz	
cellar	'sɛlə(r	'sɛlə
cellars	'sɛləz	'sɛləz
cement	sɪ'mɛnt	
cements	sɪ'mɛnts	
cemented	sɪ'mɛntɪd	
cementing	sɪ'mɛntɪŋ	
cent	sɛnt	
cents	sɛnts	
centigrade	'sɛntɪgreɪd	

Traditional Spelling	Received Pronunciation	American Variants
centimeter (*Amer.*)		
centimetre	'sɛntɪmiˑtə(r	'sɛntɪmiˑtə
centimeters (*Amer.*)		
centimetres	'sɛntɪmiˑtəz	'sɛntɪmiˑtəz
central	'sɛntrəl	
centrally	'sɛntrəlɪ	
center (*Amer.*)		
centre	'sɛntə(r	'sɛntə
centres	'sɛntəz	sɛntəz
century	'sɛntʃurɪ, 'sɛntjəri	
centuries	'sɛntʃurɪz	
	'sɛntjərɪz	
ceremonial	sɛrɪ'mounjəl	
	sɛrɪ'mounɪəl	
ceremonious	sɛri'mounjəs	
	sɛrɪ'mounɪəs	
ceremony	'sɛrɪmənɪ	
ceremonies	'sɛrɪmənɪz	
certain	'səˑtn̩	'səətn̩
certainly	'səˑtn̩lɪ	'səətn̩lɪ
certainty	'səˑtn̩tɪ	'səətn̩tɪ
certificate	sə'tɪfɪkɪt	səə'tɪfɪkɪt
certificates	sə'tɪfɪkɪts	səə'tɪfɪkɪts
Ceylon	sɪ'lɒn	
chain	tʃeɪn	
chains	tʃeɪnz	
chained	tʃeɪnd	
chaining	'tʃeɪnɪŋ	
chair	tʃɛə(r	tʃɛə
chairs	tʃɛəz	tʃɛəz
chairman	'tʃɛəmən	'tʃɛəmən
chairmen	'tʃɛəmən	'tʃɛəmən
chalk	tʃɔˑk	
challenge	'tʃæləndʒ, 'tʃælɪndʒ	
challenges	'tʃæləndʒɪz	
	'tʃælɪndʒɪz	
challenged	'tʃæləndʒd	
	'tʃælɪndʒd	
challenging	'tʃæləndʒɪŋ	
	'tʃælɪndʒɪŋ	
champion	'tʃæmpɪən	
champions	'tʃæmpɪənz	
chance	tʃɑˑns	tʃaˑns
chances	'tʃɑˑnsɪz	'tʃaˑnsɪz
change	tʃeɪndʒ	
changes	'tʃeɪndʒɪz	
changed	tʃeɪndʒd	

Traditional Spelling	Received Pronunciation	American Variants
changing	ˈtʃeɪndʒɪŋ	
changeable	ˈtʃeɪndʒəbl̩	
channel	ˈtʃænl̩	
channels	ˈtʃænl̩z	
chap	tʃæp	
chaps	tʃæps	
chapel	ˈtʃæpl̩	
chapels	ˈtʃæpl̩z	
chapter	ˈtʃæptə(r	ˈtʃæptə
chapters	ˈtʃæptəz	ˈtʃæptəz
character	ˈkærɪktə(r	ˈkærɪktə
characters	ˈkærɪktəz	ˈkærɪktəz
characteristic	kærɪktəˈrɪstɪk	
characteristics	kærɪktəˈrɪstɪks	
charcoal	ˈtʃɑˑkoul	ˈtʃɑəkoul
charge	tʃɑˑdʒ	tʃɑədʒ
charges	ˈtʃɑˑdʒɪz	ˈtʃɑədʒɪz
charged	ˈtʃɑˑdʒd	ˈtʃɑədʒd
charging	ˈtʃɑˑdʒɪŋ	ˈtʃɑədʒɪŋ
charitable	tʃærɪtəbl̩	
charitably	tʃærɪtəblɪ	
charity	tʃærɪtɪ	
charities	tʃærɪtɪz	
Charles	tʃɑˑlz	tʃɑəlz
charm	tʃɑˑm	tʃɑəm
charms	tʃɑˑmz	tʃɑəmz
charmed	tʃɑˑmd	tʃɑəmd
charming	ˈtʃɑˑmɪŋ	ˈtʃɑəmɪŋ
chart	tʃɑˑt	tʃɑət
charts	tʃɑˑts	tʃɑəts
chase	tʃeɪs	
chases	ˈtʃeɪsɪz	
chased	tʃeɪst	
chasing	ˈtʃeɪsɪŋ	
chat	tʃæt	
chats	tʃæts	
chatted	ˈtʃætɪd	
chatting	ˈtʃætɪŋ	
chauffeur	ʃouˈfɜˑ(r, ˈʃoufə(r	ʃouˈfɜə, ˈʃoufə
chauffeurs	ʃouˈfɜˑz, ˈʃoufəz	ʃouˈfɜəz, ˈʃoufəz
cheap	tʃiˑp	
cheaper	ˈtʃiˑpə(r	ˈtʃiˑpə
cheapest	ˈtʃiˑpɪst	
cheaply	ˈtʃiˑplɪ	
cheat	tʃiˑt	
cheats	tʃiˑts	
cheated	ˈtʃiˑtid	

Traditional Spelling	Received Pronunciation	American Variants
cheating	ˈtʃiˑtɪŋ	
check	tʃɛk	
checks	tʃɛks	
checked	tʃɛkt	
checking	tʃɛkɪŋ	
cheek	tʃiˑk	
cheeks	tʃiˑks	
cheer	tʃɪə(r	tʃɪə
cheers	tʃɪəz	tʃɪəz
cheered	tʃɪəd	tʃɪəd
cheering	ˈtʃɪərɪŋ	ˈtʃɪˑrɪŋ
cheerful	ˈtʃɪəfʊl	ˈtʃɪəfʊl
cheerfully	ˈtʃɪəfəlɪ, ˈtʃɪəfʊlɪ	ˈtʃɪəfəlɪ, ˈtʃɪəfʊlɪ
cheese	tʃiˑz	
chemical	ˈkɛmɪkəl	
chemicals	ˈkɛmɪkəlz	
chemist	ˈkɛmɪst	
chemists	ˈkɛmɪsts	
chemistry	ˈkɛmɪstrɪ	
cheque	tʃɛk	
cheques	tʃɛks	
cherry	ˈtʃɛrɪ	
cherries	ˈtʃɛrɪz	
chess	tʃɛs	
chest	tʃɛst	
chests	tʃɛsts	
chestnut	ˈtʃɛsnʌt	
chestnuts	ˈtʃɛsnʌts	
chew	tʃuˑ	
chews	tʃuˑz	
chewed	tʃuˑd	
chewing	ˈtʃuˑɪŋ	
Chicago	ʃɪˈkɑˑgoʊ	ʃɪˈkɑˑgo
chicken	ˈtʃɪkɪn	
chickens	ˈtʃɪkɪnz	
chief	tʃiˑf	
chiefs	tʃiˑfs	
chiefly	ˈtʃiˑflɪ	
child	tʃaɪld	
children	ˈtʃɪldrən ˈtʃʊldrən	
childhood	ˈtʃaɪldhʊd	
childish	ˈtʃaɪldɪʃ	
childishly	ˈtʃaɪldɪʃlɪ	
childishness	ˈtʃaɪldɪʃnɪs	
Chile	ˈtʃɪlɪ	
Chilian	ˈtʃɪlɪən	

Traditional Spelling	Received Pronunciation	American Variants
Chilians	ˈtʃɪlɪənz	
chilly	ˈtʃɪlɪ	
chillier	ˈtʃɪlɪə(r	ˈtʃɪlɪə
chilliest	ˈtʃɪlɪɪst	
chimney	ˈtʃɪmnɪ	
chimneys	ˈtʃɪmnɪz	
chin	tʃɪn	
chins	tʃɪnz	
china	ˈtʃaɪnə .	
China		
Chinese	ˈtʃaɪˈniˑz	
chip	tʃɪp	
chips	tʃɪps	
chipped	tʃɪpt	
chipping	ˈtʃɪpɪŋ	
chisel	ˈtʃɪzl̩	
chisels	ˈtʃɪzl̩z	
chivalrous	ˈʃɪvəlrəs, ˈtʃɪvəlrəs	
chivalry	ˈʃɪvəlrɪ, ˈtʃɪvəlrɪ	
chocolate	ˈtʃɒkəlɪt	ˈtʃɑkələt
chocolates	ˈtʃɒkəlɪts	ˈtʃɑkələts
choice	tʃɔɪs	
choke	tʃouk	
chokes	tʃouks	
choked	tʃoukt	
choking	ˈtʃoukɪŋ	
cholera	ˈkɒlərə	ˈkɑlərə
choose	tʃuˑz	
chooses	ˈtʃuˑzɪz	
chose	tʃouz	
chosen	tʃouzn̩	
choosing	ˈtʃuˑzɪŋ	
chop	tʃɒp	tʃɑp
chops	tʃɒps	tʃɑps
chopped	tʃɒpt	tʃɑpt
chopping	ˈtʃɒpɪŋ	ˈtʃɑpɪŋ
chopper	ˈtʃɒpə(r	ˈtʃɑpə
choppers	ˈtʃɒpəz	ˈtʃɑpəz
chop-stick	ˈtʃɒpstɪk	ˈtʃɑpstɪk
chop-sticks	ˈtʃɒpstɪks	ˈtʃɑpstɪks
chord	kɔˑd	kɔəd
chords	kɔˑdz	kɔədz
chorus	ˈkɔˑrəs	
choruses	ˈkɔˑrəsɪz	
CHOSE *from* choose	tʃouz	
Christian	ˈkrɪstjən	
Christians	ˈkrɪstjənz	

Traditional Spelling	Received Pronunciation	American Variants
Christianity	krɪstɪ'ænɪtɪ	
Christmas	'krɪsməs	
chronic	'krɒnɪk	'krɑnɪk
church	tʃɜ·tʃ	'tʃɜə·tʃ
churches	'tʃɜ·tʃɪz	'tʃɜə·tʃɪz
cider	'saɪdə(r	'saɪdə
cigar	sɪ'gɑ·(r	sɪ'gɑə
cigars	sɪ'gɑ·z	sɪ'gɑəz
cigarette	sɪgə'rɛt	
cigarettes	sɪgə'rɛts	
cinder	'sɪndə(r	'sɪndə
cinders	'sɪndəz	'sɪndəz
cinema	'sɪnɪmə	
cinemas	'sɪnɪməz	
cinematograph	sɪnɪ'mætəgrɑ·f sɪnɪ'mætəgræf	sɪnɪ'mætəgra·f
cinematographs	sɪnɪ'mætəgrɑ·fs sɪnɪ'mætəgræfs	sɪnɪ'mætəgra·fs
circle	'sɜ·kl̩	'sɜəkl̩
circles	'sɜ·kl̩z	'sɜəkl̩z
circuit	'sɜ·kɪt	'sɜəkɪt
circuits	'sɜ·kɪts	'sɜəkɪts
circular	'sɜ·kjʊlə(r	'sɜəkjʊlə
circulars	'sɜ·kjʊləz	'sɜəkjʊləz
circulation	sɜkjʊ'leɪʃən	sɜəkjʊ'leɪʃən
circulations	sɜkjʊ'leɪʃənz	sɜəkjʊ'leɪʃənz
circumference	sə'kʌmfərəns	sə'kʌmfərəns
circumferences	sə'kʌmfərənsɪz	sə'kʌmfərənsɪz
circumstance	'sɜ·kəmstəns	'sɜəkəmstæns
circumstances	'sɜ·kəmstənsɪz	'sɜəkəmstænsɪz
citizen	'sɪtɪzn̩	
citizens	'sɪtɪzn̩z	
city	'sɪtɪ	
cities	'sɪtɪz	
civil	'sɪvɪl	
civilly	'sɪvɪlɪ	
civilian	sɪ'vɪljən	
civilians	sɪ'vɪljənz	
civilization	sɪvɪlaɪ'zeɪʃən sɪvɪlɪ'zeɪʃən	
civilizations	sɪvɪlaɪ'zeɪʃənz sɪvɪlɪ'zeɪʃənz	
civilize	'sɪvɪlaɪz	
civilizes	'sɪvɪlaɪzɪz	
civilized	'sɪvɪlaɪzd	
civilizing	'sɪvɪlaɪzɪŋ	
claim	kleɪm	

Traditional Spelling	Received Pronunciation	American Variants
claims	kleɪmz	
claimed	kleɪmd	
claiming	ˈkleɪmɪŋ	
clap	klæp	
claps	klæps	
clapped	klæpt	
clapping	ˈklæpɪŋ	
clarify	ˈklærɪfaɪ	
clarifies	ˈklærifaɪz	
clarified	ˈklærifaɪd	
clarifying	ˈklærifaɪɪŋ	
class	klɑ·s	kla·s, klæs
classes	ˈklɑ·sɪz	ˈkla·sɪz, klæsɪz
classic	ˈklæsɪk	
classics	ˈklæsɪks	
classical	ˈklæsɪkəl	
classification	klæsɪfɪˈkeɪʃən	
classifications	klæsɪfɪˈkeɪʃənz	
classify	ˈklæsɪfaɪ	
classifies	ˈklæsɪfaɪz	
classified	ˈklæsɪfaɪd	
classifying	ˈklæsɪfaɪɪŋ	
clause	klɔ·z	
clauses	ˈklɔ·zɪz	
clay	kleɪ	
clean	kli·n	
cleaner	ˈkli·nə(r	ˈkli·nə
cleanest	ˈkli·nɪst	
cleans	kli·nz	
cleaned	kli·nd	
cleaning	ˈkli·nɪŋ	
clear	klɪə(r	klɪə
clearer	ˈklɪərə(r	ˈklɪ·rə
clearest	ˈklɪərɪst	ˈklɪ·rɪst
clearly	ˈklɪəlɪ	ˈklɪəlɪ
clergyman	ˈklɜ·ʤɪmən	ˈklɜəʤɪmən
clergymen	ˈklɜ·ʤɪmən	ˈklɜəʤɪmən
clerk	klɑ·k	klɜək
clerks	klɑ·ks	klɜəks
clever	ˈklɛvə(r	ˈklɛvə
cleverer	ˈklɛvərə(r	ˈklɛvərə
cleverest	ˈklɛvərɪst	
cleverly	ˈklɛvəlɪ	ˈklɛvəlɪ
cleverness	ˈklɛvənɪs	ˈklɛvənɪs
cliff	klɪf	
cliffs	klɪfs	
climate	ˈklaɪmɪt	

Traditional Spelling	Received Pronunciation	American Variants
climates	ˈklaɪmɪts	
climb	klaɪm	
climbs	klaɪmz	
climbed	klaɪmd	
climbing	ˈklaɪmɪŋ	
cling	klɪŋ	
clings	klɪŋz	
clung	klʌŋ	
clinging	ˈklɪŋɪŋ	
cloak	kloʊk	
cloaks	kloʊks	
cloak-room	ˈkloʊkrum ˈkloʊkrʊm	
cloak-rooms	ˈkloʊkrumz ˈkloʊkrʊmz	
clock	klɒk	klɑk
clocks	klɒks	klɑks
close, *noun*	kloʊz	
close, *adj.*	kloʊs	
closer	ˈkloʊsə(r	ˈkloʊsə
closest	ˈkloʊsɪst	
close, *verb.*	kloʊz	
closes	ˈkloʊzɪz	
closed	kloʊzd	
closing	ˈkloʊzɪŋ	
closely	ˈkloʊslɪ	
cloth	klɔθ, klɒθ	
cloths	klɔˑðz, klɔðz, klɔθs, klɒθs	
clothes	kloʊz, kloʊðz	
cloud	klaʊd	
clouds	klaʊdz	
cloudy	ˈklaʊdɪ	
club	klʌb	
clubs	klʌbz	
clumsy	ˈklʌmzɪ	
clumsier	ˈklʌmzɪə(r	ˈklʌmzɪə
clumsiest	ˈklʌmzɪɪst	
clumsily	ˈklʌmzɪlɪ	
CLUNG *from* cling	klʌŋ	
coach	koʊtʃ	
coaches	ˈkoʊtʃɪz	
coal	koʊl	
coals	koʊlz	
coarse	kɔˑs, kɔəs	koəs
coarser	ˈkɔˑsə(r, ˈkɔəsə(r	ˈkoəsə
coarsest	ˈkɔˑsɪst, ˈkɔəsɪst	ˈkoəsɪst

Traditional Spelling	Received Pronunciation	American Variants
coarsely	'kɔ·slɪ, 'kɔəslɪ	'koəslɪ
coast	koʊst	
coasts	koʊsts	
coat	koʊt	
coats	koʊts	
cock	kɒk	kɑk
cocks	kɒks	kɑks
cocoa	'koʊkoʊ	
coco(a)nut	'koʊkənʌt	
coco(a)nuts	'koʊkənʌts	
code	koʊd	
codes	koʊdz	
coerce	koʊ'ɜ·s	koʊ'ɜəs
coerces	koʊ'ɜ·sɪz	koʊ'ɜəsɪz
coerced	koʊ'ɜ·st	koʊ'ɜəst
coercing	koʊ'ɜ·sɪŋ	koʊ'ɜəsɪŋ
coffee	'kɒfɪ	
coffin	'kɒfɪn	'kɑfɪn
coffins	'kɒfɪnz	'kɑfɪnz
coil	kɔɪl	
coils	kɔɪlz	
coiled	kɔɪld	
coiling	'kɔɪlɪŋ	
coincide	koʊɪn'saɪd	
coincides	koʊɪn'saɪdz	
coincided	koʊɪn'saɪdɪd	
coinciding	koʊɪn'saɪdɪŋ	
coincidence	koʊ'ɪnsɪdᵊns	
coincidences	koʊ'ɪnsɪdᵊnsɪz	
coin	kɔɪn	
coins	kɔɪnz	
cold	koʊld	
colder	'koʊldə(r	'koʊldə
coldest	'koʊldɪst	
colds	koʊldz	
coldly	'koʊldlɪ	
coldness	'koʊldnɪs	
collaborate	kə'læbəreɪt	
collaborates	kə'læbəreɪts	
collaborated	kə'læbəreɪtɪd	
collaborating	kə'læbəreɪtɪŋ	
collaborator	kə'læbəreɪtə(r	kə'læbəreɪtə
collaborators	kə'læbəreɪtəz	kə'læbəreɪtəz
collaboration	kəlæbə'reɪʃᵊn	
collapse	kə'læps	
collapses	kə'læpsɪz	
collapsed	kə'læpst	

Traditional Spelling	Received Pronunciation	American Variants
collapsing	kə'læpsɪŋ	
collar	'kɒlə(r	'kɑlə
collars	'kɒləz	'kɑləz
colleague	'kɒlig	'kɑlig
colleagues	'kɒligz	'kɑligz
collect	kə'lɛkt	
collects	kə'lɛkts	
collected	kə'lɛktɪd	
collecting	kə'lɛktɪŋ	
collector	kə'lɛktə(r	kə'lɛktə
collectors	kə'lɛktəz	kə'lɛktəz
collection	kə'lɛkʃən	
collections	kə'lɛkʃənz	
collective	kə'lɛktɪv	
collectively	kə'lɛktɪvlɪ	
college	'kɒlɪʤ	'kɑlɪʤ
colleges	'kɒlɪʤɪz	'kɑlɪʤɪz
collide	kə'laɪd	
collides	kə'laɪdz	
collided	kə'laɪdɪd	
colliding	kə'laɪdɪŋ	
collision	kə'lɪʒən	
collisions	kə'lɪʒənz	
colloquial	kə'loukwɪəl	
colloquially	kə'loukwɪəlɪ	
colloquialism	kə'loukwɪəlɪzṃ	
colloquialisms	kə'loukwɪəlɪzṃz	
Colombia	kə'lʌmbɪə	
Colombian	kə'lʌmbɪən	
Colombians	kə'lʌmbɪənz	
colon	'koulən	
colons	'koulənz	
colonel	'kɜ·nḷ	'kɜənḷ
colonels	'kɜ·nḷz	'kɜənḷz
colonial	kə'lounjəl	
colonials	kə'lounjəlz	
colonist	'kɒlənɪst	'kɑlənɪst
colonists	'kɒlənɪsts	'kɑlənɪsts
colonization	kɒlənaɪ'zeɪʃən	kɑlənaɪ'zeɪʃən
colonize	'kɒlənaɪz	'kɑlənaɪz
colonizes	'kɒlənaɪzɪz	'kɑlənaɪzɪz
colonized	'kɒlənaɪzd	'kɑlənaɪzd
colonizing	'kɒlənaɪzɪŋ	'kɑlənaɪzɪŋ
colony	'kɒlənɪ	
colonies	'kɒlənɪz	
color (*Amer.*)		
colour	'kʌlə(r	'kʌlə

Traditional Spelling	Received Pronunciation	American Variants
colors (*Amer.*)		
colours	ˈkʌləz	ˈkʌləz
colored (*Amer.*)		
coloured	ˈkʌləd	ˈkʌləd
coloring (*Amer.*)		
colouring	ˈkʌlərɪŋ	
column	ˈkɒləm	
columns	ˈkɒləmz	
comb	koʊm	
combs	koʊmz	
combed	koʊmd	
combing	ˈkoʊmɪŋ	
combination	kɒmbɪˈneɪʃən	kɑmbɪˈneɪʃən
combinations	kɒmbɪˈneɪʃənz	kɑmbɪˈneɪʃənz
combine	kəmˈbaɪn	
combines	kəmˈbaɪnz	
combined	kəmˈbaɪnd	
combining	kəmˈbaɪnɪŋ	
combustion	kəmˈbʌstʃən	
come	kʌm	
comes	kʌmz	
came	keɪm	
coming	ˈkʌmɪŋ	
comedian	kəˈmiˑdjən kəˈmiˑdɪən	
comedians	kəˈmiˑdjənz kəˈmiˑdɪənz	
comedy	ˈkɒmɪdɪ	ˈkɑmɪdɪ
comedies	ˈkɒmɪdɪz	ˈkɑmɪdɪz
comet	ˈkɒmɪt	
comets	ˈkɒmɪts	
comfort	ˈkʌmfət	ˈkʌmfət
comforts	ˈkʌmfəts	ˈkʌmfəts
comforted	ˈkʌmfətɪd	ˈkʌmfətɪd
comforting	ˈkʌmfətɪŋ	ˈkʌmfətɪŋ
comfortable	ˈkʌmfətəbl̩	ˈkʌmfətəbl̩
comfortably	ˈkʌmfətəblɪ	ˈkʌmfətəblɪ
comic	ˈkɒmɪk	ˈkɑmɪk
comical	ˈkɒmɪkəl	ˈkɑmɪkəl
comma	ˈkɒmə	ˈkɑmə
commas	ˈkɒməz	ˈkɑməz
command	kəˈmɑˑnd	kəˈmaˑnd
commands	kəˈmɑˑndz	kəˈmaˑndz
commanded	kəˈmɑˑndɪd	kəˈmaˑndɪd
commanding	kəˈmɑˑndɪŋ	kəˈmaˑndɪŋ
commander	kəˈmɑˑndə(r	kəˈmaˑndə
commanders	kəˈmɑˑndəz	kəˈmaˑndəz

Traditional Spelling	Received Pronunciation	American Variants
commandment	kə'mɑ·ndmənt	kə'ma·ndmənt
commandments	kə'mɑ·ndmənts	kə'ma·ndmənts
commemorate	kə'mɛməreɪt	
commemorates	kə'mɛməreɪts	
commemorated	kə'mɛməreɪtɪd	
commemorating	kə'mɛməreɪtɪŋ	
commemoration	kəmɛmə'reɪʃən	
commemorations	kəmɛmə'reɪʃənz	
commence	kə'mɛns	
commences	kə'mɛnsɪz	
commenced	kə'mɛnst	
commencing	kə'mɛnsing	
comment	'kɒmɛnt	'kamɛnt
comments	'kɒmɛnts	'kamɛnts
commented	'kɒmɛntɪd	'kamɛntɪd
commenting	'kɒmɛntɪŋ	'kamɛntɪŋ
commerce	'kɒmɜs, 'kɒməs	'kamɜəs, 'kaməs
commercial	kə'mɜ·ʃəl	kə'mɜəʃəl
commercially	kə'mɜ·ʃəlɪ	kə'mɜəʃəlɪ
commission	kə'mɪʃən	
commissions	kə'mɪʃənz	
commit	kə'mɪt	
commits	kə'mɪts	
committed	kə'mɪtɪd	
committing	kə'mɪtɪŋ	
committee	kə'mɪtɪ	
committees	kə'mɪtɪz	
common	'kɒmən	'kamən
commoner	'kɒmənə(r	'kamənə
commonest	'kɒmənɪst	'kamənɪst
commonly	'kɒmənlɪ	'kamənlɪ
common-sense	'kɒmən'sɛns	'kamən'sɛns
commotion	kə'moʊʃən	
communicate	kə'mju·nɪkeɪt	kə'mju·nɪket
communicates	kə'mju·nɪkeɪts	kə'mju·nɪkets
communicated	kə'mju·nɪkeɪtɪd	kə'mju·nɪketɪd
communicating	kə'mju·nɪkeɪtɪŋ	kə'mju·nɪketɪŋ
communication	kəmju·nɪ'keɪʃən	
communications	kəmju·nɪ'keɪʃənz	
communism	'kɒmjʊnɪzṃ	'kamjʊnɪzṃ
communist	'kɒmjʊnɪst	'kamjʊnɪst
communists	'kɒmjʊnɪsts	'kamjʊnɪsts
community	kə'mju·nɪtɪ	
communities	kə'mju·nɪtɪz	
compact, *adj.*	kəm'pækt	
companion	kəm'pænjən	
companions	kəm'pænjənz	

Traditional Spelling	Received Pronunciation	American Variants
company	ˈkʌmpənɪ	
companies	ˈkʌmpənɪz	
comparable	ˈkɒmpərəbl̩	ˈkampərəbl̩
comparably	ˈkɒmpərəblɪ	ˈkampərəblɪ
comparative	kəmˈpærətɪv	
comparatives	kəmˈpærətɪvz	
comparatively	kəmˈpærətɪvlɪ	
compare	kəmˈpɛə(r	kəmˈpɛə
compares	kəmˈpɛəz	kəmˈpɛəz
compared	kəmˈpɛəd	kəmˈpɛəd
comparing	kəmˈpɛərɪŋ	kəmˈpɛ·rɪŋ
comparison	kəmˈpærɪsən kəmˈpærɪzən	
comparisons	kəmˈpærɪsənz kəmˈpærɪzənz	
compartment	kəmˈpɑ·tmənt	kəmˈpɑətmənt
compartments	kəmˈpɑ·tmənts	kəmˈpɑətmənts
compass	ˈkʌmpəs	
compasses	ˈkʌmpəsɪz	
compatible	kəmˈpætɪbl̩	
compel	kəmˈpɛl	
compels	kəmˈpɛlz	
compelled	kəmˈpɛld	
compelling	kəmˈpɛlɪŋ	
compensate	ˈkɒmpənseɪt ˈkɒmpɛnseɪt	ˈkampənseɪt
compensates	ˈkɒmpənseɪts ˈkɒmpɛnseɪts	ˈkampənseɪts
compensated	ˈkɒmpənseɪtɪd ˈkɒmpɛnseɪtɪd	ˈkampənseɪtɪd
compensating	ˈkɒmpənseɪtɪŋ ˈkɒmpɛnseɪtɪŋ	ˈkampənseɪtɪŋ
compensation	kɒmpənˈseɪʃən kɒmpɛnˈseɪʃən	kampənˈseɪʃən
compensations	kɒmpənˈseɪʃənz kɒmpɛnˈseɪʃənz	kampənˈseɪʃənz
compete	kəmˈpi·t	
competes	kəmˈpi·ts	
competed	kəmˈpi·tɪd	
competing	kəmˈpi·tɪŋ	
competence	ˈkɒmpɪtəns	ˈkampɪtəns
competent	ˈkɒmpɪtənt	ˈkampɪtənt
competition	kɒmpɪˈtɪʃən	kampɪˈtɪʃən
competitions	kɒmpɪˈtɪʃənz	kampɪˈtɪʃənz
competitive	kəmˈpɛtɪtɪv	
competitor	kəmˈpɛtɪtə(r	kəmˈpɛtɪtə
competitors	kəmˈpɛtɪtəz	kəmˈpɛtɪtəz

Traditional Spelling	Received Pronunciation	American Variants
compile	kəm'paɪl	
compiles	kəm'paɪlz	
compiled	kəm'paɪld	
compiling	kəm'paɪlɪŋ	
compiler	kəm'paɪlə(r	kəm'paɪlə
compilers	kəm'paɪləz	kəm'paɪləz
complain	kəm'pleɪn	
complains	kəm'pleɪnz	
complained	kəm'pleɪnd	
complaining	kəm'pleɪnɪŋ	
complaint	kəm'pleɪnt	
complaints	kəm'pleɪnts	
complement	'kɒmplɪmənt	'kɑmplɪmənt
complements	'kɒmplɪmənts	'kɑmplɪmənts
complete	kəm'pliˑt	
complicate	'kɒmplɪkeɪt	'kɑmplɪkeɪt
complicates	'kɒmplɪkeɪts	'kɑmplɪkeɪts
complicated	'kɒmplɪkeɪtɪd	'kɑmplɪkeɪtɪd
complicating	'kɒmplɪkeɪtɪŋ	'kɑmplɪkeɪtɪŋ
complication	kɒmplɪ'keɪʃən	kɑmplɪ'keɪʃən
complications	kɒmplɪ'keɪʃənz	kɑmplɪ'keɪʃənz
compliment, *noun*	'kɒmplɪmənt	'kɑmplɪmənt
compliments	'kɒmplɪmənts	'kɑmplɪmənts
compliment, *verb*	'kɒmplɪmɛnt	'kɑmplɪmɛnt
compliments	'kɒmplɪmɛnts	'kɑmplɪmɛnts
complimented	'kɒmplɪmɛntɪd	'kɑmplɪmɛntɪd
complimenting	'kɒmplɪmɛntɪŋ	'kɑmplɪmɛntɪŋ
complimentary	kɒmplɪ'mɛntərɪ	'kɑmplɪmɛntərɪ
comply	kəm'plaɪ	
complies	kəm'plaɪz	
complied	kəm'plaɪd	
complying	kəm'plaɪɪŋ	
compose	kəm'poʊz	
composes	kəm'poʊzɪz	
composed	kəm'poʊzd	
composing	kəm'poʊzɪŋ	
composer	kəm'poʊzə(r	kəm'poʊzə
composers	kəm'poʊzəz	kəm'poʊzəz
composition	kɒmpə'zɪʃən	kɑmpə'zɪʃən
compositions	kɒmpə'zɪʃənz	kɑmpə'zɪʃənz
compound	'kɒmpaʊnd	'kɑmpaʊnd
compounds	'kɒmpaʊndz	'kɑmpaʊndz
compress	kəm'prɛs	
compresses	kəm'prɛsɪz	
compressed	kəm'prɛst	
compressing	kəm'prɛsɪŋ	
compromise	'kɒmprəmaɪz	'kɑmprəmaɪz

Traditional Spelling	Received Pronunciation	American Variants
compromises	ʹkɒmprəmaɪzɪz	ʹkɑmprəmaɪzɪz
compromised	ʹkɒmprəmaɪzd	ʹkɑmprəmaɪzd
compromising	ʹkɒmprəmaɪzɪŋ	ʹkɑmprəmaɪzɪŋ
compulsory	kəmʹpʌlsərɪ	
concave	ʹkɒnʹkeɪv	ʹkɑnʹkeɪv
conceal	kənʹsiːl	
conceals	kənʹsiːlz	
concealed	kənʹsiːld	
concealing	kənʹsiːlɪŋ	
concede	kənʹsiːd	
concedes	kənʹsiːdz	
conceded	kənʹsiːdɪd	
conceding	kənʹsiːdɪŋ	
conceit	kənʹsiːt	
conceited	kənʹsiːtɪd	
conceivable	kənʹsiːvəbl̩	
conceivably	kənʹsiːvəblɪ	
conceive	kənʹsiːv	
conceives	kənʹsiːvz	
conceived	kənʹsiːvd	
conceiving	kənʹsiːvɪŋ	
concentration	kɒnsənʹtreɪʃən kɒnsɛnʹtreɪʃən	kɑnsənʹtreɪʃən
concentrations	kɒnsənʹtreɪʃn̩z kɒnsɛnʹtreɪʃn̩z	kɑnsənʹtreɪʃənz
concept	ʹkɒnsɛpt	ʹkɑnsɛpt
concepts	ʹkɒnsɛpts	ʹkɑnsɛpts
concern	kənʹsɜːn	kənʹsɜən
concerns	kənʹsɜːnz	kənʹsɜənz
concerned	kənʹsɜːnd	kəbʹsɜənd
concerning	kənʹsɜːnɪŋ	kənʹsɜənɪŋ
concert, ***noun***	ʹkɒnsət	ʹkɑnsət
concerts	ʹkɒnsəts	ʹkɑnsəts
conciliate	kənʹsɪlɪeɪt	
conciliates	kənʹsɪlɪeɪts	
conciliated	kənʹsɪlɪeɪtɪd	
conciliating	kənʹsɪlɪeɪtɪŋ	
concise	kənʹsaɪs	
concisely	kənʹsaɪslɪ	
conciseness	kənʹsaɪsnɪs	
conclude	kənʹkluːd	
concludes	kənʹkluːdz	
concluded	kənʹkluːdɪd	
concluding	kənʹkluːdɪŋ	
conclusion	kənʹkluːʒən	
conclusions	kənʹkluːʒənz	

Traditional Spelling	Received Pronunciation	American Variants
concrete	ʹkɒnkriːt, ʹkɒŋkrit	ʹkɑnkriːt
concur	kənʹkɜː	kənʹkɜə
concurs	kənʹkɜːz	kənʹkɜəz
concurred	kənʹkɜːd	kənʹkɜəd
concurring	kənʹkɜːrɪŋ	
condemn	kənʹdɛm	
condemns	kənʹdɛmz	
condemned	kənʹdɛmd	
condemning	kənʹdɛmɪŋ	
condemnation	kɒndɛmʹneɪʃən kɒndəmʹneɪʃən	kɑndɛmʹneɪʃən
condemnations	kɒndɛmʹneɪʃənz kɒndəmʹneɪʃənz	kɑndɛmʹneɪʃənz
condense	kənʹdɛns	
condenses	kənʹdɛnsɪz	
condensed	kənʹdɛnst	
condensing	kənʹdɛnsɪŋ	
condition	kənʹdɪʃən	
conditions	kənʹdɪʃənz	
conditional	kənʹdɪʃənəl	
conditionally	kənʹdɪʃnəlɪ	
conduct, ***noun***	ʹkɒndʌkt, ʹkɒndəkt	ʹkɑndʌkt, ʹkɑndəkt
conduct, *verb*	kənʹdʌkt	
conducts	kənʹdʌkts	
conducted	kənʹdʌktɪd	
conducting	kənʹdʌktɪŋ	
conductor	kənʹdʌktə(r	kənʹdʌktə
conductors	kənʹdʌktəz	kənʹdʌktəz
cone	koʊn	
cones	koʊnz	
confectionery	kənʹfɛkʃənərɪ	kənʹfɛkʃənɛrɪ
confederation	kənfɛdəʹreɪʃən	
confederations	kənfɛdəʹreɪʃənz	
confer	kənʹfɜː(r	kənʹfɜə
confers	kənʹfɜːz	kənʹfɜəz
conferred	kənʹfɜːd	kənʹfɜəd
conferring	kənʹfɜːrɪŋ	
conference	ʹkɒnfərəns	ʹkɑnfərəns
conferences	ʹkɒnfərənsɪz	ʹkɑnfərənsɪz
confess	kənʹfɛs	
confesses	kənʹfɛsɪz	
confessed	kənʹfɛst	
confessing	kənʹfɛsɪŋ	
confession	kənʹfɛʃən	
confessions	kənʹfɛʃənz	
confide	kənʹfaɪd	
confides	kənʹfaɪdz	

Traditional Spelling	Received Pronunciation	American Variants
confided	kən'faɪdɪd	
confiding	kən'faɪdɪŋ	
confidence	'kɒnfɪdəns	'kɑnfɪdəns
confident	'kɒnfɪdənt	'kɑnfɪdənt
confidently	'kɒnfɪdəntlɪ	'kɑnfɪdəntlɪ
confidential	kɒnfɪ'dɛnʃəl	kɑnfɪ'dɛnʃəl
confidentially	kɒnfɪ'dɛnʃəlɪ	kɑnfɪ'dɛnʃəlɪ
confine	kən'faɪn	
confines	kən'faɪnz	
confined	kən'faɪnd	
confining	kən'faɪnɪŋ	
confirm	kən'fɜ·m	kən'fɜəm
confirms	kən'fɜ·mz	kən'fɜəmz
confirmed	kən'fɜ·md	kən'fɜəmd
confirming	kən'fɜ·mɪŋ	
confirmation	kɒnfə'meɪʃən	kɑnfə'meɪʃən
confirmations	kɒnfə'meɪʃənz	kɑnfə'meɪʃənz
confiscate	'kɒnfɪskeɪt	'kɑnfɪskeɪt
confiscates	'kɒnfɪskeɪts	'kɑnfɪskeɪts
confiscated	'kɒnfɪskeɪtɪd	'kɑnfɪskeɪtɪd
confiscating	'kɒnfɪskeɪtɪŋ	'kɑnfɪskeɪtɪŋ
confiscation	kɒnfɪs'keɪʃən	kɑnfɪs'keɪʃən
conflict, *noun*	'kɒnflɪkt	'kɑnflɪkt
conflicts	'kɒnflɪkts	'kɑnflɪkts
conflict, *verb*	kən'flɪkt	
conflicts	kən'flɪkts	
conflicted	kən'flɪktɪd	
conflicting	kən'flɪktɪŋ	
conform	kən'fɔ·m	kən'fɔəm
conforms	kən'fɔ·mz	kən'fɔəmz
conformed	kən'fɔ·md	kən'fɔəmd
conforming	kən'fɔ·mɪŋ	kən'fɔəmɪŋ
conformity	kən'fɔ·mɪtɪ	kən'fɔəmɪtɪ
confront	kən'frʌnt	
confronts	kən'frʌnts	
confronted	kən'frʌntɪd	
confronting	kən'frʌntɪŋ	
confuse	kən'fju·z	
confuses	kən'fju·zɪz	
confused	kən'fju·zd	
confusing	kən'fju·zɪŋ	
confusion	kən'fju·ʒən	
confusions	kən'fju·ʒənz	
congestion	kən'ʤɛstʃən	
Congo	'kɒŋgoʊ	
congratulate	kən'grætjʊleɪt	
congratulates	kən'grætjʊleɪts	

Traditional Spelling	Received Pronunciation	American Variants
congratulated	kən'grætjuleɪtɪd	
congratulating	kən'grætjuleɪtɪŋ	
congratulation	kəngrætju'leɪʃən	
congratulations	kəngrætju'leɪʃənz	
congregation	kɒŋgrɪ'geɪʃən	kaŋgrɪ'geɪʃən
congregations	kɒŋgrɪ'geɪʃənz	kaŋgrɪ'geɪʃənz
congregational	kɒŋgrɪ'geɪʃənl̩	kaŋgrɪ'geɪʃənl̩
congress	'kɒŋgrɛs	'kaŋgrɪs
congresses	'kɒŋgrɛsɪz	'kaŋgrɪsɪz
conical	'kɒnɪkəl	'kanɪkəl
conjecture	kən'ʤɛktʃə(r	kən'ʤɛktʃɔ
conjectures	kən'ʤɛktʃəz	kən'ʤɛktʃəz
conjectured	kən'ʤɛktʃəd	kən'ʤɛktʃəd
conjecturing	kən'ʤɛktʃərɪŋ	
conjoint	'kɒnʤɔɪnt, kən'ʤɔɪnt	'kanʤɔɪnt
conjointly	'kɒnʤɔɪntlɪ kən'ʤɔɪntlɪ	'kanʤɔɪntlɪ
conjugal	'kɒnʤugəl	'kanʤugəl
conjugate	'kɒnʤugeɪt	'kanʤugeɪt
conjugates	'kɒnʤugeɪts	'kanʤugeɪts
conjugated	'kɒnʤugeɪtɪd	'kanʤugeɪtɪd
conjugating	'kɒnʤugeɪtɪŋ	'kanʤugeɪtɪŋ
conjugation	kɒnʤu'geɪʃən	kanʤu'geɪʃən
conjugations	kɒnʤu'geɪʃənz	kanʤu'geɪʃənz
conjunction	kən'ʤʌŋkʃən	
conjunctions	kən'ʤʌŋkʃənz	
conjunctive	kən'ʤʌŋktɪv	
conjunctively	kən'ʤʌŋktɪvlɪ	
conjure	'kʌnʤə(r	'kʌnʤə, 'kanʤə
conjures	'kʌnʤəz	'kʌnʤəz, 'kanʤəz
conjured	'kʌnʤəd	'kʌnʤəd, 'kanʤəd
conjuring	'kʌnʤərɪŋ	'kanʤərɪŋ
conjurer	'kʌnʤərə(r	'kʌnʤərə
conjurers	'kʌnʤərəz	'kʌnʤərəz
connect	kə'nɛkt	
connects	kə'nɛkts	
connected	kə'nɛktɪd	
connecting	kə'nɛktɪŋ	
connectedly	kə'nɛktɪdlɪ	
connection	kə'nɛkʃən	
connections	kə'nɛkʃənz	
connective	kə'nɛktɪv	
connexion	kə'nɛkʃən	
connexions	kə'nɛkʃənz	
connivance	kə'naɪvəns	
connive	kə'naɪv	
connives	kə'naɪvz	

Traditional Spelling	Received Pronunciation	American Variants
connived	kə'naɪvd	
conniving	kə'naɪvɪŋ	
connotation	kɒnoʊ'teɪʃən	kɑnoʊ'teɪʃən
connotations	kɒnoʊ'teɪʃənz	kɑnoʊ'teɪʃənz
conquer	'kɒŋkə(r	'kɑŋkə
conquers	'kɒŋkəz	'kɑŋkəz
conquered	'kɒŋkəd	'kɑŋkəd
conquering	'kɒŋkərɪŋ	'kɑŋkərɪŋ
conqueror	'kɒŋkərə(r	'kɑŋkərə
conquerors	'kɒŋkərəz	'kɑŋkərəz
conquest	'kɒŋkwɛst	'kɑŋkwɛst
conquests	'kɒŋkwɛsts	'kɑŋkwɛsts
conscience	'kɒnʃəns	'kɑnʃəns
consciences	'kɒnʃənsɪz	'kɑnʃənsɪz
conscientious	kɒnʃɪ'ɛnʃəs	kɑnʃɪ'ɛnʃəs
conscientiously	kɒnʃɪ'ɛnʃəslɪ	kɑnʃɪ'ɛnʃəslɪ
conscientiousness	kɒnʃɪ'ɛnʃəsnɪs	kɑnʃɪ'ɛnʃəsnɪs
conscious	'kɒnʃəs	'kɑnʃəs
consciously	'kɒnʃəslɪ	'kɑnʃəslɪ
consciousness	'kɒnʃəsnɪs	'kɑnʃəsnɪs
conscript	'kɒnskrɪpt	'kɑnskrɪpt
conscripts	'kɒnskrɪpts	'kɑnskrɪpts
conscription	kən'skrɪpʃən	
consecutive	kən'sɛkjutɪv	
consecutively	kən'sɛkjutɪvlɪ	
consent	kən'sɛnt	
consents	kən'sɛnts	
consented	kən'sɛntɪd	
consenting	kən'sɛntɪŋ	
consequence	'kɒnsɪkwəns	'kɑnsɪkwəns
consequences	'kɒnsɪkwənsɪz	'kɑnsɪkwənsɪz
consequent	'kɒnsɪkwənt	'kɑnsɪkwənt
consequently	'kɒnsɪkwəntlɪ	'kɑnsɪkwəntlɪ
conservatism	kən'sɜˑvətɪzm̩	kən'sɜəvətɪzm̩
conservative	kən'sɜˑvətɪv	kən'sɜəvətɪv
conservatives	kən'sɜˑvətɪvz	kən'sɜəvətɪvz
consider	kən'sɪdə(r	kən'sɪdə
considers	kən'sɪdəz	kən'sɪdəz
considered	kən'sɪdəd	kən'sɪdəd
considering	kən'sɪdərɪŋ	
considerable	kən'sɪdərəbl̩	
considerably	kən'sɪdərəblɪ	
considerate	kən'sɪdərɪt	
considerately	kən'sɪdərɪtlɪ	
consideration	kənsɪdə'reɪʃən	
considerations	kənsɪdə'reɪʃənz	
consign	kən'saɪn	

Traditional Spelling	Received Pronunciation	American Variants
consigns	kən'saɪnz	
consigned	kən'saɪnd	
consigning	kən'saɪnɪŋ	
consigner	kən'saɪnə	
consigners	kən'saɪnəz	
consignment	kən'saɪnmənt	
consignments	kən'saɪnmənts	
consist	kən'sɪst	
consists	kən'sɪsts	
consisted	kən'sɪstɪd	
consisting	kən'sɪstɪŋ	
consistency	kən'sɪstənsɪ	
consistent	kən'sɪstənt	
consistently	kən'sɪstəntlɪ	
consolation	kɒnsə'leɪʃən	kɑnsə'leɪʃən
consolations	kɒnsə'leɪʃənz	kɑnsə'leɪʃənz
console	kən'soul	
consoles	kən'soulz	
consoled	kən'sould	
consoling	kən'soulɪŋ	
consonant	'kɒnsənənt	'kɑnsənənt
consonants	'kɒnsənənts	'kɑnsənənts
conspicuous	kən'spɪkjuəs	
conspicuously	kən'spɪkjuəslɪ	
conspiracy	kən'spɪrəsɪ	
conspiracies	kən'spɪrəsɪz	
conspirator	kən'spɪrətə(r	kən'spɪrətə
conspirators	kən'spɪrətəz	kən'spɪrətəz
conspire	kən'spaɪə(r	kən'spaɪə
conspires	kən'spaɪəz	kən'spaɪəz
conspired	kən'spaɪəd	kən'spaɪəd
conspiring	kən'spaɪərɪŋ	kən'spaɪrɪŋ
constable	'kʌnstəbl̩	
constables	'kʌnstəbl̩z	
constancy	'kɒnstənsɪ	'kɑnstənsɪ
constant	'kɒnstənt	'kɑnstənt
Constantinople	kɒn'stæntɪ'noupl̩	
constantly	'kɒnstəntlɪ	'kɑnstəntlɪ
consternation	kɒnstɜ'neɪʃən	kɒnstɜə'neɪʃən
constitute	'kɒnstɪtjut	'kɑnstɪtjut
constitutes	'kɒnstɪtjuts	'kɑnstɪtjuts
constituted	'kɒnstɪtjutɪd	'kɑnstɪtjutɪd
constituting	'kɒnstɪtjutɪŋ	'kɑnstɪtjutɪŋ
constitution	kɒnstɪ'tju·ʃən	kɑnstɪ'tju·ʃən
constitutions	kɒnstɪ'tju·ʃənz	kɑnstɪ'tju·ʃənz
constitutional	kɒnstɪ'tju·ʃənəl	kɑnstɪ'tju·ʃənəl
constitutionally	kɒnstɪ'tju·ʃənəlɪ	kɑnstɪ'tju·ʃənəlɪ

Traditional Spelling	Received Pronunciation	American Variants
construct	kən'strʌkt	
constructs	kən'strʌkts	
constructed	kən'strʌktɪd	
constructing	kən'strʌktɪŋ	
constructor	kən'strʌktə(r	kən'strʌktə
constructors	kən'strʌktəz	kən'strʌktəz
construction	kən'strʌkʃən	
constructions	kən'strʌkʃənz	
constructive	kən'strʌktɪv	
constructively	kən'strʌktɪvlɪ	
consul	'kɒnsḷ	'kɑnsḷ
consuls	'kɒnsḷz	'kɑnsḷz
consular	'kɒnsjʊlə(r	'kɑnsʊlə
consulate	'kɒnsjʊlɪt	'kɑnsʊlɪt
consulates	'kɒnsjʊlɪts	'kɑnsʊlɪts
consult	kən'sʌlt	
consults	kən'sʌlts	
consulted	kən'sʌltɪd	
consulting	kən'sʌltɪŋ	
consultation	kɒnsḷ'teɪʃən	kɑnsḷ'teɪʃən
consultations	kɒnsḷ'teɪʃənz	kɑnsḷ'teɪʃənz
consume	kən'sjuːm	
consumes	kən'sjuːmz	
consumed	kən'sjuːmd	
consuming	kən'sjuːmɪŋ	
consumer	kən'sjuːmə(r	kən'sjuːmə
consumers	kən'sjuːməz	kən'sjuːməz
consumption	kən'sʌmpʃən	
contact	'kɒntækt	'kɑntækt
contacts	'kɒntækts	'kɑntækts
contagion	kən'teɪʤən	
contagious	kən'teɪʤəs	
contain	kən'teɪn	
contains	kən'teɪnz	
contained	kən'teɪnd	
containing	kən'teɪnɪŋ	
contaminate	kən'tæmɪneɪt	
contaminates	kən'tæmɪneɪts	
contaminated	kən'tæmɪneɪtɪd	
contaminating	kən'tæmɪneɪtɪŋ	
contamination	kəntæmɪ'neɪʃən	
contemplate	'kɒntɛmpleɪt 'kɒntəmpleɪt	'kɑntɛmpleɪt
contemplates	'kɒntɛmpleɪts 'kɒntəmpleɪts	'kɑntɛmpleɪts
contemplated	'kɒntɛmpleɪtɪd 'kɒntəmpleɪtɪd	'kɑntɛmpleɪtɪd

Traditional Spelling	Received Pronunciation	American Variants
contemplating	'kɒntɛmpleɪtɪŋ 'kɒntəmpleɪtɪŋ	'kɑntɛmpleɪtɪŋ
contemplation	kɒntɛm'pleɪʃən kɒntəm'pleɪʃən	kɑntɛm'pleɪʃən
contemporary	kən'tɛmpərərɪ	kən'tɛmpərɛrɪ
contemporaries	kən'tɛmpərərɪz	kən'tɛmpərɛrɪz
contempt	kən'tɛm*p*t	
contemptible	kən'tɛm*p*təbl̩	
contemptibly	kən'tɛm*p*təblɪ	
contemptuous	kən'tɛm*p*tjʊəs	
contemptuously	kən'tɛm*p*tjʊəslɪ	
contend	kən'tɛnd	
contends	kən'tɛndz	
contended	kən'tɛndɪd	
contending	kən'tɛndɪŋ	
content, ***noun***	'kɒntɛnt	'kɑntɛnt
contents	'kɒntɛnts	'kɑntɛnts
content, ***verb, adj.***	kən'tɛnt	
contents	kən'tɛnts	
contented	kən'tɛntɪd	
contenting	kən'tɛntɪŋ	
contentment	kən'tɛntmənt	
contention	kən'tɛnʃən	
contentions	kən'tɛnʃənz	
contentious	kən'tɛnʃəs	
contest, ***noun***	'kɒntɛst	'kɑntɛst
contests	'kɒntɛsts	'kɑntɛsts
contest, ***verb***	kən'tɛst	
contests	kən'tɛsts	
contested	kən'tɛstɪd	
contesting	kən'tɛstɪŋ	
context	'kɒntɛkst	'kɑntɛkst
contexts	'kɒntɛksts	'kɑntɛksts
continent	'kɒntɪnənt	'kɑntɪnənt
continents	'kɒntɪnənts	'kɑntɪnənts
continental	kɒntɪ'nɛntl̩	kɑntɪ'nɛntl̩
contingent	kən'tɪndʒənt	
contingents	kən'tɪndʒənts	
continual	kən'tɪnjʊəl	
continually	kən'tɪnjʊəlɪ	
continuation	kəntɪnjʊ'eɪʃən	
continuations	kəntɪnjʊ'eɪʃənz	
continue	kən'tɪnju	
continues	kən'tɪnjuz	
continued	kən'tɪnjud	
continuing	kən'tɪnjʊɪŋ	
continuity	kɒntɪ'njuˑɪtɪ	kɑntɪ'njuˑɪtɪ

Traditional Spelling	Received Pronunciation	American Variants
continuous	kən'tɪnjʊəs	
continuously	kən'tɪnjʊəslɪ	
contortion	kən'tɔ·ʃən	kən'tɔəʃən
contortions	kən'tɔ·ʃənz	kən'tɔəʃənz
contract, *noun*	'kɒntrækt	'kɑntrækt
contracts	'kɒntrækts	'kɑntrækts
contract, *verb*	kən'trækt	
contracts	kən'trækts	
contracted	kən'træktɪd	
contracting	kən'træktɪŋ	
contraction	kən'trækʃən	
contractions	kən'trækʃənz	
contractor	kən'træktə(r	kən'træktə
contractors	kən'træktəz	kən'træktəz
contradict	kɒntrə'dɪkt	kɑntrə'dɪkt
contradicts	kɒntrə'dɪkts	kɑntrə'dɪkts
contradicted	kɒntrə'dɪktɪd	kɑntrə'dɪktɪd
contradicting	kɒntrə'dɪktɪŋ	kɑntrə'dɪktɪŋ
contradiction	kɒntrə'dɪkʃən	kɑntrə'dɪkʃən
contradictions	kɒntrə'dɪkʃənz	kɑntrə'dɪkʃənz
contradictory	kɒntrə'dɪktərɪ	kɑntrə'dɪktərɪ
contrarily	'kɒntrərɪlɪ	'kɑntrərɪlɪ
contrary	'kɒntrərɪ	'kɑntrɛrɪ
contraries	'kɒntrərɪz	'kɑntrɛrɪz
contrast, *noun*	'kɒntrɑst, 'kɒntræst	'kɑntrast
contrasts	'kɒntrɑsts 'kɒntræsts	'kɑntrasts
contrast, *verb*	kən'trɑ·st kən'træst	'kən'tra·st
contrasts	kən'trɑ·sts, kən'træsts	kən'tra·sts
contrasted	kən'trɑ·sted kən'træstɪd	kən'tra·stɪd
contrasting	kən'trɑ·stɪŋ kən'træstɪŋ	kən'tra·stɪŋ
contribute	kən'trɪbjut	
contributes	kən'trɪbjʊts	
contributed	kən'trɪbjʊtɪd	
contributing	kən'trɪbjʊtɪŋ	
contribution	kɒntrɪ'bju·ʃən	kɑntrɪ'bju·ʃən
contributions	kɒntrɪ'bju·ʃənz	kɑntrɪ'bju·ʃənz
contributor	kən'trɪbjʊtə(r	kən'trɪbjʊtə
contributors	kən'trɪbjʊtəz	kən'trɪbjʊtəz
contrivance	kən'traɪvəns	
contrivances	kən'traɪvənsɪz	
contrive	kən'traɪv	
contrives	kən'traɪvz	

Traditional Spelling	Received Pronunciation	American Variants
contrived	kən'traɪvd	
contriving	kən'traɪvɪŋ	
control	kən'troʊl	
controls	kən'troʊlz	
controlled	kən'troʊld	
controlling	kən'troʊlɪŋ	
controller	kən'troʊlə(r	kən'troʊlə
controllers	kən'troʊləz	kən'troʊləz
controversial	kɒntrə'vɜ·ʃəl	kɑntrə'vɜəʃəl
controversy	'kɒntrəvɜsɪ	'kɑntrəvɜəsɪ
controversies	'kɒntrəvɜsɪz	'kɑntrəvɜəsɪz
conundrum	kə'nʌndrəm	
conundrums	kə'nʌndrəmz	
convalescence	kɒnvə'lɛsn̩s	kɑnvə'lɛsn̩s
convalescent	kɒnvə'lɛsn̩t	kɑnvə'lɛsn̩t
convenience	kən'vi·njəns	
conveniences	kən'vi·njənsɪz	
convenient	kən'vi·njənt	
conveniently	kən'vi·njəntlɪ	
convent	'kɒnvənt, 'kɒnvɛnt	'kɑnvɛnt
convents	'kɒnvənts 'kɒnvɛnts	'kɑnvɛnts
convention	kən'vɛnʃən	
conventions	kən'vɛnʃənz	
conventional	kən'vɛnʃənl̩	
conventionally	kən'vɛnʃənl̩ɪ	
converge	kən'vɜ·ʤ	kən'vɜəʤ
converges	kən'vɜ·ʤɪz	kən'vɜəʤɪz
converged	kən'vɜ·ʤd	kən'vɜəʤd
converging	kən'vɜ·ʤɪŋ	kən'vɜəʤɪŋ
conversation	kɒnvə'seɪʃən	kɑnvə'seɪʃən
conversations	kɒnvə'seɪʃəns	kɑnvə'seɪʃənz
conversational	kɒnvə'seɪʃənl̩	
conversationally	kɒnvə'seɪʃənl̩ɪ	
converse, *noun*	'kɒnvɜs	'kɑnvɜəs
converse, *verb*	kən'vɜ·s	kən'vɜəs
converses	kən'vɜ·sɪz	kən'vɜəsɪz
conversed	kən'vɜ·st	kən'vɜəst
conversing	kən'vɜ·sɪŋ	kən'vɜəsɪŋ
conversion	kən'vɜ·ʃn̩	kən'vɜəʃn̩
conversions	kən'vɜ·ʃn̩z	kən'vɜəʃn̩z
convert, *noun*	'kɒnvɜt	'kɑnvɜət
converts	'kɒnvɜts	'kɑnvɜəts
convert, *verb*	kən'vɜ·t	kən'vɜət
converts	kən'vɜ·ts	kən'vɜəts
converted	kən'vɜ·tɪd	kən'vɜətɪd
converting	kən'vɜ·tɪŋ	kən'vɜətɪŋ

Traditional Spelling	Received Pronunciation	American Variants
convex	ˈkɒnˈvɛks	ˈkɑnˈvɛks
convey	kənˈveɪ	
conveys	kənˈveɪz	
conveyed	kənˈveɪd	
conveying	kənˈveɪɪŋ	
conveyance	kənˈveɪəns	
conveyances	kənˈveɪənsɪz	
convict, ***noun***	ˈkɒnvɪkt	ˈkɑnvɪkt
convicts	ˈkɒnvɪkts	ˈkɑnvɪkts
convict, *verb*	kənˈvɪkt	
convicts	kənˈvɪkts	
convicted	kənˈvɪktɪd	
convicting	kənˈvɪktɪŋ	
conviction	kənˈvɪkʃən	
convictions	kənˈvɪkʃənz	
convince	kənˈvɪns	
convinces	kənˈvɪnsɪz	
convinced	kənˈvɪnst	
convincing	kənˈvɪnsɪŋ	
convivial	kənˈvɪvɪəl	
convulsion	kənˈvʌlʃən	
convulsions	kənˈvʌlʃənz	
cook	kʊk	
cooks	kʊks	
cooked	kʊkt	
cooking	ˈkʊkɪŋ	
cookery	ˈkʊkərɪ	
cool	kuˑl	
cooler	ˈkuˑlə(r	ˈkuˑlə
coolest	ˈkuˑlɪst	
coolly	ˈkuˑllɪ	
coolness	ˈkuˑlnɪs	kuˑlnəs
co-operate	koʊˈɒpəreɪt	koʊˈɑpəreɪt
co-operates	koʊˈɒpəreɪts	koʊˈɑpəreɪts
co-operated	koʊˈɒpəreɪtɪd	koʊˈɑpəreɪtɪd
co-operating	koʊˈɒpəreɪtɪŋ	koʊˈɑpəreɪtɪŋ
co-operator	koʊˈɒpəreɪtə(r	koʊˈɑpəreɪtə
co-operators	koʊˈɒpəreɪtəz	koʊˈɑpəreɪtəz
co-operation	koʊɒpəˈreɪʃən	koʊɑpəˈreɪʃən
co-ordinate	koʊˈɔˑdɪneɪt	koʊˈɔədɪneɪt
co-ordinates	koʊˈɔˑdɪneɪts	koʊˈɔədɪneɪts
co-ordinated	koʊˈɔˑdɪneɪtɪd	koʊˈɔədɪneɪtɪd
co-ordinating	koʊˈɔˑdɪneɪtɪŋ	koʊˈɔədɪneɪtɪŋ
Copenhagen	ˈkoʊpn̩ˈheɪgən	
copper	ˈkɒpə(r	ˈkɑpə
copy	ˈkɒpɪ	ˈkɑpɪ
copies	ˈkɒpɪz	ˈkɑpɪz

Traditional Spelling	Received Pronunciation	American Variants
copied	ˈkɒpɪd	ˈkɑpɪd
copying	ˈkɒpɪɪŋ	ˈkɑpɪɪŋ
copyright	ˈkɒpɪraɪt	ˈkɑpɪraɪt
coral	ˈkɒrəl	
cord	kɔˑd	kɔəd
cords	kɔˑdz	kɔədz
cordial	ˈkɔˑdjəl, ˈkɔˑdɪəl	ˈkɔəʤəl, ˈkɔədɪəl
cordially	ˈkɔˑdjəlɪ, ˈkɔˑdɪəlɪ	ˈkɔədɪəlɪ
core	kɔˑ(r, kɔə(r	koə
cores	kɔˑz, kɔəz	koəz
cork	kɔˑk	kɔək
corks	kɔˑks	kɔəks
cork-screw	ˈkɔˑkskruˑ	ˈkɔəkskruˑ
cork-screws	ˈkɔˑkskruˑz	ˈkɔəkskruˑz
corn	kɔˑn	kɔən
corns	kɔˑnz	kɔənz
corner	ˈkɔˑnə(r	ˈkɔənə
corners	ˈkɔˑnəz	ˈkɔənəz
corollary	kəˈrɒlərɪ	ˈkɒrəlɛrɪ
corollaries	kəˈrɒlərɪz	ˈkɒrəlɛrɪz
coronation	kɒrəˈneɪʃən	
coronations	kɒrəˈneɪʃənz	
corporal	ˈkɔˑpərəl	ˈkɔəpərəl
corporals	ˈkɔˑpərəlz	ˈkɔəpərəlz
corporation	kɔˑpəˈreɪʃən	kɔəpəˈreɪʃən
corporations	kɔˑpəˈreɪʃənz	kɔəpəˈreɪʃənz
corps, *sing.*	kɔə, kɔˑ	koə
corps, *plu.*	kɔəz, kɔˑz	koəz
corpse	kɔˑps	kɔəps
corpses	ˈkɔˑpsɪz	ˈkɔəpsɪz
correct	kəˈrɛkt	
corrects	kəˈrɛkts	
corrected	kəˈrɛktɪd	
correcting	kəˈrɛktɪŋ	
correction	kəˈrɛkʃən	
corrections	kəˈrɛkʃənz	
correctly	kəˈrɛktlɪ	
correctness	kəˈrɛktnɪs	
corrector	kəˈrɛktə(r	kəˈrɛktə
correctors	kəˈrɛktəz	kəˈrɛktəz
corrective	kəˈrɛktɪv	
correlate	ˈkɒrɪleɪt	
correlates	ˈkɒrɪleɪts	
correlated	ˈkɒrɪleɪtɪd	
correlating	ˈkɒrɪleɪtɪŋ	
correlation	kɒrɪˈleɪʃən	
correlations	kɒrɪˈleɪʃənz	

Traditional Spelling	Received Pronunciation	American Variants
correspond	kɒrɪs'pɒnd	kɒrɪs'pɑnd
corresponds	kɒrɪs'pɒndz	kɑrɪs'pɑndz
corresponded	kɒrɪs'pɒndɪd	kɒrɪs'pɑndɪd
corresponding	kɒrɪs'pɒndɪŋ	kɒrɪs'pɑndɪŋ
correspondence	kɒrɪs'pɒndəns	kɒrɪs'pɑndəns
correspondingly	kɒrɪs'pɒndɪŋlɪ	kɒrɪs'pɑndɪŋlɪ
corridor	'kɒrɪdɔ(r	'kɒrɪdɔə, kɒrɪdə
corridors	'kɒrɪdɔz	'kɒrɪdɔəz, kɒrɪdəz
corroborate	kə'rɒbəreɪt	kə'rɑbəreɪt
corroborates	kə'rɒbəreɪts	kə'rɑbəreɪts
corroborated	kə'rɒbəreɪtɪd	kə'rɑbəreɪtɪd
corroborating	kə'rɒbəreɪtɪŋ	kə'rɑbəreɪtɪŋ
corroboration	kərɒbə'reɪʃən	kərɑbə'reɪʃən
corrupt	kə'rʌpt	
corrupts	kə'rʌpts	
corrupted	kə'rʌptɪd	
corrupting	kə'rʌptɪŋ	
corruption	kə'rʌpʃən	
corruptly	kə'rʌptlɪ	
corset	'kɔˑsɪt	'kɔəsɪt
corsets	'kɔˑsɪts	'kɔəsɪts
cosmopolitan	kɒzmə'pɒlɪtən	kɑzmə'pɑlɪtən
cost	kɔst, kɒst	
costs	kɔsts, kɒsts	
costing	'kɔstɪŋ, 'kɒstɪŋ	
costly	'kɔstlɪ, 'kɒstlɪ	
costume	'kɒstjum	'kɑstjum
costumes	'kɒstjumz	'kɑstjumz
cosy	'kouzɪ	
cosier	'kouzɪə(r	'kouzɪə
cosiest	'kouzɪɪst	
cosily	'kouzɪlɪ	
cot	kɒt	kɑt
cots	kɒts	kɑts
cottage	'kɒtɪʤ	'kɑtɪʤ
cottages	'kɒtɪʤɪz	'kɑtɪʤɪz
cotton	'kɒtn̩	'kɑtn̩
cough	kɒf	
coughs	kɒfs	
coughed	kɒft	
coughing	'kɒfɪŋ	
COULD *from* can	kud *s.f.*, kəd *w.f.*	
council	'kaʊnsl̩	
councils	'kaʊnsl̩z	
councillor	'kaʊnsɪlə(r	'kaʊnsɪlə
councillors	'kaʊnsɪləz	'kaʊnsɪləz
counsel	'kaʊnsl̩	

Traditional Spelling	Received Pronunciation	American Variants
counsels	'kaʊnslz	
counsellor	'kaʊnsələ(r	'kaʊnsələ
counsellors	'kaʊnsələz	'kaʊnsələz
count	kaʊnt	
counts	kaʊnts	
counted	'kaʊntɪd	
counting	'kaʊntɪŋ	
countenance	'kaʊntɪnəns	
countenances	'kaʊntɪnənsɪz	
counter	'kaʊntə(r	'kaʊntə
counters	'kaʊntəz	'kaʊntəz
counterbalance	kaʊntə'bæləns	kaʊntə'bæləns
counterbalances	kaʊntə'bælənsɪz	kaʊntə'bælənsɪz
counterbalanced	kaʊntə'bælənst	kaʊntə'bælənst
counterbalancing	kaʊntə'bælənsɪŋ	kaʊntə'bælənsɪŋ
countermand	kaʊntə'mɑ·nd	kaʊntə'ma·nd
countermands	kaʊntə'mɑ·ndz	kaʊntə'ma·ndz
countermanded	kaʊntə'mɑ·ndɪd	kaʊntə'ma·ndɪd
countermanding	kaʊntə'mɑ·ndɪŋ	kaʊntə'ma·ndɪŋ
countess	'kaʊntɪs	
countesses	'kaʊntɪsɪz	
countless	'kaʊntlɪs	
country	'kʌntrɪ	
countries	'kʌntrɪz	
countryman	'kʌntrɪmən	
countrymen	'kʌntrɪmən	
couple	'kʌpl	
couples	'kʌplz	
coupled	'kʌpld	
coupling	'kʌplɪŋ	
courage	'kʌrɪʤ	'kɜrɪʤ
courageous	kə'reɪʤəs	
courageously	kə'reɪʤəslɪ	
course	kɔ·s	koəs
courses	'kɔ·sɪz	'koəsɪz
court	kɔ·t, kɔət	koət
courts	kɔ·ts, kɔəts	koəts
courteous	'kɜ·tjəs, 'kɜ·tɪəs	'kɜətjəs, 'kɜətɪəs
courteously	'kɜ·tjəslɪ, 'kɜ·tɪəslɪ	'kɜətjəslɪ, 'kɜətɪəslɪ
courtesy	'kɜ·tɪsɪ	'kɜətɪsɪ
courtesies	'kɜ·tɪsɪz	'kɜətɪsɪz
cousin	'kʌzn	
cousins	'kʌznz	
cover	'kʌvə(r	'kʌvə
covers	'kʌvəz	'kʌvəz
covered	'kʌvəd	'kʌvəd
covering	'kʌvərɪŋ	

Traditional Spelling	Received Pronunciation	American Variants
cow	kaʊ	
cows	kaʊz	
coward	ˈkaʊəd	ˈkaʊəd
cowards	ˈkaʊədz	ˈkaʊədz
cowardice	ˈkaʊədɪs	ˈkaʊədɪs
cowardly	ˈkaʊədlɪ	ˈkaʊədlɪ
crab	kræb	
crabs	kræbz	
crack	kræk	
cracks	kræks	
cracked	krækt	
cracking	ˈkrækɪŋ	
cradle	ˈkreɪdl̩	
cradles	ˈkreɪdl̩z	
craft	krɑˑft	kraˑft, kræft
crafts	krɑˑfts	kraˑfts, kræfts
craftily	ˈkrɑˑftɪlɪ	ˈkraˑftɪlɪ, kræftɪlɪ
crafty	ˈkrɑˑftɪ	ˈkraˑftɪ, kræftɪ
cram	kræm	
crams	kræmz	
crammed	kræmd	
cramming	ˈkræmɪŋ	
cramp	kræmp	
crane	kreɪn	
cranes	kreɪnz	
crank	kræŋk	
cranks	kræŋks	
crash	kræʃ	
crashes	ˈkræʃɪz	
crashed	ˈkræʃt	
crashing	ˈkræʃɪŋ	
crater	ˈkreɪtə(r	ˈkreɪtə
craters	ˈkreɪtəz	ˈkreɪtəz
crave	kreɪv	
craves	kreɪvz	
craved	kreɪvd	
craving	ˈkreɪvɪŋ	
cravings	ˈkreɪvɪŋz	
crawl	krɔˑl	
crawls	krɔˑlz	
crawled	krɔˑld	
crawling	ˈkrɔˑlɪŋ	
crazy	ˈkreɪzɪ	
crazier	ˈkreɪzɪə(r	ˈkreɪzɪə
craziest	ˈkreɪzɪɪst	
cream	kriˑm	
crease	kriˑs	

Traditional Spelling	Received Pronunciation	American Variants
creases	ˈkriˑsɪz	
create	krɪˈeɪt	
creates	krɪˈeɪts	
created	krɪˈeɪtɪd	
creating	krɪˈeɪtɪŋ	
creation	krɪˈeɪʃən	
creations	krɪˈeɪʃənz	
creative	krɪˈeɪtɪv	
creator	krɪˈeɪtə(r	krɪˈeɪtə
creators	krɪˈeɪtəz	krɪˈeɪtəz
creature	ˈkriˑtʃə(r	ˈkriˑtʃə
creatures	ˈkriˑtʃəz	ˈkriˑtʃəz
credential	krɪˈdenʃəl	
credentials	krɪˈdenʃəlz	
credible	ˈkredɪbl̩	
credibly	ˈkredɪblɪ	
credit	ˈkredɪt	
credits	ˈkredɪts	
credited	ˈkredɪtɪd	
crediting	ˈkredɪtɪŋ	
creditable	ˈkredɪtəbl̩	
creditably	ˈkredɪtəblɪ	
creditor	ˈkredɪtə(r	ˈkredɪtə
creditors	ˈkredɪtəz	ˈkredɪtəz
credulity	krɪˈdjuˑlɪtɪ	
credulous	ˈkredjuləs	
creed	kriˑd	
creeds	kriˑdz	
creep	kriˑp	
creeps	kriˑps	
crept	krept	
creeping	ˈkriˑpɪŋ	
creeper	ˈkriˑpə(r	ˈkriˑpə
creepers	ˈkriˑpəz	ˈkriˑpəz
cremate	krɪˈmeɪt	
cremates	krɪˈmeɪts	
cremated	krɪˈmeɪtɪd	
cremating	krɪˈmeɪtɪŋ	
cremation	krɪˈmeɪʃən	
CREPT *from* creep	krept	
crescent	ˈkresn̩t, ˈkrezn̩t	
crescents	ˈkresn̩ts, ˈkrezn̩ts	
crest	krest	
crests	krests	
crew	kruˑ	
crews	kruˑz	
CREW *from* crow	kruˑ	

Traditional Spelling	Received Pronunciation	American Variants
cricket	ˈkrɪkɪt	
crime	kraɪm	
crimes	kraɪmz	
criminal	ˈkrɪmɪnl̩	
criminals	ˈkrɪmɪnl̩z	
crimson	ˈkrɪmzn̩	
cripple	ˈkrɪpl̩	
cripples	ˈkrɪpl̩z	
crippled	ˈkrɪpl̩d	
crippling	ˈkrɪplɪŋ, ˈkrɪpl̩ɪŋ	
critic	ˈkrɪtɪk	
critics	ˈkrɪtɪks	
critical	ˈkrɪtɪkəl	
critically	ˈkrɪtɪkəlɪ	
criticism	ˈkrɪtɪsɪzm̩	
criticisms	ˈkrɪtɪsɪzm̩z	
criticize	ˈkrɪtɪsaɪz	
criticizes	ˈkrɪtɪsaɪzɪz	
criticized	ˈkrɪtɪsaɪzd	
criticizing	ˈkrɪtɪsaɪzɪŋ	
critique	krɪˈtiˑk	
critiques	krɪˈtiˑks	
crockery	ˈkrɒkərɪ	ˈkrɑkərɪ
crocodile	ˈkrɒkədaɪl	ˈkrɑkədaɪl
crocodiles	ˈkrɒkədaɪlz	ˈkrɑkədaɪlz
crooked	ˈkrʊkɪd	
crookedly	ˈkrʊkɪdlɪ	
crop	krɒp	krɑp
crops	krɒps	krɑps
cropped	krɒpt	krɑpt
cropping	ˈkrɒpɪŋ	ˈkrɑpɪŋ
cross	krɔs, krɒs	krɔˑs, krɑs
crosser	ˈkrɔsə(r, ˈkrɒsə(r	krɔsə, krɒsə
crossest	ˈkrɔsɪst, ˈkrɒsɪst	
crosses	ˈkrɔsɪz, ˈkrɒsɪz	
crossed	krɔst, krɒst	
crossing	ˈkrɔsɪŋ, ˈkrɒsɪŋ	
crossings	ˈkrɔsɪŋz, ˈkrɒsɪŋz	
crossly	ˈkrɔslɪ, ˈkrɒslɪ	
crossness	ˈkrɔsnɪs, ˈkrɒsnɪs	
crouch	kraʊtʃ	
crouches	ˈkraʊtʃɪz	
crouched	kraʊtʃt	
crouching	ˈkraʊtʃɪŋ	
crow	kroʊ	
crows	kroʊz	
crowed	kroʊd	

Traditional Spelling	Received Pronunciation	American Variants
crowing	ˈkrouɪŋ	
crowd	kraud	
crowds	kraudz	
crowded	ˈkraudɪd	
crowding	ˈkraudɪŋ	
crown	kraun	
crowns	kraunz	
crowned	kraund	
crowning	ˈkraunɪŋ	
crude	kruˑd	
cruder	ˈkruˑdə(r	ˈkruˑdə
crudest	ˈkruˑdɪst	
crudely	ˈkruˑdlɪ	
crudeness	ˈkruˑdnɪs	
cruel	ˈkruəl, ˈkruɪl	
crueller	ˈkruələ(r, kruɪlə(r	ˈkruələ
cruellest	ˈkruəlɪst, ˈkruɪlɪst	
cruelly	ˈkruəlɪ, ˈkruɪlɪ	
cruelness	ˈkruəlnɪs, ˈkruɪlnɪs	
cruelty	ˈkruəltɪ	
cruelties	ˈkruəltɪz	
cruise	kruˑz	
cruises	ˈkruˑzɪz	
cruised	kruˑzd	
cruising	ˈkruˑzɪŋ	
cruiser	ˈkruˑzə(r	ˈkruˑzə
cruisers	ˈkruˑzəz	ˈkruˑzəz
crumb	krʌm	
crumbs	krʌmz	
crumble	ˈkrʌmbl̩	
crumbles	ˈkrʌmbl̩z	
crumbled	ˈkrʌmbl̩d	
crumbling	ˈkrʌmblɪŋ	
crumple	ˈkrʌmpl̩	
crumples	ˈkrʌmpl̩z	
crumpled	ˈkrʌmpl̩d	
crumpling	ˈkrʌmplɪŋ	
crush	krʌʃ	
crushes	ˈkrʌʃɪz	
crushed	krʌʃt	
crushing	ˈkrʌʃɪŋ	
crust	krʌst	
crusts	krʌsts	
cry	kraɪ	
cries	kraɪz	
cried	kraɪd	
crying	ˈkraɪɪŋ	

Traditional Spelling	Received Pronunciation	American Variants
crystal	ˈkrɪstl̩	
crystals	ˈkrɪstl̩z	
Cuba	ˈkjuˑbə	
Cuban	ˈkjuˑbən	
Cubans	ˈkjuˑbənz	
cube	kjuˑb	
cubes	kjuˑbz	
cubic	ˈkjuˑbɪk	
cuff	kʌf	
cuffs	kʌfs	
cultivate	ˈkʌltɪveɪt	
cultivates	ˈkʌltɪveɪts	
cultivated	ˈkʌltɪveɪtɪd	
cultivating	ˈkʌltɪveɪtɪŋ	
cultivation	kʌltɪˈveɪʃən	
culture	ˈkʌltʃə(r	ˈkʌltʃə
cultures	ˈkʌltʃəz	ˈkʌltʃəz
cultured	ˈkʌltʃəd	ˈkʌltʃəd
cumbrous	ˈkʌmbrəs	
cunning	ˈkʌnɪŋ	
cunningly	ˈkʌnɪŋlɪ	
cup	kʌp	
cups	kʌps	
cupboard	ˈkʌbəd	ˈkʌbəd
cupboards	ˈkʌbədz	ˈkʌbədz
cupful	ˈkʌpful	
cupfuls	ˈkʌpfulz	
curable	ˈkjuərəbl̩	ˈkjuˑrəbl̩
curate	ˈkjuərɪt	ˈkjuˑrɪt
curates	ˈkjuərɪts	ˈkjuˑrɪts
cure	kjuə(r	kjuə
cures	kjuəz	kjuəz
cured	kjuəd	kjuəd
curing	ˈkjuərɪŋ	ˈkjuˑrɪŋ
curio	ˈkjuərɪou	ˈkjuˑrɪou
curios	ˈkjuərɪouz	ˈkjuˑrɪouz
curiosity	kjuərɪˈɒsɪtɪ	kjuˑrɪˈɑsɪtɪ
curiosities	kjuərɪˈɒsɪtɪz	kjuˑrɪˈɑsɪtɪz
curious	ˈkjuərɪəs	kjuˑrɪəs
curiously	ˈkjuərɪəslɪ	kjuˑrɪəslɪ
curl	kɜˑl	kɜəl
curls	kɜˑlz	kɜəlz
curled	kɜˑld	kɜəld
curling	ˈkɜˑlɪŋ	ˈkɜəlɪŋ
currant	ˈkʌrənt	ˈkɜrənt
currants	ˈkʌrənts	ˈkɜrənts
current	ˈkʌrənt	

Traditional Spelling	Received Pronunciation	American Variants
currents	ˈkʌrənts	
currently	ˈkʌrəntlɪ	
curse	kɜˑs	kɜəs
curses	ˈkɜˑsɪz	ˈkɜəsɪz
cursed	kɜˑst	kɜəst
cursing	ˈkɜˑsɪŋ	ˈkɜəsɪŋ
cursed, *adj.*	ˈkɜˑsɪd	ˈkɜəsɪd
curt	kɜˑt	kɜət
curter	ˈkɜˑtə(r	ˈkɜətə
curtest	ˈkɜˑtɪst	ˈkɜətɪst
curtain	ˈkɜˑtn̩	ˈkɜətn̩
curtains	ˈkɜˑtn̩z	ˈkɜətn̩z
curtly	ˈkɜˑtlɪ	ˈkɜətlɪ
curve	kɜˑv	kɜəv
curves	kɜˑvz	kɜəvz
curved	kɜˑvd	kɜəvd
curving	ˈkɜˑvɪŋ	ˈkɜəvɪŋ
cushion	ˈkʊʃɪn	
cushions	ˈkʊʃɪnz	
custom	ˈkʌstəm	
customs	ˈkʌstəmz	
customer	ˈkʌstəmə(r	ˈkʌstəmə
customers	ˈkʌstəməz	ˈkʌstəməz
custom-house	ˈkʌstəmhaʊs	
custom-houses	ˈkʌstəmhaʊzɪz	
cut	kʌt	
cuts	kʌts	
cutting	ˈkʌtɪŋ	
cutter	ˈkʌtə(r	ˈkʌtə
cutters	ˈkʌtəz	ˈkʌtəz
cycle	ˈsaɪkl̩	
cycles	ˈsaɪkl̩z	
cycled	ˈsaɪkl̩d	
cycling	ˈsaɪklɪŋ	
cyclist	ˈsaɪklɪst	
cyclists	ˈsaɪklɪsts	
cylinder	ˈsɪlɪndə(r	ˈsɪlɪndə
cylinders	ˈsɪlɪndəz	ˈsɪlɪndəz
cynic	ˈsɪnɪk	
cynics	ˈsɪnɪks	
cynical	ˈsɪnɪkəl	
cynically	ˈsɪnɪkəlɪ	

D

Traditional Spelling	Received Pronunciation	American Variants
D	di·	
D's	di·z	
daily	ˈdeılı	
dainty	ˈdeıntı	
dainties	ˈdeıntız	
daintier	ˈdeıntıə(r	ˈdeıntıə
daintiest	ˈdeıntııst	
daintily	ˈdeıntılı	
dairy	ˈdɛərı	ˈdɛ·rı
dairies	ˈdɛərız	ˈdɛ·rız
dam	dæm	
dams	dæmz	
damage	ˈdæmıʤ	
damages	ˈdæmıʤız	
damaged	ˈdæmıʤd	
damaging	ˈdæmıʤıŋ	
damp	dæmp	
damper	ˈdæmpə(r	ˈdæmpə
dampest	ˈdæmpıst	
dampness	ˈdæmpnıs	
dance	dɑ·ns	da·ns
dances	ˈdɑ·nsiz	ˈda·nsız
danced	dɑ·nst	da·nst
dancing	ˈdɑ·nsıŋ	ˈda·nsıŋ
dancer	ˈdɑ·nsə(r	ˈda·nsə
dancers	ˈdɑ·nsəz	ˈda·nsəz
Dane	deın	
Danes	deınz	
danger	ˈdeınʤə(r	ˈdeınʤə
dangers	ˈdeınʤəz	ˈdeınʤəz
dangerous	ˈdeınʤərəs	
dangerously	ˈdeınʤərəslı	
Danish	ˈdeınıʃ	
dare	dɛə(r	dɛə
dares	dɛəz	dɛəz
dared	dɛəd	dɛəd
daring	ˈdɛərıŋ	ˈdɛ·rıŋ
daren't	dɛənt	dɛənt
daring, *adj*	ˈdɛərıŋ	ˈdɛ·rıŋ
daringly	ˈdɛərıŋlı	ˈdɛ·rıŋlı
dark	dɑ·k	dɑək
darker	ˈdɑ·kə(r	ˈdɑəkə
darkest	ˈdɑ·kıst	ˈdɑəkıst
darkness	ˈdɑ·knıs	ˈdɑəknıs
darken	ˈdɑ·kən	ˈdɑəkən

Traditional Spelling	Received Pronunciation	American Variants
darkens	'dɑ·kənz	'dɑəkənz
darkened	'dɑ·kənd	dɑəkənd
darkening	'dɑ·kənɪŋ	'dɑəkənɪŋ
darling	'dɑ·lɪŋ	'dɑəlɪŋ
darlings	'dɑ·lɪŋz	'dɑəlɪŋz
dart	dɑ·t	dɑət
darts	dɑ·ts	dɑəts
darted	'dɑ·tɪd	'dɑətɪd
darting	'dɑ·tɪŋ	'dɑətɪŋ
dash	dæʃ	
dashes	'dæʃɪz	
dashed	dæʃt	
dashing	'dæʃɪŋ	
date	deɪt	
dates	deɪts	
dated	'deɪtɪd	
dating	'deɪtɪŋ	
daughter	'dɔ·tə(r	'dɔ·tə
daughters	'dɔ·təz	'dɔ·təz
daughter-in-law	'dɔ·tərɪnlɔ	
daughters-in-law	'dɔ·təzɪnlɔ	'dɔ·təzɪnlɔ
dawn	dɔ·n	
dawns	dɔ·nz	
dawned	dɔ·nd	
dawning	'dɔ·nɪŋ	
day	deɪ	
days	deɪz	
daylight	'deɪlaɪt	
daytime	'deɪtaɪm	
dazzle	'dæzl̩	
dazzles	'dæzl̩z	
dazzled	'dæzl̩d	
dazzling	'dæzl̩ɪŋ	
dead	dɛd	
deaden	'dɛdn̩	
deadens	'dɛdn̩z	
deadened	'dɛdn̩d	
deadening	'dɛdn̩ɪŋ	
deadly	'dɛdlɪ	
deaf	dɛf	
deafer	'dɛfə(r	'dɛfə
deafest	'dɛfɪst	
deafness	'dɛfnɪs	
deafen	'dɛfn̩	
deafens	'dɛfn̩z	
deafened	'dɛfn̩d	
deafening	'dɛfn̩ɪŋ	

Traditional Spelling	Received Pronunciation	American Variants
deal	diˑl	
deals	diˑlz	
dealt	dɛlt	
dealing	ˈdiˑlɪŋ	
dealer	ˈdiˑlə(r	ˈdiˑlɚ
dealers	ˈdiˑləz	ˈdiˑlɚz
dealings	ˈdiˑlɪŋz	
dear	dɪə	dɪɚ
dearer	ˈdɪərə(r	ˈdɪˑrɚ
dearest	ˈdɪərɪst	ˈdɪˑrɪst
dearly	ˈdɪəlɪ	ˈdɪɚlɪ
dearness	ˈdɪənɪs	ˈdɪɚnɪs
death	dɛθ	
deaths	dɛθs	
debate	dɪˈbeɪt	
debates	dɪˈbeɪts	
debated	dɪˈbeɪtɪd	
debating	dɪˈbeɪtɪŋ	
debt	dɛt	
debts	dɛts	
debtor	ˈdɛtə(r	ˈdɛtɚ
debtors	ˈdɛtəz	ˈdɛtɚz
decay	dɪˈkeɪ	
decays	dɪˈkeɪz	
decayed	dɪˈkeɪd	
decaying	dɪˈkeɪɪŋ	
deceased, *adj*	dɪˈsiˑst	
deceit	dɪˈsiˑt	
deceitful	dɪˈsiˑtfʊl	
deceive	dɪˈsiˑv	
deceives	dɪˈsiˑvz	
deceived	dɪˈsiˑvd	
deceiving	dɪˈsiˑvɪŋ	
December	dɪˈsɛmbə(r	dɪˈsɛmbɚ
decent	ˈdiˑsənt	
decently	ˈdiˑsəntlɪ	
deception	dɪˈsɛpʃən	
deceptions	dɪˈsɛpʃənz	
deceptive	dɪˈsɛptɪv	
decide	dɪˈsaɪd	
decides	dɪˈsaɪdz	
decided	dɪˈsaɪdɪd	
deciding	dɪˈsaɪdɪŋ	
decidedly	dɪˈsaɪdɪdlɪ	
decimal	ˈdɛsɪməl	
decimals	ˈdɛsɪməlz	
decipher	dɪˈsaɪfə(r	dɪˈsaɪfɚ

Traditional Spelling	Received Pronunciation	American Variants
deciphers	dɪˈsaɪfəz	dɪˈsaɪfəz
deciphered	dɪˈsaɪfəd	dɪˈsaɪfəd
deciphering	dɪˈsaɪfərɪŋ	
decision	dɪˈsɪʒən	
decisions	dɪˈsɪʒənz	
decisive	dɪˈsaɪsɪv	
decisively	dɪˈsaɪsɪvlɪ	
deck	dɛk	
decks	dɛks	
declaration	dɛkləˈreɪʃən	
declarations	dɛkləˈreɪʃənz	
declare	dɪˈklɛə	dɪˈklɛə
declares	dɪˈklɛəz	dɪˈklɛəz
declared	dɪˈklɛəd	dɪˈklɛəd
declaring	dɪˈklɛərɪŋ	dɪˈklɛ·rɪŋ
declension	dɪˈklɛnʃən	
declensions	dɪˈklɛnʃənz	
decline	dɪˈklaɪn	
declines	dɪˈklaɪnz	
declined	dɪˈklaɪnd	
declining	dɪˈklaɪnɪŋ	
decompose	di·kəmˈpoʊz	
decomposes	di·kəmˈpoʊzɪz	
decomposed	dikəmˈpoʊzd	
decomposing	di·kəmˈpoʊzɪŋ	
decomposition	dikɒmpəˈzɪʃən	dikɑmpəˈzɪʃən
decorate	ˈdɛkəreɪt	
decorates	ˈdɛkəreɪts	
decorated	ˈdɛkəreɪtɪd	
decorating	ˈdɛkəreɪtɪŋ	
decorator	ˈdɛkəreɪtə(r	ˈdɛkəreɪtə
decorators	ˈdɛkəreɪtəz	ˈdɛkəreɪtəz
decoration	dɛkəˈreɪʃən	
decorations	dɛkəˈreɪʃənz	
decorative	ˈdɛkərətɪv	ˈdɛkəreɪtɪv
decoratively	ˈdɛkərətɪvlɪ	ˈdɛkəreɪtɪvlɪ
decrease, *noun*	ˈdi·kris, diˈkri·s	
decrease, *verb*	diˈkri·s, dɪˈkri·s	
decreases	diˈkri·sɪz, dɪˈkri·sɪz	
decreased	diˈkri·st, dɪˈkri·st	
decreasing	diˈkri·sɪŋ, dɪˈkri·sɪŋ	
decreasingly	diˈkri·sɪŋlɪ, dɪˈkri·sɪŋlɪ	
decree	dɪˈkri·	
decrees	dɪˈkri·z	
dedicate	ˈdɛdɪkeɪt	
dedicates	ˈdɛdɪkeɪts	
dedicated	ˈdɛdɪkeɪtɪd	

Traditional Spelling	Received Pronunciation	American Variants
dedicating	ˈdɛdɪkeɪtɪŋ	
dedication	dɛdɪˈkeɪʃən	
dedications	dɛdɪˈkeɪʃənz	
deduce	dɪˈdju·s	
deduces	dɪˈdju·sɪz	
deduced	dɪˈdju·st	
deducing	dɪˈdju·sɪŋ	
deduct	dɪˈdʌkt	
deducts	dɪˈdʌkts	
deducted	dɪˈdʌktɪd	
deducting	dɪˈdʌktɪŋ	
deduction	dɪˈdʌkʃən	
deductions	dɪˈdʌkʃənz	
deed	di·d	
deeds	di·dz	
deep	di·p	
deeper	ˈdi·pə(r	ˈdi·pə
deepest	ˈdi·pɪst	
deeply	ˈdi·plɪ	
deepen	ˈdi·pən	
deepens	ˈdi·pənz	
deepened	ˈdi·pənd	
deepening	ˈdi·pənɪŋ	
deer	dɪə(r	dɪə
default	dɪˈfɔ·lt, dɪˈfɒlt	
defaulter	dɪˈfɔ·ltə(r, dɪˈfɒltə(r	dɪˈfɔ·ltə
defaulters	dɪˈfɔ·ltəz, dɪˈfɒltəz	dɪˈfɔ·ltəz
defeat	dɪˈfi·t	
defeats	dɪˈfi·ts	
defeated	dɪˈfi·tɪd	
defeating	dɪˈfi·tɪŋ	
defect	dɪˈfɛkt, ˈdiˈfɛkt	
defects	dɪˈfɛkts, ˈdiˈfɛkts	
defective	dɪˈfɛktɪv	
defectively	dɪˈfɛktɪvlɪ	
defence	dɪˈfɛns	
defences	dɪˈfɛnsɪz	
defenceless	dɪˈfɛnslɪs	
defend	dɪˈfɛnd	
defends	dɪˈfɛndz	
defended	dɪˈfɛndɪd	
defending	dɪˈfɛndɪŋ	
defender	dɪˈfɛndə(r	dɪˈfɛndə
defenders	dɪˈfɛndəz	dɪˈfɛndəz
defendant	dɪˈfɛndənt	
defendants	dɪˈfɛndənts	
defensive	dɪˈfɛnsɪv	

Traditional Spelling	Received Pronunciation	American Variants
defer	dɪ'fɜ·(r	dɪ'fɜə
defers	dɪ'fɜ·z	dɪ'fɜəz
deferred	dɪ'fɜ·d	dɪ'fɜəd
deferring	dɪ'fɜ·rɪŋ	
deference	'dɛfərəns	
defiance	dɪ'faɪəns	
defiant	dɪ'faɪənt	
defiantly	dɪ'faɪəntlɪ	
deficiency	dɪ'fɪʃənsɪ	
deficiencies	dɪ'fɪʃənsɪz	
deficient	dɪ'fɪʃənt	
deficit	'dɛfɪsɪt 'di·fɪsɪt	
deficits	'dɛfɪsɪts 'dɪ·fɪsɪts	
define	dɪ'faɪn	
defines	dɪ'faɪnz	
defined	dɪ'faɪnd	
defining	dɪ'faɪnɪŋ	
definite	'dɛfɨnɪt	
definitely	'dɛfɨnɪtlɪ	
definition	dɛfɪ'nɪʃən	
definitions	dɛfɪ'nɪʃənz	
deform	dɪ'fɔ·m	dɪ'fɔəm
deforms	dɪ'fɔ·mz	dɪ'fɔəmz
deformed	dɪ'fɔ·md	dɪ'fɔəmd
deforming	dɪ'fɔ·mɪŋ	dɪ'fɔəmɪŋ
deformity	dɪ'fɔ·mɪtɪ	dɪ'fɔəmɪtɪ
deformities	dɪ'fɔ·mɪtɪz	dɪ'fɔəmɪtɪz
defraud	dɪ'frɔ·d	
defrauds	dɪ'frɔ·dz	
defrauded	dɪ'frɔ·dɪd	
defrauding	dɪ'frɔ·dɪŋ	
defy	dɪ'faɪ	
defies	dɪ'faɪz	
defied	dɪ'faɪd	
defying	dɪ'faɪɪŋ	
degenerate, *adj.*	dɪ'ʤenərɪt	
degradation	degrə'deɪʃən	
degrade	dɪ'greɪd	
degrades	dɪ'greɪdz	
degraded	dɪ'greɪdɪd	
degrading	dɪ'greɪdɪŋ	
degree	dɪ'gri·	
degrees	dɪ'gri·z	
deject	dɪ'ʤɛkt	
dejects	dɪ'ʤɛkts	

Traditional Spelling	Received Pronunciation	American Variants
dejected	dɪ'dʒɛktɪd	
dejecting	dɪ'dʒɛktɪŋ	
dejection	dɪ'dʒɛkʃən	
delay	dɪ'leɪ	
delays	dɪ'leɪz	
delayed	dɪ'leɪd	
delaying	dɪ'leɪɪŋ	
delegate, *noun*	'dɛlɪgɪt, 'dɛlɪgeɪt	
delegates	'dɛlɪgɪts, 'dɛlɪgeɪts	
delegate, *verb*	'dɛlɪgeɪt	
delegates	'dɛlɪgeɪts	
delegated	'dɛlɪgeɪtɪd	
delegating	'dɛlɪgeɪtɪŋ	
delegation	dɛlɪ'geɪʃən	
delegations	dɛlɪ'geɪʃənz	
deliberate, *adj.*	dɪ'lɪbərɪt	
deliberately	dɪ'lɪbərɪtlɪ	
deliberate, *verb*	dɪ'lɪbəreɪt	
deliberates	dɪ'lɪbəreɪts	
deliberated	dɪ'lɪbəreɪtɪd	
deliberating	dɪ'lɪbəreɪtɪŋ	
deliberation	dɪlɪbə'reɪʃən	
deliberations	dɪlɪbə'reɪʃənz	
delicacy	'dɛlɪkəsɪ	
delicacies	'dɛlɪkəsɪz	
delicate	'dɛlɪkɪt	
delicately	'dɛlɪkɪtlɪ	
delicious	dɪ'lɪʃəs	
deliciously	dɪ'lɪʃəslɪ	
delight	dɪ'laɪt	
delights	dɪ'laɪts	
delighted	dɪ'laɪtɪd	
delighting	dɪ'laɪtɪŋ	
delightful	dɪ'laɪtful	
delightfully	dɪ'laɪtfəlɪ, dɪ'laɪtfulɪ	
delirious	dɪ'lɪrɪəs	
deliriously	dɪ'lɪrɪəslɪ	
deliver	dɪ'lɪvə(r	dɪ'lɪvə
delivers	dɪ'lɪvəz	dɪ'lɪvəz
delivered	dɪ'lɪvəd	dɪ'lɪvəd
delivering	dɪ'lɪvərɪŋ	
deliverance	dɪ'lɪvərəns	
deliverances	dɪ'lɪvərənsɪz	
delivery	dɪ'lɪvərɪ	
deliveries	dɪ'lɪvərɪz	
delude	dɪ'ljuˑd	
deludes	dɪ'ljuˑdz	

Traditional Spelling	Received Pronunciation	American Variants
deluded	dɪˈljuˑdɪd	
deluding	dɪˈljuˑdɪŋ	
deluge	ˈdɛljuʤ	
deluges	ˈdɛljuʤɪz	
delusion	dɪˈljuˑʒən	
delusions	dɪˈljuˑʒənz	
demand	dɪˈmɑˑnd	dɪˈmaˑnd
demands	dɪˈmɑˑndz	dɪˈmaˑndz
demanded	dɪˈmɑˑndɪd	dɪˈmaˑndɪd
demanding	dɪˈmɑˑndɪŋ	dɪˈmaˑndɪŋ
democracy	dɪˈmɒkrəsɪ	dɪˈmɑkrəsɪ
democracies	dɪˈmɒkrəsɪz	dɪˈmɑkrəsɪz
democrat	ˈdɛməkræt	
democrats	ˈdɛməkræts	
democratic	dɛməˈkrætɪk	
democratically	dɛməˈkrætɪkəlɪ	
demolish	dɪˈmɒlɪʃ	dɪˈmɑlɪʃ
demolishes	dɪˈmɒlɪʃɪz	dɪˈmɑlɪʃɪz
demolished	dɪˈmɒlɪʃt	dɪˈmɑlɪʃt
demolishing	dɪˈmɒlɪʃɪŋ	dɪˈmɑlɪʃɪŋ
demonstrate	ˈdɛmənstreɪt	
demonstrates	ˈdɛmənstreɪts	
demonstrated	ˈdɛmənstreɪtɪd	
demonstrating	ˈdɛmənstreɪtɪŋ	
demonstration	dɛmənsˈtreɪʃən	
demonstrations	dɛmənsˈtreɪʃənz	
demonstrative	dɪˈmɒnstrətɪv	dɪˈmɑnstrətɪv
demoralize	dɪˈmɒrəlaɪz	
demoralizes	dɪˈmɒrəlaɪzɪz	
demoralized	dɪˈmɒrəlaɪzd	
demoralizing	dɪˈmɒrəlaɪzɪŋ	
den	dɛn	
dens	dɛnz	
denial	dɪˈnaɪəl	
denials	dɪˈnaɪəlz	
Denmark	ˈdɛnmɑˑk	ˈdɛnmɑək
dense	dɛns	
denser	ˈdɛnsə(r	ˈdɛnsə
densest	ˈdɛnsɪst	
densely	ˈdɛnslɪ	
density	ˈdɛnsɪtɪ	
dentist	ˈdɛntɪst	
dentists	ˈdɛntɪsts	
deny	dɪˈnaɪ	
denies	dɪˈnaɪz	
denied	dɪˈnaɪd	
denying	dɪˈnaɪɪŋ	

Traditional Spelling	Received Pronunciation	American Variants
depart	dɪ'pɑ·t	dɪ'pɑət
departs	dɪ'pɑ·ts	dɪ'pɑəts
departed	dɪ'pɑ·tɪd	dɪ'pɑətɪd
departing	dɪ'pɑ·tɪŋ	dɪ'pɑətɪŋ
department	dɪ'pɑ·tmənt	dɪpɑətmənt
departments	dɪ'pɑ·tmənts	dɪ'pɑətmənts
departure	dɪ'pɑ·tʃə(r	dɪ'pɑətʃə
departures	dɪ'pɑ·tʃəz	dɪ'pɑətʃəz
depend	dɪ'pɛnd	
depends	dɪ'pɛndz	
depended	dɪ'pɛndɪd	
depending	dɪ'pɛndɪŋ	
dependant	dɪ'pɛndənt	
dependants	dɪ'pɛndənts	
deplorable	dɪ'plɔ·rəbl̩	dɪ'plo·rəbl̩
deplorably	dɪ'plɔ·rəblɪ	dɪ'plo·rəblɪ
deplore	dɪ'plɔ·, dɪ'plɔə	dɪ'ploə
deplores	dɪplɔ·z, dɪ'plɔəz	dɪ'ploəz
deplored	dɪ'plɔ·d, dɪ'plɔəd	dɪ'ploəd
deploring	dɪ'plɔ·rɪŋ, dɪ'plɔərɪŋ	dɪ'plo·rɪŋ
deport	dɪ'pɔ·t	dɪ'poət
deports	dɪ'pɔ·ts	dɪ'poəts
deported	dɪ'pɔ·tɪd	dɪ'poətɪd
deporting	dɪ'pɔ·tɪŋ	dɪ'poətɪŋ
deportation	dipɔ'teɪʃən	dipoə'teɪʃən
deportations	dipɔ'teɪʃənz	dipoə'teɪʃənz
deposit	dɪ'pɒzɪt	dɪ'pɑzɪt
deposits	dɪ'pɒzɪts	dɪ'pɑzɪts
deposited	dɪ'pɒzɪtɪd	dɪ'pɑzɪtɪd
depositing	dɪ'pɒzɪtɪŋ	dɪ'pɑzɪtɪŋ
depositor	dɪ'pɒzɪtə(r	dɪ'pɑzɪtə
depositors	dɪ'pɒzɪtəz	dɪ'pɑzɪtəz
depot	'dɛpoʊ, 'di·poʊ	
depots	'dɛpoʊz, 'di·poʊz	
deprave	dɪpreɪv	
depraves	dɪ'preɪvz	
depraved	dɪ'preɪvd	
depraving	dɪ'preɪvɪŋ	
depravity	dɪ'prævɪtɪ	
depress	dɪ'prɛs	
depresses	dɪ'prɛsɪz	
depressed	dɪ'prɛst	
depressing	dɪ'prɛsɪŋ	
depression	dɪ'prɛʃən	
depressions	dɪ'prɛʃənz	
deprivation	dɛprɪ'veɪʃən	
deprivations	dɛprɪ'veɪʃənz	

Traditional Spelling	Received Pronunciation	American Variants
deprive	dɪ'praɪv	
deprives	dɪ'praɪvz	
deprived	dɪ'praɪvd	
depriving	dɪ'praɪvɪŋ	
depth	dɛpθ	
depths	dɛpθs	
deputation	dɛpju'teɪʃən	
deputations	dɛpju'teɪʃənz	
depute	dɪ'pju·t	
deputes	dɪ'pju·ts	
deputed	dɪ'pju·tɪd	
deputing	dɪ'pju·tɪŋ	
deputy	'dɛpjutɪ	
deputies	'dɛpjutɪz	
derivation	dɛrɪ'veɪʃən	
derivations	dɛrɪ'veɪʃənz	
derivative	dɪ'rɪvətɪv	
derivatives	dɪ'rɪvətɪvz	
derive	dɪ'raɪv	
derives	dɪ'raɪvz	
derived	dɪ'raɪvd	
deriving	dɪ'raɪvɪŋ	
descend	dɪ'sɛnd	
descends	dɪ'sɛndz	
descended	dɪ'sɛndɪd	
descending	dɪ'sɛndɪŋ	
descendant	dɪ'sɛndənt	
descendants	dɪ'sɛndənts	
descent	dɪ'sɛnt	
descents	dɪ'sɛnts	
describe	dɪs'kraɪb	
describes	dɪs'kraɪbz	
described	dɪs'kraɪbd	
describing	dɪs'kraɪbɪŋ	
description	dɪs'krɪpʃən	
descriptions	dɪs'krɪpʃənz	
descriptive	dɪs'krɪptiv	
desecrate	'dɛsɪkreɪt	
desecrates	'dɛsɪkreɪts	
desecrated	'dɛsɪkreɪtɪd	
desecrating	'dɛsɪkreɪtɪŋ	
desecration	dɛsɪ'kreɪʃən	
desecrations	dɛsɪ'kreɪʃənz	
desert, *noun*	'dɛzət	'dɛzət
deserts	'dɛzəts	'dɛzəts
desert, *verb*	dɪ'zɜ·t	dɪ'zɜət
deserts	dɪ'zɜ·ts	dɪ'zɜəts

Traditional Spelling	Received Pronunciation	American Variants
deserted	dɪˈzɜ·tɪd	dɪˈzɜətɪd
deserting	dɪˈzɜ·tɪŋ	dɪˈsɜətɪŋ
deserter	dɪˈzɜ·tə(r	dɪˈzɜətə
deserters	dɪˈzɜ·təz	dɪˈzɜətəz
desertion	dɪˈzɜ·ʃən	dɪˈzɜəʃən
desertions	dɪˈzɜ·ʃənz	dɪˈzɜəʃənz
deserve	dɪˈzɜ·v	dɪˈzɜəv
deserves	dɪˈzɜ·vz	dɪˈzɜəvz
deserved	dɪˈzɜ·vd	dɪˈzɜəvd
deserving	dɪˈzɜ·vɪŋ	dɪˈzɜəvɪŋ
deservedly	dɪˈzɜ·vɪdlɪ	dɪˈzɜəvɪdlɪ
design	dɪˈzaɪn	
designs	dɪˈzaɪnz	
designed	dɪˈzaɪnd	
designing	dɪˈzaɪnɪŋ	
designer	dɪˈzaɪnə(r	dɪˈzaɪnə
designers	dɪˈzaɪnəz	dɪˈzaɪnəz
designate	ˈdɛzɪgneɪt	
designates	ˈdɛzɪgneɪts	
designated	ˈdɛzɪgneɪtɪd	
designating	ˈdɛzɪgneɪtɪŋ	
designation	dɛzɪgˈneɪʃən	
designations	dɛzɪgˈneɪʃənz	
desirability	dɪzaɪərəˈbɪlɪtɪ	dɪzaɪrəˈbɪlɪtɪ
desirable	dɪˈzaɪərəbl̩	dɪˈzaɪrəbl̩
desirably	dɪˈzaɪərəblɪ	dɪˈzaɪrəblɪ
desire	dɪˈzaɪə(r	dɪˈzaɪə
desires	dɪˈzaɪəz	dɪˈzaɪəz
desired	dɪˈzaɪəd	dɪˈzaɪəd
desiring	dɪˈzaɪərɪŋ	dɪˈzaɪrɪŋ
desirous	dɪˈzaɪərəs	dɪˈzaɪrəs
desk	dɛsk	
desks	dɛsks	
desolate	ˈdɛsəlɪt	
despair	dɪsˈpɛə(r	dɪsˈpɛə
despairs	dɪsˈpɛəz	dɪsˈpɛəz
despaired	dɪsˈpɛəd	dɪsˈpɛəd
despairing	dɪsˈpɛərɪŋ	dɪsˈpɛ·rɪŋ
despatch	dɪsˈpætʃ	
despatches	dɪsˈpætʃɪz	
despatched	dɪsˈpætʃt	
despatching	dɪsˈpætʃɪŋ	
desperate	ˈdɛspərɪt	
desperately	ˈdɛspərɪtlɪ	
desperation	dɛspəˈreɪʃən	
despise	dɪsˈpaɪz	
despises	dɪsˈpaɪzɪz	

Traditional Spelling	Received Pronunciation	American Variants
despised	dɪs'paɪzd	
despising	dɪs'paɪzɪŋ	
despite	dɪs'paɪt	
dessert	dɪ'zɜ·t	dɪ'zɜət
destination	dɛstɪ'neɪʃən	
destinations	dɛstɪ'neɪʃənz	
destiny	'dɛstɪnɪ	
destinies	'dɛstɪnɪz	
destitute	'dɛstɪtjut	
destitution	dɛstɪ'tju·ʃən	
destroy	dɪs'trɔɪ	
destroys	dɪs'trɔɪz	
destroyed	dɪs'trɔɪd	
destroying	dɪs'trɔɪɪŋ	
destroyer	dɪs'trɔɪə(r	dɪs'trɔɪə
destroyers	dɪs'trɔɪəz	dɪs'trɔɪəz
destructible	dɪs'trʌktəbḷ	
destruction	dɪs'trʌkʃən	
destructive	dɪs'trʌktiv	
destructively	dɪs'trʌktɪvlɪ	
destructiveness	dɪs'trʌktɪvnɪs	
detach	dɪ'tætʃ	
detaches	dɪ'tætʃɪz	
detached	dɪ'tætʃt	
detaching	dɪ'tætʃɪŋ	
detachment	dɪ'tætʃmənt	
detail, ***noun***	'di·teɪl, dɪ'teɪl	
details	'di·teɪlz, dɪ'teɪlz	
detail, ***verb***	dɪ'teɪl	
details	dɪ'teɪlz	
detailed	dɪ'teɪld	
detailing	dɪ'teɪlɪŋ	
detain	dɪ'teɪn	
detains	dɪ'teɪnz	
detained	dɪ'teɪnd	
detaining	dɪ'teɪnɪŋ	
detect	dɪ'tɛkt	
detects	dɪ'tɛkts	
detected	dɪ'tɛktɪd	
detecting	dɪ'tɛktɪŋ	
detection	dɪ'tɛkʃən	
detective	dɪ'tɛktɪv	
detectives	dɪ'tɛktɪvz	
deter	dɪ'tɜ·(r	dɪ'tɜə
deters	dɪ'tɜ·z	dɪ'tɜəz
deterred	dɪ'tɜ·d	dɪ'tɜəd
deterring	dɪ'tɜ·rɪŋ	

Traditional Spelling	Received Pronunciation	American Variants
deteriorate	dɪ'tɪərɪəreɪt	dɪ'tɪ·rɪəreɪt
deteriorates	dɪ'tɪərɪəreɪts	dɪ'tɪ·rɪəreɪts
deteriorated	dɪ'tɪərɪəreɪtɪd	dɪ'tɪ·rɪəreɪtɪd
deteriorating	dɪ'tɪərɪəreɪtɪŋ	dɪ'tɪ·rɪəreɪtɪŋ
deterioration	dɪtɪərɪə'reɪʃən	dɪtɪ·rɪə'reɪʃən
determinative	dɪ't·ɜmɪneɪtɪv	dɪ'tɜəmɪneɪtɪv
	dɪ'tɜ·mɪnətɪv	dɪ'tɜəmɪnətɪv
determine	dɪ'tɜ·mɪn	dɪ'tɜəmɪn
determines	dɪ'tɜ·mɪnz	dɪ'tɜəmɪnz
determined	dɪ'tɜ·mɪnd	dɪ'tɜəmɪnd
determining	dɪ'tɜ·mɪnɪŋ	dɪ'tɜəmɪnɪŋ
detest	dɪ'tɛst	
detests	dɪ'tɛsts	
detested	dɪ'tɛstɪd	
detesting	dɪ'tɛstɪŋ	
detestable	dɪ'tɛstəbl̩	
detestably	dɪ'tɛstəblɪ	
detestation	ditɛs'teɪʃən	
detract	dɪ'trækt	
detracts	dɪ'trækts	
detracted	dɪ'træktɪd	
detracting	dɪ'træktɪŋ	
detriment	'dɛtrɪmənt	
detrimental	dɛtrɪ'mɛntəl	
devastate	'dɛvəsteɪt	
devastates	'dɛvəsteɪts	
devastated	'dɛvəsteɪtɪd	
devastating	'dɛvəsteɪtɪŋ	
devastation	dɛvəs'teɪʃən	
develop	dɪ'vɛləp	
develops	dɪ'vɛləps	
developed	dɪ'vɛləpt	
developing	dɪ'vɛləpɪŋ	
developer	dɪ'vɛləpə(r	dɪ'vɛləpə
developers	dɪ'vɛləpəz	dɪ'vɛləpəz
development	dɪ'vɛləpmənt	
developments	dɪ'vɛləpmənts	
deviate	'di·vɪeɪt	
deviates	'di·vɪeɪts	
deviated	'di·vɪeɪtɪd	
deviating	'di·vɪeɪtɪŋ	
deviation	divɪ'eɪʃən	
deviations	divɪ'eɪʃənz	
device	dɪ'vaɪs	
devices	dɪ'vaɪsɪz	
devil	'dɛvɪl	
devils	'dɛvɪlz	

Traditional Spelling	Received Pronunciation	American Variants
devious	ˈdiˑvɪəs	
deviously	ˈdiˑvɪəslɪ	
devise	dɪˈvaɪz	
devises	dɪˈvaɪzɪz	
devised	dɪˈvaɪzd	
devising	dɪˈvaɪzɪŋ	
devoid	dɪˈvɔɪd	
devote	dɪˈvout	
devotes	dɪˈvouts	
devoted	dɪˈvoutɪd	
devoting	dɪˈvoutɪŋ	
devotedly	dɪˈvoutɪdlɪ	
devotion	dɪˈvouʃən	
devotions	dɪˈvouʃənz	
devour	dɪˈvaʊə(r	dɪˈvaʊə
devours	dɪˈvaʊəz	dɪˈvaʊəz
devoured	dɪˈvaʊəd	dɪˈvaʊəd
devouring	dɪˈvaʊərɪŋ	dɪˈvaʊrɪŋ
devout	dɪˈvaʊt	
devouter	dɪˈvaʊtə(r	dɪˈvaʊtə
devoutest	dɪˈvaʊtɪst	
devoutly	dɪˈvaʊtlɪ	
dew	djuˑ	
diabolical	daɪəˈbɒlɪkəl	daɪəˈbɑlɪkəl
diabolically	daɪəˈbɒlikəlɪ	daɪəˈbɑlɪkəlɪ
diacritic	daɪəˈkrɪtɪk	
diacritics	daɪəˈkrɪtɪks	
diacritical	daɪəˈkrɪtɪkəl	
diagnose	ˈdaɪəgnouz	ˈdaɪəgnous
diagnoses	ˈdaɪəgnouzɪz	ˈdaɪəgnousɪz
diagnosed	ˈdaɪəgnouzd	ˈdaɪəgnoust
diagnosing	ˈdaɪəgnouzɪŋ	ˈdaɪəgnousɪŋ
diagnosis	daɪəgˈnousɪs	
diagnoses	daɪəgˈnousiz	
diagonal	daɪˈægənl̩	
diagonals	daɪˈægənl̩z	
diagonally	daɪˈægənəlɪ	
diagram	ˈdaɪəgræm	
diagrams	ˈdaɪəgræmz	
dial	ˈdaɪəl	
dials	ˈdaɪəlz	
dialect	ˈdaɪəlɛkt	
dialects	ˈdaɪəlɛkts	
dialectal	daɪəˈlɛktl̩	
dialogue	ˈdaɪəlɒg	
dialogues	ˈdaɪəlɒgz	
diameter	daɪˈæmɪtə(r	daɪˈæmɪtə

Traditional Spelling	Received Pronunciation	American Variants
diameters	daɪ'æmɪtəz	daɪ'æmɪtəz
diametrical	daɪə'mɛtrɪkəl	
diametrically	daɪə'mɛtrɪkəlɪ	
diamond	'daɪəmənd	
diamonds	'daɪəməndz	
diary	'daɪərɪ	
diaries	'daɪərɪz	
dictate, *verb*	dɪk'teɪt	
dictates	dɪk'teɪts	
dictated	dɪk'teɪtɪd	
dictating	dɪk'teɪtɪŋ	
dictator	dɪk'teɪtə(r	dɪk'teɪtə
dictators	dɪk'teɪtəz	dɪk'teɪtəz
dictation	dɪk'teɪʃən	
dictionary	'dɪkʃənərɪ	'dɪkʃənɛrɪ
dictionaries	'dɪkʃənərɪz	'dɪkʃənɛrɪz
DID *from* do	dɪd	
DIDN'T *from* did not	'dɪdn̩t	
die	daɪ	
dies	daɪz	
died	daɪd	
dying	'daɪɪŋ	
diet	'daɪət	
diets	'daɪəts	
differ	'dɪfə(r	'dɪfə
differs	'dɪfəz	'dɪfəz
differed	'dɪfəd	'dɪfəd
differing	'dɪfərɪŋ	
difference	'dɪfrəns	
differences	'dɪfrənsɪz	
different	'dɪfrənt	
differently	'dɪfrəntlɪ	
difficult	'dɪfɪkəlt	
difficulty	'dɪfɪkəltɪ	
difficulties	'dɪfɪkəltɪz	
dig	dɪg	
digs	dɪgz	
dug	dʌg	
digging	'dɪgɪŋ	
digest, *noun*	'daɪʤɛst	
digests	'daɪʤɛsts	
digest, *verb*	dɪ'ʤɛst, daɪ'ʤɛst	
digests	dɪ'ʤɛsts, daɪ'ʤɛsts	
digested	di'ʤɛstɪd daɪ'ʤɛstɪd	
digesting	dɪ'ʤɛstɪŋ daɪ'ʤɛstɪŋ	

Traditional Spelling	Received Pronunciation	American Variants
digestible	dɪˈdʒɛstəbl̩	
	daɪˈdʒɛstəbl̩	
digestion	dɪˈdʒɛstʃən	
	daɪˈdʒɛstʃən	
digestions	dɪˈdʒɛstʃənz	
	daɪˈdʒɛstʃənz	
dignify	ˈdɪgnɪfaɪ	
dignifies	ˈdɪgnɪfaɪz	
dignified	ˈdɪgnɪfaɪd	
dignifying	ˈdɪgnɪfaɪɪŋ	
dignity	ˈdɪgnɪtɪ	
dignities	ˈdɪgnɪtɪz	
dilemma	dɪˈlɛmə, daɪˈlɛmə	
dilemmas	dɪˈlɛməz, daɪˈlɛməz	
diligence	ˈdɪlɪdʒəns	
diligent	ˈdɪlɪdʒənt	
diligently	ˈdɪlɪdʒəntlɪ	
dilute	daɪˈljuˑt, dɪˈljuˑt	
dilutes	daɪˈljuˑts, dɪˈljuˑts	
diluted	daɪˈljuˑtɪd	
	dɪˈljuˑtɪd	
diluting	daɪˈljuˑtɪŋ	
	dɪˈljuˑtɪŋ	
dim	dɪm	
dimmer	ˈdɪmə(r	ˈdɪmə
dimmest	ˈdɪmɪst	
dime	daɪm	
dimes	daɪmz	
dimly	ˈdɪmlɪ	
dimness	ˈdɪmnɪs	
dimension	dɪˈmɛnʃən	
	daɪˈmɛnʃən	
dimensions	dɪˈmɛnʃənz	
	daɪˈmɛnʃənz	
diminish	dɪˈmɪnɪʃ	
diminishes	dɪˈmɪnɪʃɪz	
diminished	dɪˈmɪnɪʃt	
diminishing	dɪˈmɪnɪʃɪŋ	
diminution	dɪmɪˈnjuˑʃən	
diminutions	dɪmɪˈnjuˑʃənz	
dine	daɪn	
dines	daɪnz	
dined	daɪnd	
dining	ˈdaɪnɪŋ	
diner	ˈdaɪnə(r	ˈdaɪnə
diners	ˈdaɪnəz	ˈdaɪnəz
dingy	ˈdɪndʒɪ	

Traditional Spelling	Received Pronunciation	American Variants
dining-room	ˈdaɪnɪŋrʊm	
	ˈdaɪnɪŋrum	
dining-rooms	ˈdaɪnɪŋrʊmz	
	ˈdaɪnɪŋrumz	
dinner	ˈdɪnə(r	ˈdɪnə
dinners	ˈdɪnəz	ˈdɪnəz
dint	dɪnt	
dip	dɪp	
dips	dɪps	
dipped	dɪpt	
dipping	ˈdɪpɪŋ	
diphthong	ˈdɪfθɒŋ	
diphthongs	ˈdɪfθɒŋz	
diploma	dɪˈploʊmə	
diplomas	dɪˈploʊməz	
diplomacy	dɪˈploʊməsɪ	
diplomat	ˈdɪploʊmæt	
	ˈdɪpləmæt	
diplomats	ˈdɪploʊmæts	
	ˈdɪpləmæts	
diplomatic	dɪploʊˈmætɪk	
	dɪpləˈmætɪk	
diplomatically	dɪploʊˈmætɪkəlɪ	
	dɪpləˈmætɪkəlɪ	
diplomatist	dɪˈploʊmətɪst	
diplomatists	dɪˈploʊmətɪsts	
direct	dɪˈrɛkt, daɪˈrɛkt	
directs	dɪˈrɛkts, daɪˈrɛkts	
directed	dɪˈrɛktɪd, daɪˈrɛktɪd	
directing	dɪˈrɛktɪŋ, daɪˈrɛktɪŋ	
director	dɪˈrɛktə(r, daɪˈrɛktə(r	dɪˈrɛktə, daɪˈrɛktə
directors	dɪˈrɛktəz, daɪˈrɛktəz	dɪˈrɛktəz, daɪˈrɛktəz
direction	dɪˈrɛkʃən, daɪˈrɛkʃən	
directions	dɪˈrɛkʃənz	
	daɪˈrɛkʃənz	
directly	dɪˈrɛktlɪ, daɪˈrɛktlɪ	
directory	dɪˈrɛktərɪ, daɪˈrɛktərɪ	
directories	dɪˈrɛktərɪz	
	daɪˈrɛktərɪz	
dirt	dɜˑt	dɜət
dirty	ˈdɜˑtɪ	ˈdɜətɪ
dirtier	ˈdɜˑtɪə(r	ˈdɜətɪə
dirtiest	ˈdɜˑtɪɪst	ˈdɜətɪɪst
dirties	ˈdɜˑtɪz	ˈdɜətɪz
dirtied	ˈdɜˑtɪd	ˈdɜətɪd
dirtying	ˈdɜˑtɪɪŋ	ˈdɜətɪɪŋ
disadvantage	dɪsədˈvɑˑntɪʤ	dɪsədˈvaˑntɪʤ

Traditional Spelling	Received Pronunciation	American Variants
disadvantages	dɪsəd'vɑːntɪdʒɪz	dɪsəd'væːntɪdʒɪz
disadvantageous	dɪsædvɑn'teɪdʒəs dɪsædvən'teɪdʒəs	dɪsædvæn'teɪdʒəs
disagree	dɪsə'griː	
disagrees	dɪsə'griːz	
disagreed	dɪsə'griːd	
disagreeing	dɪsə'griːɪŋ	
disagreement	dɪsə'griːmənt	
disagreements	dɪsə'griːmənts	
disagreeable	dɪsə'grɪəbl̩	
disagreeably	dɪsə'grɪəblɪ	
disappear	dɪsə'pɪə(r	dɪsə'pɪɚ
disappears	dɪsə'pɪəz	dɪsə'pɪɚz
disappeared	dɪsə'pɪəd	dɪsə'pɪɚd
disappearing	dɪsə'pɪərɪŋ	dɪsə'pɪːrɪŋ
disappearance	dɪsə'pɪərəns	dɪsə'pɪːrəns
disappearances	dɪsə'pɪərənsɪz	dɪsə'pɪːrənsɪz
disappoint	dɪsə'pɔɪnt	
disappoints	dɪsə'pɔɪnts	
disappointed	dɪsə'pɔɪntɪd	
disappointing	dɪsə'pɔɪntɪŋ	
disappointment	dɪsə'pɔɪntmənt	
disappointments	dɪsə'pɔɪntmənts	
disapproval	dɪsə'pruːvl̩	
disapprove	dɪsə'pruːv	
disapproves	dɪsə'pruːvz	
disapproved	dɪsə'pruːvd	
disapproving	dɪsə'pruːvɪŋ	
disarm	dɪs'ɑːm	dɪs'ɑɚm
disarms	dɪs'ɑːmz	dɪs'ɑɚmz
disarmed	dɪs'ɑːmd	dɪs'ɑɚmd
disarming	dɪs'ɑːmɪŋ	dɪs'ɑɚmɪŋ
disarmament	dɪs'ɑːməmənt	dɪs'ɑɚməmənt
disarrange	'dɪsə'reɪndʒ	
disarranges	'dɪsə'reɪndʒɪz	
disarranged	'dɪsə'reɪndʒd	
disarranging	'dɪsə'reɪndʒɪŋ	
disaster	dɪ'zɑːstə(r	dɪ'zæːstɚ
disasters	dɪ'zɑːstəz	dɪ'zæːstɚz
disastrous	dɪ'zɑːstrəs	dɪ'zæːstrəs
disastrously	dɪ'zɑːstrəslɪ	dɪ'zæːstrəslɪ
disbelief	'dɪsbɪ'liːf	
disbelieve	'dɪsbɪ'liːv	
disbelieves	'dɪsbɪ'liːvz	
disbelieved	'dɪsbɪ'liːvd	
disbelieving	'dɪsbɪ'liːvɪŋ	
disc	dɪsk	

Traditional Spelling	Received Pronunciation	American Variants
discs	dɪsks	
discharge	dɪs'tʃɑ·ʤ	dɪs'tʃɑəʤ
discharges	dɪs'tʃɑ·ʤɪz	dɪs'tʃɑəʤɪz
discharged	dɪs'tʃɑ·ʤd	dɪs'tʃɑəʤd
discharging	dɪs'tʃɑ·ʤɪŋ	dɪs'tʃɑəʤɪŋ
disciple	dɪ'saɪpl̩	
disciples	dɪ'saɪpl̩z	
discipline	'dɪsɪplɪn	
disciplines	'dɪsɪplɪnz	
disciplined	'dɪsɪplɪnd	
disciplining	'dɪsɪplɪnɪŋ	
disciplinary	'dɪsɪplɪnərɪ	'dɪsɪplɪnɛrɪ
disclaim	dɪs'kleɪm	
disclaims	dɪs'kleɪmz	
disclaimed	dɪs'kleɪmd	
disclaiming	dɪs'kleɪmɪŋ	
disclose	dɪs'klouz	
discloses	dɪs'klouzɪz	
disclosed	dɪs'klouzd	
disclosing	dɪs'klouzɪŋ	
disclosure	dɪs'klouʒə(r	dɪs'klouʒɚ
disclosures	dɪs'klouʒəz	dɪs'klouʒɚz
discomfort	dɪs'kʌmfət	dɪs'kʌmfɚt
discomforts	dɪs'kʌmfəts	dɪs'kʌmfɚts
discomforted	dɪs'kʌmfətɪd	dɪs'kʌmfɚtɪd
discomforting	dɪs'kʌmfətɪŋ	dɪs'kʌmfɚtɪŋ
disconcert	dɪskən'sɜ·t	dɪskən'sɜɚt
disconcerts	dɪskən'sɜ·ts	dɪskən'sɜɚts
disconcerted	dɪskən'sɜ·tɪd	dɪskən'sɜɚtɪd
disconcerting	dɪskən'sɜ·tɪŋ	dɪskən'sɜɚtɪŋ
disconnect	'dɪskə'nɛkt	
disconnects	'dɪskə'nɛkts	
disconnected	'dɪskə'nɛktɪd	
disconnecting	'dɪskə'nɛktɪŋ	
discontent	'dɪskən'tɛnt	
discontented	'dɪskən'tɛntɪd	
discontinue	'dɪskən'tɪnju	
discontinues	'dɪskən'tɪnjuz	
discontinued	'dɪskən'tɪnjud	
discontinuing	'dɪskən'tɪnjuɪŋ	
discord, *noun*	'dɪskɔ·d	'dɪskɔɚd
discords	'dɪskɔ·dz	'dɪskɔɚdz
discount, *noun*	'dɪskaʊnt	
discounts	'dɪskaʊnts	
discount, *verb*	dɪs'kaʊnt, 'dɪskaʊnt	
discounts	dɪs'kaʊnts 'dɪskaʊnts,	

Traditional Spelling	Received Pronunciation	American Variants
discounted	dɪs'kaʊntɪd	
	'dɪskaʊntɪd	
discounting	dɪs'kaʊntɪŋ	
	'dɪskaʊntɪŋ	
discourage	dɪs'kʌrɪʤ	dɪs'kɝ·rɪʤ
discourages	dɪs'kʌrɪʤɪz	dɪs'kɝ·rɪʤɪz
discouraged	dɪs'kʌrɪʤd	dɪs'kɝ·rɪʤd
discouraging	dɪs'kʌrɪʤɪŋ	dɪs'kɝ·rɪʤɪŋ
discouragement	dɪs'kʌrɪʤmənt	dɪs'kɝ·rɪʤmənt
discouragements	dɪs'kʌrɪʤmənts	dɪs'kɝ·rɪʤmənts
discourse, *noun*	'dɪskɔs	'dɪskoəs
discourses	'dɪskɔsɪz	'dɪskoəsɪz
discourteous	dɪs'kɜ·tjəs	dɪs'kɝətɪəs
	dɪs'kɜ·tɪəs	
discourteously	dɪs'kɜ·tjəslɪ	dɪs'kɝətɪəslɪ
	dɪs'kɜ·tɪəslɪ	
discourtesy	dɪs'kɜ·tɪsɪ	dɪs'kɝətɪsɪ
discover	dɪs'kʌvə(r	dɪs'kʌvɚ
discovers	dɪs'kʌvəz	dɪs'kʌvɚz
discovered	dɪs'kʌvəd	dɪs'kʌvɚd
discovering	dɪs'kʌvərɪŋ	
discoverer	dɪs'kʌvərə(r	dɪs'kʌvərɚ
discoverers	dɪs'kʌvərəz	dɪs'kʌvərɚz
discovery	dɪs'kʌvərɪ	
discoveries	dɪs'kʌvərɪz	
discredit	dɪs'krɛdɪt	
discredits	dɪs'krɛdɪts	
discredited	dɪs'krɛdɪtɪd	
discrediting	dɪs'krɛdɪtɪŋ	
discreditable	dɪs'krɛdɪtəbl̩	
discreet	dɪs'kri·t	
discreetly	dɪs'kri·tlɪ	
discretion	dɪs'krɛʃən	
discriminate, *verb*	dɪs'krɪmɪneɪt	
discriminates	dɪs'krɪmɪneɪts	
discriminated	dɪs'krɪmɪneɪtɪd	
discriminating	dɪs'krɪmɪneɪtɪŋ	
discrimination	dɪskrɪmɪ'neɪʃən	
discuss	dɪs'kʌs	
discusses	dɪs'kʌsɪz	
discussed	dɪs'kʌst	
discussing	dɪs'kʌsɪŋ	
discussion	dɪs'kʌʃən	
discussions	dɪs'kʌʃənz	
disdain	dɪs'deɪn	
disdains	dɪs'deɪnz	
disdained	dɪs'deɪnd	

Traditional Spelling	Received Pronunciation	American Variants
disdaining	dɪs'deɪnɪŋ	
disdainful	dɪs'deɪnful	
disdainfully	dɪs'deɪnfəlɪ dɪs'deɪnfulɪ	
disease	dɪ'ziˑz	
diseases	dɪ'ziˑzɪz	
diseased	dɪ'ziˑzd	
disengage	'dɪsɪn'geɪʤ	
disengages	'dɪsɪn'geɪʤɪz	
disengaged	'dɪsɪn'geɪʤd	
disengaging	'dɪsɪn'geɪʤɪŋ	
disfavour	'dɪs'feɪvə(r	'dɪs'feɪvə
disfigure	dɪs'fɪgə(r	dɪs'fɪgjə
disfigures	dɪs'fɪgəz	dɪs'fɪgjəz
disfigured	dɪs'fɪgəd	dɪs'fɪgjəd
disfiguring	dɪs'fɪgərɪŋ	
disfigurement	dɪs'fɪgəmənt	dɪs'fɪgjəmənt
disfigurements	dɪs'fɪgəments	dɪs'fɪgjəmənts
disgrace	dɪs'greɪs	
disgraces	dɪs'greɪsɪz	
disgraced	dɪs'greɪst	
disgracing	dɪs'greɪsɪŋ	
disgraceful	dɪs'greɪsful	
disgracefully	dɪs'greɪsfəlɪ	
disguise	dɪs'gaɪz	
disguises	dɪs'gaɪzɪz	
disguised	dɪs'gaɪzd	
disguising	dɪs'gaɪzɪŋ	
disgust	dɪs'gʌst	
disgusts	dɪs'gʌsts	
disgusted	dɪs'gʌstɪd	
disgusting	dɪs'gʌstɪŋ	
dish	dɪʃ	
dishes	'dɪʃɪz	
dishearten	dɪs'hɑˑtn̩	dɪs'hɑətn̩
disheartens	dɪs'hɑˑtn̩z	dɪs'hɑətn̩z
disheartened	dɪs'hɑˑtn̩d	dɪs'hɑətn̩d
disheartening	dɪs'hɑˑtn̩ɪŋ	dɪs'hɑətn̩ɪŋ
dishonest	dɪs'ɒnɪst	dɪs'ɑnɪst
dishonestly	dɪs'ɒnɪstlɪ	dɪs'ɑnɪstlɪ
dishonesty	dɪs'ɒnɪstɪ	dɪs'ɑnɪstɪ
dishonour	dɪs'ɒnə(r	dɪs'ɑnə
dishonours	dɪs'ɒnəz	dɪs'ɑnəz
dishonoured	dɪs'ɒnəd	dɪs'ɑnəd
dishonouring	dɪs'ɒnərɪŋ	dɪs'ɑnərɪŋ
dishonourable	dɪs'ɒnərəbl̩	dɪs'ɑnərəbl̩
dishonourably	dɪs'ɒnərəblɪ	dɪs'ɑnərəblɪ

Traditional Spelling	Received Pronunciation	American Variants
disinclination	dɪsɪnklɪ'neɪʃən	
disinclined	'dɪsɪn'klaɪnd	
disinfect	'dɪsɪn'fɛkt	
disinfects	'dɪsɪn'fɛkts	
disinfected	'dɪsɪn'fɛktɪd	
disinfecting	'dɪsɪn'fɛktɪŋ	
disinfectant	dɪsɪn'fɛktənt	
disinfectants	dɪsɪn'fɛktənts	
disinterested	dɪs'ɪntərɪstɪd	
disinterestedly	dɪs'ɪntərɪstɪdlɪ	
disinterestedness	dɪs'ɪntərɪstɪdnɪs	
disk	dɪsk	
disks	dɪsks	
dislike	dɪs'laɪk	
dislikes	dɪs'laɪks	
disliked	dɪs'laɪkt	
disliking	dɪs'laɪkɪŋ	
disloyal	'dɪs'lɔɪəl	
disloyalty	'dɪs'lɔɪəltɪ	
dismal	'dɪzməl	
dismally	'dɪzməlɪ	
dismiss	dɪs'mɪs	
dismisses	dɪs'mɪsɪz	
dismissed	dɪs'mɪst	
dismissing	dɪs'mɪsɪŋ	
dismissal	dɪs'mɪsḷ	
dismissals	dɪs'mɪsḷz	
dismount	'dɪs'maʊnt	
dismounts	'dɪs'maʊnts	
dismounted	'dɪs'maʊntɪd	
dismounting	'dɪs'maʊntɪŋ	
disobedience	dɪsə'bi·djəns dɪsə'bi·dɪəns	
disobedient	dɪsə'bi·djənt dɪsə'bi·dɪənt	
disobey	'dɪsə'beɪ	
disobeys	'dɪsə'beɪz	
disobeyed	'dɪsə'beɪd	
disobeying	'dɪsə'beɪɪŋ	
disobliging	'dɪsə'blaɪʤɪŋ	
disorder	dɪs'ɔ·də(r	dɪs'ɔədə
disorders	dɪs'ɔ·dəz	dɪs'ɔədəz
disordered	dɪs'ɔ·dəd	dɪs'ɔədəd
disordering	dɪs'ɔ·dərɪŋ	dɪs'ɔədərɪŋ
disorderly	dɪs'ɔ·dəlɪ	dɪs'ɔədəlɪ
dispatch	dɪs'pætʃ	
dispatches	dɪs'pætʃɪz	

Traditional Spelling	Received Pronunciation	American Variants
dispatched	dɪs'pætʃt	
dispatching	dɪs'pætʃɪŋ	
dispel	dɪs'pɛl	
dispels	dɪs'pɛlz	
dispelled	dɪs'pɛld	
dispelling	dɪs'pɛlɪŋ	
dispense	dɪs'pɛns	
dispenses	dɪs'pɛnsɪz	
dispensed	dɪs'pɛnst	
dispensing	dɪs'pɛnsɪŋ	
disperse	dɪs'pɜˑs	dɪs'pɜəs
disperses	dɪs'pɜˑsɪz	dɪs'pɜəsɪz
dispersed	dɪs'pɜˑst	dɪs'pɜəst
dispersing	dɪs'pɜˑsɪŋ	dɪs'pɜəsɪŋ
displace	dɪs'pleɪs	
displaces	dɪs'pleɪsɪz	
displaced	dɪs'pleɪst	
displacing	dɪs'pleɪsɪŋ	
display	dɪs'pleɪ	
displays	dɪs'pleɪz	
displayed	dɪs'pleɪd	
displaying	dɪs'pleɪɪŋ	
displease	dɪs'pliˑz	
displeases	dɪs'pliˑzɪz	
displeased	dɪs'pliˑzd	
displeasing	dɪs'pliˑzɪŋ	
displeasure	dɪs'plɛʒə(r	dɪs'plɛʒə
dispose	dɪs'poʊz	
disposes	dɪs'poʊzɪz	
disposed	dɪs'poʊzd	
disposing	dɪs'poʊzɪŋ	
disposition	dɪspə'zɪʃən	
dispositions	dɪspə'zɪʃənz	
disproportion	'dɪsprə'pɔˑʃən	'dɪsprə'poəʃən
disproportioned	'dɪsprə'pɔˑʃənd	'dɪsprə'poəʃənd
disproportional	dɪsprə'pɔˑʃənl̩	dɪsprə'poəʃənl̩
disproportionally	dɪsprə'pɔˑʃənl̩ɪ	dɪsprə'poəʃənl̩ɪ
disproportionate	dɪsprə'pɔˑʃənɪt	dɪsprə'poəʃənɪt
disproportionately	dɪsprə'pɔˑʃənɪtlɪ	dɪsprə'poəʃənɪtlɪ
disprove	'dɪs'pruˑv	
disproves	'dɪs'pruˑvz	
disproved	'dɪs'pruˑvd	
disproving	'dɪs'pruˑvɪŋ	
disputable	'dɪspjʊtəbl̩	
dispute	dɪs'pjuˑt	
disputes	dɪs'pjuˑts	
disputed	dɪs'pjuˑtɪd	

Traditional Spelling	Received Pronunciation	American Variants
disputing	dɪs'pju·tɪŋ	
disqualification	dɪskwɒlɪfɪ'keɪʃən	dɪskwɑlɪfɪ'keɪʃən
disqualifications	dɪskwɒlɪfɪ'keɪʃənz	dɪskwɑlɪfɪ'keɪʃənz
disqualify	dɪs'kwɒlɪfaɪ	dɪs'kwɑlɪfaɪ
disqualifies	dɪs'kwɒlɪfaɪz	dɪs'kwɑlɪfaɪz
disqualified	dɪs'kwɒlɪfaɪd	dɪs'kwɑlɪfaɪd
disqualifying	dɪs'kwɒlɪfaɪɪŋ	dɪs'kwɑlɪfaɪɪŋ
disregard	'dɪsrɪ'gɑ·d	'dɪsrɪ'gɑəd
disregards	'dɪsrɪ'gɑ·dz	'dɪsrɪ'gɑədz
disregarded	'dɪsrɪ'gɑ·dɪd	'dɪsrɪ'gɑədɪd
disregarding	'dɪsrɪ'gɑ·dɪŋ	'dɪsrɪ'gɑədɪŋ
disreputable	dɪs'rɛpjʊtəbl̩	
disreputably	dɪs'rɛpjʊtəblɪ	
disrepute	'dɪsrɪ'pju·t	
disrespect	'dɪsrɪs'pɛkt	
disrespectful	dɪsrɪs'pɛktfʊl	
disrespectfully	dɪsrɪs'pɛktfəlɪ	
dissatisfaction	'dɪssætɪs'fækʃən	
dissatisfy	'dɪs'sætɪsfaɪ	
dissatisfies	'dɪs'sætɪsfaɪz	
dissatisfied	'dɪs'sætɪsfaɪd	
dissatisfying	'dɪs'sætɪsfaɪɪŋ	
dissect	dɪ'sɛkt	
dissects	dɪ'sɛkts	
dissected	dɪ'sɛktɪd	
dissecting	dɪ'sɛktɪŋ	
dissension	dɪ'sɛnʃən	
dissensions	dɪ'sɛnʃənz	
dissent	dɪ'sɛnt	
dissents	dɪ'sɛnts	
dissented	dɪ'sɛntɪd	
dissenting	dɪ'sɛntɪŋ	
dissenter	dɪ'sɛntə(r	dɪ'sɛntə
dissenters	dɪ'sɛntəz	dɪ'sɛntəz
dissimilar	'dɪs'sɪmɪlə(r	'dɪs'sɪmɪlə
dissimilarity	'dɪssɪmɪ'lærɪtɪ	
dissimilarities	'dɪssɪmɪ'lærɪtɪz	
dissipate	'dɪsɪpeɪt	
dissipates	'dɪsɪpeɪts	
dissipated	'dɪsɪpeɪtɪd	
dissipating	'dɪsɪpeɪtɪŋ	
dissipation	dɪsɪ'peɪʃən	
dissipations	dɪsɪ'peɪʃənz	
dissolute	'dɪsəljut	
dissolutely	'dɪsəljutlɪ	
dissolution	dɪsə'lju·ʃən	
dissolutions	dɪsə'lju·ʃənz	

Traditional Spelling	Received Pronunciation	American Variants
dissolve	dɪ'zɒlv	dɪ'zɑlv
dissolves	dɪ'zɒlvz	dɪ'zɑlvz
dissolved	dɪ'zɒlvd	dɪ'zɑlvd
dissolving	dɪ'zɒlvɪŋ	dɪ'zɑlvɪŋ
dissuade	dɪ'sweɪd	
dissuades	dɪ'sweɪdz	
dissuaded	dɪ'sweɪdɪd	
dissuading	dɪ'sweɪdɪŋ	
distance	'dɪstəns	
distances	'dɪstənsɪz	
distant	'dɪstənt	
distantly	'dɪstəntlɪ	
distil	dɪs'tɪl	
distils	dɪs'tɪlz	
distilled	dɪs'tɪld	
distilling	dɪs'tɪlɪŋ	
distinct	dɪs'tɪŋkt	
distinctly	dɪs'tɪŋktlɪ	
distinctness	dɪs'tɪŋktnɪs	
distinction	dɪs'tɪŋkʃən	
distinctions	dɪs'tɪŋkʃənz	
distinctive	dɪs'tɪŋktɪv	
distinguish	dɪs'tɪŋgwɪʃ	
distinguishes	dɪs'tɪŋgwɪʃɪz	
distinguished	dɪs'tɪŋgwɪʃt	
distinguishing	dɪs'tɪŋgwɪʃɪŋ	
distort	dɪs'tɔ·t	dɪs'tɔət
distorts	dɪs'tɔ·ts	dɪs'tɔəts
distorted	dɪs'tɔ·tɪd	dɪs'tɔətɪd
distorting	dɪs'tɔ·tɪŋ	dɪs'tɔətɪŋ
distortion	dɪs'tɔ·ʃən	dɪs'tɔəʃən
distract	dɪs'trækt	
distracts	dɪs'trækts	
distracted	dɪs'træktɪd	
distracting	dɪs'træktɪŋ	
distress	dɪs'trɛs	
distresses	dɪs'trɛsɪz	
distressed	dɪs'trɛst	
distressing	dɪs'trɛsɪŋ	
distribute	dɪs'trɪbjut 'dɪstrɪbjut	
distributes	dɪs'trɪbjuts 'dɪstrɪbjuts	
distributed	dɪs'trɪbjutɪd 'dɪstrɪbjutɪd	
distributing	dɪs'trɪbjutɪŋ 'dɪstrɪbjutɪŋ	

Traditional Spelling	Received Pronunciation	American Variants
distribution	dɪstrɪ'bjuːʃən	
district	'dɪstrɪkt	
districts	'dɪstrɪkts	
distrust	dɪs'trʌst	
distrusts	dɪs'trʌsts	
distrusted	dɪs'trʌstɪd	
distrusting	dɪs'trʌstɪŋ	
distrustful	dɪs'trʌstful	
disturb	dɪs'tɜːb	dɪs'tɜəb
disturbs	dɪs'tɜːbz	dɪs'tɜəbz
disturbed	dɪs'tɜːbd	dɪs'tɜəbd
disturbing	dɪs'tɜːbɪŋ	dɪs'tɜəbɪŋ
disturbance	dɪs'tɜːbəns	dɪs'tɜəbəns
disturbances	dɪs'tɜːbənsɪz	dɪs'tɜəbənsɪz
disuse, ***noun***	'dɪs'juːs	
ditch	dɪtʃ	
ditches	'dɪtʃɪz	
ditto	'dɪtoʊ	
dive	daɪv	
dives	daɪvz	
dived	daɪvd	
diving	'daɪvɪŋ	
diver	'daɪvə(r	'daɪvə
divers	'daɪvəz	'daɪvəz
diverge	daɪ'vɜːdʒ, dɪ'vɜːdʒ	daɪ'vɜədʒ, dɪ'vɜədʒ
diverges	daɪ'vɜːdʒɪz dɪ'vɜːdʒɪz	daɪ'vɜədʒɪz dɪ'vɜədʒɪz
diverged	daɪ'vɜːdʒd dɪ'vɜːdʒd	daɪ'vɜədʒd dɪ'vɜədʒd
diverging	daɪ'vɜːdʒɪŋ dɪ'vɜːdʒɪŋ	daɪ'vɜədʒɪŋ dɪ'vɜədʒɪŋ
divergence	daɪ'vɜːdʒəns dɪ'vɜːdʒəns	daɪ'vɜədʒəns dɪ'vɜədʒəns
divergences	daɪ'vɜːdʒənsɪz dɪ'vɜːdʒənsɪz	daɪ'vɜədʒənsɪz dɪ'vɜədʒənsɪz
divergency	daɪ'vɜːdʒənsɪ dɪ'vɜːdʒənsɪ	daɪ'vɜədʒənsɪ dɪ'vɜədʒənsɪ
divergent	daɪ'vɜːdʒənt dɪ'vɜːdʒənt	daɪ'vɜədʒənt dɪ'vɜədʒənt
diverse	daɪ'vɜːs, dɪ'vɜːs	daɪ'vɜəs, dɪ'vɜəs
diversely	daɪ'vɜːslɪ, dɪ'vɜːslɪ	daɪ'vɜəslɪ, dɪ'vɜəslɪ
diversity	daɪ'vɜːsɪtɪ, dɪ'vɜːsɪtɪ	daɪ'vɜəsɪtɪ, dɪ'vɜəsɪtɪ
divide	dɪ'vaɪd	
divides	dɪ'vaɪdz	
divided	dɪ'vaɪdɪd	
dividing	dɪ'vaɪdɪŋ	
divine	dɪ'vaɪn	

Traditional Spelling	Received Pronunciation	American Variants
divinely	dɪ'vaɪnlɪ	
divinity	dɪ'vɪnɪtɪ	
divinities	dɪ'vɪnɪtɪz	
divisible	dɪ'vɪzɪbl̩, dɪ'vɪzəbl̩	
division	dɪ'vɪʒən	
divisions	dɪ'vɪʒənz	
divisional	dɪ'vɪʒənl̩	
divorce	dɪ'vɔ·s	dɪ'voəs
divorces	dɪ'vɔ·sɪz	dɪ'voəsɪz
divorced	dɪ'vɔ·st	dɪ'voəst
divorcing	dɪ'vɔ·sɪŋ	dɪ'voəsɪŋ
dizzy	'dɪzɪ	
dizziness	'dɪzɪnɪs	
do	du· *s.f.*, dʊ, də *w.fs.*	
does	dʌz *s.f.*, dəz *w.f.*	
did	dɪd *s.f.*, dɪd *w.f.*	
done	dʌn	
doing	'du·ɪŋ	
docile	'dousaɪl, 'dɒsaɪl	'dɒsɪl
dock	dɒk	dɑk
docks	dɒks	dɑks
dockyard	'dɒkjɑ·d	'dɑkjɑəd
dockyards	'dɒkjɑ·dz	'dɑkjɑədz
doctor	'dɒktə(r	'dɑktə
doctors	'dɒktəz	'dɑktəz
doctrine	'dɒktrɪn	'dɑktrɪn
doctrines	'dɒktrɪnz	'dɑktrɪnz
document	'dɒkjumənt	'dɑkjumənt
documents	'dɒkjumənts	'dɑkjumənts
dodge	dɒʤ	dɑʤ
dodges	'dɒʤɪz	'dɑʤɪz
dodged	dɒʤd	dɑʤd
dodging	'dɒʤɪŋ	'dɑʤɪŋ
DOES *from* do	dʌz *s.f.*, dəz *w.f.*	
DOESN'T *from* do	'dʌznt̩	
dog	dɒg	
dogs	dɒgz	
dogma	'dɒgmə	
dogmas	'dɒgməz	
dogmatic	dɒg'mætɪk	
doings	'du·ɪŋz	
doll	dɒl	dɑl
dolls	dɒlz	dɑlz
dollar	'dɒlə(r	'dɑlə
dollars	'dɒləz	'dɑləz
domain	dou'meɪn, də'meɪn	

Traditional Spelling	Received Pronunciation	American Variants
domains	douˈmeɪnz	
	dəˈmeɪnz	
dome	doum	
domes	doumz	
domestic	dəˈmɛstɪk	
dominate	ˈdɒmɪneɪt	ˈdɑmɪneɪt
dominates	ˈdɒmɪneɪts	ˈdɑmɪneɪts
dominated	ˈdɒmɪneɪtɪd	ˈdɑmɪneɪtɪd
dominating	ˈdɒmɪneɪtɪŋ	ˈdɑmɪnatɪŋ
domination	dɒmɪˈneɪʃən	dɑmɪˈneɪʃən
dominations	dɒmɪˈneɪʃənz	dɑmɪˈneɪʃənz
dominion	dəˈmɪnjən	
dominions	dəˈmɪnjənz	
donation	douˈneɪʃən	
donations	douˈneɪʃənz	
DONE *from* do	dʌn	
donkey	ˈdɒŋkɪ	
donkeys	ˈdɒŋkɪz	
DON'T *from* do	dount	
door	dɔˑ(r, dɔə(r	dɔə
doors	dɔˑz, dɔəz	dɔəz
dormitory	ˈdɔˑmɪtrɪ	ˈdɔəmɪtorɪ
dormitories	ˈdɔˑmɪtrɪz	ˈdɔəmɪtorɪz
Dorothy	ˈdɒrəθɪ	
dose	dous	
doses	ˈdousɪz	
dot	dɒt	dɑt
dots	dɒts	dɑts
dotted	ˈdɒtɪd	ˈdɑtɪd
dotting	ˈdɒtɪŋ	ˈdɑtɪŋ
double	ˈdʌbl̩	
doubles	ˈdʌbl̩z	
doubled	ˈdʌbl̩d	
doubling	ˈdʌblɪŋ, ˈdʌbl̩ɪŋ	
doubly	ˈdʌblɪ	
doubt	daut	
doubts	dauts	
doubted	ˈdautɪd	
doubting	ˈdautɪŋ	
doubtful	ˈdautful	
doubtfully	ˈdautfulɪ, dautfəlɪ	
doubtless	ˈdautlɪs	
doubtlessly	ˈdautlɪslɪ	
dough	dou	
dove	dʌv	
doves	dʌvz	
down	daun	

Traditional Spelling	Received Pronunciation	American Variants
down-hearted	ˈdaʊnˈhɑˑtɪd	ˈdaʊnˈhɑətɪd
downstairs	ˈdaʊnˈstɛəz	ˈdaʊnˈstɛəz
downward	ˈdaʊnwəd	ˈdaʊnwəd
downwards	ˈdaʊnwədz	ˈdaʊnwədz
doze	doʊz	
dozes	ˈdoʊzɪz	
dozed	doʊzd	
dozing	ˈdoʊzɪŋ	
dozen	ˈdʌzn̩	
dozens	ˈdʌzn̩z	
draft	drɑˑft	draˑft
drafts	drɑˑfts	draˑfts
drafted	ˈdrɑˑftɪd	ˈdraˑftɪd
drafting	ˈdrɑˑftɪŋ	ˈdraˑftɪŋ
drag	dræg	
drags	drægz	
dragged	drægd	
dragging	ˈdrægɪŋ	
drain	dreɪn	
drains	dreɪnz	
drained	dreɪnd	
draining	ˈdreɪnɪŋ	
drama	ˈdrɑˑmə	
dramas	ˈdrɑˑməz	
dramatic	drəˈmætɪk	
dramatically	drəˈmætɪkəlɪ	
DRANK *from* drink	dræŋk	
draper	ˈdreɪpə(r	ˈdreɪpə
drapers	ˈdreɪpəz	ˈdreɪpəz
draught	drɑˑft	draˑft
draughts	drɑˑfts	draˑfts
draughty	ˈdrɑˑftɪ	ˈdraˑftɪ
draw	drɔˑ	
draws	drɔˑz	
drew	druˑ	
drawn	drɔˑn	
drawing	ˈdrɔˑɪŋ	
drawer, ***person who draws***	ˈdrɔˑə(r	ˈdrɔˑə
drawers	ˈdrɔˑəz	ˈdrɔˑəz
drawer, ***sliding box***	drɔˑ(r, ˈdrɔə(r	drɔə
drawers	drɔˑz, ˈdrɔəz	ˈdrɔəz
drawing-room	ˈdrɔɪŋrʊm ˈdrɔɪŋrum ˈdrɔˑɪŋrʊm ˈdrɔˑɪŋrum	

Traditional Spelling	Received Pronunciation	American Variants
drawing-rooms	ˈdrɔɪŋrʊmz	
	ˈdrɔɪŋrumz	
	ˈdrɔˑɪŋrʊmz	
	ˈdrɔˑɪŋrumz	
DRAWN *from* draw	drɔˑn	
dread	drɛd	
dreads	drɛdz	
dreaded	ˈdrɛdɪd	
dreading	ˈdrɛdɪŋ	
dreadful	ˈdrɛdfʊl	
dreadfully	ˈdrɛdfʊlɪ, ˈdrɛdfəlɪ	
dream	driˑm	
dreams	driˑmz	
dreamed	drɛm*p*t, driˑmd	
dreamt	drɛm*p*t	
dreaming	ˈdriˑmɪŋ	
dreamer	ˈdriˑmə(r	ˈdriˑmə
dreamers	ˈdriˑməz	ˈdriˑməz
dreary	ˈdrɪərɪ	drɪˑrɪ
drearier	ˈdrɪərɪə(r	ˈdrɪˑrɪə
dreariest	ˈdrɪərɪɪst	drɪˑrɪɪst
dress	drɛs	
dresses	ˈdrɛsɪz	
dressed	drɛst	
dressing	ˈdrɛsɪŋ	
dresser	ˈdrɛsə(r	ˈdrɛsə
dressers	ˈdrɛsəz	ˈdrɛsəz
DREW *from* draw	druˑ	
DRIED *from* dry	draɪd	
DRIES *from* dry	draɪz	
drift	drɪft	
drifts	drɪfts	
drifted	ˈdrɪftɪd	
drifting	ˈdrɪftɪŋ	
drill	drɪl	
drills	drɪlz	
drilled	drɪld	
drilling	ˈdrɪlɪŋ	
drily (=*dryly*)	ˈdraɪlɪ	
drink	drɪŋk	
drinks	drɪŋks	
drank	dræŋk	
drunk	drʌŋk	
drinking	ˈdrɪŋkɪŋ	
drip	drɪp	
drips	drɪps	
dripped	drɪpt	

Traditional Spelling	Received Pronunciation	American Variants
dripping	ˈdrɪpɪŋ	
drive	ˈdraɪv	
drives	draɪvz	
drove	droʊv	
driven	ˈdrɪvn̩	
driving	ˈdraɪvɪŋ	
driver	ˈdraɪvə(r	ˈdraɪvə
drivers	ˈdraɪvəz	ˈdraɪvəz
drop	drɒp	drɑp
drops	drɒps	drɑps
dropped	drɒpt	drɑpt
dropping	ˈdrɒpɪŋ	ˈdrɑpɪŋ
DROVE *from* drive	droʊv	
drown	draʊn	
drowns	draʊnz	
drowned	draʊnd	
drowning	ˈdraʊnɪŋ	
drudgery	ˈdrʌʤərɪ	
drug	drʌg	
drugs	drʌgz	
druggist	ˈdrʌgɪst	
druggists	ˈdrʌgɪsts	
drum	drʌm	
drums	drʌmz	
DRUNK *from* drink	drʌŋk	
drunken	ˈdrʌŋkən	
drunkenness	ˈdrʌŋkənnɪs	
dry	draɪ	
drier	ˈdraɪə(r	ˈdraɪə
driest	ˈdraɪɪst	
dries	draɪz	
dried	draɪd	
drying	ˈdraɪɪŋ	
dryly	draɪlɪ	
dryness	ˈdraɪnɪs	
duchess	ˈdʌʧɪs	
duchesses	ˈdʌʧɪsɪz	
duck	dʌk	
ducks	dʌks	
duel	djuˑəl	
DUG *from* dig	dʌg	
duke	djuˑk	
dukes	djuˑks	
dull	dʌl	
duller	ˈdʌlə(r	ˈdʌlə
dullest	ˈdʌlɪst	
dullness	ˈdʌlnɪs	
duly	ˈdjuˑlɪ	

Traditional Spelling	Received Pronunciation	American Variants
dumb	dʌm	
dumbness	ˈdʌmnɪs	
duplicate, *noun*	ˈdjuˑplɪkɪt	
duplicates	ˈdjuˑplɪkɪts	
duplicate, *verb*	ˈdjuˑplɪkeɪt	
duplicates	ˈdjuˑplɪkeɪts	
duplicated	ˈdjuˑplɪkeɪtɪd	
duplicating	ˈdjuˑplikeɪtɪŋ	
duplicity	djuˈplɪsɪtɪ	
durability	djʊərəˈbɪlɪtɪ	djuˑrəˈbɪlɪtɪ
durable	ˈdjʊərəbl̩	ˈdjuˑrəbl̩
duration	djʊəˈreɪʃən	djuˑˈreɪʃən
during	ˈdjʊərɪŋ	ˈdjuˑrɪŋ
dusk	dʌsk	
dust	dʌst	
dusts	dʌsts	
dusted	ˈdʌstɪd	
dusting	ˈdʌstɪŋ	
dusty	ˈdʌstɪ	
Dutch	dʌtʃ	
Dutchman	ˈdʌtʃmən	
Dutchmen	ˈdʌtʃmən	
duty	ˈdjuˑtɪ	
duties	ˈdjuˑtɪz	
dwarf	dwɔˑf	dwɔəf
dwarfs	dwɔˑfs	dwɔəfs
dye	daɪ	
dyes	daɪz	
dyed	daɪd	
dyeing	ˈdaɪɪŋ	
DYING *from* die	ˈdaɪɪŋ	
dynamo	ˈdaɪnəmoʊ	
dynamos	ˈdaɪnəmoʊz	

The phonetic value of the symbol [ɪ].

When this symbol stands for the *e* of traditional spelling, its phonetic value is variable and very unstable. In slow and careful speech, it approximates to [ɛ], in rapid speech either to the *i* of *inspect* or to the *a* of *ago*. In the case of slow and careful speech, usage in England and America is practically identical; in rapid speech the vowel tends rather towards the *i* of *inspect* in England, and towards the *a* of *ago* in America.

Such entries as [ɪˈfɛkt] are therefore to be interpreted in the following sense—

[ɪ'fɛkt.] This is the more normal pronunciation of users of Received Pronunciation, either in England or in America.

[ə'fɛkt] or a form intermediate between [ə'fɛkt] and [ɛ'fɛkt]. These forms are characteristic of American speakers, and are also heard in the speech of users of Received Pronunciation.

[ɛ'fɛkt]. This form is frequently heard in the case of slow and careful speech, both in England and in America, but especially in America.

E

Traditional Spelling	Received Pronunciation	American Variants
E	iˑ	
E's	iˑz	
each	iˑtʃ	
eager	'iˑgə(r	'iˑgə
eagerly	'iˑgəlɪ	'iˑgəlɪ
eagerness	'iˑgənɪs	'iˑgənɪs
eagle	'iˑgl̩	
eagles	'iˑgl̩z	
ear	ɪə(r	ɪə
ears	ɪəz	ɪəz
early	'ɜˑlɪ	'ɜəlɪ
earlier	'ɜˑlɪə(r	'ɜəlɪə
earliest	'ɜˑlɪɪst	'ɜəlɪɪst
earn	ɜˑn	ɜən
earns	ɜˑnz	ɜənz
earned	ɜˑnd, ɜˑnt	ɜənd
earnt	ɜˑnt	ɜənt
earning	'ɜˑnɪŋ	'ɜənɪŋ
earnest	'ɜˑnɪst	'ɜənɪst
earnestly	'ɜˑnɪstlɪ	'ɜənɪstlɪ
earnestness	'ɜˑnɪstnɪs	'ɜənɪstnɪs
earnings	'ɜˑnɪŋz	'ɜənɪŋz
earth	ɜˑθ	ɜəθ
earthquake	'ɜˑθkweɪk	'ɜəθkweɪk
earthquakes	'ɜˑθkweɪks	'ɜəθkweɪks
ease	iˑz	
easily	'iˑzɪlɪ	
east	iˑst	
Easter	'iˑstə(r	'iˑstə
easterly	'iˑstəlɪ	'iˑstəlɪ
eastern	'iˑstən	'iˑstən
eastward	'iˑstwəd	'iˑstwəd
eastwardly	'iˑstwədlɪ	'iˑstwədlɪ
easy	'iˑzɪ	
easier	'iˑsɪə(r	'iˑzɪə
easiest	'iˑzɪɪst	

Traditional Spelling	Received Pronunciation	American Variants
eat	iˑt	
eats	iˑts	
ate	ɛt	eɪt
eaten	ˈiˑtn̩	
eating	ˈiˑtɪŋ	
eccentric	ɪkˈsɛntrɪk	
eccentricity	ɛksɛnˈtrɪsɪtɪ ɛksənˈtrɪsɪtɪ	
eccentricities	ɛksɛnˈtrɪsɪtɪz ɛksənˈtrɪsɪtɪz	
echo	ˈɛkoʊ	
echoes	ˈɛkoʊz	
echoed	ˈɛkoʊd	
echoing	ˈɛkoʊɪŋ	
eclipse	ɪˈklɪps	
eclipses	ɪˈklɪpsɪz	
economic	ikəˈnɒmɪk ɛkəˈnɒmɪk	ɛkəˈnɑmɪk
economical	ikəˈnɒmikəl ɛkəˈnɒmɪkəl	ɛkəˈnɑmɪkəl
economically	ikəˈnɒmɪkəlɪ ɛkəˈnɒmɪkəlɪ	ɛkəˈnɑmɪkəlɪ
economics	ikəˈnɒmɪks ɛkəˈnɒmɪks	ɛkəˈnɑmɪks
economize	ɪˈkɒnəmaɪz	ɪˈkɑnəmaɪz
economizes	ɪˈkɒnəmaɪzɪz	ɪˈkɑnəmaɪzɪz
economized	ɪˈkɒnəmaɪzd	ɪˈkɑnəmaɪzd
economizing	ɪˈkɒnəmaɪzɪŋ	ɪˈkɑnəmaɪzɪŋ
economy	ɪˈkɒnəmɪ	ɪˈkɑnəmɪ
economies	ɪˈkɒnəmɪz	ɪˈkɑnəmɪz
edge	ɛʤ	
edges	ˈɛʤɪz	
edgeways	ˈɛʤweɪz	
edit	ˈɛdɪt	
edits	ˈɛdɪts	
edited	ˈɛdɪtɪd	
editing	ˈɛdɪtɪŋ	
edition	ɪˈdɪʃən	
editions	ɪˈdɪʃənz	
editor	ˈɛdɪtə(r	ˈɛdɪtə
editors	ˈɛdɪtəz	ˈɛdɪtəz
editorial	ɛdɪˈtɔˑrɪəl	ɛdɪˈtoˑrɪəl
editorials	ɛdɪˈtɔˑrɪəlz	ɛdɪˈtoˑrɪəlz
educate	ˈɛdjʊkeɪt	
educates	ˈɛdjʊkeɪts	
educated	ˈɛdjʊkeɪtɪd	
educating	ˈɛdjʊkeɪtɪŋ	

Traditional Spelling	Received Pronunciation	American Variants
education	ɛdjʊ'keɪʃən	
educational	ɛdjʊ'keɪʃənl̩	
educationist	ɛdjʊ'keɪʃənɪst	
educationists	ɛdjʊ'keɪʃənɪsts	
educator	'ɛdjʊkeɪtə(r	'ɛdjʊkeɪtə
educators	'ɛdjʊkeɪtəz	'ɛdjʊkeɪtəz
Edward	'ɛdwəd	'ɛdwəd
eel	iˑl	
eels	iˑlz	
effect	ɪ'fɛkt	
effects	ɪ'fɛkts	
effected	ɪ'fɛktɪd	
effecting	ɪ'fɛktɪŋ	
effective	ɪ'fɛktɪv	
effectively	ɪ'fɛktɪvlɪ	
effectual	ɪ'fɛktjʊəl	
effectually	ɪ'fɛktjʊəlɪ	
effeminate	ɪ'fɛmɪnɪt	
efficacious	ɛfɪ'keɪʃəs	
efficaciously	ɛfɪ'keɪʃəslɪ	
efficacy	'ɛfɪkəsɪ	
efficiency	ɪ'fɪʃənsɪ	
efficient	ɪ'fɪʃənt	
efficiently	ɪ'fɪʃəntlɪ	
effort	'ɛfət	'ɛfət
efforts	'ɛfəts	'ɛfəts
egg	ɛg	
eggs	ɛgz	
egotism	'ɛgoʊtɪzm̩	'iˑgətɪzm̩
egotist	'ɛgoʊtɪst	'iˑgətɪst
egotists	'ɛgoʊtɪsts	'i'gətɪsts
egotistic	ɛgoʊ'tɪstɪk	igə'tɪstɪk
egotistically	ɛgoʊ'tɪstɪkəlɪ	igə'tɪstɪkəlɪ
Egypt	'iˑʤɪpt	
Egyptian	ɪ'ʤɪpʃən	
Egyptians	ɪ'ʤɪpʃənz	
eh	eɪ, ɛˑ,	
eight	eɪt	
eighteen	'eɪ'tiˑn	
eighteenth	'eɪ'tiˑnθ	
eighteenths	'eɪ'tiˑnθs	
eighth	eɪtθ	
eighths	eɪtθs	
eighty	'eɪtɪ	
eightieth	'eɪtɪɪθ	
eightieths	'eɪtɪɪθs	
either	'aɪðə(r, 'iˑðə(r	'iˑðə

Traditional Spelling	Received Pronunciation	American Variants
elaborate, *adj.*	ɪ'læbərɪt	
elaborately	ɪ'læbərɪtlɪ	
elaborate, *verb*	ɪ'læbəreɪt	
elaborates	ɪ'læbəreɪts	
elaborated	ɪ'læbəreɪtɪd	
elaborating	ɪ'læbəreɪtɪŋ	
elapse	ɪ'læps	
elapses	ɪ'læpsɪz	
elapsed	ɪ'læpst	
elapsing	ɪ'læpsɪŋ	
elastic	ɪ'læstɪk, ɪ'lɑstɪk	
elasticity	ɪlæs'tɪsɪtɪ, ilæs'tɪsɪtɪ	
elbow	'ɛlbou	
elbows	'ɛlbouz	
elder	'ɛldə(r	'ɛldə
elders	'ɛldəz	'ɛldəz
elderly	'ɛldəlɪ	
eldest	'ɛldɪst	
elect	ɪ'lɛkt	
elects	ɪ'lɛkts	
elected	ɪ'lɛktɪd	
electing	ɪ'lɛktɪŋ	
election	ɪ'lɛkʃən	
elections	ɪ'lɛkʃənz	
elector	ɪ'lɛktə(r	ɪ'lɛktə
electors	ɪ'lɛktəz	ɪ'lɛktəz
electric	ɪ'lɛktrɪk	
electrically	ɪ'lɛktrɪkəlɪ	
electrician	ɪlɛk'trɪʃən	
electricians	ɪlɛk'trɪʃənz	
electricity	ɪlɛk'trɪsɪtɪ	
electron	ɪ'lɛktrɒn	ɪ'lɛktrɑn
electrons	ɪ'lɛktrɒnz	ɪ'lɛktrɑnz
elegance	'ɛlɪgəns	
elegant	'ɛlɪgənt	
elegantly	'ɛlɪgəntlɪ	
element	'ɛlɪmənt	
elements	'ɛlɪmənts	
elementary	ɛlɪ'mentərɪ	
elephant	'ɛlɪfənt	
elephants	'ɛlɪfənts	
elevate	'ɛlɪveɪt	
elevates	'ɛlɪveɪts	
elevated	'ɛliveɪtɪd	
elevating	'ɛlɪveɪtɪŋ	
elevation	ɛlɪ'veɪʃən	
elevations	ɛlɪ'veɪʃənz	

Traditional Spelling	Received Pronunciation	American Variants
elevator	'ɛlɪveɪtə(r	'ɛlɪveɪtə
elevators	'ɛlɪveɪtəz	'ɛlɪveɪtəz
eleven	ɪ'lɛvn̩	
eleventh	ɪ'lɛvn̩θ	
elevenths	ɪ'lɛvn̩θs	
eligible	'ɛlɪʤəbl̩	
eliminate	ɪ'lɪmɪneɪt	
eliminates	ɪ'lɪmɪneɪts	
eliminated	ɪ'lɪmɪneɪtɪd	
eliminating	ɪ'lɪmɪneɪtɪŋ	
elimination	ɪlɪmɪ'neɪʃən	
eliminations	ɪlɪmɪ'neɪʃənz	
elision	ɪ'lɪʒən	
elisions	ɪ'lɪʒənz	
Elizabeth	ɪ'lɪzəbəθ	
ellipse	ɪ'lɪps	
ellipses	ɪ'lɪpsɪz	
elliptic	ɪ'lɪptɪk	
elliptical	ɪ'lɪptɪkəl	
elocution	ɛlə'kju·ʃən	
elocutionist	ɛlə'kju·ʃənɪst	
elocutionists	ɛlə'kju·ʃənɪsts	
eloquence	'ɛləkwəns	
eloquent	'ɛləkwənt	
eloquently	'ɛləkwəntlɪ	
else	ɛls	
elsewhere	'ɛls'*h*wɛə(r	'ɛls'hwɛə
'em, *weak form of* them	əm	
emancipate	ɪ'mænsɪpeɪt	
emancipates	ɪ'mænsɪpeɪts	
emancipated	ɪ'mænsɪpeɪtɪd	
emancipating	ɪ'mænsɪpeɪtɪŋ	
emancipation	ɪmænsɪ'peɪʃən	
embankment	ɪm'bæŋkmənt	
embark	ɪm'bɑ·k	ɪm'bɑək
embarks	ɪm'bɑ·ks	ɪm'bɑəks
embarked	ɪm'bɑ·kt	ɪm'bɑəkt
embarking	ɪm'bɑ·kɪŋ	ɪm'bɑəkɪŋ
embarrass	ɪm'bærəs	
embarrasses	ɪm'bærəsɪz	
embarrassed	ɪm'bærəst	
embarrassing	ɪm'bærəsɪŋ	
embarrassment	ɪm'bærəsmənt	
embassy	'ɛmbəsɪ	
embassies	'ɛmbəsɪz	
emblem	'ɛmbləm	
emblems	'ɛmbləmz	

Traditional Spelling	Received Pronunciation	American Variants
embody	ɪm'bɒdɪ	ɪm'bɑdɪ
embodies	ɪm'bɒdɪz	ɪm'bɑdɪz
embodied	ɪm'bɒdɪd	ɪm'bɑdɪd
embodying	ɪm'bɒdɪɪŋ	ɪm'bɑdɪɪŋ
embodiment	ɪm'bɒdɪmənt	ɪm'bɑdɪmənt
embodiments	ɪm'bɒdɪmənts	ɪm'bɑdɪmənts
embroider	ɪm'brɔɪdə(r	ɪm'brɔɪdə
embroiders	ɪm'brɔɪdəz	ɪm'brɔɪdəz
embroidered	ɪm'brɔɪdəd	ɪm'brɔɪdəd
embroidering	ɪm'brɔɪdərɪŋ	
embroidery	ɪm'brɔɪdərɪ	
embroideries	ɪm'brɔɪdərɪz	
emerald	'ɛmərəld	
emeralds	'ɛmərəldz	
emergency	ɪ'mɜ·dʒənsɪ	ɪ'mɜədʒənsɪ
emergencies	ɪ'mɜ·dʒənsɪz	ɪ'mɜədʒənsɪz
emigrant	'ɛmɪgrənt	
emigrants	'ɛmɪgrənts	
emigrate	'ɛmɪgreɪt	
emigrates	'ɛmɪgreɪts	
emigrated	'ɛmɪgreɪtɪd	
emigrating	'ɛmɪgreɪtɪŋ	
emigration	ɛmɪ'greɪʃən	
eminence	'ɛmɪnəns	
eminent	'ɛmɪnənt	
eminently	'ɛmɪnəntlɪ	
Emma	'ɛmə	
emotion	ɪ'moʊʃən	
emotions	ɪ'moʊʃənz	
emotional	ɪ'moʊʃənəl	
emotionally	ɪ'moʊʃənəlɪ	
emperor	'ɛmpərə(r	'ɛmpərə
emperors	'ɛmpərəz	'ɛmpərəz
emphasis	'ɛmfəsɪs	
emphasize	'ɛmfəsaɪz	
emphasizes	'ɛmfəsaɪzɪz	
emphasized	'ɛmfəsaɪzd	
emphasizing	'ɛmfəsaɪzɪŋ	
emphatic	ɪm'fætɪk	
emphatically	ɪm'fætɪkəlɪ	
empire	'ɛmpaɪə(r	'ɛmpaɪə
empires	'ɛmpaɪəz	'ɛmpaɪəz
employ	ɪm'plɔɪ	
employs	ɪm'plɔɪz	
employed	ɪm'plɔɪd	
employing	ɪm'plɔɪɪŋ	
employer	ɪm'plɔɪə(r	ɪm'plɔɪə

Traditional Spelling	Received Pronunciation	American Variants
employers	ɪm'plɔɪəz	ɪm'plɔɪəz
employment	ɪm'plɔɪmənt	
empty	'ɛm*p*tɪ	
empties	'ɛm*p*tɪz	
emptied	'ɛm*p*tɪd	
emptying	'ɛm*p*tɪɪŋ	
emptiness	'ɛm*p*tɪnɪs	
enable	ɪ'neɪbl̩	
enables	ɪ'neɪbl̩z	
enabled	ɪ'neɪbl̩d	
enabling	ɪ'neɪblɪŋ	
enamel	ɪ'næməl	
encamp	ɪn'kæmp	
encamps	ɪn'kæmps	
encamped	ɪn'kæmpt	
encamping	ɪn'kæmpɪŋ	
encampment	ɪn'kæmpmənt	
encampments	ɪn'kæmpmənts	
enclose	ɪn'klouz	
encloses	ɪn'klouzɪz	
enclosed	ɪn'klouzd	
enclosing	ɪn'klouzɪŋ	
enclosure	ɪn'klouʒə(r	ɪn'klouʒɚ
enclosures	ɪn'klouʒəz	ɪn'klouʒɚz
encounter	ɪn'kaʊntə(r	ɪn'kaʊntɚ
encounters	ɪn'kaʊntəz	ɪn'kaʊntɚz
encountered	ɪn'kaʊntəd	ɪn'kaʊntɚd
encountering	ɪn'kaʊntərɪŋ	
encourage	ɪn'kʌrɪʤ	ɪn'kɜrɪʤ
encourages	ɪn'kʌrɪʤɪz	ɪn'kɜrɪʤɪz
encouraged	ɪn'kʌrɪʤd	ɪn'kɜrɪʤd
encouraging	ɪn'kʌrɪʤɪŋ	ɪn'kɜrɪʤɪŋ
encouragement	ɪn'kʌrɪʤmənt	ɪn'kɜrɪʤmənt
encyclopædia	ɛnsaɪklə'pi·dɪə ɛnsaɪklou'pi·dɪə	
encyclopædias	ɛnsaɪklə'pi·dɪəz ɛnsaɪklou'pi·dɪəz	
end	ɛnd	
ends	ɛndz	
ended	'ɛndɪd	
ending	'ɛndɪŋ	
endeavour	ɪn'dɛvə(r	ɪn'dɛvɚ
endeavor (*Amer.*)		
endeavours	ɪn'dɛvəz	ɪn'dɛvɚz
endeavors (*Amer.*)		
endeavoured	ɪn'dɛvəd	ɪn'dɛvɚd
endeavored (*Amer.*)		

Traditional Spelling	Received Pronunciation	American Variants
endeavouring	ɪn'dɛvərɪŋ	
endeavoring (*Amer.*)		
ending	'ɛndɪŋ	
endings	'ɛndɪŋz	
endless	'ɛndlɪs	
endlessly	'ɛndlɪslɪ	
endorse	ɪn'dɔ·s	ɪn'dɔəs
endorses	ɪn'dɔ·sɪz	ɪn'dɔəsɪz
endorsed	ɪn'dɔ·st	ɪn'dɔəst
endorsing	ɪn'dɔ·sɪŋ	ɪn'dɔəsɪŋ
endorsement	ɪn'dɔ·smənt	ɪn'dɔəsmənt
endorsements	ɪn'dɔ·smənts	ɪn'dɔəsmənts
endow	ɪn'daʊ	
endows	ɪn'daʊz	
endowed	ɪn'daʊd	
endowing	ɪn'daʊɪŋ	
endowment	ɪn'daʊmənt	
endowments	ɪn'daʊmənts	
endure	ɪn'djʊə(r	ɪn'djʊə
endures	ɪn'djʊəz	ɪn'djʊəz
endured	ɪn'djʊəd	ɪn'djʊəd
enduring	ɪn'djʊərɪŋ	ɪn'djʊ·rɪŋ
endurance	ɪn'djʊərəns	ɪn'djʊ·rəns
endways	'ɛndweɪz	
enemy	'ɛnɪmɪ	
enemies	'ɛnɪmɪz	
energetic	ɛnə'ʤɛtɪk	
energetically	ɛnæ'ʤɛtɪkəlɪ	
energy	'ɛnəʤɪ	'ɛnəʤɪ
energies	'ɛnəʤɪz	'ɛnəʤɪz
enforce	ɪn'fɔ·s	ɪn'foəs
enforces	ɪn'fɔ·sɪz	ɪn'foəsɪz
enforced	ɪn'fɔ·st	ɪn'foəst
enforcing	ɪn'fɔ·sɪŋ	ɪn'foəsɪŋ
enforcement	ɪn'fɔ·smənt	ɪn'foəsmənt
engage	ɪn'geɪʤ	
engages	ɪn'geɪʤɪz	
engaged	ɪn'geɪʤd	
engaging	ɪn'geɪʤɪŋ	
engagement	ɪn'geɪʤmənt	
engagements	ɪn'geɪʤmənts	
engine	'ɛnʤɪn	
engines	'ɛnʤɪnz	
engineer	ɛnʤɪ'nɪə(r	ɛnʤɪ'nɪə
engineers	ɛnʤɪ'nɪəz	ɛnʤɪnɪəz
engineering	ɛnʤɪ'nɪərɪŋ	ɛnʤɪ'nɪ·rɪŋ
England	'ɪŋglənd	

Traditional Spelling	Received Pronunciation	American Variants
English	ˈɪŋglɪʃ	
Englishman	ˈɪŋglɪʃmən	
Englishmen	ˈɪŋglɪʃmən	
Englishwoman	ˈɪŋglɪʃwʊmən	
Englishwomen	ˈɪŋglɪʃwɪmɪn	
engrave	ɪnˈgreɪv	
engraves	ɪnˈgreɪvz	
engraved	ɪnˈgreɪvd	
engraver	ɪnˈgreɪvə(r	ɪnˈgreɪvɚ
engravers	ɪnˈgreɪvəz	ɪnˈgreɪvɚz
engraving	ɪnˈgreɪvɪŋ	
engravings	ɪnˈgreɪvɪŋz	
enjoy	ɪnˈʤɔɪ	
enjoys	ɪnˈʤɔɪz	
enjoyed	ɪnˈʤɔɪd	
enjoying	ɪnˈʤɔɪɪŋ	
enjoyment	ɪnˈʤɔɪmənt	
enjoyable	ɪnˈʤɔɪəbl̩	
enlarge	ɪnˈlɑˑʤ	ɪnˈlɑɚʤ
enlarges	ɪnˈlɑˑʤɪz	ɪnˈlɑɚʤɪz
enlarged	ɪnˈlɑˑʤd	ɪnˈlɑɚʤd
enlarging	ɪnˈlɑˑʤɪŋ	ɪnˈlɑɚʤɪŋ
enlargement	ɪnˈlɑˑʤmənt	ɪnˈlɑɚʤmənt
enlargements	ɪnˈlɑˑʤmənts	ɪnˈlɑɚʤmənts
enlighten	ɪnˈlaɪtn̩	
enlightens	ɪnˈlaɪtn̩z	
enlightened	ɪnˈlaɪtn̩d	
enlightening	ɪnˈlaɪtn̩ɪŋ	
enlightenment	ɪnˈlaɪtn̩mənt	
enlist	ɪnˈlɪst	
enlists	ɪnˈlɪsts	
enlisted	ɪnˈlɪstɪd	
enlisting	ɪnˈlɪstɪŋ	
enmity	ˈɛnmɪtɪ	
enormous	ɪˈnɔˑməs	ɪˈnɔɚməs
enormously	ɪˈnɔˑməslɪ	ɪˈnɔɚməslɪ
enough	ɪˈnʌf	
enquire	ɪnˈkwaɪə(r	ɪnˈkwaɪɚ
enquires	ɪnˈkwaɪəz	ɪnˈkwaɪɚz
enquired	ɪnˈkwaɪəd	ɪnˈkwaɪɚd
enquiring	ɪnˈkwaɪərɪŋ	ɪnˈkwaɪrɪŋ
enquirer	ɪnˈkwaɪərə(r	ɪnˈkwaɪrɚ
enquirers	ɪnˈkwaɪərəz	ɪnˈkwaɪrɚz
enquiry	ɪnˈkwaɪərɪ	
enquiries	ɪnˈkwaɪərɪz	
enrage	ɪnˈreɪʤ	
enrages	ɪnˈreɪʤɪz	

Traditional Spelling	Received Pronunciation	American Variants
enraged	ɪn'reɪdʒd	
enraging	ɪn'reɪdʒɪŋ	
enrich	ɪn'rɪtʃ	
enriches	ɪn'rɪtʃɪz	
enriched	ɪn'rɪtʃt	
enriching	ɪn'rɪtʃɪŋ	
enrol	ɪn'roul	
enrols	ɪn'roulz	
enrolled	ɪn'rould	
enrolling	ɪn'roulɪŋ	
enrolment	ɪn'roulmənt	
ensure	ɪn'ʃuə(r, ɪn'ʃɔə(r	ɪn'ʃuə
ensures	ɪn'ʃuəz, ɪn'ʃɔəz	ɪn'ʃuəz
ensured	ɪn'ʃuəd, ɪn'ʃɔəd	ɪn'ʃuəd
ensuring	ɪn'ʃuərɪŋ, ɪn'ʃɔərɪŋ	ɪn'ʃuˑrɪŋ
entangle	ɪn'tæŋgl̩	
entangles	ɪn'tæŋgl̩z	
entangled	ɪn'tæŋgl̩d	
entangling	ɪn'tæŋglɪŋ	
	ɪn'tæŋgl̩ɪŋ	
enter	'ɛntə(r	'ɛntə
enters	'ɛntəz	'ɛntəz
entered	'ɛntəd	'ɛntəd
entering	'ɛntərɪŋ	
enterprise	'ɛntəpraɪz	'ɛntəpraɪz
enterprises	'ɛntəpraɪzɪz	'ɛntəpraɪzɪz
entertain	ɛntə'teɪn	ɛntə'teɪn
entertains	ɛntə'teɪnz	ɛntə'teɪnz
entertained	ɛntə'teɪnd	ɛntə'teɪnd
entertaining	ɛntə'teɪnɪŋ	ɛntə'teɪnɪŋ
entertainment	ɛntə'teɪnmənt	ɛntə'teɪnmənt
entertainments	ɛntə'teɪnmənts	ɛntə'teɪnmənts
enthusiasm	ɪn'θjuˑzɪæzm̩	
enthusiast	ɪn'θjuˑzɪæst	
enthusiasts	ɪn'θjuˑzɪæsts	
enthusiastic	ɪnθjuzɪ'æstɪk	
enthusiastically	ɪnθjuzɪ'æstɪkəlɪ	
entire	ɪn'taɪə(r	ɪn'taɪə
entirely	ɪn'taɪəlɪ	ɪn'taɪəlɪ
entirety	ɪn'taɪətɪ	ɪn'taɪətɪ
entitle	ɪn'taɪtl̩	
entitles	ɪn'taɪtl̩z	
entitled	ɪn'taɪtl̩d	
entitling	ɪn'taɪtlɪŋ, ɪn'taɪtl̩ɪŋ	
entomology	ɛntə'mɒlədʒɪ	ɛntə'mɑlədʒɪ
entrance	'ɛntrəns	
entrances	'ɛntrənsɪz	
entrust	ɪn'trʌst	

Traditional Spelling	Received Pronunciation	American Variants
entrusts	ɪn'trʌsts	
entrusted	ɪn'trʌstɪd	
entrusting	ɪn'trʌstɪŋ	
entry	'ɛntrɪ	
entries	'ɛntrɪz	
envelope, ***noun***	'ɛnvɪloup 'ɛnvəloup 'ɒnvəloup	
envelopes	'ɛnvɪloups 'ɛnvəloups 'ɒnvəloups	
envious	'ɛnvɪəs	
enviously	'ɛnvɪəslɪ	
environment	ɪn'vaɪərənmənt	ɪn'vaɪrənmənt
environments	ɪn'vaɪərənmənts	ɪn'vaɪrənmənt
environs	'ɛnvɪrənz ɪn'vaɪərənz	ɪn'vaɪrənz
envy	'ɛnvɪ	
envies	'ɛnvɪz	
envied	'ɛnvɪd	
envying	'ɛnvɪɪŋ	
epidemic	ɛpɪ'dɛmɪk	
epidemics	ɛpɪ'dɛmɪks	
episode	'ɛpɪsoud	
episodes	'ɛpɪsoudz	
epoch	'iˑpɒk	'iˑpɑk
epochs	'iˑpɒks	'iˑpɑks
equal	'iˑkwəl	
equals	'iˑkwəlz	
equalled	'iˑkwəld	
equalling	'iˑkwəlɪŋ	
equality	i'kwɒlɪtɪ ɪ'kwɒlɪtɪ	i'kwɑlɪtɪ ɪ'kwɑlɪtɪ
equally	'iˑkwəlɪ	
equation	ɪ'kweɪʃən	
equations	ɪ'kweɪʃənz	
equator	ɪ'kweɪtə(r	ɪ'kweɪtə
equip	ɪ'kwɪp	
equips	ɪ'kwɪps	
equipped	ɪ'kwɪpt	
equipping	ɪ'kwɪpɪŋ	
equipment	ɪ'kwɪpmənt	
equivalent	ɪ'kwɪvələnt	
equivalents	ɪ'kwɪvələnts	
erase	ɪ'reɪz, ɪ'reɪs	
erases	ɪ'reɪzɪz, ɪ'reɪsɪz	
erased	ɪ'reɪzd, ɪ'reɪst	

Traditional Spelling	Received Pronunciation	American Variants
erasing	ɪ'reɪzɪŋ, ɪ'reɪsɪŋ	
eraser	ɪ'reɪzə(r, ɪ'reɪsə(r	ɪ'reɪsə
erasers	ɪ'reɪzəz, ɪ'reɪsəz	ɪ'reɪsəz
erect	ɪ'rɛkt	
Ernest	'ɜ·nɪst	'ɜənɪst
err	ɜ·(r	ɜə
errs	ɜ·z	ɜəz
erred	ɜ·d	ɜəd
erring	ɜ·rɪŋ	
errand	'ɛrənd	
errands	'ɛrəndz	
erratic	ɪ'rætɪk	
erroneous	ɪ'rounjəs, ɪ'rounɪəs	
erroneously	ɪ'rounjəslɪ, ɪ'rounɪəslɪ	
error	'ɛrə(r	ɛrə
errors	'ɛrəz	'ɛrəz
erudite	'ɛrudaɪt, 'i·rudaɪt	
erudition	ɛru'dɪʃən, iru'dɪʃən	
erupt	ɪ'rʌpt	
erupts	ɪ'rʌpts	
erupted	ɪ'rʌptɪd	
erupting	ɪ'rʌptɪŋ	
eruption	ɪ'rʌpʃən	
eruptions	ɪ'rʌpʃənz	
escalator	'ɛskəleɪtə(r	'ɛskəleɪtə
escalators	'ɛskəleɪtəz	'ɛskəleɪtəz
escape	ɪs'keɪp	
escapes	ɪs'keɪps	
escaped	ɪs'keɪpt	
escaping	ɪs'keɪpɪŋ	
escort, ***noun***	'ɛskɔ·t	'ɛskɔət
escorts	'ɛskɔ·ts	'ɛskɔəts
escort, ***verb***	ɪs'kɔ·t	ɪs'kɔət
escorts	ɪs'kɔ·ts	ɪs'kɔəts
escorted	ɪs'kɔ·tɪd	ɪs'kɔətɪd
escorting	ɪs'kɔ·tɪŋ	ɪs'kɔətɪŋ
especially	ɪs'pɛʃəlɪ	
esquire	ɪs'kwaɪə(r	ɪs'kwaɪə
essay, ***noun***	'ɛseɪ	
essays	'ɛseɪz	
essence	'ɛsn̩s	
essential	ɪ'sɛnʃəl	
essentially	ɪ'sɛnʃəlɪ	
establish	ɪs'tæblɪʃ	
establishes	ɪs'tæblɪʃɪz	
established	ɪs'tæblɪʃt	
establishing	ɪs'tæblɪʃɪŋ	

Traditional Spelling	Received Pronunciation	American Variants
establishment	ɪs'tæblɪʃmənt	
establishments	ɪs'tæblɪʃmənts	
esteem	ɪs'tiˑm	
esteems	ɪs'tiˑmz	
esteemed	ɪs'tiˑmd	
esteeming	ɪs'tiˑmɪŋ	
estimate, *noun*	'ɛstɪmɪt, 'ɛstɪmeɪt	
estimates	'ɛstɪmɪts, 'ɛstɪmeɪts	
estimate, *verb*	'ɛstɪmeɪt	
estimates	'ɛstɪmeɪts	
estimated	'ɛstɪmeɪtɪd	
estimating	'ɛstɪmeɪtɪŋ	
estimation	ɛstɪ'meɪʃən	
etc. = etcetera	ɪt'sɛtrə, ɛt'sɛtrə	
eternal	ɪ'tɜˑnəl	ɪ'tɜɚnəl
eternally	ɪ'tɜˑnəlɪ	ɪ'tɜɚnəlɪ
eternity	ɪ'tɜˑnɪtɪ	ɪ'tɜɚnɪtɪ
Ethel	'ɛθl̩	
ether	'iˑθə(r	'iˑθɚ
ethics	'ɛθɪks	
etiquette	ɛtɪ'kɛt, 'ɛtɪkɛt	
etymological	ɛtɪmə'lɒʤɪkəl	ɛtɪmə'lɑʤɪkəl
etymologically	ɛtɪmə'lɒʤɪkəlɪ	ɛtɪmə'lɑʤɪkəlɪ
etymologist	ɛtɪ'mɒləʤɪst	ɛtɪ'mɑləʤɪst
etymologists	ɛtɪ'mɒləʤɪsts	ɛtɪ'mɑləʤɪsts
etymology	ɛtɪ'mɒləʤɪ	ɛtɪ'mɑləʤɪ
Europe	'jʊərəp	juˑrəp
European	jʊərə'piˑən	jurə'piˑən
Europeans	jʊərə'piˑənz	jurə'piˑənz
evaporate	ɪ'væpəreɪt	
evaporates	ɪ'væpəreɪts	
evaporated	ɪ'væpəreɪtɪd	
evaporating	ɪ'væpəreɪtɪŋ	
evaporation	ɪvæpə'reɪʃən	
evasive	ɪ'veɪsɪv	
even	'iˑvn̩	
evening	'iˑvnɪŋ	
evenings	'iˑvnɪŋz	
evenly	'iˑvn̩lɪ	
event	ɪ'vɛnt	
events	ɪ'vɛnts	
eventful	ɪ'vɛntful	
eventual	ɪ'vɛntjuəl	
eventually	ɪ'vɛntjuəlɪ	
ever	'ɛvə(r	'ɛvɚ
every	'ɛvrɪ	
everybody	'ɛvrɪbɒdɪ	'ɛvrɪbɑdɪ

Traditional Spelling	Received Pronunciation	American Variants
everyday	ˈɛvrɪˈdeɪ	
everyone	ˈɛvrɪwʌn	
everything	ˈɛvrɪθɪŋ	
everywhere	ˈɛvrɪhwɛə(r	ˈɛvrɪhwɛə
evidence	ˈɛvɪdəns	
evident	ˈɛvɪdənt	
evidently	ˈɛvɪdəntlɪ	
evil	ˈiˑvɪl	
evils	ˈiˑvɪlz	
evolution	ivəˈljuˑʃən, ɛvəˈljuˑʃən	
ex-, *prefix meaning* former	ɛks	
exact	ɪgˈzækt	
exactly	ɪgˈzæktlɪ	
exaggerate	ɪgˈzædʒəreɪt	
exaggerates	ɪgˈzædʒəreɪts	
exaggerated	ɪgˈzædʒəreɪtɪd	
exaggerating	ɪgˈzædʒəreɪtɪŋ	
exaggeration	ɪgzædʒəˈreɪʃən	
exaltation	ɛgzɔlˈteɪʃən	
examination	ɪgzæmɪˈneɪʃən	
examinations	ɪgzæmɪˈneɪʃənz	
examine	ɪgˈzæmɪn	
examines	ɪgˈzæmɪnz	
examined	ɪgˈzæmɪnd	
examining	ɪgˈzæmɪnɪŋ	
examiner	ɪgˈzæmɪnə(r	ɪgˈzæmɪnə
examiners	ɪgˈzæmɪnəz	ɪgˈzæmɪnəz
example	ɪgˈzɑˑmpl̩	ɪgˈzaˑmpl̩
examples	ɪgˈzɑˑmpl̩z	ɪgˈzaˑmpl̩z
exasperate	ɪgˈzɑˑspəreɪt ɪgˈzæspəreɪt	ɪgˈzaˑspəreɪt
exasperates	ɪgˈzɑˑspəreɪts ɪgˈzæspəreɪts	ɪgˈzaˑspəreɪts
exasperated	ɪgˈzɑˑspəreɪtɪd ɪgˈzæspəreɪtɪd	ɪgˈzaˑspəreɪtɪd
exasperating	ɪgˈzɑˑspəreɪtɪŋ ɪgˈzæspəreɪtɪŋ	ɪgˈzaˑspəreɪtɪŋ
exasperation	ɪgzɑspəˈreɪʃən ɪgzæspəˈreɪʃən	ɪgzaspəˈreɪʃən
excavate	ˈɛkskəveɪt	
excavates	ˈɛkskəveɪts	
excavated	ˈɛkskəveɪtɪd	
excavating	ˈɛkskəveɪtɪŋ	
excavation	ɛkskəˈveɪʃən	
excavations	ɛkskəˈveɪʃənz	
exceed	ɪkˈsiˑd	

Traditional Spelling	Received Pronunciation	American Variants
exceeds	ɪk'siˑdz	
exceeded	ɪk'siˑdɪd	
exceeding	ɪk'siˑdɪŋ	
exceedingly	ɪk'siˑdɪŋlɪ	
excel	ɪk'sɛl	
excels	ɪk'sɛlz	
excelled	ɪk'sɛld	
excelling	ɪk'sɛlɪŋ	
excellence	'ɛksələns	
excellency	'ɛksələnsɪ	
excellencies	'ɛksələnsɪz	
excellent	'ɛksələnt	
excellently	'ɛksələntlɪ	
except	ɪk'sɛpt	
excepts	ɪk'sɛpts	
excepted	ɪk'sɛptɪd	
excepting	ɪk'sɛptɪŋ	
exception	ɪk'sɛpʃən	
exceptions	ɪk'sɛpʃənz	
exceptional	ɪk'sɛpʃənəl	
exceptionally	ɪk'sɛpʃənəlɪ	
excess	ɪk'sɛs	
excessive	ɪk'sɛsɪv	
exchange	ɪks'tʃeɪnʤ	
exchanges	ɪks'tʃeɪnʤɪz	
exchanged	ɪks'tʃeɪnʤd	
exchanging	ɪks'tʃeɪnʤɪŋ	
excite	ɪk'saɪt	
excites	ɪk'saɪts	
excited	ɪk'saɪtɪd	
exciting	ɪk'saɪtɪŋ	
excitement	ɪk'saɪtmənt	
exclaim	ɪks'kleɪm	
exclaims	ɪks'kleɪmz	
exclaimed	ɪks'kleɪmd	
exclaiming	ɪk'skleɪmɪŋ	
exclamation	ɛksklə'meɪʃən	
exclamations	ɛksklə'meɪʃənz	
exclamatory	ɪks'klæmətərɪ	ɪks'klæmətorɪ
exclude	ɪks'kluˑd	
excludes	ɪks'kluˑdz	
excluded	ɪks'kluˑdɪd	
excluding	ɪks'kluˑdɪŋ	
exclusion	ɪks'kluˑʒən	
exclusive	ɪks'kluˑsɪv	
exclusively	ɪks'kluˑsɪvlɪ	
excursion	ɪks'kɜˑʃən	ɪks'kɜəʃən, ɪks'kɜəʒən

Traditional Spelling	Received Pronunciation	American Variants
excursions	ɪks'kɜˑʃənz	ɪks'kɜəʃənz ɪks'kɜəʒənz
excursionist	ɪks'kɜˑʃənɪst	ɪks'kɜəʃənɪst ɪks'kɜəʒənɪst
excursionists	ɪks'kɜˑʃənɪsts	ɪks'kɜəʃənɪsts ɪks'kɜəʒənɪsts
excusable	ɪks'kjuˑzəbl̩	
excusably	ɪks'kjuˑzəblɪ	
excuse, *noun*	ɪks'kjuˑs	
excuses	ɪks'kjuˑsɪz	
excuse, *verb*	ɪks'kjuˑz	
excuses	ɪks'kjuˑzɪz	
excused	ɪks'kjuˑzd	
excusing	ɪks'kjuˑzɪŋ	
execute	'ɛksɪkjut	
executes	'ɛksɪkjuts	
executed	'ɛksɪkjutɪd	
executing	'ɛksɪkjutɪŋ	
execution	ɛksɪ'kjuˑʃən	
executions	ɛksɪ'kjuˑʃənz	
executioner	ɛksɪ'kjuˑʃənə(r	ɛksɪ'kjuˑʃənə
executioners	ɛksɪ'kjuˑʃənəz	ɛksɪ'kjuˑʃənəz
executive	ɪg'zɛkjutɪv	
executor	ɪg'zɛkjutə(r	ɪg'zɛkjutə
executors	ɪg'zɛkjutəz	ɪg'zɛkjutəz
exemplify	ɪg'zɛmplɪfaɪ	
exemplifies	ɪg'zɛmplɪfaɪz	
exemplified	ɪg'zɛmplɪfaɪd	
exemplifying	ɪg'zɛmplɪfaɪɪŋ	
exempt	ɪg'zɛm*p*t	
exempts	ɪg'zɛm*p*ts	
exempted	ɪg'zɛm*p*tɪd	
exempting	ɪg'zɛm*p*tɪŋ	
exemption	ɪg'zɛm*p*ʃən	
exemptions	ɪg'zɛm*p*ʃənz	
exercise	'ɛksəsaɪz	'ɛksəsaɪz
exercises	'ɛksəsaɪzɪz	'ɛksəsaɪzɪz
exercised	'ɛksəsaɪzd	'ɛksəsaɪzd
exercising	'ɛksəsaɪzɪŋ	'ɛksəsaɪzɪŋ
exert	ɪg'zɜˑt	ɪg'zɜət
exerts	ɪg'zɜˑts	ɪg'zɜəts
exerted	ɪg'zɜˑtɪd	ɪg'zɜətɪd
exerting	ɪg'zɜˑtɪŋ	ɪg'zɜətɪŋ
exertion	ɪg'zɜˑʃən	ɪg'zɜəʃən
exertions	ɪg'zɜˑʃənz	ɪg'zɜəʃənz
exhaust	ɪg'zɔˑst	
exhausts	ɪg'zɔˑsts	

Traditional Spelling	Received Pronunciation	American Variants
exhausted	ɪg'zɔˑstɪd	
exhausting	ɪg'zɔˑstɪŋ	
exhaustion	ɪg'zɔˑstʃən	
exhaustive	ɪg'zɔˑstɪv	
exhaustively	ɪg'zɔˑstɪvlɪ	
exhibit	ɪg'zɪbɪt	
exhibits	ɪg'zɪbɪts	
exhibited	ɪg'zɪbɪtɪd	
exhibiting	ɪg'zɪbɪtɪŋ	
exhibitor	ɪg'zɪbɪtə(r	ɪg'zɪbɪtɚ
exhibitors	ɪg'zɪbɪtəz	ɪg'zɪbɪtɚz
exhibition	ɛksɪ'bɪʃən	
exhibitions	ɛksɪ'bɪʃənz	
exhilarate	ɪg'zɪləreɪt	
exhilarates	ɪg'zɪləreɪts	
exhilarated	ɪg'zɪləreɪtɪd	
exhilarating	ɪg'zɪləreɪtɪŋ	
exhilaration	ɪg'zɪlə'reɪʃən	
exile	'ɛksaɪl, 'ɛgzaɪl	
exiles	'ɛksaɪlz, 'ɛgzaɪlz	
exist	ɪg'zɪst	
exists	ɪg'zɪsts	
existed	ɪg'zɪstɪd	
existing	ɪg'zɪstɪŋ	
existence	ɪg'zɪstəns	
existences	ɪg'zɪstənsɪz	
exit	'ɛksɪt	
exits	'ɛksɪts	
exonerate	ɪg'zɒnəreɪt	ɪg'zɑnəreɪt
exonerates	ɪg'zɒnəreɪts	ɪg'zɑnəreɪts
exonerated	ɪg'zɒnəreɪtɪd	ɪg'zɑnəreɪtɪd
exonerating	ɪg'zɒnəreɪtɪŋ	ɪg'zɑnəreɪtɪŋ
exotic	ɛk'sɒtɪk, ɛk'zɒtɪk ɛg'zɒtɪk	ɛk'sɑtɪk, ɛk'zɑtɪk ɛg'zɑtɪk
expand	ɪks'pænd	
expands	ɪks'pændz	
expanded	ɪks'pændɪd	
expanding	ɪks'pændɪŋ	
expansion	ɪks'pænʃən	
expect	ɪks'pɛkt	
expects	ɪks'pɛkts	
expected	ɪks'pɛktɪd	
expecting	ɪks'pɛktɪŋ	
expectation	ɛkspɛk'teɪʃən	
expectations	ɛkspɛk'teɪʃənz	
expedient	ɪks'piˑdjənt ɪks'piˑdɪənt	

Traditional Spelling	Received Pronunciation	American Variants
expedients	ɪks'piˑdjənts	
	ɪks'piˑdɪənts	
expedition	ɛkspɪ'dɪʃən	
expeditions	ɛkspɪ'dɪʃənz	
expel	ɪks'pɛl	
expels	ɪks'pɛlz	
expelled	ɪks'pɛld	
expelling	ɪks'pɛlɪŋ	
expend	ɪks'pɛnd	
expends	ɪks'pɛndz	
expended	ɪks'pɛndɪd	
expending	ɪks'pɛndɪŋ	
expenditure	ɪks'pɛnditʃə(r	ɪks'pɛndɪtʃə
expense	ɪks'pɛns	
expenses	ɪks'pɛnsɪz	
expensive	ɪks'pɛnsɪv	
expensively	ɪks'pɛnsɪvlɪ	
experience	ɪks'pɪərɪəns	ɪks'pɪˑrɪəns
experiences	ɪks'pɪərɪənsɪz	ɪks'pɪˑrɪənsɪz
experienced	ɪks'pɪərɪənst	ɪks'pɪˑrɪənst
experiencing	ɪks'pɪərɪənsɪŋ	ɪks'pɪˑrɪənsɪŋ
experiment, *noun*	ɪks'pɛrɪmənt	
experiments	ɪks'pɛrɪmənts	
experiment, *verb*	ɪks'pɛrɪmɛnt	
experiments	ɪks'pɛrɪmɛnts	
experimented	ɪks'pɛrɪmɛntɪd	
experimenting	ɪks'pɛrɪmɛntɪŋ	
experimental	ɛkspɛrɪ'mɛntl̩	
	ɪkspɛrɪ'mɛntl̩	
experimentally	ɛkspɛrɪ'mɛntəlɪ	
	ɪkspɛrɪ'mɛntəlɪ	
expert, *noun*	'ɛkspɜt	'ɛkspɜət
experts	'ɛkspɜts	'ɛkspɜəts
expert, *adj.*	ɪks'pɜˑt, 'ɛkspɜt	ɪks'pɜət, 'ɛkspɜət
expertly	ɪks'pɜˑtlɪ, 'ɛkspɜtlɪ	ɪks'pɜətlɪ, 'ɛkspɜətlɪ
expiration	ɛkspɪ'reɪʃən	
expire	ɪks'paɪə(r	ɪks'paɪə
expires	ɪks'paɪəz	ɪks'paɪəz
expired	ɪks'paɪəd	ɪks'paɪəd
expiring	ɪks'paɪərɪŋ	ɪks'paɪrɪŋ
expiry	ɪks'paɪərɪ	
explain	ɪks'pleɪn	
explains	ɪks'pleɪnz	
explained	ɪks'pleɪnd	
explaining	ɪks'pleɪnɪŋ	
explainable	ɪks'pleɪnəbl̩	
explanation	ɛksplə'neɪʃən	

Traditional Spelling	Received Pronunciation	American Variants
explanations	ɛksplɔ'neɪʃənz	
explanatory	ɪks'plænətərɪ	ɪks'plænətorɪ
explicit	ɪks'plɪsɪt	
explicitly	ɪks'plɪsɪtlɪ	
explode	ɪks'ploʊd	
explodes	ɪks'ploʊdz	
exploded	ɪks'ploʊdɪd	
exploding	ɪks'ploʊdɪŋ	
exploration	ɛksplɔ'reɪʃən ɛksplə'reɪʃən	
explorations	ɛksplɔ'reɪʃənz ɛksplə'reɪʃənz	
explore	ɪks'plɔ·(r, ɪks'plɔə(r	ɪks'ploə
explores	ɪks'plɔ·z, ɪks'plɔəz	ɪks'ploəz
explored	ɪks'plɔ·d, ɪks'plɔəd	ɪks'ploəd
exploring	ɪks'plɔ·rɪŋ ɪks'plɔərɪŋ	ɪks'plo·rɪŋ
explorer	ɪks'plɔ·rə(r ɪks'plɔərə(r	ɪks'plo·rə
explorers	ɪks'plɔ·rəz ɪks'plɔərəz	ɪks'plo·rəz
explosion	ɪks'ploʊʒən	
explosions	ɪks'ploʊʒənz	
explosive	ɪks'ploʊsɪv	
explosives	ɪks'ploʊsɪvz	
export, *noun*	'ɛkspɔt	'ɛkspoət
exports	'ɛkspɔts	'ɛkspoəts
export, *verb*	ɪks'pɔ·t	ɪks'poət
exports	ɪks'pɔ·ts	ɪks'poəts
exported	ɪks'pɔ·tɪd	ɪks'poətɪd
exporting	ɪks'pɔ·tɪŋ	ɪks'poətɪŋ
exporter	ɪks'pɔ·tə(r	ɪks'poətə
exporters	ɪks'pɔ·təz	ɪks'poətəz
exportation	ɛkspɔ'teɪʃən	ɛkspoə'teɪʃən
expose	ɪks'poʊz	
exposes	ɪks'poʊzɪz	
exposed	ɪks'poʊzd	
exposing	ɪks'poʊzɪŋ	
exposure	ɪks'poʊʒə(r	ɪks'poʊʒə
exposures	ɪks'poʊʒəz	ɪks'poʊʒəz
express	ɪks'prɛs	
expresses	ɪks'prɛsɪz	
expressed	ɪks'prɛst	
expressing	ɪks'prɛsɪŋ	
expression	ɪks'prɛʃən	
expressions	ɪks'prɛʃənz	
expressive	ɪks'prɛsɪv	

Traditional Spelling	Received Pronunciation	American Variants
exquisite	'ɛkskwɪzɪt	
exquisitely	'ɛkskwɪzɪtlɪ	
extend	ɪks'tɛnd	
extends	ɪks'tɛndz	
extended	ɪks'tɛndɪd	
extending	ɪks'tɛndɪŋ	
extension	ɪks'tɛnʃən	
extensions	ɪks'tɛnʃənz	
extensive	ɪks'tɛnsɪv	
extensively	ɪks'tɛnsɪvlɪ	
extent	ɪks'tɛnt	
exterior	ɪks'tɪərɪə(r	ɪks'tɪːrɪə
exterminate	ɪks'tɜːmɪneɪt	ɪks'tɜəmɪneɪt
exterminates	ɪks'tɜːmɪneɪts	ɪks'tɜəmɪneɪts
exterminated	ɪks'tɜːmɪneɪtɪd	ɪks'tɜəmɪneɪtɪd
exterminating	ɪks'tɜːmɪneɪtɪŋ	ɪks'tɜəmɪneɪtɪŋ
external	ɪks'tɜːnl̩	ɪks'tɜənl̩
externally	ɪks'tɜːnəlɪ	ɪks'tɜənəlɪ
extinct	ɪks'tɪŋ*k*t	
extortionate	ɪks'tɔːʃənɪt	ɪks'tɔəʃənɪt
extra	'ɛkstrə	
extras	'ɛkstrəz	
extract, *noun*	'ɛkstrækt	
extracts	'ɛkstrækts	
extract, *verb*	ɪks'trækt	
extracts	ɪks'trækts	
extracted	ɪks'træktɪd	
extracting	ɪks'træktɪŋ	
extraordinarily	ɪks'trɔːd*ɪ*nrɪlɪ ɪks'trɔːd*ɪ*n*ə*rɪlɪ ɛkstr*ə*'ɔːd*ɪ*nrɪlɪ ɛkstr*ə*'ɔːd*ɪ*n*ə*rɪlɪ	ɪks'trɔədɪnɛrɪlɪ ɛkstr*ə*'ɔədɪnɛrɪlɪ
extraordinary	ɪks'trɔːd*ɪ*nrɪ ɪkstrə'ɔːd*ɪ*n*ə*rɪ ɛkstr*ə*'ɔːd*ɪ*nrɪ ɛkstr*ə*'ɔːd*ɪ*n*ə*rɪ	ɪkstrə'ɔədɪnɛrɪ ɛkstr*ə*'ɔədɪnɛrɪ
extravagance	ɪks'trævɪgəns ɪks'trævəgəns	
extravagant	ɪks'trævɪgənt ɪks'trævəgənt	
extreme	ɪks'triːm	
extremes	ɪks'triːmz	
extremely	ɪks'triːmlɪ	
extremity	ɪks'trɛmɪtɪ	
extremities	ɪks'trɛmɪtɪz	
eye	aɪ	
eyes	aɪz	

Traditional Spelling	Received Pronunciation	American Variants
eyeglass	ʹaɪglɑs	ʹaɪglas
eyeglasses	aɪglɑsɪz	ʹaɪglasɪz

F

F	ɛf	
F's	ɛfs	
fable	ʹfeɪbl̩	
fables	ʹfeɪbl̩z	
face	feɪs	
faces	ʹfeɪsɪz	
faced	feɪst	
facing	ʹfeɪsɪŋ	
facilitate	fəʹsɪlɪteɪt	
facilitates	fəʹsɪlɪteɪts	
facilitated	fəʹsɪlɪteɪtɪd	
facilitating	fəʹsɪlɪteɪtɪŋ	
facility	fəʹsɪlɪtɪ	
facilities	fəʹsɪlɪtɪz	
fact	fækt	
facts	fækts	
factor	ʹfæktə(r	ʹfæktə
factors	ʹfæktəz	ʹfæktəz
factory	ʹfæktərɪ	
factories	ʹfæktərɪz	
fade	feɪd	
fades	feɪdz	
faded	ʹfeɪdɪd	
fading	ʹfeɪdɪŋ	
Fahrenheit	ʹfærənhaɪt, ʹfɑ·rənhaɪt	ʹfa·rənhaɪt
fail	feɪl	
fails	feɪlz	
failed	feɪld	
failing	ʹfeɪlɪŋ	
failings	ʹfeɪlɪŋz	
failure	ʹfeɪljə(r	ʹfeɪljə
failures	ʹfeɪljəz	ʹfeɪljəz
faint	feɪnt	
faints	feɪnts	
fainted	ʹfeɪntɪd	
fainting	ʹfeɪntɪŋ	
faintly	ʹfeɪntlɪ	
faintness	ʹfeɪntnɪs	
fair	fɛə(r	fɛə
fairer	ʹfɛərə(r	ʹfɛ·rə

Traditional Spelling	Received Pronunciation	American Variants
fairest	ˈfɛərɪst	ˈfɛ·rɪst
fairly	ˈfɛəlɪ	ˈfɛəlɪ
fairness	ˈfɛənɪs	ˈfɛənɪs
fairy	ˈfɛərɪ	ˈfɛ·rɪ
fairies	ˈfɛərɪz	ˈfɛ·rɪz
faith	feɪθ	
faiths	feɪθs	
faithful	ˈfeɪθfʊl	
faithfully	feɪθfʊlɪ, ˈfeɪθfəlɪ	
fall	fɔ·l	
falls	fɔ·lz	
fell	fɛl	
fallen	ˈfɔ·lən	
falling	ˈfɔ·lɪŋ	
fallacy	ˈfæləsɪ	
fallacies	ˈfæləsɪz	
false	fɔls, fɒls	
falser	ˈfɔlsə(r, ˈfɒlsə(r	ˈfɔlsə, ˈfɒlsə
falsest	ˈfɔlsɪst, ˈfɒlsɪst	
falsely	ˈfɔlslɪ, ˈfɒlslɪ	
fame	feɪm	
familiar	fəˈmɪljə(r	fəˈmɪljə
familiarity	fəmɪlɪˈærɪtɪ	
familiarities	fəmɪlɪˈærɪtɪz	
familiarize	fəˈmɪljəraɪz	
familiarizes	fəˈmɪljəraɪzɪz	
familiarized	fəˈmɪljəraɪzd	
familiarizing	fəˈmɪljəraɪzɪŋ	
familiarly	fəˈmɪljəlɪ	fəˈmɪljəlɪ
family	ˈfæmɪlɪ	
families	ˈfæmɪlɪz	
famine	ˈfæmɪn	
famines	ˈfæmɪnz	
famous	ˈfeɪməs	
famously	ˈfeɪməslɪ	
fan	fæn	
fans	fænz	
fanned	fænd	
fanning	ˈfænɪŋ	
fanatic	fəˈnætɪk	
fanatics	fəˈnætɪks	
fanaticism	fəˈnætɪsɪzṃ	
fancy	ˈfænsɪ	
fancies	ˈfænsɪz	
fancied	ˈfænsɪd	
fancying	ˈfænsɪɪŋ	
fantastic	fænˈtæstɪk	

Traditional Spelling	Received Pronunciation	American Variants
fantastically	fæn'tæstɪkəlɪ	
far	fɑ·(r	fɑə
fare	fɛə(r	fɛə
fares	fɛəz	fɛəz
farewell	'fɛə'wɛl	'fɛə'wɛl
farewells	'fɛə'wɛlz	'fɛə'wɛlz
farm	fɑ·m	fɑəm
farms	fɑ·mz	fɑəmz
farmer	'fɑ·mə(r	'fɑəmə
farmers	'fɑ·məz	'fɑəməz
farming	'fɑ·mɪŋ	'fɑəmɪŋ
farther	'fɑ·ðə(r	'fɑəðə
farthest	'fɑ·ðɪst	'fɑəðɪst
fascinate	'fæsɪneɪt	
fascinates	'fæsɪneɪts	
fascinated	'fæsɪneɪtɪd	
fascinating	'fæsɪneɪtɪŋ	
fascination	fæsɪ'neɪʃən	
fascinations	fæsɪ'neɪʃənz	
fashion	'fæʃən	
fashions	'fæʃənz	
fashionable	'fæʃənəbl̩	
fashionably	'fæʃənəblɪ	
fast	fɑ·st	fa·st
faster	'fɑ·stə(r	'fa·stə
fastest	'fɑ·stɪst	'fa·stɪst
fasten	'fɑ·sn̩	'fa·sn̩
fastens	'fɑ·sn̩z	'fa·sn̩z
fastened	'fɑ·sn̩d	'fa·sn̩d
fastening	'fɑ·sn̩ɪŋ	'fa·sn̩ɪŋ
fat	fæt	
fatter	'fætə(r	'fætə
fattest	'fætɪst	
fatal	'feɪtl̩	
fatally	'feɪtəlɪ	
fate	feɪt	
father	'fɑ·ðə(r	'fɑ·ðə
fathers	'fɑ·ðəz	'fɑ·ðəz
fatigue	fə'ti·g	
faucet	'fɔ·sɪt	
faucets	'fɔ·sɪts	
fault	fɔ·lt, fɒlt	
faults	fɔ·lts, fɒlts	
faultless	'fɔ·ltlɪs, 'fɒltlɪs	
faultlessly	'fɔ·ltlɪslɪ, 'fɒltlɪslɪ	
faulty	'fɔ·ltɪ, 'fɒltɪ	
favor (*Amer.*)		

Traditional Spelling	Received Pronunciation	American Variants
favour	ˈfeɪvə(r	ˈfeɪvə
favors (*Amer.*)		
favours	ˈfeɪvəz	ˈfeɪvəz
favored (*Amer.*)		
favoured	ˈfeɪvəd	ˈfeɪvəd
favoring (*Amer.*)		
favouring	ˈfeɪvərɪŋ	
favorable (*Amer.*)		
favourable	ˈfeɪvərəbl̩	
favorably (*Amer.*)		
favourably	ˈfeɪvərəblɪ	
favorite (*Amer.*)		
favourite	ˈfeɪvərɪt	
favorites (*Amer.*)		
favourites	ˈfeɪvərɪts	
fear	fɪə(r	fɪə
fears	fɪəz	fɪəz
feared	fɪəd	fɪəd
fearing	ˈfɪərɪŋ	ˈfɪ·rɪŋ
fearful	ˈfɪəful	ˈfɪəful
fearfully	fɪəfulɪ, ˈfɪəfəlɪ	ˈfɪəfulɪ, ˈfɪəfəlɪ
feast	fi·st	
feasts	fi·sts	
feather	ˈfɛðə(r	ˈfɛðə
feathers	ˈfɛðəz	ˈfɛðəz
feature	ˈfi·tʃə(r	ˈfi·tʃə
features	ˈfi·tʃəz	ˈfi·tʃəz
February	ˈfɛbrʊərɪ	ˈfɛbrʊɛrɪ
FED *from* feed	fɛd	
fee	fi·	
fees	fi·z	
feed	fi·d	
feeds	fi·dz	
fed	fɛd	
feeding	ˈfi·dɪŋ	
feel	fi·l	
feels	fi·lz	
felt	fɛlt	
feeling	ˈfi·lɪŋ	
feelings	ˈfi·lɪŋz	
FEET *plur. of* foot	fi·t	
FELL *from* fall	fɛl	
fellow	ˈfɛloʊ	
fellows	ˈfɛloʊz	
felt	fɛlt	
FELT *from* feel	fɛlt	
female	ˈfi·meɪl	

Traditional Spelling	Received Pronunciation	American Variants
females	ˈfiˑmeɪlz	
feminine	ˈfɛmɪnɪn	
fence	fɛns	
fences	ˈfɛnsiz	
ferocious	fəˈroʊʃəs	
ferry	ˈfɛrɪ	
ferries	ˈfɛrɪz	
fertile	ˈfɜˑtaɪl	ˈfɜətɪl
festival	ˈfɛstɪvḷ, ˈfɛstəvḷ	
festivals	ˈfɛstɪvḷz, ˈfɛstəvḷz	
festivity	fɛsˈtɪvɪtɪ	
festivities	fɛsˈtɪvɪtɪz	
fetch	fɛtʃ	
fetches	ˈfɛtʃɪz	
fetched	fɛtʃt	
fetching	ˈfɛtʃɪŋ	
feudal	ˈfjuˑdəl	
fever	ˈfiˑvə(r	ˈfiˑvə
feverish	ˈfiˑvərɪʃ	
feverishly	ˈfiˑvərɪʃlɪ	
few	fjuˑ	
fewer	ˈfjuˑə(r	ˈfjuˑə
fewest	ˈfjuˑɪst	
fickle	ˈfɪkḷ	
fiction	ˈfɪkʃən	
fictitious	fɪkˈtɪʃəs	
fidget	ˈfɪdʒɪt	
fidgets	ˈfɪdʒɪts	
fidgeted	ˈfɪdʒɪtɪd	
fidgeting	ˈfɪdʒɪtɪŋ	
fidgety	ˈfɪdʒɪtɪ	
field	fiˑld	
fields	fiˑldz	
fierce	fɪəs	fɪəs
fiercer	ˈfɪəsə(r	ˈfɪəsə
fiercest	ˈfɪəsɪst	ˈfɪəsɪst
fiercely	ˈfɪəslɪ	ˈfɪəslɪ
fierceness	ˈfɪəsnɪs	ˈfɪəsnɪs
fifteen	ˈfɪfˈtiˑn	
fifteenth	ˈfɪfˈtiˑnθ	
fifteenths	ˈfɪfˈtiˑnθs	
fifth	fɪf*t*θ	
fifths	fɪf*t*θs	
fifty	ˈfɪftɪ	
fiftieth	ˈfɪftɪɪθ	
fiftieths	ˈfɪftɪɪθs	
fig	fɪg	

Traditional Spelling	Received Pronunciation	American Variants
figs	fɪgz	
fight	faɪt	
fights	faɪts	
fought	fɔ·t	
fighting	'faɪtɪŋ	
fighter	'faɪtə(r	'faɪtə
fighters	'faɪtəz	'faɪtəz
figure	'fɪgə(r	'fɪgjə
figures	'fɪgəz	'fɪgjəz
file	faɪl	
files	faɪlz	
fill	fɪl	
fills	fɪlz	
filled	fɪld	
filling	'fɪlɪŋ	
film	fɪlm	
films	fɪlmz	
filter	'fɪltə(r	'fɪltə
filters	'fɪltəz	'fɪltəz
filthy	'fɪlθɪ	
fin	fɪn	
fins	fɪnz	
final	'faɪnl̩	
finally	'faɪnəlɪ	
finance	fɪ'næns, faɪ'næns	
finances	fɪ'nænsɪz, faɪ'nænsɪz	
financial	fɪ'nænʃəl, faɪ'nænʃəl	
financially	fɪ'nænʃəlɪ, faɪ'nænʃəlɪ	
find	faɪnd	
finds	faɪndz	
found	faʊnd	
finding	'faɪndɪŋ	
finder	'faɪndə(r	'faɪndə
finders	'faɪndəz	'faɪndəz
fine	faɪn	
finer	'faɪnə(r	'faɪnə
finest	'faɪnɪst	
finely	'faɪnlɪ	
fineness	'faɪnnɪs	
finger	'fɪŋgə(r	'fɪŋgə
fingers	'fɪŋgəz	'fɪŋgəz
finish	'fɪnɪʃ	
finishes	'fɪnɪʃɪz	
finished	'fɪnɪʃt	
finishing	'fɪnɪʃɪŋ	
finite	'faɪnaɪt	
fir	fɜ·(r	fɜə·

Traditional Spelling	Received Pronunciation	American Variants
firs	fɜ·z	fɜəz
fire	′faɪə(r	′faɪə
fires	′faɪəz	′faɪəz
fired	′faɪəd	′faɪəd
firing	′faɪərɪŋ	
fireworks	′faɪəwɜks	′faɪəwɜəks
firm	fɜ·m	fɜəm
firms	fɜ·mz	fɜəmz
firmer	′fɜ·mə(r	′fɜəmə
firmest	′fɜ·mɪst	′fɜəmɪst
firmly	′fɜ·mlɪ	′fɜəmlɪ
firmness	′fɜ·mnɪs	′fɜəmnɪs
first	fɜ·st	fɜəst
first-class	′fɜ·st′klɑ·s	′fɜəst′kla·s
firstly	′fɜ·stlɪ	′fɜəstlɪ
fish	fɪʃ	
fishes	′fɪʃɪz	
fished	fɪʃt	
fishing	′fɪʃɪŋ	
fisherman	′fɪʃəmən	′fɪʃəmən
fishermen	′fɪʃəmən	′fɪʃəmən
fist	fɪst	
fists	fɪsts	
fit	fɪt	
fitter	′fɪtə(r	′fɪtə
fittest	′fɪtɪst	
fits	fɪts	
fitted	′fɪtɪd	
fitting	′fɪtɪŋ	
fitness	′fɪtnɪs	
five	faɪv	
fix	fɪks	
fixes	′fɪksɪz	
fixed	fɪkst	
fixing	′fɪksɪŋ	
flag	flæg	
flags	flægz	
flake	fleɪk	
flakes	fleɪks	
flame	fleɪm	
flames	fleɪmz	
flannel	′flænḷ	
flannels	′flænḷz	
flap	flæp	
flaps	flæps	
flapped	flæpt	
flapping	′flæpɪŋ	

Traditional Spelling	Received Pronunciation	American Variants
flash	flæʃ	
flashes	ˈflæʃɪz	
flashed	flæʃt	
flashing	ˈflæʃɪŋ	
flask	flɑˑsk	flaˑsk
flasks	flɑˑsks	flaˑsks
flat	flæt	
flatter	ˈflætə(r	ˈflætə
flattest	ˈflætɪst	
flatness	ˈflætnɪs	
flatten	ˈflætn̩	
flattens	ˈflætn̩z	
flattened	ˈflætn̩d	
flattening	ˈflætn̩ɪŋ	
flatter	ˈflætə(r	ˈflætə
flatters	ˈflætəz	ˈflætəz
flattered	ˈflætəd	ˈflætəd
flattering	ˈflætərɪŋ	
flatterer	ˈflætərə(r	ˈflætərə
flatterers	ˈflætərəz	ˈflætərəz
flavour	ˈfleɪvə(r	ˈfleɪvə
flavours	ˈfleɪvəz	ˈfleɪvəz
flaw	flɔˑ	
flaws	flɔˑz	
flea	fliˑ	
fleas	fliˑz	
fleet	fliˑt	
fleets	fliˑts	
flesh	flɛʃ	
FLEW *from* fly	fluˑ	
flexible	ˈflɛksɪbl̩, ˈflɛksəbl̩	
flight	flaɪt	
flights	flaɪts	
fling	flɪŋ	
flings	flɪŋz	
flung	flʌŋ	
flinging	ˈflɪŋɪŋ	
flint	flɪnt	
float	flout	
floats	flouts	
floated	ˈfloutɪd	
floating	ˈfloutɪŋ	
flock	flɒk	flɑk
flocks	flɒks	flɑks
flood	flʌd	
floods	flʌdz	
flooded	ˈflʌdɪd	

Traditional Spelling	Received Pronunciation	American Variants
flooding	ˈflʌdɪŋ	
floor	flɔˑ(r, flɔə(r	floə
floors	flɔˑz, flɔəz	floəz
flour	ˈflaʊə(r	ˈflaʊə
flourish	ˈflʌrɪʃ	ˈflɜrɪʃ
flourishes	ˈflʌrɪʃɪz	ˈflɜrɪʃɪz
flourished	ˈflʌrɪʃt	ˈflɜrɪʃt
flourishing	ˈflʌrɪʃɪŋ	ˈflɜrɪʃɪŋ
flow	floʊ	
flows	floʊz	
flowed	floʊd	
flowing	ˈfloʊɪŋ	
flower	ˈflaʊə(r	ˈflaʊə
flowers	ˈflaʊəz	flaʊəz
FLOWN *from* fly	floʊn	
fluctuate	ˈflʌktjʊeɪt	
fluctuates	ˈflʌktjʊeɪts	
fluctuated	ˈflʌktjʊeɪtɪd	
fluctuating	ˈflʌktjʊeɪtɪŋ	
fluency	ˈfluˑənsɪ	
fluent	ˈfluˑənt	
fluently	ˈfluˑəntlɪ	
fluid	ˈfluˑɪd	
fluids	ˈfluˑɪdz	
FLUNG *from* fling	flʌŋ	
flute	fluˑt	
flutes	fluˑts	
fly	flaɪ	
flies	flaɪz	
flew	fluˑ	
flown	floʊn	
flying	ˈflaɪɪŋ	
fog	fɒg	
fogs	fɒgz	
foggy	ˈfɒgɪ	
fold	foʊld	
folds	foʊldz	
folded	ˈfoʊldɪd	
folding	ˈfoʊldɪŋ	
folder	ˈfoʊldə(r	ˈfoʊldə
folders	ˈfoʊldəz	ˈfoʊldəz
folk	foʊk	
folks	foʊks	
follow	ˈfɒloʊ	ˈfɑloʊ
follows	ˈfɒloʊz	ˈfɑloʊz
followed	ˈfɒloʊd	ˈfɑloʊd
following	ˈfɒloʊɪŋ	ˈfɑloʊɪŋ

Traditional Spelling	Received Pronunciation	American Variants
follower	ˈfɒlouə(r	ˈfɑlouə
followers	ˈfɒlouəz	ˈfɑlouəz
folly	ˈfɒlɩ	ˈfɑlɩ
fond	fɒnd	fɑnd
fonder	ˈfɒndə(r	ˈfɑndə
fondest	ˈfɒndɩst	ˈfɑndɩst
fondly	ˈfɒndlɩ	ˈfɑndlɩ
fondness	ˈfɒndnɩs	ˈfɑndnɩs
food	fuˑd	
foods	fuˑdz	
fool	fuˑl	
fools	fuˑlz	
foolish	ˈfuˑlɩʃ	
foolishly	ˈfuˑlɩʃlɩ	
foot	fʊt	
feet	fiˑt	
football	ˈfʊtbɔl	
for	fɔˑ(r *s.f.*, fə(r *w.f.*	fɔə *s.f.*, fə *w.f.*
force	fɔˑs	foəs
forces	ˈfɔˑsɩz	ˈfoəsɩz
forced	fɔˑst	foəst
forcing	ˈfɔˑsɩŋ	ˈfoəsɩŋ
ford	fɔˑd	foəd
fords	fɔˑdz	foədz
foreground	ˈfɔˑgraʊnd ˈfɔəgraʊnd	ˈfoəgraʊnd
forehead	ˈfɒrɩd, ˈfɒrəd	
foreheads	ˈfɒrɩdz, ˈfɒrədz	
foreign	ˈfɒrən, ˈfɒrɩn	
foreigner	ˈfɒrənə(r, ˈfɒrɩnə(r	ˈfɒrənə, ˈfɒrɩnə
foreigners	ˈfɒrənəz, ˈfɒrɩnəz	ˈfɒrənəz, ˈfɒrɩnəz
foresee	fɔˈsiˑ, fɔəˈsiˑ	foəˈsiˑ
foresees	fɔˈsiˑz, fɔəˈsiˑz	foəˈsiˑz
foresaw	fɔˈsɔˑ, fɔəˈsɔˑ	foəˈsɔˑ
foreseen	fɔˈsiˑn	foəˈsiˑn
foreseeing	fɔˈsiˑɩŋ	foəˈsiˑɩŋ
forest	ˈfɒrɩst	ˈfɑrɩst
forests	ˈfɒrɩsts	ˈfɑrɩsts
forfeit	ˈfɔˑfɩt	ˈfoəfɩt
forfeits	ˈfɔˑfɩts	ˈfɔəfɩts
forfeited	ˈfɔˑfɩtɩd	ˈfɔəfɩtɩd
forfeiting	ˈfɔˑfɩtɩŋ	ˈfɔəfɩtɩŋ
FORGAVE *from* forgive	fəˈgeɩv	fəˈgeɩv
forge	fɔˑʤ	foəʤ
forges	ˈfɔˑʤɩz	ˈfoəʤɩz
forged	fɔˑʤd	foəʤd

Traditional Spelling	Received Pronunciation	American Variants
forging	ˈfɔˑʤɪŋ	ˈfoəʤɪŋ
forgery	ˈfɔˑʤərɪ	ˈfoəʤərɪ
forgeries	ˈfɔˑʤərɪz	ˈfoəʤərɪz
forget	fəˈgɛt	fəˈgɛt
forgets	fəˈgɛts	fəˈgɛts
forgot	fəˈgɒt	fəˈgɑt
forgotten	fəˈgɒtn̩	fəˈgɑtn̩
forgetting	fəˈgɛtɪŋ	fəˈgɛtɪŋ
forgetful	fəˈgɛtful	fəˈgɛtful
forgetfulness	fəˈgɛtfulnɪs fəˈgɛtfəlnɪs	fəˈgɛtfulnɪs
forgive	fəˈgɪv	fəˈgɪv
forgives	fəˈgɪvz	fəˈgɪvz
forgave	fəˈgeɪv	fəˈgeɪv
forgiven	fəˈgɪvn̩	fəˈgɪvn̩
forgiving	fəˈgɪvɪŋ	fɔˈgɪvɪŋ
forgiveness	fəˈgɪvnɪs	fəˈgɪvnɪs
FORGOT *from* forget	fəˈgɒt	fəˈgɑt
fork	fɔˑk	fɔək
forks	fɔˑks	fɔəks
form	fɔˑm	fɔəm
forms	fɔˑmz	fɔəmz
formed	fɔˑmd	fɔəmd
forming	ˈfɔˑmɪŋ	ˈfɔəmɪŋ
formal	fɔˑməl	fɔəməl
formally	ˈfɔˑməlɪ	ˈfɔəməlɪ
former	ˈfɔˑmə(r	ˈfɔəmə
formerly	ˈfɔˑməlɪ, ˈfɔˑməlɪ	ˈfɔəməlɪ
formula	ˈfɔˑmjulə	ˈfɔəmjulə
formulæ	ˈfɔˑmjuli	ˈfɔəmjuli
formulas	ˈfɔˑmjuləz	ˈfɔəmjuləz
fort	fɔˑt	fɔət
forts	fɔˑts	fɔəts
forthcoming	fɔθˈkʌmɪŋ	fɔəθˈkʌmɪŋ
fortieth	ˈfɔˑtɪɪθ	ˈfɔətɪɪθ
fortification	fɔtɪfɪˈkeɪʃən	fɔətɪfɪˈkeɪʃən
fortifications	fɔtɪfɪˈkeɪʃənz	fɔətɪfɪˈkeɪʃənz
fortify	ˈfɔˑtɪfaɪ	ˈfɔətɪfaɪ
fortifies	ˈfɔˑtɪfaɪz	ˈfɔətɪfaɪz
fortified	ˈfɔˑtɪfaɪd	ˈfɔətɪfaɪd
fortifying	ˈfɔˑtɪfaɪɪŋ	ˈfɔətɪfaɪɪŋ
fortnight	ˈfɔˑtnaɪt	ˈfɔətnaɪt
fortnightly	ˈfɔˑtnaɪtlɪ	ˈfɔətnaɪtlɪ
fortress	ˈfɔˑtrɪs	ˈfɔətrɪs
fortresses	ˈfɔˑtrɪsɪz	ˈfɔətrɪsɪz
fortunate	ˈfɔˑʧn̩ɪt	ˈfɔəʧn̩ɪt
fortunately	ˈfɔˑʧn̩ɪtlɪ	ˈfɔəʧn̩ɪtlɪ

Traditional Spelling	Received Pronunciation	American Variants
fortune	′fɔ·tʃən	′fɔətʃən
fortunes	′fɔ·tʃənz	′fɔətʃənz
forty	′fɔ·tɪ	′fɔətɪ
forward	′fɔ·wəd	′fɔəwəd
forwards	′fɔ·wədz	′fɔəwədz
fossil	′fɒsɨl	′fɑsɨl
fossils	′fɒsɨlz	′fɑsɨlz
FOUGHT *from* fight	fɔ·t	
foul	faʊl	
found	faʊnd	
founds	faʊndz	
founded	′faʊndɪd	
founding	′faʊndɪŋ	
FOUND *from* find	faʊnd	
founder	′faʊndə(r	′faʊndə
founders	′faʊndəz	′faʊndəz
foundation	faʊn′deɪʃən	
foundations	faʊn′deɪʃənz	
fountain	′faʊntɪn, ′faʊntən	′faʊntn̩
fountains	′faʊntɪnz, ′faʊntənz	′faʊntn̩z
four	fɔ·(r, fɔə(r	foə
fourteen	′fɔ·′ti·n	′foə′ti·n
fourteenth	′fɔ·′ti·nθ	′foə′ti·nθ
fourteenths	′fɔ·′ti·nθs	′foə′ti·nθs
fourth	fɔ·θ, fɔəθ	foəθ
fourths	fɔ·θs, fɔəθs	foəθs
fourthly	′fɔ·θlɪ, ′fɔəθlɪ	′foəθlɪ
fowl	faʊl	
fowls	faʊlz	
fox	fɒks	fɑks
foxes	′fɒksɪz	′fɑksɪz
fraction	′frækʃən	
fractions	′frækʃənz	
fragile	′frædʒaɪl	′frædʒɪl
fragment	′frægmənt	
fragments	′frægmənts	
fragrance	′freɪgrəns	
fragrant	′freɪgrənt	
frame	freɪm	
frames	freɪmz	
framed	freɪmd	
framing	′freɪmɪŋ	
France	frɑ·ns	fra·ns
frank	fræŋk	
frankly	′fræŋklɪ	
frankness	′fræŋknɪs	′fræŋknɪs
fraud	frɔ·d	

Traditional Spelling	Received Pronunciation	American Variants
frauds	frɔˑdz	
free	friˑ	
freer	ˈfriˑə(r	ˈfriˑə
freest	ˈfriˑɪst	
freely	ˈfriˑlɪ	
freedom	ˈfriˑdəm	
freeze	friˑz	
freezes	ˈfriˑzɪz	
froze	frouz	
frozen	ˈfrouzn̩	
freezing	ˈfriˑzɪŋ	
freight	freɪt	
freights	freɪts	
French	frɛntʃ	
Frenchman	ˈfrɛntʃmən	
Frenchmen	ˈfrɛntʃmən	
frequency	ˈfriˑkwənsɪ	
frequent, ***adj.***	ˈfriˑkwənt	
frequently	ˈfriˑkwəntlɪ	
fresh	frɛʃ	
fresher	ˈfrɛʃə(r	ˈfrɛʃə
freshest	ˈfrɛʃɪst	
freshly	ˈfrɛʃlɪ	
freshness	ˈfrɛʃnɪs	
friction	ˈfrɪkʃən	
Friday	ˈfraɪdɪ	
Fridays	ˈfraɪdɪz	
FRIED *from* fry	fraɪd	
friend	frɛnd	
friends	frɛndz	
friendly	ˈfrɛndlɪ	
fright	fraɪt	
frights	fraɪts	
frighten	ˈfraɪtn̩	
frightens	ˈfraɪtn̩z	
frightened	ˈfraɪtn̩d	
frightening	ˈfraɪtn̩ɪŋ	
frightful	ˈfraɪtful	
frightfully	ˈfraɪtfulɪ, ˈfraɪtfəlɪ	
frock	frɒk	frak
frocks	frɒks	fraks
frockcoat	ˈfrɒkˈkout	ˈfrakˈkout
frockcoats	ˈfrɒkˈkouts	ˈfrakˈkouts
frog	frɒg	
frogs	frɒgz	
from	frɒm *s.f.*, frəm *w.f.*	fram *s.f.*, frəm *w.f.*
front	frʌnt	

Traditional Spelling	Received Pronunciation	American Variants
fronts	frʌnts	
frontier	ˈfrʌntjə(r, ˈfrʌntɪə(r	ˈfrʌntɪə, frʌnˈtɪə
frontiers	ˈfrʌntjəz, ˈfrʌntɪəz	ˈfrʌntɪəz, frʌnˈtɪəz
frost	frɔst, frɒst	
frown	fraʊn	
frowns	fraʊnz	
frowned	fraʊnd	
frowning	ˈfraʊnɪŋ	
FROZE *from* freeze	frouz	
FROZEN *from* freeze	frouzn̩	
fruit	fruˑt	
fruits	fruˑts	
fry	fraɪ	
fries	fraɪz	
fried	fraɪd	
frying	ˈfraɪɪŋ	
fuel	ˈfjuˑəl	
fugitive	ˈfjuˑʤɪtɪv, ˈfjuˑʤətɪv	
fugitives	ˈfjuˑʤɪtɪvz	
	ˈfjuˑʤətɪvz	
fulfil	fʊlˈfɪl	
fulfils	fʊlˈfɪlz	
fulfilled	fʊlˈfɪld	
fulfilling	fʊlˈfɪlɪŋ	
full	fʊl	
fuller	ˈfʊlə(r	ˈfʊlə
fullest	ˈfʊlɪst	
fullness	ˈfʊlnɪs	
fully	ˈfʊlɪ	
fun	fʌn	
function	ˈfʌŋ*k*ʃən	
functions	ˈfʌŋ*k*ʃənz	
functioned	ˈfʌŋ*k*ʃənd	
functioning	ˈfʌŋ*k*ʃn̩ɪŋ	
fund	fʌnd	
funds	fʌndz	
fundamental	fʌndəˈmentl̩	
fundamentals	fʌndəˈmentl̩z	
fundamentally	fʌndəˈmentəlɪ	
funeral	ˈfjuˑnərəl	
funerals	ˈfjuˑnərəlz	
funnel	ˈfʌnl̩	
funnels	ˈfʌnl̩z	
funnily	ˈfʌnɪlɪ	
funny	ˈfʌnɪ	
funnier	ˈfʌnɪə(r	ˈfʌnɪə
funniest	ˈfʌnɪɪst	

Traditional Spelling	Received Pronunciation	American Variants
fur	fɜ·(r	fɜə
furs	fɜ·z	fɜəz
furious	'fjuərɪəs	'fjʊ·rɪəs
furiously	'fjuərɪəslɪ	'fjʊ'rɪəslɪ
furnace	'fɜ·nɪs	'fɜənɪs
furnaces	'fɜ·nɪsɪz	'fɜənɪsɪz
furnish	'fɜ·nɪʃ	'fɜənɪʃ
furnishes	'fɜ·nɪʃɪz	'fɜənɪʃɪz
furnished	'fɜ·nɪʃt	'fɜənɪʃt
furnishing	'fɜ·nɪʃɪŋ	'fɜənɪʃɪŋ
furniture	'fɜ·nɪtʃə(r	'fɜənɪtʃə
furry	'fɜ·rɪ	
further	'fɜ·ðə(r	'fɜəðə
furthers	'fɜ·ðəz	'fɜəðəz
furthered	'fɜ·ðəd	'fɜəðəd
furthering	'fɜ·ðərɪŋ	'fɜəðərɪŋ
furthermore	'fɜ·ðə'mɔ(r	'fɜəðə'moə
	'fɜ·ðə'mɔə(r	
furthest	'fɜ·ðɪst	'fɜəðɪst
fury	'fjuərɪ	'fjʊ·rɪ
furies	'fjuərɪz	'fjʊ·rɪz
fuse	fju·z	
fuses	'fju·zɪz	
fused	fju·zd	
fusing	'fju·zɪŋ	
fuss	fʌs	
fussy	'fʌsɪ	
futile	'fju·taɪl	'fju·tɪl
futility	fju'tɪlɪtɪ	
future	'fju·tʃə(r	'fju·tʃə

G

Traditional Spelling	Received Pronunciation	American Variants
G	dʒi·	
G's	dʒi·z	
gaiety	'geɪətɪ, 'geɪɪtɪ	
gaily	'geɪlɪ	
gain	geɪn	
gains	geɪnz	
gained	geɪnd	
gaining	'geɪnɪŋ	
gaiter	'geɪtə(r	'geɪtə
gaiters	'geɪtəz	'geɪtəz
gale	geɪl	
gales	geɪlz	

Traditional Spelling	Received Pronunciation	American Variants
gallant, *brave*	ˈgælənt	
amourous	gəˈlænt	
gallantly, *bravely*	ˈgæləntlɪ	
amorously	gəˈlæntlɪ	
gallantry	ˈgæləntrɪ	
gallery	ˈgælərɪ	
galleries	ˈgælərɪz	
gallop	ˈgæləp	
gallops	ˈgæləps	
galloped	ˈgæləpt	
galloping	ˈgæləpɪŋ	
gamble	ˈgæmbl̩	
gambles	ˈgæmbl̩z	
gambled	ˈgæmbl̩d	
gambling	ˈgæmblɪŋ	
gambler	ˈgæmblə(r	ˈgæmblə
gamblers	ˈgæmbləz	ˈgæmbləz
game	geɪm	
games	geɪmz	
gang	gæŋ	
gangs	gæŋz	
gangway	gæŋweɪ	
gangways	gæŋweɪz	
gaol	ʤeɪl	
gaols	ʤeɪlz	
gap	gæp	
gaps	gæps	
garage	ˈgærɑʒ, gəˈrɑˑʒ	
garages	ˈgærɑʒɪz, gəˈrɑˑʒɪz	
garden	ˈgɑˑdn̩	ˈgɑədn̩
gardens	ˈgɑˑdn̩z	ˈgɑədn̩z
gardening	ˈgɑˑdn̩ɪŋ	
gardener	ˈgɑˑdn̩ə(r	ˈgɑədn̩ə
gardeners	ˈgɑˑdn̩əz	ˈgɑədn̩əz
garrison	ˈgærɪsən	
garrisons	ˈgærɪsənz	
garter	ˈgɑˑtə(r	ˈgɑətə
garters	ˈgɑˑtəz	ˈgɑətəz
gas	gæs	
gases	ˈgæsɪz	
gaseous	ˈgeɪzɪəs, ˈgæzɪəs, ˈgæzjəs, ˈgæsɪəs, ˈgeɪsjəs, ˈgæsjəs	
gasoline	gæsəˈliˑn, ˈgæsəlin	
gasp	gɑˑsp	gaˑsp
gasps	gɑˑsps	gaˑsps
gasped	gɑˑspt	gaˑspt

Traditional Spelling	Received Pronunciation	American Variants
gasping	ˈgɑˑspɪŋ	ˈgaˑspɪŋ
gate	geɪt	
gates	geɪts	
gateway	ˈgeɪtweɪ	
gateways	ˈgeɪtweɪz	
gather	ˈgæðə(r	ˈgæðə
gathers	ˈgæðəz	ˈgæðəz
gathered	ˈgæðəd	ˈgæðəd
gathering	ˈgæðərɪŋ	
gatherings	ˈgæðərɪŋz	
gaudy	ˈgɔˑdɪ	
gauge	geɪʤ	
gauges	ˈgeɪʤɪz	
gauze	gɔˑz	
GAVE *from* give	geɪv	
gay	geɪ	
gayer	ˈgeɪə(r	ˈgeɪə
gayest	ˈgeɪɪst	
gayety (*Amer.*)	ˈgeɪətɪ, ˈgeɪɪtɪ	
gaze	geɪz	
gazes	ˈgeɪzɪz	
gazed	geɪzd	
gazing	ˈgeɪzɪŋ	
GEESE, *plur. of* goose	giˑs	
gender	ˈʤendə(r	ˈʤendə
genders	ˈʤendəz	ˈʤendəz
general	ʤenərəl	
generals	ˈʤenərəlz	
generally	ˈʤenərəlɪ	
generation	ʤenəˈreɪʃən	
generations	ʤenəˈreɪʃənz	
generosity	ʤenɔˈrɒsɪtɪ	ʤenəˈrɑsɪtɪ
generous	ˈʤenərəs	
generously	ˈʤenərəslɪ	
genial	ˈʤiˑnjəl	
genially	ˈʤiˑnjəlɪ	
genius	ˈʤiˑnjəs	
geniuses	ˈʤiˑnjəsɪz	
gentle	ˈʤentl̩	
gentler	ˈʤentlə(r	ˈʤentlə
gentlest	ˈʤentlɪst	
gently	ˈʤentlɪ	
gentleman	ˈʤentl̩mən	
gentlemen	ˈʤentl̩mən	
genuine	ˈʤenjuɪn	
genuinely	ˈʤenjuɪnlɪ	
genuineness	ˈʤenjuɪnnɪs	

Traditional Spelling	Received Pronunciation	American Variants
geographical	dʒioʊ'græfɪkəl	
	dʒiə'græfɪkəl	
geographically	dʒioʊ'græfɪkəlɪ	
	dʒiə'græfɪkəlɪ	
geography	dʒi'ɒgrəfɪ	dʒi'ɑgrəfɪ
geological	dʒioʊ'lɒdʒɪkəl	dʒioʊ'lɑdʒɪkəl
	dʒiə'lɒdʒɪkəl	dʒiə'lɑdʒɪkəl
geologist	dʒi'ɒlədʒɪst	dʒi'ɑlədʒɪst
geologists	dʒi'ɒlədʒɪsts	dʒi'ɑlədʒɪsts
geology	dʒi'ɒlədʒɪ	dʒi'ɑlədʒɪ
geometrical	dʒioʊ'mɛtrɪkəl	
	dʒiə'mɛtrɪkəl	
geometrically	dʒioʊ'mɛtrɪkəlɪ	
	dʒiə'mɛtrɪkəlɪ	
geometry	dʒi'ɑmɪtrɪ	dʒi'ɑmɪtrɪ
germ	dʒɜ·m	dʒɝm
germs	dʒɜ·mz	dʒɝmz
German	'dʒɜ·mən	'dʒɝmən
Germans	'dʒɜ·mənz	'dʒɝmənz
Germany	'dʒɜ·mənɪ	'dʒɝmənɪ
gesture	'dʒɛstʃə(r	'dʒɛstʃɚ
gestures	'dʒɛstʃəz	'dʒɛstʃɚz
get	gɛt	
gets	gɛts	
got	gɒt	gɑt
gotten	'gɒtn̩	'gɑtn̩
getting	'gɛtɪŋ	
ghastly	'gɑ·stlɪ	'ga·stlɪ
ghost	goʊst	
ghosts	goʊsts	
giant	'dʒaɪənt	
giants	'dʒaɪənts	
giddy	'gɪdɪ	
giddiness	'gɪdɪnɪs	
gift	gɪft	
gifts	gɪfts	
gifted	'gɪftɪd	
gin	dʒɪn	
ginger	'dʒɪndʒə(r	'dʒɪndʒɚ
gipsy	'dʒɪpsɪ	
gipsies	'dʒɪpsɪz	
giraffe	dʒɪ'rɑ·f	dʒɪ'ra·f
giraffes	dʒɪ'rɑ·fs	dʒɪ'ra·fs
girder	'gɜ·də(r	'gɝdɚ
girders	'gɜ·dəz	'gɝdɚz
girl	gɜ·l	gɝl
girls	gɜ·lz	gɝlz

Traditional Spelling	Received Pronunciation	American Variants
gist	ʤɪst	
give	gɪv	
gives	gɪvz	
gave	geɪv	
given	ˈgɪvn̩	
giving	ˈgɪvɪŋ	
glad	glæˑd	
gladder	ˈglædə(r, ˈglæˑdə(r	ˈglædə
gladdest	ˈglædɪst, ˈglæˑdɪst	
gladly	ˈglæˑdlɪ	
gladness	ˈglæˑdnɪs	
glance	glɑˑns	glaˑns
glances	ˈglɑˑnsɪz	ˈglaˑnsɪz
glanced	ˈglɑˑnst	ˈglaˑnst
glancing	ˈglɑˑnsɪŋ	ˈglaˑnsɪŋ
glass	glɑˑs	glaˑs
glasses	ˈglɑˑsɪz	ˈglaˑsɪz
glassful	ˈglɑˑsful	ˈglaˑsful
glassfuls	ˈglɑˑsfulz	ˈglaˑsfulz
glassy	ˈglɑˑsɪ	ˈglaˑsɪ
gleam	gliˑm	
gleams	gliˑmz	
gleamed	gliˑmd	
gleaming	ˈgliˑmɪŋ	
glide	glaɪd	
glides	glaɪdz	
glided	ˈglaɪdɪd	
gliding	ˈglaɪdɪŋ	
glimpse	ˈglɪmps	
glimpses	ˈglɪmpsɪz	
glitter	ˈglɪtə(r	ˈglɪtə
glitters	ˈglɪtəz	ˈglɪtəz
glittered	ˈglɪtəd	ˈglɪtəd
glittering	ˈglɪtərɪŋ	
globe	gloʊb	
globes	gloʊbz	
gloom	gluˑm	
gloomy	ˈgluˑmɪ	
glorify	ˈglɔˑrɪfaɪ	ˈgloˑrɪfaɪ
glorifies	ˈglɔˑrɪfaɪz	ˈgloˑrɪfaɪz
glorified	ˈglɔˑrɪfaɪd	ˈgloˑrɪfaɪd
glorifying	ˈglɔˑrɪfaɪɪŋ	ˈgloˑrɪfaɪɪŋ
glorious	ˈglɔˑrɪəs	ˈgloˑrɪəs
gloriously	ˈglɔˑrɪəslɪ	ˈgloˑrɪəslɪ
glory	ˈglɔˑrɪ	ˈgloˑrɪ
glories	ˈglɔˑrɪz	ˈgloˑrɪz
glove	glʌv	

Traditional Spelling	Received Pronunciation	American Variants
gloves	glʌvz	
glue	gluˑ	
glues	gluˑz	
glued	gluˑd	
gluing	′gluˑɪŋ	
glycerine	′glɪsə′riˑn, ′glɪsərɪn	
gnaw	nɔˑ	
gnaws	nɔˑz	
gnawed	nɔˑd	
gnawing	′nɔˑɪŋ	
go	goʊ	
goes	goʊz	
went	wɛnt	
gone	gɒn, gɔn	
going	′goʊɪŋ	
goal	goʊl	
goals	goʊlz	
goat	goʊt	
goats	goʊts	
god	gɒd	gɑd
gods	gɒdz	gɑdz
godchild	′gɒdtʃaɪld	′gɑdtʃaɪld
godchildren	′gɒdtʃɪldrən	′gɑdtʃɪldrən
goddess	′gɒdɪs	′gɑdɪs
goddesses	′gɒdɪsɪz	′gɑdɪsɪz
godfather	′gɒdfɑðə(r	′gɑdfaðə
godfathers	′gɒdfɑðəz	′gɑdfaðəz
godmother	′gɒdmʌðə(r	′gɑdmʌðə
godmothers	′gɒdmʌðəz	′gɑdmʌðəz
gold	goʊld	
golden	′goʊldn̩	
goldfish	′goʊldfɪʃ	
goldfishes	′goʊldfɪʃɪz	
golf	gɒlf, gɒf	
golfer	′gɒlfə(r	′gɒlfə
golfers	′gɒlfəz	′gɒlfəz
GONE *from* go	gɒn, gɔn	
gong	gɒŋ	
gongs	gɒŋz	
good	gʊd	
good-bye	′gʊd′baɪ	
good-evening, *on meeting*	gʊd′iˑvnɪŋ	
on parting	′gʊd′iˑvnɪŋ	
good-humor (*Amer.*)		
good-humour	′gʊd′*h*juˑmə(r gʊd′*h*juˑmə(r	′gʊd′hjuˑmə gʊd′hjuˑmə

Traditional Spelling	Received Pronunciation	American Variants
good-humored (*Am.*)		
good-humoured	'gʊd'*h*ju·məd	'gʊd'hju·məd
	gʊd'*h*ju·məd	gʊd'hju·məd
goodish	'gʊdɪʃ	
good-morning, *on meeting*	gʊd'mɔ·nɪŋ	gʊd'mɔənɪŋ
on parting	'gʊd'mɔ·nɪŋ	'gʊd'mɔənɪŋ
good-nature	'gʊd'neɪtʃə(r	'gʊd'neɪtʃə
good-natured	'gʊd'neɪtʃəd	'gʊd'neɪtʃəd
goodness	'gʊdnɪs	
good-night	'gʊd'naɪt	
goods	gʊdz	
goodwill	'gʊd'wɪl	
goose	gu·s	
geese	gi·s	
gorge	gɔ·dʒ	gɔədʒ
gorges	'gɔ·dʒɪz	'gɔədʒɪz
gorilla	gə'rɪlə	
gorillas	gə'rɪləz	
gospel	'gɒspəl	'gɑspl̩
gospels	'gɒspəlz	'gɑspl̩z
gossip	'gɒsɪp	'gɑsɪp
gossips	'gɒsɪps	'gɑsɪps
gossiped	'gɒsɪpt	'gɑsɪpt
gossiping	'gɒsɪpɪŋ	'gɑsɪpɪŋ
GOT *from* get	gɒt	' gɑt
GOTTEN *from* get	'gɒtn̩	'gɑtn̩
gouge	gaʊdʒ	
gouges	'gaʊdʒɪz	
gouged	gaʊdʒd	
gouging	'gaʊdʒɪŋ	
govern	'gʌvən, 'gʌvn̩	'gʌvən
governs	'gʌvənz	'gʌvənz
governed	'gʌvənd	'gʌvənd
governing	'gʌvənɪŋ	'gʌvənɪŋ
governess	'gʌvənɪs	'gʌvənɪs
governesses	'gʌvənɪsɪz	'gʌvənɪsɪz
government	'gʌvənmənt	'gʌvənmənt
governments	'gʌvənmənts	'gʌvənmənts
governor	'gʌvənə(r	'gʌvənə
governors	'gʌvənəz	'gʌvənəz
grab	græb	
grabs	græbz	
grabbed	'græbd	
grabbing	'græbɪŋ	
grace	greɪs	
graceful	'greɪsfʊl	

Traditional Spelling	Received Pronunciation	American Variants
gracefully	'greɪsfʊlɪ, 'greɪsf*ə*lɪ	
gracious	'greɪʃəs	
graciously	'greɪʃəslɪ	
grade	greɪd	
grades	greɪdz	
graded	'greɪdɪd	
grading	'greɪdɪŋ	
gradual	'grædjʊəl	
gradually	'grædjʊəlɪ	
graduate, *noun*	'grædjʊɪt	
graduates	'grædjʊɪts	
graduate, *verb*	'grædjʊeɪt	'grædjʊɪt
graduates	'grædjʊeɪts	'grædjʊɪts
graduated	'grædjʊeɪtɪd	'grædjʊɪtɪd
graduating	'grædjʊeɪtɪŋ	'grædjʊɪtɪŋ
graduation	'grædjʊ'eɪʃ*ə*n	
graft	grɑ·ft	gra·ft
grafts	grɑ·fts	gra·fts
grafted	'grɑ·ftɪd	'gra·ftɪd
grafting	'grɑ·ftɪŋ	'gra·ftɪŋ
grain	greɪn	
grains	greɪnz	
gram	græm	
grams	græmz	
grammar	'græmə(r	'græmə
grammars	'græməz	'græməz
grammarian	grə'mɛərɪən	grə'mɛ·rɪən
grammarians	grə'mɛərɪənz	grə'mɛ·rɪənz
grammatical	grə'mætɪk*ə*l	
grammatically	grə'mætɪk*ə*lɪ	
gramophone	'græməfoʊn	
gramophones	'græməfoʊnz	
grand	grænd	
grander	'grændə(r	'grændə
grandest	'grændɪst	
grandly	'grændlɪ	
grandchild	'græn*d*tʃaɪld	
grandchildren	'græn*d*tʃɪldrən	
granddaughter	'græn*d*dɔtə(r	'græn*d*dɔtə
granddaughters	'græn*d*dɔtəz	'græn*d*dɔtəz
grandeur	'grændʒə(r 'grændjə(r	'grændʒə
grandfather	'græn*d*fɑðə(r	'græn*d*fɑðə
grandfathers	'græn*d*fɑðəz	'græn*d*fɑðəz
grandmother	'græn*d*mʌðə(r	'græn*d*mʌðə
grandmothers	'græn*d*mʌðəz	'græn*d*mʌðəz
grandparent	'græn*d*pɛər*ə*nt	'græn*d*pɛ·r*ə*nt

Traditional Spelling	Received Pronunciation	American Variants
grandparents	ˈgrændpɛərənts	ˈgrændpɛˑrənts
grandson	ˈgrændsʌn	
grandsons	ˈgrændsʌnz	
granite	ˈgrænɪt	
grant	grɑˑnt	graˑnt
grants	grɑˑnts	graˑnts
granted	ˈgrɑˑntɪd	ˈgraˑntɪd
granting	ˈgrɑˑntɪŋ	ˈgraˑntɪŋ
grape	greɪp	
grapes	greɪps	
graph	græf, grɑˑf	graˑf
graphs	græfs, grɑˑfs	graˑfs
graphic	ˈgræfɪk	
grasp	grɑˑsp	graˑsp
grasps	grɑˑsps	graˑsps
grasped	grɑˑspt	graˑspt
grasping	ˈgrɑˑspɪŋ	ˈgraˑspɪŋ
grass	grɑˑs	graˑs
grasses	ˈgrɑˑsɪz	ˈgraˑsɪz
grassy	ˈgrɑˑsɪ	ˈgraˑsɪ
grateful	ˈgreɪtfʊl	
gratefully	ˈgreɪtfʊlɪ, ˈgreɪtfəlɪ	
gratification	grætɪfɪˈkeɪʃən	
gratify	ˈgrætɪfaɪ	
gratifies	ˈgrætɪfaɪz	
gratified	ˈgrætɪfaɪd	
gratifying	ˈgrætɪfaɪɪŋ	
gratis	ˈgreɪtɪs	
gratitude	ˈgrætɪtjud	
grave	greɪv	
graves	greɪvz	
graver	ˈgreɪvə(r	ˈgreɪvə
gravest	ˈgreɪvɪst	
gravely	ˈgreɪvlɪ	
gravel	ˈgrævəl	
gravitate	ˈgrævɪteɪt	
gravitates	ˈgrævɪteɪts	
gravitated	ˈgrævɪteɪtɪd	
gravitating	ˈgrævɪteɪtɪŋ	
gravitation	grævɪˈteɪʃən	
gravity	ˈgrævɪtɪ	
gravy	ˈgreɪvɪ	
gray	greɪ	
grayer	ˈgreɪə(r	ˈgreɪə
grayest	ˈgreɪɪst	
gray-haired	ˈgreɪˈhɛəd	ˈgreɪˈhɛəd
gray-headed	ˈgreɪˈhɛdɪd	

Traditional Spelling	Received Pronunciation	American Variants
grease, ***noun***	griˑs	
greases	ˈgriˑsɪz	
grease, ***verb***	griˑz	
greases	ˈgriˑzɪz	
greased	griˑzd	
greasing	ˈgriˑzɪŋ	
greasy	ˈgriˑzɪ, ˈgriˑsɪ	
great	greɪt	
greater	ˈgreɪtə(r	ˈgreɪtə
greatest	ˈgreɪtɪst	
greatly	ˈgreɪtlɪ	
greatness	ˈgreɪtnɪs	
Greece	griˑs	
greedy	griˑdɪ	
greedier	ˈgriˑdɪə(r	ˈgriˑdɪə
greadiest	ˈgriˑdɪɪst	
greedily	ˈgriˑdɪlɪ	
greediness	ˈgriˑdɪnɪs	
Greek	griˑk	
Greeks	griˑks	
green	griˑn	
greener	ˈgriˑnə(r	ˈgriˑnə
greenest	ˈgriˑnɪst	
greenness	ˈgriˑnnɪs	
greengrocer	ˈgriˑngrousə(r	ˈgriˑngrousə
greengrocers	ˈgriˑngrousəz	ˈgriˑngrousəz
greenish	ˈgriˑnɪʃ	
greet	griˑt	
greets	griˑts	
greeted	ˈgriˑtɪd	
greeting	ˈgriˑtɪŋ	
greetings	ˈgriˑtɪŋz	
GREW *from* grow	gruˑ	
grey	greɪ	
greyer	ˈgreɪə(r	ˈgreɪə
greyest	ˈgreɪɪst	
greyness	ˈgreɪnɪs	
grey-haired	ˈgreɪˈhɛəd	ˈgreɪˈhɛəd
grey-headed	ˈgreɪˈhɛdɪd	
greyish	ˈgreɪɪʃ	
grief	griˑf	
grievance	ˈgriˑvəns	
grievances	ˈgriˑvənsɪz	
grieve	griˑv	
grieves	griˑvz	
grieved	griˑvd	
grieving	ˈgriˑvɪŋ	

Traditional Spelling	Received Pronunciation	American Variants
grimace	grɪ'meɪs	
grimaces	grɪ'meɪsiz	
grimy	'graɪmɪ	
grin	grɪn	
grins	grɪnz	
grinned	grɪnd	
grinning	'grɪnɪŋ	
grind	graɪnd	
grinds	graɪndz	
ground	graʊnd	
grinding	'graɪndɪŋ	
grip	grɪp	
grips	grɪps	
gripped	grɪpt	
gripping	'grɪpɪŋ	
grit	grɪt	
gritty	'grɪtɪ	
groan	groʊn	
groans	groʊnz	
groaned	groʊnd	
groaning	'groʊnɪŋ	
grocer	'groʊsə(r	'groʊsə
grocers	'groʊsəz	'groʊsəz
grocery	'groʊsərɪ	
groceries	'groʊsərɪz	
groom	grʊm, gru·m	
grooms	grʊmz, gru·mz	
groove	gru·v	
grooves	gru·vz	
grooved	gru·vd	
grope	groʊp	
gropes	groʊps	
groped	groʊpt	
groping	'groʊpɪŋ	
gross	groʊs	
grossly	'groʊslɪ	
ground	graʊnd	
grounds	graʊndz	
grounded	'graʊndɪd	
grounding	'graʊndɪŋ	
GROUND *from* grind	graʊnd	
ground-floor	'graʊnd'flɔ·(r 'graʊnd'flɔə(r	'graʊn*d*'floə
groundless	'graʊndlɪs	
groundlessly	'graʊndlɪslɪ	
groundwork	'graʊndwɜk	'graʊndwɜək
group	gru·p	

Traditional Spelling	Received Pronunciation	American Variants
groups	gruˑps	
grouped	gruˑpt	
grouping	′gruˑpɪŋ	
grove	groʊv	
groves	groʊvz	
grow	groʊ	
grows	groʊz	
grew	gruˑ	
grown	groʊn	
growing	′groʊɪŋ	
grower	′groʊə(r	′groʊə
growers	′groʊəz	′groʊəz
growl	graʊl	
growls	graʊlz	
growled	graʊld	
growling	′graʊlɪŋ	
growth	groʊθ	
growths	groʊθs	
grudge	grʌʤ	
grudges	′grʌʤɪz	
gruff	grʌf	
gruffly	′grʌflɪ	
gruffness	′grʌfnɪs	
grumble	′grʌmbḷ	
grumbles	′grʌmbḷz	
grumbled	′grʌmbḷd	
grumbling	′grʌmblɪŋ	
grumbler	′grʌmblə(r	′grʌmblə
grumblers	′grʌmbləz	′grʌmbləz
grunt	grʌnt	
grunts	grʌnts	
grunted	′grʌntɪd	
grunting	′grʌntɪŋ	
guarantee	gærən′tiˑ	
guarantees	gærən′tiˑz	
guaranteed	gærən′tiˑd	
guaranteeing	gærən′tiˑɪŋ	
guard	gɑˑd	gɑəd
guards	gɑˑdz	gɑədz
guarded	′gɑˑdɪd	′gɑədɪd
guarding	′gɑˑdɪŋ	′gɑədɪŋ
guardian	′gɑˑdjən, ′gɑˑdɪən	′gɑədjən, ′gɑədɪən
guess	gɛs	
guesses	′gɛsɪz	
guessed	gɛst	
guessing	′gɛsɪŋ	
guesser	′gɛsə(r	′gɛsə

Traditional Spelling	Received Pronunciation	American Variants
guessers	ˈgɛsəz	ˈgɛsəz
guesswork	ˈgɛswɜk	ˈgɛswɜək
guest	gɛst	
guests	gɛsts	
guidance	ˈgaɪdn̩s	
guide	gaɪd	
guides	gaɪdz	
guided	ˈgaɪdɪd	
guiding	ˈgaɪdɪŋ	
guilt	gɪlt	
guilty	ˈgɪltɪ	
guiltier	ˈgɪltɪə(r	ˈgɪltɪə
guiltiest	ˈgɪltɪɪst	
guiltily	ˈgɪltɪlɪ	
gulf	gʌlf	
gulfs	gʌlfs	
gum	gʌm	
gums	gʌmz	
gummed	gʌmd	
gumming	ˈgʌmɪŋ	
gun	gʌn	
guns	gʌnz	
gunner	ˈgʌnə(r	ˈgʌnə
gunners	ˈgʌnəz	ˈgʌnəz
gunpowder	ˈgʌnpaʊdə(r	ˈgʌnpaʊdə
gust	gʌst	
gusts	gʌsts	
gutter	ˈgʌtə(r	ˈgʌtə
gutters	ˈgʌtəz	ˈgʌtəz
gymnasium	ʤɪmˈneɪzjəm ʤɪmˈneɪzɪəm	
gymnasiums	ʤɪmˈneɪzjəmz ʤɪmˈneɪzɪəmz	
gymnast	ˈʤɪmnæst	
gymnasts	ˈʤɪmnæsts	
gymnastic, *adj.*	ʤɪmˈnæstɪk	
gymnastics, *noun*	ʤɪmˈnæstɪks	
gyroscope	ˈgaɪərəskoʊp ˈʤaɪərəskoʊp	
gyroscopes	ˈgaɪərəskoʊps ˈʤaɪərəskoʊps	

Traditional Spelling	Received Pronunciation	American Variants

H

H	eɪtʃ	
H's	ˈeɪtʃɪz	
ha	hɑ·	
habit	ˈhæbɪt	
habits	ˈhæbɪts	
habitual	həˈbɪtjuəl, hæˈbɪtjuəl	
habitually	həˈbɪtjuəlɪ, hæˈbɪtjuəlɪ	
HAD *from* have	hæd *s.f.*, *h*əd, d *w.fs.*	
HADN'T	ˈhædn̩t	
hail	heɪl	
hair	hɛə(r	hɛə
hairs	hɛəz	hɛəz
hairbrush	ˈhɛəbrʌʃ	ˈhɛəbrʌʃ
hairbrushes	ˈhɛəbrʌʃɪz	ˈhɛəbrʌʃɪz
hairy	ˈhɛərɪ	ˈhɛ·rɪ
half	hɑ·f	ha·f
halves	hɑ·vz	ha·vz
half-a-crown	ˈhɑ·fəˈkraʊn	ˈha·fəˈkraʊn
half-a-dozen	ˈhɑ·fəˈdʌzn̩	ˈha·fəˈdʌzn̩
half-an-hour	ˈhɑ·fəˈnaʊə(r	ˈha·fəˈnaʊə
half-crown	ˈhɑ·fˈkraʊn	ˈha·fˈkraʊn
half-crowns	ˈhɑ·fˈkraʊnz	ˈha·fˈkraʊnz
half-dozen	ˈhɑ·fˈdʌzn̩	ˈha·fˈdʌzn̩
half-dozens	ˈhɑ·fˈdʌzn̩z	ˈha·fˈdʌzn̩z
half-hearted	ˈhɑ·fˈhɑ·tɪd	ˈha·fˈhɑətɪd
half-heartedly	ˈhɑ·fˈhɑ·tɪdlɪ	ˈha·fˈhɑətɪdlɪ
half-hour	ˈhɑ·fˈaʊə(r	ˈha·fˈaʊə
half-hours	ˈhɑ·fˈaʊəz	ˈha·fˈaʊəz
half-length	ˈhɑ·fˈleŋ*k*θ	ˈha·fˈleŋ*k*θ
half-measure	ˈhɑ·fˈmɛʒə(r	ˈha·fˈmɛʒə
half-measures	ˈhɑ·fˈmɛʒəz	ˈha·fˈmɛʒəz
half-pay	ˈhɑ·fˈpeɪ	ˈha·fˈpeɪ
half-penny	ˈheɪpənɪ	
half-pennies	ˈheɪpənɪz	
half-pence	ˈheɪpəns	
half-price	ˈhɑ·fˈpraɪs	ˈha·fˈpraɪs
half-time	ˈhɑ·fˈtaɪm	ˈha·fˈtaɪm
half-way	ˈhɑ·fˈweɪ	ˈha·fˈweɪ
half-yearly	ˈhɑ·fˈjɜ·lɪ	ˈha·fˈjɪəlɪ
hall	hɔ·l	
halls	hɔ·lz	
hallo(a)	həˈlou,ˈhʌˈlou,ˈhæˈlou	
halt	hɔlt, hɒlt	

Traditional Spelling	Received Pronunciation	American Variants
halts	hɔlts, hɒlts	
halted	ˈhɔltɪd, ˈhɒltɪd	
halting	ˈhɔltɪŋ, ˈhɒltɪŋ	
haltingly	ˈhɔltɪŋlɪ, ˈhɒltɪŋlɪ	
halve	hɑˑv	haˑv
halves	hɑˑvz	haˑvz
halved	hɑˑvd	haˑvd
halving	ˈhɑˑvɪŋ	ˈhaˑvɪŋ
ham	hæm	
hams	hæmz	
hammer	ˈhæmə(r	ˈhæmə
hammers	ˈhæməz	ˈhæməz
hammered	ˈhæməd	ˈhæməd
hammering	ˈhæmərɪŋ	
hammock	ˈhæmək	
hammocks	ˈhæməks	
hand	hænd	
hands	hændz	
handed	ˈhændɪd	
handing	ˈhændɪŋ	
hand-bag	ˈhæn*d*bæg	
hand-bags	ˈhæn*d*bægz	
handful	ˈhæn*d*fʊl	
handfuls	ˈhæn*d*fʊlz	
handicap	ˈhændɪkæp	
handicaps	ˈhændɪkæps	
handicapped	ˈhændɪkæpt	
handicapping	ˈhændɪkæpɪŋ	
handkerchief	ˈhæŋkəʧɪʃ	
handkerchiefs	ˈhæŋkəʧɪfs	
handle	ˈhændl̩	
handles	ˈhændl̩z	
handled	ˈhændl̩d	
handling	ˈhændl̩ɪŋ	
handsome	ˈhænsəm	
handsomer	ˈhænsəmə(r	ˈhænsəmə
handsomest	ˈhænsəmɪst	
handsomely	ˈhænsəmlɪ	
handy	ˈhændɪ	
handier	ˈhændɪə(r	ˈhændɪə
handiest	ˈhændɪɪst	
hang	hæŋ	
hangs	hæŋz	
hanged	hæŋd	
hung	hʌŋ	
hanging	ˈhæŋɪŋ	
happen	hæpən	

Traditional Spelling	Received Pronunciation	American Variants
happens	hæpənz	
happened	hæpənd	
happening	ˈhæpənɪŋ	
happenings	ˈhæpənɪŋz	
happy	ˈhæpɪ	
happier	ˈhæpɪə(r	ˈhæpɪə
happiest	ˈhæpɪɪst	
happily	ˈhæpɪlɪ	
happiness	ˈhæpɪnɪs	
harass	ˈhærəs	
harasses	ˈhærəsɪz	
harassed	ˈhærəst	
harassing	ˈhærəsɪŋ	
harbor (*Amer.*)		
harbour	ˈhɑˑbə(r	ˈhɑəbə
harbors (*Amer.*)		
harbours	ˈhɑˑbəz	ˈhɑəbəz
hard	hɑˑd	hɑəd
harder	ˈhɑˑdə(r	ˈhɑədə
hardest	ˈhɑˑdɪst	ˈhɑədɪst
harden	ˈhɑˑdn̩	ˈhɑədn̩
hardens	ˈhɑˑdn̩z	ˈhɑədn̩z
hardened	ˈhɑˑdn̩d	ˈhɑədn̩d
hardening	ˈhɑˑdn̩ɪŋ	ˈhɑədn̩ɪŋ
hardly	ˈhɑˑdlɪ	ˈhɑədlɪ
hardness	ˈhɑˑdnɪs	ˈhɑədnɪs
hardship	ˈhɑˑdʃɪp	ˈhɑədʃɪp
hardships	ˈhɑˑdʃɪps	ˈhɑədʃɪps
hardy	ˈhɑˑdɪ	ˈhɑədɪ
hare	hɛə(r	hɛə
hares	hɛəz	hɛəz
harm	hɑˑm	hɑəm
harms	hɑˑmz	hɑəmz
harmed	hɑˑmd	hɑəmd
harming	ˈhɑˑmɪŋ	ˈhɑəmɪŋ
harmful	ˈhɑˈmful	ˈhɑəmful
harmfully	ˈhɑˑmfəlɪ	ˈhɑəmfəlɪ
harmless	ˈhɑˑmlɪs	ˈhɑəmlɪs
harmlessly	ˈhɑˑmlɪslɪ	ˈhɑəmlɪslɪ
harmonious	hɑˈmounjəs hɑˈmounɪəs	hɑəˈmounjəs hɑəˈmounɪəs
harmoniously	hɑˈmounjəslɪ hɑˈmounɪəslɪ	hɑəˈmounjəslɪ hɑəˈmounɪəslɪ
harmony	ˈhɑˑmənɪ	ˈhɑəmənɪ
harmonies	ˈhɑˑmənɪz	ˈhɑəmənɪz
harness	ˈhɑˑnɪs	ˈhɑənɪs
harnesses	ˈhɑˑnɪsɪz	ˈhɑənɪsɪz

Traditional Spelling	Received Pronunciation	American Variants
harp	hɑˑp	hɑəp
harps	hɑˑps	hɑəps
harsh	hɑˑʃ	hɑəʃ
harsher	ˈhɑˑʃə(r	ˈhɑəʃə
harshest	ˈhɑˑʃɪst	ˈhɑəʃɪst
harshly	ˈhɑˑʃlɪ	ˈhɑəʃlɪ
harshness	ˈhɑˑʃnɪs	ˈhɑəʃnɪs
harvest	ˈhɑˈvɪst	ˈhɑəvɪst
harvests	ˈhɑˑvɪsts	ˈhɑəvɪsts
harvested	ˈhɑˑvɪstɪd	ˈhɑəvɪstɪd
harvesting	ˈhɑˑvɪstɪŋ	ˈhɑəvɪstɪŋ
harvester	ˈhɑˑvɪstə(r	ˈhɑəvɪstə
harvesters	ˈhɑˑvɪstəz	ˈhɑəvɪstəz
HAS *from* have	hæz *s.f.*, *h*əz, z *w.fs.*	
HASN'T	ˈhæzn̩t	
haste	heɪst	
hasty	ˈheɪstɪ	
hastily	ˈheɪstɪlɪ	
hat	hæt	
hats	hæts	
hate	heɪt	
hates	heɪts	
hated	ˈheɪtɪd	
hating	ˈheɪtɪŋ	
hatred	ˈheɪtrɪd	
hatter	ˈhætə(r	ˈhætə
hatters	ˈhætəz	ˈhætəz
haughty	ˈhɔˑtɪ	
haughtily	ˈhɔˑtɪlɪ	
haul	hɔˑl	
hauls	hɔˑlz	
hauled	hɔˑld	
hauling	ˈhɔˑlɪŋ	
haunt	hɔˑnt	
haunts	hɔˑnts	
haunted	ˈhɔˑntɪd	
haunting	ˈhɔˑntɪŋ	
have	hæv *s.f.*, *h*əv, v *w.fs.*	
has	hæz *s.f.*, *h*əz, z *w.fs.*	
had	hæd *s.f.*, *h*əd, d *w.fs.*	
having	ˈhævɪŋ	
haven't	ˈhævn̩t	
havoc	ˈhævək	
hay	heɪ	
hazy	ˈheɪzɪ	
he	hiˑ *s.f.*, *h*i *w.f.*	
head	hɛd	

Traditional Spelling	Received Pronunciation	American Variants
heads	hɛdz	
headache	ˈhɛdeɪk	
headaches	ˈhɛdeɪks	
heading	ˈhɛdɪŋ	
headings	ˈhɛdɪŋz	
headmaster	ˈhɛdˈmɑˑstə(r	ˈhɛdˈmaˑstə
headmasters	ˈhɛdˈmɑˑstəz	ˈhɛdˈmaˑstəz
headway	ˈhɛdweɪ	
heal	hiˑl	
heals	hiˑlz	
healed	hiˑld	
healing	ˈhiˑlɪŋ	
health	hɛlθ	
healths	hɛlθs	
healthy	ˈhɛlθɪ	
healthier	ˈhɛlθɪə(r	ˈhɛlθɪə
healthiest	ˈhɛlθɪɪst	
healthily	ˈhɛlθɪlɪ	
heap	hiˑp	
heaps	hiˑps	
heaped	hiˑpt	
heaping	ˈhiˑpɪŋ	
hear	hɪə(r	hɪə
hears	hɪəz	hɪəz
heard	hɜˑd	hɜəd
hearing	ˈhɪərɪŋ	ˈhɪˑrɪŋ
hearer	ˈhɪərə(r	ˈhɪˑrə
hearers	ˈhɪərəz	ˈhɪˑrəz
heart	hɑˑt	hɑət
hearts	hɑˑts	hɑəts
heart-breaking	ˈhɑˑtbreɪkɪŋ	ˈhɑətbreɪkɪŋ
heart-broken	ˈhɑˑtbroukən	ˈhɑətbroukən
hearth	hɑˑθ	hɑəθ
heartless	ˈhɑˑtlɪs	ˈhɑətlɪs
heartlessly	ˈhɑˑtlɪslɪ	ˈhɑətlɪslɪ
hearty	ˈhɑˑtɪ	ˈhɑətɪ
heartier	ˈhɑˑtɪə(r	ˈhɑətɪə
heartiest	ˈhɑˑtɪɪst	ˈhɑətɪɪst
heartily	ˈhɑˑtɪlɪ	ˈhɑətɪlɪ
heartiness	ˈhɑˑtɪnɪs	ˈhɑətɪnɪs
heat	hiˑt	
heats	hiˑts	
heated	ˈhiˑtɪd	
heating	ˈhiˑtɪŋ	
heath	hiˑθ	
heave	hiˑv	
heaves	hiˑvz	

Traditional Spelling	Received Pronunciation	American Variants
heaved	hiˑvd	
heaving	ˈhiˑvɪŋ	
heaven	ˈhɛvn̩	
heavens	ˈhɛvn̩z	
heavy	ˈhɛvɪ	
heavier	ˈhɛvɪə(r	ˈhɛvɪə
heaviest	ˈhɛvɪɪst	
heavily	ˈhɛvɪlɪ	
heaviness	ˈhɛvɪnɪs	
Hebrew	ˈhiˑbru	
Hebrews	ˈhiˑbruz	
hedge	ˈhɛʤ	
hedges	ˈhɛʤɪz	
heel	hiˑl	
heels	hiˑlz	
height	haɪt	
heights	haɪts	
heighten	ˈhaɪtn̩	
heightens	ˈhaɪtn̩z	
heightened	ˈhaɪtn̩d	
heightening	ˈhaɪtn̩ɪŋ	
heir	ɛə(r	ɛə
heirs	ɛəz	ɛəz
heiress	ˈɛərɪs	ˈɛˑrɪs
heiresses	ˈɛərɪsɪz	ˈɛˑrɪsɪz
HELD *from* hold	hɛld	
hell	hɛl	
helm	hɛlm	
helms	hɛlmz	
helmet	ˈhɛlmɪt	
helmets	ˈhɛlmɪts	
help	hɛlp	
helps	hɛlps	
helped	hɛlpt	
helping	ˈhɛlpɪŋ	
helper	ˈhɛlpə(r	ˈhɛlpə
helpers	ˈhɛlpəz	ˈhɛlpəz
helpful	ˈhɛlpful	
helpfully	ˈhɛlpfulɪ, ˈhɛlpfəlɪ	
helpless	ˈhɛlplɪs	
helplessly	ˈhɛlplɪslɪ	
helplessness	ˈhɛlplɪsnɪs	
hemisphere	ˈhɛmɪsfɪə(r	ˈhɛmɪsfɪə
hemispheres	ˈhɛmɪsfɪəz	ˈhɛmɪsfɪəz
hen	hɛn	
hens	hɛnz	
hence	hɛns	

Traditional Spelling	Received Pronunciation	American Variants
Henry	ˈhɛnrɪ	
her	hɜ·(r *s.f.*, *hə w.f.*	hɜə *s.f.*, *hə w.f.*
herb	hɜ·b	ɜəb
herbs	hɜ·bz	ɜəbz
herd	hɜ·d	hɜəd
herds	hɜ·dz	hɜədz
here	hɪə(r	hɪə
hereabout	ˈhɪərəbaʊt	ˈhɪ·rəbaʊt
hereabouts	ˈhɪərəbaʊts	ˈhɪ·rəbaʊts
hereafter	hɪəˈrɑ·ftə(r hjəˈrɑ·ftə(r	hɪˈra·ftə
hereby	ˈhɪəˈbaɪ	ˈhɪəˈbaɪ
hereditary	hɪˈrɛdɪtərɪ	
heredity	hɪˈrɛdɪtɪ	
heresy	ˈhɛrəsɪ, ˈhɛrɪsɪ	
heresies	ˈhɛrəsɪz, ˈhɛrɪsɪz	
herewith	ˈhɪəˈwɪð, ˈhɪəˈwɪθ	ˈhɪəˈwɪð, ˈhɪəˈwɪθ
hero	ˈhɪərou	ˈhɪ·rou
heroes	ˈhɪərouz	ˈhɪ·rouz
heroic	hɪˈrouɪk	
heroically	hɪˈrouɪkəlɪ	
heroine	ˈhɛrouɪn	
heroines	ˈhɛrouɪnz	
heroism	ˈhɛrouɪzm̩	
herring	ˈhɛrɪŋ	
herrings	ˈhɛrɪŋz	
hers	hɜ·z	hɜəz
herself, *emph. pro.*	hɜˈsɛlf	hɜəsɛlf
herself, *reflex. pro.*	*h*əˈsɛlf	*h*əˈsɛlf
hesitate	ˈhɛzɪteɪt	
hesitates	ˈhɛzɪteɪts	
hesitated	ˈhɛzɪteɪtɪd	
hesitating	ˈhɛzɪteɪtɪŋ	
hesitation	hɛzɪˈteɪʃən	
heterogeneous	ˈhɛtərouˈʤi·njəs ˈhɛtərəˈʤi·njəs	
hi	haɪ	
hide	haɪd	
hides	haɪdz	
hid	hɪd	
hidden	ˈhɪdn̩	
hiding	ˈhaɪdɪŋ	
hideous	ˈhɪdɪəs, ˈhɪdjəs	
hideously	ˈhɪdɪəslɪ, ˈhɪdjəslɪ	
high	haɪ	
higher	ˈhaɪə(r	ˈhaɪə
highest	ˈhaɪɪst	

Traditional Spelling	Received Pronunciation	American Variants
highly	'haɪlɪ	
high-handed	'haɪ'hændɪd	
highness	'haɪnɪs	
highnesses	'haɪnɪsɪz	
high-road	'haɪ'roʊd	
high-roads	'haɪ'roʊdz	
hill	hɪl	
hills	hɪlz	
hilly	'hɪlɪ	
hillier	'hɪlɪə(r	'hɪlɪə
hilliest	'hɪlɪɪst	
hilliness	'hɪlɪnɪs	
him	hɪm *s.f.*, *h*ɪm *w.f.*	
himself, *emph. pro.*	hɪm'sɛlf	
himself, *reflex. pro.*	*h*ɪm'sɛlf	
hinder	'hɪndə(r	'hɪndə
hinders	'hɪndəz	'hɪndəz
hindered	'hɪndəd	'hɪndəd
hindering	'hɪnd*ə*rɪŋ	
hindrance	'hɪndrəns	
hindrances	'hɪndrənsɪz	
hinge	hɪnʤ	
hinges	'hɪnʤɪz	
hint	hɪnt	
hints	hɪnts	
hinted	'hɪntɪd	
hinting	'hɪntɪŋ	
hip	hɪp	
hips	hɪps	
hippopotamus	hɪpə'pɒtəməs	hɪpə'pɑtəməs
hippopotami	hɪpə'pɒtəmaɪ	hɪpə'pɑtəmaɪ
hippopotamuses	hɪpə'pɒtəməsɪz	hɪpə'pɑtəməsɪz
hire	'haɪə(r	'haɪə
hires	'haɪəz	'haɪəz
hired	'haɪəd	'haɪəd
hiring	'haɪərɪŋ	
his	hɪz *s.f.*, *h*ɪz *w.f.*	
historian	hɪs'tɔ·rɪən	
historians	hɪs'tɔ·rɪənz	
historical	hɪs'tɒrɪk*ə*l	
historically	hɪs'tɒrɪk*ə*lɪ	
history	'hɪst*ə*rɪ	
histories	'hɪst*ə*rɪz	
hit	hɪt	
hits	hɪts	
hitting	'hɪtɪŋ	
hitherto	'hɪðə'tu·	'hɪðə'tu·

Traditional Spelling	Received Pronunciation	American Variants
hoard	hɔːd, hɔəd	hoəd
hoards	hɔːdz, hɔədz	hoədz
hoarded	ˈhɔːdɪd, ˈhɔədɪd	ˈhoədɪd
hoarding	ˈhɔːdɪŋ, ˈhɔədɪŋ	ˈhoədɪŋ
hoarse	hɔːs, hɔəs	hoəs
hoarsely	ˈhɔːslɪ, ˈhɔəslɪ	ˈhoəslɪ
hoarseness	ˈhɔːsnɪs, ˈhɔəsnɪs	ˈhoəsnɪs
hoax	hoʊks	
hoaxes	ˈhoʊksɪz	
hoaxed	ˈhoʊkst	
hoaxing	ˈhoʊksɪŋ	
hobby	ˈhɒbɪ	ˈhɑbɪ
hobbies	hɒbɪz	ˈhɑbɪz
hoist	hɔɪst	
hoists	hɔɪsts	
hoisted	ˈhɔɪstɪd	
hoisting	ˈhɔɪstɪŋ	
hold	hoʊld	
holds	hoʊldz	
held	hɛld	
holding	ˈhoʊldɪŋ	
holder	ˈhoʊldə(r	ˈhoʊldə
holders	ˈhoʊldəz	ˈhoʊldəz
hole	hoʊl	
holes	hoʊlz	
holiday	ˈhɒlədɪ, ˈhɒlɪdɪ, ˈhɒlɪdeɪ	ˈhɑlədɪ, ˈhɑlɪdɪ, ˈhɑlɪdeɪ
holidays	ˈhɒlədɪz, ˈhɒlɪdɪz, ˈhɒlɪdeɪz	ˈhɑlədɪz, ˈhɑlɪdɪz, ˈhɑlɪdeɪz
Holland	ˈhɒlənd	ˈhɑlənd
hollow	ˈhɒloʊ	ˈhɑloʊ
hollows	ˈhɒloʊz	ˈhɑloʊz
hollower	ˈhɒloʊə(r	ˈhɑloʊə
hollowest	ˈhɒloʊɪst	ˈhɑloʊɪst
holy	ˈhoʊlɪ	
holier	ˈhoʊlɪə(r	ˈhoʊlɪə
holiest	ˈhoʊlɪɪst	
holiness	ˈhoʊlɪnɪs	
home	hoʊm	
homes	hoʊmz	
homeless	ˈhoʊmlɪs	
homely	ˈhoʊmlɪ	
honest	ˈɒnɪst	ˈɑnɪst
honestly	ˈɒnɪstlɪ	ˈɑnɪstlɪ
honesty	ˈɒnɪstɪ	ˈɑnɪstɪ
honey	ˈhʌnɪ	
honorary	ˈɒnərərɪ	ˈɑnərɛrɪ

Traditional Spelling	Received Pronunciation	American Variants
honor (*Amer.*)		
honour	ˈɒnə(r	ˈɑnə
honors (*Amer.*)		
honours	ˈɒnəz	ˈɑnəz
honored (*Amer.*)		
honoured	ˈɒnəd	ˈɑnəd
honoring (*Amer.*)		
honouring	ˈɒnərɪŋ	ˈɑnərɪŋ
honorable (*Amer.*)		
honourable	ˈɒnᵊrəbl̩	ˈɑnᵊrəbl̩
honorably (*Amer.*)		
honourably	ˈɒnᵊrəblɪ	ˈɑnᵊrəblɪ
hood	hʊd	
hoods	hʊdz	
hoof	huˑf	
hoofs	huˑfs	
hooves	huˑvz	
hook	hʊk	
hooks	hʊks	
hooked	hʊkt	
hooking	ˈhʊkɪŋ	
hoop	huˑp	
hoops	huˑps	
hoot	huˑt	
hoots	huˑts	
hooted	ˈhuˑtɪd	
hooting	ˈhuˑtɪŋ	
hop	hɒp	hɑp
hops	hɒps	hɑps
hopped	hɒpt	hɑpt
hopping	ˈhɒpɪŋ	ˈhɑpɪŋ
hope	hoʊp	
hopes	hoʊps	
hoped	hoʊpt	
hoping	ˈhoʊpɪŋ	
hopeful	ˈhoʊpfʊl	
hopefully	ˈhoʊpfʊlɪ, ˈhoʊpfᵊlɪ	
hopeless	ˈhoʊplɪs	
hopelessly	ˈhoʊplɪslɪ	
horizon	həˈraɪzn̩	
horizons	həˈraɪzn̩z	
horizontal	hɒrɪˈzɒntl̩	
horizontally	hɒrɪˈzɒntᵊlɪ	
horn	hɔˑn	hɔən
horns	hɔˑnz	hɔənz
horny	ˈhɔˑnɪ	ˈhɔənɪ
horrible	ˈhɒrɪbl̩, ˈhɒrəbl̩	

Traditional Spelling	Received Pronunciation	American Variants
horribly	ˈhɒrɪblɪ, ˈhɒrəblɪ	
horror	ˈhɒrə(r	ˈhɒrə
horse	hɔˑs	hɔəs
horses	ˈhɔˑsɪz	ˈhɔəsɪz
horseman	ˈhɔˑsmən	ˈhɔəsmən
horsemen	ˈhɔˑsmən	ˈhɔəsmən
horse-shoe	ˈhɔˑsʃu, ˈhɔˑʃʃu	ˈhɔəsʃu, ˈhɔəʃʃu
horse-shoes	ˈhɔˑsʃuz, ˈhɔˑʃʃuz	ˈhɔəsʃuz, ˈhɔəʃʃuz
hose	houz	
hoses	ˈhouzɪz	
hospitable	ˈhɒspɪtəbl̩	ˈhɑspɪtəbl̩
hospitably	ˈhɒspɪtəblɪ	ˈhɑspɪtəblɪ
hospital	ˈhɒspɪtl̩	ˈhɑspɪtl̩
hospitals	ˈhɒspɪtl̩z	ˈhɑspɪtl̩z
hospitality	hɒspɪˈtælɪtɪ	hɑspɪˈtælɪtɪ
host	houst	
hosts	housts	
hostage	ˈhɒstɪʤ	ˈhɑstɪʤ
hostages	ˈhɒstɪʤɪz	ˈhɑstɪʤɪz
hostel	ˈhɒstəl	ˈhɑstl̩
hostels	ˈhɒstəlz	ˈhɑstl̩z
hostess	ˈhoustɪs	
hostesses	ˈhoustɪsɪz	
hostile	ˈhɒstaɪl	ˈhɑstɪl
hostility	hɒsˈtɪlɪtɪ	hɑsˈtɪlɪtɪ
hostilities	hɒsˈtɪlɪtɪz	hɑsˈtɪlɪtɪz
hot	hɒt	hɑt
hotter	ˈhɒtə(r	ˈhɑtə
hottest	ˈhɒtɪst	ˈhɑtɪst
hotly	ˈhɒtlɪ	ˈhɑtlɪ
hotel	*h*ouˈtɛl	
hotels	*h*ouˈtɛlz	
hothouse	ˈhɒthaʊs	ˈhɑthaʊs
hothouses	ˈhɒthaʊsɪz	ˈhɑthaʊsɪz
hound	haʊnd	
hounds	haʊndz	
hour	aʊə(r	aʊə
hours	aʊəz	aʊəz
hourly	ˈaʊəlɪ	ˈaʊəlɪ
house	haʊs	
houses	ˈhaʊzɪz	
household	ˈhaʊs*h*ould	
households	ˈhaʊs*h*ouldz	
housekeeper	ˈhaʊskipə(r	ˈhaʊskipə
housekeepers	ˈhaʊskipəz	ˈhaʊskipəz
housemaid	ˈhaʊsmeɪd	
housemaids	ˈhaʊsmeɪdz	

Traditional Spelling	Received Pronunciation	American Variants
hovel	ˈhɒvl̩, ˈhʌvl̩	ˈhɑvl̩
hovels	ˈhɒvl̩z, ˈhʌvl̩z	ˈhɑvl̩z
hover	ˈhɒvə(r, ˈhʌvə(r	ˈhɑvə, ˈhʌvə
hovers	ˈhɒvəz, ˈhʌvəz	ˈhɑvəz, ˈhʌvəz
hovered	ˈhɒvəd, ˈhʌvəd	ˈhɑvəd, ˈhʌvəd
hovering	ˈhɒvərɪŋ, ˈhʌvərɪŋ	ˈhɑvərɪŋ, ˈhʌvərɪŋ
how	haʊ	
however	haʊˈɛvə(r	haʊˈɛvə
howl	haʊl	
howls	haʊlz	
howled	haʊld	
howling	ˈhaʊlɪŋ	
huddle	ˈhʌdl̩	
huddles	ˈhʌdl̩z	
huddled	ˈhʌdl̩d	
huddling	ˈhʌdl̩ɪŋ	
hug	hʌg	
hugs	hʌgz	
hugged	hʌgd	
hugging	ˈhʌgɪŋ	
huge	hjuˑʤ	
hugeness	ˈhjuˑʤnɪs	
hullo	ˈhʌˈloʊ	
hum	hʌm	
hums	hʌmz	
hummed	hʌmd	
humming	ˈhʌmɪŋ	
human	ˈhjuˑmən	
humanly	ˈhjuˑmənlɪ	
humane	hjuˈmeɪn	
humanely	hjuˈmeɪnlɪ	
humanity	hjuˑmænɪtɪ	
humble	ˈhʌmbl̩	
humbler	ˈhʌmblə(r	ˈhʌmblə
humblest	ˈhʌmblɪst	
humbly	ˈhʌmblɪ	
humiliate	hjuˈmɪlɪeɪt	
humiliates	hjuˈmɪlɪeɪts	
humiliated	hjuˈmɪlɪeɪtɪd	
humiliating	hjuˈmɪlɪeɪtɪŋ	
humiliation	hjumɪlɪˈeɪʃən	
humiliations	hjumɪlɪˈeɪʃənz	
humility	hjuˈmɪlɪtɪ	
humorist	ˈ*h*juˑmərɪst	
humorists	ˈ*h*juˑmərɪsts	
humorous	ˈ*h*juˑmərəs	
humorously	ˈ*h*juˑmərəslɪ	

Traditional Spelling	Received Pronunciation	American Variants
humor (*Amer.*)		
humour	ˈ*h*juˑmə(r	ˈhjuˑmə
humors (*Amer.*)		
humours	ˈ*h*juˑməz	ˈhjuˑməz
humored (*Amer.*)		
humoured	ˈ*h*juˑməd	ˈhjuˑməd
humoring (*Amer.*)		
humouring	ˈ*h*juˑmərɪŋ	
hump	hʌmp	
humps	hʌmps	
hunchback	ˈhʌntʃbæk	
hunchbacks	ˈhʌntʃbæks	
hunchbacked	ˈhʌntʃbækt	
hundred	ˈhʌndrəd	
	ˈhʌndrɪd	
hundreds	ˈhʌndrədz	
	ˈhʌndrɪdz	
hundredth	ˈhʌndrədθ	
	ˈhʌndrətθ	
	ˈhʌndrɪdθ	
	ˈhʌndrɪtθ	
hundredths	ˈhʌndrədθs	
	ˈhʌndrətθs	
	ˈhʌndrɪdθs	
	ˈhʌndrɪtθs	
hundredweight	ˈhʌndrədweɪt	
	ˈhʌndrɪdweɪt	
hundredweights	ˈhʌndrədweɪts	
	ˈhʌndrɪdweɪts	
HUNG *from* hang	hʌŋ	
Hungarian	hʌŋˈgɛərɪən	hʌŋˈgɛˑrɪən
Hungarians	hʌŋˈgɛərɪənz	hʌŋˈgɛˑrɪənz
Hungary	ˈhʌŋgərɪ	
hunger	ˈhʌŋgə(r	ˈhʌŋgə
hungry	ˈhʌŋgrɪ	
hungrier	ˈhʌŋgrɪə(r	ˈhʌŋgrɪə
hungriest	ˈhʌŋgrɪɪst	
hungrily	ˈhʌŋgrɪlɪ	
hunt	hʌnt	
hunts	hʌnts	
hunted	ˈhʌntɪd	
hunting	ˈhʌntɪŋ	
hunter	ˈhʌntə(r	ˈhʌntə
hunters	ˈhʌntəz	ˈhʌntəz
huntsman	ˈhʌntsmən	
huntsmen	ˈhʌntsmən	
hurl	hɜˑl	hɜəl

Traditional Spelling	Received Pronunciation	American Variants
hurls	hɜˑlz	hɜəlz
hurled	hɜˑld	hɜəld
hurling	ˈhɜˑlɪŋ	ˈhɜəlɪŋ
hurrah	hʊˈrɑˑ, hʊˈreɪ	
hurry	ˈhʌrɪ	ˈhɜrɪ
hurries	ˈhʌrɪz	ˈhɜrɪz
hurried	ˈhʌrɪd	ˈhɜrɪd
hurrying	ˈhʌrɪɪŋ	ˈhɜrɪɪŋ
hurriedly	ˈhʌrɪdlɪ	ˈhɜrɪdlɪ
hurt	hɜˑt	hɜət
hurts	hɜˑts	hɜəts
hurting	ˈhɜˑtɪŋ	ˈhɜətɪŋ
husband	ˈhʌzbənd	
husbands	ˈhʌzbəndz	
hush, *verb*	hʌʃ	
hushes	ˈhʌʃɪz	
hushed	hʌʃt	
hushing	ˈhʌʃɪŋ	
hush, *interj.*	hʌʃ, ʃ	
hustle	ˈhʌsl̩	
hustles	ˈhʌsl̩z	
hustled	ˈhʌsl̩d	
hustling	ˈhʌsl̩ɪŋ	
hut	hʌt	
huts	hʌts	
hydrogen	ˈhaɪdrəʤən	
hygiene	ˈhaɪʤin, ˈhaɪʤɪin	
hygienic	haɪʤɪˈɛnɪk, haɪˈʤiˑnɪk	
hymn	hɪm	
hymns	hɪmz	
hyphen	ˈhaɪfn̩	
hyphens	ˈhaɪfn̩z	
hypnotic	hɪpˈnɒtɪk	hɪpˈnɑtɪk
hypnotism	ˈhɪpnətɪzm̩	
hypnotize	ˈhɪpnətaɪz	
hypnotizes	ˈhɪpnətaɪzɪz	
hypnotized	ˈhɪpnətaɪzd	
hypnotizing	ˈhɪpnətaɪzɪŋ	
hypocrisy	hɪˈpɒkrɪsɪ	hɪˈpɑkrɪsɪ
hypocrite	ˈhɪpəkrɪt	
hypocrites	ˈhɪpəkrɪts	
hypothesis	haɪˈpɒθɪsɪs haɪˈpɒθəsɪs	haɪˈpɑθɪsɪs haɪˈpɑθəsɪs
hypotheses	haɪˈpɒθɪsiˑz haɪˈpɒθəsiˑz	haɪˈpɑθɪsiˑz haɪˈpɑθəsiˑz

I

Traditional Spelling	Received Pronunciation	American Variants
I	aɪ	
I's	aɪz	
ice	aɪs	
ices	ˈaɪsɪz	
iceberg	ˈaɪsbɜg	ˈaɪsbɜɚg
icebergs	ˈaɪsbɜgz	ˈaɪsbɜɚgz
ice-cream	aɪsˈkri·m	
Iceland	ˈaɪslənd	
icicle	ˈaɪsɪkḷ	
icicles	ˈaɪsɪkḷz	
icy	ˈaɪsɪ	
idea	aɪˈdɪə	
ideas	aɪˈdɪəz	
ideal	aɪˈdi·əl, aɪˈdɪəl	
ideals	aɪˈdi·əlz, aɪˈdɪəlz	
idealism	aɪˈdi·əlɪzṃ, aɪˈdɪəlɪzṃ	
idealist	aɪˈdi·əlɪst, aɪˈdɪəlɪst	
idealists	aɪˈdi·əlɪsts aɪˈdɪəlɪsts	
ideally	aɪˈdi·əlɪ, aɪˈdɪəlɪ	
identical	aɪˈdɛntɪkəl	
identically	aɪˈdɛntɪkəlɪ	
identification	aɪdɛntɪfɪˈkeɪʃən	
identifications	aɪdɛntɪfɪˈkeɪʃənz	
identify	aɪˈdɛntɪfaɪ	
identifies	aɪˈdɛntɪfaɪz	
identified	aɪˈdɛntɪfaɪd	
identifying	aɪˈdɛntɪfaɪɪŋ	
identity	aɪˈdɛntɪtɪ	
identities	aɪˈdɛntɪtɪz	
idiocy	ˈɪdɪəsɪ	
idiom	ˈɪdɪəm, ˈɪdjəm	
idioms	ˈɪdɪəmz, ˈɪdjəmz	
idiomatic	ɪdɪəˈmætɪk	
idiomatically	ɪdɪəˈmætɪkəlɪ	
idiot	ˈɪdɪət, ˈɪdjət	
idiots	ˈɪdɪəts, ˈɪdjəts	
idiotic	ɪdɪˈɒtɪk	ɪdɪˈɑtɪk
idle	ˈaɪdḷ	
idly	ˈaɪdlɪ	
idleness	ˈaɪdḷnɪs	
idol	ˈaɪdḷ	
idols	ˈaɪdḷz	
i.e.	ˈaɪˈi· [ˈðæt ˈɪz]	
if	ɪf *s.f.*, ɪf *w.f.*	

Traditional Spelling	Received Pronunciation	American Variants
ignition	ɪg'nɪʃən	
ignominious	ɪgnə'mɪnjəs	
ignominiously	ɪgnə'mɪnjəslɪ	
ignorance	'ɪgnərəns	
ignorant	'ɪgnərənt	
ignorantly	'ɪgnərəntlɪ	
ignore	ɪg'nɔ·(r, ɪg'nɔə(r	ɪg'noə
ignores	ɪg'nɔ·z, ɪg'nɔəz	ɪg'noəz
ignored	ɪg'nɔ·d, ɪg'nɔəd	ɪg'noəd
ignoring	ɪg'nɔ·rɪŋ, ɪg'nɔərɪŋ	ɪg'no·rɪŋ
ill	ɪl	
ill-bred	'ɪl'brɛd	
illegal	ɪ'li·gəl	
illegally	ɪ'li·gəlɪ	
illegibility	ɪlɛʤɪ'bɪlɪtɪ	
illegible	ɪ'lɛʤɪbl̩	
illegibly	ɪ'lɛʤɪblɪ	
illegitimate	ɪlɪ'ʤɪtɪmɪt	
illegitimately	ɪlɪ'ʤɪtɪmɪtlɪ	
illness	'ɪlnɪs	
illnesses	'ɪlnɪsɪz	
illogical	ɪ'lɒʤɪkəl	ɪ'lɑʤɪkəl
illogically	ɪ'lɒʤɪkəlɪ	ɪ'lɑʤɪkəlɪ
ill-treat	ɪl'tri·t	
ill-treats	ɪl'tri·ts	
ill-treated	ɪl'tri·tɪd	
ill-treating	ɪl'tri·tɪŋ	
ill-treatment	ɪl'tri·tmənt	
illuminate	ɪ'lju·mɪneɪt	
illuminates	ɪ'lju·mɪneɪts	
illuminated	ɪ'lju·mɪneɪtɪd	
illuminating	ɪ'lju·mɪneɪtɪŋ	
illumination	ɪljumɪ'neɪʃən	
illuminations	ɪljumɪ'neɪʃənz	
ill-used	'ɪl'ju·zd	
illusion	ɪ'lju·ʒn̩	
illusions	ɪ'lju·ʒn̩z	
illusive	ɪ'lju·sɪv	
illusory	ɪ'lju·sərɪ	
illustrate	'ɪləstreɪt	
illustrates	'ɪləstreɪts	
illustrated	'ɪləstreɪtɪd	
illustrating	'ɪləstreɪtɪŋ	
illustration	ɪləs'treɪʃən	
illustrations	ɪləs'treɪʃənz	
ill-will	'ɪl'wɪl	
image	'ɪmɪʤ	

Traditional Spelling	Received Pronunciation	American Variants
images	ˈɪmɪʤɪz	
imaginable	ɪˈmæʤɪnəbl̩	
imaginary	ɪˈmæʤɪnərɪ	ɪˈmæʤɪnɛrɪ
imagination	ɪmæʤɪˈneɪʃən	
imaginations	ɪmæʤɪˈneɪʃənz	
imaginative	ɪˈmæʤɪnətɪv	
imagine	ɪˈmæʤɪn	
imagines	ɪˈmæʤɪnz	
imagined	ɪˈmæʤɪnd	
imagining	ɪˈmæʤɪnɪŋ	
imaginings	ɪˈmæʤɪnɪŋz	
imitable	ˈɪmɪtəbl̩	
imitate	ˈɪmɪteɪt	
imitates	ˈɪmɪteɪts	
imitated	ˈɪmɪteɪtɪd	
imitating	ˈɪmɪteɪtɪŋ	
imitator	ˈɪmɪteɪtə(r	ˈɪmɪteɪtɚ
imitators	ˈɪmɪteɪtəz	ˈɪmɪteɪtɚz
imitation	ɪmɪˈteɪʃən	
imitations	ɪmɪˈteɪʃənz	
imitative	ˈɪmɪteɪtɪv, ˈɪmɪtətɪv	
immaterial	ɪməˈtɪərɪəl	ɪməˈtɪ·rɪəl
immediate	ɪˈmi·djət	
immediately	ɪˈmi·djətlɪ	
immense	ɪˈmɛns	
immensely	ɪˈmɛnslɪ	
immensity	ɪˈmɛnsɪtɪ	
immigrant	ˈɪmɪgrənt	
immigrants	ˈɪmɪgrənts	
immigrate	ˈɪmɪgreɪt	
immigrates	ˈɪmɪgreɪts	
immigrated	ˈɪmɪgreɪtɪd	
immigrating	ˈɪmɪgreɪtɪŋ	
immigration	ɪmɪˈgreɪʃən	
immigrations	ɪmɪˈgreɪʃənz	
immoral	ɪˈmɒrəl	
immorality	†ɪməˈrælɪtɪ	
immortal	ɪˈmɔ·tl̩	ɪˈmɔɚtl̩
immortally	ɪˈmɔ·təlɪ	ɪˈmɔɚtəlɪ
immortality	ɪmɔˈtælɪtɪ	ɪmɔɚˈtælɪtɪ
impair	ɪmˈpɛə(r	ɪmˈpɛɚ
impairs	ɪmˈpɛəz	ɪmˈpɛɚz
impaired	ɪmˈpɛəd	ɪmˈpɛɚd
impairing	ɪmˈpɛərɪŋ	ɪmˈpɛ·rɪŋ
impart	ɪmˈpɑ·t	ɪmˈpɑɚt

† See Note **30**, p. xxxv. in Introduction.

Traditional Spelling	Received Pronunciation	American Variants
imparts	ɪm'pɑ·ts	ɪm'pɑəts
imparted	ɪm'pɑ·tɪd	ɪm'pɑətɪd
imparting	ɪm'pɑ·tɪŋ	ɪm'pɑətɪŋ
impartial	ɪm'pɑ·ʃəl	ɪm'pɑəʃəl
impartially	ɪm'pɑ·ʃəlɪ	ɪm'pɑəʃəlɪ
impartiality	ɪmpɑʃɪ'ælɪtɪ	ɪmpɑəʃɪ'ælɪtɪ
impatience	ɪm'peɪʃəns	
impatient	ɪm'peɪʃənt	
impatiently	ɪm'peɪʃəntlɪ	
imperative	ɪm'pɛrətɪv	
imperceptible	ɪmpə'sɛptəbl̩	ɪmpə'sɛptəbl̩
	ɪmpə'sɛptɪbl̩	ɪmpə'sɛptɪbl̩
imperceptibly	ɪmpə'sɛptəblɪ	ɪmpə'sɛptəblɪ
	ɪmpə'sɛptɪblɪ	ɪmpə'sɛptɪblɪ
imperfect	ɪm'pɜ·fɪkt	ɪm'pɜəfɪkt
imperfectly	ɪm'pɜ'fɪktlɪ	ɪm'pɜəfɪktlɪ
imperial	ɪm'pɪərɪəl	ɪm'pɪ·rɪəl
impersonal	ɪm'pɜ·sən̩	ɪm'pɜəsən̩
impersonally	ɪm'pɜ·sənᵊlɪ	ɪm'pɜəsənᵊlɪ
impersonate	ɪm'pɜ·səneɪt	ɪm'pɜəsəneɪt
impersonates	ɪm'pɜ·səneɪts	ɪm'pɜəsəneɪts
impersonated	ɪm'pɜ·səneɪtɪd	ɪm'pɜəsəneɪtɪd
impersonating	ɪm'pɜ·səneɪtɪŋ	ɪm'pɜəsəneɪtɪŋ
impertinence	ɪm'pɜ·tɪnəns	ɪm'pɜətɪnəns
impertinent	ɪm'pɜ·tɪnənt	ɪm'pɜətɪnənt
impetuosity	ɪmpɛtjʊ'ɒsɪtɪ	ɪmpɛtjʊ'ɑsɪtɪ
impetuous	ɪm'pɛtjʊəs	
impetuously	ɪm'pɛtjʊəslɪ	
impiety	ɪm'paɪətɪ	
impious	'ɪmpɪəs, 'ɪmpjəs	
impiously	'ɪmpɪəslɪ, 'ɪmpjəslɪ	
implication	ɪmplɪ'keɪʃən	
implications	ɪmplɪ'keɪʃənz	
implore	ɪm'plɔ·(r, ɪm'plɔə(r	ɪm'ploə
implores	ɪm'plɔ·z, ɪm'plɔəz	ɪm'ploəz
implored	ɪm'plɔ·d, ɪm'plɔəd	ɪm'ploəd
imploring	ɪm'plɔ·rɪŋ	ɪm'plo·rɪŋ
	ɪm'plɔərɪŋ	
imply	ɪm'plaɪ	
implies	ɪm'plaɪz	
implied	ɪm'plaɪd	
implying	ɪm'plaɪɪŋ	
impolite	†ɪmpə'laɪt	
impolitely	†ɪmpə'laɪtlɪ	
impoliteness	†ɪmpə'laɪtnɪs	
import, *noun*	'ɪmpɔt	'ɪmpoət
imports	'ɪmpɔts	'ɪmpoəts

† See Note 30, p. xxxv. in Introduction.

Traditional Spelling	Received Pronunciation	American Variants
import, *verb*	ɪm'pɔˑt	ɪm'poət
imports	ɪm'pɔˑts	ɪm'poəts
imported	ɪm'pɔˑtɪd	ɪm'poətɪd
importing	ɪm'pɔˑtɪŋ	ɪm'poətɪŋ
importer	ɪm'pɔˑtə(r	ɪm'poətə
importers	ɪm'pɔˑtəz	ɪm'poətəz
importance	ɪm'pɔˑtəns	ɪm'poətəns
important	ɪm'pɔˑtənt	ɪm'poətənt
importation	ɪmpɔ'teɪʃən	ɪmpoə'teɪʃən
importations	ɪmpɔ'teɪʃənz	ɪmpoə'teɪʃənz
impose	ɪm'pouz	
imposes	ɪm'pouzɪz	
imposed	ɪm'pouzd	
imposing, *adj. & verb*	ɪm'pouzɪŋ	
imposition	ɪmpə'zɪʃən	
impossibility	ɪmpɒsə'bɪlɪtɪ ɪmpɒsɪ'bɪlɪtɪ	ɪmpɑsə'bɪlɪtɪ ɪmpɑsɪ'bɪlɪtɪ
impossibilities	ɪmpɒsə'bɪlɪtɪz ɪmpɒsɪ'bɪlɪtɪz	ɪmpɑsə'bɪlɪtɪz ɪmpɑsɪ'bɪlɪtɪz
impossible	ɪm'pɒsəbl̩, ɪm'pɒsɪbl̩	ɪm'pɑsəbl̩, ɪm'pɑsɪbl̩
impossibly	ɪm'pɒsəblɪ, ɪm'pɒsɪblɪ	ɪm'pɑsəblɪ, ɪm'pɑsɪblɪ
impostor	ɪm'pɒstə(r	ɪm'pɑstə
impostors	ɪm'pɒstəz	ɪm'pɑstəz
imposture	ɪm'pɒstʃə(r	ɪm'pɑstʃə
impostures	ɪm'pɒstʃəz	ɪm'pɑstʃəz
impracticable	ɪm'præktɪkəbl̩	
impregnable	ɪm'prɛgnəbl̩	
impress	ɪm'prɛs	
impresses	ɪm'prɛsɪz	
impressed	ɪm'prɛst	
impressing	ɪm'prɛsɪŋ	
impression	ɪm'prɛʃən	
impressions	ɪm'prɛʃənz	
impressionable	ɪm'prɛʃənəbl̩	
impressive	ɪm'prɛsɪv	
impressively	ɪm'prɛsɪvlɪ	
imprison	ɪm'prɪzn̩	
imprisons	ɪm'prɪzn̩z	
imprisoned	ɪm'prɪzn̩d	
imprisoning	ɪm'prɪzn̩ɪŋ	
imprisonment	ɪm'prɪzn̩mənt	
imprisonments	ɪm'prɪzn̩mənts	
improbability	ɪmprɒbə'bɪlɪtɪ	ɪmprɑbə'bɪlɪtɪ
improbable	ɪm'prɒbəbl̩	ɪm'prɑbəbl̩
improper	ɪm'prɒpə(r	ɪm'prɑpə
improperly	ɪm'prɒpəlɪ	ɪm'prɑpəlɪ
improvable	ɪm'pruˑvəbl̩	

Traditional Spelling	Received Pronunciation	American Variants
improve	ɪm'pru·v	
improves	ɪm'pru·vz	
improved	ɪm'pru·vd	
improving	ɪm'pru·vɪŋ	
improvement	ɪm'pru·vmənt	
improvements	ɪm'pru·vmənts	
improvise	†'ɪmprəvaɪz	
improvises	†'ɪmprəvaɪzɪz	
improvised	†'ɪmprəvaɪzd	
improvising	†'ɪmprəvaɪzɪŋ	
imprudence	ɪm'pru·dəns	
imprudent	ɪm'pru·dənt	
imprudently	ɪm'pru·dəntlɪ	
impudence	'ɪmpjudəns	
impudent	'ɪmpjudənt	
impudently	'ɪmpjudəntlɪ	
impulse	'ɪmpʌls	
impulses	'ɪmpʌlsɪz	
impulsive	ɪm'pʌlsɪv	
impulsively	ɪm'pʌlsɪvlɪ	
impure	ɪm'pjuə(r	ɪm'pjʊə
impurely	ɪm'pjuəlɪ	ɪm'pjʊəlɪ
impurity	ɪm'pjuərɪtɪ	ɪm'pjʊ·rɪtɪ
impurities	ɪm'pjuərɪtɪz	ɪm'pjʊ·rɪtɪz
in	ɪn *s.f.*, ɪn *w.f.*	
inability	ɪnə'bɪlɪtɪ	
inaccuracy	ɪ'nækjurəsɪ	
inaccurate	ɪ'nækjurɪt	
inaccurately	ɪ'nækjurɪtlɪ	
inaction	ɪ'nækʃən	
inactive	ɪ'næktɪv	
inactively	ɪ'næktɪvlɪ	
inactivity	ɪnæk'tɪvɪtɪ	
inadequacy	ɪ'nækdɪkwəsɪ	
inadequate	ɪ'nækdɪkwɪt	
inadequately	ɪ'nædɪkwɪtlɪ	
inadmissible	ɪnəd'mɪsəbl̩	
	ɪnəd'mɪsɪbl̩	
inapplicable	ɪ'næplɪkəbl̩	
inappreciable	ɪnə'pri·ʃɪəbl̩	
	ɪnə'pri·ʃjəbl̩	
inappropriate	ɪnə'prouprɪɪt	
inappropriately	ɪnə'prouprɪɪtlɪ	
inappropriateness	ɪnə'prouprɪɪtnɪs	
inattention	ɪnə'tɛnʃən	

† See Note 30, p. xxxv. in Introduction.

Q

Traditional Spelling	Received Pronunciation	American Variants
inattentive	ɪnə'tɛntɪv	
inaudibility	ɪnɔdə'bɪlɪtɪ	
inaudible	ɪ'nɔ·dəbḷ, ɪ'nɔ·dɪbḷ	
inaudibly	ɪ'nɔ·dəblɪ, ɪ'nɔ·dɪblɪ	
inaugurate	ɪ'nɔ·gjureɪt	
inaugurates	ɪ'nɔ·gjureɪts	
inaugurated	ɪ'nɔ·gjureɪtɪd	
inaugurating	ɪ'nɔ·gjureɪtɪŋ	
inauguration	ɪnɔgju'reɪʃən	
inaugurations	ɪnɔgju'reɪʃənz	
inauspicious	ɪnɔs'pɪʃəs	
inauspiciously	ɪnɔs'pɪʃəslɪ	
inborn	'ɪn'bɔ·n, 'ɪn'bɔən	'ɪn'bɔən
incalculable	ɪn'kælkjuləbḷ	
incalculably	ɪn'kælkjuləblɪ	
incandescence	ɪnkæn'dɛsṇs ɪnkən'dɛsṇs	
incandescent	ɪnkæn'dɛsṇt ɪnkən'dɛsṇt	
incapability	ɪnkeɪpə'bɪlɪtɪ	
incapable	ɪn'keɪpəbḷ	
incapacity	ɪnkə'pæsɪtɪ	
incense	'ɪnsɛns	
incentive	ɪn'sɛntɪv	
incentives	ɪn'sɛntɪvz	
incessant	ɪn'sɛsənt	
incessantly	ɪn'sɛsəntlɪ	
inch	ɪntʃ	
inches	'ɪntʃɪz	
incident	'ɪnsɪdənt	
incidents	'ɪnsɪdənts	
incidental	ɪnsɪ'dɛntḷ	
incidentally	ɪnsɪ'dɛntəlɪ	
incite	ɪn'saɪt	
incites	ɪn'saɪts	
incited	ɪn'saɪtɪd	
inciting	ɪn'saɪtɪŋ	
incivility	ɪnsɪ'vɪlɪtɪ	
inclination	ɪnklɪ'neɪʃən	
inclinations	ɪnklɪ'neɪʃənz	
incline	ɪn'klaɪn	
inclines	ɪn'klaɪnz	
inclined	ɪn'klaɪnd	
inclining	ɪn'klaɪnɪŋ	
inclose, *etc.* *See* enclose, *etc.*		
include	ɪn'klu·d	

Traditional Spelling	Received Pronunciation	American Variants
includes	ɪn'kluˑdz	
included	ɪn'kluˑdɪd	
including	ɪn'kluˑdɪŋ	
inclusion	ɪn'kluˑʒən, ɪŋ'kluˑʒən	
inclusions	ɪn'kluˑʒənz	
	ɪŋ'kluˑʒənz	
inclusive	ɪn'kluˑsɪv, ɪŋ'kluˑsɪv	
inclusively	ɪn'kluˑsɪvlɪ	
	ɪŋ'kluˑsɪvlɪ	
incognito	ɪn'kɒgnɪtoʊ	ɪn'kagnɪto
incoherence	ɪnkoʊ'hɪərəns	ɪnkoʊ'hɪˑrəns
incoherent	ɪnkoʊ'hɪərənt	ɪnkoʊ'hɪˑrənt
incoherently	ɪnkoʊ'hɪərəntlɪ	ɪnkoʊ'hɪˑrəntlɪ
incombustible	ɪnkəm'bʌstəbl̩	
	ɪnkəm'bʌstɪbl̩	
income	'ɪnkʌm, 'ɪnkəm̩	
	'ɪŋkəm	
incomes	'ɪnkʌmz, 'ɪnkəmz	
	'ɪŋkəmz	
incommensurable	ɪnkə'mɛnsjərəbl̩	
	ɪnkə'mɛnʃərəbl̩	
	ɪŋkə'mɛnʃərəbl̩	
incomparable	ɪn'kɒmpərəbl̩	ɪn'kampərəbl̩
	ɪŋ'kɒmpərəbl̩	ɪŋ'kampərəbl̩
incomparably	ɪn'kɒmpərəblɪ	ɪn'kampərəblɪ
	ɪŋ'kɒmpərəblɪ	ɪŋ'kampərəblɪ
incompatibility	ɪnkəmpætə'bɪlɪtɪ	
	ɪnkəmpætɪ'bɪlɪtɪ	
incompatible	ɪnkəm'pætəbl̩	
	ɪnkəm'pætɪbl̩	
incompetence	ɪn'kɒmpɪtəns	ɪn'kampɪtəns
	ɪŋ'kɒmpɪtəns	ɪŋ'kampɪtəns
incompetent	ɪn'kɒmpɪtənt	ɪn'kampɪtənt
	ɪŋ'kɒmpɪtənt	ɪŋ'kampɪtənt
incomplete	ɪnkəm'pliˑt	
incompletely	ɪnkəm'pliˑtlɪ	
incompleteness	ɪnkəm'pliˑtnɪs	
incomprehensible	ɪnkɒmprɪ'hɛnsəbl̩	ɪnkamprɪ'hɛnsəbl̩
	ɪnkɒmprɪ'hɛnsɪbl̩	ɪnkamprɪ'hɛnsɪbl̩
inconceivable	ɪnkən'siˑvəbl̩	
inconclusive	ɪnkən'kluˑsɪv	
incongruity	ɪnkɒŋ'gruˑɪtɪ	ɪnkaŋ'gruˑɪtɪ
	ɪŋkɒŋ'gruˑɪtɪ	ɪŋkaŋ'gruˑɪtɪ
incongruous	ɪn'kɒŋgrʊəs	ɪn'kaŋgrʊəs
	ɪŋ'kɒŋgrʊəs	ɪŋ'kaŋgrʊəs
inconsiderable	ɪnkən'sɪdərəbl̩	
inconsiderate	ɪnkən'sɪdərɪt	

Traditional Spelling	Received Pronunciation	American Variants
inconsiderately	ɪnkən'sɪdərɪtlɪ	
inconsistency	ɪnkən'sɪstənsɪ	
inconsistencies	ɪnkən'sɪstənsɪz	
inconsistent	ɪnkən'sɪstənt	
inconsistently	ɪnkən'sɪstəntlɪ	
inconspicuous	ɪnkən'spɪkjuəs	
inconspicuously	ɪnkən'spɪkjuəslɪ	
incontestable	ɪnkən'tɛstəbḷ	
incontestably	ɪnkən'tɛstəblɪ	
inconvenience	ɪnkən'viˑnjəns	
inconveniences	ɪnkən'viˑnjənsɪz	
inconvenienced	ɪnkən'viˑnjənst	
inconveniencing	ɪnkən'viˑnjənsɪŋ	
inconvenient	ɪnkən'viˑnjənt	
inconveniently	ɪnkən'viˑnjəntlɪ	
incorporate	ɪn'kɔˑpəreɪt ɪŋ'kɔˑpəreɪt	ɪn'kɔəpəreɪt ɪŋ'kɔəpəreɪt
incorporates	ɪn'kɔˑpəreɪts ɪŋ'kɔˑpəreɪts	ɪn'kɔəpəreɪts ɪŋ'kɔəpəreɪts
incorporated	ɪn'kɔˑpəreɪtɪd ɪŋ'kɔˑpəreɪtɪd	ɪn'kɔəpəreɪtɪd ɪŋ'kɔəpəreɪtɪd
incorporating	ɪn'kɔˑpəreɪtɪŋ ɪŋ'kɔˑpəreɪtɪŋ	ɪn'kɔəpəreɪtɪŋ ɪŋ'kɔəpəreɪtɪŋ
incorporation	ɪnkɔpə'reɪʃən ɪŋkɔpə'reɪʃən	ɪnkɔəpə'reɪʃən ɪŋkɔəpə'reɪʃənz
incorrect	ɪnkə'rɛkt	
incorrectly	ɪnkə'rɛktlɪ	
incorrectness	ɪnkə'rɛktnɪs	
incorrigible	ɪn'kɒrɪʤəbḷ ɪn'kɒrɪʤɪbḷ	
incorrigibly	ɪn'kɒrɪʤəblɪ ɪn'kɒrɪʤɪblɪ	
increase, *noun*	'ɪnkris, 'ɪŋkris	
increases	'ɪnkrisɪz, 'ɪŋkrisɪz	
increase, *verb*	ɪn'kriˑs, ɪŋ'kriˑs	
increases	ɪn'kriˑsɪz, ɪŋ'kriˑsɪz	
increased	ɪn'kriˑst, ɪŋ'kriˑst	
increasing	ɪn'kriˑsɪŋ, ɪŋ'kriˑsɪŋ	
incredibility	ɪnkrɛdɪ'bɪlɪtɪ ɪŋkrɛdɪ'bɪlɪtɪ	
incredible	ɪn'krɛdəbḷ, ɪn'krɛdɪbḷ ɪŋ'krɛdəbḷ, ɪŋ'krɛdɪbḷ	
incredibly	ɪn'krɛdəblɪ, ɪn'krɛdɪblɪ ɪŋ'krɛdəblɪ, ɪŋ'krɛdɪblɪ	
incredulity	ɪnkrɪ'djuˑlɪtɪ ɪŋkrɪ'djuˑlɪtɪ	

Traditional Spelling	Received Pronunciation	American Variants
incredulous	ɪn'krɛdjʊləs ɪŋ'krɛdjʊləs	
incredulously	ɪn'krɛdjʊləslɪ ɪŋ'krɛdjʊləslɪ	
incur	ɪn'kɜ·(r, ɪŋ'kɜ·(r	ɪn'kɜə, ɪŋ'kɜə
incurs	ɪn'kɜ·z, ɪŋ'kɜ·z	ɪn'kɜəz, ɪŋ'kɜəz
incurred	ɪn'kɜ·d, ɪŋ'kɜ·d	ɪn'kɜəd, ɪŋ'kɜəd
incurring	ɪn'kɜ·rɪŋ, ɪŋ'kɜ·rɪŋ	
incurable	ɪn'kjʊərəbl̩	ɪn'kjʊ·rəbl̩
indebted	ɪn'dɛtɪd	
indebtedness	ɪn'dɛtɪdnɪs	
indecency	ɪn'di·sənsɪ	
indecent	ɪn'di·sənt	
indecently	ɪn'di·səntlɪ	
indecision	ɪndɪ'sɪʒən	
indecisive	ɪndɪ'saɪsɪv	
indecisively	ɪndɪ'saɪsɪvlɪ	
indecisiveness	ɪndɪ'saɪsɪvnɪs	
indeed	ɪn'di·d	
indefatigable	ɪndɪ'fætɪgəbl̩	
indefatigably	ɪndɪ'fætɪgəblɪ	
indefinite	ɪn'dɛfɪnɪt	
indefinitely	ɪn'dɛfɪnɪtlɪ	
indefiniteness	ɪn'dɛfɪnɪtnɪs	
indemnity	ɪn'dɛmnɪtɪ	
indemnities	ɪn'dɛmnɪtɪz	
independence	ɪndɪ'pɛndəns	
independent	ɪndɪ'pɛndənt	
independently	ɪndɪ'pɛndəntlɪ	
indescribable	ɪndɪs'kraɪbəbl̩	
indescribably	ɪndɪs'kraɪbəblɪ	
indestructible	ɪndɪs'trʌktəbl̩ ɪndɪs'trʌktɪbl̩	
index	'ɪndɛks	
indexes	'ɪndɛksɪz	
indices	'ɪndɪsiz	
India	'ɪndjə	
Indian	'ɪndjən	
Indians	'ɪndjənz	
india-rubber	'ɪndjə'rʌbə(r	'ɪndjə'rʌbə
indicate	'ɪndɪkeɪt	
indicates	'ɪndɪkeɪts	
indicated	'ɪndɪkeɪtɪd	
indicating	'ɪndɪkeɪtɪŋ	
indication	ɪndɪ'keɪʃən	
indications	ɪndɪ'keɪʃənz	
indicative	ɪn'dɪkətɪv	

Traditional Spelling	Received Pronunciation	American Variants
indict	ɪn'daɪt	
indicts	ɪn'daɪts	
indicted	ɪn'daɪtɪd	
indicting	ɪn'daɪtɪŋ	
indictment	ɪn'daɪtmənt	
indictments	ɪn'daɪtmənts	
indifference	ɪn'dɪfərəns	
indifferent	ɪn'dɪfərənt	
indifferently	ɪn'dɪfərəntlɪ	
indigestible	ɪndɪ'ʤɛstəbl̩ ɪndɪ'ʤɛstɪbl̩	
indigestion	ɪndɪ'ʤɛstʃən	
indignant	ɪn'dɪgnənt	
indignantly	ɪn'dɪgnəntlɪ	
indignation	ɪndɪg'neɪʃən	
indignity	ɪn'dɪgnɪtɪ	
indignities	ɪn'dɪgnɪtɪz	
indigo	'ɪndɪgoʊ	
indirect	ɪndɪ'rɛkt, ɪndə'rɛkt ɪndaɪ'rɛkt	
indirectly	ɪndɪ'rɛktlɪ, ɪndə'rɛktlɪ ɪndaɪ'rɛktlɪ	
indirectness	ɪndɪ'rɛktnɪs ɪndə'rɛktnɪs ɪndaɪ'rɛktnɪs	
indiscreet	ɪndɪs'kri·t	
indiscreetly	ɪndɪs'kri·tlɪ	
indiscretion	ɪndɪs'krɛʃən	
indiscretions	ɪndɪs'krɛʃənz	
indiscriminate	ɪndɪs'krɪmɪnɪt	
indiscriminately	ɪndɪs'krɪmɪnɪtlɪ	
indispensability	'ɪndɪspɛnsə'bɪlɪtɪ	
indispensable	ɪndɪs'pɛnsəbl̩	
indisputable	ɪn'dɪspjutəbl̩	
indisputably	ɪn'dɪspjutəblɪ	
indistinct	ɪndɪs'tɪŋ*k*t	
indistinctly	ɪndɪs'tɪŋ*k*tlɪ	
indistinguishable	ɪndɪs'tɪŋgwɪʃəbl̩	
individual	ɪndɪ'vɪdjʊəl	
individuals	ɪndɪ'vɪdjʊəlz	
individually	ɪndɪ'vɪdjʊəlɪ	
individuality	'ɪndɪvɪdjʊ'ælɪtɪ	
individualities	'ɪndɪvɪdjʊ'ælɪtɪz	
indivisibility	'ɪndɪvɪzɪ'bɪlɪtɪ 'ɪndɪvɪzə'bɪlɪtɪ	
indivisible	ɪndɪ'vɪzəbl̩ ɪndɪ'vɪzɪbl̩	

Traditional Spelling	Received Pronunciation	American Variants
indivisibly	ɪndɪ'vɪzəblɪ	
	ɪndɪ'vɪzɪblɪ	
indolence	'ɪndələns	
indolent	'ɪndələnt	
indomitable	ɪn'dɒmɪtəbḷ	ɪn'dɑmɪtəbḷ
indoor	'ɪndɔ·(r, 'ɪndɔə(r	'ɪndoə
indoors	'ɪn'dɔ·z, 'ɪn'dɔəz	'ɪn'doəz
induce	ɪn'dju·s	
induces	ɪn'dju·sɪz	
induced	ɪn'dju·st	
inducing	ɪn'dju·sɪŋ	
inducement	ɪn'dju·smənt	
inducements	ɪn'dju·smənts	
induction	ɪn'dʌkʃən	
inductive	ɪn'dʌktɪv	
inductively	ɪn'dʌktɪvlɪ	
indulge	ɪn'dʌlʤ	
indulges	ɪn'dʌlʤɪz	
indulged	ɪn'dʌlʤd	
indulging	ɪn'dʌlʤɪŋ	
indulgence	ɪn'dʌlʤəns	
indulgences	ɪn'dʌlʤənsɪz	
indulgent	ɪn'dʌlʤənt	
indulgently	ɪn'dʌlʤəntlɪ	
industrial	ɪn'dʌstrɪəl	
industrially	ɪn'dʌstrɪəlɪ	
industrious	ɪn'dʌstrɪəs	
industriously	ɪn'dʌstrɪəslɪ	
industry	'ɪndəstrɪ	
industries	'ɪndəstrɪz	
ineffective	ɪnɪ'fɛktɪv	
ineffectively	ɪnɪ'fɛktɪvlɪ	
ineffectual	ɪnɪ'fɛktjʊəl	
ineffectually	ɪnɪ'fɛktjʊəlɪ	
inefficacious	ɪnɛfɪ'keɪʃəs	
inefficacy	ɪ'nɛfɪkəsɪ	
inefficiency	ɪnɪ'fɪʃənsɪ	
inefficient	ɪnɪ'fɪʃənt	
inefficiently	ɪnɪ'fɪʃəntlɪ	
ineligibility	ɪnɛlɪʤə'bɪlɪtɪ	
	ɪnɛlɪʤɪ'bɪlɪtɪ	
ineligible	ɪ'nɛlɪʤəbḷ, ɪ'nɛlɪʤɪbḷ	
inequality	ɪnɪ'kwɒlɪtɪ	ɪnɪ'kwɑlɪtɪ
inequalities	ɪnɪ'kwɒlɪtɪz	ɪnɪ'kwɑlɪtɪz
inert	ɪ'nɜ·t	ɪ'nɜət
inertia	ɪ'nɜ·ʃɪə, ɪ'nɜ·ʃjə	ɪ'nɜəʃɪə, ɪ'nɜəʃjə
inestimable	ɪ'nɛstɪməbḷ	

Traditional Spelling	Received Pronunciation	American Variants
inevitability	ɪnɛvɪtə'bɪlɪtɪ	
inevitable	ɪ'nɛvɪtəbl̩	
inevitably	ɪ'nɛvɪtəblɪ	
inexact	ɪnɪg'zækt	
inexactness	ɪnɪg'zæktnɪs	
inexcusable	ɪnɪks'kju·zəbl̩	
inexhaustible	ɪnɪg'zɔ·stəbl̩	
	ɪnɪg'zɔ·stɪbl̩	
inexhaustibly	ɪnɪg'zɔ·stəblɪ	
	ɪnɪg'zɔ·stɪblɪ	
inexpediency	ɪnɪks'pi·djənsɪ	
inexpedient	ɪnɪks'pi·djənt	
inexpediently	ɪnɪks'pi·djəntlɪ	
inexpensive	ɪnɪks'pɛnsɪv	
inexperience	ɪnɪks'pɪərɪəns	ɪnɪks'pɪ·rɪəns
infallibility	ɪnfælə'bɪlɪtɪ	
	ɪnfælɪ'bɪlɪtɪ	
infallible	ɪn'fæləbl̩, ɪn'fælɪbl̩	
infallibly	ɪn'fæləblɪ, ɪn'fælɪblɪ	
infamous	'ɪnfəməs	
infamously	'ɪnfəməslɪ	
infamy	'ɪnfəmɪ	
infancy	'ɪnfənsɪ	
infant	'ɪnfənt	
infants	'ɪnfənts	
infantry	'ɪnfəntrɪ	
infatuate	ɪn'fætjueɪt	
infatuates	ɪn'fætjueɪts	
infatuated	ɪn'fætjueɪtɪd	
infatuating	ɪn'fætjueɪtɪŋ	
infatuation	ɪnfætju'eɪʃən	
infect	ɪn'fɛkt	
infects	ɪn'fɛkts	
infected	ɪn'fɛktɪd	
infecting	ɪn'fɛktɪŋ	
infection	ɪn'fɛkʃən	
infections	ɪn'fɛkʃənz	
infectious	ɪn'fɛkʃəs	
infer	ɪn'fɜ·(r	ɪn'fɜə
infers	ɪn'fɜ·z	ɪn'fɜəz
inferred	ɪn'fɜ·d	ɪn'fɜəd
inferring	ɪn'fɜ·rɪŋ	
inference	'ɪnfərəns	
inferences	'ɪnfərənsɪz	
inferior	ɪn'fɪərɪə(r	ɪn'fɪ·rɪə
inferiors	ɪn'fɪərɪəz	ɪn'fɪ·rɪəz
inferiority	ɪnfɪərɪ'ɒrɪtɪ	ɪnfɪ·rɪ'ɒrɪtɪ

Traditional Spelling	Received Pronunciation	American Variants
infidel	ˈɪnfɪdəl	
infidels	ˈɪnfɪdəlz	
infidelity	ɪnfɪˈdɛlɪtɪ	
infinite	ˈɪnfɪnɪt	
infinitely	ˈɪnfɪnɪtlɪ	
infinitive	ɪnˈfɪnɪtɪv	
infinitives	ɪnˈfɪnɪtɪvz	
infinity	ɪnˈfɪnɪtɪ	
infirm	ɪnˈfɜˑm	ɪnˈfɜəm
infirmly	ɪnˈfɜˑmlɪ	ɪnˈfmɜəlɪ
infirmity	ɪnˈfɜˑmɪtɪ	ɪnˈfɜəmɪtɪ
infirmities	ɪnˈfɜˑmɪtɪz	ɪnˈfɜəmɪtɪz
inflamation	ɪnfləˈmeɪʃən	
inflate	ɪnˈfleɪt	
inflates	ɪnˈfleɪts	
inflated	ɪnˈfleɪtɪd	
inflating	ɪnˈfleɪtɪŋ	
inflation	ɪnˈfleɪʃən	
inflect	ɪnˈflɛkt	
inflects	ɪnˈflɛkts	
inflected	ɪnˈflɛktɪd	
inflecting	ɪnˈflɛktɪŋ	
inflection	ɪnˈflɛkʃən	
inflections	ɪnˈflɛkʃənz	
inflectional	ɪnˈflɛkʃənəl	
inflexible	ɪnˈflɛksəbl̩ ɪnˈflɛksɪbl̩	
inflexibly	ɪnˈflɛksəblɪ ɪnˈflɛksɪblɪ	
inflexion	ɪnˈflɛkʃən	
inflexions	ɪnˈflɛkʃənz	
inflexional	ɪnˈflɛkʃənəl	
inflict	ɪnˈflɪkt	
inflicts	ɪnˈflɪkts	
inflicted	ɪnˈflɪktɪd	
inflicting	ɪnˈflɪktɪŋ	
influence	ˈɪnflʊəns	
influences	ˈɪnflʊənsɪz	
influenced	ˈɪnflʊənst	
influencing	ˈɪnflʊənsɪŋ	
influential	ɪnflʊˈɛnʃəl	
influentially	ɪnflʊˈɛnʃəlɪ	
influenza	ɪnflʊˈɛnzə	
inform	ɪnˈfɔˑm	ɪnˈfɔəm
informs	ɪnˈfɔˑmz	ɪnˈfɔəmz
informed	ɪnˈfɔˑmd	ɪnˈfɔəmd
informing	ɪnˈfɔˑmɪŋ	ɪnˈfɔəmɪŋ

Traditional Spelling	Received Pronunciation	American Variants
informer	ɪn'fɔ·mə(r	ɪn'fɔəmə
informers	ɪn'fɔ·məz	ɪn'fɔəməz
informal	ɪn'fɔ·məl	ɪn'fɔəməl
informally	ɪn'fɔ·məlɪ	ɪn'fɔəməlɪ
information	ɪnfə'meɪʃən	ɪnfə'meɪʃən
infringe	ɪn'frɪnʤ	
infringes	ɪn'frɪnʤɪz	
infringed	ɪn'frɪnʤd	
infringing	ɪn'frɪnʤɪŋ	
ingenious	ɪn'ʤi·njəs	
ingeniously	ɪn'ʤi·njəslɪ	
ingenuity	ɪnʤɪ'nju·ɪtɪ ɪnʤə'nju·ɪtɪ	
ingrained	'ɪn'greɪnd	
ingratitude	ɪn'grætɪtjud	
ingredient	ɪn'gri·dɪənt	
ingredients	ɪn'gri·dɪənts	
inhabit	ɪn'hæbɪt	
inhabits	ɪn'hæbɪts	
inhabited	ɪn'hæbɪtɪd	
inhabiting	ɪn'hæbɪtɪŋ	
inhabitable	ɪn'hæbɪtəbḷ	
inhabitant	ɪn'hæbɪtənt	
inhabitants	ɪn'hæbɪtənts	
inhale	ɪn'heɪl	
inhales	ɪn'heɪlz	
inhaled	ɪn'heɪld	
inhaling	ɪn'heɪlɪŋ	
inherit	ɪn'herɪt	
inherits	ɪn'herɪts	
inherited	ɪn'herɪtɪd	
inheriting	ɪn'herɪtɪŋ	
inhospitable	ɪn'hɒspɪtəbḷ	ɪn'hɑspɪtəbḷ
inhospitably	ɪn'hɒspɪtəblɪ	ɪn'hɑspɪtəblɪ
inhuman	ɪn'hju·mən	
inhumane	ɪnhju'meɪn	
inhumanity	ɪnhju·mænɪtɪ	
iniquitous	ɪ'nɪkwɪtəs	
iniquitously	ɪ'nɪkwɪtəslɪ	
iniquity	ɪ'nɪkwɪtɪ	
iniquities	ɪ'nɪkwɪtɪz	
initial	ɪ'nɪʃəl	
initials	ɪ'nɪʃəlz	
initially	ɪ'nɪʃəlɪ	
initiate	ɪ'nɪʃɪeɪt	
initiates	ɪ'nɪʃɪeɪts	
initiated	ɪ'nɪʃɪeɪtɪd	

Traditional Spelling	Received Pronunciation	American Variants
initiating	ɪ'nɪʃɪeɪtɪŋ	
initiation	ɪnɪʃɪ'eɪʃən	
initiations	ɪnɪʃɪ'eɪʃənz	
initiative	ɪ'nɪʃɪətɪv, ɪ'nɪʃjətɪv	
inject	ɪn'ʤɛkt	
injects	ɪn'ʤɛkts	
injected	ɪn'ʤɛktɪd	
injecting	ɪn'ʤɛktɪŋ	
injection	ɪn'ʤɛkʃən	
injections	ɪn'ʤɛkʃənz	
injurious	ɪn'ʤuərɪəs	
injuriously	ɪn'ʤuərɪəslɪ	
injury	'ɪnʤərɪ	
injuries	'ɪnʤərɪz	
injustice	ɪn'ʤʌstɪs	
ink	ɪŋk	
inks	ɪŋks	
ink-bottle	'ɪŋkbɒtl̩	'ɪŋkbɑtl̩
ink-bottles	'ɪŋkbɒtl̩z	'ɪŋkbɑtl̩z
ink-pot	'ɪŋkpɒt	'ɪŋkpɑt
ink-pots	'ɪŋkpɒts	'ɪŋkpɑts
ink-stand	'ɪŋkstænd	
ink-stands	'ɪŋkstændz	
inland	'ɪnlənd, 'ɪnlænd	
inmost	'ɪnmoust, 'ɪnməst	
inn	ɪn	
inns	ɪnz	
inner	'ɪnə(r	'ɪnə
innermost	'ɪnəmoust, 'ɪnəməst	'ɪnəmoust, 'ɪnəməst
inn-keeper	'ɪnkiˑpə(r	'ɪnkiˑpə
inn-keepers	'ɪnkiˑpəz	'ɪnkiˑpəz
innocence	†'ɪnəsəns	
innocent	†'ɪnəsənt	
innocently	†'ɪnəsəntlɪ	
innovate	†'ɪnəveɪt	
innovates	†'ɪnəveɪts	
innovated	†'ɪnəveɪtɪd	
innovating	†'ɪnəveɪtɪŋ	
innovator	†'ɪnəveɪtə(r	'ɪnəveɪtə
innovators	†'ɪnəveɪtəz	'ɪnəveɪtəz
innovation	†ɪnə'veɪʃən	
innovations	†ɪnə'veɪʃənz	
innumerable	ɪ'njuˑmərəbl̩	
inoculate	ɪ'nɒkjuleɪt	ɪ'nɑkjuleɪt
inoculates	ɪ'nɒkjuleɪts	ɪ'nɑkjuleɪts

† See Note 30, p. xxxv. in Introduction.

Traditional Spelling	Received Pronunciation	American Variants
inoculated	ɪ'nɒkjuleɪtɪd	ɪ'nɑkjuleɪtɪd
inoculating	ɪ'nɒkjuleɪtɪŋ	ɪ'nɑkjuleɪtɪŋ
inoculation	ɪnɒkju'leɪʃən	ɪnɑkju'leɪʃən
inoculations	ɪnɒkju'leɪʃənz	ɪnɑkju'leɪʃənz
inoffensive	ɪnə'fɛnsɪv	
inoffensively	ɪnə'fɛnsɪvlɪ	
inopportune	ɪ'nɒpətjun	ɪ'nɑpətjun
inorganic	ɪnɔ'gænɪk	ɪnɔə'gænɪk
inquest	'ɪnkwɛst, 'ɪŋkwɛst	
inquests	'ɪnkwɛsts 'ɪŋkwɛsts	
inquire	ɪn'kwaɪə(r	ɪn'kwaɪə
inquires	ɪn'kwaɪəz	ɪn'kwaɪəz
inquired	ɪn'kwaɪəd	ɪn'kwaɪəd
inquiring	ɪn'kwaɪərɪŋ	ɪn'kwaɪrɪŋ
inquirer	ɪn'kwaɪərə(r	ɪn'kwaɪrə
inquirers	ɪn'kwaɪərəz	ɪn'kwaɪrəz
inquiry	ɪn'kwaɪərɪ	ɪn'kwaɪrɪ
inquiries	ɪn'kwaɪərɪz	ɪn'kwaɪrɪz
inquisitive	ɪn'kwɪzɪtɪv ɪn'kwɪzətɪv	
insane	ɪn'seɪn	
insanely	ɪn'seɪnlɪ	
insanity	ɪn'sænɪtɪ	
inscribe	ɪn'skraɪb	
inscribes	ɪn'skraɪbz	
inscribed	ɪn'skraɪbd	
inscribing	ɪn'skraɪbɪŋ	
inscription	ɪns'krɪpʃən	
inscriptions	ɪns'krɪpʃənz	
insect	'ɪnsɛkt	
insects	'ɪnsɛkts	
insecure	ɪnsɪ'kjuə(r	ɪnsɪ'kjuə
insecurely	ɪnsɪ'kjuəlɪ	ɪnsɪ'kjuəlɪ
insecurity	ɪnsɪ'kjuərɪtɪ	ɪnsɪ'kjuˑrɪtɪ
insensibility	ɪnsɛnsə'bɪlɪtɪ ɪnsɛnsɪ'bɪlɪtɪ	
insensible	ɪn'sɛnsəbl̩ ɪn'sɛnsɪbl̩	
insensibly	ɪn'sɛnsəblɪ ɪn'sɛnsɪblɪ	
inseparable	ɪn'sɛpərəbl	
inseparably	ɪn'sɛpərəblɪ	
insert	ɪn'sɜˑt	ɪn'sɜət
inserts	ɪn'sɜˑts	ɪn'sɜəts
inserted	ɪn'sɜˑtɪd	ɪn'sɜətɪd
inserting	ɪn'sɜˑtɪŋ	ɪn'sɜətɪŋ

Traditional Spelling	Received Pronunciation	American Variants
insertion	ɪn'sɜ·ʃən	ɪn'sɝʃən
insertions	ɪn'sɜ·ʃənz	ɪn'sɝʃənz
inside	'ɪn'saɪd	
insides	'ɪn'saɪdz	
insight	'ɪnsaɪt	
insignificance	ɪnsɪg'nɪfɪkəns	
insignificant	ɪnsɪg'nɪfɪkənt	
insignificantly	ɪnsɪg'nɪfɪkəntlɪ	
insincere	ɪnsɪn'sɪə(r	ɪnsɪn'sɪɚ
insincerely	ɪnsɪn'sɪəlɪ	ɪnsɪn'sɪɚlɪ
insincerity	ɪnsɪn'sɛrɪtɪ	
insinuate	ɪn'sɪnjueɪt	
insinuates	ɪn'sɪnjueɪts	
insinuated	ɪn'sɪnjʊeɪtɪd	
insinuating	ɪn'sɪnjʊeɪtɪŋ	
insinuation	ɪnsɪnju'eɪʃən	
insinuations	ɪnsɪnju'eɪʃənz	
insipid	ɪn'sɪpɪd	
insist	ɪn'sɪst	
insists	ɪn'sɪsts	
insisted	ɪn'sɪstɪd	
insisting	ɪn'sɪstɪŋ	
insistence	ɪn'sɪstəns	
insistent	ɪn'sɪstənt	
insistently	ɪn'sɪstəntlɪ	
insolence	†'ɪnsələns	
insolent	†'ɪnsələnt	
insolently	†'ɪnsələntlɪ	
insoluble	ɪn'sɒljubl̩	ɪn'sɑljubl̩
insomnia	ɪn'sɒmnɪə	ɪn'sɑmnɪə
inspect	ɪn'spɛkt	
inspects	ɪn'spɛkts	
inspected	ɪn'spɛktɪd	
inspecting	ɪn'spɛktɪŋ	
inspector	ɪn'spɛktə(r	ɪn'spɛktɚ
inspectors	ɪn'spɛktəz	ɪn'spɛktɚz
inspection	ɪn'spɛkʃən	
inspections	ɪn'spɛkʃənz	
inspiration	ɪnspə'reɪʃən ɪnspɪ'reɪʃən	
inspirations	ɪnspə'reɪʃənz ɪnspɪ'reɪʃənz	
inspire	ɪn'spaɪə(r	ɪn'spaɪɚ
inspires	ɪn'spaɪəz	ɪn'spaɪɚz
inspired	ɪn'spaɪəd	ɪn'spaɪɚd

† See Note 30, p. xxxv. in Introduction.

Traditional Spelling	Received Pronunciation	American Variants
inspiring	ɪn'spaɪərɪŋ	ɪn'spaɪrɪŋ
instability	ɪnstə'bɪlɪtɪ	
install	ɪn'stɔ·l	
installs	ɪn'stɔ·lz	
installed	ɪn'stɔ·ld	
installing	ɪn'stɔ·lɪŋ	
installation	†ɪnstə'leɪʃən	
installations	†ɪnstə'leɪʃənz	
installment (*Amer.*)		
instalment	ɪn'stɔ·lmənt	
installments (*Amer.*)		
instalments	ɪn'stɔ·lmənts	
instance	'ɪnstəns	
instances	'ɪnstənsɪz	
instant	'ɪnstənt	
instants	'ɪnstənts	
instantly	'ɪnstəntlɪ	
instantaneous	ɪnstən'teɪnjəs	
instantaneously	ɪnstən'teɪnjəslɪ	
instead	ɪns'ted	
instigate	'ɪnstɪgeɪt	
instigates	'ɪnstɪgeɪts	
instigated	'ɪnstɪgeɪtɪd	
instigating	'ɪnstɪgeɪtɪŋ	
instigation	ɪnstɪ'geɪʃən	
instinct	'ɪnstɪŋkt	
instincts	'ɪnstɪŋkts	
instinctive	ɪns'tɪŋktɪv	
instinctively	ɪns'tɪŋktɪvlɪ	
institute	'ɪnstɪtjut	
institutes	'ɪnstɪtjuts	
instituted	'ɪnstɪtjutɪd	
instituting	'ɪnstɪtjutɪŋ	
institution	ɪnstɪ'tju·ʃən	
institutions	ɪnstɪ'tju·ʃənz	
instruct	ɪns'trʌkt	
instructs	ɪns'trʌkts	
instructed	ɪns'trʌktɪd	
instructing	ɪns'trʌktɪŋ	
instructor	ɪns'trʌktə(r	ɪns'trʌktə
instructors	ɪns'trʌktəz	ɪns'trʌktəz
instruction	ɪns'trʌkʃən	
instructions	ɪns'trʌkʃənz	
instructive	ɪns'trʌktɪv	
instructively	ɪns'trʌktɪvlɪ	

† See Note 30, p. xxxv. in Introduction.

Traditional Spelling	Received Pronunciation	American Variants
instrument	ˈɪnstrʊmənt	
	ˈɪnstrəmənt	
instruments	ˈɪnstrʊmənts	
	ˈɪnstrəmənts	
instrumental	ɪnstrʊˈmɛntl̩	
	ɪnstrəˈmɛntl̩	
insubordination	ˈɪnsəbɔdɪˈneɪʃən	ˈɪnsəbɔədɪˈneɪʃən
insufficient	ɪnsəˈfɪʃənt	
insufficiently	ɪnsəˈfɪʃəntlɪ	
insult, *noun*	ˈɪnsʌlt	
insults	ˈɪnsʌlts	
insult, *verb*	ɪnˈsʌlt	
insults	ɪnˈsʌlts	
insulted	ɪnˈsʌltɪd	
insulting	ɪnˈsʌltɪŋ	
insuperable	ɪnˈsjuˑpərəbl̩	
	ɪnˈsuˑpərəbl̩	
insupportable	ɪnsəˈpɔˑtəbl̩	ɪnsəˈpɔətəbl̩
insure	ɪnˈʃʊə(r, ɪnˈʃɔə(r	ɪnˈʃʊə
insures	ɪnˈʃʊəz, ɪnˈʃɔəz	ɪnˈʃʊəz
insured	ɪnˈʃʊəd, ɪnˈʃɔəd	ɪnˈʃʊəd
insuring	ɪnˈʃʊərɪŋ, ɪnˈʃɔərɪŋ	ɪnˈʃʊˑrɪŋ
insurance	ɪnˈʃʊərəns, ɪnˈʃɔˑrəns	ɪnˈʃʊˑrəns
insusceptibility	ˈɪnsəsɛptəˈbɪlɪtɪ	
	ˈɪnsəsɛptɪˈbɪlɪtɪ	
insusceptible	ɪnsəˈsɛptəbl̩	
	ɪnsəˈsɛptɪbl̩	
intact	ɪnˈtækt	
integral	ˈɪntɪgrəl	
integrity	ɪnˈtɛgrɪtɪ	
intellect	ˈɪntɪlɛkt	
intellects	ˈɪntɪlɛkts	
intellectual	ɪntɪˈlɛktjʊəl	
	ɪntɪˈlɛkʧʊəl	
intellectually	ɪntɪˈlɛktjʊəlɪ	
	ɪntɪˈlɛkʧʊəlɪ	
intelligence	ɪnˈtɛlɪʤəns	
intelligences	ɪnˈtɛlɪʤənsɪz	
intelligent	ɪnˈtɛlɪʤənt	
intelligently	ɪnˈtɛlɪʤəntlɪ	
intelligibility	ɪntɛlɪʤəˈbɪlɪtɪ	
	ɪntɛlɪʤɪˈbɪlɪtɪ	
intelligible	ɪnˈtɛlɪʤəbl̩	
	ɪnˈtɛlɪʤɪbl̩	
intelligibly	ɪnˈtɛlɪʤəblɪ	
	ɪnˈtɛlɪʤɪblɪ	
intemperance	ɪnˈtɛmpərəns	

Traditional Spelling	Received Pronunciation	American Variants
intemperate	ɪn'tempərɪt	
intemperately	ɪn'tempərɪtlɪ	
intend	ɪn'tend	
intends	ɪn'tendz	
intended	ɪn'tendɪd	
intending	ɪn'tendɪŋ	
intense	ɪn'tens	
intensely	ɪn'tenslɪ	
intensify	ɪn'tensɪfaɪ	
intensifies	ɪn'tensɪfaɪz	
intensified	ɪn'tensɪfaɪd	
intensifying	ɪn'tensɪfaɪɪŋ	
intensity	ɪn'tensɪtɪ	
intensive	ɪn'tensɪv	
intensively	ɪn'tensɪvlɪ	
intent	ɪn'tent	
intention	ɪn'tenʃən	
intentions	ɪn'tenʃənz	
intentional	ɪn'tenʃənl̩	
intentionally	ɪn'tenʃənl̩ɪ	
inter-, *prefix*	ɪntə(r, 'ɪntə(r	ɪntɚ, 'ɪntɚ
intercept	ɪntə'sept	ɪntɚ'sept
intercepts	ɪntə'septs	ɪntɚ'septs
intercepted	ɪntə'septɪd	ɪntɚ'septɪd
intercepting	ɪntə'septɪŋ	ɪntɚ'septɪŋ
intercourse	'ɪntəkɔːs, 'ɪntəkɔəs	'ɪntɚkoɚs, 'ɪntɜɚkoɚs
interest	'ɪntrɪst, 'ɪntərəst	
interests	'ɪntrɪsts, 'ɪntərəsts	
interested	'ɪntrɪstɪd 'ɪntərəstɪd	
interesting	'ɪntrɪstɪŋ 'ɪntərəstɪŋ	
interfere	ɪntə'fɪə(r	ɪntɚ'fɪɚ
interferes	ɪntə'fɪəz	ɪntɚ'fɪɚz
interfered	ɪntə'fɪəd	ɪntɚ'fɪɚd
interfering	ɪntə'fɪərɪŋ	ɪntɚ'fɪːrɪŋ
interference	ɪntə'fɪərəns	ɪntɚ'fɪːrəns
interferences	ɪntə'fɪərənsɪz	ɪntɚ'fɪːrənsɪz
interior	ɪn'tɪərɪə(r	ɪn'tɪːrɪɚ
interjection	ɪntə'dʒekʃən	ɪntɚ'dʒekʃən
interjections	ɪntə'dʒekʃənz	ɪntɚ'dʒekʃənz
intermediary	ɪntə'miːdɪərɪ ɪntə'miːdjərɪ	ɪntɚ'miːdɪerɪ
intermediate	ɪntə'miːdɪɪt ɪntə'miːdjət	ɪntɚ'miːdɪɪt ɪntɚ'miːdjət
intermission	ɪntə'mɪʃən	ɪntɚ'mɪʃən
internal	ɪn'təːnəl	ɪn'tɝnəl

Traditional Spelling	Received Pronunciation	American Variants
internally	ɪn'tɜ·nəlɪ	ɪn'tɜənəlɪ
international	ɪntə'næʃn̩l̩	ɪntə'næʃn̩l̩
internationally	ɪntə'næʃn̩əlɪ	ɪntə'næʃn̩əlɪ
internationalism	ɪntə'næʃn̩əlɪzm̩	ɪntə'næʃn̩əlɪzm̩
interpret	ɪn'tɜ·prɪt	ɪn'tɜəprɪt
interprets	ɪn'tɜ·prɪts	ɪn'tɜəprɪts
interpreted	ɪn'tɜ·prɪtɪd	ɪn'tɜəprɪtɪd
interpreting	ɪn'tɜ·prɪtɪŋ	ɪn'tɜəprɪtɪŋ
interpreter	ɪn'tɜ·prɪtə(r	ɪn'tɜəprɪtə
interpreters	ɪn'tɜ·prɪtəz	ɪn'tɜəprɪtəz
interpretation	ɪntɜprɪ'teɪʃən	ɪntɜəprɪ'teɪʃən
interpretations	ɪntɜprɪ'teɪʃənz	ɪntɜəprɪ'teɪʃənz
interrogation	ɪnterə'geɪʃən	
interrogative	ɪntə'rɒgətɪv	ɪntə'rɑgətɪv
interrogatives	ɪntə'rɒgətɪvz	ɪntə'rɑgətɪvz
interrogatively	ɪntə'rɒgətɪvlɪ	ɪntə'rɑgətɪvlɪ
interrupt	ɪntə'rʌpt	
interrupts	ɪntə'rʌpts	
interrupted	ɪntə'rʌptɪd	
interrupting	ɪntə'rʌptɪŋ	
interruption	ɪntə'rʌpʃən	
interruptions	ɪntə'rʌpʃənz	
interval	'ɪntəvəl	'ɪntəvəl
intervals	'ɪntəvəlz	'ɪntəvəlz
intervene	ɪntə'vi·n	ɪntə'vi·n
intervenes	ɪntə'vi·nz	ɪntə'vi·nz
intervened	ɪntə'vi·nd	ɪntə'vi·nd
intervening	ɪntə'vi·nɪŋ	ɪntə'vi·nɪŋ
interview	'ɪntəvju	'ɪntəvju
interviews	'ɪntəvjuz	'ɪntəvjuz
interviewed	'ɪntəvjud	'ɪntəvjud
interviewing	'ɪntəvjuɪŋ	'ɪntəvjuɪŋ
interviewer	'ɪntəvjuə(r	'ɪntəvjuə
interviewers	'ɪntəvjuəz	'ɪntəvjuəz
intimacy	'ɪntɪməsɪ	
intimate, *adj.*	'ɪntɪmɪt	
intimate	'ɪntɪmeɪt	
intimates	'ɪntɪmeɪts	
intimated	'ɪntɪmeɪtɪd	
intimating	'ɪntɪmeɪtɪŋ	
intimately	'ɪntɪmɪtlɪ	
intimation	ɪntɪ'meɪʃən	
intimidate	ɪn'tɪmɪdeɪt	
intimidates	ɪn'tɪmɪdeɪts	
intimidated	ɪn'tɪmɪdeɪtɪd	
intimidating	ɪn'tɪmɪdeɪtɪŋ	
intimidation	ɪntɪmɪ'deɪʃən	

Traditional Spelling	Received Pronunciation	American Variants
into	ˈɪntu *s.f.*	
	ɪntə, ɪntʊ *w.fs.*	
intolerable	ɪnˈtɒlərəbl̩	ɪnˈtɑlərəbl̩
intolerably	ɪnˈtɒlərəblɪ	ɪnˈtɑlərəblɪ
intolerance	ɪnˈtɒlərəns	ɪnˈtɑlərəns
intolerant	ɪnˈtɒlərənt	ɪnˈtɑlərənt
intolerantly	ɪnˈtɒlərəntlɪ	ɪnˈtɑlərəntlɪ
intonation	ɪntoʊˈneɪʃən	
	ɪntəˈneɪʃən	
intonations	ɪntoʊˈneɪʃənz	
	ɪntəˈneɪʃənz	
intone	ɪnˈtoʊn	
intones	ɪnˈtoʊnz	
intoned	ɪnˈtoʊnd	
intoning	ɪnˈtoʊnɪŋ	
intoxicant	ɪnˈtɒksɪkənt	ɪnˈtɑksɪkənt
intoxicants	ɪnˈtɒksɪkənts	ɪnˈtɑksɪkənts
intoxicate	ɪnˈtɒksɪkeɪt	ɪnˈtɑksɪkeɪt
intoxicates	ɪnˈtɒksɪkeɪts	ɪnˈtɑksɪkeɪts
intoxicated	ɪnˈtɒksɪkeɪtɪd	ɪnˈtɑksɪkeɪtɪd
intoxicating	ɪnˈtɒksɪkeɪtɪŋ	ɪnˈtɑksɪkeɪtɪŋ
intoxication	ɪntɒksɪˈkeɪʃən	ɪntɑksɪˈkeɪʃən
intransitive	ɪnˈtrɑˑnsɪtɪv	ɪnˈtraˑnsɪtɪv
	ɪnˈtrænsɪtɪv	
intransitively	ɪnˈtrɑˑnsɪtɪvlɪ	ɪnˈtraˑnsɪtɪvlɪ
	ɪnˈtrænsɪtɪvlɪ	
intricacy	ˈɪntrɪkəsɪ	
intricacies	ˈɪntrɪkəsɪz	
intricate	ˈɪntrɪkɪt	
intricately	ˈɪntrɪkɪtlɪ	
introduce	ɪntrəˈdjuˑs	
introduces	ɪntrəˈdjuˑsɪz	
introduced	ɪntrəˈdjuˑst	
introducing	ɪntrəˈdjuˑsɪŋ	
introduction	ɪntrəˈdʌkʃən	
introductions	ɪntrəˈdʌkʃənz	
intrude	ɪnˈtruˑd	
intrudes	ɪnˈtruˑdz	
intruded	ɪnˈtruˑdɪd	
intruding	ɪnˈtruˑdɪŋ	
intruder	ɪnˈtruˑdə(r	ɪnˈtruˑdə
intruders	ɪnˈtruˑdəz	ɪnˈtruˑdəz
intrusion	ɪnˈtruˑʒən	
intrusions	ɪnˈtruˑʒənz	
intuition	ɪntjuˈɪʃən	
invade	ɪnˈveɪd	
invades	ɪnˈveɪdz	

Traditional Spelling	Received Pronunciation	American Variants
invaded	ɪn'veɪdɪd	
invading	ɪn'veɪdɪŋ	
invader	ɪn'veɪdə(r	ɪn'veɪdə
invaders	ɪn'veɪdəz	ɪn'veɪdəz
invalid, *noun*	'ɪnvəlid	'ɪnvəlɪd
invalid, *adj.*	ɪn'vælɪd	
invalidate	ɪn'vælɪdeɪt	
invalidates	ɪn'vælɪdeɪts	
invalidated	ɪn'vælɪdeɪtɪd	
invalidating	ɪn'vælɪdeɪtɪŋ	
invaluable	ɪn'væljuəbl̩	
invariability	ɪnvɛərɪə'bɪlɪtɪ	ɪnvɛ·rɪə'bɪlɪtɪ
invariable	ɪn'vɛərɪəbl̩	ɪn'vɛ·rɪəbl̩
invariably	ɪn'vɛərɪəblɪ	ɪn'vɛ·rɪəblɪ
invasion	ɪn'veɪʒən	
invasions	ɪn'veɪʒənz	
invent	ɪn'vɛnt	
invents	ɪn'vɛnts	
invented	ɪn'vɛntɪd	
inventing	ɪn'vɛntɪŋ	
inventor	ɪn'vɛntə(r	ɪn'vɛntə
inventors	ɪn'vɛntəz	ɪn'vɛntəz
invention	ɪn'vɛnʃən	
inventions	ɪn'vɛnʃənz	
inventive	ɪn'vɛntɪv	
inventory	'ɪnvəntrɪ	'ɪnvəntorɪ
inventories	'ɪnvəntrɪz	'ɪnvəntorɪz
inverse	'ɪn'vɜ·s	'ɪn'vɜəs
inversely	'ɪn'vɜ·slɪ	'ɪn'vɜəslɪ
inversion	ɪn'vɜ·ʃən	ɪn'vɜəʃən
inversions	ɪn'vɜ·ʃənz	ɪn'vɜəʃənz
invert	ɪn'vɜ·t	ɪn'vɜət
inverts	ɪn'vɜ·ts	ɪn'vɜəts
inverted	ɪn'vɜ·tɪd	ɪn'vɜətɪd
inverting	ɪn'vɜ·tɪŋ	ɪn'vɜətɪŋ
invest	ɪn'vɛst	
invests	ɪn'vɛsts	
invested	ɪn'vɛstɪd	
investing	ɪn'vɛstɪŋ	
investor	ɪn'vɛstə(r	ɪn'vɛstə
investors	ɪn'vɛstəz	ɪn'vɛstəz
investigate	ɪn'vɛstɪgeɪt	
investigates	ɪn'vɛstɪgeɪts	
investigated	ɪn'vɛstɪgeɪtɪd	
investigating	ɪn'vɛstɪgeɪtɪŋ	
investigation	ɪnvɛstɪ'geɪʃən	
investigations	ɪnvɛstɪ'geɪʃənz	

Traditional Spelling	Received Pronunciation	American Variants
investment	ɪn'vestmənt	
investments	ɪn'vestmənts	
invigorate	ɪn'vɪgəreɪt	
invigorates	ɪn'vɪgəreɪts	
invigorated	ɪn'vɪgəreɪtɪd	
invigorating	ɪn'vɪgəreɪtɪŋ	
invincible	ɪn'vɪnsəbḷ, ɪn'vɪnsɪbḷ	
invisibility	ɪnvɪzə'bɪlɪtɪ ɪnvɪzɪ'bɪlɪtɪ	
invisible	ɪn'vɪzəbḷ, ɪn'vɪzɪbḷ	
invisibly	ɪn'vɪzəblɪ, ɪn'vɪzɪblɪ	
invitation	ɪnvɪ'teɪʃən	
invitations	ɪnvɪ'teɪʃənz	
invite	ɪn'vaɪt	
invites	ɪn'vaɪts	
invited	ɪn'vaɪtɪd	
inviting	ɪn'vaɪtɪŋ	
invitingly	ɪn'vaɪtɪŋlɪ	
invoice	'ɪnvɔɪs	
invoices	'ɪnvɔɪsɪz	
involuntary	ɪn'vɒləntərɪ	ɪn'vɑlənterɪ
involuntarily	ɪn'vɒləntərɪlɪ	ɪn'vɑlənterɪlɪ
involve	ɪn'vɒlv	ɪn'vɑlv
involves	ɪn'vɒlvz	ɪn'vɑlvz
involved	ɪn'vɒlvd	ɪn'vɑlvd
involving	ɪn'vɒlvɪŋ	ɪn'vɑlvɪŋ
inward	'ɪnwəd	'ɪnwəd
inwards	'ɪnwədz	'ɪnwədz
inwardly	'ɪnwədlɪ	'ɪnwədlɪ
iodine	'aɪədaɪn, 'aɪədin	
Ireland	'aɪələnd	'aɪələnd
Irish	'aɪərɪʃ	'aɪrɪʃ
Irishman	'aɪərɪʃmən	'aɪrɪʃmən
Irishmen	'aɪərɪʃmən	'aɪrɪʃmən
irksome	'ɜːksəm	'ɜəksəm
iron	'aɪən	'aɪən
irons	'aɪənz	'aɪənz
ironed	'aɪənd	'aɪənd
ironing	'aɪənɪŋ	'aɪənɪŋ
ironical	aɪə'rɒnɪkəl	aɪ'rɑnɪkəl
ironically	aɪə'rɒnɪkəlɪ	aɪ'rɑnɪkəlɪ
irony, *noun*	'aɪərənɪ	'aɪrənɪ
irony, *adj.* (=ironlike)	'aɪənɪ	'aɪənɪ
irrational	ɪ'ræʃənḷ	
irrationally	ɪ'ræʃənəlɪ	
irreconcilable	ɪ'rekənsaɪləbḷ	

Traditional Spelling	Received Pronunciation	American Variants
irrefutable	ɪ'rɛfjutəbl̩	
irrefutably	ɪ'rɛfjutəblɪ	
irregular	ɪ'rɛgjulə(r	ɪ'rɛgjulə
irregularly	ɪ'rɛgjuləlɪ	ɪ'rɛgjuləlɪ
irregularity	ɪrɛgju'lærɪtɪ	
irregularities	ɪrɛgju'lærɪtɪz	
irrelevance	ɪ'rɛlɪvəns	
irrelevant	ɪ'rɛlɪvənt	
irrelevantly	ɪ'rɛlɪvəntlɪ	
irreligious	ɪrɪ'lɪʤəs	
irreparable	ɪ'rɛpərəbl̩	
irreparably	ɪ'rɛpərəblɪ	
irresistible	ɪrɪ'zɪstəbl̩ ɪrɪ'zɪstɪbl̩	
irresistibly	ɪrɪ'zɪstəblɪ ɪrɪ'zɪstɪblɪ	
irrespective	ɪrɪs'pɛktɪv	
irresponsibility	ɪrɪspɒnsə'bɪlɪtɪ ɪrɪspɒnsɪ'bɪlɪtɪ	ɪrɪspɑnsə'bɪlɪtɪ ɪrɪspɑnsɪ'bɪlɪtɪ
irresponsible	ɪrɪs'pɒnsəbl̩ ɪrɪs'pɒnsɪbl̩	ɪrɪs'pɑnsɪbl̩ ɪrɪs'pɑnsɪbl̩
irresponsibly	ɪrɪs'pɒnsəblɪ ɪrɪs'pɒnsɪblɪ	ɪrɪs'pɑnsəblɪ ɪrɪs'pɑnsɪblɪ
irresponsive	ɪrɪs'pɒnsɪv	ɪrɪs'pɑnsɪv
irresponsively	ɪrɪs'pɒnsɪvlɪ	ɪrɪs'pɑnsɪvlɪ
irresponsiveness	ɪrɪs'pɒnsɪvnɪs	ɪrɪs'pɑnsɪvnɪs
irreverence	ɪ'rɛvərəns	
irreverent	ɪ'rɛvərənt	
irreverently	ɪ'rɛvərəntlɪ	
irrevocable	ɪ'rɛvəkəbl̩	
irrevocably	ɪ'rɛvəkəblɪ	
irrigate	'ɪrɪgeɪt	
irrigates	'ɪrɪgeɪts	
irrigated	'ɪrɪgeɪtɪd	
irrigating	'ɪrɪgeɪtɪŋ	
irrigation	ɪrɪ'geɪʃən	
irritable	'ɪrɪtəbl̩	
irritably	'ɪrɪtəblɪ	
irritate	'ɪrɪteɪt	
irritates	'ɪrɪteɪts	
irritated	'ɪrɪteɪtɪd	
irritating	'ɪrɪteɪtɪŋ	
irritation	ɪrɪ'teɪʃən	
IS *from* be	ɪz *s.f.*, ɪz, z, s *w.fs.*	
island	'aɪlənd	
islands	'aɪləndz	
isle	aɪl	

Traditional Spelling	Received Pronunciation	American Variants
isles	aɪlz	
ISN'T *from* be	'ɪzn̩t	
isolate	'aɪsəleɪt, 'aɪsouleɪt	'ɪsəleɪt, 'ɪsouleɪt
isolates	'aɪsəleɪts, 'aɪsouleɪts	'ɪsəleɪts, 'ɪsouleɪts
isolated	'aɪsəleɪtɪd 'aɪsouleɪtɪd	'ɪsəleɪtɪd 'ɪsouleɪtɪd
isolating	'aɪsəleɪtɪŋ 'aɪsouleɪtɪŋ	'ɪsəleɪtɪŋ 'ɪsouleɪtɪŋ
isolation	aɪsə'leɪʃən, aɪsou'leɪʃən	ɪsə'leɪʃən, ɪsou'leɪʃən
issue	'ɪsju, 'ɪʃju	
issues	'ɪsjuz, 'ɪʃjuz	
issued	'ɪsjud, 'ɪʃjud	
issuing	'ɪsjuɪŋ, 'ɪʃjuɪŋ	
Italian	ɪ'tæljən	
Italians	ɪ'tæljənz	
italic	ɪ'tælɪk	
italics	ɪ'tælɪks	
Italy	'ɪtəlɪ	
itch	ɪʧ	
itches	'ɪʧɪz	
itched	'ɪʧt	
itching	'ɪʧɪŋ	
item	'aɪtəm	
items	'aɪtəmz	
its	ɪts *s.f.*, ɪts *w.f.*	
itself	ɪt'sɛlf	
ivory	'aɪvərɪ	
ivy	'aɪvɪ	

J

Traditional Spelling	Received Pronunciation	American Variants
J	ʤeɪ	
J's	ʤeɪz	
jacket	'ʤækɪt	
jackets	'ʤækɪts	
Jacob	'ʤeɪkəb	
jail	ʤeɪl	
jails	ʤeɪlz	
am, *noun*	ʤæm	
jams	ʤæmz	
am, *verb*	ʤæm	
jams	ʤæmz	
jammed	ʤæmd	
jamming	'ʤæmɪŋ	
James	ʤeɪmz	

Traditional Spelling	Received Pronunciation	American Variants
Jane	ʤeɪn	
janitor	ˈʤænɪtə(r	ˈʤænɪtə
janitors	ˈʤænɪtəz	ˈʤænɪtəz
January	ˈʤænjʊərɪ	ˈʤænjʊɛrɪ
Japan	ʤəˈpæn	
Japanese	ʤæpəˈniˑz	ʤæpəˈniˑs
jar	ʤɑˑ(r	ʤɑə
jars	ʤɑˑz	ʤɑəz
Java	ˈʤɑˑvə	
jaw	ʤɔˑ	
jaws	ʤɔˑz	
jealous	ˈʤɛləs	
jealously	ˈʤɛləslɪ	
jealousy	ˈʤɛləsɪ	
jealousies	ˈʤɛləsɪz	
jelly	ˈʤɛlɪ	
jellies	ˈʤɛlɪz	
jerk	ʤɜˑk	ʤɝk
jerks	ʤɜˑks	ʤɝks
jerked	ʤɜˑkt	ʤɝkt
jerking	ˈʤɜˑkɪŋ	ˈʤɝkɪŋ
Jew	ʤuˑ	
Jews	ʤuˑz	
jewel	ʤuɪl, ʤuᵊl	
jewels	ʤuɪlz, ʤuᵊlz	
jeweller	ˈʤuɪlə(r, ˈʤuələ(r	ˈʤuɪlə, ˈʤuələ
jewellers	ˈʤuɪləz, ˈʤuələz	ˈʤuɪləz, ˈʤuələz
jewellery	ˈʤuɪlrɪ, ˈʤuᵊlrɪ	
Jewish	ˈʤuɪʃ	
job	ʤɒb	ʤɑb
jobs	ʤɒbz	ʤɑbz
jocular	ˈʤɒkjʊlə(r	ˈʤɑkjʊlə
jog	ʤɒg	ʤɑg
jogs	ʤɒgz	ʤɑgz
jogged	ʤɒgd	ʤɑgd
jogging	ˈʤɒgɪŋ	ˈʤɑgɪŋ
John	ʤɒn	ʤɑn
join	ʤɔɪn	
joins	ʤɔɪnz	
joined	ʤɔɪnd	
joining	ˈʤɔɪnɪŋ	
joint	ʤɔɪnt	
joints	ʤɔɪnts	
jointly	ˈʤɔɪntlɪ	
joke	ʤoʊk	
jokes	ʤoʊks	
joked	ʤoʊkt	

Traditional Spelling	Received Pronunciation	American Variants
joking	ˈʤoukɪŋ	
jokingly	ˈʤoukɪŋlɪ	
jolly	ˈʤɒlɪ	ˈʤalɪ
jollier	ˈʤɒlɪə(r	ˈʤalɪə
jolliest	ˈʤɒlɪɪst	ˈʤalɪɪst
jolt	ʤoult	
jolts	ʤoults	
jolted	ˈʤoultɪd	
jolting	ˈʤoultɪŋ	
Joseph	ˈʤouzɪf	
jot	ʤɒt	ʤat
jots	ʤɒts	ʤats
jotted	ˈʤɒtɪd	ˈʤatɪd
jotting	ˈʤɒtɪŋ	ˈʤatɪŋ
journal	ˈʤɜˑnl̩	ˈʤɜənl̩
journals	ˈʤɜˑnl̩z	ˈʤɜənl̩z
journalism	ˈʤɜˑnəlɪzm̩	ˈʤɜənəlɪzm̩
journalist	ˈʤɜˑnəlɪst	ˈʤɜənəlɪst
journalists	ˈʤɜˑnəlɪsts	ˈʤɜənəlɪsts
journalistic	ʤɜnəˈlɪstɪk	ʤɜənəˈlɪstɪk
journey	ˈʤɜˑnɪ	ˈʤɜənɪ
journeys	ˈʤɜˑnɪz	ˈʤɜənɪz
jovial	ˈʤouvjəl, ˈʤouvɪəl	
jovially	ˈʤouvjəlɪ, ˈʤouvɪəlɪ	
joviality	ʤouvɪˈælɪtɪ	
joy	ʤɔɪ	
joys	ʤɔɪz	
joyful	ˈʤɔɪful	
joyfully	ˈʤɔɪfulɪ, ˈʤɔɪfəlɪ	
judge	ʤʌʤ	
judges	ˈʤʌʤɪz	
judged	ʤʌʤd	
judging	ˈʤʌʤɪŋ	
judg(e)ment	ˈʤʌʤmənt	
judg(e)ments	ˈʤʌʤmənts	
judicial	ʤuˈdɪʃəl	
judicious	ʤuˈdɪʃəs	
judiciously	ʤuˈdɪʃəslɪ	
jug	ʤʌg	
jugs	ʤʌgs	
juggle	ˈʤʌgl̩	
juggles	ˈʤʌgl̩z	
juggled	ˈʤʌgl̩d	
juggling	ˈʤʌglɪŋ	
juggler	ˈʤʌglə(r	ˈʤʌglə
jugglers	ˈʤʌgləz	ˈʤʌgləz
juice	ʤuˑs	

Traditional Spelling	Received Pronunciation	American Variants
juices	ˈʤuˑsɪz	
juicy	ˈʤuˑsɪ	
July	ʤuˈlaɪ	
jumble	ˈʤʌmbḷ	
jumbles	ˈʤʌmbḷz	
jumbled	ˈʤʌmbḷd	
jumbling	ˈʤʌmblɪŋ	
jump	ʤʌmp	
jumps	ʤʌmps	
jumped	ʤʌm*p*t	
jumping	ˈʤʌmpɪŋ	
junction	ˈʤʌŋ*k*ʃən	
junctions	ˈʤʌŋ*k*ʃənz	
juncture	ˈʤʌŋ*k*ʧə(r	ˈʤʌŋ*k*ʧə
junctures	ˈʤʌŋ*k*ʧəz	ˈʤʌŋ*k*ʧəz
June	ʤuˑn	
jungle	ˈʤʌŋgḷ	
jungles	ˈʤʌŋgḷz	
junior	ˈʤuˑnjə(r	ˈʤuˑnjə
juniors	ˈʤuˑnjəz	ˈʤuˑnjəz
jury	ˈʤʊərɪ	ˈʤʊˑrɪ
juries	ˈʤʊərɪz	ˈʤʊˑrɪz
just	ʤʌst	
justly	ˈʤʌstlɪ	
justness	ˈʤʌstnɪs	
justice	ˈʤʌstɪs	
justifiable	ˈʤʌstɪfaɪəbḷ ʤʌstɪˈfaɪəbḷ	
justification	ʤʌstɪfɪˈkeɪʃən	
justifications	ʤʌstɪfɪˈkeɪʃənz	
justify	ˈʤʌstɪfaɪ	
justifies	ˈʤʌstɪfaɪz	
justified	ˈʤʌstɪfaɪd	
justifying	ˈʤʌstɪfaɪɪŋ	
jut	ʤʌt	
juts	ʤʌts	
jutted	ˈʤʌtɪd	
jutting	ˈʤʌtɪŋ	
juvenile	ˈʤuˑvɪnaɪl, ˈʤuˑvənaɪl	ˈʤuˑvɪnḷ, ˈʤuˑvənḷ

K

Traditional Spelling	Received Pronunciation	American Variants
K	keɪ	
K's	keɪz	
kangaroo	kæŋgəˈruˑ	
kangaroos	kæŋgəˈruˑz	

Traditional Spelling	Received Pronunciation	American Variants
Kate	keɪt	
Katherine	ˈkæθərɪn	
Kathleen	ˈkæθlin, kæθˈliˑn	
keen	kiˑn	
keener	ˈkiˑnə(r	ˈkiˑnə
keenest	ˈkiˑnɪst	
keenly	ˈkiˑnlɪ	
keenness	ˈkiˑnnɪs	
keep	kiˑp	
keeps	kiˑps	
kept	kɛpt	
keeping	ˈkiˑpɪŋ	
keeper	ˈkiˑpə(r	ˈkiˑpə
keepers	ˈkiˑpəz	ˈkiˑpəz
kernel	ˈkɜˑnl̩	ˈkɜənl̩
kernels	ˈkɜˑnl̩z	ˈkɜənl̩z
kerosene	ˈkɛrəsiˑn	
kettle	ˈkɛtl̩	
kettles	ˈkɛtl̩z	
key	kiˑ	
keys	kiˑz	
keyboard	ˈkiˑbɔd, ˈkiˑbɔəd	ˈkiˑboəd
keyboards	ˈkiˑbɔdz, ˈkiˑbɔədz	ˈkiˑboədz
kick	kɪk	
kicks	kɪks	
kicked	kɪkt	
kicking	ˈkɪkɪŋ	
kid	kɪd	
kidnap	ˈkɪdnæp	
kidnaps	ˈkɪdnæps	
kidnapped	ˈkɪdnæpt	
kidnapping	ˈkɪdnæpɪŋ	
kidney	ˈkɪdnɪ	
kidneys	ˈkɪdnɪz	
kill	kɪl	
kills	kɪlz	
killed	kɪld	
killing	ˈkɪlɪŋ	
kilogram (*Amer.*)		
kilogramme	ˈkɪləgræm	
kilograms (*Amer.*)		
kilogrammes	ˈkɪləgræmz	
kilometer (*Amer.*)		
kilometre	ˈkɪləˈmiˑtə(r	ˈkɪlɔˈmiˑtə
kilometers (*Amer.*)		
kilometres	ˈkɪləˈmiˑtəz	ˈkɪləˈmiˑtəz
kimono	ˈkɪmənou, kɪˈmounou	

Traditional Spelling	Received Pronunciation	American Variants
kimonos	ˈkɪmənouz	
	kɪˈmounouz	
kind	kaɪnd	
kinds	kaɪndz	
kinder	ˈkaɪndə(r	ˈkaɪndɚ
kindest	ˈkaɪndɪst	
kindly	ˈkaɪndlɪ	
kindness	ˈkaɪndnɪs	
kindergarten	ˈkɪndəgɑtn̩	ˈkɪndɚgɑɚtn̩
kindergartens	ˈkɪndəgɑtn̩z	ˈkɪndɚgɑɚtn̩z
king	kɪŋ	
kings	kɪŋz	
kingdom	ˈkɪŋdəm	
kingdoms	ˈkɪŋdəmz	
kiss	kɪs	
kisses	ˈkɪsɪz	
kissed	kɪst	
kissing	ˈkɪsɪŋ	
kitchen	ˈkɪtʃɪn, ˈkɪtʃən	
kitchens	ˈkɪtʃɪnz, ˈkɪtʃənz	
kite	kaɪt	
kites	kaɪts	
kitten	ˈkɪtn̩	
kittens	ˈkɪtn̩z	
knack	næk	
knacks	næks	
knapsack	ˈnæpsæk	
knapsacks	ˈnæpsæks	
knee	niˑ	
knees	niˑz	
kneel	niˑl	
kneels	niˑlz	
kneeled	nɛlt, niˑld	
knelt	nɛlt	
kneeling	ˈniˑlɪŋ	
KNEW *from* know	njuˑ	
knife	naɪf	
knives	naɪvz	
knight	naɪt	
knights	naɪts	
knighthood	ˈnaɪthud	
knighthoods	ˈnaɪthudz	
knit	nɪt	
knits	nɪts	
knitted	ˈnɪtɪd	
knitting	ˈnɪtɪŋ	
knob	nɒb	nɑb

Traditional Spelling	Received Pronunciation	American Variants
knobs	nɒbz	nɑbz
knock	nɒk	nɑk
knocks	nɒks	nɑks
knocked	nɒkt	nɑkt
knocking	ˈnɒkɪŋ	ˈnɑkɪŋ
knocker	ˈnɒkə(r	ˈnɑkə
knockers	ˈnɒkəz	ˈnɑkəz
knot	nɒt	nɑt
knots	nɒts	nɑts
knotted	ˈnɒtɪd	ˈnɑtɪd
knotting	ˈnɒtɪŋ	ˈnɑtɪŋ
know	noʊ	
knows	noʊz	
knew	njuˑ	
known	noʊn	
knowing, *adj. & verb*	ˈnoʊɪŋ	
knowingly	ˈnoʊɪŋlɪ	
knowledge	ˈnɒlɪʤ	ˈnɑlɪʤ
knuckle	ˈnʌkl̩	
knuckles	ˈnʌkl̩z	
Korea	†kəˈrɪə	

L

L	ɛl	
L's	ɛlz	
label	ˈleɪbl̩	
labels	ˈleɪbl̩z	
labelled	ˈleɪbl̩d	
labelling	ˈleɪblɪŋ	
laboratory	ˈlæbərətərɪ, ləˈbɒrətərɪ	ˈlæbərətorɪ
laboratories	ˈlæbərətərɪz ləˈbɒrətərɪz	ˈlæbərətorɪz
laborious	ləˈbɔˑrɪəs	
laboriously	ləˈbɔˑrɪəslɪ	
labor (*Amer.*)		
labour	ˈleɪbə(r	ˈleɪbə
labors (*Amer.*)		
labours	ˈleɪbəz	ˈleɪbəz
labored (*Amer.*)		
laboured	ˈleɪbəd	ˈleɪbəd
laboring (*Amer.*)		
labouring	ˈleɪbərɪŋ	

† See Note **30**, p. xxxv. in Introduction.

Traditional Spelling	Received Pronunciation	American Variants
laborer (*Amer.*)		
labourer	ˈleɩbərə(r	ˈleɩbərə
laborers (*Amer.*)		
labourers	ˈleɩbərəz	ˈleɩbərəz
lace	leɩs	
laces	ˈleɩsɩz	
laced	leɩst	
lacing	ˈleɩsɩŋ	
lack	læk	
lacquer	ˈlækə(r	ˈlækə
lad	læd	
lads	lædz	
ladder	ˈlædə(r	ˈlædə
ladders	ˈlædəz	ˈlædəz
lady	ˈleɩdɩ	
ladies	ˈleɩdɩz	
lag	læg	
lags	lægz	
lagged	lægd	
lagging	ˈlægɩŋ	
LAID *from* lay	leɩd	
lake	leɩk	
lakes	leɩks	
lamb	læm	
lambs	læmz	
lame	leɩm	
lamer	ˈleɩmə(r	ˈleɩmə
lamest	ˈleɩmɩst	
lamely	ˈleɩmlɩ	
lamp	læmp	
lamps	læmps	
land	lænd	
lands	lændz	
landed	ˈlændɩd	
landing	ˈlændɩŋ	
landings	ˈlændɩŋz	
landlady	ˈlæn*d*leɩdɩ	
landladies	ˈlæn*d*leɩdɩz	
landlord	ˈlæn*d*lɔd	ˈlæn*d*lɔəd
landlords	ˈlæn*d*lɔdz	ˈlæn*d*lɔədz
landmark	ˈlæn*d*mɑk	ˈlæn*d*mɑək
landmarks	ˈlæn*d*mɑks	ˈlæn*d*mɑəks
landscape	ˈlæn*d*skeɩp	
landscapes	ˈlæn*d*skeɩps	
lane	leɩn	
lanes	leɩnz	
language	ˈlæŋgwɩʤ	

Traditional Spelling	Received Pronunciation	American Variants
languages	ˈlæŋgwɪʤɪz	
lantern	ˈlæntən	ˈlæntən
lanterns	ˈlæntənz	ˈlæntənz
lap	læp	
laps	læps	
lapse	læps	
lapses	ˈlæpsɪz	
lapsed	læpst	
lapsing	ˈlæpsɪŋ	
large	lɑˑʤ	lɑəʤ
larger	ˈlɑˑʤə(r	ˈlɑəʤə
largest	ˈlɑˑʤɪst	ˈlɑəʤɪst
largely	ˈlɑˑʤlɪ	ˈlɑəʤlɪ
last	lɑˑst	laˑst
lasts	lɑˑsts	laˑsts
lasted	ˈlɑˑstɪd	ˈlaˑstɪd
lasting	ˈlɑˑstɪŋ	ˈlaˑstɪŋ
lastly	ˈlɑˑstlɪ	ˈlaˑstlɪ
latch	lætʃ	
latches	ˈlætʃɪz	
late	leɪt	
later	ˈleɪtə(r	ˈleɪtə
latest	ˈleɪtɪst	
lately	ˈleɪtlɪ	
lateness	ˈleɪtnɪs	
lather	lɑˑðə(r	laˑðə
Latin	ˈlætɪn	
latitude	ˈlætɪtjud	
latitudes	ˈlætɪtjudz	
latter	ˈlætə(r	ˈlætə
latterly	ˈlætəlɪ	ˈlætəlɪ
laugh	lɑˑf	laˑf
laughs	lɑˑfs	laˑfs
laughed	lɑˑft	laˑft
laughing	ˈlɑˑfɪŋ	ˈlaˑfɪŋ
laughingly	ˈlɑˑfɪŋlɪ	ˈlaˑfɪŋlɪ
laughable	ˈlɑˑfəbl̩	ˈlaˑfəbl̩
laughter	ˈlɑˑftə(r	ˈlaˑftə
launch	lɔˑntʃ, lɑˑntʃ	lɔˑntʃ, laˑntʃ
launches	ˈlɔˑntʃɪz, lɑˑntʃɪz	ˈlɔˑntʃɪz, ˈlaˑntʃɪz
launched	lɔˑntʃt, lɑˑntʃt	lɔˑntʃt, laˑntʃt
launching	ˈlɔˑntʃɪŋ, ˈlɑˑntʃɪŋ	ˈlɔˑntʃɪŋ, ˈlaˑntʃɪŋ
laundress	ˈlɔˑndrɪs, ˈlɑˑndrɪs	ˈlɔˑndrɪs, ˈlaˑndrɪs
laundresses	ˈlɔˑndrɪsɪz, ˈlɑˑndrɪsɪz	ˈlɔˑndrɪsɪz, ˈlaˑndrɪsɪz
laundry	ˈlɔˑndrɪ, ˈlɑˑndrɪ	ˈlɔˑndrɪ, ˈlaˑndrɪ
laundries	ˈlɔˑndrɪz, ˈlɑˑndrɪz	ˈlɔˑndrɪz, ˈlaˑndrɪz
laurel	ˈlɒrəl	

Traditional Spelling	Received Pronunciation	American Variants
laurels	ˈlɒrəlz	
lava	ˈlɑˑvə	
lavatory	ˈlævətərɪ	ˈlævətorɪ
lavatories	ˈlævətərɪz	ˈlævətorɪz
law	lɔˑ	
laws	lɔˑz	
lawful	ˈlɔˑfʊl	
lawfully	ˈlɔˑfʊlɪ, ˈlɔˑfəlɪ	
lawn	lɔˑn	
lawns	lɔˑnz	
law-suit	ˈlɔˑsjut	
law-suits	ˈlɔˑsjuts	
lawyer	ˈlɔˑjə(r, ˈlɔɪə(r	ˈlɔˑjə
lawyers	ˈlɔˑjəz, ˈlɔɪəz	ˈlɔˑjəz
lax	læks	
lay	leɪ	
lays	leɪz	
laid	leɪd	
laying	ˈleɪɪŋ	
layer	leɪə(r, lɛə(r	leɪə
layers	leɪəz, lɛəz	leɪəz
lazy	ˈleɪzɪ	
lazier	ˈleɪzɪə(r	ˈleɪzɪə
laziest	ˈleɪzɪɪst	
lazily	ˈleɪzɪlɪ	
laziness	ˈleɪzɪnɪs	
lead, *the metal*	lɛd	
lead, *conduct*	liˑd	
leads	liˑdz	
led	lɛd	
leading	ˈliˑdɪŋ	
leader	ˈliˑdə(r	ˈliˑdə
leaders	ˈliˑdəz	ˈliˑdəz
leaf	liˑf	
leaves	liˑvz	
leaflet	ˈliˑflɪt	
leaflets	ˈliˑflɪts	
league	liˑg	
leagues	liˑgz	
leak	liˑk	
leaks	liˑks	
leaked	liˑkt	
leaking	ˈliˑkɪŋ	
lean	liˑn	
leaner	ˈliˑnə(r	ˈliˑnə
leanest	ˈliˑnɪst	
leans	liˑnz	

Traditional Spelling	Received Pronunciation	American Variants
leaned	lɛnt, liˑnd	
leant	lɛnt	
leaning	ˈliˑnɪŋ	
learn	lɜˑn	lɜən
learns	lɜˑnz	lɜənz
learned	lɜˑnt, lɜˑnd	lɜənt, lɜənd
learnt	lɜˑnt	lɜənt
learning	ˈlɜˑnɪŋ	ˈlɜənɪŋ
learner	ˈlɜˑnə(r	ˈlɜənə
learners	ˈlɜˑnəz	ˈlɜənəz
learned, *adj.*	ˈlɜˑnɪd	ˈlɜənd
learnedly	ˈlɜˑnɪdlɪ	ˈlɜənɪdlɪ
lease	liˑs	
leases	ˈliˑsɪz	
least	liˑst	
leather	ˈlɛðə(r	ˈlɛðə
leave	liˑv	
leaves	liˑvz	
left	lɛft	
leaving	ˈliˑvɪŋ	
lecture	ˈlɛktʃə(r	ˈlɛktʃə
lectures	ˈlɛktʃəz	ˈlɛktʃəz
lectured	ˈlɛktʃəd	ˈlɛktʃəd
lecturing	ˈlɛktʃərɪŋ	
lecturer	ˈlɛktʃərə(r	ˈlɛktʃərə
lecturers	ˈlɛktʃərəz	ˈlɛktʃərəz
LED *from* lead	lɛd	
ledge	lɛdʒ	
ledges	ˈlɛdʒɪz	
ledger	ˈlɛdʒə(r	ˈlɛdʒə
ledgers	ˈlɛdʒəz	ˈlɛdʒəz
left	lɛft	
left-handed	ˈlɛftˈhændɪd	
leg	lɛg	
legs	lɛgz	
legacy	ˈlɛgəsɪ	
legal	ˈliˑgəl	
legally	ˈliˑgəlɪ	
legation	lɪˈgeɪʃən lɛˈgeɪʃən	
legations	lɪˈgeɪʃənz lɛˈgeɪʃənz	
legend	ˈlɛdʒənd	ˈliˑdʒənd
legends	ˈlɛdʒəndz	ˈliˑdʒəndz
legging	ˈlɛgɪŋ	
leggings	ˈlɛgɪŋz	
legibility	lɛdʒɪˈbɪlɪtɪ, lɛdʒəˈbɪlɪtɪ	

Traditional Spelling	Received Pronunciation	American Variants
legible	ˈlɛdʒɪbl̩, ˈlɛdʒəbl̩	
legibly	ˈlɛdʒɪblɪ, ˈlɛdʒəblɪ	
legislation	lɛdʒɪsˈleɪʃən	
legitimate	lɪˈdʒɪtɪmɪt	
legitimately	lɪˈdʒɪtɪmɪtlɪ	
leisure	ˈlɛʒə(r	ˈlɛʒə,ˈliˑʒə
lemon	ˈlɛmən	
lemons	ˈlɛmənz	
lemonade	lɛməˈneɪd	
lend	lɛnd	
lends	lɛndz	
lent	lɛnt	
lending	ˈlɛndɪŋ	
lender	ˈlɛndə(r	ˈlɛndə
lenders	ˈlɛndəz	ˈlɛndəz
length	lɛŋ*k*θ	
lengths	lɛŋ*k*θs	
lengthen	ˈlɛŋ*k*θən	
lengthens	ˈlɛŋ*k*θənz	
lengthened	ˈlɛŋ*k*θənd	
lengthening	ˈlɛŋ*k*θənɪŋ	
lengthways	ˈlɛŋ*k*θweɪz	
lengthwise	lɛŋ*k*θwaɪz	
lengthy	ˈlɛŋ*k*θɪ	
lens	lɛnz	
lenses	ˈlɛnzɪz	
LENT *from* lend	lɛnt	
leopard	ˈlɛpəd	ˈlɛpəd
leopards	ˈlɛpədz	ˈlɛpədz
less	lɛs	
lessen	ˈlɛsn̩	
lessens	ˈlɛsn̩z	
lessened	ˈlɛsn̩d	
lessening	ˈlɛsnɪŋ	
lesson	ˈlɛsn̩	
lessons	ˈlɛsn̩z	
let	lɛt	
lets	ˈlɛts	
letting	ˈlɛtɪŋ	
letter	ˈlɛtə(r	ˈlɛtə
letters	ˈlɛtəz	ˈlɛtəz
letterbox	ˈlɛtəbɒks	ˈlɛtəbɑks
letterboxes	lɛtəbɒksɪz	ˈlɛtəbɑksɪz
level	ˈlɛvl̩	
levels	ˈlɛvl̩z	
leveled (*Amer.*)		
levelled	ˈlɛvl̩d	

Traditional Spelling	Received Pronunciation	American Variants
leveling (*Amer.*)		
levelling	ˈlɛvəlɪŋ	
lever	ˈliˑvə(r	ˈliˑvə, ˈlɛvə
levers	ˈliˑvəz	ˈliˑvəz, ˈlɛvəz
leverage	ˈliˑvərɪʤ	ˈlɛvərɪʤ
liability	laɪəˈbɪlɪtɪ	
liabilities	laɪəˈbɪlɪtɪz	
liable	ˈlaɪəbl̩	
liar	ˈlaɪə(r	ˈlaɪə
liars	ˈlaɪəz	ˈlaɪəz
libel	ˈlaɪbəl	
libels	ˈlaɪbəlz	
libeled (*Amer.*)		
libelled	ˈlaɪbəld	
libeling (*Amer.*)		
libelling	ˈlaɪbəlɪŋ	
libelous (*Amer.*)		
libellous	ˈlaɪbələs	
liberal	ˈlɪbərəl	
liberals	ˈlɪbərəlz	
liberally	ˈlɪbərəlɪ	
liberality	lɪbəˈrælɪtɪ	
liberate	ˈlɪbəreɪt	
liberates	ˈlɪbəreɪts	
liberated	ˈlɪbəreɪtɪd	
liberating	ˈlɪbəreɪtɪŋ	
liberation	lɪbəˈreɪʃən	
liberty	ˈlɪbətɪ	ˈlɪbətɪ
liberties	ˈlɪbətɪz	ˈlɪbətɪz
librarian	laɪˈbrɛərɪən	laɪˈbrɛˑrɪən
librarians	laɪˈbrɛərɪənz	laɪˈbrɛˑrɪənz
library	ˈlaɪbrərɪ	ˈlaɪbrɛrɪ
libraries	ˈlaɪbrərɪz	ˈlaɪbrɛrɪz
licence	ˈlaɪsəns	
licences	ˈlaɪsənsɪz	
lick	lɪk	
licks	lɪks	
licked	lɪkt	
licking	ˈlɪkɪŋ	
lid	lɪd	
lids	lɪdz	
lie	laɪ	
lies	laɪz	
lied	laɪd	
lay	leɪ	
lying	ˈlaɪɪŋ	
lieutenant	lɛfˈtɛnənt	luˈtɛnənt

Traditional Spelling	Received Pronunciation	American Variants
lieutenants	lɛf'tɛnənts	lu'tɛnənts
life	laɪf	
lives	laɪvz	
lifetime	'laɪftaɪm	
lifetimes	'laɪftaɪmz	
lift	lɪft	
lifts	lɪfts	
lifted	'lɪftɪd	
lifting	'lɪftɪŋ	
light	laɪt	
lighter	'laɪtə(r	'laɪtə
lightest	'laɪtɪst	
lights	laɪts	
lighted	'laɪtɪd	
lit	lɪt	
lighting	'laɪtɪŋ	
lighten	'laɪtn̩	
lightens	'laɪtn̩z	
lightened	'laɪtn̩d	
lightening	'laɪtn̩ɪŋ, 'laɪtnɪŋ	
light-hearted	'laɪt'hɑːtɪd	'laɪt'hɑətɪd
light-heartedly	'laɪt'hɑːtɪdlɪ	'laɪt'hɑətɪdlɪ
lighthouse	'laɪthaʊs	
lighthouses	'laɪthaʊzɪz	
lightly	'laɪtlɪ	
lightness	'laɪtnɪs	
lightning	'laɪtnɪŋ	
like	laɪk	
likes	laɪks	
liked	'laɪkt	
liking	'laɪkɪŋ	
likelihood	'laɪklɪhʊd	
likely	'laɪklɪ	
likeness	'laɪknɪs	
lily	'lɪlɪ	
lilies	'lɪlɪz	
limb	lɪm	
limbs	lɪmz	
lime	laɪm	
limit	'lɪmɪt	
limits	'lɪmɪts	
limited	'lɪmɪtɪd	
limiting	'lɪmɪtɪŋ	
limitation	lɪmɪ'teɪʃən	
limitations	lɪmɪ'teɪʃənz	
limp	lɪmp	
limper	'lɪmpə(r	'lɪmpə

Traditional Spelling	Received Pronunciation	American Variants
limpest	ˈlɪmpɪst	
limps	lɪmps	
limped	lɪm*p*t	
limping	ˈlɪmpɪŋ	
limply	ˈlɪmplɪ	
line	laɪn	
lines	laɪnz	
lined	ˈlaɪnd	
lining	ˈlaɪnɪŋ	
linen	ˈlɪnɪn	
liner	ˈlaɪnə(r	ˈlaɪnə
liners	ˈlaɪnəz	ˈlaɪnəz
linguist	ˈlɪŋgwɪst	
linguists	ˈlɪŋgwɪsts	
linguistic	lɪŋˈgwɪstɪk	
linguistics	lɪŋˈgwɪstɪks	
lining	ˈlaɪnɪŋ	
linings	ˈlaɪnɪŋz	
link	lɪŋk	
links	lɪŋks	
linked	lɪŋ*k*t	
linking	lɪŋkɪŋ	
lion	ˈlaɪən	
lions	ˈlaɪənz	
lip	lɪp	
lips	lɪps	
liquid	ˈlɪkwɪd	
liquids	ˈlɪkwɪdz	
lisp	lɪsp	
lisps	lɪsps	
lisped	lɪspt	
lisping	ˈlɪspɪŋ	
list	lɪst	
lists	lɪsts	
listen	ˈlɪsn̩	
listens	ˈlɪsn̩z	
listened	ˈlɪsn̩d	
listening	ˈlɪsnɪŋ	
listener	ˈlɪsnə(r	ˈlɪsnə
listeners	ˈlɪsnəz	ˈlɪsnəz
LIT *from* light	lɪt	
literal	ˈlɪtərəl	
literally	ˈlɪtərəlɪ	
literature	ˈlɪtərɪtʃə(r	ˈlɪtərɪtʃə
	ˈlɪtərɪtʃʊə(r	ˈlɪtərɪtʃʊə
	ˈlɪtərətʃə(r	ˈlɪtərətʃə
	ˈlɪtərətjʊə(r	ˈlɪtərətjʊə

Traditional Spelling	Received Pronunciation	American Variants
literatures	'lɪtərɪtʃəz	'lɪtərɪtʃəz
	'lɪtərɪtʃuəz	'lɪtərɪtʃuəz
	'lɪtərətʃəz	'lɪtərətʃəz
	'lɪtərətjuəz	'lɪtərətjuəz
lithograph	'lɪθəgræf, 'lɪθəgrɑf	'lɪθəgraf
lithographs	'lɪθəgræfs	'lɪθəgrafs
	'lɪθəgrɑfs	
lithography	lɪ'θɒgrəfɪ	lɪ'θɑgrəfɪ
liter (*Amer.*)		
litre	'liːtə(r	'liːtə
liters (*Amer.*)		
litres	'liːtəz	'liːtəz
little	'lɪtl̩	
live, *adj.*	laɪv	
live, *verb*	lɪv	
lives	lɪvz	
lived	'lɪvd	
living	'lɪvɪŋ	
lively	'laɪvlɪ	
liver	'lɪvə(r	'lɪvə
livers	'lɪvəz	'lɪvəz
Liverpool	'lɪvəpul	'lɪvəpul
LIVES, *plur. of* life	laɪvz	
LIVES *from* live	lɪvz	
load	loʊd	
loads	loʊdz	
loaded	'loʊdɪd	
loading	'loʊdɪŋ	
loaf	loʊf	
loaves	loʊvz	
loan	loʊn	
loans	loʊnz	
loathe	loʊð	
loathes	loʊðz	
loathed	loʊðd	
loathing	'loʊðɪŋ	
lobster	'lɒbstə(r	'lɑbstə
lobsters	'lɒbstəz	'lɑbstəz
local	'loʊkəl	
locally	'loʊkəlɪ	
locality	loʊ'kælɪtɪ	
localities	loʊ'kælɪtɪz	
locate	loʊ'keɪt	'loʊkeɪt
locates	loʊ'keɪts	'loʊkeɪts
located	loʊ'keɪtɪd	'loʊkeɪtɪd
locating	loʊ'keɪtɪŋ	'loʊkeɪtɪŋ
location	loʊ'keɪʃən	

Traditional Spelling	Received Pronunciation	American Variants
locations	loʊ'keɪʃənz	
lock	lɒk	lɑk
locks	lɒks	lɑks
locked	lɒkt	lɑkt
locking	'lɒkɪŋ	'lɑkɪŋ
lockout	'lɒk'aʊt	'lɑk'aʊt
lockouts	'lɒk'aʊts	'lɑk'aʊts
locomotive	'loʊkə'moʊtɪv	
locomotives	'loʊkə'moʊtɪvz	
lodge	lɒʤ	lɑʤ
lodges	'lɒʤɪz	'lɑʤɪz
lodged	'lɒʤd	'lɑʤd
lodging	'lɒʤɪŋ	'lɑʤɪŋ
lodger	'lɒʤə(r	'lɑʤə
lodgers	'lɒʤəz	'lɑʤəz
lodging	'lɒʤɪŋ	'lɑʤɪŋ
lodgings	'lɒʤɪŋz	'lɑʤɪŋz
lofty	'lɔˑftɪ, 'lɒftɪ	
log	lɒg	lɑg
logs	lɒgz	lɑgz
logarithm	'lɒgərɪθm̩ 'lɒgərɪðm̩	'lɑgərɪðm̩
logarithms	'lɒgərɪθm̩z 'lɒgərɪðm̩z	'lɑgərɪðm̩z
logic	'lɒʤɪk	'lɑʤɪk
logical	'lɒʤɪkəl	'lɑʤɪkəl
logically	'lɒʤɪkəlɪ	'lɑʤɪkəlɪ
logician	loʊ'ʤɪʃən, lɒ'ʤɪʃən	
logicians	loʊ'ʤɪʃənz lɒ'ʤɪʃənz	
London	'lʌndən	
lonely	'loʊnlɪ	
lonelier	'loʊnlɪə(r 'loʊnljə(r	'loʊnlɪə 'loʊnljə
loneliest	'loʊnlɪɪst 'loʊnljɪst	
loneliness	'loʊnlɪnɪs	
long	lɒŋ	
longer	'lɒŋgə(r	
longest	'lɒŋgɪst	
longs	lɒŋz	
longed	lɒŋd	
longing	'lɒŋɪŋ	
longings	'lɒŋɪŋz	
longitude	'lɒnʤɪtjud	'lɑnʤɪtjud
longitudes	'lɒnʤɪtjudz	'lɑnʤɪtjudz
look	lʊk	

Traditional Spelling	Received Pronunciation	American Variants
looks	lʊks	
looked	lʊkt	
looking	ˈlʊkɪŋ	
looking-glass	ˈlʊkɪŋglɑs	ˈlʊkɪŋglas
looking-glass	ˈlʊkɪŋglɑsɪz	ˈlʊkɪŋglasɪz
look-out	ˈlʊkˈaʊt	
loop	luˑp	
loops	luˑps	
loose	luˑs	
looser	ˈluˑsə(r	ˈluˑsə
loosest	ˈluˑsɪst	
loosely	ˈluˑslɪ	
loosen	ˈluˑsn̩	
loosens	ˈluˑsn̩z	
loosened	ˈluˑsn̩d	
loosening	ˈluˑsnɪŋ	
looseness	ˈluˑsnɪs	
loquacious	louˈkweɪʃəs ləˈkweɪʃəs	
lord	lɔˑd	lɔəd
lords	lɔˑdz	lɔədz
lordship	ˈlɔˑdʃɪp	ˈlɔədʃɪp
lordships	ˈlɔˑdʃɪps	ˈlɔədʃɪps
lose	luˑz	
loses	ˈluˑzɪz	
lost	lɔˑst, lɒst	
losing	ˈluˑzɪŋ	
loser	ˈluˑzə(r	ˈluˑzə
losers	ˈluˑzɔz	ˈluˑzəz
loss	lɔˑs, lɒs	
losses	ˈlɔˑsɪz, ˈlɒsɪz	
lot	lɒt	lɑt
lots	lɒts	lɑts
lottery	ˈlɒtərɪ	ˈlɑtərɪ
lotteries	ˈlɒtərɪz	ˈlɑtərɪz
lotus	ˈloutəs	
loud	laʊd	
louder	ˈlaʊdə(r	ˈlaʊdə
loudest	ˈlaʊdɪst	
loudly	ˈlaʊdlɪ	
loudness	ˈlaʊdnɪs	
lovable	ˈlʌvəbl̩	
love	lʌv	
loves	lʌvz	
loved	lʌvd	
loving	ˈlʌvɪŋ	
lover	ˈlʌvə(r	ˈlʌvə

Traditional Spelling	Received Pronunciation	American Variants
lovers	ˈlʌvəz	ˈlʌvəz
lovely	ˈlʌvlɪ	
lovelier	ˈlʌvlɪə(r	ˈlʌvlɪə
loveliest	ˈlʌvlɪɪst	
loveliness	ˈlʌvlɪnɪs	
lovingly	ˈlʌvɪŋlɪ	
low	loʊ	
lower	ˈloʊə(r	ˈloʊə
lowest	ˈloʊɪst	
lower	ˈloʊə(r	ˈloʊə
lowers	ˈloʊəz	ˈloʊəz
lowered	ˈloʊəd	ˈloʊəd
lowering	ˈloʊərɪŋ	
lowness	ˈloʊnɪs	
loyal	ˈlɔɪᵊl	
loyally	ˈlɔɪəlɪ	
loyalty	ˈlɔɪᵊltɪ	
lubricate	ˈljuˑbrɪkeɪt	
lubricates	ˈljuˑbrɪkeɪts	
lubricated	ˈljuˑbrɪkeɪtɪd	
lubricating	ˈljuˑbrɪkeɪtɪŋ	
lubrication	ljubrɪˈkeɪʃən	
luck	lʌk	
lucky	ˈlʌkɪ	
luckier	ˈlʌkɪə(r	ˈlʌkɪə
luckiest	ˈlʌkɪɪst	
luckily	ˈlʌkɪlɪ	
lucrative	ˈljuˑkrətɪv	
ludicrous	ˈljuˑdɪkrəs	
luggage	ˈlʌgɪʤ	
lumber	ˈlʌmbə(r	ˈlʌmbə
lump	lʌmp	
lumps	lʌmps	
lunacy	ˈljuˑnəsɪ	
lunar	ˈljuˑnə(r	ˈljuˑnə
lunatic	ˈljuˑnᵊtɪk	
lunatics	ˈljuˑnᵊtɪks	
lunch	lʌntʃ	
lunches	ˈlʌntʃɪz	
lunched	ˈlʌntʃt	
lunching	ˈlʌntʃɪŋ	
luncheon	ˈlʌntʃən, ˈlʌnʃən	
luncheons	ˈlʌntʃənz, ˈlʌnʃənz	
lung	lʌŋ	
lungs	lʌŋz	
lurch	lɜˑtʃ	lɜətʃ
lurches	ˈlɜˑtʃɪz	ˈlɜətʃɪz

Traditional Spelling	Received Pronunciation	American Variants
lurched	lɜ·ʧt	lɜəʧt
lurching	ˈlɜ·ʧɪŋ	ˈlɜəʧɪŋ
luxuriant	lʌkˈsjʊərɪənt	
	lʌgˈzjʊərɪənt	
	lʌgˈʒʊərɪənt	lʌgˈʒʊ·rɪənt
luxurious	lʌkˈsjʊərɪəs	
	lʌgˈzjʊərɪəs	
	lʌgˈʒʊərɪəs	lʌgˈʒʊ·rɪəs
luxuriously	lʌkˈsjʊərɪəslɪ	
	lʌgˈzjʊərɪəslɪ	
	lʌgˈʒʊərɪəslɪ	lʌgˈʒʊ·rɪəslɪ
luxury	ˈlʌkʃʊrɪ, ˈlʌkʃərɪ	
	ˈlʌksjʊrɪ, ˈlʌksjərɪ	
luxuries	ˈlʌkʃʊrɪz, ˈlʌkʃərɪz	
	ˈlʌksjʊrɪz, ˈlʌksjərɪz	
LYING *from* lie	ˈlaɪɪŋ	

M

Traditional Spelling	Received Pronunciation	American Variants
M	ɛm	
M's	ɛmz	
Mabel	ˈmeɪbl̩	
machine	məˈʃi·n	
machines	məˈʃi·nz	
mad	mæ·d	
madder	ˈmæ·də(r, ˈmædə(r	ˈmæ·də, ˈmædə
maddest	ˈmæ·dɪst, ˈmædɪst	
madam	ˈmædəm	
madden	ˈmædn̩	
maddens	ˈmædn̩z	
maddened	ˈmædn̩d	
maddening	ˈmædn̩ɪŋ	
MADE *from* make	meɪd	
madly	ˈmæ·dlɪ, ˈmædlɪ	
madness	ˈmæ·dnɪs, ˈmædnɪs	
Madras	məˈdræs, məˈdrɑ·s	
magazine	ˈmægəˈzi·n	
magazines	ˈmægəˈzi·nz	
magic	ˈmæʤɪk	
magical	ˈmæʤɪkl̩	
magically	ˈmæʤɪkəlɪ	
magician	məˈʤɪʃən	
magicians	məˈʤɪʃənz	
magistrate	ˈmæʤɪstrɪt	
	ˈmæʤɪstreɪt	
	ˈmæʤɪstrɛt	

Traditional Spelling	Received Pronunciation	American Variants
magistrates	ˈmæʤɪstrɪts	
	ˈmæʤɪstreɪts	
	ˈmæʤɪstrɛts	
magnanimity	mægnəˈnɪmɪtɪ	
magnanimous	mægˈnænɪməs	
	məgˈnænɪməs	
magnanimously	mægˈnænɪməslɪ	
	məgˈnænɪməslɪ	
magnet	ˈmægnɪt	
magnets	ˈmægnɪts	
magnetic	mægˈnɛtɪk	
	məgˈnɛtɪk	
magnetism	ˈmægnɪtɪzm̩	
magnetize	ˈmægnɪtaɪz	
magnetizes	ˈmægnɪtaɪzɪz	
magnetized	ˈmægnɪtaɪzd	
magnetizing	ˈmægnɪtaɪzɪŋ	
magnificence	mægˈnɪfɪsn̩s	
	məgˈnɪfɪsn̩s	
magnificent	mægˈnɪfɪsn̩t	
	məgˈnɪfɪsn̩t	
magnificently	mægˈnɪfɪsn̩tlɪ	
	məgˈnɪfɪsn̩tlɪ	
magnify	ˈmægnɪfaɪ	
magnifies	ˈmægnɪfaɪz	
magnified	ˈmægnɪfaɪd	
magnifying	ˈmægnɪfaɪɪŋ	
magnifier	ˈmægnɪfaɪə(r	ˈmægnɪfaɪə
magnifiers	ˈmægnɪfaɪəz	ˈmægnɪfaɪəz
mahogany	məˈhɒgənɪ	məˈhɑgənɪ
Mahommedan	məˈhɒmɪdən	məˈhɑmɪdən
Mahommedans	məˈhɒmɪdənz	məˈhɑmɪdənz
maid	meɪd	
maids	meɪdz	
mail	meɪl	
mails	meɪlz	
mailed	meɪld	
mailing	ˈmeɪlɪŋ	
main	meɪn	
mainly	ˈmeɪnlɪ	
mainland	ˈmeɪnˈlænd	
	ˈmeɪnlənd	
mainspring	ˈmeɪnsprɪŋ	
mainsprings	ˈmeɪnsprɪŋz	
maintain	meɪnˈteɪn	
maintains	meɪnˈteɪnz	
maintained	meɪnˈteɪnd	

Traditional Spelling	Received Pronunciation	American Variants
maintaining	meɪn'teɪnɪŋ	
maintenance	'meɪntɪnəns	
majestic	mə'ʤestɪk	
majestically	mə'ʤestɪkəlɪ	
majesty	'mæʤɪstɪ, 'mæʤəstɪ	
majesties	'mæʤɪstɪz 'mæʤəstɪz	
major	'meɪʤə(r	'meɪʤə
majors	'meɪʤəz	'meɪʤəz
majority	mə'ʤɒrɪtɪ	
majorities	mə'ʤɒrɪtɪz	
make	meɪk	
makes	meɪkz	
made	meɪd	
making	'meɪkɪŋ	
makeshift	'meɪkʃɪft	
makeshifts	'meɪkʃɪfts	
maker	'meɪkə(r	'meɪkə
makers	'meɪkəz	'meɪkəz
Malay	mə'leɪ	'meɪleɪ
Malays	mə'leɪz	'meɪleɪz
male	meɪl	
males	meɪlz	
malice	'mælɪs	
malicious	mə'lɪʃəs	
maliciously	mə'lɪʃəslɪ	
malignant	mə'lɪgnənt	
malt	mɔlt, mɒlt	
Malta	'mɔˑltə, 'mɒltə	
mammal	'mæməl	
mammals	'mæməlz	
man	mæn	
men	men	
manage	'mænɪʤ	
manages	'mænɪʤɪz	
managed	'mænɪʤd	
managing	'mænɪʤɪŋ	
manageable	'mænɪʤəbḷ	
management	'mænɪʤmənt	
manager	'mænɪʤə(r	'mænɪʤə
managers	'mænɪʤəz	'mænɪʤəz
Manchester	'mæntʃɪstə(r	'mæntʃɪstə, 'mæntʃestə
Manchuria	mæn'tʃʊərɪə	mæn'tʃuˑrɪə
mandarin	'mændərɪn mændə'riˑn	
mandarins	'mændərɪnz mændə'riˑnz	

Traditional Spelling	Received Pronunciation	American Variants
mandate	ˈmændeɪt, ˈmændɪt	
mandates	ˈmændeɪts	
	ˈmændɪts	
mandoline	†ˈmændəlin	
	†mændəˈliˑn	
mandolines	†ˈmændəlinz	
	†mændəˈliˑnz	
maneuver (*Amer.*)	məˈnuˑvə(r	məˈnuˑvə
(*See* manœuvre)	məˈnjuˑvə(r	məˈnjuˑvə
maneuvers	məˈnuˑvəz	məˈnuˑvəz
	məˈnjuˑvəz	məˈnjuˑvəz
maneuvered	məˈnuˑvəd	məˈnuˑvəd
	məˈnjuˑvəd	məˈnjuˑvəd
maneuvering	məˈnuˑvərɪŋ	
	məˈnjuˑvərɪŋ	
mangle	mæŋgl̩	
mangles	mæŋgl̩z	
mangled	mæŋgl̩d	
mangling	ˈmæŋglɪŋ	
manhood	ˈmænhud	
mania	ˈmeɪnɪə, ˈmeɪnjə	
manias	ˈmeɪnɪəz, ˈmeɪnjəz	
manifest	ˈmænɪfɛst	
manifests	ˈmænɪfɛsts	
manifested	ˈmænɪfɛstɪd	
manifesting	ˈmænɪfɛstɪŋ	
manifestation	mænɪfɛsˈteɪʃən	
	mænɪfəsˈteɪʃən	
manifestations	mænɪfɛsˈteɪʃənz	
	mænɪfəsˈteɪʃənz	
Manila	məˈnɪlə	
mankind	mænˈkaɪnd	
manly	ˈmænlɪ	
manner	ˈmænə(r	ˈmænə
manners	ˈmænəz	ˈmænəz
manœuvre (*English*)	məˈnuˑvə(r	məˈnuˑvə
(*See* maneuver)	məˈnjuˑvə(r	məˈnjuˑvə
manœuvres	məˈnuˑvəz	məˈnuˑvəz
	məˈnjuˑvəz	məˈnjuˑvəz
manœuvred	məˈnuˑvəd	məˈnuˑvəd
	məˈnjuˑvəd	məˈnjuˑvəd
manœuvring	məˈnuˑvərɪŋ	
	məˈnjuˑvərɪŋ	
man-of-war	ˈmænəvˈwɔə(r	mænəvˈwɔə
men-of-war	ˈmɛnəvˈwɔə(r	ˈmɛnəvˈwɔə

† See Note 30, p. xxxv. in Introduction.

Traditional Spelling	Received Pronunciation	American Variants
manufactory	mænju'fæktərɪ	
manufactories	mænju'fæktərɪz	
manufacture	mænju'fækʧə(r	mænju'fækʧə
manufactures	mænju'fækʧəz	mænju'fækʧəz
manufactured	mænju'fækʧəd	mænju'fækʧəd
manufacturing	mænju'fækʧərɪŋ	
manufacturer	mænju'fækʧərə(r	mænju'fækʧərə
manufacturers	mænju'fækʧərəz	mænju'fækʧərəz
manuscript	'mænjuskrɪpt	
manuscripts	'mænjuskrɪpts	
many	'mɛnɪ	
map	mæp	
maps	mæps	
mapped	mæpt	
mapping	'mæpɪŋ	
maple	'meɪpl̩	
maples	'meɪpl̩z	
marble	'mɑ·bl̩	'mɑəbl̩
marbles	'mɑ·bl̩z	'mɑəbl̩z
march	mɑ·ʧ	mɑəʧ
marches	'mɑ·ʧɪz	'mɑəʧɪz
marched	mɑ·ʧt	mɑəʧt
marching	'mɑ·ʧɪŋ	'mɑəʧɪŋ
mare	mɛə(r	mɛə
mares	mɛəz	mɛəz
Margaret	'mɑ·gərɪt	'mɑəgərɪt
margin	'mɑ·ʤɪn	'mɑəʤɪn
margins	'mɑ·ʤɪnz	'mɑəʤɪnz
marine	mə'ri·n	
mark	mɑ·k	mɑək
marks	mɑ·ks	mɑəks
marked	mɑ·kt	mɑəkt
marking	'mɑ·kɪŋ	'mɑəkɪŋ
market	'mɑ·kɪt	'mɑəkɪt
markets	'mɑ·kɪts	'mɑəkɪts
marketed	'mɑ·kɪtɪd	'mɑəkɪtɪd
marketing	'mɑ·kɪtɪŋ	'mɑəkɪtɪŋ
marketable	'mɑ·kɪtəbl̩	'mɑəkɪtəbl̩
markings	'mɑ·kɪŋz	'mɑəkɪŋz
marmalade	'mɑ·məleɪd	'mɑəməleɪd
marquis	'mɑ·kwɪs	'mɑəkwɪs
marquises	'mɑ·kwɪsɪz	'mɑəkwɪsɪz
marriage	'mærɪʤ	
marriages	'mærɪʤɪz	
marry	'mærɪ	
marries	'mærɪz	
married	'mærɪd	

Traditional Spelling	Received Pronunciation	American Variants
marrying	ˈmærɪɪŋ	
Marseilles	mɑˈseɪlz	mɑəˈseɪlz
marsh	mɑːʃ	mɑəʃ
marshes	ˈmɑːʃɪz	ˈmɑəʃɪz
marshal	ˈmɑːʃəl	ˈmɑəʃəl
marshals	ˈmɑːʃəlz	ˈmɑəʃəlz
martyr	ˈmɑːtə(r	ˈmɑətə
martyrs	ˈmɑːtəz	ˈmɑətəz
marvel	ˈmɑːvl̩	ˈmɑəvl̩
marvels	ˈmɑːvl̩z	ˈmɑəvl̩z
marvellous	ˈmɑːvɨləs	ˈmɑəvɨləs
marvellously	ˈmɑːvɨləslɪ	ˈmɑəvɨləslɪ
Mary	ˈmɛərɪ	ˈmɛːrɪ
masculine	ˈmæskjʊlɪn	
mask	mɑːsk	maːsk
masks	mɑːsks	maːsks
mason	ˈmeɪsn̩	
masons	ˈmeɪsn̩z	
masonry	ˈmeɪsn̩rɪ	
masquerade	mɑskəˈreɪd	
	mæskəˈreɪd	
masquerades	mɑskəˈreɪdz	
	mæskəˈreɪdz	
masqueraded	mɑskəˈreɪdɪd	
	mæskəˈreɪdɪd	
masquerading	mɑskəˈreɪdɪŋ	
	mæskəˈreɪdɪŋ	
mass	mæs	
masses	ˈmæsɪz	
Massachusetts	mæsəˈʧuːsɛts	
	mæsəˈʧuːsɪts	
massacre	ˈmæsəkə(r	ˈmæsəkə
massacres	ˈmæsəkəz	ˈmæsəkəz
massacred	ˈmæsəkəd	ˈmæsəkəd
massacring	ˈmæsəkərɪŋ	
massage	mæˈsɑːʒ	
	ˈmæsɑʒ	
massages	mæˈsɑːʒɪz	
	ˈmæsɑʒɪz	
massaged	mæˈsɑːʒd	
	ˈmæsɑʒd	
massaging	mæˈsɑːʒɪŋ	
	ˈmæsɑʒɪŋ	
massive	ˈmæsɪv	
mast	mɑːst	maːst
masts	mɑːsts	maːsts
master	ˈmɑːstə(r	ˈmaːstə

Traditional Spelling	Received Pronunciation	American Variants
masters	'mɑ·stəz	'mɑ·stəz
mastered	'mɑ·stəd	'ma·stəd
mastering	'mɑ·stərɪŋ	'ma·stərɪŋ
masterful	'mɑ·stəfʊl	'ma·stəful
masterly	'mɑ·stəlɪ	'ma·stəlɪ
masterpiece	'mɑ·stəpis	'ma·stəpis
masterpieces	'mɑ·stəpisɪz	'ma·stəpisɪz
mastery	'mɑ·stərɪ	'ma·stərɪ
mat	mæt	
mats	mæts	
match	mætʃ	
matches	'mætʃɪz	
matched	mætʃt	
matching	'mætʃɪŋ	
match-box	'mætʃbɒks	'mætʃbɑks
match-boxes	'mætʃbɒksɪz	'mætʃbɑksɪz
matchless	'mætʃlɪs	
mate	meɪt	
mates	meɪts	
material	mə'tɪərɪəl	mə'tɪ·rɪəl
materials	mə'tɪərɪəlz	mə'tɪ·rɪəlz
materialism	mə'tɪərɪəlɪzm̩	mə'tɪ·rɪəlɪzm̩
materialist	mə'tɪərɪəlɪst	mə'tɪ·rɪəlɪst
materialists	mə'tɪərɪəlɪsts	mə'tɪ·rɪəlɪsts
materialistic	mətɪərɪə'lɪstɪk	mətɪrɪə'lɪstɪk
materially	mə'tɪərɪəlɪ	mə'tɪ·rɪəlɪ
maternal	mə'tɜ·nl̩	mə'tɜənl̩
mathematical	mæθɪ'mætɪkəl mæθə'mætɪkəl	
mathematically	mæθɪ'mætɪkəlɪ mæθə'mætɪkəlɪ	
mathematician	mæθɪmə'tɪʃən mæθəmə'tɪʃən	
mathematicians	mæθɪmə'tɪʃənz mæθəmə'tɪʃənz	
mathematics	mæθɪ'mætɪks mæθə'mætɪks	
matriculate	mə'trɪkjʊleɪt	
matriculates	mə'trɪkjʊleɪts	
matriculated	mə'trɪkjʊleɪtɪd	
matriculating	mə'trɪkjʊleɪtɪŋ	
matriculation	mətrɪkjʊ'leɪʃən	
matriculations	mətrɪkjʊ'leɪʃənz	
matter	'mætə(r	'mætə
matters	'mætəz	'mætəz
mattered	'mætəd	'mætəd
mattering	'mætərɪŋ	

Traditional Spelling	Received Pronunciation	American Variants
Matthew	ʹmæθju	
matting	ʹmætɪŋ	
mattress	ʹmætrɪs	
mattresses	ʹmætrɪsɪz	
mauve	moʊv	
maxim	ʹmæksɪm	
maxims	ʹmæksɪmz	
may	meɪ	
mayn't	meɪnt	
might	maɪt	
mightn't	maɪtn̩t	
May	meɪ	
maybe	ʹmeɪʹbiˑ	
mayor	mɛə(r	meɪə
mayors	mɛəz	meɪəz
me	miˑ *s.f.*, mi, mɪ *w.fs.*	
meadow	ʹmɛdoʊ	
meadows	ʹmɛdoʊz	
meal	miˑl	
meals	miˑlz	
mean	miˑn	
meaner	ʹmiˑnə(r	ʹmiˑnə
meanest	ʹmiˑnɪst	
means	miˑnz	
meant	mɛnt	
meaning	ʹmiˑnɪŋ	
meanings	ʹmiˑnɪŋz	
meanly	ʹmiˑnlɪ	
meanness	ʹmiˑnnɪs	
means, *noun*	miˑnz	
meantime	ʹmiˑnʹtaɪm	
meanwhile	ʹmiˑnʹ*h*waɪl	
measurable	ʹmɛʒərəbl̩	
measure	ʹmɛʒə(r	ʹmɛʒə
measures	ʹmɛʒəz	ʹmɛʒəz
measured	ʹmɛʒəd	ʹmɛʒəd
measuring	ʹmɛʒərɪŋ	
measurement	ʹmɛʒəmənt	ʹmɛʒəmənt
measurements	ʹmɛʒəmənts	ʹmɛʒəmənts
meat	miˑt	
mechanic	mɪʹkænɪk	
mechanics	mɪʹkænɪks	
mechanical	mɪʹkænɪkəl	
mechanically	mɪʹkænɪkəlɪ	
mechanism	ʹmɛkənɪzm̩	
mechanisms	ʹmɛkənɪzm̩z	
medal	ʹmɛdl̩	

Traditional Spelling	Received Pronunciation	American Variants
medals	'mɛdl̩z	
meddle	'mɛdl̩	
meddles	'mɛdl̩z	
meddled	'mɛdl̩d	
meddling	'mɛdlɪŋ, 'mɛdl̩ɪŋ	
meddler	'mɛdlə(r, 'mɛdl̩ə(r	'mɛdlə
meddlers	'mɛdləz, 'mɛdl̩əz	'mɛdləz
mediæval	mɛdɪ'i·vl̩, midɪ'i·vl̩	
medical	'mɛdɪkəl	
medically	'mɛdɪkəlɪ	
medicinal	mɪ'dɪsɪnl̩	
medicinally	mɪ'dɪsɪnəlɪ	
medicine	'mɛdɪsɪn	
medicines	'mɛdɪsɪnz	
medieval	mɛdɪ'i·vl̩, midɪ'i·vl̩	
meditate	'mɛdɪteɪt	
meditates	'mɛdɪteɪts	
meditated	'mɛdɪteɪtɪd	
meditating	'mɛdɪteɪtɪŋ	
meditation	mɛdɪ'teɪʃən	
meditations	mɛdɪ'teɪʃənz	
Mediterranean	mɛdɪtə'reɪnjən	
medium	'mi·dɪəm, 'mi·djəm	
media	'mi·dɪə	
mediums	'mi·dɪəmz 'mi·djəmz	
meek	mi·k	
meeker	'mi·kə(r	'mi·kə
meekest	'mi·kɪst	
meekly	'mi·klɪ	
meekness	'mi·knɪs	
meet	mi·t	
meets	mi·ts	
met	mɛt	
meeting	'mi·tɪŋ	
meetings	'mi·tɪŋz	
melancholy	†'mɛlənkəlɪ †'mɛləŋkəlɪ	'mɛlənkɑlɪ
Melbourne	'mɛlbən, 'mɛlbɔn	'mɛlbən, 'mɛlboən
melodious	mɪ'loʊdjəs	
melody	†'mɛlədɪ	
melodies	†'mɛlədɪz	
melon	'mɛlən	
melons	'mɛlənz	
melt	mɛlt	

† See Note 30, p. xxxv. in Introduction.

T

Traditional Spelling	Received Pronunciation	American Variants
melts	mɛlts	
melted	ˈmɛltɪd	
melting	ˈmɛltɪŋ	
member	ˈmɛmbə(r	ˈmɛmbə
members	ˈmɛmbəz	ˈmɛmbəz
memorable	†ˈmɛmərəbl̩	
memorize	†ˈmɛməraɪz	
memorizes	†ˈmɛməraɪzɪz	
memorized	†ˈmɛməraɪzd	
memorizing	†ˈmɛməraɪzɪŋ	
memory	†ˈmɛmərɪ	
memories	†ˈmɛmərɪz	
MEN, *plur. of* man	mɛn	
menagerie	mɪˈnæʤərɪ mɪˈnɑːʤərɪ	
menageries	mɪˈnæʤərɪz mɪˈnɑːʤərɪz	
mend	mɛnd	
mends	mɛndz	
mended	ˈmɛndɪd	
mending	ˈmɛndɪŋ	
MEN-OF-WAR, *plur. of* man-of-war	ˈmɛnəvˈwɔə(r	ˈmɛnəvˈwɔə
mental	ˈmɛntl̩	
mentally	ˈmɛntəlɪ	
mentality	mɛnˈtælɪtɪ	
mention	ˈmɛnʃən	ˈmɛntʃən
mentions	ˈmɛnʃənz	ˈmɛntʃənz
mentioned	ˈmɛnʃənd	ˈmɛntʃənd
mentioning	ˈmɛnʃənɪŋ	ˈmɛntʃənɪŋ
mercenary	ˈmɜːsɪnərɪ	ˈmɜəsɪnɛrɪ
merchant	ˈmɜːʧənt	ˈmɜəʧənt
merchants	ˈmɜːʧənts	ˈmɜəʧənts
merciful	ˈmɜːsɪful	ˈmɜəsɪful
mercifully	ˈmɜːsɪfulɪ, ˈmɜːsɪfəlɪ	ˈmɜəsɪfulɪ, ˈmɜəsɪfəlɪ
merciless	ˈmɜːsɪlɪs	ˈmɜəsɪlɪs
mercilessly	ˈmɜːsɪlɪslɪ	ˈmɜəsɪlɪslɪ
mercury	ˈmɜːkjurɪ, ˈmɜːkjərɪ	ˈmɜəkjurɪ, ˈmɜəkjərɪ
mercy	ˈmɜːsɪ	ˈmɜəsɪ
mercies	ˈmɜːsɪz	ˈmɜəsɪz
mere	mɪə(r	mɪə
merest	mɪərɪst	ˈmɪːrɪst
merely	ˈmɪəlɪ	ˈmɪəlɪ
meridian	mɪˈrɪdɪən, mɪˈrɪdjən	

† See Note 30, p. xxxv. in Introduction.

Traditional Spelling	Received Pronunciation	American Variants
meridians	mɪ'rɪdɪənz	
	mɪ'rɪdjənz	
merit	'merɪt	
merits	'merɪts	
merry	'merɪ	
merrier	'merɪə(r	'merɪə
merriest	'merɪɪst	
merrily	'merɪlɪ	
mess	mes	
messes	'mesɪz	
message	'mesɪʤ	
messages	'mesɪʤɪz	
messenger	'mesɪnʤə(r	'mesɪnʤə
messengers	'mesɪnʤəz	'mesɪnʤəz
Messrs.	'mesəz, 'mesjəz	'mesəz
messy	'mesɪ	
MET *from* meet	met	
metal	'metḷ	
metals	'metḷz	
metallic	mɪ'tælɪk	
metaphor	'metəfə(r	'metəfə
metaphors	'metəfəz	'metəfəz
metaphoric	metə'fɒrɪk	
metaphorically	metə'fɒrɪkəlɪ	
meter	'mi·tə(r	'mi·tə
meters	'mi·təz	'mi·təz
method	'meθəd	
methods	'meθədz	
methodical	mɪ'θɒdɪkəl	mɪ'θɑdɪkḷ
methodically	mɪ'θɒdɪkəlɪ	mɪ'θɑdɪkəlɪ
methodist	'meθədɪst	
methodists	'meθədɪsts	
metre	'mi·tə(r	'mi·tə
metres	'mi·təz	'mi·təz
metric	'metrɪk	
Mexican	'meksɪkən	
Mexicans	'meksɪkənz	
Mexico	'meksɪkoʊ	
MICE, *plur. of* mouse	maɪs	
Michael	'maɪkəl	
Michigan	'mɪʃɪgən	
microbe	'maɪkroʊb	
microbes	'maɪkroʊbz	
microscope	'maɪkrəskoʊp	
microscopes	'maɪkrəskoʊps	
microscopic	maɪkrəs'kɒpɪk	maɪkrəs'kɑpɪk
microscopically	maɪkrəs'kɒpɪkəlɪ	maɪkrəs'kɑpɪkəlɪ

Traditional Spelling	Received Pronunciation	American Variants
mid-, *prefix*	mɪd	
mid-day	ˈmɪddeɪ	
middle	ˈmɪdl̩	
middles	ˈmɪdl̩z	
middle-aged	ˈmɪdl̩ˈeɪʤd	
midnight	ˈmɪdnaɪt	
midsummer	ˈmɪdsʌmə(r	ˈmɪdsʌmə
midway	ˈmɪdˈweɪ	
MIGHT *from* may	maɪt	
MIGHTN'T *from* may	ˈmaɪtn̩t	
mightily	ˈmaɪtɪlɪ	
mighty	ˈmaɪtɪ	
mightier	ˈmaɪtɪə(r	ˈmaɪtɪə
mightiest	ˈmaɪtɪɪst	
mild	maɪld	
milder	ˈmaɪldə(r	ˈmaɪldə
mildest	ˈmaɪldɪst	
mildew	ˈmɪldju	
mildews	ˈmɪldjuz	
mildewed	ˈmɪldjud	
mildewing	ˈmɪldjuɪŋ	
mildly	ˈmaɪldlɪ	
mildness	ˈmaɪldnɪs	
mile	maɪl	
miles	maɪlz	
militarism	ˈmɪlɪtərɪzm̩	
militarist	ˈmɪlɪtərɪst	
militarists	ˈmɪlɪtərɪsts	
military	ˈmɪlɪtərɪ	ˈmɪlɪterɪ
milk	mɪlk	
mill	mɪl	
mills	mɪlz	
miller	ˈmɪlə(r	ˈmɪlə
millers	ˈmɪləz	ˈmɪləz
million	ˈmɪljən	
millions	ˈmɪljənz	
millionaire	ˈmɪljəˈnɛə(r	ˈmɪljəˈnɛə
millionaires	ˈmɪljəˈnɛəz	ˈmɪljəˈnɛəz
millionth	ˈmɪljənθ	
millionths	ˈmɪljənθs	
mimic	ˈmɪmɪk	
mimics	ˈmɪmɪks	
mimicked	ˈmɪmɪkt	
mimicking	ˈmɪmɪkɪŋ	
mimicry	ˈmɪmɪkrɪ	
mind	maɪnd	
minds	maɪndz	

Traditional Spelling	Received Pronunciation	American Variants
minded	'maɪndɪd	
minding	'maɪndɪŋ	
mindful	'maɪndfʊl	
mine	maɪn	
mines	maɪnz	
mined	maɪnd	
mining	'maɪnɪŋ	
miner	'maɪnə(r	'maɪnə
miners	'maɪnəz	'maɪnəz
mineral	'mɪnᵊrəl	
minerals	'mɪnᵊrəlz	
minimum	'mɪnɪməm	
minima	'mɪnɪmə	
minister	'mɪnɪstə(r	'mɪnɪstə
ministers	'mɪnɪstəz	'mɪnɪstəz
ministry	'mɪnɪstrɪ	
ministries	'mɪnɪstrɪz	
minor	'maɪnə(r	'maɪnə
minority	mɪ'nɒrɪtɪ, maɪ'nɒrɪtɪ	
minorities	mɪ'nɒrɪtɪz maɪ'nɒrɪtɪz	
minus	'maɪnəs	
minute, ***noun***	'mɪnɪt	
minutes	'mɪnɪts	
minute, ***adj.***	maɪ'nju·t, mɪ'nju·t	
minutest	maɪ'nju·tɪst mɪ'nju·tɪst	
minutely	maɪ'nju·tlɪ, mɪ'nju·tlɪ	
minuteness	maɪ'nju·tnɪs mɪ'nju·tnɪs	
miracle	'mɪrəkl̩, 'mɪrɪkl̩	
miracles	'mɪrəkl̩z, 'mɪrɪkl̩z	
miraculous	maɪ'rækjʊləs mɪ'rækjʊləs	
miraculously	maɪ'rækjʊləslɪ mɪ'rækjʊləslɪ	
mirror	'mɪrə(r	'mɪrə
mirrors	'mɪrəz	'mɪrəz
mis-, ***prefix***	mɪs-	
misbehave	'mɪsbɪ'heɪv	
misbehaves	'mɪsbɪ'heɪvz	
misbehaved	'mɪsbɪ'heɪvd	
misbehaving	'mɪsbɪ'heɪvɪŋ	
miscalculate	'mɪs'kælkjʊleɪt	
miscalculates	'mɪs'kælkjʊleɪts	
miscalculated	'mɪs'kælkjʊleɪtɪd	
miscalculating	'mɪs'kælkjʊleɪtɪŋ	

Traditional Spelling	Received Pronunciation	American Variants
miscalculation	′mɪskælkjʊ′leɪʃən	
miscalculations	′mɪskælkjʊ′leɪʃənz	
miscellaneous	mɪsə′leɪnjəs	
	mɪsɪ′leɪnjəs	
mischief	′mɪsʧɪf	
mischievous	′mɪsʧɪvəs	
mischievously	′mɪsʧɪvəslɪ	
misconception	′mɪskən′sɛpʃən	
misconceptions	′mɪskən′sɛpʃənz	
misconduct, *noun*	′mɪs′kɒndəkt	′mɪs′kɑndəkt
miser	′maɪzə(r	′maɪzə
misers	′maɪzəz	′maɪzəz
miserly	′maɪzəlɪ	′maɪzəlɪ
miserable	′mɪzərəbl̩	
miserably	′mɪzərəblɪ	
misery	′mɪzərɪ	
misfortune	mɪs′fɔ·ʧən	mɪs′fɔəʧən
misfortunes	mɪs′fɔ·ʧənz	mɪs′fɔəʧənz
misgovern	′mɪs′gʌvən	′mɪs′gʌvən
misgoverns	′mɪs′gʌvənz	′mɪs′gʌvənz
misgoverned	′mɪs′gʌvənd	′mɪs′gʌvənd
misgoverning	′mɪs′gʌvənɪŋ	′mɪs′gʌvənɪŋ
misgovernment	′mɪs′gʌvənmənt	′mɪs′gʌvənmənt
misguided, *adj.*	′mɪs′gaɪdɪd	
misinform	′mɪsɪn′fɔ·m	′mɪsɪn′fɔəm
misinforms	′mɪsɪn′fɔ·mz	′mɪsɪn′fɔəmz
misinformed	′mɪsɪn′fɔ·md	′mɪsɪn′fɔəmd
misinforming	′mɪsɪn′fɔ·mɪŋ	′mɪsɪn′fɔəmɪŋ
misinterpret	′mɪsɪn′tɜ·prɪt	′mɪsɪn′tɜəprɪt
misinterprets	′mɪsɪn′tɜ·prɪts	′mɪsɪn′tɜəprɪts
misinterpreted	′mɪsɪn′tɜ·prɪtɪd	′mɪsɪn′tɜəprɪtɪd
misinterpreting	′mɪsɪn′tɜ·prɪtɪŋ	′mɪsɪn′tɜəprɪtɪŋ
misinterpretation	′mɪsɪntɜprɪ′teɪʃən	′mɪsɪntɜəprɪ′teɪʃən
misinterpretations	′mɪsɪntɜprɪ′teɪʃənz	′mɪsɪntɜəprɪ′teɪʃənz
mislay	′mɪs′leɪ	
mislays	′mɪs′leɪz	
mislaid	′mɪs′leɪd	
mislaying	′mɪs′leɪɪŋ	
mislead	′mɪs′li·d	
misleads	′mɪs′li·dz	
misled	′mɪs′lɛd	
misleading	′mɪs′li·dɪŋ	
mismanage	′mɪs′mænɪʤ	
mismanages	′mɪs′mænɪʤɪz	
mismanaged	′mɪs′mænɪʤd	
mismanaging	′mɪs′mænɪʤɪŋ	
mismanagement	′mɪs′mænɪʤmənt	

Traditional Spelling	Received Pronunciation	American Variants
misprint	'mɪs'prɪnt	
misprints	'mɪs'prɪnts	
mispronounce	'mɪsprə'naʊns	
mispronounces	'mɪsprə'naʊnsɪz	
mispronounced	'mɪsprə'naʊnst	
mispronouncing	'mɪsprə'naʊnsɪŋ	
mispronunciation	'mɪsprənʌnsɪ'eɪʃən	
mispronunciations	'mɪsprənʌnsɪ'eɪʃənz	
misread	'mɪs'riˑd	
misreads	'mɪs'riˑdz	
misread	'mɪs'rɛd	
misreading	'mɪs'riˑdɪŋ	
misrepresent	'mɪsrɛprɪ'zɛnt	
misrepresents	'mɪsrɛprɪ'zɛnts	
misrepresented	'mɪsrɛprɪ'zɛntɪd	
misrepresenting	'mɪsrɛprɪ'zɛntɪŋ	
misrepresentation	'mɪsrɛprɪzɛn'teɪʃən 'mɪsrɛprɪzən'teɪʃən	
misrepresentations	'mɪsrɛprɪzɛn'teɪʃənz 'mɪsrɛprɪzən'teɪʃənz	
Miss	mɪs *s.f.*, mɪs *w.f.*	
miss	mɪs	
misses	'mɪsɪz	
missed	'mɪst	
missing, *adj.*	'mɪsɪŋ	
mission	'mɪʃən	
missions	'mɪʃənz	
missionary	'mɪʃənərɪ	'mɪʃənɛrɪ
missionaries	'mɪʃənərɪz	'mɪʃənɛrɪz
misspell	'mɪs'spɛl	
misspells	'mɪs'spɛlz	
misspelled	'mɪs'spɛlt	
misspelt	'mɪs'spɛlt	
misspelling	'mɪs'spɛlɪŋ	
misspellings	'mɪs'spɛlɪŋz	
mist	mɪst	
mists	mɪsts	
mistake	mɪs'teɪk	
mistakes	mɪs'teɪks	
mistook	mɪs'tʊk	
mistaken	mɪs'teɪkən	
mistaking	mɪs'teɪkɪŋ	
mistakenly	mɪs'teɪkənlɪ	
mistranslate	'mɪstrɑns'leɪt 'mɪstræns'leɪt	'mɪstrans'leɪt
mistranslates	'mɪstrɑns'leɪts 'mɪstræns'leɪts	'mɪstrans'leɪts

Traditional Spelling	Received Pronunciation	American Variants
mistranslated	ˈmɪstrɑnsˈleɪtɪd ˈmɪstrænsˈleɪtɪd	ˈmɪstransˈleɪtɪd
mistranslating	ˈmɪstrɑnsˈleɪtɪŋ ˈmɪstrænsˈleɪtɪŋ	ˈmɪstransˈleɪtɪŋ
mistranslation	ˈmɪstrɑnsˈleɪʃən ˈmɪstrænsˈleɪʃən	ˈmɪstransˈleɪʃən
mistranslations	ˈmɪstrɑnsˈleɪʃənz ˈmɪstrænsˈleɪʃənz	ˈmɪstransˈleɪʃənz
mistress	ˈmɪstrɪs	
mistresses	ˈmɪstrɪsɪz	
mistrust	ˈmɪsˈtrʌst	
mistrusts	ˈmɪsˈtrʌsts	
mistrusted	ˈmɪsˈtrʌstɪd	
mistrusting	ˈmɪsˈtrʌstɪŋ	
misty	ˈmɪstɪ	
misunderstand	ˈmɪsʌndəˈstænd	ˈmɪsʌndəˈstænd
misunderstands	ˈmɪsʌndəˈstændz	ˈmɪsʌndəˈstændz
misunderstood	ˈmɪsʌndəˈstʊd	ˈmɪsʌndəˈstʊd
misunderstanding	ˈmɪsʌndəˈstændɪŋ	ˈmɪsʌndəˈstændɪŋ
misunderstandings	ˈmɪsʌndəˈstændɪŋz	ˈmɪsʌndəˈstændɪŋz
misuse, *noun*	ˈmɪsˈju·s	
misuse, *verb*	ˈmɪsˈju·z	
misuses	ˈmɪsˈju·zɪz	
misused	ˈmɪsˈju·zd	
misusing	ˈmɪsˈju·zɪŋ	
mix	mɪks	
mixes	ˈmɪksɪz	
mixed	mɪkst	
mixing	ˈmɪksɪŋ	
mixture	ˈmɪkstʃə(r	ˈmɪkstʃə
mixtures	ˈmɪkstʃəz	ˈmɪkstʃəz
mob	mɒb	mɑb
mobs	mɒbz	mɑbz
mobilization	moʊbɪlaɪˈzeɪʃən	
mobilizations	moʊbɪlaɪˈzeɪʃənz	
mobilize	ˈmoʊbɪlaɪz	
mobilizes	ˈmoʊbɪlaɪzɪz	
mobilized	ˈmoʊbɪlaɪzd	
mobilizing	ˈmoʊbɪlaɪzɪŋ	
mock	mɒk	mɑk
mocks	mɒks	mɑks
mocked	mɒkt	mɑkt
mocking	ˈmɒkɪŋ	ˈmɑkɪŋ
mockery	ˈmɒkərɪ	ˈmɑkərɪ
model	ˈmɒdl̩	ˈmɑdl̩
models	ˈmɒdl̩z	ˈmɑdl̩z
modelled	ˈmɒdl̩d	ˈmɑdl̩d

Traditional Spelling	Received Pronunciation	American Variants
modelling	ˈmɒdl̩ɪŋ	ˈmɑdl̩ɪŋ
moderate, *adj.*	ˈmɒdərɪt	ˈmɑdərɪt
moderate, *verb*	ˈmɒdəreɪt	ˈmɑdəreɪt
moderates	ˈmɒdəreɪts	ˈmɑdəreɪts
moderated	ˈmɒdəreɪtɪd	ˈmɑdəreɪtɪd
moderating	ˈmɒdəreɪtɪŋ	ˈmɑdəreɪtɪŋ
moderately	ˈmɒdərɪtlɪ	ˈmɑdərɪtlɪ
moderation	mɒdəˈreɪʃən	mɑdəˈreɪʃən
modern	ˈmɒdən	ˈmɑdən
modest	ˈmɒdɪst	ˈmɑdɪst
modestly	ˈmɒdɪstlɪ	ˈmɑdɪstlɪ
modesty	ˈmɒdɪstɪ	ˈmɑdɪstɪ
modification	mɒdɪfɪˈkeɪʃən	mɑdɪfɪˈkeɪʃən
modifications	mɒdɪfɪˈkeɪʃənz	mɑdɪfɪˈkeɪʃənz
modify	ˈmɒdɪfaɪ	ˈmɑdɪfaɪ
modifies	ˈmɒdɪfaɪz	ˈmɑdɪfaɪz
modified	ˈmɒdɪfaɪd	ˈmɑdɪfaɪd
modifying	ˈmɒdɪfaɪɪŋ	ˈmɑdɪfaɪɪŋ
modifier	ˈmɒdɪfaɪə(r	ˈmɑdɪfaɪə
modifiers	ˈmɒdɪfaɪəz	ˈmɑdɪfaɪəz
Mohammedan	məˈhɒmɪdən moʊˈhæmɪdən	
Mohammedans	məˈhɒmɪdənz moʊˈhæmɪdənz	
moist	mɔɪst	
moister	ˈmɔɪstə(r	ˈmɔɪstə
moistest	ˈmɔɪstɪst	
moisten	ˈmɔɪsn̩	
moistens	ˈmɔɪsn̩z	
moistened	ˈmɔɪsn̩d	
moistening	ˈmɔɪsnɪŋ, ˈmɔɪsn̩ɪŋ	
moistness	ˈmɔɪstnɪs	
moisture	ˈmɔɪstʃə(r	ˈmɔɪstʃə
mold, *Amer.*	moʊld	
molds	moʊldz	
molded	ˈmoʊldɪd	
molding	ˈmoʊldɪŋ	
moldy (*Amer.*)	ˈmoʊldɪ	
molecule	ˈmoʊlɪkjul, ˈmɒlɪkjul	ˈmɑlɪkjul
molecules	ˈmoʊlɪkjulz ˈmɒlɪkjulz	ˈmɑlɪkjulz
moment	ˈmoʊmənt	
moments	ˈmoʊmənts	
monarch	ˈmɒnək	ˈmɑnək
monarchs	ˈmɒnəks	ˈmɑnəks
monarchy	ˈmɒnəkɪ	ˈmɑnəkɪ
monarchies	ˈmɒnəkɪz	ˈmɑnəkɪz

Traditional Spelling	Received Pronunciation	American Variants
monastery	ˈmɒnəstrɪ	ˈmɑnəsterɪ
monasteries	ˈmɒnəstrɪz	ˈmɑnəsterɪz
Monday	ˈmʌndɪ	
Mondays	ˈmʌndɪz	
money	ˈmʌnɪ	
Mongolia	mɒŋˈgouljə mɒŋˈgoulɪə	mɑŋˈgouljə mɑŋˈgoulɪə
Mongolian	mɒŋˈgouljən mɑŋˈgoulɪən	mɑŋˈgouljən mɑŋˈgoulɪən
monk	mʌŋk	
monks	mʌŋks	
monkey	ˈmʌŋkɪ	
monkeys	ˈmʌŋkɪz	
monopolize	məˈnɒpəlaɪz	məˈnɑpəlaɪz
monopolizes	məˈnɒpəlaɪzɪz	məˈnɑpəlaɪzɪz
monopolized	məˈnɒpəlaɪzd	məˈnɑpəlaɪzd
monopolizing	məˈnɒpəlaɪzɪŋ	məˈnɑpəlaɪzɪŋ
monopoly	məˈnɒpəlɪ	məˈnɑpəlɪ
monopolies	məˈnɒpəlɪz	məˈnɑpəlɪz
monosyllabic	ˈmɒnəsɪˈlæbɪk	ˈmɑnəsɪˈlæbɪk
monosyllable	ˈmɒnəsɪləbl̩	ˈmɑnəsɪləbl̩
monosyllables	ˈmɒnəsɪləbl̩z	ˈmɑnəsɪləbl̩z
monotonous	məˈnɒtənəs	məˈnɑtənəs
monotonously	məˈnɒtənəslɪ	məˈnɑtənəslɪ
monotony	məˈnɒtənɪ	məˈnɑtənɪ
monster	ˈmɒnstə(r	ˈmɑnstə
monsters	ˈmɒnstəz	ˈmɑnstəz
monstrosity	mɒnsˈtrɒsɪtɪ	mɑnsˈtrɑsɪtɪ
monstrosities	mɒnsˈtrɒsɪtɪz	mɑnsˈtrɑsɪtɪz
monstrous	ˈmɒnstrəs	ˈmɑnstrəs
month	mʌnθ	
months	mʌnθs	
monthly	ˈmʌnθlɪ	
Montreal	mɒntrɪˈɔ·l	mɑntrɪˈɔ·l
monument	ˈmɒnjumənt ˈmɒnjəmənt	
monuments	ˈmɒnjumənts ˈmɒnjəmənts	
mood	mu·d	
moods	mu·dz	
moon	mu·n	
moonlight	ˈmu·nlaɪt	
moor	mɔə(r, mɔ·(r, muə(r	muə
moors	mɔəz, mɔ·z, muəz	muəz
moored	mɔəd, mɔ·d, muəd	muəd
mooring	ˈmɔərɪŋ, ˈmɔ·rɪŋ ˈmuərɪŋ	ˈmu·rɪŋ

Traditional Spelling	Received Pronunciation	American Variants
moral	ʼmɒrəl	
morality	†məʼrælɪtɪ	
morally	ʼmɒrəlɪ	
morals	ʼmɒrəlz	
morbid	ʼmɔ·bɪd	ʼmɔəbɪd
more	mɔ·(r, mɔə(r	mɔə
moreover	mɔ·rouvə(r	mɔʊʼrouvə
morning	ʼmɔ·nɪŋ	ʼmɔənɪŋ
mornings	ʼmɔ·nɪŋz	ʼmɔənɪŋz
Morocco	məʼrɒkou	məʼrɑkou
mortal	ʼmɔ·tl̩	ʼmɔətl̩
mortals	ʼmɔ·tl̩z	ʼmɔətl̩z
mortality	mɔ·tælɪtɪ	mɔəʼtælɪtɪ
mortally	ʼmɔ·təlɪ	ʼmɔətəlɪ
mortified	ʼmɔ·tɪfaɪd	ʼmɔətɪfaɪd
Moscow	ʼmɒskou	ʼmɑskou
mosquito	məsʼki·tou mɒsʼki·tou	
mosquitoes	məsʼki·touz mɒsʼki·touz	
moss	mɒs	
most	moust	
mostly	ʼmoustlɪ	
moth	mɒθ, mɔθ	
moths	mɒθs, mɔθs, mɔ·ðz	
mother	ʼmʌðə(r	ʼmʌðə
mothers	ʼmʌðəz	ʼmʌðəz
mother-in-law	ʼmʌðərɪnlɔ	
mother-in-laws *or*	ʼmʌðərɪnlɔz	
mothers-in-law	ʼmʌðəzɪnlɔ	ʼmʌðəzɪnlɔ
motion	ʼmouʃən	
motions	ʼmouʃənz	
motive	ʼmoutɪv	
motives	ʼmoutɪvz	
motor	ʼmoutə(r	ʼmoutə
motors	ʼmoutəz	ʼmoutəz
motor-car	ʼmoutəkɑ(r	ʼmoutəkɑə
motor-cars	ʼmoutəkɑz	ʼmoutəkɑəz
motto	ʼmɒtou	ʼmɑtou
mottos	ʼmɒtouz	ʼmɑtouz
mould	mould	
moulds	mouldz	
moulded	ʼmouldɪd	
moulding	ʼmouldɪŋ	
mouldy	ʼmouldɪ	

† See Note 30, p. xxxv. in Introduction.

Traditional Spelling	Received Pronunciation	American Variants
mount	maʊnt	
mounts	maʊnts	
mounted	ˈmaʊntɪd	
mounting	ˈmaʊntɪŋ	
mountain	ˈmaʊntɪn	
mountains	ˈmaʊntɪnz	
mountainous	ˈmaʊntɪnəs	
mourn	mɔ·n, mɔən	moən
mourns	mɔ·nz, mɔənz	moənz
mourned	mɔ·nd, mɔənd	moənd
mourning	ˈmɔ·nɪŋ, ˈmɔənɪŋ	ˈmoənɪŋ
mourner	ˈmɔ·nə(r, ˈmɔənə(r	ˈmoənə
mourners	ˈmɔ·nəz, ˈmɔənəz	ˈmoənəz
mouse	maʊs	
mice	maɪs	
moustache	məsˈtɑ·ʃ, mʊsˈtɑ·ʃ	məsˈta·ʃ, mʊsˈta·ʃ
moustaches	məsˈtɑ·ʃɪz	məsˈta·ʃɪz
	mʊsˈtɑ·ʃɪz	mʊsˈta·ʃɪz
mouth	maʊθ	
mouths	maʊðz	
mouthful	ˈmaʊθfʊl	
mouthfuls	ˈmaʊθfʊlz	
movable	ˈmu·vəbl̩	
move	mu·v	
moves	mu·vz	
moved	mu·vd	
moving	ˈmu·vɪŋ	
movement	ˈmu·vmənt	
movements	ˈmu·vmənts	
Mr.	ˈmɪstə(r	ˈmɪstə
Mrs.	ˈmɪsɪz	
much	mʌʧ	
mud	mʌd	
muddle	ˈmʌdl̩	
muddles	ˈmʌdl̩z	
muddled	ˈmʌdl̩d	
muddling	ˈmʌdlɪŋ, ˈmʌdl̩ɪŋ	
muddy	ˈmʌdɪ	
mule	mju·l	
mules	mju·lz	
multiple	ˈmʌltɪpl̩	
multiples	ˈmʌltɪpl̩z	
multiplication	mʌltɪplɪˈkeɪʃən	
multiply	ˈmʌltɪplaɪ	
multiplies	ˈmʌltɪplaɪz	
multiplied	ˈmʌltɪplaɪd	
multiplying	ˈmʌltɪplaɪɪŋ	

Traditional Spelling	Received Pronunciation	American Variants
mumble	ˈmʌmbl̩	
mumbles	ˈmʌmbl̩z	
mumbled	ˈmʌmbl̩d	
mumbling	ˈmʌmblɪŋ	
	ˈmʌmbl̩ɪŋ	
mummy	ˈmʌmɪ	
mummies	ˈmʌmɪz	
municipal	mjuˈnɪsɪpəl	
murder	ˈmɜˑdə(r	ˈmɜədə
murders	ˈmɜˑdəz	ˈmɜədəz
murdered	ˈmɜˑdəd	ˈmɜədəd
murdering	ˈmɜˑdərɪŋ	ˈmɜədərɪŋ
murderer	ˈmɜˑdərə(r	ˈmɜədərə
murderers	ˈmɜˑdərəz	ˈmɜədərəz
murmur	ˈmɜˑmə(r	ˈmɜəmə
murmurs	ˈmɜˑməz	ˈmɜəməz
murmured	ˈmɜˑməd	ˈmɜəməd
murmuring	ˈmɜˑmərɪŋ	ˈmɜəmərɪŋ
muscle	ˈmʌsl̩	
muscles	ˈmʌsl̩z	
muscular	ˈmʌskjʊlə(r	ˈmʌskjʊlə
	ˈmʌskjələ(r	ˈmʌskjələ
museum	mjuˈziˑəm	
	mjuˈzɪəm	
museums	mjuˈziˑəmz	
	mjuˈzɪəmz	
mushroom	ˈmʌʃrʊm	
mushrooms	ˈmʌʃrʊmz	
music	ˈmjuˑzɪk	
musical	ˈmjuˑzɪkəl	
musically	ˈmjuˑzɪkəlɪ	
musician	mjuˈzɪʃən	
musicians	mjuˈzɪʃənz	
muslin	ˈmʌzlɪn	
must	mʌst *s.f.*,	
	məs*t*, ms*t* *w.fs.*	
mustn't	ˈmʌsn̩*t*	
mustard	ˈmʌstəd	ˈmʌstəd
mutton	ˈmʌtn̩	
mutual	ˈmjuˑtjʊəl	
mutually	ˈmjuˑtjʊəlɪ	
muzzle	ˈmʌzl̩	
muzzles	ˈmʌzl̩z	
muzzled	ˈmʌzl̩d	
muzzling	ˈmʌzlɪŋ, ˈmʌzl̩ɪŋ	
my	maɪ *s.f.*,	
	mɪ *occ. w.f.*	

Traditional Spelling	Received Pronunciation	American Variants
myself	maɪ'sɛlf *s.f.*	
	mɪ'sɛlf *w.f.*	
mysterious	mɪs'tɪərɪəs	mɪs'tɪ·rɪəs
mysteriously	mɪs'tɪərɪəslɪ	mɪs'tɪ·rɪəslɪ
mystery	'mɪstərɪ	
mysteries	'mɪstərɪz	
myth	mɪθ, maɪθ	
myths	mɪθs, maɪθs	

N

Traditional Spelling	Received Pronunciation	American Variants
N	ɛn	
N's	ɛnz	
nail	neɪl	
nails	neɪlz	
nailed	neɪld	
nailing	'neɪlɪŋ	
naked	'neɪkɪd	
name	neɪm	
names	neɪmz	
named	neɪmd	
naming	'neɪmɪŋ	
nameless	'neɪmlɪs	
namely	'neɪmlɪ	
napkin	'næpkɪn	
napkins	'næpkɪnz	
narrative	'nærətɪv	
narratives	'nærətɪvz	
narrow	'nærou	
narrower	'nærouə(r	'nærouə
narrowest	'nærouɪst	
narrows	'nærouz	
narrowed	'næroud	
narrowing	'nærouɪŋ	
narrowly	'nærouli	
narrow-minded	'nærou'maɪndɪd	
narrowness	'nærounɪs	
nasal	'neɪzəl	
nasty	'nɑ·stɪ	'na·stɪ
nastier	'nɑ·stɪə(r	'na·stɪə
nastiest	'nɑ·stɪɪst	'na·stɪɪst
nastily	'nɑ·stɪlɪ	'na·stɪlɪ
nastiness	'nɑ·stɪnɪs	'na·stɪnɪs
nation	'neɪʃən	
nations	'neɪʃənz	
national	'næʃənl̩	

Traditional Spelling	Received Pronunciation	American Variants
nationally	'næʃn̩əlɪ	
nationalism	'næʃənəlɪzm̩	
nationality	næʃə'nælɪtɪ	
nationalities	næʃə'nælɪtɪz	
native	'neɪtɪv	
natives	'neɪtɪvz	
natural	'nætʃərəl	
naturally	'nætʃərəlɪ	
naturalist	'nætʃurəlɪst 'nætʃərəlɪst	
naturalists	'nætʃurəlɪsts 'nætʃərəlɪsts	
naturalization	nætʃurəlaɪ'zeɪʃən nætʃərəlaɪ'zeɪʃən	
naturalize	'nætʃurəlaɪz 'nætʃərəlaɪz	
naturalizes	'nætʃurəlaɪzɪz 'nætʃərəlaɪzɪz	
naturalized	'nætʃurəlaɪzd 'nætʃərəlaɪzd	
naturalizing	'nætʃurəlaɪzɪŋ 'nætʃərəlaɪzɪŋ	
nature	'neɪtʃə(r	'neɪtʃə
natures	'neɪtʃəz	'neɪtʃəz
naught	nɔ·t	
naughts	nɔ·ts	
naughty	'nɔ·tɪ	
naughtier	'nɔ·tɪə(r	'nɔ·tɪə
naughtiest	'nɔ·tɪɪst	
naughtily	'nɔ·tɪlɪ	
naughtiness	'nɔ·tɪnɪs	
nautical	'nɔ·tɪkəl	
naval	'neɪvəl	
navigable	'nævɪgəbl̩	
navigate	'nævɪgeɪt	
navigates	'nævɪgeɪts	
navigated	'nævɪgeɪtɪd	
navigating	'nævɪgeɪtɪŋ	
navigation	nævɪ'geɪʃən	
navigator	'nævɪgeɪtɔ(r	'nævɪgeɪtə
navigators	'neɪvɪgeɪtəz	'nævɪgeɪtəz
navy	'neɪvɪ	
navies	'neɪvɪz	
near	nɪə(r	nɪə
nearer	'nɪərə(r	'nɪ·rə]
nearest	'nɪərɪst	'nɪ·rɪst
nears	nɪəz	nɪəz

Traditional Spelling	Received Pronunciation	American Variants
neared	nɪəd	nɪəd
nearing	ˈnɪərɪŋ	ˈnɪˑrɪŋ
nearly	ˈnɪəlɪ	ˈnɪəlɪ
nearness	ˈnɪənɪs	ˈnɪənɪs
near-sighted	ˈnɪəˈsaɪtɪd	ˈnɪəˈsaɪtɪd
neat	niˑt	
neater	ˈniˑtə(r	ˈniˑtə
neatest	ˈniˑtɪst	
neatly	ˈniˑtlɪ	
neatness	ˈniˑtnɪs	
necessarily	ˈnɛsɪsərɪlɪ, ˈnɛsəsərɪlɪ ˈnɛsɪsɛrɪlɪ	
necessary	ˈnɛsɪsərɪ, ˈnɛsəsərɪ ˈnɛsɪsɛrɪ	
necessaries	ˈnɛsɪsərɪz, ˈnɛsəsərɪz ˈnɛsɪsɛrɪz	
necessitate	nɪˈsɛsɪteɪt	
necessitates	nɪˈsɛsɪteɪts	
necessitated	nɪˈsɛsɪteɪtɪd	
necessitating	nɪˈsɛsɪteɪtɪŋ	
necessity	nɪˈsɛsɪtɪ	
necessities	nɪˈsɛsɪtɪz	
neck	nɛk	
necks	nɛks	
necklace	ˈnɛklɪs	
necklaces	ˈnɛklɪsɪz	
neck-tie	ˈnɛktaɪ	
neck-ties	ˈnɛktaɪz	
need	niˑd	
needs	niˑdz	
needed	ˈniˑdɪd	
needing	ˈniˑdɪŋ	
needn't	ˈniˑdn̩t	
needful	ˈniˑdfʊl	
needle	ˈniˑdl̩	
needles	ˈniˑdl̩z	
needless	ˈniˑdlɪs	
needlessly	ˈniˑdlɪslɪ	
needlework	ˈniˑdl̩wɜk	ˈniˑdl̩wɜək
NEEDN'T *from* need	ˈniˑdn̩t	
negative	ˈnɛgətɪv	
negatives	ˈnɛgətɪvz	
negatively	ˈnɛgətɪvlɪ	
neglect	nɪˈglɛkt	
neglects	nɪˈglɛkts	
neglected	nɪˈglɛktɪd	
neglecting	nɪˈglɛktɪŋ	

Traditional Spelling	Received Pronunciation	American Variants
neglectful	nɪ'glɛktful	
neglectfully	nɪ'glɛktfulɪ nɪ'glɛktfəlɪ	
negligence	'nɛglɪʤəns	
negligent	'nɛglɪʤənt	
negligently	'nɛglɪʤəntlɪ	
negligible	'nɛglɪʤɪbl̩	
negotiate	nɪ'gouʃɪeɪt	
negotiates	nɪ'gouʃɪeɪts	
negotiated	nɪ'gouʃɪeɪtɪd	
negotiating	nɪ'gouʃɪeɪtɪŋ	
negotiation	nɪgouʃɪ'eɪʃən	
negotiations	nɪgouʃɪ'eɪʃənz	
negress	'niˑgrɪs	
negresses	'niˑgrɪsɪz	
negro	'niˑgrou	
negroes	'niˑgrouz	
neighbor (*Amer.*)		
neighbour	'neɪbə(r	'neɪbə
neighbors (*Amer.*)		
neighbours	'neɪbəz	'neɪbəz
neighborhood (*Amer.*)		
neighbourhood	'neɪbəhud	'neɪbəhud
neighborhoods (*Am.*)		
neighbourhoods	'neɪbəhudz	'neɪbəhudz
neighborly (*Amer.*)		
neighbourly	'neɪbəlɪ	'neɪbəlɪ
neither	'naɪðə(r, 'niˑðə(r	'naɪðə, 'niˑðə
Nellie *or* **Nelly**	'nɛlɪ	
nephew	'nɛvju, 'nɛfju	
nephews	'nɛvjuz, 'nɛfjuz	
nerve	nɜˑv	nɜəv
nerves	nɜˑvz	nɜəvz
nervous	'nɜˑvəs	'nɜəvəs
nervously	'nɜˑvəslɪ	'nɜəvəslɪ
nest	nɛst	
nests	nɛsts	
net	nɛt	
nets	nɛts	
Netherlands	'nɛðələndz	'nɛðələndz
netting	'nɛtɪŋ	
neuralgia	njuə'rælʤjə njɔə'rælʤjə	
neuter	'njuˑtə(r	'njuˑtə
neuters	'njuˑtəz	'njuˑtəz
neutral	'njuˑtrəl	
neutrals	'njuˑtrəlz	

Traditional Spelling	Received Pronunciation	American Variants
neutrality	njuˈtrælɪtɪ	
never	ˈnɛvə(r	ˈnɛvə
nevertheless	nɛvəðəˈlɛs	ˈnɛvəðəˈlɛs
new	njuˑ	
newer	ˈnjuˑə(r	ˈnjuˑə
newest	ˈnjuˑɪst	
newly	ˈnjuˑlɪ	
newcomer	ˈnjuˑˈkʌmə(r	ˈnjuˑˈkʌmə
newcomers	ˈnjuˑˈkʌməz	ˈnjuˑˈkʌməz
news, *sing.*	njuˑz	
newspaper	ˈnjuˑspeɪpə(r ˈnjuˑzpeɪpə(r	ˈnjuˑspeɪpə ˈnjuˑzpeɪpə
newspapers	ˈnjuˑspeɪpəz ˈnjuˑzpeɪpəz	ˈnjuˑspeɪpəz ˈnjuˑzpeɪpəz
New York	ˈnjuˑˈjɔˑk	ˈnjuˑˈjɔək
New Zealand	njuˈziˑlənd	
next	nɛkst	
nice	naɪs	
nicer	ˈnaɪsə(r	ˈnaɪsə
nicest	ˈnaɪsɪst	
nicely	ˈnaɪslɪ	
niceness	ˈnaɪsnɪs	
nicety	ˈnaɪsɪtɪ	
niceties	ˈnaɪsɪtɪz	
Nicholas	ˈnɪkələs	
nickel	ˈnɪkl̩	
nickels	ˈnɪkl̩z	
nickname	ˈnɪkneɪm	
nicknames	ˈnɪkneɪmz	
niece	niˑs	
nieces	ˈniˑsɪz	
night	naɪt	
nights	naɪts	
nightly	ˈnaɪtlɪ	
Nile	naɪl	
nine	naɪn	
nineteen	ˈnaɪnˈtiˑn	
nineteenth	ˈnaɪnˈtiˑnθ	
nineteenths	ˈnaɪnˈtiˑnθs	
ninetieth	ˈnaɪntɪɪθ	
ninetieths	ˈnaɪntɪɪθs	
ninety	ˈnaɪntɪ	
ninth	naɪnθ	
ninths	naɪnθs	
nitrogen	ˈnaɪtrəʤən	
no	noʊ	
noble	ˈnoʊbl̩	

Traditional Spelling	Received Pronunciation	American Variants
nobles	ˈnoʊbl̩z	
nobler	ˈnoʊblə(r	ˈnoʊblə
noblest	ˈnoʊblɪst	
nobleman	ˈnoʊbl̩mən	
noblemen	ˈnoʊbl̩mən	
nobleness	ˈnoʊbl̩nɪs	
nobly	ˈnoʊblɪ	
nobody	ˈnoʊbədɪ, ˈnoʊbɒdɪ	ˈnoʊbɑdɪ
nod	nɒd	nɑd
nods	nɒdz	nɑdz
nodded	ˈnɒdɪd	ˈnɑdɪd
nodding	ˈnɒdɪŋ	ˈnɑdɪŋ
noise	nɔɪz	
noises	ˈnɔɪzɪz	
noiseless	ˈnɔɪzlɪs	
noiselessly	ˈnɔɪzlɪslɪ	
noisy	ˈnɔɪzɪ	
noisier	ˈnɔɪzɪə(r	ˈnɔɪzɪə
noisiest	ˈnɔɪzɪɪst	
noisily	ˈnɔɪzɪlɪ	
nominal	ˈnɒmɪnl̩	ˈnɑmɪnl̩
nominate	ˈnɒmɪneɪt	ˈnɑmɪneɪt
nominates	ˈnɒmɪneɪts	ˈnɑmɪneɪts
nominated	ˈnɒmɪneɪtɪd	ˈnɑmɪneɪtɪd
nominating	ˈnɒmɪneɪtɪŋ	ˈnɑmɪneɪtɪŋ
nomination	nɒmɪˈneɪʃən	nɑmɪˈneɪʃən
nominations	nɒmɪˈneɪʃənz	nɑmɪˈneɪʃənz
non, *neg. prefix*	nɒn	nɑn
none	nʌn	
nonsense	ˈnɒnsəns	ˈnɑnsəns, ˈnɑnsɛns
nonsensical	nɒnˈsɛnsɪkəl	nɑnˈsɛnsɪkəl
noon	nu·n	
noose	nu·s, nu·z	
nooses	ˈnu·sɪz, ˈnu·zɪz	
nor	nɔ·(r *s.f.*, nɔ(r *w.f.*	nɔə *s.f.*, nə *w.f.*
normal	ˈnɔ·məl	ˈnɔəməl
normally	ˈnɔ·məlɪ	ˈnɔəməlɪ
north	nɔ·θ	nɔəθ
north-east	ˈnɔ·θˈi·st	ˈnɔəθˈi·st
northerly	ˈnɔ·ðəlɪ	ˈnɔəθəlɪ
northern	ˈnɔ·ðən	ˈnɔəðən
northward	ˈnɔ·θwəd	ˈnɔəθwəd
northwards	ˈnɔ·θwədz	ˈnɔəθwədz
north-west	ˈnɔ·θˈwɛst	ˈnɔəθˈwɛst
Norway	ˈnɔ·weɪ	ˈnɔəweɪ
Norwegian	nɔˈwi·dʒən	nɔəˈwi·dʒən
Norwegians	nɔˈwi·dʒənz	nɔəˈwi·dʒənz

Traditional Spelling	Received Pronunciation	American Variants
nose	noʊz	
noses	'noʊzɪz	
not	nɒt	nɑt
	nt, *after finites ending in a vowel*	
	n̩t, *after finites ending in a consonant*	
notably	'noutəblɪ	
notation	nou'teɪʃən	
notations	nou'teɪʃənz	
note	noʊt	
notes	noʊts	
noted	'noʊtɪd	
noting	'noʊtɪŋ	
nothing	'nʌθɪŋ	
notice	'noʊtɪs	
notices	'noʊtɪsɪz	
noticed	'noʊtɪst	
noticing	'noʊtɪsɪŋ	
noticeable	'noʊtɪsəbl̩	
notification	noʊtɪfɪ'keɪʃən	
notifications	noʊtɪfɪ'keɪʃənz	
notify	'noʊtɪfaɪ	
notifies	'noʊtɪfaɪz	
notified	'noʊtɪfaɪd	
notifying	'noʊtɪfaɪɪŋ	
notion	'nouʃən	
notions	'nouʃənz	
notorious	nou'tɔ·rɪəs	nou'torɪəs
	nə'tɔ·rɪəs	nə'torɪəs
notwithstanding	nɒtwɪθ'stændɪŋ	nɑtwɪθ'stændɪŋ
	nɒtwɪð'stændɪŋ	
nought	nɔ·t	
noughts	nɔ·ts	
noun	naʊn	
nouns	naʊnz	
nourish	'nʌrɪʃ	'nɜrɪʃ
nourishes	'nʌrɪʃɪz	'nɜrɪʃɪz
nourished	'nʌrɪʃt	'nɜrɪʃt
nourishing	'nʌrɪʃɪŋ	'nɜrɪʃɪŋ
nourishment	'nʌrɪʃmənt	'nɜrɪʃmənt
novel	'nɒvəl	'nɑvəl
novels	'nɒvəlz	'nɑvəlz
novelist	'nɒvəlɪst	'nɑvəlɪst
novelists	'nɒvəlɪsts	'nɑvəlɪsts
novelty	'nɒvl̩tɪ	'nɑvl̩tɪ
novelties	'nɒvl̩tɪz	'nɑvl̩tɪz

Traditional Spelling	Received Pronunciation	American Variants
November	nə'vɛmbə(r	nə'vɛmbə
	nou'vɛmbə(r	nou'vɛmbə
novice	'nɒvɪs	'nɑvɪs
novices	'nɒvɪsɪz	'nɑvɪsɪz
now	naʊ	
nowadays	'naʊədeɪz	
nowhere	'nouhwɛə(r	
N'T = *not*	nt *after a vowel*, n̩t *after a consonant*	
nucleus	'nju·klɪəs	
nuisance	'nju·sn̩s	
nuisances	'nju·sn̩sɪz	
number	'nʌmbə(r	'nʌmbə
numbers	'nʌmbəz	'nʌmbəz
numbered	'nʌmbəd	'nʌmbəd
numbering	'nʌmbərɪŋ	
numeral	'nju·mərəl	
numerals	'nju·mərəlz	
numerical	nju'mɛrɪkəl	
numerous	'nju·mərəs	
nun	nʌn	
nuns	nʌnz	
nurse	nɜ·s	nɜəs
nurses	'nɜ·sɪz	'nɜəsɪz
nursed	nɜ·st	nɜəst
nursing	'nɜ·sɪŋ	'nɜəsɪŋ
nursery	'nɜ·sərɪ	'nɜəsərɪ
nurseries	'nɜ·sərɪz	'nɜəsərɪz
nut	nʌt	
nuts	nʌts	
nutshell	'nʌtʃɛl	
nutshells	'nʌtʃɛlz	

O

Traditional Spelling	Received Pronunciation	American Variants
O	ou	
O's	ouz	
oak	ouk	
oaks	ouks	
oar	ɔ·(r, ɔə(r	oə
oars	ɔ·z, ɔəz	oəz
oats	outs	
oath	ouθ	
oaths	ouðz, ouθs	
oatmeal	'outmil	

Traditional Spelling	Received Pronunciation	American Variants
obdurate	ˈɒbdjʊrɪt, əbˈdjʊərit	ˈɑbdjʊrɪt, ˈɑbdjʊreɪt
obdurately	ˈɒbdjʊrɪtlɪ	ˈɑbdjʊrɪtlɪ
	əbˈdjʊərɪtlɪ	ˈɑbdjʊreɪtlɪ
obedience	əˈbiˑdɪəns, oʊˈbiˑdɪəns	
	əˈbiˑdjəns, oʊˈbiˑdjəns	
obedient	əˈbiˑdɪənt, oʊˈbiˑdɪənt	
	əˈbiˑdjənt, oʊˈbiˑdjənt	
obediently	əˈbiˑdjəntlɪ	
	oʊˈbiˑdjəntlɪ	
obey	əˈbeɪ, oʊˈbeɪ	
obeys	əˈbeɪz, oʊˈbeɪz	
obeyed	əˈbeɪd, oʊˈbeɪd	
obeying	əˈbeɪɪŋ, oʊˈbeɪɪŋ	
object, ***noun***	ˈɒbʤɪkt	ˈɑbʤɪkt
objects	ˈɒbʤɪkts	ˈɑbʤɪkts
object, *verb*	†əbˈʤɛkt	
objects	†əbˈʤɛkts	
objected	†əbˈʤɛktɪd	
objecting	†əbˈʤɛktɪŋ	
objection	†əbˈʤɛkʃən	
objections	†əbˈʤɛkʃənz	
objectionable	†əbˈʤɛkʃənəbḷ	
objective	†əbˈʤɛktɪv	
objectively	†əbˈʤɛktɪvlɪ	
objector	†əbˈʤɛktə(r	†əbˈʤɛktə
objectors	†əbˈʤɛktəz	†əbˈʤɛktəz
obligation	ɒblɪˈgeɪʃən	ɑblɪˈgeɪʃən
obligations	ɒblɪˈgeɪʃənz	ɑblɪˈgeɪʃənz
obligatory	ˈɒblɪgətərɪ	ˈɑblɪgətorɪ
	ˈɒblɪgeɪtərɪ	ˈɑblɪgeɪtorɪ
	†əˈblɪgətərɪ	†əˈblɪgətorɪ
oblige	†əˈblaɪʤ	
obliges	†əˈblaɪʤɪz	
obliged	†əˈblaɪʤd	
obliging	†əˈblaɪʤɪŋ	
obligingly	†əˈblaɪʤɪŋlɪ	
oblique	†əˈbliˑk	
obliterate	†əˈblɪtəreɪt	
obliterates	†əˈblɪtəreɪts	
obliterated	†əˈblɪtəreɪtɪd	
obliterating	†əˈblɪtəreɪtɪŋ	
oblivious	†əˈblɪvɪəs	
oblong	ˈɒblɒŋ	ˈɑblɒŋ
oblongs	ˈɒblɒŋz	ˈɒblɒŋz
obnoxious	†əbˈnɒkʃəs	†əbˈnɑkʃəs

† See Note 30, p. xxxv. in Introduction.

Traditional Spelling	Received Pronunciation	American Variants
obnoxiously	†əb'nɒkʃəslɪ	†əb'nɑkʃəslɪ
obscene	†əb'siˑn	
obscure	†əb'skjuə(r	†əb'skjuɚ
obscurer	†əb'skjuərə(r	†əb'skjuˑrɚ
obscurest	†əb'skjuərɪst	†əb'skjuˑrɪst
obscures	†əb'skjuəz	†əb'skjuɚz
obscured	†əb'skjuəd	†əb'skjuɚd
obscuring	†əb'skjuərɪŋ	†əb'skjuˑrɪŋ
obscurely	†əb'skjuəlɪ	†əb'skjuɚlɪ
obscurity	†əb'skjuərɪtɪ	†əb'skjuˑrɪtɪ
observance	†əb'zɜˑvəns	†əb'zɝvəns
observant	†əb'zɜˑvənt	†əb'zɝvənt
observation	ɒbzə'veɪʃən	ɑbzɚ'veɪʃən
observations	ˌɒbzə'veɪʃənz	ɑbzɚ'veɪʃənz
observe	†əb'zɜˑv	†əb'zɝv
observes	†əb'zɜˑvz	†əb'zɝvz
observed	†əb'zɜˑvd	†əb'zɝvd
observing	†əb'zɜˑvɪŋ	†əb'zɝvɪŋ
observer	†əb'zɜˑvə(r	†əb'zɝvɚ
observers	†əb'zɜˑvəz	†əb'zɝvɚz
obsolete	†'ɒbsəliˑt	†'ɑbsəliˑt
obstacle	'ɒbstəkl̩	'ɑbstəkl̩
obstacles	'ɒbstəkl̩z	'ɑbstəkl̩z
obstinacy	'ɑbstɪnəsɪ	'ɑbstɪnəsɪ
obstinate	'ɒbstɪnɪt	'ɑbstɪnɪt
obstinately	'ɒbstɪnɪtlɪ	'ɑbstɪnɪtlɪ
obstruct	†əb'strʌkt	
obstructs	†əb'strʌkts	
obstructed	†əb'strʌktɪd	
obstructing	†əb'strʌktɪŋ	
obstruction	†əb'strʌkʃən	
obstructions	†əb'strʌkʃənz	
obtain	†əb'teɪn	
obtains	†əb'teɪnz	
obtained	†əb'teɪnd	
obtaining	†əb'teɪnɪŋ	
obtainable	†əb'teɪnəbl̩	
obtuse	†əb'tjuˑs	
obviate	'ɒbvɪeɪt	'ɑbvɪeɪt
obviates	'ɒbvɪeɪts	'ɑbvɪeɪts
obviated	'ɒbvɪeɪtɪd	'ɑbvɪeɪtɪd
obviating	'ɒbvɪeɪtɪŋ	'ɑbvɪeɪtɪŋ
obvious	'ɒbvɪəs 'ɒbvjəs	'ɑbvɪəs 'ɑbvjəs
obviously	ɒbvɪəslɪ, 'ɒbvjəslɪ	'ɑbvɪəslɪ, 'ɑbvjəslɪ

† See Note **30**, p. **xxxv.** in Introduction.

Traditional Spelling	Received Pronunciation	American Variants
obviousness	ˈɒbvɪəsnɪs, ˈɒbvjəsnɪs	ˈɑbvɪəsnɪs, ˈɑbvjəsnɪs
occasion	†əˈkeɪʒən	
occasions	†əˈkeɪʒənz	
occasioned	†əˈkeɪʒənd	
occasioning	†əˈkeɪʒənɪŋ	
occasional	†əˈkeɪʒənl̩	
occasionally	†əˈkeɪʒənəlɪ	
occupant	ˈɒkjupənt	ˈɑkjupənt
occupants	ˈɒkjupənts	ˈɑkjupənts
occupation	ɒkjuˈpeɪʃən	ɑkjuˈpeɪʃən
occupations	ɒkjuˈpeɪʃənz	ɑkjuˈpeɪʃənz
occupy	ˈɒkjupaɪ	ˈɑkjupaɪ
occupies	ˈɒkjupaɪz	ˈɑkjupaɪz
occupied	ˈɒkjupaɪd	ˈɑkjupaɪd
occupying	ˈɒkjupaɪɪŋ	ˈɑkjupaɪɪŋ
occupier	ˈɒkjupaɪə(r	ˈɑkjupaɪə
occupiers	ˈɒkjupaɪəz	ˈɑkjupaɪəz
occur	†əˈkɜː(r	†əˈkɜə
occurs	†əˈkɜːz	†əˈkɜəz
occurred	†əˈkɜːd	†əˈkɜəd
occurring	†əˈkɜːrɪŋ	
occurrence	†əˈkʌrəns, †əˈkɜːrəns	
occurrences	†əˈkʌrənsɪz †əˈkɜːrənsɪz	
ocean	ˈouʃən	
oceans	ˈouʃənz	
o'clock	†əˈklɒk	†əˈklɑk
October	ɒkˈtoubə(r	ɑkˈtoubə
oculist	ˈɒkjulɪst	ˈɑkjulɪst
oculists	ˈɒkjulɪsts	ˈɑkjulɪsts
odd	ɒd	ɑd
odder	ˈɒdə(r	ˈɑdə
oddest	ˈɒdɪst	ˈɑdɪst
oddly	ˈɒdlɪ	ˈɑdlɪ
oddness	ˈɒdnɪs	ˈɑdnɪs
odds	ɒdz	ɑdz
odor (*Amer.*) **odour**	ˈoudə(r	ˈoudə
odors (*Amer.*) odours	ˈoudəz	ˈoudəz
odorless (*Amer.*) **odourless**	ˈoudəlɪs	ˈoudəlɪs
of	ɒv *s.f.*, əv, v *w.fs.*,	ɑv *s.f.*
off	ɔːf, ɔf, ɒf	
offence	†əˈfɛns	

† See Note **30**, p. xxxv. in Introduction.

Traditional Spelling	Received Pronunciation	American Variants
offences	†ə'fɛnsɪz	
offend	†ə'fɛnd	
offends	†ə'fɛndz	
offended	†ə'fɛndɪd	
offending	†ə'fɛndɪŋ	
offender	†ə'fɛndə(r	†ə'fɛndə
offenders	†ə'fɛndəz	†ə'fɛndəz
offensive	†ə'fɛnsɪv	
offensively	†ə'fɛnsɪvlɪ	
offer	'ɒfə(r	'ɒfə
offers	'ɒfəz	'ɒfəz
offered	'ɒfəd	'ɒfəd
offering	'ɒfərɪŋ	'ɒfərɪŋ
offerings	'ɒfərɪŋz	'ɒfərɪŋz
off-hand	'ɔ·f'hænd	
office	'ɒfɪs	
offices	'ɒfɪsɪz	
officer	'ɒfɪsə(r	'ɑfɪsə
officers	'ɒfɪsəz	'ɑfɪsəz
official	†ə'fɪʃəl	
officials	†ə'fɪʃəlz	
officially	†ə'fɪʃəlɪ	
officiate	†ə'fɪʃɪeɪt	
officiates	†ə'fɪʃɪeɪts	
officiated	†ə'fɪʃɪeɪtɪd	
officiating	†ə'fɪʃɪeɪtɪŋ	
officious	†ə'fɪʃəs	
officiously	†ə'fɪʃəslɪ	
officiousness	†ə'fɪʃəsnɪs	
often	'ɔ·fn̩, 'ɔfn̩, 'ɒfn̩	'ɑfn̩
oh	oʊ	
oil	ɔɪl	
oils	ɔɪlz	
oiled	ɔɪld	
oiling	'ɔɪlɪŋ	
oily	'ɔɪlɪ	
ointment	'ɔɪntmənt	
old	oʊld	
older	'oʊldə(r	'oʊldə
oldest	'oʊldɪst	
old-fashioned	'oʊld-fæʃənd	
oldish	'oʊldɪʃ	
omelet(te)	'ɒmlɪt	'ɑməlɪt
omelet(te)s	'ɒmlɪts	'ɑməlɪts
omission	ə'mɪʃən, oʊ'mɪʃən	

† See Note **30**, p. xxxv. in Introduction.

Traditional Spelling	Received Pronunciation	American Variants
omissions	ə'mɪʃənz, oʊ'mɪʃənz	
omit	ə'mɪt, oʊ'mɪt	
omits	ə'mɪts, oʊ'mɪts	
omitted	ə'mɪtɪd, oʊ'mɪtɪd	
omitting	ə'mɪtɪŋ, oʊ'mɪtɪŋ	
omnibus	'ɒmnɪbəs	'ɑmnɪbəs
omnibuses	'ɒmnɪbəsɪz	'ɑmnɪbəsɪz
omnipotence	ɒm'nɪpətəns	ɑm'nɪpətəns
omnipotent	ɒm'nɪpətənt	ɑm'nɪpətənt
omnipotently	ɒm'nɪpətəntlɪ	ɑm'nɪpətəntlɪ
on	ɒn	ɑn
once	wʌns	
one	wʌn	
ones	wʌnz	
oneself	wʌn'sɛlf	
onesided	'wʌn'saɪdɪd	
onion	'ʌnjən	
onions	'ʌnjənz	
onlooker	'ɒnlukə(r	'ɑnlukə
onlookers	'ɒnlukəz	'ɑnlukəz
only	'ounlɪ	
onward	'ɒnwəd	'ɑnwəd
onwards	'ɒnwədz	'ɑnwədz
ooze	uːz	
oozes	'uːzɪz	
oozed	uːzd	
oozing	'uːzɪŋ	
open	'oupən	
opens	'oupənz	
opened	'oupənd	
opening	'oupnɪŋ	
openings	'oupnɪŋz	
opener	'oupnə(r	'oupnə
openers	'oupnəz	'oupnəz
openly	'oupn̩lɪ	
opera	'ɒpərə	'ɑpərə
operas	'ɒpərəz	'ɑpərəz
operate	'ɒpəreɪt	'ɑpəreɪt
operates	'ɒpəreɪts	'ɑpəreɪts
operated	'ɒpəreɪtɪd	'ɑpəreɪtɪd
operating	'ɒpəreɪtɪŋ	'ɑpəreɪtɪŋ
operator	'ɒpəreɪtə(r	'ɑpəreɪtə
operators	'ɒpəreɪtəz	'ɑpəreɪtəz
operatic	ɒpə'rætɪk	ɑpə'rætɪk
operation	ɒpə'reɪʃən	ɑpə'reɪʃən
operations	ɒpə'reɪʃənz	ɑpə'reɪʃənz
opinion	†ə'pɪnjən	

Traditional Spelling	Received Pronunciation	American Variants
opinions	†ə'pɪnjənz	
opium	'oupɪəm	
opponent	†ə'pounənt	
opponents	†ə'pounənts	
opportune	'ɒpətjun	'apətjun
opportunely	'ɒpətjunlɪ	'apətjunlɪ
	ɒpə'tju·nlɪ	apə'tju·nlɪ
opportunity	ɒpə'tju·nɪtɪ	apə'tju·nɪtɪ
opportunities	ɒpə'tju·nɪtɪz	apə'tju·nɪtɪz
oppose	†ə'pouz	
opposes	†ə'pouzɪz	
opposed	†ə'pouzd	
opposing	†ə'pouzɪŋ	
opposite	'ɒpəzɪt	'apəzɪt
opposition	ɒpə'zɪʃən	apə'zɪʃən
oppress	†ə'prɛs	
oppresses	†ə'prɛsɪz	
oppressed	†ə'prɛst	
oppressing	†ə'prɛsɪŋ	
oppressor	†ə'prɛsə(r	†ə'prɛsə
oppressors	†ə'prɛsəz	†ə'prɛsəz
oppression	†ə'prɛʃən	
oppressive	†ə'prɛsɪv	
optical	'ɒptɪkəl	'aptɪkḷ
optimism	'ɒptɪmɪzm̩	'aptɪmɪzm̩
optimist	'ɒptɪmɪst	'aptɪmɪst
optimists	'ɒptɪmɪsts	'aptɪmɪsts
optimistic	ɒptɪ'mɪstɪk	aptɪ'mɪstɪk
option	'ɒpʃən	'apʃən
options	'ɒpʃənz	'apʃənz
optional	'ɒpʃənḷ	'apʃənḷ
optionally	'ɒpʃənəlɪ	'apʃn̩əlɪ
or	ɔ·(r, ə(r	ɔə, ə
oral	'ɔ·rəl	'orəl
orally	'ɔ·rəlɪ	'orəlɪ
orange	'ɒrɪnʤ, 'ɒrənʤ	
oranges	'ɒrɪnʤɪz, 'ɒrənʤɪz	
orator	'ɒrətə(r, 'ɒrɪtə(r	
orators	'ɒrətəz, 'ɒrɪtəz	
oratorical	ɒrə'tɒrɪkəl	
orchard	'ɔ·ʧəd	'ɔəʧəd
orchards	'ɔ·ʧədz	'ɔəʧədz
orchestra	'ɔ·kɪstrə	'ɔəkɪstrə
orchestras	'ɔ·kɪstrəz	'ɔəkɪstrəz
ordain	ɔ'deɪn	ɔə'deɪn

† See Note 30, p. xxxv. in Introduction.

Traditional Spelling	Received Pronunciation	American Variants
ordains	ɔˈdeɪnz	ɔəˈdeɪnz
ordained	ɔˈdeɪnd	ɔəˈdeɪnd
ordaining	ɔˈdeɪnɪŋ	ɔəˈdeɪnɪŋ
ordeal	ɔˈdiˑəl, ˈɔˑdiəl	ˈɔədiəl
ordeals	ɔˈdiˑəlz, ˈɔˑdiəlz	ˈɔədiəlz
order	ˈɔˑdə(r	ˈɔədə
orders	ˈɔˑdəz	ˈɔədəz
ordered	ˈɔˑdəd	ˈɔədəd
ordering	ˈɔˑdərɪŋ	ˈɔədərɪŋ
orderly	ˈɔˑdəlɪ	ˈɔədəlɪ
ordinal	ˈɔˑdɪnl̩	ˈɔədɪnl̩
ordinals	ˈɔˑdɪnl̩z	ˈɔədɪnl̩z
ordinary	ˈɔˑdɪnrɪ	ˈɔədɪnɛrɪ
ordinarily	ˈɔˑdɪnərɪlɪ	ˈɔədɪnɛrɪlɪ
ore	ɔˑ(r, ɔə(r	oə
ores	ɔˑz, ɔəz	oəz
organ	ˈɔˑgən	ˈɔəgən
organs	ˈɔˑgənz	ˈɔəgənz
organic	ɔˈgænɪk	ɔəˈgænɪk
organically	ɔˈgænɪkəlɪ	ɔəˈgænɪkəlɪ
organist	ˈɔˑgənɪst	ˈɔəgənɪst
organists	ˈɔˑgənɪsts	ˈɔəgənɪsts
organization	ɔgənaɪˈzeɪʃən ɔgənɪˈzeɪʃən	ɔəgənaɪˈzeɪʃən ɔəgənɪˈzeɪʃən
organizations	ɔgənaɪˈzeɪʃənz ɔgənɪˈzeɪʃənz	ɔəgənaɪˈzeɪʃənz ɔəgənɪˈzeɪʃənz
organize	ˈɔˑgənaɪz	ˈɔəgənaɪz
organizes	ˈɔˑgənaɪzɪz	ˈɔəgənaɪzɪz
organized	ˈɔˑgənaɪzd	ˈɔəgənaɪzd
organizing	ˈɔˑgənaɪzɪŋ	ˈɔəgənaɪzɪŋ
organizer	ˈɔˑgənaɪzə(r	ˈɔəgənaɪzə
organizers	ˈɔˑgənaɪzəz	ˈɔəgənaɪzəz
orient	ˈɔˑrɪənt, ˈɒrɪənt	ˈorɪənt
oriental	ɔrɪˈɛntl̩, ɒrɪˈɛntl̩	orɪˈɛntl̩
orientals	ɔrɪˈɛntl̩z, ɒrɪˈɛntl̩z	orɪˈɛntl̩z
origin	ˈɒrɪʤɪn	ˈɑrɪʤɪn
origins	ˈɒrɪʤɪnz	ˈɑrɪʤɪnz
original	†əˈrɪʤɪnl̩	
originally	†əˈrɪʤɪnəlɪ	
originality	†ərɪʤɪˈnælɪtɪ	
originate	†əˈrɪʤɪneɪt	
originates	†əˈrɪʤɪneɪts	
originated	†əˈrɪʤɪneɪtɪd	
originating	†əˈrɪʤɪneɪtɪŋ	
ornament, ***noun***	ˈɔˑnəmənt	ˈɔənəmənt

† See Note 30, p. xxxv. in Introduction.

Traditional Spelling	Received Pronunciation	American Variants
ornaments	ˈɔˑnəmənts	ˈɔənəmənts
ornamental	ɔnəˈmentl̩	ɔənəˈmentl̩
orphan	ˈɔˑfn̩	ˈɔəfn̩
orphans	ˈɔˑfn̩z	ˈɔəfn̩z
orthodox	ˈɔˑθədɒks	ˈɔəθədɑks
orthographic	ɔθəˈgræfɪk	ɔəθəˈgræfɪk
orthographically	ɔθəˈgræfɪkəlɪ	ɔəθəˈgræfɪkəlɪ
ostrich	ˈɒstrɪtʃ	
ostriches	ˈɒstrɪtʃɪz	
other	ˈʌðə(r	ˈʌðə
others	ˈʌðəz	ˈʌðəz
otherwise	ˈʌðəwaɪz	ˈʌðəwaɪz
ought	ɔˑt	
oughtn't	ˈɔˑtn̩t	
ounce	aʊns	
ounces	ˈaʊnsɪz	
our	ˈaʊə(r	ˈaʊə
ours	ˈaʊəz	ˈaʊəz
ourself	aʊəˈsɛlf	aʊəˈsɛlf
ourselves	aʊəˈsɛlvz	aʊəˈsɛlvz
out	aʊt	
outbreak	ˈaʊtbreɪk	
outbreaks	ˈaʊtbreɪks	
outcome	ˈaʊtkʌm	
outdoor	ˈaʊtdɔ(r, ˈaʊtdɔə(r	ˈaʊtdoə
outdoors	ˈaʊtˈdɔˑz, ˈaʊtˈdɔəz	ˈaʊtˈdoəz
outer	ˈaʊtə(r	ˈaʊtə
outfit	ˈaʊtfɪt	
outfits	ˈaʊtfɪts	
outing	ˈaʊtɪŋ	
outings	ˈaʊtɪŋz	
outlaw	ˈaʊtlɔ	
outlaws	ˈaʊtlɔz	
outlay	ˈaʊtleɪ	
outlet	ˈaʊtlɛt, ˈaʊtlɪt	
outlets	ˈaʊtlɛts, ˈaʊtlɪts	
outline	ˈaʊtlaɪn	
outlines	ˈaʊtlaɪnz	
outlined	ˈaʊtlaɪnd	
outlining	ˈaʊtlaɪnɪŋ	
outlive	aʊtˈlɪv	
outlives	aʊtˈlɪvz	
outlived	aʊtˈlɪvd	
outliving	aʊtˈlɪvɪŋ	
outlook	ˈaʊtlʊk	
outlooks	ˈaʊtlʊks	
outlying	ˈaʊtlaɪɪŋ	

Traditional Spelling	Received Pronunciation	American Variants
out-of-doors	′aʊtəv′dɔˑz ′aʊtəv′dɔəz	′aʊtəv′doəz
out-of-the-way	′aʊtə*v*ðə′weɪ	
outpost	′aʊtpoʊst	
outposts	′aʊtpoʊsts	
output	′aʊtpʊt	
outrageous	aʊt′reɪʤəs	
outrageously	aʊt′reɪʤəslɪ	
outright	′aʊt′raɪt	
outset	′aʊtsɛt	
outside	′aʊt′saɪd	
outsides	′aʊt′saɪdz	
outsider	′aʊt′saɪdə(r	′aʊt′saɪdə
outsiders	′aʊt′saɪdəz	′aʊt′saɪdəz
outskirt	′aʊtskɜt	′aʊtskɜət
outskirts	′aʊtskɜts	′aʊtskɜəts
outspoken	aʊt′spoʊkən	
outstanding	aʊt′stændɪŋ	
outward	′aʊtwəd	′aʊtwəd
outwardly	′aʊtwədlɪ	′aʊtwədlɪ
outwards	′aʊtwədz	′aʊtwədz
outweigh	aʊt′weɪ	
outweighs	aʊt′weɪz	
outweighed	aʊt′weɪd	
outweighing	aʊt′weɪɪŋ	
oven	′ʌvn̩	
ovens	′ʌvn̩z	
over	′oʊvə(r	′oʊvə
overbearing	oʊvə′bɛərɪŋ	oʊvə′bɛˑrɪŋ
overboard	′oʊvə′bɔˑd, ′oʊvə′bɔəd	′oʊvə′boəd
overburden	oʊvə′bɜˑdn̩	oʊvə′bɜədn̩
overburdens	oʊvə′bɜˑdn̩z	oʊvə′bɜədn̩z
overburdened	oʊvə′bɜˑdn̩d	oʊvə′bɜədn̩d
overburdening	oʊvə′bɜˑdnɪŋ	oʊvə′bɜədnɪŋ
overcharge, *noun & verb*	′oʊvə′ʧɑˑʤ	′oʊvə′ʧɑəʤ
overcharges	′oʊvə′ʧɑˑʤɪz	′oʊvə′ʧɑəʤɪz
overcharged	′oʊvə′ʧɑˑʤd	′oʊvə′ʧɑəʤd
overcharging	′oʊvə′ʧɑˑʤɪŋ	′oʊvə′ʧɑəʤɪŋ
overcoat	′oʊvəkoʊt	′oʊvəkoʊt
overcoats	′oʊvəkoʊts	′oʊvəkoʊts
overcome	oʊvə′kʌm	oʊvə′kʌm
overcomes	oʊvə′kʌmz	oʊvə′kʌmz
overcame	oʊvə′keɪm	oʊvə′keɪm
overcoming	oʊvə′kʌmɪŋ	oʊvə′kʌmɪŋ
over-confidence	′oʊvə′kɒnfɪdəns	′oʊvə′kɑnfɪdəns
over-confident	′oʊvə′kɒnfɪdənt	′oʊvə′kɑnfɪdənt

Traditional Spelling	Received Pronunciation	American Variants
overdo	ouvə'du·	ouvə'du·
overdoes	ouvə'dʌz	ouvə'dʌz
overdid	ouvə'dɪd	ouvə'dɪd
overdone	ouvə'dʌn	ouvə'dʌn
overdoing	ouvə'du·ɪŋ	ouvə'du·ɪŋ
overdose	'ouvə'dous	'ouvə'dous
	'ouvədous	'ouvədous
overdue	ouvə'dju·	ouvədju·
overestimate	'ouvə'ʳɛstɪmeɪt	'ouvə'ɛstɪmeɪt
overestimates	'ouvə'ʳɛstɪmeɪts	'ouvə'ɛstɪmeɪts
overestimated	'ouvə'ʳɛstɪmeɪtɪd	'ouvə'ɛstɪmeɪtɪd
overestimating	'ouvə'ʳɛstɪmeɪtɪŋ	'ouvə'ɛstɪmeɪtɪŋ
overflow, ***noun***	'ouvəflou	'ouvəflou
overhang	'ouvə'hæŋ	'ouvə'hæŋ
overhangs	'ouvə'hæŋz	'ouvə'hæŋz
overhung	'ouvə'hʌŋ	'ouvə'hʌŋ
overhanging	'ouvə'hæŋɪŋ	'ouvə'hæŋɪŋ
overhaul	ouvə'hɔ·l	ouvə'hɔ·l
overhauls	ouvə'hɔ·lz	ouvə'hɔ·lz
overhauled	ouvə'hɔ·ld	ouvə'hɔ·ld
overhauling	ouvə'hɔ·lɪŋ	ouvə'hɔ·lɪŋ
overhear	ouvə'hɪə(r	ouvə'hɪə
overhears	ouvə'hɪəz	ouvə'hɪəz
overheard	ouvə'hɜ·d	ouvə'hɜəd
overhearing	ouvə'hɪərɪŋ	ouvə'hɪ·rɪŋ
overlap	ouvə'læp	ouvə'læp
overlaps	ouvə'læps	ouvə'læps
overlapped	ouvə'læpt	ouvə'læpt
overlapping	ouvə'læpɪŋ	ouvə'læpɪŋ
overload	'ouvə'loud	'ouvə'loud
overloads	'ouvə'loudz	'ouvə'loudz
overloaded	'ouvə'loudɪd	'ouvə'loudɪd
overloading	'ouvə'loudɪŋ	'ouvə'loudɪŋ
overlook	ouvə'luk	ouvə'luk
overlooks	ouvə'luks	ouvə'luks
overlooked	ouvə'lukt	ouvə'lukt
overlooking	ouvə'lukɪŋ	ouvə'lukɪŋ
overmuch	'ouvə'mʌtʃ, 'ouvəmʌtʃ	'ouvə'mʌtʃ, 'ouvəmʌtʃ
overnight	'ouvə'naɪt	'ouvə'naɪt
overreach	ouvə'ri·tʃ	
overreaches	ouvə'ri·tʃɪz	
overreached	ouvə'ri·tʃt	
overreaching	ouvə'ri·tʃɪŋ	
override	ouvə'raɪd	
overrides	ouvə'raɪdz	
overrode	ouvə'roud	
overridden	ouvə'rɪdn̩	

Traditional Spelling	Received Pronunciation	American Variants
overriding	ouvəˈraɪdɪŋ	
overrule	ouvəˈruˑl	
overrules	ouvəˈruˑlz	
overruled	ouvəˈruˑld	
overruling	ouvəˈruˑlɪŋ	
overrun	ouvəˈrʌn	
overruns	ouvəˈrʌnz	
overran	ouvəˈræn	
overrunning	ouvəˈrʌnɪŋ	
oversea	ˈouvəˈsiˑ	ˈouvəˈsiˑ
overseas	ˈouvəˈsiˑz	ˈouvəˈsiˑz
overshadow	ouvəˈʃædou	ouvəˈʃædou
overshadows	ouvəˈʃædouz	ouvəˈʃædouz
overshadowed	ouvəˈʃædoud	ouvəˈʃædoud
overshadowing	ouvəˈʃædouɪŋ	ouvəˈʃædouɪŋ
overshoot	ˈouvəˈʃuˑt	ˈouvəˈʃuˑt
overshoots	ˈouvəˈʃuˑts	ˈouvəˈʃuˑts
overshot	ˈouvəˈʃɒt	ˈouvəˈʃɑt
overshooting	ˈouvəˈʃuˑtɪŋ	ˈouvəˈʃuˑtɪŋ
oversight	ˈouvəsaɪt	ˈouvəsaɪt
oversights	ˈouvəsaɪts	ˈouvəsaɪts
overstate	ˈouvəˈsteɪt	ˈouvəˈsteɪt
overstates	ˈouvəˈsteɪts	ˈouvəˈsteɪts
overstated	ˈouvəˈsteɪtɪd	ˈouvəˈsteɪtɪd
overstating	ˈouvəˈsteɪtɪŋ	ˈouvəˈsteɪtɪŋ
overstep	ˈouvəˈstɛp	ˈouvəˈstɛp
oversteps	ˈouvəˈstɛps	ˈouvəˈstɛps
overstepped	ˈouvəˈstɛpt	ˈouvəˈstɛpt
overstepping	ˈouvəˈstɛpɪŋ	ˈouvəˈstɛpɪŋ
overtake	ouvəˈteɪk	ouvəˈteɪk
overtakes	ouvəˈteɪks	ouvəˈteɪks
overtook	ouvəˈtuk	ouvəˈtuk
overtaken	ouvəˈteɪkən	ouvəˈteɪkən
overtaking	ouvəˈteɪkɪŋ	ouvəˈteɪkɪŋ
overtax	ˈouvəˈtæks	ˈouvəˈtæks
overtaxes	ˈouvəˈtæksɪz	ˈouvəˈtæksɪz
overtaxed	ˈouvəˈtækst	ˈouvəˈtækst
overtaxing	ˈouvəˈtæksɪŋ	ˈouvəˈtæksɪŋ
overthrow, *noun*	ˈouvəθrou	ˈouvəθrou
overthrow, *verb*	ouvəˈθrou	ouvəˈθrou
overthrows	ouvəˈθrouz	ouvəˈθrouz
overthrew	ouvəˈθruˑ	ouvəˈθruˑ
overthrown	ouvəˈθroun	ouvəˈθroun
overthrowing	ouvəˈθrouɪŋ	ouvəˈθrouɪŋ
overtime	ˈouvətaɪm	ˈouvətaɪm
overture	ˈouvətjuə(r ˈouvətʃuə(r	ˈouvətjuə ˈouvətʃuə

Traditional Spelling	Received Pronunciation	American Variants
overtures	'ouvətjuəz	'ouvətjuəz
	'ouvətʃuəz	'ouvətʃuəz
overturn	ouvə'tɜ·n	ouvə'tɜən
overturns	ouvə'tɜ·nz	ouvə'tɜənz
overturned	ouvə'tɜ·nd	ouvə'tɜənd
overturning	ouvə'tɜ·nɪŋ	ouvə'tɜənɪŋ
overweight	'ouvə'weɪt	'ouvə'weɪt
overwhelm	ouvə'*h*welm	ouvə'hwelm
overwhelms	ouvə'*h*wɛlmz	ouvə'hwɛlmz
overwhelmed	ouvə'*h*wɛlmd	ouvə'hwɛlmd
overwhelming	ouvə'*h*wɛlmɪŋ	ouvə'hwɛlmɪŋ
overwhelmingly	ouvə'*h*wɛlmɪŋlɪ	ouvə'hwɛlmɪŋlɪ
overwork, *noun & verb*	'ouvə'wɜ·k	'ouvə'wɜək
overworks	'ouvə'wɜ·ks	'ouvə'wɜəks
overworked	'ouvə'wɜ·kt	'ouvə'wɜəkt
overworking	'ouvə'wɜ·kɪŋ	'ouvə'wɜəkɪŋ
owe	ou	
owes	ouz	
owed	oud	
owing	'ouɪŋ	
owing to	'ouɪŋ tu *s.f.*	
	'ouɪŋ tʊ, 'ouɪŋ tə *w.fs.*	
owl	aʊl	
owls	aʊlz	
own	oun	
owns	ounz	
owned	ound	
owning	'ounɪŋ	
owner	'ounə(r	'ounə
owners	'ounəz	'ounəz
ownership	'ounəʃɪp	'ounəʃɪp
ox	ɒks	ɑks
oxen	'ɒksn̩	'ɑksn̩
Oxford	'ɒksfəd	'ɑksfəd
oxygen	'ɒksɪʤən, 'ɒkzɪʤən	'ɑksɪʤən, 'ɑkzɪʤən
oyster	'ɔɪstə(r	'ɔɪstə
oysters	'ɔɪstəz	'ɔɪstəz

P

Traditional Spelling	Received Pronunciation	American Variants
P	pi·	
P's	pi·z	
pace	peɪs	
paces	'peɪsɪz	
pacific	pə'sɪfɪk	

Traditional Spelling	Received Pronunciation	American Variants
pacify	ˈpæsɪfaɪ	
pacifies	ˈpæsɪfaɪz	
pacified	ˈpæsɪfaɪd	
pacifying	ˈpæsɪfaɪɪŋ	
pack	pæk	
packs	pæks	
packed	pækt	
packing	ˈpækɪŋ	
package	ˈpækɪʤ	
packages	ˈpækɪʤɪz	
packet	ˈpækɪt	
packets	ˈpækɪts	
pad	pæd	
pads	pædz	
padded	ˈpædɪd	
padding	ˈpædɪŋ	
paddle	ˈpædl̩	
paddles	ˈpædl̩z	
paddled	ˈpædl̩d	
paddling	ˈpædlɪŋ	
page	peɪʤ	
pages	ˈpeɪʤɪz	
PAID *from* pay	peɪd	
pail	peɪl	
pails	peɪlz	
pailful	ˈpeɪlful	
pailfuls	ˈpeɪlfulz	
pain	peɪn	
pains	peɪnz	
pained	peɪnd	
paining	ˈpeɪnɪŋ	
painful	ˈpeɪnful	
painfully	ˈpeɪnfulɪ, ˈpeɪnfəlɪ	
painless	ˈpeɪnlɪs	
painlessly	ˈpeɪnlɪslɪ	
painstaking	ˈpeɪnzteɪkɪŋ	
paint	peɪnt	
paints	peɪnts	
painted	ˈpeɪntɪd	
painting	ˈpeɪntɪŋ	
painter	ˈpeɪntə(r	ˈpeɪntə
painters	ˈpeɪntəz	ˈpeɪntəz
painting	ˈpeɪntɪŋ	
paintings	ˈpeɪntɪŋz	
pair	pɛə(r	pɛə
pairs	pɛəz	pɛəz
pajamas (*Amer.*)	pəˈʤɑ·məz	pəˈʤa·məz

Traditional Spelling	Received Pronunciation	American Variants
palace	'pælɪs, 'pæləs	
palaces	'pælɪsɪz, 'pæləsɪz	
palate	'pælɪt, 'pælət	
palates	'pælɪts, 'pæləts	
palatial	pə'leɪʃəl, pə'leɪʃjəl	
pale	peɪl	
paler	'peɪlə(r	'peɪlə
palest	'peɪlɪst	
paleness	'peɪlnɪs	
palm	pɑ·m	pa·m
palms	pɑ·mz	pa·mz
palpitation	pælpɪ'teɪʃən	
paltry	'pɔ·ltrɪ, 'pɒltrɪ	
pamphlet	'pæmflɪt	
pamphlets	'pæmflɪts	
pan	pæn	
pans	pænz	
pane	peɪn	
panes	peɪnz	
panel	'pænl̩	
panels	'pænl̩z	
panic	'pænɪk	
panics	'pænɪks	
panorama	pænə'rɑ·mə	pænə'ra·mə
panoramas	pænə'rɑ·məz	pænə'ra·məz
paper	'peɪpə(r	'peɪpə
papers	'peɪpəz	'peɪpəz
parachute	pærə'ʃu·t, 'pærəʃut	
parachutes	pærə'ʃu·ts 'pærəʃuts	
parade	pə'reɪd	
parades	pə'reɪdz	
paradise	'pærədaɪs	
paradox	'pærədɒks	'pærədɑks
paradoxes	'pærədɒksɪz	'pærədɑksɪz
paradoxical	pærə'dɒksɪkəl	pærə'dɑksɪkəl
paraffin	'pærəfɪn, 'pærəfin	
paragraph	'pærəgrɑf	'pærəgraf
paragraphs	'pærəgrɑfs	'pærəgrafs
parallel	'pærəlɛl, 'pærələl	
parallels	'pærəlɛlz, 'pærələlz	
paralyse	'pærəlaɪz	
paralyses	'pærəlaɪzɪz	
paralysed	'pærəlaɪzd	
paralysing	'pærəlaɪzɪŋ	
paralysis	pə'rælɪsɪs	
paraphrase	'pærəfreɪz	

Traditional Spelling	Received Pronunciation	American Variants
paraphrases	ˈpærəfreɪzɪz	
paraphrased	ˈpærəfreɪzd	
paraphrasing	ˈpærəfreɪzɪŋ	
parasite	ˈpærəsaɪt	
parasites	ˈpærəsaɪts	
parasol	ˈpærəˈsɒl	
parasols	ˈpærəˈsɒlz	
parcel	ˈpɑˑsl̩	ˈpɑəsl̩
parcels	ˈpɑˑsl̩z	ˈpɑəsl̩z
parchment	ˈpɑˑtʃmənt	ˈpɑətʃmənt
pardon	ˈpɑˑdn̩	ˈpɑədn̩
pardons	ˈpɑˑdn̩z	ˈpɑədn̩z
pardoned	ˈpɑˑdn̩d	ˈpɑədn̩d
pardoning	ˈpɑˑdnɪŋ	ˈpɑədnɪŋ
pardonable	ˈpɑˑdnəbl̩	ˈpɑədnəbl̩
pardonably	ˈpɑˑdnəblɪ	ˈpɑədnəblɪ
parent	ˈpɛərənt	ˈpɛˑrənt
parents	ˈpɛərənts	ˈpɛˑrənts
parenthesis	pəˈrɛnθɪsɪs pəˈrɛnθəsɪs	
parentheses	pəˈrɛnθɪsiz pəˈrɛnθəsiz	
Paris	ˈpærɪs	
parish	ˈpærɪʃ	
parishes	ˈpærɪʃɪz	
Parisian	pəˈrɪzjən, pəˈrɪzɪən	
Parisians	pəˈrɪzjənz pəˈrɪzɪənz	
park	pɑˑk	pɑək
parks	pɑˑks	pɑəks
parliament	ˈpɑˑləmənt ˈpɑˑlɪmənt	ˈpɑələmənt ˈpɑəlɪmənt
parliaments	ˈpɑˑləmənts ˈpɑˑlɪmənts	ˈpɑələmənts ˈpɑəlɪmənts
parliamentary	pɑləˈmɛntərɪ pɑlɪˈmɛntərɪ	pɑələˈmɛntərɪ pɑəlɪˈmɛntərɪ
parlor (*Amer.*) **parlour**	ˈpɑˑlə(r	ˈpɑələ
parlors (*Amer.*) parlours	ˈpɑˑləz	ˈpɑələz
parody	ˈpærədɪ	
parodies	ˈpærədɪz	
parrot	ˈpærət	
parrots	ˈpærəts	
part	pɑˑt	pɑət
parts	pɑˑts	pɑəts
parted	ˈpɑˑtɪd	ˈpɑətɪd

Traditional Spelling	Received Pronunciation	American Variants
parting	ˈpɑ·tɪŋ	ˈpɑətɪŋ
partial	ˈpɑ·ʃəl	ˈpɑəʃəl
partially	ˈpɑ·ʃəlɪ	ˈpɑəʃəlɪ
partiality	pɑʃɪˈælɪtɪ	pɑəʃɪˈælɪtɪ
participate	pɑˈtɪsɪpeɪt	pɑəˈtɪsɪpeɪt
participates	pɑˈtɪsɪpeɪts	pɑəˈtɪsɪpeɪts
participated	pɑˈtɪsɪpeɪtɪd	pɑəˈtɪsɪpeɪtɪd
participating	pɑˈtɪsɪpeɪtɪŋ	pɑəˈtɪsɪpeɪtɪŋ
participation	pɑtɪsɪˈpeɪʃən	pɑətɪsɪˈpeɪʃən
participle	ˈpɑ·tɪsɪpl̩	pɑətɪsɪpl̩
participles	ˈpɑ·tɪsɪpl̩z	ˈpɑətɪsɪpl̩z
particle	ˈpɑ·tɪkl̩	ˈpɑətɪkl̩
particles	ˈpɑ·tɪkl̩z	ˈpɑətɪkl̩z
particular	pəˈtɪkjulə(r pəˈtɪkjələ(r	pəˈtɪkjulə pəˈtɪkjələ
particulars	pəˈtɪkjuləz pəˈtɪkjələz	pəˈtɪkjuləz pəˈtɪkjələz
particularly	pəˈtɪkjuləlɪ pəˈtɪkjələlɪ	pəˈtɪkjuləlɪ pəˈtɪkjələlɪ
parting	ˈpɑ·tɪŋ	ˈpɑətɪŋ
partings	ˈpɑ·tɪŋz	ˈpɑətɪŋz
partition	pɑˈtɪʃən, pəˈtɪʃən	pɑəˈtɪʃən, pəˈtɪʃən
partitions	pɑˈtɪʃənz, pəˈtɪʃənz	pɑəˈtɪʃənz, pəˈtɪʃən
partly	ˈpɑ·tlɪ	ˈpɑətlɪ
partner	ˈpɑ·tnə(r	ˈpɑətnə
partners	ˈpɑ·tnəz	ˈpɑətnəz
party	ˈpɑ·tɪ	ˈpɑətɪ
parties	ˈpɑ·tɪz	ˈpɑətɪz
pass	pɑ·s	pa·s
passes	ˈpɑ·sɪz	ˈpa·sɪz
passed	ˈpɑ·st	pa·st
passing	ˈpɑ·sɪŋ	ˈpa·sɪŋ
passable	ˈpɑ·səbl̩	ˈpa·səbl̩
passably	ˈpɑ·səblɪ	ˈpa·səblɪ
passage	ˈpæsɪʤ	
passages	ˈpæsɪʤɪz	
passenger	ˈpæsɪnʤə(r	ˈpæsɪnʤə
passengers	ˈpæsɪnʤəz	ˈpæsɪnʤəz
passer-by	ˈpɑ·səˈbaɪ	ˈpa·səˈbaɪ
passers-by	ˈpɑ·səzˈbaɪ	ˈpa·səzˈbaɪ
passion	ˈpæʃən	
passions	ˈpæʃənz	
passionate	ˈpæʃənɪt	
passionately	ˈpæʃənɪtlɪ	
passive	ˈpæsɪv	
passively	ˈpæsɪvlɪ	
passport	ˈpɑ·spɔt	ˈpa·spoət

Traditional Spelling	Received Pronunciation	American Variants
passports	ˈpɑ·spɔts	ˈpa·spoəts
past	pɑ·st	pa·st
paste	peɪst	
pastes	peɪsts	
pasted	ˈpeɪstɪd	
pasting	ˈpeɪstɪŋ	
pastime	ˈpɑ·staɪm, ˈpæstaɪm	ˈpa·staɪm
pastimes	ˈpɑ·staɪmz ˈpæstaɪmz	ˈpa·staɪmz
pastry	ˈpeɪstrɪ	
pat	pæt	
pats	pæts	
patted	ˈpætɪd	
patting	ˈpætɪŋ	
patch	pætʃ	
patches	ˈpætʃɪz	
patched	pætʃt	
patching	ˈpætʃɪŋ	
patchy	ˈpætʃɪ	
patent	ˈpeɪtənt, ˈpætənt	
patents	ˈpeɪtənts, ˈpætənts	
patented	ˈpeɪtəntɪd ˈpætəntɪd	
patenting	ˈpeɪtəntɪŋ ˈpætəntɪŋ	
paternal	pəˈtə·nl̩	pəˈtɜən l̩
path	pɑ·θ	pa·θ
paths	pɑ·ðz	pa·ðz
pathetic	pəˈθɛtɪk	
pathway	ˈpɑ·θweɪ	ˈpa·θweɪ
pathways	ˈpɑ·θweɪz	ˈpa·θweɪz
patience	ˈpeɪʃəns	
patient	ˈpeɪʃənt	
patients	ˈpeɪʃənts	
patiently	ˈpeɪʃəntlɪ	
patriot	ˈpeɪtrɪət, ˈpætrɪət	
patriots	ˈpeɪtrɪəts, ˈpætrɪəts	
patriotic	pætrɪˈɒtɪk peɪtrɪˈɒtɪk	pætrɪˈɑtɪk peɪtrɪˈɑtɪk
patriotically	pætrɪˈɒtɪkəlɪ peɪtrɪˈɒtɪkəlɪ	pætrɪˈɑtɪkəlɪ peɪtrɪˈɑtɪkəlɪ
patriotism	ˈpætrɪətɪzm̩ ˈpeɪtrɪətɪzm̩	
patrol	pəˈtroʊl	

‡ British usage tends towards [ˈpeɪtənt], and American usage towards [ˈpætənt].

Traditional Spelling	Received Pronunciation	American Variants
patrols	pəˈtroulz	
patrolled	pəˈtrould	
patrolling	pəˈtroulɪŋ	
patron	ˈpeɪtrən, ˈpætrən	
patrons	ˈpeɪtrənz, ˈpætrənz	
patronage	ˈpætrənɪʤ	ˈpeɪtrənɪʤ
patronize	ˈpætrənaɪz	ˈpeɪtrənaɪz
patronizes	ˈpætrənaɪzɪz	ˈpeɪtrənaɪzɪz
patronized	ˈpætrənaɪzd	ˈpeɪtrənaɪzd
patronizing	ˈpætrənaɪzɪŋ	ˈpeɪtrənaɪzɪŋ
pattern	ˈpætən	
patterns	ˈpætənz	
Paul	pɔˑl	
pauper	ˈpɔˑpə(r	ˈpɔˑpə
paupers	ˈpɔˑpəz	ˈpɔˑpəz
pause	pɔˑz	
pauses	ˈpɔˑzɪz	
paused	pɔˑzd	
pausing	ˈpɔˑzɪŋ	
pave	peɪv	
paves	peɪvz	
paved	peɪvd	
paving	ˈpeɪvɪŋ	
pavement	ˈpeɪvmənt	
pavements	ˈpeɪvmənts	
pavilion	pəˈvɪljən	
pavilions	pəˈvɪljənz	
paw	pɔˑ	
paws	pɔˑz	
pay	peɪ	
pays	peɪz	
paid	peɪd	
paying	ˈpeɪɪŋ	
payable	ˈpeɪəbḷ	
payment	ˈpeɪmənt	
payments	ˈpeɪmənts	
pea	piˑ	
peas	piˑz	
peace	piˑs	
peaceful	ˈpiˑsful	
peacefully	ˈpiˑsfulɪ, ˈpiˑsfəlɪ	
peach	piˑʧ	
peaches	ˈpiˑʧɪz	
peacock	ˈpiˑkɒk	ˈpiˑkɑk
peacocks	ˈpiˑkɒks	ˈpiˑkɑks
peak	piˑk	
peaks	piˑks	

Traditional Spelling	Received Pronunciation	American Variants
peanut	ˈpiˑnʌt	
peanuts	ˈpiˑnʌts	
pear	pɛə(r	pɛə
pears	pɛəz	pɛəz
pearl	pɜˑl	pɜəl
pearls	pɜˑlz	pɜəlz
peasant	ˈpɛzənt	
peasants	ˈpɛzənts	
pebble	ˈpɛbl̩	
pebbles	ˈpɛbl̩z	
peck	pɛk	
pecks	pɛks	
pecked	pɛkt	
pecking	ˈpɛkɪŋ	
peculiar	pɪˈkjuˑljə(r	pɪˈkjuˑljə
peculiarly	pɪˈkjuˑljəlɪ	pɪˈkjuˑljəlɪ
peculiarity	pikjulɪˈærɪtɪ	
peculiarities	pɪkjulɪˈærɪtɪz	
pedal	ˈpɛdl̩	
pedals	ˈpɛdl̩z	
pedalled	ˈpɛdl̩d	
pedalling	ˈpɛdl̩ɪŋ	
pedant	ˈpɛdənt	
pedants	ˈpɛdənts	
pedantic	pɪˈdæntɪk, pɛˈdæntɪk	
pedantically	pɪˈdæntɪkəlɪ pɛˈdæntɪkəlɪ	
pedantry	ˈpɛdəntrɪ	
peel	piˑl	
peels	piˑlz	
peeled	piˑld	
peeling	ˈpiˑlɪŋ	
peep	piˑp	
peeps	piˑps	
peeped	piˑpt	
peeping	ˈpiˑpɪŋ	
peer	pɪə(r	pɪə
peers	pɪəz	pɪəz
peerage	ˈpɪərɪʤ	ˈpɪˑrɪʤ
peerages	ˈpɪərɪʤɪz	ˈpɪˑrɪʤɪz
peeress	ˈpɪərɪs, ˈpɪərɛs	ˈpɪˑrɪs, ˈpɪˑrɛs
peeresses	ˈpɪərɪsɪz, ˈpɪərɛsɪz	ˈpɪˑrɪsɪz, ˈpɪˑrɛsɪz
peerless	ˈpɪəlɪs	ˈpɪəlɪs
peerlessly	ˈpɪəlɪslɪ	ˈpɪəlɪslɪ
peevish	ˈpiˑvɪʃ	
peevishly	ˈpiˑvɪʃlɪ	
peg	pɛg	

Traditional Spelling	Received Pronunciation	American Variants
pegs	pɛgz	
Pekin	pi'kɪn	
Peking	pi'kɪŋ	
pelican	'pɛlɪkən	
pelicans	'pɛlɪkənz	
pen	pɛn	
pens	pɛnz	
penned	pɛnd	
penning	'pɛnɪŋ	
penal	'piːnl̩	
penalty	'pɛnl̩tɪ	
penalties	'pɛnl̩tɪz	
PENCE, *plur. of* penny	pɛns	
pencil	'pɛnsl̩	
pencils	'pɛnsl̩z	
pencilled	'pɛnsl̩d	
pencilling	'pɛnsəlɪŋ	
pending	'pɛndɪŋ	
pendulum	'pɛndjuləm 'pɛndjələm	
pendulums	'pɛndjuləmz 'pɛndjələmz	
penetrate	'pɛnɪtreɪt	
penetrates	'pɛnɪtreɪts	
penetrated	'pɛnɪtreɪtɪd	
penetrating	'pɛnɪtreɪtɪŋ	
peninsula	pɪ'nɪnsjulə pə'nɪnsjulə	
peninsulas	pɪ'nɪnsjuləz pə'nɪnsjuləz	
penitence	'pɛnɪtəns	
penitent	'pɛnɪtənt	
penitently	'pɛnɪtəntlɪ	
penmanship	'pɛnmənʃɪp	
penniless	'pɛnɪlɪs	
penny	'pɛnɪ	
pennies	'pɛnɪz	
pence	'pɛns	
pension	'pɛnʃən	
pensions	'pɛnʃənz	
pensioned	'pɛnʃənd	
pensioning	'pɛnʃənɪŋ	
people	'piːpl̩	
peoples	'piːpl̩z	
peopled	'piːpl̩d	
pepper	'pɛpə(r	'pɛpə

Traditional Spelling	Received Pronunciation	American Variants
per	pɜ· *s.f.*, pə *w.f.*	pɜə *s.f.*, pə *w.f.*
perceive	pə'si·v, pɜ'si·v	pə'si·v, pɜə'si·v
perceives	pə'si·vz, pɜ'si·vz	pə'si·vz, pɜə'si·vz
perceived	pə'si·vd, pɜ'si·vd	pə'si·vd, pɜə'si·vd
perceiving	pə'si·vɩŋ, pɜ'si·vɩŋ	pə'si·vɩŋ, pɜə'si·vɩŋ
per cent.	pə'sɛnt, pɜ'sɛnt	pə'sɛnt, pɜə'sɛnt
percentage	pə'sɛntɩʤ, pɜ'sɛntɩʤ	pə'sɛntɩʤ, pɜə'sɛntɩʤ
perception	pə'sɛpʃən, pɜ'sɛpʃən	pə'sɛpʃən, pɜə'sɛpʃən
perceptions	pə'sɛpʃənz pɜ'sɛpʃənz	pə'sɛpʃənz pɜə'sɛpʃənz
perch	pɜ·ʧ	pɜəʧ
perches	'pɜ·ʧɩz	'pɜəʧɩz
perched	pɜ·ʧt	pɜəʧt
perching	'pɜ·ʧɩŋ	'pɜəʧɩŋ
Percy	'pɜ·sɩ	'pɜəsɩ
peremptory	pə'rɛm*p*tərɩ 'pɛrəm*p*tərɩ	 'pɛrəm*p*torɩ
perfect, *adj.*	'pɜ·fɩkt	'pɜəfɩkt
perfect, *verb*	pə'fɛkt, 'pɜ·fɩkt	pə'fɛkt, 'pɜəfɩkt
perfects	pə'fɛkts, 'pɜ·fɩkts	pə'fɛkts, 'pɜəfɩkts
perfected	pə'fɛktɩd, 'pɜ·fɩktɩd	pə'fɛktɩd, 'pɜəfɩktɩd
perfecting	pə'fɛktɩŋ, 'pɜ·fɩktɩŋ	pə'fɛktɩŋ, 'pɜəfɩktɩŋ
perfection	pə'fɛkʃən, pɜ'fɛkʃən	pə'fɛkʃən, pɜə'fɛkʃən
perfectly	'pɜ·fɩk*t*lɩ	'pɜəfɩk*t*lɩ
perforate	'pɜ·fəreɩt	'pɜəfəreɩt
perforates	'pɜ·fəreɩts	'pɜəfəreɩts
perforated	'pɜ·fəreɩtɩd	'pɜəfəreɩtɩd
perforating	'pɜ·fəreɩtɩŋ	'pɜəfəreɩtɩŋ
perforation	pɜfə'reɩʃən	pɜəfə'reɩʃən
perform	pə'fɔ·m	pə'fɔəm
performs	pə'fɔ·mz	pə'fɔəmz
performed	pə'fɔ·md	pə'fɔəmd
performing	pə'fɔ·mɩŋ	pə'fɔəmɩŋ
performer	pə'fɔ·mə(r	pə'fɔəmə
performers	pə'fɔ·məz	pə'fɔəməz
perfume, *noun*	'pɜ·fjum	'pɜəfjum
perfumes	'pɜ·fjumz	'pɜəfjumz
perfume, *verb*	pə'fju·m, 'pɜ·fjum	pə'fju·m, 'pɜəfjum
perfumes	pə'fju·mz 'pɜ·fjumz	pə'fju·mz 'pɜəfjumz
perfumed	pə'fju·md 'pɜ·fjumd	pə'fju·md 'pɜəfjumd
perfuming	pə'fju·mɩŋ 'pɜ·fjumɩŋ	pə'fju·mɩŋ 'pɜəfjumɩŋ
perhaps	pə'hæps, præps	pə'hæps
peril	'pɛrɩl	
perils	'pɛrɩlz	

Traditional Spelling	Received Pronunciation	American Variants
period	'pɪərɪəd	'pɪ·rɪəd
periods	'pɪərɪədz	'pɪ·rɪədz
periodical	pɪərɪ'ɒdɪkəl	pɪ·rɪ'ɑdɪkəl
periodicals	pɪərɪ'ɒdɪkəlz	pɪ·rɪ'ɑdɪkəlz
periodically	pɪərɪ'ɒdɪkəlɪ	pɪ·rɪ'ɑdɪkəlɪ
perish	'pɛrɪʃ	
perishes	'pɛrɪʃɪz	
perished	'pɛrɪʃt	
perishing	'pɛrɪʃɪŋ	
permanent	'pɜ·mənənt 'pɜ·mɪnənt	'pɜəmənənt 'pɜəmɪnənt
permanently	'pɜ·mənəntlɪ 'pɜ·mɪnəntlɪ	'pɜəmənəntlɪ 'pɜəmɪnəntlɪ
permissible	pə'mɪsəbḷ, pɜ'mɪsəbḷ pə'mɪsɪbḷ, pɜ'mɪsɪbḷ	pə'mɪsəbḷ, pɜəmɪsəbḷ pə'mɪsɪbḷ, pɜəmɪsɪbḷ
permission	pə'mɪʃən, pɜ'mɪʃən	pə'mɪʃən, pɜə'mɪʃən
permit, *noun*	'pɜ·mɪt	'pɜəmɪt
permits	'pɜ·mɪts	'pɜəmɪts
permit, *verb*	pə'mɪt, pɜ'mɪt	pə'mɪt, pɜəmɪt
permits	pə'mɪts, pɜ'mɪts	pə'mɪts, pɜə'mɪts
permitted	pə'mɪtɪd, pɜ'mɪtɪd	pə'mɪtɪd, pɜə'mɪtɪd
permitting	pə'mɪtɪŋ, pɜ'mɪtɪŋ	pə'mɪtɪŋ, pɜə'mɪtɪŋ
pernicious	pɜ'nɪʃəs	pə'nɪʃəs
peroration	†pɛrə'reɪʃən	
perorations	†pɛrə'reɪʃənz	
perpendicular	pɜpən'dɪkjulə(r	pɜəpən'dɪkjulə
perpendicularly	pɜpən'dɪkjuləlɪ	pɜəpən'dɪkjuləlɪ
perpetual	pə'pɛtjuəl, pɜ'pɛtjuəl	pə'pɛtjuəl, pɜə'pɛtjuəl
perpetually	pə'pɛtjuəlɪ, pɜ'pɛtjuəlɪ	pə'pɛtjuəlɪ, pɜə'pɛtjuəl
perplex	pə'plɛks, pɜ'plɛks	pə'plɛks, pɜə'plɛks
perplexes	pə'plɛksɪz pɜ'plɛksɪz	pə'plɛksɪz pɜə'plɛksɪz
perplexed	pə'plɛkst pɜ'plɛkst	pə'plɛkst pɜə'plɛkst
perplexing	pə'plɛksɪŋ pɜ'plɛksɪŋ	pə'plɛksɪŋ pɜə'plɛksɪŋ
perplexingly	pə'plɛksɪŋlɪ pɜ'plɛksɪŋlɪ	pə'plɛksɪŋlɪ pɜə'plɛksɪŋlɪ
perplexity	pə'plɛksɪtɪ pɜ'plɛksɪtɪ	pə'plɛksɪtɪ pɜə'plɛksɪtɪ
perplexities	pə'plɛksɪtɪz pɜ'plɛksɪtɪz	pə'plɛksɪtɪz pɜə'plɛksɪtɪz
persecute	'pɜ·sɪkjut	'pɜəsɪkjut
persecutes	'pɜ·sɪkjuts	'pɜəsɪkjuts
persecuted	'pɜ·sɪkjutɪd	'pɜəsɪkjutɪd

† See Note 30, p. xxxv. in Introduction.

Traditional Spelling	Received Pronunciation	American Variants
persecuting	ˈpɜ·sɪkjutɪŋ	ˈpɜəsɪkjutɪŋ
persecutor	ˈpɜ·sɪkjutə(r	ˈpɜəsɪkjutə
persecutors	ˈpɜ·sɪkjutəz	ˈpɜəsɪkjutəz
persecution	pɜsɪˈkju·ʃən	pɜəsɪˈkju·ʃən
persecutions	pɜsɪˈkju·ʃənz	pɜəsɪˈkju·ʃənz
persevere	pɜsɪˈvɪə(r	pɜəsɪˈvɪə
perseveres	pɜsɪˈvɪəz	pɜəsɪˈvɪəz
persevered	pɜsɪˈvɪəd	pɜəsɪˈvɪəd
persevering	pɜsɪˈvɪərɪŋ	pɜəsɪˈvɪ·rɪŋ
Persia	ˈpɜ·ʃə	ˈpɜəʃə
Persian	ˈpɜ·ʃən	ˈpɜəʃən
Persians	ˈpɜ·ʃənz	ˈpɜəʃənz
persist	pəˈsɪst, pɜˈsɪst	pəˈsɪst, pɜəˈsɪst
persists	pəˈsɪsts, pɜˈsɪsts	pəˈsɪsts, pɜəˈsɪsts
persisted	pəˈsɪstɪd, pɜˈsɪstɪd	pəˈsɪstɪd, pɜəˈsɪstɪd
persisting	pəˈsɪstɪŋ, pɜˈsɪstɪŋ	pəˈsɪstɪŋ, pɜəˈsɪstɪŋ
persistence	pəˈsɪstəns, pɜˈsɪstəns	pəˈsɪstəns, pɜəˈsɪstəns
persistent	pəˈsɪstənt, pɜˈsɪstənt	pəˈsɪstənt, pɜəˈsɪstənt
persistently	pəˈsɪstəntlɪ pɜˈsɪstəntlɪ	pəˈsɪstəntlɪ pɜəˈsɪstəntlɪ
person	ˈpɜ·sn̩	ˈpɜəsn̩
persons	ˈpɜ·sn̩z	ˈpɜəsn̩z
personal	ˈpɜ·sənl̩	ˈpɜəsənl̩
personally	ˈpɜ·snəlɪ	ˈpɜəsnəlɪ
personality	pɜsəˈnælɪtɪ	pɜəsəˈnælɪtɪ
perspective	pəˈspɛktɪv	pɜəˈspɛktɪv
perspiration	pɜspəˈreɪʃən	pɜəspəˈreɪʃən
perspire	pəsˈpaɪə(r, pɜsˈpaɪə(r	pəsˈpaɪə, pɜəsˈpaɪə
perspires	pəsˈpaɪəz, pɜsˈpaɪəz	pəsˈpaɪəz, pɜəsˈpaɪəz
perspired	pəsˈpaɪəd, pɜsˈpaɪəd	pəsˈpaɪəd, pɜəsˈpaɪəd
perspiring	pəsˈpaɪərɪŋ pɜsˈpaɪərɪŋ	pəsˈpaɪrɪŋ pɜəsˈpaɪrɪŋ
persuade	pəˈsweɪd, pɜˈsweɪd	pəˈsweɪd, pɜəˈsweɪd
persuades	pəˈsweɪdz pɜˈsweɪdz	pəˈsweɪdz pɜəˈsweɪdz
persuaded	pəˈsweɪdɪd pɜˈsweɪdɪd	pəˈsweɪdɪd pɜəˈsweɪdɪd
persuading	pəˈsweɪdɪŋ pɜˈsweɪdɪŋ	pəˈsweɪdɪŋ pɜəˈsweɪdɪŋ
persuasion	pəˈsweɪʒən pɜˈsweɪʒən	pəˈsweɪʒən pɜəˈsweɪʒən
persuasive	pəˈsweɪsɪv pɜˈsweɪsɪv	pəˈsweɪsɪv pɜəsweɪsɪv
Peru	pəˈru·	
Peruvian	pəˈru·vɪən	
Peruvians	pəˈru·vɪənz	
pessimism	ˈpɛsɪmɪzm̩	

Traditional Spelling	Received Pronunciation	American Variants
pessimist	'pɛsɪmɪst	
pessimists	'pɛsɪmɪsts	
pessimistic	pɛsɪ'mɪstɪk	
pessimistically	pɛsɪ'mɪstɪkəlɪ	
pest	pɛst	
pests	pɛsts	
pester	'pɛstə(r	'pɛstə
pesters	'pɛstəz	'pɛstəz
pestered	'pɛstəd	'pɛstəd
pestering	'pɛstərɪŋ	
pet	pɛt	
pets	pɛts	
petted	'pɛtɪd	
petting	'pɛtɪŋ	
petal	'pɛtl̩	
petals	'pɛtl̩z	
Peter	'pi·tə(r	'pi·tə
petition	pɪ'tɪʃən, pə'tɪʃən	
petitions	pɪ'tɪʃənz, pə'tɪʃənz	
petitioned	pɪ'tɪʃənd, pə'tɪʃənd	
petitioning	pɪ'tɪʃənɪŋ, pə'tɪʃənɪŋ	
petrol	'pɛtrɒl, 'pɛtrəl	pɪ'troul, 'pɛtrɑl
petroleum	pɪ'troulɪəm pɪ'trouljəm	
petticoat	'pɛtɪkout	
petticoats	'pɛtɪkouts	
petty	'pɛtɪ	
pettiness	'pɛtɪnɪs	
petulant	'pɛtjulənt	
petulantly	'pɛtjuləntlɪ	
phantom	'fæntəm	
phantoms	'fæntəmz	
pharmaceutic	fɑmə'sju·tɪk	fɑəmə'sju·tɪk
pharmacist	'fɑ·məsɪst	'fɑəməsɪst
pharmacists	'fɑ·məsɪsts	'fɑəməsɪsts
pharmacy	'fɑ·məsɪ	'fɑəməsɪ
pharmacies	'fɑ·məsɪz	'fɑəməsɪz
phase	feɪz	
phases	'feɪzɪz	
pheasant	'fɛzn̩t	
pheasants	'fɛzn̩ts	
phenomenon	fɪ'nɒmɪnən	fɪ'nɑmɪnən
phenomena	fɪ'nɒmɪnə	fɪ'nɑmɪnə
Philadelphia	fɪlə'dɛlfɪə	
philanthropic	fɪlən'θrɒpɪk	fɪlən'θrɑpɪk
Philip	'fɪlɪp	
Philippine	fɪlɪ'pi·n, fɪlɪ'paɪn	

Traditional Spelling	Received Pronunciation	American Variants
Philippines	fılı'piˑnz, fılı'paınz	
philological	fılə'lɒʤıkəl	fılə'lɑʤıkəl
philologically	fılə'lɒʤıkəlı	fılə'lɑʤıkəlı
philologist	fı'lɒləʤıst	fı'lɑləʤıst
philologists	fı'lɒləʤısts	fı'lɑləʤısts
philology	fı'lɒləʤı	fı'lɑləʤı
philosopher	fı'lɒsəfə(r	fı'lɑsəfə
philosophers	fı'lɒsəfəz	fı'lɑsəfəz
philosophical	fılə'sɒfıkəl	fılə'sɑfıkəl
philosophically	fılə'sɒfıkəlı	fılə'sɑfıkəlı
philosophy	fı'lɒsəfı	fı'lɑsəfı
philosophies	fı'lɒsəfız	fı'lɑsəfız
phonetic	fə'nɛtık, foʊ'nɛtık	
phonetically	fə'nɛtıkəlı foʊ'nɛtıkəlı	
phonetician	foʊnı'tıʃən, fɒnı'tıʃən	
phoneticians	foʊnı'tıʃənz fɒnı'tıʃənz	
phonetics	fə'nɛtıks, foʊ'nɛtıks	
phonograph	'foʊnəgræf 'foʊnəgrɑf	 'foʊnəgraf
phonographs	'foʊnəgræfs 'foʊnəgrɑfs	 'foʊnəgrafs
photo	'foʊtoʊ	
photos	'foʊtoʊz	
photograph	'foʊtəgrɑf, 'foʊtəgræf	'foʊtəgraf
photographs	'foʊtəgrɑfs 'foʊtəgræfs	'foʊtəgrafs
photographer	fə'tɒgrəfə(r	fə'tɑgrəfə
photographers	fə'tɒgrəfəz	fə'tɑgrəfəz
photographic	foʊtə'græfık	
photography	fə'tɒgrəfı	fə'tɑgrəfı
phrase	freız	
phrases	'freızız	
physic	'fızık	
physical	'fızıkəl	
physically	'fızıkəlı	
physician	fı'zıʃən	
physicians	fı'zıʃənz	
physicist	'fızısıst	
physicists	'fızısısts	
physics	'fızıks	
physiological	fızıə'lɒʤıkəl	fızıə'lɑʤıkəl
physiologically	fızıə'lɒʤıkəlı	fızıə'lɑʤıkəlı
physique	fı'ziˑk	
pianist	'piənıst, pı'ænıst	
pianists	'piənısts, pı'ænısts	

Traditional Spelling	Received Pronunciation	American Variants
piano	pɪ'ænoʊ, 'pjænoʊ	
pianos	pɪ'ænoʊz, 'pjænoʊz	
pick	pɪk	
picks	pɪks	
picked	pɪkt	
picking	'pɪkɪŋ	
pickle	'pɪkl̩	
pickles	'pɪkl̩z	
pickled	'pɪkl̩d	
pickling	'pɪklɪŋ	
pictorial	pɪk'tɔ·rɪəl	
pictorially	pɪk'tɔ·rɪəlɪ	
picture	'pɪktʃə(r	'pɪktʃə
pictures	'pɪktʃəz	'pɪktʃəz
picturesque	pɪktʃə'rɛsk	
picturesquely	pɪktʃə'rɛsklɪ	
pie	paɪ	
pies	paɪz	
piece	pi·s	
pieces	'pi·sɪz	
pieced	pi·st	
piecing	'pi·sɪŋ	
pier	pɪə(r	pɪə
piers	pɪəz	pɪəz
pierce	pɪəs	pɪəs
pierces	'pɪəsɪz	'pɪəsɪz
pierced	pɪəst	pɪəst
piercing	'pɪəsɪŋ	'pɪəsɪŋ
piety	'paɪətɪ, 'paɪɪtɪ	
pig	pɪg	
pigs	pɪgz	
pigeon	'pɪʤɪn, 'pɪʤən	
pigeons	'pɪʤɪnz, 'pɪʤənz	
pile	paɪl	
piles	paɪlz	
piled	paɪld	
piling	'paɪlɪŋ	
pilgrim	'pɪlgrɪm	
pilgrims	'pɪlgrɪmz	
pilgrimage	'pɪlgrɪmɪʤ	
pilgrimages	'pɪlgrɪmɪʤɪz	
pill	pɪl	
pills	pɪlz	
pillar	'pɪlə(r	'pɪlə
pillars	'pɪləz	'pɪləz
pillow	'pɪloʊ	
pillows	'pɪloʊz	

Traditional Spelling	Received Pronunciation	American Variants
pilot	ˈpaɪlət	
pilots	ˈpaɪləts	
piloted	ˈpaɪlətɪd	
piloting	ˈpaɪlətɪŋ	
pimple	ˈpɪmpl̩	
pimples	ˈpɪmpl̩z	
pin	pɪn	
pins	pɪnz	
pinned	pɪnd	
pinning	ˈpɪnɪŋ	
pinch	pɪntʃ	
pinches	ˈpɪntʃɪz	
pinched	pɪntʃt	
pinching	ˈpɪntʃɪŋ	
pine	paɪn	
pines	paɪnz	
pink	pɪŋk	
pint	paɪnt	
pints	paɪnts	
pioneer	paɪəˈnɪə(r	paɪəˈnɪə
pioneers	paɪəˈnɪəz	paɪəˈnɪəz
pious	ˈpaɪəs	
piously	ˈpaɪəslɪ	
pip	pɪp	
pips	pɪps	
pipe	paɪp	
pipes	paɪps	
piracy	ˈpaɪərəsɪ	ˈpaɪrəsɪ
pirate	ˈpaɪərət	ˈpaɪrət
pirates	ˈpaɪərəts	ˈpaɪrəts
pistol	ˈpɪstl̩	
pistols	ˈpɪstl̩z	
piston	ˈpɪstən	
pistons	ˈpɪstənz	
pit	pɪt	
pits	pɪts	
pitch	pɪtʃ	
pitches	ˈpɪtʃɪz	
pitched	pɪtʃt	
pitching	ˈpɪtʃɪŋ	
pitiable	ˈpɪtɪəbl̩	
pitiful	ˈpɪtɪful	
pitifully	ˈpɪtɪfulɪ, ˈpɪtɪfəlɪ	
pitiless	ˈpɪtɪlɪs	
pitilessly	ˈpɪtɪlɪslɪ	
pity	ˈpɪtɪ	
pities	ˈpɪtɪz	

Traditional Spelling	Received Pronunciation	American Variants
pitied	'pɪtɪd	
pitying	'pɪtɪɪŋ	
placard	'plækɑd	'plækɑəd
placards	'plækɑdz	'plækɑədz
place	pleɪs	
places	'pleɪsɪz	
placed	pleɪst	
placing	'pleɪsɪŋ	
plague	pleɪg	
plagues	pleɪgz	
plagued	pleɪgd	
plaguing	'pleɪgɪŋ	
plain	pleɪn	
plains	pleɪnz	
plainer	'pleɪnə(r	'pleɪnə
plainest	'pleɪnɪst	
plainly	'pleɪnlɪ	
plaintiff	'pleɪntɪf	
plaintiffs	'pleɪntɪfs	
plan	plæn	
plans	plænz	
planned	plænd	
planning	'plænɪŋ	
plane	pleɪn	
planes	pleɪnz	
planet	'plænɪt	
planets	'plænɪts	
plank	'plæŋk	
planks	'plæŋks	
plant	plɑ·nt	pla·nt
plants	plɑ·nts	pla·nts
planted	'plɑ·ntɪd	'pla·ntɪd
planting	'plɑ·ntɪŋ	'pla·ntɪŋ
planter	'plɑ·ntə(r	'pla·ntə
planters	'plɑ·ntəz	'pla·ntəz
plantation	plæn'teɪʃən	
plantations	plæn'teɪʃənz	
plaster	'plɑ·stə(r	'pla·stə
plasters	'plɑ·stəz	'pla·stəz
plate	pleɪt	
plates	pleɪts	
plateau	'plætoʊ	
plateaus	'plætoʊz	
plateaux	'plætoʊ	
plateful	'pleɪtfʊl	
platefuls	'pleɪtfʊlz	
platform	'plætfɔm	'plætfɔəm

Traditional Spelling	Received Pronunciation	American Variants
platforms	ˈplætfɔmz	ˈplætfɔəmz
play	pleɪ	
plays	pleɪz	
played	pleɪd	
playing	ˈpleɪɪŋ	
player	ˈpleɪə(r	ˈpleɪə
players	ˈpleɪəz	ˈpleɪəz
playful	ˈpleɪful	
playfully	ˈpleɪfulɪ, ˈpleɪfəlɪ	
plaything	ˈpleɪθɪŋ	
playthings	ˈpleɪθɪŋz	
plea	pliˑ	
pleas	pliˑz	
plead	pliˑd	
pleads	pliˑdz	
pleaded	ˈpliˑdɪd	
pleading	ˈpliˑdɪŋ	
pleasant	ˈplɛzn̩t	
pleasanter	ˈplɛzn̩tə(r	ˈplɛzn̩tə
pleasantest	ˈplɛzn̩tɪst	
pleasantly	ˈplɛzn̩tlɪ	
please	pliˑz	
pleases	ˈpliˑzɪz	
pleased	pliˑzd	
pleasing	ˈpliˑzɪŋ	
pleasingly	ˈpliˑzɪŋlɪ	
pleasure	ˈplɛʒə(r	ˈplɛʒə
pleasures	ˈplɛʒəz	ˈplɛʒəz
pledge	plɛʤ	
pledges	ˈplɛʤɪz	
pledged	ˈplɛʤd	
pledging	ˈplɛʤɪŋ	
plentiful	ˈplɛntɪful	
plentifully	ˈplɛntɪfulɪ; ˈplɛntɪfəlɪ	
plenty	ˈplɛntɪ	
plight	plaɪt	
plights	plaɪts	
plot	plɒt	plɑt
plots	plɒts	plɑts
plotted	ˈplɒtɪd	ˈplɑtɪd
plotting	ˈplɒtɪŋ	ˈplɑtɪŋ
plough	plaʊ	
ploughs	plaʊz	
ploughed	plaʊd	
ploughing	ˈplaʊɪŋ	
pluck	plʌk	
plucky	ˈplʌkɪ	

Traditional Spelling	Received Pronunciation	American Variants
plug	plʌg	
plugs	plʌgz	
plum	plʌm	
plums	plʌmz	
plume	pluˑm	
plumes	pluˑmz	
plump	plʌmp	
plunder	ˈplʌndə(r	ˈplʌndə
plunders	ˈplʌndəz	ˈplʌndəz
plundered	ˈplʌndəd	ˈplʌndəd
plundering	ˈplʌndərɪŋ	
plunderer	ˈplʌndərə(r	ˈplʌndərə
plunderers	ˈplʌndərəz	ˈplʌndərəz
plunge	plʌnʤ	
plunges	ˈplʌnʤɪz	
plunged	plʌnʤd	
plunging	ˈplʌnʤɪŋ	
plural	ˈplʊərəl	ˈpluˑrəl
plurals	ˈplʊərəlz	ˈpluˑrəlz
plus	plʌs	
p.m.	ˈpiˑˈɛm	
pneumatic	njuˈmætɪk	
pneumonia	njuˈmoʊnjə	
pocket	ˈpɒkɪt	ˈpɑkɪt
pockets	ˈpɒkɪts	ˈpɑkɪts
pocketed	ˈpɒkɪtɪd	ˈpɑkɪtɪd
pocketing	ˈpɒkɪtɪŋ	ˈpɑkɪtɪŋ
pocketful	ˈpɒkɪtfʊl	ˈpɑkɪtfʊl
pocketfuls	ˈpɒkɪtfʊlz	ˈpɑkɪtfʊlz
poem	ˈpoʊɪm	
poems	ˈpoʊɪmz	
poet	ˈpoʊɪt	
poets	ˈpoʊɪts	
poetic	poʊˈɛtɪk	
poetically	poʊˈɛtɪkəlɪ	
poetry	ˈpoʊɪtrɪ, ˈpɔɪtrɪ	
point	pɔɪnt	
points	pɔɪnts	
pointed	ˈpɔɪntɪd	
pointing	ˈpɔɪntɪŋ	
pointer	ˈpɔɪntə(r	ˈpɔɪntə
pointers	ˈpɔɪntəz	ˈpɔɪntəz
pointless	ˈpɔɪntlɪs	
poison	ˈpɔɪzn̩	
poisons	ˈpɔɪzn̩z	
poisoned	ˈpɔɪzn̩d	
poisoning	ˈpɔɪznɪŋ, ˈpɔɪzn̩ɪŋ	

Traditional Spelling	Received Pronunciation	American Variants
poisonous	ˈpɔɪznəs, ˈpɔɪzn̩əs	
poke	pouk	
pokes	pouks	
poked	poukt	
poking	ˈpoukɪŋ	
Poland	ˈpoulənd	
polar	ˈpoulə(r	ˈpoulə
pole	poul	
poles	poulz	
Pole	poul	
Poles	poulz	
police	pəˈliˑs, pouˈliˑs	
policeman	pəˈliˑsmən pouˈliˑsmən	
policemen	pəˈliˑsmən pouˈliˑsmən	
policy	ˈpɒlɪsɪ, ˈpɒləsɪ	ˈpalɪsɪ, ˈpaləsɪ
policies	ˈpɒlɪsɪz, ˈpɒləsɪz	ˈpalɪsɪz, ˈpaləsɪz
polish	ˈpɒlɪʃ	ˈpalɪʃ
polishes	ˈpɒlɪʃɪz	ˈpalɪʃɪz
polished	ˈpɒlɪʃt	ˈpalɪʃt
polishing	ˈpɒlɪʃɪŋ	ˈpalɪʃɪŋ
Polish, *adj.*	ˈpoulɪʃ	
polite	pəˈlaɪt, pouˈlaɪt	
politely	pəˈlaɪtlɪ, pouˈlaɪtlɪ	
politeness	pəˈlaɪtnɪs, pouˈlaɪtnɪs	
political	pəˈlɪtɪkəl	
politician	pɒlɪˈtɪʃən	palɪˈtɪʃən
politicians	pɒlɪˈtɪʃənz	palɪˈtɪʃənz
Polynesia	pɒlɪˈniˑzɪə	palɪˈniˑzɪə
pomp	pɒmp	pamp
pompous	ˈpɒmpəs	ˈpampəs
pond	pɒnd	pand
ponds	pɒndz	pandz
ponder	ˈpɒndə(r	ˈpandə
ponders	ˈpɒndəz	ˈpandəz
pondered	ˈpɒndəd	ˈpandəd
pondering	ˈpɒndərɪŋ	ˈpandərɪŋ
ponderous	ˈpɒndərəs	ˈpandərəs
pony	ˈpounɪ	
ponies	ˈpounɪz	
pool	puˑl	
pools	puˑlz	
pooled	puˑld	
pooling	ˈpuˑlɪŋ	
poor	puə(r, pɔə(r	puə
poorer	ˈpuərə(r, ˈpɔərə(r	ˈpuˑrə

Traditional Spelling	Received Pronunciation	American Variants
poorest	ˈpuərɪst, ˈpɔərɪst	ˈpuˑrɪst
poorly	ˈpuəlɪ, ˈpɔəlɪ	ˈpuəlɪ
poorness	ˈpuənɪs, ˈpɔənɪs	ˈpuənɪs
pope	poup	
popes	poups	
popular	ˈpɒpjulə(r, ˈpɒpjələ(r	ˈpɑpjulə, ˈpɑpjələ
popularity	pɒpjuˈlærɪtɪ pɒpjəˈlærɪtɪ	pɑpjuˈlærɪtɪ pɑpjəˈlærɪtɪ
popularize (s)	ˈpɒpjuləraɪz ˈpɒpjələraɪz	ˈpɑpjuləraɪz ˈpɑpjələraɪz
popularizes	ˈpɒpjuləraɪzɪz ˈpɒpjələraɪzɪz	ˈpɑpjuləraɪzɪz ˈpɑpjələraɪzɪz
popularized	ˈpɒpjuləraɪzd ˈpɒpjələraɪzd	ˈpɑpjuləraɪzd ˈpɑpjələraɪzd
popularizing	ˈpɒpjuləraɪzɪŋ ˈpɒpjələraɪzɪŋ	ˈpɑpjuləraɪzɪŋ ˈpɑpjələraɪzɪŋ
popularly	ˈpɒpjuləlɪ, ˈpɒpjələlɪ	ˈpɑpjuləlɪ, ˈpɑpjələlɪ
population	pɒpjuˈleɪʃən	pɑpjuˈleɪʃən
populations	pɒpjuˈleɪʃənz	pɑpjuˈleɪʃənz
porcelain	ˈpɔˑslɪn, ˈpɔˑsleɪn	ˈpɔəslɪn
porch	pɔˑtʃ	poətʃ
porches	ˈpɔˑtʃɪz	ˈpoətʃɪz
pore	pɔˑ(r, pɔə(r	poə
pores	pɔˑz, pɔəz	poəz
pork	pɔˑk	poək
porridge	ˈpɒrɪdʒ	ˈpɑrɪdʒ
port	pɔˑt	poət
ports	pɔˑts	poəts
portable	ˈpɔˑtəbḷ	ˈpoətəbḷ
porter	ˈpɔˑtə(r	ˈpoətə
porters	ˈpɔˑtəz	ˈpoətəz
portfolio	pɔtˈfoulɪou	poətˈfoulɪou
portfolios	pɔtˈfoulɪouz	poətˈfoulɪouz
portion	ˈpɔˑʃən	ˈpoəʃən
portions	ˈpɔˑʃənz	ˈpoəʃənz
portmanteau	pɔtˈmæntou	poətˈmæntou
portmanteaus	pɔtˈmæntouz	poətˈmæntouz
portrait	ˈpɔˑtrɪt	ˈpoətrɪt
portraits	ˈpɔˑtrɪts	ˈpoətrɪts
Portsmouth	ˈpɔˑtsməθ	ˈpoətsməθ
Portugal	ˈpɔˑtjugəl, ˈpɔˑtʃugəl	ˈpoətjugəl, ˈpoətʃugəl
Portuguese	pɔtjuˈgiˑz pɔtʃuˈgiˑz	poətjuˈgiˑz poətʃuˈgiˑz poətjuˈgiˑs poətʃuˈgiˑs
pose	pouz	
poses	ˈpouzɪz	

Traditional Spelling	Received Pronunciation	American Variants
posed	pouzd	
posing	'pouzɪŋ	
position	†pə'zɪʃən	
positions	†pə'zɪʃənz	
positive	'pɒzətɪv, 'pɒzɪtɪv	'pazətɪv, 'pazɪtɪv
positively	'pɒzətɪvlɪ, 'pɒzɪtɪvlɪ	'pazətɪvlɪ, 'pazɪtɪvlɪ
possess	†pə'zɛs	
possesses	†pə'zɛsɪz	
possessed	†pə'zɛst	
possessing	†pə'zɛsɪŋ	
possession	†pə'zɛʃən	
possessions	†pə'zɛʃənz	
possessive	†pə'zɛsɪv	
possessives	†pə'zɛsɪvz	
possessor	†pə'zɛsə(r	pə'zɛsə
possessors	†pə'zɛsəz	pə'zɛsəz
possibility	pɒsɪ'bɪlɪtɪ pɒsə'bɪlɪtɪ	pasɪ'bɪlɪtɪ pasə'bɪlɪtɪ
possibilities	pɒsɪ'bɪlɪtɪz pɒsə'bɪlɪtɪz	pasɪ'bɪlɪtɪz pasə'bɪlɪtɪz
possible	'pɒsɪbl̩, 'pɒsəbl̩	'pasɪbl̩, 'pasəbl̩
possibly	'pɒsɪblɪ, 'pɒsəblɪ	'pasɪblɪ, 'pasəblɪ
post	poust	
posts	pousts	
posted	'poustɪd	
posting	'poustɪŋ	
postage	'poustɪdʒ	
postages	'poustɪdʒɪz	
postal	'poustəl	
postcard	'pous*t*kad	'pous*t*kaəd
postcards	'pous*t*kadz	'pous*t*kaədz
poster	'poustə(r	'poustə
posters	'poustəz	'poustəz
postman	'pous*t*mən	
postmen	'pous*t*mən	
postmark	'pous*t*mak	'pous*t*maək
postmarks	'pous*t*maks	'pous*t*maəks
postmaster	'pous*t*mastə(r	'pous*t*mastə
postmasters	'pous*t*mastəz	'pous*t*mastəz
post-office	'poustɒfɪs	'poustafɪs
post-offices	'poustɒfɪsɪz	'poustafɪsɪz
postpone	pous*t*'poun pəs'poun	
postpones	pous*t*'pounz pəs'pounz	

† See Note 30, p. xxxv. in Introduction.

Traditional Spelling	Received Pronunciation	American Variants
postponed	poust'pound pəs'pound	
postponing	poust'pounɪŋ pəs'pounɪŋ	
postponement	poust'pounmənt pəs'pounmənt	
postponements	poust'pounmənts pəs'pounmənts	
postscript	'pousskrɪpt	
postscripts	'pousskrɪpts	
pot	pɒt	pɑt
pots	pɒts	pɑts
potato	†pə'teɪtou	
potatos	†pə'teɪtouz	
pottery	'pɒtərɪ	'pɑtərɪ
pouch	pautʃ	
pouches	'pautʃɪz	
poultry	'poultrɪ	
pound	paund	
pounds	paundz	
pour	pɔ·(r, pɔə(r	pɔə
pours	pɔ·z, pɔəz	pɔəz
poured	pɔ·d, pɔəd	pɔəd
pouring	'pɔ·rɪŋ, 'pɔərɪŋ	'pɔ·rɪŋ
poverty	'pɒvətɪ	'pɑvətɪ
powder	'paudə(r	'paudə
powders	'paudəz	'paudəz
powdered	'paudəd	'paudəd
powdering	'paudərɪŋ	
power	'pauə(r	'pauə
powers	'pauəz	'pauəz
powerful	'pauəful	'pauəful
powerfully	'pauəfulɪ, 'pauəfəlɪ	'pauəfulɪ, 'pauəfəl
powerless	'pauəlɪs	'pauəlɪs
practicability	præktɪkə'bɪlɪtɪ	
practicable	'præktɪkəbl̩	
practicably	'præktɪkəblɪ	
practical	'præktɪkəl	
practically, *in a practical manner*	'præktɪkəlɪ	
practically, *very nearly*	'præktɪklɪ	
practice, *noun*	'præktɪs	
practices	'præktɪsɪz	
practise, *verb*	'præktɪs	

† See Note 30, p. xxxv. in Introduction.

Traditional Spelling	Received Pronunciation	American Variants
practises	ˈpræktɪsɪz	
practised	ˈpræktɪst	
practising	ˈpræktɪsɪŋ	
Prague	preɪg, prɑˑg	
prairie	ˈprɛərɪ	ˈprɛˑrɪ
prairies	ˈprɛərɪz	ˈprɛˑrɪz
praise	preɪz	
praises	ˈpreɪzɪz	
praised	preɪzd	
praising	ˈpreɪzɪŋ	
praiseworthy	ˈpreɪzwɜðɪ	ˈpreɪzwɜəðɪ
pray	preɪ	
prays	preɪz	
prayed	preɪd	
praying	ˈpreɪɪŋ	
prayer	ˈprɛə(r	ˈprɛə
prayers	ˈprɛəz	ˈprɛəz
preach	priˑtʃ	
preaches	ˈpriˑtʃɪz	
preached	priˑtʃt	
preaching	ˈpriˑtʃɪŋ	
preacher	ˈpriˑtʃə(r	ˈpriˑtʃə
preachers	ˈpriˑtʃəz	ˈpriˑtʃəz
prearrange	ˈpriˑəˈreɪndʒ	
prearranges	ˈpriˑəˈreɪndʒɪz	
prearranged	ˈpriˑəˈreɪndʒd	
prearranging	ˈpriˑəˈreɪndʒɪŋ	
precaution	prɪˈkɔˑʃən	
precautions	prɪˈkɔˑʃənz	
precede	ˈpriˑˈsiˑd	
precedes	ˈpriˑˈsiˑdz	
preceded	ˈpriˑˈsiˑdɪd	
preceding	ˈpriˑˈsiˑdɪŋ	
precedence	priˈsiˑdəns, ˈprɛsɪdəns	
precedent	ˈprɛsɪdənt	
precedents	ˈprɛsɪdənts	
precious	ˈprɛʃəs	
preciously	ˈprɛʃəslɪ	
precipice	ˈprɛsɪpɪs	
precipices	ˈprɛsɪpɪsɪz	
precise	prɪˈsaɪs, prəˈsaɪs	
precisely	prɪˈsaɪslɪ, prəˈsaɪslɪ	
precision	prɪˈsɪʒən	
preclude	prɪˈkluˑd	
precludes	prɪˈkluˑdz	
precluded	prɪˈkluˑdɪd	
precluding	prɪˈkluˑdɪŋ	

Traditional Spelling	Received Pronunciation	American Variants
precocious	prɪˈkoʊʃəs	
predecessor	ˈpriˑdɪsɛsə(r pridɪˈsɛsə(r	ˈpriˑdɪsɛsə pridɪˈsɛsə ˈprɛdɪsɛsə prɛdɪˈsɛsə
predecessors	ˈpriˑdɪsɛsəz pridɪˈsɛsəz	ˈpriˑdɪsɛsəz ˈprɛdɪsɛsəz pridɪˈsɛsəz prɛdɪˈsɛsəz
predicament	prɪˈdɪkəmənt prəˈdɪkəmənt	
predicaments	prɪˈdɪkəmənts prəˈdɪkəmənts	
predicate	ˈprɛdɪkɪt, ˈprɛdɪkeɪt	
predicates	ˈprɛdɪkɪts ˈprɛdɪkeɪts	
predict	prɪˈdɪkt, prəˈdɪkt	
predicts	prɪˈdɪkts, prəˈdɪkts	
predicted	prɪˈdɪktɪd prəˈdɪktɪd	
predicting	prɪˈdɪktɪŋ prəˈdɪktɪŋ	
prediction	prɪˈdɪkʃən prəˈdɪkʃən	
predictions	prɪˈdɪkʃənz prəˈdɪkʃənz	
predominate	prɪˈdɒmɪneɪt	prɪˈdɑmɪneɪt
predominates	prɪˈdɒmɪneɪts	prɪˈdɑmɪneɪts
predominated	prɪˈdɒmɪneɪtɪd	prɪˈdɑmɪneɪtɪd
predominating	prɪˈdɒmɪneɪtɪŋ	prɪˈdɑmɪneɪtɪŋ
preface	ˈprɛfɪs	
prefaces	ˈprɛfɪsɪz	
prefaced	ˈprɛfɪst	
prefacing	ˈprɛfɪsɪŋ	
prefer	prɪˈfɜˑ(r	prɪˈfɜə
prefers	prɪˈfɜˑz	prɪˈfɜəz
preferred	prɪˈfɜˑd	prɪˈfɜəd
preferring	prɪˈfɜˑrɪŋ	
preferable	ˈprɛfərəbḷ	
preferably	ˈprɛfərəblɪ	
preference	ˈprɛfərəns	
preferences	ˈprɛfərənsɪz	
prefix	ˈpriˑfɪks	
prefixes	ˈpriˑfɪksɪz	
prehistoric	ˈpriˑhɪsˈtɒrɪk	ˈpriˑhɪsˈtɑrɪk
prejudice	ˈprɛʤudɪs, ˈprɛʤədɪs	

Traditional Spelling	Received Pronunciation	American Variants
prejudices	ˈprɛʤudɪsɪz	
	ˈprɛʤədɪsɪz	
prejudiced	ˈprɛʤudɪst	
	ˈprɛʤədɪst	
prejudicing	ˈprɛʤudɪsɪŋ	
	ˈprɛʤədɪsɪŋ	
prejudicial	prɛʤuˈdɪʃəl	
	prɛʤəˈdɪʃəl	
preliminary	prɪˈlɪmɪnərɪ	prɪˈlɪmɪnɛrɪ
	prəˈlɪmɪnərɪ	prəˈlɪmɪnɛrɪ
preliminaries	prɪˈlɪmɪnərɪz	prɪˈlɪmɪnɛrɪz
	prəˈlɪmɪnərɪz	prəˈlɪmɪnɛrɪz
prelude	ˈprɛljud	ˈpriˑljud
preludes	ˈprɛljudz	ˈpriˑljudz
premature	prɛməˈtjʊə(r	prɛməˈtjʊə
	priməˈtjʊə(r	priməˈtjʊə
prematurely	prɛməˈtjʊəlɪ	prɛməˈtjʊəlɪ
	priməˈtjʊəlɪ	priməˈtjʊəlɪ
premeditate	priˈmɛdɪteɪt	
premeditates	priˈmɛdɪteɪts	
premeditated	priˈmɛdɪteɪtɪd	
premeditating	priˈmɛdɪteɪtɪŋ	
premeditation	primɛdɪˈteɪʃən	
premier	ˈprɛmjə(r	ˈprɛmjə
premiers	ˈprɛmjəz	ˈprɛmjəz
premises	ˈprɛmɪsɪz	
premium	ˈpriˑmɪəm	
premiums	ˈpriˑmɪəmz	
preparation	prɛpəˈreɪʃən	
preparations	prɛpəˈreɪʃənz	
preparatory	prɪˈpærətərɪ	prɪˈpæretorɪ
prepare	prɪˈpɛə(r	prɪˈpɛə
prepares	prɪˈpɛəz	prɪˈpɛəz
prepared	prɪˈpɛəd	prɪˈpɛəd
preparing	prɪˈpɛərɪŋ	prɪˈpɛˑrɪŋ
preposition	prɛpəˈzɪʃən	
prepositions	prɛpəˈzɪʃənz	
preposterous	prɪˈpɒstərəs	prɪˈpɑstərəs
	prəˈpɒstərəs	prəˈpɑstərəs
prescribe	prɪsˈkraɪb	
prescribes	prɪsˈkraɪbz	
prescribed	prɪsˈkraɪbd	
prescribing	prɪsˈkraɪbɪŋ	
prescription	prɪsˈkrɪpʃən	
	prəsˈkrɪpʃən	
prescriptions	prɪsˈkrɪpʃənz	
	prəsˈkrɪpʃənz	

Traditional Spelling	Received Pronunciation	American Variants
presence	ˈprɛzn̩s	
presences	ˈprɛzn̩sɪz	
present, *noun*	ˈprɛzn̩t	
presents	ˈprɛzn̩ts	
present, *verb*	prɪˈzɛnt	
presents	prɪˈzɛnts	
presented	prɪˈzɛntɪd	
presenting	prɪˈzɛntɪŋ	
presentable	prɪˈzɛntəbl̩ prəˈzɛntəbl̩	
presentation	prɛzənˈteɪʃən prɛzɛnˈteɪʃən	
presentations	prɛzənˈteɪʃənz prɛzɛnˈteɪʃənz	
presently	ˈprɛzn̩tlɪ	
preserve	prɪˈzɜˑv	prɪˈzɜəv
preserves	prɪˈzɜˑvz	prɪˈzɜəvz
preserved	prɪˈzɜˑvd	prɪˈzɜəvd
preserving	prɪˈzɜˑvɪŋ	prɪˈzɜəvɪŋ
preserver	prɪˈzɜˑvə(r	prɪˈzɜəvə
preservers	prɪˈzɜˑvəz	prɪˈzɜəvəz
preside	prɪˈzaɪd	
presides	prɪˈzaɪdz	
presided	prɪˈzaɪdɪd	
presiding	prɪˈzaɪdɪŋ	
presidency	ˈprɛzɪdənsɪ	
president	ˈprɛzɪdənt	
presidents	ˈprɛzɪdənts	
presidential	prɛzɪˈdɛnʃəl	
press	prɛs	
presses	ˈprɛsɪz	
pressed	prɛst	
pressing	ˈprɛsɪŋ	
pressingly	ˈprɛsɪŋlɪ	
pressure	ˈprɛʃə(r	ˈprɛʃə
presume	prɪˈzjuˑm	
presumes	prɪˈzjuˑmz	
presumed	prɪˈzjuˑmd	
presuming	prɪˈzjuˑmɪŋ	
pretence	prɪˈtɛns	
pretences	prɪˈtɛnsɪz	
pretend	prɪˈtɛnd	
pretends	prɪˈtɛndz	
pretended	prɪˈtɛndɪd	
pretending	prɪˈtɛndɪŋ	
pretentious	prɪˈtɛnʃəs	
preterite	ˈprɛtərɪt	

Traditional Spelling	Received Pronunciation	American Variants
preterites	'prɛtərɪts	
pretext	'pri·tɛkst	
pretexts	'pri·tɛksts	
Pretoria	prɪ'tɔ·rɪə	
pretty	'prɪtɪ	
prettier	'prɪtɪə(r	
prettiest	'prɪtɪɪst	
prettily	'prɪtɪlɪ	
prettiness	'prɪtɪnɪs	
prevail	prɪ'veɪl	
prevails	prɪ'veɪlz	
prevailed	prɪ'veɪld	
prevailing	prɪ'veɪlɪŋ	
prevalence	'prɛvələns	
prevalent	'prɛvələnt	
prevent	prɪ'vɛnt	
prevents	prɪ'vɛnts	
prevented	prɪ'vɛntɪd	
preventing	prɪ'vɛntɪŋ	
prevention	prɪ'vɛnʃən	
previous	'pri·vɪəs, 'pri·vjəs	
previously	'pri·vɪəslɪ, 'pri·vjəslɪ	
prey	preɪ	
preys	preɪz	
preyed	preɪd	
preying	'preɪɪŋ	
price	praɪs	
prices	'praɪsɪz	
priceless	'praɪslɪs	
prick	prɪk	
pricks	prɪks	
pricked	prɪkt	
pricking	'prɪkɪŋ	
prickly	'prɪklɪ	
pride	praɪd	
priest	pri·st	
priests	pri·sts	
prig	prɪg	
prigs	prɪgz	
prim	prɪm	
primary	'praɪmərɪ	
prime minister	'praɪm'mɪnɪstə(r	'praɪm 'mɪnɪstə
prime ministers	'praɪm 'mɪnɪstəz	'praɪm 'mɪnɪstəz
primer	'praɪmə(r, 'prɪmə(r	'praɪmə, 'prɪmə
primers	'praɪməz, 'prɪməz	'praɪməz, 'prɪməz
primitive	'prɪmɪtɪv	
primitively	'prɪmɪtɪvlɪ	

Traditional Spelling	Received Pronunciation	American Variants
primly	ˈprɪmlɪ	
primness	ˈprɪmnɪs	
primrose	ˈprɪmrouz	
primroses	ˈprɪmrouzɪz	
prince	prɪns	
princes	ˈprɪnsɪz	
princess	ˈprɪnˈsɛs	
princesses	ˈprɪnˈsɛsɪz	
principal	ˈprɪnsɪpəl, ˈprɪnsəpəl	
principals	ˈprɪnsɪpəlz ˈprɪnsəpəlz	
principally	ˈprɪnsɪpəlɪ, ˈprɪnsəpəlɪ	
principle	ˈprɪnsɪpl̩, ˈprɪnsəpl̩	
principles	ˈprɪnsɪpl̩z ˈprɪnsəpl̩z	
print	prɪnt	
prints	prɪnts	
printed	ˈprɪntɪd	
printing	ˈprɪntɪŋ	
printer	ˈprɪntə(r	ˈprɪntə
printers	ˈprɪntəz	ˈprɪntəz
prism	ˈprɪzm̩	
prisms	ˈprɪzm̩z	
prison	ˈprɪzn̩	
prisons	ˈprɪzn̩z	
prisoner	ˈprɪzn̩ə(r, ˈprɪznə(r	ˈprɪzn̩ə
prisoners	ˈprɪzn̩əz, ˈprɪznəz	ˈprɪzn̩əz
privacy	ˈpraɪvəsɪ, ˈprɪvəsɪ	
private	ˈpraɪvɪt	
privately	ˈpraɪvɪtlɪ	
privilege	ˈprɪvɪlɪʤ	
privileges	ˈprɪvɪlɪʤɪz	
prize	praɪz	
prizes	ˈpraɪzɪz	
prized	praɪzd	
prizing	ˈpraɪzɪŋ	
pro	prou	
probability	prɒbəˈbɪlɪtɪ	prɑbəˈbɪlɪtɪ
probabilities	prɒbəˈbɪlɪtɪz	prɑbəˈbɪlɪtɪz
probable	ˈprɒbəbl̩	ˈprɑbəbl̩
probably	ˈprɒbəblɪ	ˈprɑbəblɪ
problem	ˈprɒbləm	ˈprɑbləm
problems	ˈprɒbləmz	ˈprɑbləmz
procedure	†prəˈsiˑʤə(r †prəˈsiˑdjə(r	prəˈsiˑʤə prəˈsiˑdjuə

† See Note 30, p. xxxv. in Introduction.

Traditional Spelling	Received Pronunciation	American Variants
procedures	†prə'si·dʒəz †prə'si·djəz	prə'si·dʒəz prə'si·djʊəz
proceed	†prə'si·d	
proceeds	†prə'si·dz	
proceeded	†prə'si·dɪd	
proceeding	†prə'si·dɪŋ	
proceedings	†prə'si·dɪŋz	
proceeds, *noun*	'prousidz	
process	'prousεs, 'prousɪs 'prɒsεs, 'prɒsɪs	'prasεs, 'prasɪs
processes	'prousεsɪz 'prousɪsɪz 'prɒsεsɪz 'prɒsɪsɪz	 'prasεsɪz 'prɒsɪsɪz
procession	†prə'sεʃən	
processions	†prə'sεʃənz	
proclaim	†prə'kleɪm	
proclaims	†prə'kleɪmz	
proclaimed	†prə'kleɪmd	
proclaiming	†prə'kleɪmɪŋ	
proclamation	prɒklə'meɪʃən	praklə'meɪʃən
proclamations	prɒklə'meɪʃənz	praklə'meɪʃənz
procure	†prə'kjʊə(r	prə'kjʊə
procures	†prə'kjʊəz	prə'kjʊəz
procured	†prə'kjʊəd	prə'kjʊəd
procuring	†prə'kjʊərɪŋ	prə'kjʊ·rɪŋ
produce, *noun*	'prɒdjus	'pradjus
produce, *verb*	†prə'dju·s	
produces	†prə'dju·sɪz	
produced	†prə'dju·st	
producing	†prə'dju·sɪŋ	
product	'prɒdəkt, 'prɒdʌkt	'pradəkt, 'pradʌkt
products	'prɒdəkts 'prɒdʌkts	'pradəkts 'pradʌkts
production	†prə'dʌkʃən	
productions	†prə'dʌkʃənz	
productive	†prə'dʌktɪv	
productively	†prə'dʌktɪvlɪ	
profess	†prə'fεs	
professes	†prə'fεsɪz	
professed	†prə'fεst	
professing	†prə'fεsɪŋ	
profession	†prə'fεʃən	
professions	†prə'fεʃənz	
professional	†prə'fεʃənl̩	

† See Note 30, p. xxxv. in Introduction.

Traditional Spelling	Received Pronunciation	American Variants
professor	†prə'fɛsə(r	prə'fɛsə
professors	†prə'fɛsəz	prə'fɛsəz
proficiency	†prə'fɪʃənsɪ	
proficient	†prə'fɪʃənt	
proficiently	†prə'fɪʃəntlɪ	
profit	'prɒfɪt	'prɑfɪt
profits	'prɒfɪts	'prɑfɪts
profited	'prɒfɪtɪd	'prɑfɪtɪd
profiting	'prɒfɪtɪŋ	'prɑfɪtɪŋ
profitable	'prɒfɪtəbḷ	'prɑfɪtəbḷ
profitably	'prɒfɪtəblɪ	'prɑfɪtəblɪ
profound	†prə'faʊnd	
profoundly	†prə'faʊndlɪ	
program (*Amer.*)	'prougræm	
programs (*Amer.*)	'prougræmz	
programme	'prougræm	
programmes	'prougræmz	
progress, ***noun***	'prougrɛs, 'prɒgrɛs	'prɑgrɛs
progress, ***verb***	†prə'grɛs	
progresses	†prə'grɛsɪz	
progressed	†prə'grɛst	
progressing	†prə'grɛsɪŋ	
progressive	†prə'grɛsɪv	
progressively	†prə'grɛsɪvlɪ	
prohibit	†prə'hɪbɪt	
prohibits	†prə'hɪbɪts	
prohibited	†prə'hɪbɪtɪd	
prohibiting	†prə'hɪbɪtɪŋ	
prohibition	prou*h*ɪ'bɪʃən	
prohibitive	†prə'hɪbɪtɪv	
project, ***noun***	'prɒdʒɛkt, 'prɒdʒɪkt	'prɑdʒɛkt, 'prɑdʒɪkt
projects	'prɒdʒɛkts 'prɒdʒɪkts	'prɑdʒɛkts 'prɑdʒɪkts
project, ***verb***	†prə'dʒɛkt	
projects	†prə'dʒɛkts	
projected	†prə'dʒɛktɪd	
projecting	†prə'dʒɛktɪŋ	
projection	†prə'dʒɛkʃən	
projections	†prə'dʒɛkʃənz	
proletarian	proulɪ'tɛərɪən	proulɪ'tɛ·rɪən
prolog (*Amer.*) **prologue**	'proulɒg	'proulɑg
prologs (*Amer.*) prologues	'proulɒgz	'proulɑgz
prolong	†prə'lɒŋ	

† See Note 30, p. xxxv. in Introduction.

Traditional Spelling	Received Pronunciation	American Variants
prolongs	†prəˈlɒŋz	
prolonged	†prəˈlɒŋd	
prolonging	†prəˈlɒŋɪŋ	
prominence	ˈprɒmɪnəns	ˈprɑmɪnəns
prominent	ˈprɒmɪnənt	ˈprɑmɪnənt
prominently	ˈprɒmɪnəntlɪ	ˈprɑmɪnəntlɪ
promise	ˈprɒmɪs	ˈprɑmɪs
promises	ˈprɒmɪsɪz	ˈprɑmɪsɪz
promised	ˈprɒmɪst	ˈprɑmɪst
promising	ˈprɒmɪsɪŋ	ˈprɑmɪsɪŋ
promote	prəˈmoʊt	
promotes	prəˈmoʊts	
promoted	prəˈmoʊtɪd	
promoting	prəˈmoʊtɪŋ	
promotion	prəˈmoʊʃ*ə*n	
promotions	prəˈmoʊʃ*ə*nz	
prompt	prɒm*p*t	prɑm*p*t
prompter	ˈprɒm*p*tə(r	ˈprɑm*p*tə
promptest	ˈprɒm*p*tɪst	ˈprɑm*p*tɪst
prompts	prɒm*p*ts	prɑm*p*ts
prompted	ˈprɒm*p*tɪd	ˈprɑm*p*tɪd
prompting	ˈprɒm*p*tɪŋ	ˈprɑm*p*tɪŋ
promptly	ˈprɒm*p*tlɪ	ˈprɑm*p*tlɪ
promptness	ˈprɒm*p*tnɪs	ˈprɑm*p*tnɪs
prong	prɒŋ	
prongs	prɒŋz	
pronoun	ˈproʊnaʊn	
pronouns	ˈproʊnaʊnz	
pronounce	†prəˈnaʊns	
pronounces	†prəˈnaʊnsɪz	
pronounced	†prəˈnaʊnst	
pronouncing	†prəˈnaʊnsɪŋ	
pronunciation	†prənʌnsɪˈeɪʃ*ə*n	
pronunciations	†prənʌnsɪˈeɪʃ*ə*nz	
proof	pruˑf	
proofs	pruˑfs	
propaganda	prɒpəˈgændə	prɑpəˈgændə
propagate	ˈprɒpəgeɪt	ˈprɑpəˈgeɪt
propagates	ˈprɒpəgeɪts	ˈprɑpəˈgeɪts
propagated	ˈprɒpəgeɪtɪd	ˈprɑpəˈgeɪtɪd
propagating	ˈprɒpəgeɪtɪŋ	ˈprɑpəˈgeɪtɪŋ
propel	prəˈpɛl	
propels	prəˈpɛlz	
propelled	prəˈpɛld	
propelling	prəˈpɛlɪŋ	

† See Note 30, p. xxxv. in Introduction.

Traditional Spelling	Received Pronunciation	American Variants
propeller	†prə'pɛlə(r	prə'pɛlə
propellers	†prə'pɛləz	prə'pɛləz
proper	'prɒpə(r	'prɑpə
properly	'prɒpəlɪ	'prɑpəlɪ
property	'prɒpətɪ	'prɑpətɪ
properties	'prɒpətɪz	'prɑpətɪz
prophecy	'prɒfɪsɪ, 'prɒfɪsaɪ	'prɑfɪsɪ, 'prɑfɪsaɪ
prophecies	'prɒfɪsɪz, 'prɒfɪsaɪz	'prɑfɪsɪz, 'prɑfɪsaɪz
prophesy	'prɒfɪsaɪ	'prɑfɪsaɪ
prophesies	'prɒfɪsaɪz	'prɑfɪsaɪz
prophesied	'prɒfɪsaɪd	'prɑfɪsaɪd
prophesying	'prɒfɪsaɪɪŋ	'prɑfɪsaɪɪŋ
prophet	'prɒfɪt, 'prɒfɛt	'prɑfɪt, 'prɑfɛt
prophets	'prɒfɪts, 'prɒfɛts	'prɑfɪts, 'prɑfɛts
proportion	†prə'pɔ·ʃən	prə'poəʃən
proportions	†prə'pɔ·ʃənz	prə'poəʃənz
proportionate	†prə'pɔ·ʃənɪt	prə'poəʃənɪt
proportionately	†prə'pɔ·ʃənɪtlɪ	prə'poəʃənɪtlɪ
proposal	†prə'pouzəl	
proposals	†prə'pouzəlz	
propose	†prə'pouz	
proposes	†prə'pouzɪz	
proposed	†prə'pouzd	
proposing	†prə'pouzɪŋ	
proposer	†prə'pouzə(r	prə'pouzə
proposers	†prə'pouzəz	prə'pouzəz
proposition	prɒpə'zɪʃən	prɑpə'zɪʃən
propositions	prɒpə'zɪʃənz	prɑpə'zɪʃənz
proprietor	†prə'praɪətə(r	prə'praɪətə
proprietors	†prə'praɪətəz	prə'praɪətəz
proprietress	†prə'praɪətrɪs	prə'praɪətrɪs
proprietresses	†prə'praɪətrɪsɪz	prə'praɪətrɪsɪz
prosaic	prou'zeɪɪk, prə'zeɪɪk	
prose	prouz	
prosecute	'prɒsɪkjut	'prɑsɪkjut
prosecutes	'prɒsɪkjuts	'prɑsɪkjuts
prosecuted	'prɒsɪkjutɪd	'prɑsɪkjutɪd
prosecuting	'prɒsɪkjutɪŋ	'prɑsɪkjutɪŋ
prosecution	prɒsɪ'kju·ʃən	prɑsɪ'kju·ʃən
prosecutions	prɒsɪ'kju·ʃənz	prɑsɪ'kju·ʃənz
prospect, ***noun***	'prɒspɛkt	'prɑspɛkt
prospects	'prɒspɛkts	'prɑspɛkts
prospectus	†prəs'pɛktəs	
prospectuses	†prəs'pɛktəsɪz	
prosper	'prɒspə(r	'prɑspə

† See Note 30, p. xxxv. in Introduction.

Y

Traditional Spelling	Received Pronunciation	American Variants
prospers	ˈprɒspəz	ˈprɑspəz
prospered	ˈprɒspəd	ˈprɑspəd
prospering	ˈprɒspərɪŋ	ˈprɑspərɪŋ
prosperity	prɒsˈpɛrɪtɪ	prɑsˈpɛrɪtɪ
prosperous	ˈprɒspərəs	ˈprɑspərəs
prosperously	ˈprɒspərəslɪ	ˈprɑspərəslɪ
protect	†prəˈtɛkt	
protects	†prəˈtɛkts	
protected	†prəˈtɛktɪd	
protecting	†prəˈtɛktɪŋ	
protection	†prəˈtɛkʃən	
protective	†prəˈtɛktɪv	
protector	†prəˈtɛktə(r	prəˈtɛktə
protectors	†prəˈtɛktəz	prəˈtɛktəz
protectorate	†prəˈtɛktərɪt	
protectorates	†prəˈtɛktərɪts	
protest, *noun*	ˈproʊtɛst	
protests	ˈproʊtɛsts	
protest, *verb*	†prəˈtɛst	
protests	†prəˈtɛsts	
protested	†prəˈtɛstɪd	
protesting	†prəˈtɛstɪŋ	
protestant	ˈprɒtɪstənt	ˈprɑtɪstənt
protestants	ˈprɒtɪstənts	ˈprɑtɪstənts
proud	praʊd	
prouder	ˈpraʊdə(r	ˈpraʊdə
proudest	ˈpraʊdɪst	
proudly	ˈpraʊdlɪ	
prove	pruˑv	
proves	pruˑvz	
proved	pruˑvd	
proving	ˈpruˑvɪŋ	
proverb	ˈprɒvəb, ˈprɒvɜb	ˈprɑvəb, ˈprɑvɜəb
proverbs	ˈprɒvəbz, ˈprɒvɜbz	ˈprɑvəbz, ˈprɑvɜəbz
proverbial	†prəˈvɜˑbɪəl	prəˈvɜəbɪəl
proverbially	†prəˈvɜˑbɪəlɪ †prəˈvɜˑbjəlɪ	prəˈvɜəbɪəlɪ
provide	†prəˈvaɪd	
provides	†prəˈvaɪdz	
provided	†prəˈvaɪdɪd	
providing	†prəˈvaɪdɪŋ	
providence	ˈprɒvɪdəns	ˈprɑvɪdəns
provident	ˈprɒvɪdənt	ˈprɑvɪdənt
providently	ˈprɒvɪdəntlɪ	ˈprɑvɪdəntlɪ
providential	prɒvɪˈdɛnʃəl	prɑvɪˈdɛnʃəl

† See Note **30**, p. xxxv. in Introduction.

Traditional Spelling	Received Pronunciation	American Variants
providentially	prɒvɪ'denʃəlɪ	prɑvɪ'denʃəlɪ
province	'prɒvɪns	'prɑvɪns
provinces	'prɒvɪnsɪz	'prɑvɪnsɪz
provincial	†prə'vɪnʃəl	
provision	†prə'vɪʒən	
provisions	†prə'vɪʒənz	
provisional	†prə'vɪʒənl̩	
provisionally	†prə'vɪʒənəlɪ	
provocation	prɒvə'keɪʃən	prɑvə'keɪʃən
provocations	prɒvə'keɪʃənz	prɑvə'keɪʃənz
provoke	†prə'vouk	
provokes	†prə'vouks	
provoked	†prə'voukt	
provoking	†prə'voukɪŋ	
prudence	'pruˑdəns	
prudent	'pruˑdənt	
prudently	'pruˑdəntlɪ	
prune	pruˑn	
prunes	pruˑnz	
Prussia	'prʌʃə	
Prussian	'prʌʃən	
Prussians	'prʌʃənz	
psychological	saɪkə'lɒʤɪkəl	saɪkə'lɑʤɪkəl
psychologically	saɪkə'lɒʤɪkəlɪ	saɪkə'lɑʤɪkəlɪ
psychologist	saɪ'kɒləʤɪst	saɪ'kɑləʤɪst
psychologists	saɪ'kɒləʤɪsts	saɪ'kɑləʤɪsts
psychology	saɪ'kɒləʤɪ	saɪ'kɑləʤɪ
public	'pʌblɪk	
publication	pʌblɪ'keɪʃən	
publications	pʌblɪ'keɪʃənz	
publicity	pʌb'lɪsɪtɪ, pəb'lɪsɪtɪ	
publicly	'pʌblɪklɪ	
publish	'pʌblɪʃ	
publishes	'pʌblɪʃɪz	
published	'pʌblɪʃt	
publishing	'pʌblɪʃɪŋ	
publisher	'pʌblɪʃə(r	'pʌblɪʃə
publishers	'pʌblɪʃəz	'pʌblɪʃəz
pudding	'pudɪŋ	
puddings	'pudɪŋz	
puddle	'pʌdl̩	
puddles	'pʌdl̩z	
puff	pʌf	
puffs	pʌfs	
puffed	pʌft	

† See Note 30, p. xxxv. in Introduction.

Traditional Spelling	Received Pronunciation	American Variants
puffing	ˈpʌfɪŋ	
pull	pʊl	
pulls	pʊlz	
pulled	pʊld	
pulling	ˈpʊlɪŋ	
pulp	pʌlp	
pulpit	ˈpʊlpɪt	
pulpits	ˈpʊlpɪts	
pulse	pʌls	
pulses	ˈpʌlsɪz	
pump	pʌmp	
pumps	pʌmps	
pumped	pʌm*p*t	
pumping	ˈpʌmpɪŋ	
pun	pʌn	
puns	pʌnz	
punned	pʌnd	
punning	ˈpʌnɪŋ	
punch	pʌntʃ	
punches	ˈpʌntʃɪz	
punched	pʌntʃt	
punching	ˈpʌntʃɪŋ	
punctual	ˈpʌŋ*k*tjʊəl	
	ˈpʌŋ*k*tʃʊəl	
punctuality	pʌŋ*k*tjʊˈælɪtɪ	
	pʌŋ*k*tʃʊˈælɪtɪ	
punctually	ˈpʌŋ*k*tjʊəlɪ	
	ˈpʌŋ*k*tʃʊəlɪ	
punctuate	ˈpʌŋ*k*tjʊeɪt	
	ˈpʌŋ*k*tʃʊeɪt	
punctuates	ˈpʌŋ*k*tjʊeɪts	
	ˈpʌŋ*k*tʃʊeɪts	
punctuated	ˈpʌŋ*k*tjʊeɪtɪd	
	ˈpʌŋ*k*tʃʊeɪtɪd	
punctuating	ˈpʌŋ*k*tjʊeɪtɪŋ	
	ˈpʌŋ*k*tʃʊeɪtɪŋ	
punctuation	pʌŋ*k*tjʊˈeɪʃən	
	pʌŋ*k*tʃʊˈeɪʃən	
puncture	ˈpʌŋktʃə(r	ˈpʌŋktʃɚ
punctures	ˈpʌŋktʃəz	ˈpʌŋktʃɚz
punctured	ˈpʌŋktʃəd	ˈpʌŋktʃɚd
puncturing	ˈpʌŋktʃərɪŋ	
punish	ˈpʌnɪʃ	
punishes	ˈpʌnɪʃɪz	
punished	ˈpʌnɪʃt	
punishing	ˈpʌnɪʃɪŋ	
punishable	ˈpʌnɪʃəbl̩	

Traditional Spelling	Received Pronunciation	American Variants
punishment	'pʌnɪʃmənt	
punishments	'pʌnɪʃmənts	
pupil	'pjuˑpɨl	
pupils	'pjuˑpɨlz	
puppy	'pʌpɪ	
puppies	'pʌpɪz	
purchase	'pɜˑtʃɪs	'pɜətʃɪs
purchases	'pɜˑtʃɪsɪz	'pɜətʃɪsɪz
purchased	'pɜˑtʃɪst	'pɜətʃɪst
purchasing	'pɜˑtʃɪsɪŋ	'pɜətʃɪsɪŋ
purchaser	'pɜˑtʃəsə(r	'pɜətʃəsə
purchasers	'pɜˑtʃəsəz	'pɜətʃəsəz
pure	pjʊə(r	pjʊə
purer	'pjʊərə(r	'pjʊˑrə
purest	'pjʊərɪst	'pjʊˑrɪst
purely	'pjʊəlɪ	'pjʊəlɪ
pureness	'pjʊənɪs	'pjʊənɪs
purify	'pjʊərɪfaɪ	'pjʊˑrɪfaɪ
purifies	'pjʊərɪfaɪz	'pjʊˑrɪfaɪz
purified	'pjʊərɪfaɪd	'pjʊˑrɪfaɪd
purifying	'pjʊərɪfaɪɪŋ	'pjʊˑrɪfaɪɪŋ
purity	'pjʊərɪtɪ	'pjʊˑrɪtɪ
purple	'pɜˑpl̩	'pɜəpl̩
purpose	'pɜˑpəs	'pɜəpəs
purposes	'pɜˑpəsɪz	'pɜəpəsɪz
purposely	'pɜˑpəslɪ	'pɜəpəslɪ
purse	pɜˑs	pɜəs
purses	'pɜˑsɪz	'pɜəsɪz
pursue	pə'sjuˑ, pɜ'sjuˑ	pə'sjuˑ, pɜə'sjuˑ
pursues	pə'sjuˑz, pɜ'sjuˑz	pə'sjuˑz, pɜə'sjuˑz
pursued	pə'sjuˑd, pɜ'sjuˑd	pə'sjuˑd, pɜə'sjuˑd
pursuing	pə'sjuˑɪŋ, pɜ'sjuˑɪŋ	pə'sjuˑɪŋ, pɜə'sjuˑɪŋ
pursuer	pə'sjuˑə(r, pɜ'sjuˑə(r	pə'sjuˑə, pɜə'sjuˑə
pursuers	pə'sjuˑəz, pɜ'sjuˑəz	pə'sjuˑəz, pɜə'sjuˑəz
pursuit	pə'sjuˑt, pɜ'sjuˑt	pə'sjuˑt, pɜə'sjuˑt
pursuits	pə'sjuˑts, pɜ'sjuˑts	pə'sjuˑts, pɜə'sjuˑts
push	pʊʃ	
pushes	'pʊʃɪz	
pushed	pʊʃt	
pushing	'pʊʃɪŋ	
put	pʊt	
puts	pʊts	
putting	'pʊtɪŋ	
putty	'pʌtɪ	
putties	'pʌtɪz	
puzzle	'pʌzl̩	
puzzles	'pʌzl̩z	

Traditional Spelling	Received Pronunciation	American Variants
puzzled	ˈpʌzḷd	
puzzling	ˈpʌzlɪŋ	
pyjamas	pəˈʤɑˑməz	(*See* pajamas)
	pɪˈʤɑˑməz	
	paɪˈʤɑˑməz	
pyramid	ˈpɪrəmɪd	
pyramids	ˈpɪrəmɪdz	

Q

Traditional Spelling	Received Pronunciation	American Variants
Q	kjuˑ	
Q's	kjuˑz	
quaint	kweɪnt	
quainter	ˈkweɪntə(r	ˈkweɪntə
quaintest	ˈkweɪntɪst	
quaintly	ˈkweɪntlɪ	
quaintness	ˈkweɪntnɪs	
qualification	kwɒlɪfɪˈkeɪʃən	kwɑlɪfɪˈkeɪʃən
qualifications	kwɒlɪfɪˈkeɪʃənz	kwɒlɪfɪˈkeɪʃənz
qualify	ˈkwɒlɪfaɪ	ˈkwɑlɪfaɪ
qualifies	ˈkwɒlɪfaɪz	ˈkwɑlɪfaɪz
qualified	ˈkwɒlɪfaɪd	ˈkwɑlɪfaɪd
qualifying	ˈkwɒlɪfaɪɪŋ	ˈkwɑlɪfaɪɪŋ
quality	ˈkwɒlɪtɪ	ˈkwɑlɪtɪ
qualities	ˈkwɒlɪtɪz	ˈkwɑlɪtɪz
quantity	ˈkwɒntɪtɪ	ˈkwɑntɪtɪ
quantities	ˈkwɒntɪtɪz	ˈkwɑntɪtɪz
quarantine	ˈkwɒrəntin	
quarrel	ˈkwɒrəl	
quarrels	ˈkwɒrəlz	
quarrelled	ˈkwɒrəld	
quarrelling	ˈkwɒrəlɪŋ	
quarrelsome	ˈkwɒrəlsəm	
quarry	ˈkwɒrɪ	
quarries	ˈkwɒrɪz	
quart, *measure of capacity*	kwɔˑt	kwɔət
quarts	kwɔˑts	kwɔəts
quarter	ˈkwɔˑtə(r	ˈkwɔətə
quarters	ˈkwɔˑtəz	ˈkwɔətəz
quay	kiˑ	
quays	kiˑz	
Quebec	kwɪˈbɛk, kwəˈbɛk	
queen	kwiˑn	
queens	kwiˑnz	

Traditional Spelling	Received Pronunciation	American Variants
queer	kwɪə(r	kwɪə
queerer	ˈkwɪərə(r	ˈkwɪˑrə
queerest	ˈkwɪərɪst	ˈkwɪˑrɪst
queerly	ˈkwɪəlɪ	ˈkwɪəlɪ
quench	kwɛntʃ	
quenches	ˈkwɛntʃɪz	
quenched	kwɛntʃt	
quenching	ˈkwɛntʃɪŋ	
query	ˈkwɪərɪ	ˈkwɪˑrɪ
queries	ˈkwɪərɪz	ˈkwɪˑrɪz
queried	ˈkwɪərɪd	ˈkwɪˑrɪd
querying	ˈkwɪərɪɪŋ	ˈkwɪˑrɪɪŋ
question	ˈkwɛstʃən	
questions	ˈkwɛstʃənz	
questioned	ˈkwɛstʃənd	
questioning	ˈkwɛstʃənɪŋ	
questionable	ˈkwɛstʃənəbl̩	
questionably	ˈkwɛstʃənəblɪ	
queue	kjuˑ	
queues	kjuˑz	
quibble	ˈkwɪbl̩	
quibbles	ˈkwɪbl̩z	
quibbled	ˈkwɪbl̩d	
quibbling	ˈkwɪblɪŋ, ˈkwɪbl̩ɪŋ	
quick	kwɪk	
quicker	ˈkwɪkə(r	ˈkwɪkə
quickest	ˈkwɪkɪst	
quickly	ˈkwɪklɪ	
quickness	ˈkwɪknɪs	
quick-tempered	ˈkwɪkˈtɛmpəd	ˈkwɪkˈtɛmpəd
quick-witted	ˈkwɪkˈwɪtɪd	
quiet	ˈkwaɪət	
quieter	ˈkwaɪətə(r	ˈkwaɪətə
quietest	ˈkwaɪətɪst	
quietly	ˈkwaɪətlɪ	
quietness	ˈkwaɪətnɪs	
quilt	kwɪlt	
quilts	kwɪlts	
quinine	kwɪˈniˑn, ˈkwɪnin	
quit	kwɪt	
quits	kwɪts	
quitted	ˈkwɪtɪd	
quitting	ˈkwɪtɪŋ	
quite	kwaɪt	
quits	kwɪts	
quotation	kwouˈteɪʃən	
quotations	kwouˈteɪʃənz	

Traditional Spelling	Received Pronunciation	American Variants
quote	kwout	
quotes	kwouts	
quoted	'kwoutɪd	
quoting	'kwoutɪŋ	

R

Traditional Spelling	Received Pronunciation	American Variants
R	ɑ·(r	ɑə
R's	ɑ·z	ɑəz
rabbit	'ræbɪt	
rabbits	'ræbɪts	
race	reɪs	
races	'reɪsɪz	
raced	reɪst	
racing	'reɪsɪŋ	
racial	'reɪʃjəl, 'reɪʃəl	
rack	ræk	
racks	ræks	
radiance	'reɪdɪəns, 'reɪdjəns	
radiant	'reɪdɪənt, 'reɪdjənt	
radiantly	'reɪdɪəntlɪ, 'reɪdjəntlɪ	
radiate	'reɪdɪeɪt, 'reɪdjeɪt	
radiates	'reɪdɪeɪts, 'reɪdjeɪts	
radiated	'reɪdɪeɪtɪd 'reɪdjeɪtɪd	
radiating	'reɪdɪeɪtɪŋ 'reɪdjeɪtɪŋ	
radiation	reɪdɪ'eɪʃən	
radiator	'reɪdɪeɪtə(r	'reɪdɪeɪtə
radiators	'reɪdɪeɪtəz	'reɪdɪeɪtəz
radical	'rædɪkəl	
radicals	'rædɪkəlz	
radically	'rædɪkəlɪ	
radium	'reɪdɪəm, 'reɪdjəm	
radius	'reɪdɪəs, 'reɪdjəs	
radii	'reɪdɪaɪ	
raft	rɑ·ft	ra·ft
rafts	rɑ·fts	ra·fts
rag	ræg	
rags	rægz	
rage	reɪʤ	
rages	'reɪʤɪz	
raged	'reɪʤd	
raging	'reɪʤɪŋ	
ragged	'rægɪd	

Traditional Spelling	Received Pronunciation	American Variants
raggedness	ˈrægɪdnɪs	
raid	reɪd	
raids	reɪdz	
raided	ˈreɪdɪd	
raiding	ˈreɪdɪŋ	
raider	ˈreɪdə(r	ˈreɪdə
raiders	ˈreɪdəz	ˈreɪdəz
rail	reɪl	
rails	reɪlz	
railing	ˈreɪlɪŋ	
railings	ˈreɪlɪŋz	
railroad	ˈreɪlroʊd	
railroads	ˈreɪlroʊdz	
railway	ˈreɪlweɪ	
railways	ˈreɪlweɪz	
rain	reɪn	
rains	reɪnz	
rained	reɪnd	
raining	ˈreɪnɪŋ	
rainy	ˈreɪnɪ	
rainier	ˈreɪnɪə(r	ˈreɪnɪə
rainiest	ˈreɪnɪɪst	
raise	reɪz	
raises	ˈreɪzɪz	
raised	reɪzd	
raising	ˈreɪzɪŋ	
raisin	ˈreɪzn̩	
raisins	ˈreɪzn̩z	
rake	reɪk	
rakes	reɪks	
raked	reɪkt	
raking	ˈreɪkɪŋ	
rally	ˈrælɪ	
rallies	ˈrælɪz	
rallied	ˈrælɪd	
rallying	ˈrælɪɪŋ	
Ralph	rælf, rɑˑf, rɑlf, reɪf	raˑf, raˑlf
ram	ræm	
rams	ræmz	
rammed	ræmd	
ramming	ˈræmɪŋ	
ramble	ˈræmbl̩	
rambles	ˈræmbl̩z	
rambled	ˈræmbl̩d	
rambling	ˈræmblɪŋ	
ramification	ræmɪfɪˈkeɪʃən	
ramifications	ræmɪfɪˈkeɪʃənz	

Traditional Spelling	Received Pronunciation	American Variants
RAN *from* run	ræn	
ranch	ræntʃ, rɑˑntʃ	raˑntʃ
ranches	ˈræntʃɪz, ˈrɑˑntʃɪz	ˈraˑntʃɪz
random	ˈrændəm	
RANG *from* ring	ræŋ	
range	reɪndʒ	
ranges	ˈreɪndʒɪz	
ranged	reɪndʒd	
ranging	ˈreɪndʒɪŋ	
rank	ræŋk	
ranks	ræŋks	
ranked	ræŋ*k*t	
ranking	ˈræŋkɪŋ	
ransack	ˈrænˈsæk	
ransacks	ˈrænˈsæks	
ransacked	ˈrænˈsækt	
ransacking	ˈrænˈsækɪŋ	
ransom	ˈrænsəm	
ransoms	ˈrænsəmz	
ransomed	ˈrænsəmd	
ransoming	ˈrænsəmɪŋ	
rap	ræp	
raps	ræps	
rapped	ræpt	
rapping	ˈræpɪŋ	
rapid	ˈræpɪd	
rapidly	ˈræpɪdlɪ	
rapidity	rəˈpɪdɪtɪ, ræˈpɪdɪtɪ	
rare	rɛə(r	rɛə
rarer	ˈrɛərə(r	ˈrɛˑrə
rarest	ˈrɛərɪst	ˈrɛˑrɪst
rarely	ˈrɛəlɪ	ˈrɛəlɪ
rareness	ˈrɛənɪs	ˈrɛənɪs
rascal	ˈrɑˑsk*ə*l	ˈraˑsk*ə*l
rascals	ˈrɑˑsk*ə*lz	ˈraˑsk*ə*lz
rash	ræʃ	
rashly	ˈræʃlɪ	
rat	ræt	
rats	ræts	
rate	reɪt	
rates	reɪts	
rather	ˈrɑˑðə(r	ˈraˑðə
ratification	rætɪfɪˈkeɪʃ*ə*n	
ratifications	rætɪfɪˈkeɪʃ*ə*nz	
ratify	ˈrætɪfaɪ	
ratifies	ˈrætɪfaɪz	
ratified	ˈrætɪfaɪd	

Traditional Spelling	Received Pronunciation	American Variants
ratifying	'rætɪfaɪɪŋ	
ratio	'reɪʃɪoʊ, 'reɪʃjoʊ	
ratios	'reɪʃɪoʊz, 'reɪʃjoʊz	
ration	'ræʃən	
rations	'ræʃənz	
rationed	'ræʃənd	
rationing	'ræʃənɪŋ	
rational	'ræʃənl̩	
rationally	'ræʃənəlɪ	
rattle	'rætl̩	
rattles	'rætl̩z	
rattled	'rætl̩d	
rattling	'rætlɪŋ	
rattlesnake	'rætl̩sneɪk	
rattlesnakes	'rætl̩sneɪks	
ravage	'rævɪdʒ	
ravages	'rævɪdʒɪz	
ravaged	'rævɪdʒd	
ravaging	'rævɪdʒɪŋ	
rave	reɪv	
raves	reɪvz	
raved	reɪvd	
raving	'reɪvɪŋ	
raven	'reɪvn̩	
ravens	'reɪvn̩z	
raw	rɔˑ	
rawer	'rɔˑə(r	'rɔˑə
rawest	'rɔˑɪst	
rawly	'rɔˑlɪ	
rawness	'rɔˑnɪs	
ray	reɪ	
rays	reɪz	
razor	'reɪzə(r	'reɪzə
razors	'reɪzəz	'reɪzəz
re-, *affix*	riˑ-, rɪ- (*rarely* rə-)	
reach	riˑtʃ	
reaches	'riˑtʃɪz	
reached	riˑtʃt	
reaching	'riˑtʃɪŋ	
react	ri'ækt, rɪ'ækt	
reacts	ri'ækts, rɪ'ækts	
reacted	ri'æktɪd, rɪ'æktɪd	
reacting	ri'æktɪŋ, rɪ'æktɪŋ	
reaction	ri'ækʃən, rɪ'ækʃən	
reactions	ri'ækʃənz, rɪ'ækʃənz	
reactionary	ri'ækʃənərɪ rɪ'ækʃənərɪ	ri'ækʃənɛrɪ

Traditional Spelling	Received Pronunciation	American Variants
reactionaries	ri'ækʃənərɪz rɪ'ækʃənərɪz	ri'ækʃənɛrɪz
read	riˑd	
reads	riˑdz	
read	rɛd	
reading	'riˑdɪŋ	
readable	'riˑdəbl̩	
reader	'riˑdə(r	'riˑdə
readers	'riˑdəz	'riˑdəz
ready	'rɛdɪ	
readier	'rɛdɪə(r	'rɛdɪə
readiest	'rɛdɪɪst	
readily	'rɛdɪlɪ	
readiness	'rɛdɪnɪs	
real	'riˑəl, rɪəl	
realism	'riˑəlɪzm̩, 'rɪəlɪzm̩	
realist	'riˑəlɪst, 'rɪəlɪst	
realists	'riˑəlɪsts, 'rɪəlɪsts	
realistic	riə'lɪstɪk, rɪə'lɪstɪk	
realistically	riə'lɪstɪkəlɪ rɪə'lɪstɪkəlɪ	
reality	ri'ælɪtɪ, rɪ'ælɪtɪ	
realities	ri'ælɪtɪz, rɪ'ælɪtɪz	
realization	riəlaɪ'zeɪʃən riəlɪ'zeɪʃən	
realize	'riˑəlaɪz	
realizes	'riˑəlaɪzɪz	
realized	'riˑəlaɪzd	
realizing	'riˑəlaɪzɪŋ	
really	'rɪəlɪ	
reap	riˑp	
reaps	riˑps	
reaped	riˑpt	
reaping	'riˑpɪŋ	
reappear	'riˑə'pɪə(r, rɪə'pɪə(r	'riˑə'pɪə, 'rɪə'pɪə
reappears	'riˑə'pɪəz, rɪə'pɪəz	'riˑə'pɪəz, 'rɪə'pɪəz
reappeared	'riˑə'pɪəd, rɪə'pɪəd	'riˑə'pɪəd, 'rɪə'pɪəd
reappearing	'riˑə'pɪərɪŋ 'rɪə'pɪərɪŋ	'riˑə'pɪˑrɪŋ 'riə'pɪˑrɪŋ
reappoint	'riˑə'pɔɪnt, rɪə'pɔɪnt	
reappoints	'riˑə'pɔɪnts rɪə'pɔɪnts	
reappointed	'riˑə'pɔɪntɪd rɪə'pɔɪntɪd	
reappointing	'riˑə'pɔɪntɪŋ rɪə'pɔɪntɪŋ	
rear	'rɪə(r	'rɪə

Traditional Spelling	Received Pronunciation	American Variants
rearrange	'ri·ə'reɪnʤ, rɪə'reɪnʤ	
rearranges	'ri·ə'reɪnʤɪz	
	rɪə'reɪnʤɪz	
rearranged	'ri·ə'reɪnʤd	
	rɪə'reɪnʤd	
rearranging	'ri·ə'reɪnʤɪŋ	
	rɪə'reɪnʤɪŋ	
rearrangement	'ri·ə'reɪnʤmənt	
	rɪə'reɪnʤmənt	
rearrangements	'ri·ə'reɪnʤmənt	
	rɪə'reɪnʤmənts	
reason	'ri·zn̩	
reasons	'ri·zn̩z	
reasoned	'ri·zn̩d	
reasoning	'ri·zənɪŋ	
reasonings	'ri·zənɪŋz	
reasonable	'ri·zn̩əbl̩	
reasonableness	'ri·znəbl̩nɪs	
reasonably	'ri·znəblɪ	
reassemble	'ri·ə'sɛmbl̩, rɪə'sɛmbl̩	
reassembles	'ri·ə'sɛmbl̩z	
	rɪə'sɛmbl̩z	
reassembled	'ri·ə'sɛmbl̩d	
	rɪə'sɛmbl̩d	
reassembling	'ri·ə'sɛmblɪŋ	
	rɪə'sɛmblɪŋ	
reassert	'ri·ə'sɜ·t, rɪə'sɜ·t	'ri·ə'sɜət
reasserts	'ri·ə'sɜ·ts, rɪə'sɜ·ts	'ri·ə'sɜəts
reasserted	'ri·ə'sɜ·tɪd	'ri·ə'sɜətɪd
	rɪə'sɜ·tɪd	
reasserting	'ri·ə'sɜ·tɪŋ	'ri·ə'sɜətɪŋ
	rɪə'sɜ·tɪŋ	
reassure	riə'ʃʊə(r, rɪə'ʃɔə(r	riə'ʃʊə
reassures	riə'ʃʊəz, rɪə'ʃɔəz	riə'ʃʊəd
reassured	riə'ʃʊəd, rɪə'ʃɔəd	riə'ʃʊəd
reassuring	riə'ʃʊərɪŋ, rɪə'ʃɔərɪŋ	riə'ʃʊ·rɪŋ
rebel, ***noun***	'rɛbl̩	
rebels	'rɛbl̩z	
rebel	rɪ'bɛl	
rebels	rɪ'bɛlz	
rebelled	rɪ'bɛld	
rebelling	rɪ'bɛlɪŋ	
rebellion	rɪ'bɛljən	
rebellions	rɪ'bɛljənz	
rebellious	rɪ'bɛljəs	
rebelliously	rɪ'bɛljəslɪ	
rebuild	'ri·'bɪld	

Traditional Spelling	Received Pronunciation	American Variants
rebuilds	ˈriˑˈbɪldz	
rebuilt	ˈriˑˈbɪlt	
rebuilding	ˈriˑˈbɪldɪŋ	
rebuke	rɪˈbjuˑk	
rebukes	rɪˈbjuˑks	
rebuked	rɪˈbjuˑkt	
rebuking	rɪˈbjuˑkɪŋ	
recall	rɪˈkɔˑl	
recalls	rɪˈkɔˑlz	
recalled	rɪˈkɔˑld	
recalling	rɪˈkɔˑlɪŋ	
recapitulate	rikəˈpɪtjʊleɪt	
recapitulates	rikəˈpɪtjʊleɪts	
recapitulated	rikəˈpɪtjʊleɪtɪd	
recapitulating	rikəˈpɪtjʊleɪtɪŋ	
recapitulation	ˈriˑkəpɪtjʊˈleɪʃən	
recapitulations	ˈriˑkəpɪtjʊˈleɪʃənz	
recapture	ˈriˑˈkæptʃə(r	ˈriˑˈkæptʃə
recaptures	ˈriˑˈkæptʃəz	ˈriˑˈkæptʃəz
recaptured	ˈriˑˈkæptʃɔd	ˈriˑˈkæptʃəd
recapturing	ˈriˑˈkæptʃərɪŋ	
recast	ˈriˑˈkɑˑst	ˈriˑˈkaˑst
recasts	ˈriˑˈkɑˑsts	ˈriˑˈkaˑsts
recasting	ˈriˑˈkɑˑstɪŋ	ˈriˑˈkaˑstɪŋ
recede	rɪˈsiˑd, riˈsiˑd	
recedes	rɪˈsiˑdz, riˈsiˑdz	
receded	rɪˈsiˑdɪd, riˈsidɪd	
receding	rɪˈsiˑdɪŋ, riˈsiˑdɪŋ	
receipt	rɪˈsiˑt	
receipts	rɪˈsiˑts	
receipted	rɪˈsiˑtɪd	
receipting	rɪˈsiˑtɪŋ	
receive	rɪˈsiˑv	
receives	rɪˈsiˑvz	
received	rɪˈsiˑvd	
receiving	rɪˈsiˑvɪŋ	
receiver	rɪˈsiˑvə(r	rɪˈsiˑvə
receivers	rɪˈsiˑvəz	rɪˈsiˑvəz
recent	ˈriˑsn̩t	
recently	ˈriˑsn̩tlɪ	
receptacle	rɪˈsɛptəkl̩	
receptacles	rɪˈsɛptəkl̩z	
reception	rɪˈsɛpʃən	
receptions	rɪˈsɛpʃənz	
receptive	rɪˈsɛptɪv	
recess	rɪˈsɛs	
recesses	rɪˈsɛsɪz	

Traditional Spelling	Received Pronunciation	American Variants
recipe	ˈrɛsɪpɪ	ˈrɛsɪpi
recipes	ˈrɛsɪpɪz	ˈrɛsɪpiz
recitation	rɛsɪˈteɪʃən	
recitations	rɛsɪˈteɪʃənz	
recite	rɪˈsaɪt	
recites	rɪˈsaɪts	
recited	rɪˈsaɪtɪd	
reciting	rɪˈsaɪtɪŋ	
reckless	ˈrɛklɪs	
recklessly	ˈrɛklɪslɪ	
reckon	ˈrɛkən	
reckons	ˈrɛkənz	
reckoned	ˈrɛkənd	
reckoning	ˈrɛkənɪŋ	
recognition	rɛkəgˈnɪʃən	
recognizable	ˈrɛkəgnaɪzəbḷ rɛkəgˈnaɪzəbḷ	
recognize	ˈrɛkəgnaɪz	
recognizes	ˈrɛkəgnaɪzɪz	
recognized	ˈrɛkəgnaɪzd	
recognizing	ˈrɛkəgnaɪzɪŋ	
recollect	rɛkəˈlɛkt	
recollects	rɛkəˈlɛkts	
recollected	rɛkəˈlɛktɪd	
recollecting	rɛkəˈlɛktɪŋ	
recollection	rɛkəˈlɛkʃən	
recollections	rɛkəˈlɛkʃənz	
recommend	rɛkəˈmɛnd	
recommends	rɛkəˈmɛndz	
recommended	rɛkəˈmɛndɪd	
recommending	rɛkəˈmɛndɪŋ	
recommendation	rɛkəmɛnˈdeɪʃən	
recommendations	rɛkəmɛnˈdeɪʃənz	
reconcile	ˈrɛkənsaɪl	
reconciles	ˈrɛkənsaɪlz	
reconciled	ˈrɛkənsaɪld	
reconciling	ˈrɛkənsaɪlɪŋ	
reconciliation	rɛkənsɪlɪˈeɪʃən	
reconciliations	rɛkənsɪlɪˈeɪʃənz	
reconsider	ˈriˑkənˈsɪdə(r	ˈriˑkənˈsɪdə
reconsiders	ˈriˑkənˈsɪdəz	ˈriˑkənˈsɪdəz
reconsidered	ˈriˑkənˈsɪdəd	ˈriˑkənˈsɪdəd
reconsidering	ˈriˑkənˈsɪdərɪŋ	
record, *noun*	ˈrɛkɔd	ˈrɛkəd
records	ˈrɛkɔdz	ˈrɛkədz
record, *verb*	rɪˈkɔˑd	rɪˈkɔəd
records	rɪˈkɔˑdz	rɪˈkɔədz

Traditional Spelling	Received Pronunciation	American Variants
recorded	rɪ'kɔ·dɪd	rɪ'kɔədɪd
recording	rɪ'kɔ·dɪŋ	rɪ'kɔədɪŋ
recover, *come back to health*	rɪ'kʌvə(r	rɪ'kʌvə
recovers	rɪ'kʌvəz	rɪ'kʌvəz
recovered	rɪ'kʌvəd	rɪ'kʌvəd
recovering	rɪ'kʌvərɪŋ	
recover, *cover again*	'ri·'kʌvə(r	'ri·'kʌvə
recovers	'ri·'kʌvəz	'ri·'kʌvəz
recovered	'ri·'kʌvəd	'ri·'kʌvəd
recovering	'ri·'kʌvərɪŋ	
recovery	rɪ'kʌvərɪ	
recreation, *refreshment*	rɛkrɪ'eɪʃən	
recreations	rɛkrɪ'eɪʃənz	
recreation, *creating anew*	ri·krɪ'eɪʃən	
recreations	'ri·krɪ'eɪʃənz	
recruit	rɪ'kru·t	
recruits	rɪ'kru·ts	
recruited	rɪ'kru·tɪd	
recruiting	rɪ'kru·tɪŋ	
rectangle	'rɛktæŋgḷ	
rectangles	'rɛktæŋgḷz	
recur	rɪ'kɜ·(r	rɪ'kɜə
recurs	rɪ'kɜ·z	rɪ'kɜəz
recurred	rɪ'kɜ·d	rɪ'kɜəd
recurring	rɪ'kɜ·rɪŋ, rɪ'kʌrɪŋ	
red	rɛd	
redder	'rɛdə(r	'rɛdə
reddest	'rɛdɪst	
redness	'rɛdnɪs	
redeem	rɪ'di·m	
redeems	rɪ'di·mz	
redeemed	rɪ'di·md	
redeeming	rɪ'di·mɪŋ	
red-hot	'rɛd'hɒt	'rɛd'hɑt
redirect	'ri·dɪ'rɛkt, 'ri·daɪ'rɛkt	
redirects	'ri·dɪ'rɛkts 'ri·daɪ'rɛkts	
redirected	'ri·dɪ'rɛktɪd 'ri·daɪ'rɛktɪd	
redirecting	'ri·dɪ'rɛktɪŋ 'ri·daɪ'rɛktɪŋ	
reduce	rɪ'dju·s	
reduces	rɪ'dju·sɪz	
reduced	rɪ'dju·st	

Traditional Spelling	Received Pronunciation	American Variants
reducing	rɪ'djuˑsɪŋ	
reduction	rɪ'dʌkʃən	
reductions	rɪ'dʌkʃənz	
reed	riˑd	
reeds	riˑdz	
reef	riˑf	
reefs	riˑfs	
refer	rɪ'fɜˑ(r	rɪ'fɜə
refers	rɪ'fɜˑz	rɪ'fɜəz
referred	rɪ'fɜˑd	rɪ'fɜəd
referring	rɪ'fɜˑrɪŋ	
referee	rɛfə'riˑ	
referees	rɛfə'riˑz	
reference	'rɛfərəns	
references	'rɛfərənsɪz	
refine	rɪ'faɪn	
refines	rɪ'faɪnz	
refined	rɪ'faɪnd	
refining	rɪ'faɪnɪŋ	
refinement	rɪ'faɪnmənt	
refinements	rɪ'faɪnmənts	
reflect	rɪ'flɛkt	
reflects	rɪ'flɛkts	
reflected	rɪ'flɛktɪd	
reflecting	rɪ'flɛktɪŋ	
reflector	rɪ'flɛktə(r	rɪ'flɛktə
reflectors	rɪ'flɛktəz	rɪ'flɛktəz
reflection	rɪ'flɛkʃən	
reflections	rɪ'flɛkʃənz	
reform	rɪ'fɔˑm	rɪ'fɔəm
reforms	rɪ'fɔˑmz	rɪ'fɔəmz
reformed	rɪ'fɔˑmd	rɪ'fɔəmd
reforming	rɪ'fɔˑmɪŋ	rɪ'fɔəmɪŋ
reformer	rɪ'fɔˑmə(r	rɪ'fɔəmɔə
reformers	rɪ'fɔˑməz	rɪ'fɔəməz
reformation	†rɛfə'meɪʃən	†rɛfə'meɪʃən
reformations	†rɛfə'meɪʃənz	†rɛfə'meɪʃənz
refrain	rɪ'freɪn	
refrains	rɪ'freɪnz	
refrained	rɪ'freɪnd	
refraining	rɪ'freɪnɪŋ	
refresh	rɪ'frɛʃ	
refreshes	rɪ'frɛʃɪz	
refreshed	rɪ'frɛʃt	
refreshing	rɪ'frɛʃɪŋ	

† See Note 30, p. xxxv. in Introduction.

z

Traditional Spelling	Received Pronunciation	American Variants
refuge	'rɛfjuʤ	
refuges	'rɛfjuʤɪz	
refugee	rɛfjʊ'ʤi·	
refugees	rɛfjʊ'ʤi·z	
refund	ri'fʌnd, rɪ'fʌnd	
refunds	ri'fʌndz, rɪ'fʌndz	
refunded	ri'fʌndɪd, rɪ'fʌndɪd	
refunding	ri'fʌndɪŋ, rɪ'fʌndɪŋ	
refusal	rɪ'fju·zəl	
refusals	rɪ'fju·zəlz	
refuse, *noun*	'rɛfjus	
refuse, *verb*	rɪ'fju·z	
refuses	rɪ'fju·zɪz	
refused	rɪ'fju·zd	
refusing	rɪ'fju·zɪŋ	
refutation	rɛfjʊ'teɪʃən rɛfju'teɪʃən	
refutations	rɛfjʊ'teɪʃənz rɛfju'teɪʃənz	
refute	rɪ'fju·t	
refutes	rɪ'fju·ts	
refuted	rɪ'fju·tɪd	
refuting	rɪ'fju·tɪŋ	
regain	rɪ'geɪn, ri'geɪn	
regains	rɪ'geɪnz, ri'geɪnz	
regained	rɪ'geɪnd, ri'geɪnd	
regaining	rɪ'geɪnɪŋ, ri'geɪnɪŋ	
regard	rɪ'gɑ·d	rɪ'gɑəd
regards	rɪ'gɑ·dz	rɪ'gɑədz
regarded	rɪ'gɑ·dɪd	rɪ'gɑədɪd
regarding	rɪ'gɑ·dɪŋ	rɪ'gɑədɪŋ
regardless	rɪ'gɑ·dlɪs	rɪ'gɑədlɪs
regent	'ri·ʤənt	
regents	'ri·ʤənts	
regiment	'rɛʤɪmənt	
regiments	'rɛʤɪmənts	
region	'ri·ʤən	
regions	'ri·ʤənz	
register	'rɛʤɪstə(r	'rɛʤɪstə
registers	'rɛʤɪstəz	'rɛʤɪstəz
registered	'rɛʤɪstəd	'rɛʤɪstəd
registering	'rɛʤɪstərɪŋ	
regret	rɪ'grɛt	
regrets	rɪ'grɛts	
regretted	rɪ'grɛtɪd	
regretting	rɪ'grɛtɪŋ	
regrettable	rɪ'grɛtəbl̩	

Traditional Spelling	Received Pronunciation	American Variants
regretful	rɪ'grɛtful	
regular	'rɛgjʊlə(r, 'rɛgjələ(r	'rɛgjʊlə, 'rɛgjələ
regularly	'rɛgjʊləlɪ, 'rɛgjələlɪ	'rɛgjʊləlɪ, 'rɛgjələlɪ
regularity	rɛgjʊ'lærɪtɪ	
regulate	'rɛgjʊleɪt, 'rɛgjəleɪt	
regulates	'rɛgjʊleɪts 'rɛgjəleɪts	
regulated	'rɛgjʊleɪtɪd 'rɛgjəleɪtɪd	
regulating	'rɛgjʊleɪtɪŋ 'rɛgjəleɪtɪŋ	
regulation	rɛgjʊ'leɪʃən	
regulations	rɛgjʊ'leɪʃənz	
rehearsal	rɪ'hɜ·səl	rɪ'hɜəsəl
rehearsals	rɪ'hɜ·səlz	rɪ'hɜəsəlz
rehearse	rɪ'hɜ·s	rɪ'hɜəs
rehearses	rɪ'hɜ·sɪz	rɪ'hɜəsɪz
rehearsed	rɪ'hɜ·st	rɪ'hɜəst
rehearsing	rɪ'hɜ·sɪŋ	rɪ'hɜəsɪŋ
reign	reɪn	
reigns	reɪnz	
reigned	reɪnd	
reigning	'reɪnɪŋ	
rein	reɪn	
reins	reɪnz	
reindeer	'reɪndɪə(r	'reɪndɪə
reinforce	riɪn'fɔ·s	riɪn'foəs
reinforces	riɪn'fɔ·sɪz	riɪn'foəsɪz
reinforced	riɪn'fɔ·st	riɪn'foəst
reinforcing	riɪn'fɔ·sɪŋ	riɪn'foəsɪŋ
reject	rɪ'ʤɛkt	
rejects	rɪ'ʤɛkts	
rejected	rɪ'ʤɛktɪd	
rejecting	rɪ'ʤɛktɪŋ	
rejection	rɪ'ʤɛkʃən	
rejections	rɪ'ʤɛkʃənz	
relate	rɪ'leɪt	
relates	rɪ'leɪts	
related	rɪ'leɪtɪd	
relating	rɪ'leɪtɪŋ	
relation	rɪ'leɪʃən	
relations	rɪ'leɪʃənz	
relationship	rɪ'leɪʃn̩ʃɪp	
relative	'rɛlətɪv	
relatives	'rɛlətɪvz	
relatively	'rɛlətɪvlɪ	

Traditional Spelling	Received Pronunciation	American Variants
relax	rɪ'læks	
relaxes	rɪ'læksɪz	
relaxed	rɪ'lækst	
relaxing	rɪ'læksɪŋ	
relaxation	rilæk'seɪʃən	
release	rɪ'li·s	
releases	rɪ'li·sɪz	
released	rɪ'li·st	
releasing	rɪ'li·sɪŋ	
relent	rɪ'lɛnt	
relents	rɪ'lɛnts	
relented	rɪ'lɛntɪd	
relenting	rɪ'lɛntɪŋ	
relentless	rɪ'lɛntlɪs	
reliable	rɪ'laɪəbl̩	
reliance	rɪ'laɪəns	
reliant	rɪ'laɪənt	
relic	'rɛlɪk	
relics	'rɛlɪks	
relief	rɪ'li·f	
reliefs	rɪ'li·fs	
relieve	rɪ'li·v	
relieves	rɪ'li·vz	
relieved	rɪ'li·vd	
relieving	rɪ'li·vɪŋ	
religion	rɪ'lɪʤən	
religious	rɪ'lɪʤəs	
religiously	rɪ'lɪʤəslɪ	
relish	'rɛlɪʃ	
relishes	'rɛlɪʃɪz	
relished	'rɛlɪʃt	
relishing	'rɛlɪʃɪŋ	
reluctance	rɪ'lʌktəns	
reluctant	rɪ'lʌktənt	
reluctantly	rɪ'lʌktəntlɪ	
rely	rɪ'laɪ	
relies	rɪ'laɪz	
relied	rɪ'laɪd	
relying	rɪ'laɪɪŋ	
remain	rɪ'meɪn	
remains	rɪ'meɪnz	
remained	rɪ'meɪnd	
remaining	rɪ'meɪnɪŋ	
remainder	rɪ'meɪndə(r	rɪ'meɪndə
remainders	rɪ'meɪndəz	rɪ'meɪndəz
remark	rɪ'mɑ·k	rɪ'mɑək
remarks	rɪ'mɑ·ks	rɪ'mɑəks

Traditional Spelling	Received Pronunciation	American Variants
remarked	rɪˈmɑˑkt	rɪˈmɑəkt
remarking	rɪˈmɑˑkɪŋ	rɪˈmɑəkɪŋ
remarkable	rɪˈmɑˑkəbl̩	rɪˈmɑəkəbl̩
remarkably	rɪˈmɑˑkəblɪ	rɪˈmɑəkəblɪ
remedy	ˈrɛmɪdɪ	
remedies	ˈrɛmɪdɪz	
remedied	ˈrɛmɪdɪd	
remedying	ˈrɛmɪdɪɪŋ	
remember	rɪˈmɛmbə(r	rɪˈmɛmbə
remembers	rɪˈmɛmbəz	rɪˈmɛmbəz
remembered	rɪˈmɛmbəd	rɪˈmɛmbəd
remembering	rɪˈmɛmbərɪŋ	
remembrance	rɪˈmɛmbrəns	
remembrances	rɪˈmɛmbrənsɪz	
remind	rɪˈmaɪnd	
reminds	rɪˈmaɪndz	
reminded	rɪˈmaɪndɪd	
reminding	rɪˈmaɪndɪŋ	
reminder	rɪˈmaɪndə(r	rɪˈmaɪndə
reminders	rɪˈmaɪndəz	rɪˈmaɪndəz
reminiscence	rɛmɪˈnɪsn̩s	
reminiscences	rɛmɪˈnɪsn̩sɪz	
remiss	rɪˈmɪs	
remit	rɪˈmɪt	
remits	rɪˈmɪts	
remitted	rɪˈmɪtɪd	
remitting	rɪˈmɪtɪŋ	
remittance	rɪˈmɪtəns	
remittances	rɪˈmɪtənsɪz	
remnant	ˈrɛmnənt	
remnants	ˈrɛmnənts	
remonstrance	rɪˈmɒnstrəns	rɪˈmɑnstrəns
remonstrances	rɪˈmɒnstrənsɪz	rɪˈmɑnstrənsɪz
remonstrate	rɪˈmɒnstreɪt ˈrɛmənstreɪt	rɪˈmɑnstreɪt
remonstrates	rɪˈmɒnstreɪts ˈrɛmənstreɪts	rɪˈmɑnstreɪts
remonstrated	rɪˈmɒnstreɪtɪd ˈrɛmənstreɪtɪd	rɪˈmɑnstreɪtɪd
remonstrating	rɪˈmɒnstreɪtɪŋ ˈrɛmənstreɪtɪŋ	rɪˈmɑnstreɪtɪŋ
remorse	rɪˈmɔˑs	rɪˈmɔəs
remote	rɪˈmout	
remotely	rɪˈmoutlɪ	
removal	rɪˈmuˑvl̩	
removals	rɪˈmuˑvl̩z	
remove	rɪˈmuˑv	

Traditional Spelling	Received Pronunciation	American Variants
removes	rɪˈmuˑvz	
removed	rɪˈmuˑvd	
removing	rɪˈmuˑvɪŋ	
remunerate	rɪˈmjuˑnəreɪt	
remunerates	rɪˈmjuˑnəreɪts	
remunerated	rɪˈmjuˑnəreɪtɪd	
remunerating	rɪˈmjuˑnəreɪtɪŋ	
remuneration	rɪmjunəˈreɪʃən	
remunerative	rɪˈmjuˑnərətɪv	rɪˈmjuˑnəreɪtɪv
render	ˈrɛndə(r	ˈrɛndə
renders	ˈrɛndəz	ˈrɛndəz
rendered	ˈrɛndəd	ˈrɛndəd
rendering	ˈrɛndərɪŋ	
renew	rɪˈnjuˑ	
renews	rɪˈnjuˑz	
renewed	rɪˈnjuˑd	
renewing	rɪˈnjuˑɪŋ	
renewal	rɪˈnjuəl	
renewals	rɪˈnjuəlz	
renounce	rɪˈnaʊns	
renounces	rɪˈnaʊnsɪz	
renounced	rɪˈnaʊnst	
renouncing	rɪˈnaʊnsɪŋ	
renown	rɪˈnaʊn	
renowned	rɪˈnaʊnd	
rent	rɛnt	
rents	rɛnts	
rented	ˈrɛntɪd	
renting	ˈrɛntɪŋ	
reorganize	ˈriˑˈɔˑgənaɪz	
	rɪˈɔˑgənaɪz	rɪˈɔəgənaɪz
reorganizes	ˈriˑˈɔˑgənaɪzɪz	
	rɪˈɔˑgənaɪzɪz	rɪˈɔəgənaɪzɪz
reorganized	ˈriˑˈɔˑgənaɪzd	
	rɪˈɔˑgənaɪzd	rɪˈɔəgənaɪzd
reorganizing	ˈriˑˈɔˑgənaɪzɪŋ	
	rɪˈɔˑgənaɪzɪŋ	rɪˈɔəgənaɪzɪŋ
REPAID *from* repay	ˈriˑˈpeɪd, rɪˈpeɪd	
repair	rɪˈpɛə(r	rɪˈpɛə
repairs	rɪˈpɛəz	rɪˈpɛəz
repaired	rɪˈpɛəd	rɪˈpɛəd
repairing	rɪˈpɛərɪŋ	rɪˈpɛˑrɪŋ
reparation	rɛpəˈreɪʃən	
reparations	rɛpəˈreɪʃənz	
repay	ˈriˑˈpeɪ, rɪˈpeɪ	
repays	ˈriˑˈpeɪz, rɪˈpeɪz	
repaid	ˈriˑˈpeɪd, rɪˈpeɪd	

Traditional Spelling	Received Pronunciation	American Variants
repaying	ˈriˑˈpeɪɪŋ, rɪˈpeɪɪŋ	
repayment	ˈriˑˈpeɪmənt	
	rɪˈpeɪmənt	
repayments	ˈriˑˈpeɪmənts	
	rɪˈpeɪmənts	
repeal	rɪˈpiˑl	
repeals	rɪˈpiˑlz	
repealed	rɪˈpiˑld	
repealing	rɪˈpiˑlɪŋ	
repeat	rɪˈpiˑt	
repeats	rɪˈpiˑts	
repeated	rɪˈpiˑtɪd	
repeating	rɪˈpiˑtɪŋ	
repeatedly	rɪˈpiˑtɪdlɪ	
repeater	rɪˈpiˑtə(r	rɪˈpiˑtə
repeaters	rɪˈpiˑtəz	rɪˈpiˑtəz
repel	rɪˈpɛl	
repels	rɪˈpɛlz	
repelled	rɪˈpɛld	
repelling	rɪˈpɛlɪŋ	
repent	rɪˈpɛnt	
repents	rɪˈpɛnts	
repented	rɪˈpɛntɪd	
repenting	rɪˈpɛntɪŋ	
repentance	rɪˈpɛntəns	
repentant	rɪˈpɛntənt	
repetition	rɛpɪˈtɪʃən	
repetitions	rɛpɪˈtɪʃənz	
replace	riˑˈpleɪs, rɪˈpleɪs	
replaces	riˑˈpleɪsɪz, rɪˈpleɪsɪz	
replaced	riˑˈpleɪst, rɪˈpleɪst	
replacing	riˑˈpleɪsɪŋ, rɪˈpleɪsɪŋ	
reply	rɪˈplaɪ	
replies	rɪˈplaɪz	
replied	rɪˈplaɪd	
replying	rɪˈplaɪɪŋ	
report	rɪˈpɔˑt	rɪˈpoət
reports	rɪˈpɔˑts	rɪˈpoəts
reported	rɪˈpɔˑtɪd	rɪˈpoətɪd
reporting	rɪˈpɔˑtɪŋ	rɪˈpoətɪŋ
reporter	rɪˈpɔˑtə(r	rɪˈpoətə
reporters	rɪˈpɔˑtəz	rɪˈpoətəz
represent	rɛprɪˈzɛnt	
represents	rɛprɪˈzɛnts	
represented	rɛprɪˈzɛntɪd	
representing	rɛprɪˈzɛntɪŋ	
representative	rɛprɪˈzɛntətɪv	

Traditional Spelling	Received Pronunciation	American Variants
representatives	rɛprɪ'zɛntətɪvz	
repress	rɪ'prɛs	
represses	rɪ'prɛsɪz	
repressed	rɪ'prɛst	
repressing	rɪ'prɛsɪŋ	
repression	rɪ'prɛʃən	
reprieve	rɪ'pri·v	
reprieves	rɪ'pri·vz	
reprieved	rɪ'pri·vd	
reprieving	rɪ'pri·vɪŋ	
reprimand, *noun*	'rɛprɪmɑnd	'rɛprɪmand
reprimands	'rɛprɪmɑndz	'rɛprɪmandz
reprimand	'rɛprɪmɑnd rɛprɪ'mɑ·nd	'rɛprɪmand rɛprɪ'ma·nd
reprimands	'rɛprɪmɑndz rɛprɪ'mɑ·ndz	'rɛprɪmandz rɛprɪ'ma·ndz
reprimanded	'rɛprɪmɑndɪd rɛprɪ'mɑ·ndɪd	'rɛprɪmandɪd rɛprɪ'ma·ndɪd
reprimanding	'rɛprɪmɑndɪŋ rɛprɪ'mɑ·ndɪŋ	'rɛprɪmandɪŋ rɛprɪ'ma·ndɪŋ
reproach	rɪ'proʊtʃ	
reproaches	rɪ'proʊtʃɪz	
reproached	rɪ'proʊtʃt	
reproaching	rɪ'proʊtʃɪŋ	
reproachful	rɪ'proʊtʃful	
reproduce	'ri·prə'dju·s	
reproduces	'ri·prə'dju·sɪz	
reproduced	'ri·prə'dju·st	
reproducing	'ri·prə'dju·sɪŋ	
reproduction	'ri·prə'dʌkʃən	
reproof	rɪ'pru·f	
reproofs	rɪ'pru·fs	
reprove	rɪ'pru·v	
reproves	rɪ'pru·vz	
reproved	rɪ'pru·vd	
reproving	rɪ'pru·vɪŋ	
reptile	'rɛptaɪl	'rɛptɪl
reptiles	'rɛptaɪlz	'rɛptɪlz
republic	rɪ'pʌblɪk	
republics	rɪ'pʌblɪks	
republican	rɪ'pʌblɪkən	
republicans	rɪ'pʌblɪkənz	
repudiate	rɪ'pju·dɪeɪt	
repudiates	rɪ'pju·dɪeɪts	
repudiated	rɪ'pju·dɪeɪtɪd	
repudiating	rɪ'pju·dɪeɪtɪŋ	
repudiation	rɪpjudɪ'eɪʃən	

Traditional Spelling	Received Pronunciation	American Variants
repugnance	rɪ'pʌgnəns	
repugnant	rɪ'pʌgnənt	
repugnantly	rɪ'pʌgnəntlɪ	
repulse	rɪ'pʌls	
repulses	rɪ'pʌlsɪz	
repulsed	rɪ'pʌlst	
repulsing	rɪ'pʌlsɪŋ	
repulsion	rɪ'pʌlʃən	
repulsive	rɪ'pʌlsɪv	
repulsively	rɪ'pʌlsɪvlɪ	
repulsiveness	rɪ'pʌlsɪvnɪs	
reputable	'rɛpjʊtəbl̩	
reputation	rɛpjʊ'teɪʃən	
reputations	rɛpjʊ'teɪʃənz	
repute	rɪ'pju·t	
reputed	rɪ'pju·tɪd	
request	rɪ'kwɛst	
requests	rɪ'kwɛsts	
requested	rɪ'kwɛstɪd	
requesting	rɪ'kwɛstɪŋ	
require	rɪ'kwaɪə(r	rɪ'kwaɪɚ
requires	rɪ'kwaɪəz	rɪ'kwaɪɚz
required	rɪ'kwaɪəd	rɪ'kwaɪɚd
requiring	rɪ'kwaɪərɪŋ	
requirement	rɪ'kwaɪəmənt	rɪ'kwaɪɚmənt
requirements	rɪ'kwaɪəmənts	rɪ'kwaɪɚmənts
requisite	'rɛkwɪzɪt	
rescue	'rɛskju, 'rɛskjʊ	
rescues	'rɛskjuz, 'rɛskjʊz	
rescued	'rɛskjud, 'rɛskjʊd	
rescuing	'rɛskjʊɪŋ	
research	rɪ'sɜ·tʃ	rɪ'sɝtʃ
researches	rɪ'sɜ·tʃɪz	rɪ'sɝtʃɪz
resemblance	rɪ'zɛmbləns	
resemblances	rɪ'zɛmblənsɪz	
resemble	rɪ'zɛmbl̩	
resembles	rɪ'zɛmbl̩z	
resembled	rɪ'zɛmbl̩d	
resembling	rɪ'zɛmblɪŋ	
resent	rɪ'zɛnt	
resents	rɪ'zɛnts	
resented	rɪ'zɛntɪd	
resenting	rɪ'zɛntɪŋ	
resentful	rɪ'zɛntfʊl	
resentfully	rɪ'zɛntfʊlɪ, rɪ'zɛntfəlɪ	
resentment	rɪ'zɛntmənt	
reserve	rɪ'zɜ·v	rɪ'zɝv

Traditional Spelling	Received Pronunciation	American Variants
reserves	rɪ'zɜˑvz	rɪ'zɜəvz
reserved	rɪ'zɜˑvd	rɪ'zɜəvd
reserving	rɪ'zɜˑvɪŋ	rɪ'zɜəvɪŋ
residence	'rɛzɪdəns	
residences	'rɛzɪdənsɪz	
resign	rɪ'zaɪn	
resigns	rɪ'zaɪnz	
resigned	rɪ'zaɪnd	
resigning	rɪ'zaɪnɪŋ	
resignation	rɛsɪg'neɪʃən	
resignations	rɛsɪg'neɪʃənz	
resist	rɪ'zɪst	
resists	rɪ'zɪsts	
resisted	rɪ'zɪstɪd	
resisting	rɪ'zɪstɪŋ	
resistence	rɪ'zɪstəns	
resolute	'rɛzəlut, 'rɛzəljut	
resolutely	'rɛzəlutlɪ, 'rɛzəljutlɪ	
resolution	rɛzə'luˑʃən,rɛzə'ljuˑʃən	
resolutions	rɛzə'luˑʃənz rɛzə'ljuˑʃənz	
resolve	rɪ'zɒlv	rɪ'zɑlv
resolves	rɪ'zɒlvz	rɪ'zɑlvz
resolved	rɪ'zɒlvd	rɪ'zɑlvd
resolving	rɪ'zɒlvɪŋ	rɪ'zɑlvɪŋ
resort	rɪ'zɔˑt	rɪ'zɔət
resorts	rɪ'zɔˑts	rɪ'zɔəts
resorted	rɪ'zɔˑtɪd	rɪ'zɔətɪd
resorting	rɪ'zɔˑtɪŋ	rɪ'zɔətɪŋ
resource	rɪ'sɔˑs	rɪ'soəs
resources	rɪ'sɔˑsɪz	rɪ'soəsɪz
resourceful	rɪ'sɔˑsful	rɪ'soəsful
respect	rɪs'pɛkt	
respects	rɪs'pɛkts	
respected	rɪs'pɛktɪd	
respecting	rɪs'pɛktɪŋ	
respectable	rɪs'pɛktəbl̩	
respectably	rɪs'pɛktəblɪ	
respectful	rɪs'pɛktful	
respectfully	rɪs'pɛktfulɪ rɪs'pɛktfəlɪ	
respective	rɪs'pɛktɪv	
respectively	rɪs'pɛktɪvlɪ	
respite	'rɛspɪt, 'rɛspaɪt	
respond	rɪs'pɒnd	rɪs'pɑnd
responds	rɪs'pɒndz	rɪs'pɑndz
responded	rɪs'pɒndɪd	rɪs'pɑndɪd

Traditional Spelling	Received Pronunciation	American Variants
responding	rɪs'pɒndɪŋ	rɪs'pandɪŋ
response	rɪs'pɒns	rɪs'pans
responses	rɪs'pɒnsɪz	rɪs'pansɪz
responsibility	rɪspɒnsə'bɪlɪtɪ	rɪspansə'bɪlɪtɪ
responsibilities	rɪspɒnsə'bɪlɪtɪz	respansə'bɪlɪtɪz
responsible	rɪs'pɒnsəbl̩	rɪs'pansəbl̩
responsibly	rɪs'pɒnsəblɪ	rɪs'pansəblɪ
responsive	rɪs'pɒnsɪv	rɪs'pansɪv
rest	rɛst	
rests	rɛsts	
rested	'rɛstɪd	
resting	'rɛstɪŋ	
restaurant	'rɛstərɔŋ, 'rɛstərɒŋ	'rɛstərənt, 'rɛstərant
restaurants	'rɛstərɔŋz 'rɛstərɒŋz	'rɛstərənts 'rɛstərants
restful	'rɛstful	
restless	'rɛstlɪs	
restlessly	'rɛstlɪslɪ	
restoration	†rɛstə'reɪʃən	
restorations	†rɛstə'reɪʃənz	
restore	rɪs'tɔː(r, rɪs'tɔə(r	rɪs'toə
restores	rɪs'tɔːz, rɪs'tɔəz	rɪs'toəz
restored	rɪs'tɔːd, rɪs'tɔəd	rɪs'toəd
restoring	rɪs'tɔːrɪŋ, rɪs'tɔərɪŋ	rɪs'toːrɪŋ
restorer	rɪs'tɔːrə(r, rɪs'tɔərə(r	rɪs'toːrə
restorers	rɪs'tɔːrəz, rɪs'tɔərəz	rɪs'toːrəz
restrain	rɪs'treɪn	
restrains	rɪs'treɪnz	
restrained	rɪs'treɪnd	
restraining	rɪs'treɪnɪŋ	
restraint	rɪs'treɪnt	
restrict	rɪs'trɪkt	
restricts	rɪs'trɪkts	
restricted	rɪs'trɪktɪd	
restricting	rɪs'trɪktɪŋ	
restriction	rɪs'trɪkʃən	
restrictions	rɪs'trɪkʃənz	
result	rɪ'zʌlt	
results	rɪ'zʌlts	
resulted	rɪ'zʌltɪd	
resulting	rɪ'zʌltɪŋ	
resume	rɪ'zjuːm	
resumes	rɪ'zjuːmz	
resumed	rɪ'zjuːmd	
resuming	rɪ'zjuːmɪŋ	

† See Note 30, p. xxxv. in Introduction.

Traditional Spelling	Received Pronunciation	American Variants
retail, *adj. & adverb*	ˈriːˈteɪl	
retain	rɪˈteɪn	
retains	rɪˈteɪnz	
retained	rɪˈteɪnd	
retaining	rɪˈteɪnɪŋ	
retaliate	rɪˈtælɪeɪt	
retaliates	rɪˈtælɪeɪts	
retaliated	rɪˈtælɪeɪtɪd	
retaliating	rɪˈtælɪeɪtɪŋ	
retire	rɪˈtaɪə(r	rɪˈtaɪə
retires	rɪˈtaɪəz	rɪˈtaɪəz
retired	rɪˈtaɪəd	rɪˈtaɪəd
retiring	rɪˈtaɪərɪŋ	
retirement	rɪˈtaɪəmənt	rɪˈtaɪəmənt
retort	rɪˈtɔːt	rɪˈtɔət
retorts	rɪˈtɔːts	rɪˈtɔəts
retorted	rɪˈtɔːtɪd	rɪˈtɔətɪd
retorting	rɪˈtɔːtɪŋ	rɪˈtɔətɪŋ
retreat	rɪˈtriːt	
retreats	rɪˈtriːts	
retreated	rɪˈtriːtɪd	
retreating	rɪˈtriːtɪŋ	
return	rɪˈtɜːn	rɪˈtɜən
returns	rɪˈtɜːnz	rɪˈtɜənz
returned	rɪˈtɜːnd	rɪˈtɜənd
returning	rɪˈtɜːnɪŋ	rɪˈtɜənɪŋ
Rev.	ˈrɛvərənd, ˈrɛvərənt	
reveal	rɪˈviːl	
reveals	rɪˈviːlz	
revealed	rɪˈviːld	
revealing	rɪˈviːlɪŋ	
revelation	rɛvɪˈleɪʃən	
revelations	rɛvɪˈleɪʃənz	
revenge	rɪˈvɛndʒ	
revenges	rɪˈvɛndʒɪz	
revengeful	rɪˈvɛndʒful	
revenue	ˈrɛvɪnju	
revenues	ˈrɛvɪnjuz	
reverence	ˈrɛvərəns	
reverent	ˈrɛvərənt	
reverently	ˈrɛvərəntlɪ	
reverse	rɪˈvɜːs	rɪˈvɜəs
reverses	rɪˈvɜːsɪz	rɪˈvɜəsɪz
reversed	rɪˈvɜːst	rɪˈvɜəst
reversing	rɪˈvɜːsɪŋ	rɪˈvɜəsɪŋ
review	rɪˈvjuː	
reviews	rɪˈvjuːz	

Traditional Spelling	Received Pronunciation	American Variants
reviewed	rɪ'vju·d	
reviewing	rɪ'vju·ɪŋ	
reviewer	rɪ'vju·ə(r	rɪ'vju·ə
reviewers	rɪ'vju·əz	rɪ'vju·əz
revise	rɪ'vaɪz	
revises	rɪ'vaɪzɪz	
revised	rɪ'vaɪzd	
revising	rɪ'vaɪzɪŋ	
reviser	rɪ'vaɪzə(r	rɪ'vaɪzə
revisers	rɪ'vaɪzəz	rɪ'vaɪzəz
revision	rɪ'vɪʒən	
revisions	rɪ'vɪʒənz	
revival	rɪ'vaɪvəl	
revivals	rɪ'vaɪvəlz	
revive	rɪ'vaɪv	
revives	rɪ'vaɪvz	
revived	rɪ'vaɪvd	
reviving	rɪ'vaɪvɪŋ	
revolt	rɪ'voult	
revolts	rɪ'voults	
revolted	rɪ'voultɪd	
revolting	rɪ'voultɪŋ	
revolution	rɛvə'lu·ʃən rɛvə'lju·ʃən	
revolutions	rɛvə'lu·ʃənz rɛvə'lju·ʃənz	
revolutionary	rɛvə'lu·ʃn̩ərɪ rɛvə'lju·ʃn̩ərɪ	rɛvə'lu·ʃn̩ɛrɪ
revolutionize	rɛvə'lu·ʃn̩aɪz rɛvə'lju·ʃn̩aɪz	
revolutionizes	rɛvə'lu·ʃnaɪzɪz rɛvə'lju·ʃn̩aɪzɪz	
revolutionized	rɛvə'lu·ʃn̩aɪzd rɛvə'lju·ʃn̩aɪzd	
revolutionizing	rɛvə'lu·ʃn̩aɪzɪŋ rɛvə'lju·ʃn̩aɪzɪŋ	
revolve	rɪ'vɒlv	rɪ'vɑlv
revolves	rɪ'vɒlvz	rɪ'vɑlvz
revolved	rɪ'vɒlvd	rɪ'vɑlvd
revolving	rɪ'vɒlvɪŋ	rɪ'vɑlvɪŋ
revolver	rɪ'vɒlvə(r	rɪ'vɑlvə
revolvers	rɪ'vɒlvəz	rɪ'vɑlvəz
reward	rɪ'wɔ·d	
rewards	rɪ'wɔ·dz	
rewarded	rɪ'wɔ·dɪd	
rewarding	rɪ'wɔ·dɪŋ	
rheumati	ru'mætɪk	

Traditional Spelling	Received Pronunciation	American Variants
rheumatics	ruˈmætɪks	
rheumatism	ˈruˑmətɪzm̩	
rhinoceros	raɪˈnɒsᵊrəs	raɪˈnɑsᵊrəs
rhinoceroses	raɪˈnɒsᵊrəsɪz	raɪˈnɑsᵊrəsɪz
rhyme	raɪm	
rhymes	raɪmz	
rhymed	raɪmd	
rhyming	ˈraɪmɪŋ	
rhythm	ˈrɪðm̩, ˈrɪθm̩	
rhythms	ˈrɪðm̩z, ˈrɪθm̩z	
rib	rɪb	
ribs	rɪbz	
ribbon	ˈrɪbən	
ribbons	ˈrɪbənz	
rice	raɪs	
rich	rɪtʃ	
richer	ˈrɪtʃə(r	ˈrɪtʃə
richest	ˈrɪtʃɪst	
richly	ˈrɪtʃlɪ	
Richard	ˈrɪtʃəd	ˈrɪtʃəd
rid	rɪd	
rids	rɪdz	
ridded	ˈrɪdɪd	
ridding	ˈrɪdɪŋ	
riddance	ˈrɪdᵊns	
riddle	ˈrɪdl̩	
riddles	ˈrɪdl̩z	
ride	raɪd	
rides	raɪdz	
rode	roʊd	
ridden	ˈrɪdn̩	
riding	ˈraɪdɪŋ	
rider	ˈraɪdə(r	ˈraɪdə
riders	ˈraɪdəz	ˈraɪdəz
ridge	rɪdʒ	
ridges	ˈrɪdʒɪz	
ridicule	ˈrɪdɪkjul	
ridicules	ˈrɪdɪkjulz	
ridiculed	ˈrɪdɪkjuld	
ridiculing	ˈrɪdɪkjulɪŋ	
ridiculous	rɪˈdɪkjʊləs	
	rɪˈdɪkjələs	
ridiculously	rɪˈdɪkjʊləslɪ	
	rɪˈdɪkjələslɪ	
rifle	ˈraɪfl̩	
rifles	ˈraɪfl̩z	
Riga	ˈraɪgə, ˈriˑgə	

Traditional Spelling	Received Pronunciation	American Variants
right	raɪt	
righteous	ˈraɪtjəs, ˈraɪtʃəs	
rightful	ˈraɪtful	
rightfully	ˈraɪtfulɪ, ˈraɪtfəlɪ	
rightly	ˈraɪtlɪ	
rightness	ˈraɪtnɪs	
rights	raɪts	
rigid	ˈrɪdʒɪd	
rigidly	ˈrɪdʒɪdlɪ	
rigidity	rɪˈdʒɪdɪtɪ	
rigor (*Amer.*)	ˈrɪgə(r	ˈrɪgə
rigorous	ˈrɪgərəs	
rigorously	ˈrɪgərəslɪ	
rigour	ˈrɪgə(r	ˈrɪgə
rim	rɪm	
rims	rɪmz	
ring	rɪŋ	
rings	rɪŋz	
rang	ræŋ	
rung	rʌŋ	
ringing	ˈrɪŋɪŋ	
rinse	rɪns	
rinses	ˈrɪnsɪz	
rinsed	rɪnst	
rinsing	ˈrɪnsɪŋ	
riot	ˈraɪət	
riots	ˈraɪəts	
rioted	ˈraɪətɪd	
rioting	ˈraɪətɪŋ	
rioter	ˈraɪətə(r	ˈraɪətə
rioters	ˈraɪətəz	ˈraɪətəz
ripe	raɪp	
riper	ˈraɪpə(r	ˈraɪpə
ripest	ˈraɪpɪst	
ripen	ˈraɪpən	
ripens	ˈraɪpənz	
ripened	ˈraɪpənd	
ripening	ˈraɪpənɪŋ	
ripely	ˈraɪplɪ	
ripeness	ˈraɪpnɪs	
ripple	ˈrɪpl̩	
ripples	ˈrɪpl̩z	
rise, *noun & verb*	raɪz	
rises	ˈraɪzɪz	
rose	rouz	
risen	ˈrɪzn̩	
rising	ˈraɪzɪŋ	

Traditional Spelling	Received Pronunciation	American Variants
riser	ˈraɪzə(r	ˈraɪzə
risers	ˈraɪzəz	ˈraɪzəz
risk	rɪsk	
risks	rɪsks	
risked	rɪskt	
risking	ˈrɪskɪŋ	
risky	ˈrɪskɪ	
rival	ˈraɪvəl	
rivals	ˈraɪvəlz	
rivalled	ˈraɪvəld	
rivalling	ˈraɪvəlɪŋ	
rivalry	ˈraɪvəlrɪ	
rivalries	ˈraɪvəlrɪz	
river	ˈrɪvə(r	ˈrɪvə
rivers	ˈrɪvəz	ˈrɪvəz
road	roud	
roads	roudz	
roam	roum	
roams	roumz	
roamed	roumd	
roaming	ˈroumɪŋ	
roar	rɔˑ(r, rɔə(r	roə
roars	rɔˑz, rɔəz	roəz
roared	rɔˑd, rɔəd	roəd
roaring	ˈrɔˑrɪŋ, ˈrɔərɪŋ	ˈroˑrɪŋ
roast	roust	
roasts	rousts	
roasted	ˈroustɪd	
roasting	ˈroustɪŋ	
rob	rɒb	rɑb
robs	rɒbz	rɑbz
robbed	rɒbd	rɑbd
robbing	ˈrɒbɪŋ	ˈrɑbɪŋ
robber	ˈrɒbə(r	ˈrɑbə
robbers	ˈrɒbəz	ˈrɑbəz
robbery	ˈrɒbərɪ	ˈrɑbərɪ
robberies	ˈrɒbərɪz	ˈrɑbərɪz
robe	roub	
robes	roubz	
Robert	ˈrɒbət	ˈrɑbət
Robin	ˈrɒbɪn	ˈrɑbɪn
robust	rouˈbʌst, rəˈbʌst	
rock	rɒk	rɑk
rocks	rɒks	rɑks
rocked	rɒkt	rɑkt
rocking	ˈrɒkɪŋ	ˈrɑkɪŋ
rocky	ˈrɒkɪ	ˈrɑkɪ

Traditional Spelling	Received Pronunciation	American Variants
rod	rɒd	rɑd
rods	rɒdz	rɑdz
RODE *from* ride	roud	
rogue	roug	
rogues	rougz	
roll	roul	
rolls	roulz	
rolled	rould	
rolling	ˈroulɪŋ	
roller	ˈroulə(r	ˈroulə
rollers	ˈrouləz	ˈrouləz
Roman	ˈroumən	
Romans	ˈroumənz	
romance	rouˈmæns, rəˈmæns	
romances	rouˈmænsɪz rəˈmænsɪz	
romantic	rouˈmæntɪk rəˈmæntɪk	
romantically	rouˈmæntɪkəlɪ rəˈmæntɪkəlɪ	
Rome	roum	
roof	ruˑf	
roofs	ruˑfs	
room	ruˑm, rum	
rooms	ruˑmz, rumz	
roomy	ˈruˑmɪ, ˈrumɪ	
root	ruˑt	
roots	ruˑts	
rope	roup	
ropes	roups	
rose	rouz	
roses	ˈrouzɪz	
ROSE *from* rise	rouz	
rosy	ˈrouzɪ	
rot	rɒt	rɑt
rots	rɒts	rɑts
rotted	ˈrɒtɪd	ˈrɑtɪd
rotting	ˈrɒtɪŋ	ˈrɑtɪŋ
rotten	ˈrɒtn̩	ˈrɑtn̩
rough	rʌf	
rougher	ˈrʌfə(r	ˈrʌfə
roughest	ˈrʌfɪst	
roughly	ˈrʌflɪ	
roughness	ˈrʌfnɪs	
Roumania	ruˈmeɪnjə, ruˈmeɪnɪə	
Roumanian	ruˈmeɪnjən ruˈmeɪnɪən	

Traditional Spelling	Received Pronunciation	American Variants
Roumanians	ru'meɪnjənz	
	ru'meɪnɪənz	
round	raʊnd	
rounds	raʊndz	
rounded	'raʊndɪd	
rounding	'raʊndɪŋ	
rounder	'raʊndə(r	'raʊndə
roundest	'raʊndɪst	
roundish	'raʊndɪʃ	
roundly	'raʊndlɪ	
roundness	'raʊndnɪs	
rouse	raʊz	
rouses	'raʊzɪz	
roused	raʊzd	
rousing	'raʊzɪŋ	
routine	ru'ti·n	
row, *verb & noun*	roʊ	
rows	roʊz	
rowed	roʊd	
rowing	'roʊɪŋ	
row, *noun*	raʊ	
rows	raʊz	
rowdy	'raʊdɪ	
rower	'roʊə(r	'roʊə
rowers	'roʊəz	'roʊəz
royal	rɔɪəl	
royally	'rɔɪəlɪ, 'rɔɪllɪ	
royalty	'rɔɪəltɪ	
royalties	'rɔɪəltɪz	
rub	rʌb	
rubs	rʌbz	
rubbed	rʌbd	
rubbing	'rʌbɪŋ	
rubber	'rʌbə(r	'rʌbə
rubbish	'rʌbɪʃ	
ruby	'ru·bɪ	
rubies	'ru·bɪz	
rudder	'rʌdə(r	'rʌdə
rudders	'rʌdəz	'rʌdəz
rude	ru·d	
ruder	'ru·də(r	'ru·də
rudest	'ru·dɪst	
rudely	'ru·dlɪ	
rudeness	'ru·dnɪs	
rug	rʌg	
rugs	'rʌgz	
ruin	'ru·ɪn	

Traditional Spelling	Received Pronunciation	American Variants
ruins	ˈruˑɪnz	
ruined	ˈruˑɪnd	
ruining	ˈruˑɪnɪŋ	
ruinous	ˈruˑɪnəs	
rule	ruˑl	
rules	ruˑlz	
ruled	ruˑld	
ruling	ˈruˑlɪŋ	
ruler	ˈruˑlə(r	ˈruˑlə
rulers	ˈruˑləz	ˈruˑləz
Rumania	ruˈmeɪnjə, ruˈmeɪnɪə	
Rumanian	ruˈmeɪnjən ruˈmeɪnɪən	
Rumanians	ruˈmeɪnjənz ruˈmeɪnɪənz	
rumor (*Amer.*) **rumour**	ˈruˑmə(r	ˈruˑmə
rumors (*Amer.*) rumours	ˈruˑməz	ˈruˑməz
rumoured	ˈruˑməd	ˈruˑməd
run	rʌn	
runs	rʌnz	
ran	ræn	
running	ˈrʌnɪŋ	
RUNG *from* ring	rʌŋ	
rush	rʌʃ	
rushes	ˈrʌʃɪz	
rushed	rʌʃt	
rushing	ˈrʌʃɪŋ	
Russia	ˈrʌʃə	
Russian	ˈrʌʃən	
Russians	ˈrʌʃənz	
rust	rʌst	
rusts	rʌsts	
rusted	ˈrʌstɪd	
rusting	ˈrʌstɪŋ	
rusty	ˈrʌstɪ	
rut	rʌt	
ruts	rʌts	

S

S	ɛs	
S's	ˈɛsɪz	
sack	sæk	
sacks	sæks	
sacred	ˈseɪkrɪd	

Traditional Spelling	Received Pronunciation	American Variants
sacrifice	ˈsækrɪfaɪs	
sacrifices	ˈsækrɪfaɪsɪz	
sacrificed	ˈsækrɪfaɪst	
sacrificing	ˈsækrɪfaɪsɪŋ	
sad	sæ·d	
sadder	ˈsædə(r, ˈsæ·də(r	ˈsæ·də
saddest	ˈsædɪst, ˈsæ·dɪst	
sadly	ˈsæ·dlɪ	
sadness	ˈsæ·dnɪs	
saddle	ˈsædl̩	
saddles	ˈsædl̩z	
saddled	ˈsædl̩d	
saddling	ˈsædlɪŋ, ˈsædl̩ɪŋ	
safe	seɪf	
safes	ˈseɪfs	
safer	ˈseɪfə(r	ˈseɪfə
safest	ˈseɪfɪst	
safely	ˈseɪflɪ	
safety	ˈseɪftɪ	
SAID *from* say	sɛd	
sail	seɪl	
sails	seɪlz	
sailed	seɪld	
sailing	ˈseɪlɪŋ	
sailor	ˈseɪlə(r	ˈseɪlə
sailors	ˈseɪləz	ˈseɪləz
Saint	seɪnt *s.f.*, sən*t* *w.fs.*	
saint	seɪnt	
saints	seɪnts	
sake	seɪk	
sakes	seɪks	
salad	ˈsæləd	
salads	ˈsælədz	
salary	ˈsælərɪ	
salaries	ˈsælərɪz	
sale	seɪl	
sales	seɪlz	
saleable	ˈseɪləbl̩	
salesman	ˈseɪlzmən	
salesmen	ˈseɪlzmən	
salmon	ˈsæmən	
salt	sɔ·lt, sɒlt	
salts	sɔ·lts, sɒlts	
salted	ˈsɔ·ltɪd, ˈsɒltɪd	
saltness	ˈsɔ·ltnɪs, ˈsɒltnɪs	
salutation	sæljuˈteɪʃən	
salutations	sæljuˈteɪʃənz	

Traditional Spelling	Received Pronunciation	American Variants
salute	səˈluˑt, səˈljuˑt	
salutes	səˈluˑts, səˈljuˑts	
saluted	səˈluˑtɪd, səˈljuˑtɪd	
saluting	səˈluˑtɪŋ, səˈljuˑtɪŋ	
salvation	sælˈveɪʃən	
same	seɪm	
sample	ˈsɑˑmpl̩	ˈsaˑmpl̩
samples	ˈsɑˑmpl̩z	ˈsaˑmpl̩z
Samuel	ˈsæmjuəl	
sanction	ˈsæŋkʃən	
sanctions	ˈsæŋkʃənz	
sanctioned	ˈsæŋkʃənd	
sanctioning	ˈsæŋkʃənɪŋ	
sand	ˈsænd	
sandwich	ˈsæn*d*wɪtʃ	
sandwiches	ˈsæn*d*wɪtʃɪz ˈsæn*d*wɪdʒɪz	
sandy	ˈsændɪ	
sane	seɪn	
sanely	ˈseɪnlɪ	
San Francisco	sænfrənˈsɪskou	
SANG *from* sing	sæŋ	
sanitary	ˈsænɪtərɪ	ˈsænɪtɛrɪ
sanity	ˈsænɪtɪ	
SANK *from* sink	sæŋk	
Sarah	ˈsɛɔrə	ˈsɛˑrə
sarcasm	ˈsɑˑkæzm̩	ˈsɑəkæzm̩
sarcastic	sɑˈkæstɪk	sɑəˈkæstɪk
sarcastically	sɑˈkæstɪkəlɪ	sɑəˈkæstɪkəlɪ
sardine	ˈsɑˑˈdiˑn	ˈsɑəˈdiˑn
sardines	ˈsɑˑˈdiˑnz	ˈsɑəˈdiˑnz
sash	sæʃ	
sashes	ˈsæʃɪz	
SAT *from* sit	sæt	
satirical	səˈtɪrɪkəl	
satisfaction	sætɪsˈfækʃən	
satisfactorily	sætɪsˈfæktərɪlɪ	
satisfactory	sætɪsˈfæktərɪ	
satisfy	ˈsætɪsfaɪ	
satisfies	ˈsætɪsfaɪz	
satisfied	ˈsætɪsfaɪd	
satisfying	ˈsætɪsfaɪɪŋ	
Saturday	ˈsætədɪ	ˈsætədɪ
Saturdays	ˈsætədɪz	ˈsætədɪz
sauce	sɔˑs	
sauces	ˈsɔˑsɪz	
saucepan	ˈsɔˑspən, ˈsɔˑspæn	

Traditional Spelling	Received Pronunciation	American Variants
saucepans	ˈsɔˑspənz, ˈsɔˑspænz	
saucer	ˈsɔˑsə(r	ˈsɔˑsə
saucers	ˈsɔˑsəz	ˈsɔˑsəz
saucily	ˈsɔˑsɩlɩ	
saucy	ˈsɔˑsɩ	
sausage	ˈsɒsɩʤ	
sausages	ˈsɒsɩʤɩz	
savage	ˈsævɩʤ	
savages	ˈsævɩʤɩz	
savagely	ˈsævɩʤlɩ	
save	seɩv	
saves	seɩvz	
saved	seɩvd	
saving	ˈseɩvɩŋ	
savings	ˈseɩvɩŋz	
saw	sɔˑ	
saws	sɔˑz	
sawed	sɔˑd	
sawing	ˈsɔˑɩŋ	
say	seɩ	
says	sɛz	
said	sɛd	
saying	ˈseɩɩŋ	
sayings	ˈseɩɩŋz	
scaffold	ˈskæfəld	
scaffolds	ˈskæfəldz	
scaffolding	ˈskæfəldɩŋ	
scaffoldings	ˈskæfəldɩŋz	
scald	skɔˑld	
scalds	skɔˑldz	
scalded	ˈskɔˑldɩd	
scalding	ˈskɔˑldɩŋ	
scale	skeɩl	
scales	skeɩlz	
scaled	skeɩld	
scaling	ˈskeɩlɩŋ	
scandal	ˈskændl̩	
scandals	ˈskændl̩z	
scandalous	ˈskændələs	
scant	skænt	
scanty	ˈskæntɩ	
scar	skɑˑ(r	skɑə
scars	skɑˑz	skɑəz
scarce	skɛəs	skɛəs
scarcer	ˈskɛəsə(r	ˈskɛəsə
scarcest	ˈskɛəsɩst	ˈskɛəsɩst
scarcely	ˈskɛəslɩ	ˈskɛəslɩ

Traditional Spelling	Received Pronunciation	American Variants
scarcity	ˈskɛəsɪtɪ	ˈskɛəsɪtɪ
scarceness	ˈskɛəsnɪs	ˈskɛəsnɪs
scare	skɛə(r	ˈskɛə
scares	ˈskɛəz	ˈskɛəz
scared	ˈskɛəd	ˈskɛəd
scaring	ˈskɛərɪŋ	ˈskɛˑrɪŋ
scarf	skɑˑf	skɑəf
scarves	skɑˑvz	skɑəvz
scarlet	ˈskɑˑlɪt, ˈskɑˑlət	ˈskɑəlɪt, ˈskɑələt
scatter	ˈskætə(r	ˈskætə
scatters	ˈskætəz	ˈskætəz
scattered	ˈskætəd	ˈskætəd
scattering	ˈskætərɪŋ	
scene	siˑn	
scenes	siˑnz	
scenery	ˈsiˑnərɪ	
scent	sɛnt	
scents	sɛnts	
sceptic	ˈskɛptɪk	
sceptics	ˈskɛptɪks	
sceptical	ˈskɛptɪkəl	
sceptically	ˈskɛptɪkəlɪ	
schedule	ˈʃɛdjul	ˈskɛdjul
schedules	ˈʃɛdjulz	ˈskɛdjulz
scheduled	ˈʃɛdjuld	ˈskɛdjuld
scheduling	ˈʃɛdjulɪŋ	ˈskɛdjulɪŋ
scheme	skiˑm	
schemes	skiˑmz	
schemed	skiˑmd	
scheming	ˈskiˑmɪŋ	
scholar	ˈskɒlə(r	ˈskɑlə
scholars	ˈskɒləz	ˈskɑləz
scholarly	ˈskɒləlɪ	ˈskɑləlɪ
scholarship	ˈskɒləʃɪp	ˈskɑləʃɪp
scholarships	ˈskɒləʃɪps	ˈskɑləʃɪps
scholastic	†skəˈlæstɪk	
school	skuˑl	
schools	skuˑlz	
school-room	ˈskuˑlrum, ˈskuˑlrʊm	
school-rooms	ˈskuˑlrumz	
	ˈskuˑlrʊmz	
science	ˈsaɪəns	
sciences	ˈsaɪənsɪz	
scientific	saɪənˈtɪfɪk	
scientifically	saɪənˈtɪfɪkəlɪ	

† See Note 30, p. xxxv. in Introduction.

Traditional Spelling	Received Pronunciation	American Variants
scientist	ˈsaɪəntɪst	
scientists	ˈsaɪəntɪsts	
scissors	ˈsɪzəz	
scoff	skɒf	skɑf
scoffs	skɒfs	skɑfs
scoffed	skɒft	skɑft
scoffing	ˈskɒfɪŋ	ˈskɑfɪŋ
scoffer	ˈskɒfə(r	ˈskɑfə
scoffers	ˈskɒfəz	ˈskɑfəz
scold	skoʊld	
scolds	skoʊldz	
scolded	ˈskoʊldɪd	
scolding	ˈskoʊldɪŋ	
scope	skoʊp	
scopes	skoʊps	
scorch	skɔˑtʃ	skɔətʃ
scorches	ˈskɔˑtʃɪz	ˈskɔətʃɪz
scorched	ˈskɔˑtʃ	ˈskɔətʃ
scorching	ˈskɔˑtʃɪŋ	ˈskɔətʃɪŋ
score	skɔˑ(r, skɔə(r	skoə
scores	skɔˑz, skɔəz	skoəz
scored	skɔˑd, skɔəd	skoəd
scoring	ˈskɔˑrɪŋ, ˈskɔərɪŋ	ˈskoˑrɪŋ
scorn	skɔˑn	skɔən
scornful	ˈskɔˑnful	ˈskɔənful
scornfully	ˈskɔˑnfulɪ, ˈskɔˑnfəlɪ	ˈskɔənfulɪ, ˈskɔənfəlɪ
Scot	skɒt	skɑt
Scots	skɒts	skɑts
Scotch	skɒtʃ	skɑtʃ
Scotland	ˈskɒtlənd	ˈskɑtlənd
Scottish	ˈskɒtɪʃ	ˈskɑtɪʃ
scoundrel	ˈskaʊndrəl	
scoundrels	ˈskaʊndrəlz	
scour	ˈskaʊə(r	ˈskaʊə
scours	ˈskaʊəz	ˈskaʊəz
scoured	ˈskaʊəd	ˈskaʊəd
scouring	ˈskaʊərɪŋ	ˈskaʊrɪŋ
scout	skaʊt	
scouts	skaʊts	
scramble	ˈskræmbḷ	
scrambles	ˈskræmbḷz	
scrambled	ˈskræmbḷd	
scrambling	ˈskræmblɪŋ	
scrap	skræp	
scraps	skræps	
scrapped	skræpt	
scrapping	ˈskræpɪŋ	

Traditional Spelling	Received Pronunciation	American Variants
scrape	skreɪp	
scrapes	skreɪps	
scraped	skreɪpt	
scraping	ˈskreɪpɪŋ	
scrappy	ˈskræpɪ	
scratch	skrætʃ	
scratches	ˈskrætʃɪz	
scratched	ˈskrætʃt	
scratching	ˈskrætʃɪŋ	
scrawl	skrɔˑl	
scrawls	skrɔˑlz	
scrawled	skrɔˑld	
scrawling	ˈskrɔˑlɪŋ	
scream	skriˑm	
screams	skriˑmz	
screamed	skriˑmd	
screaming	ˈskriˑmɪŋ	
screen	skriˑn	
screens	skriˑnz	
screened	skriˑnd	
screening	ˈskriˑnɪŋ	
screw	skruˑ	
screws	skruˑz	
screwed	skruˑd	
screwing	skruɪŋ	
scribble	ˈskrɪbḷ	
scribbles	ˈskrɪbḷz	
scribbled	ˈskrɪbḷd	
scribbling	ˈskrɪblɪŋ	
scripture	ˈskrɪptʃə(r	ˈskrɪptʃə
scriptures	ˈskrɪptʃəz	ˈskrɪptʃəz
scrub	skrʌb	
scrubs	skrʌbz	
scrubbed	skrʌbd	
scrubbing	ˈskrʌbɪŋ	
scruple	ˈskruˑpḷ	
scruples	ˈskruˑpḷz	
scrupulous	ˈskruˑpjʊləs ˈskruˑpjələs	
scrupulously	ˈskruˑpjʊləslɪ ˈskruˑpjələslɪ	
scullery	ˈskʌlərɪ	
sculleries	ˈskʌlərɪz	
sculptor	ˈskʌlptə(r	ˈskʌlptə
sculptors	ˈskʌlptəz	ˈskʌlptəz
sculpture	ˈskʌlptʃə(r	ˈskʌlptʃə
sculptures	ˈskʌlptʃəz	ˈskʌlptʃəz

Traditional Spelling	Received Pronunciation	American Variants
scum	skʌm	
sea	si·	
seas	si·z	
seal	si·l	
seals	sɪ·lz	
sealed	si·ld	
sealing	ˈsi·ɪŋ	
seam	si·m	
seams	si·mz	
seaman	ˈsi·mən	
seamen	ˈsi·mən	
seaport	ˈsi·pɔt	ˈsi·poət
seaports	ˈsi·pɔts	ˈsi·poəts
search	sɜ·tʃ	sɜətʃ
searches	ˈsɜ·tʃɪz	ˈsɜətʃɪz
searched	sɜ·tʃt	sɜətʃt
searching	ˈsɜ·tʃɪŋ	ˈsɜətʃɪŋ
seasick	ˈsi·sɪk	
seasickness	ˈsi·sɪknɪs	
season	ˈsi·zn̩	
seasons	ˈsi·zn̩z	
seasonable	ˈsi·znəbl̩, ˈsi·zn̩əbl̩	
seat	si·t	
seats	si·ts	
seated	ˈsi·tɪd	
seating	ˈsi·tɪŋ	
seaworthy	ˈsi·wɜ·ðɪ	ˈsi·wɜəðɪ
seclude	sɪˈklu·d	
secluded	sɪˈklu·dɪd	
seclusion	sɪˈklu·ʒᵊn	
second	ˈsɛkᵊnd	
secondary	ˈsɛkᵊndᵊrɪ	ˈsɛkᵊndɛrɪ
secondly	ˈsɛkᵊndlɪ	
secrecy	ˈsi·krɪsɪ	
secret	ˈsi·krɪt	
secrets	ˈsi·krɪts	
secretary	ˈsɛkrətrɪ	ˈsɛkrətɛrɪ
secretaries	ˈsɛkrətrɪz	ˈsɛkrətɛrɪz
secretive	sɪˈkri·tɪv	
secretly	ˈsi·krɪtlɪ	
sect	sɛkt	
sects	sɛkts	
section	ˈsɛkʃᵊn	
sections	ˈsɛkʃᵊnz	
secure	sɪˈkjʊə(r	sɪˈkjʊə
secures	sɪˈkjʊəz	sɪˈkjʊəz
secured	sɪˈkjʊəd	sɪˈkjʊəd

Traditional Spelling	Received Pronunciation	American Variants
securing	sɪ'kjuərɪŋ	sɪ'kjuˑrɪŋ
security	sɪ'kjuərɪtɪ	sɪ'kjuˑrɪtɪ
secruities	sɪ'kjuərɪtɪz	sɪ'kjuˑrɪtɪz
see	siˑ	
sees	siˑz	
saw	sɔˑ	
seen	siˑn	
seeing	'siˑɪŋ	
seed	siˑd	
seeds	siˑdz	
seek	siˑk	
seeks	siˑks	
sought	sɔˑt	
seeking	'siˑkɪŋ	
seem	siˑm	
seems	siˑmz	
seemed	siˑmd	
seeming	'siˑmɪŋ	
seemingly	'siˑmɪŋlɪ	
SEEN *from* see	siˑn	
seesaw	'siˑ'sɔˑ	
seize	siˑz	
seizes	'siˑzɪz	
seized	siˑzd	
seizing	'siˑzɪŋ	
seizure	'siˑʒə(r	'siˑʒə
seldom	'sɛldəm	
select	sɪ'lɛkt	
selects	sɪ'lɛkts	
selected	sɪ'lɛktɪd	
selecting	sɪ'lɛktɪŋ	
selection	sɪ'lɛkʃən	
selections	sɪ'lɛkʃənz	
self	sɛlf	
selves	sɛlvz	
sell	sɛl	
sells	sɛlz	
sold	sould	
selling	'sɛlɪŋ	
seller	'sɛlə(r	'sɛlə
sellers	'sɛləz	'sɛləz
semantic	sɪ'mæntɪk	
semantics	sɪ'mæntɪks	
semi-, *prefix*	'sɛmɪ-	
semicircle	'sɛmɪsɜkl̩	'sɛmɪsɜəkl̩
semicircles	'sɛmɪsɜkl̩z	'sɛmɪsɜəkl̩z
semicolon	'sɛmɪ'koulən	

Traditional Spelling	Received Pronunciation	American Variants
semicolons	ˈsɛmɪˈkoʊlənz	
send	sɛnd	
sends	sɛndz	
sent	sɛnt	
sending	ˈsɛndɪŋ	
sender	ˈsɛndə(r	ˈsɛndə
senders	ˈsɛndəz	ˈsɛndəz
send-off	ˈsɛnˈdɔˑf, ˈsɛnˈdɒf	
senior	ˈsiˑnjə(r	ˈsiˑnjə
seniors	ˈsiˑnjəz	ˈsiˑnjəz
sensation	sɛnˈseɪʃən, sənˈseɪʃən	
sensations	sɛnˈseɪʃənz sənˈseɪʃənz	
sensational	sɛnˈseɪʃənl̩ sənˈseɪʃənl̩	
sense	sɛns	
senses	ˈsɛnsɪz	
senseless	ˈsɛnslɪs	
sensibility	sɛnsɪˈbɪlɪtɪ	
sensible	ˈsɛnsɪbl̩	
sensibly	ˈsɛnsɪblɪ	
sensitive	ˈsɛnsɪtɪv	
SENT *from* send	sɛnt	
sentence	ˈsɛntəns	
sentences	ˈsɛntənsɪz	
sentenced	ˈsɛntənst	
sentencing	ˈsɛntənsɪŋ	
sentiment	ˈsɛntɪmənt	
sentiments	ˈsɛntɪmənts	
sentimental	sɛntɪˈmɛntl̩	
sentinel	ˈsɛntɪnl̩	
sentinels	ˈsɛntɪnl̩z	
sentry	ˈsɛntrɪ	
sentries	ˈsɛntrɪz	
separable	ˈsɛpərəbl̩	
separate, *adj.*	ˈsɛpərɪt	
separately	ˈsɛpərɪtlɪ	
separate, *verb*	ˈsɛpəreɪt	
separates	ˈsɛpəreɪts	
separated	ˈsɛpəreɪtɪd	
separating	ˈsɛpəreɪtɪŋ	
separation	sɛpəˈreɪʃən	
separations	sɛpəˈreɪʃənz	
September	səpˈtɛmbə(r sɛpˈtɛmbə(r	səpˈtɛmbə sɛpˈtɛmbə
sequel	ˈsiˑkwəl	
sequels	ˈsiˑkwəlz	

Traditional Spelling	Received Pronunciation	American Variants
sequence	ˈsiːkwəns	
sequences	ˈsiːkwənsɪz	
Serb	sɜːb	sɜəb
Serbs	sɜːbz	sɜəbz
Serbia	ˈsɜːbɪə	ˈsɜəbɪə
Serbian	ˈsɜːbɪən	ˈsɜəbɪən
Serbians	ˈsɜːbɪənz	ˈsɜəbɪənz
serene	sɪˈriːn	
sergeant	ˈsɑːʤənt	ˈsɑəʤənt
sergeants	ˈsɑːʤənts	ˈsɑəʤənts
serial	ˈsɪərɪəl	ˈsiːrɪəl
serials	ˈsɪərɪəlz	ˈsiːrɪəlz
series	ˈsɪəriz, ˈsɪərɪz	ˈsiːriz, ˈsiːrɪz
serious	ˈsɪərɪəs	ˈsiːrɪəs
seriously	ˈsɪərɪəslɪ	ˈsiːrɪəslɪ
seriousness	ˈsɪərɪəsnɪs	ˈsiːrɪəsnɪs
sermon	ˈsɜːmən	ˈsɜəmən
sermons	ˈsɜːmənz	ˈsɜəmənz
servant	ˈsɜːvənt	ˈsɜəvənt
servants	ˈsɜːvənts	ˈsɜəvənts
serve	sɜːv	sɜəv
serves	sɜːvz	sɜəvz
served	sɜːvd	sɜəvd
serving	ˈsɜːvɪŋ	ˈsɜəvɪŋ
service	ˈsɜːvɪs	ˈsɜəvɪs
services	ˈsɜːvɪsɪz	ˈsɜəvɪsɪz
serviceable	ˈsɜːvɪsəbl̩	ˈsɜəvɪsəbl̩
session	ˈsɛʃən	
sessions	ˈsɛʃənz	
set	sɛt	
sets	sɛts	
setting	ˈsɛtɪŋ	
settle	ˈsɛtl̩	
settles	ˈsɛtl̩z	
settled	ˈsɛtl̩d	
settling	ˈsɛtlɪŋ, ˈsɛtl̩ɪŋ	
settlement	ˈsɛtl̩mənt	
settlements	ˈsɛtl̩mənts	
settler	ˈsɛtlə(r	ˈsɛtlə
settlers	ˈsɛtləz	ˈsɛtləz
seven	ˈsɛvn̩	
seventeen	ˈsɛvn̩ˈtiːn	
seventeenth	ˈsɛvn̩ˈtiːnθ	
seventeenths	ˈsɛvn̩ˈtiːnθs	
seventh	ˈsɛvn̩θ	
sevenths	ˈsɛvn̩θs	
seventieth	ˈsɛvn̩tɪɪθ	

Traditional Spelling	Received Pronunciation	American Variants
seventieths	ˈsɛvn̩tɪɪθs	
seventy	ˈsɛvn̩tɪ	
several	ˈsɛvrəl	
severe	sɪˈvɪə(r	sɪˈvɪə
severer	sɪˈvɪərə(r	sɪˈvɪˑrə
severest	sɪˈvɪərɪst	sɪˈvɪˑrɪst
severely	sɪˈvɪəlɪ	sɪˈvɪəlɪ
severity	sɪˈvɛrɪtɪ	
sew	sou	
sews	souz	
sewed	soud	
sewing	ˈsouɪŋ	
sex	sɛks	
sexes	ˈsɛksɪz	
sexual	ˈsɛksjuəl, ˈsɛkʃuəl	
sexually	ˈsɛksjuəlɪ, ˈsɛkʃuəlɪ	
shabby	ˈʃæbɪ	
shabbily	ˈʃæbɪlɪ	
shabbiness	ˈʃæbɪnɪs	
shade	ʃeɪd	
shades	ʃeɪdz	
shaded	ˈʃeɪdɪd	
shading	ˈʃeɪdɪŋ	
shadow	ˈʃædou	
shadows	ˈʃædouz	
shady	ˈʃeɪdɪ	
shaft	ʃɑˑft	ʃaˑft
shafts	ʃɑˑfts	ʃaˑfts
shake	ʃeɪk	
shakes	ʃeɪks	
shook	ʃuk	
shaken	ˈʃeɪkən	
shaking	ˈʃeɪkɪŋ	
shall	ʃæl *s.f.*, ʃəl *w.fs.*	
shallow	ˈʃælou	
shallower	ˈʃælouə(r	ˈʃælouə
shallowest	ˈʃælouɪst	
shallowness	ˈʃælounɪs	
sham	ʃæm	
shame	ʃeɪm	
shames	ʃeɪmz	
shamed	ʃeɪmd	
shaming	ˈʃeɪmɪŋ	
shameful	ˈʃeɪmful	
shamefully	ˈʃeɪmfulɪ, ˈʃeɪmfəlɪ	
shameless	ˈʃeɪmlɪs	
Shanghai	ˈʃæŋˈhaɪ	

Traditional Spelling	Received Pronunciation	American Variants
shan't, *shall not*	ʃɑˑnt	ʃaˑnt
shape	ʃeɪp	
shapes	ʃeɪps	
share	ʃɛə(r	ʃɛə
shares	ʃɛəz	ʃɛəz
shared	ʃɛəd	ʃɛəd
sharing	ˈʃɛərɪŋ	ˈʃɛˑrɪŋ
shark	ʃɑˑk	ʃɑək
sharks	ʃɑˑks	ʃɑəks
sharp	ʃɑˑp	ʃɑəp
sharper	ˈʃɑˑpə(r	ˈʃɑəpə
sharpest	ˈʃɑˑpɪst	ˈʃɑəpɪst
sharpen	ˈʃɑˑpən	ˈʃɑəpən
sharpens	ˈʃɑˑpənz	ˈʃɑəpənz
sharpened	ˈʃɑˑpənd	ˈʃɑəpənd
sharpening	ˈʃɑˑpənɪŋ	ˈʃɑəpənɪŋ
sharply	ˈʃɑˑplɪ	ˈʃɑəplɪ
shave	ʃeɪv	
shaves	ʃeɪvz	
shaved	ʃeɪvd	
shaving	ˈʃeɪvɪŋ	
shavings	ˈʃeɪvɪŋz	
shawl	ʃɔˑl	
shawls	ʃɔˑlz	
she	ʃiˑ, *s.f.*, ʃi, ʃɪ *w.fs.*	
shed	ʃɛd	
sheds	ʃɛdz	
shedding	ˈʃɛdɪŋ	
sheep	ʃiˑp	
sheer	ʃɪə(r	ʃɪə
sheet	ʃiˑt	
sheets	ʃiˑts	
shelf	ʃɛlf	
shelves	ʃɛlvz	
shell	ʃɛl	
shells	ʃɛlz	
shelter	ˈʃɛltə(r	ˈʃɛltə
shelters	ˈʃɛltəz	ˈʃɛltəz
sheltered	ˈʃɛltəd	ˈʃɛltəd
sheltering	ˈʃɛltərɪŋ	
shepherd	ˈʃɛpəd	ˈʃɛpəd
shepherds	ˈʃɛpədz	ˈʃɛpədz
sheriff	ˈʃɛrɪf	
sheriffs	ˈʃɛrɪfs	
shield	ʃiˑld	
shields	ʃiˑldz	
shielded	ˈʃiˑldɪd	

Traditional Spelling	Received Pronunciation	American Variants
shielding	ˈʃiˑldɪŋ	
shift	ʃɪft	
shifts	ʃɪfts	
shifted	ˈʃɪftɪd	
shifting	ˈʃɪftɪŋ	
shine	ʃaɪn	
shines	ʃaɪnz	
shined	ʃaɪnd	
shone	ʃɒn	ʃoʊn
shining	ˈʃaɪnɪŋ	
ship	ʃɪp	
ships	ʃɪps	
shipped	ʃɪpt	
shipping	ˈʃɪpɪŋ	
shipwreck	ˈʃɪprɛk	
shipwrecks	ˈʃɪprɛks	
shipwrecked	ˈʃɪprɛkt	
shirk	ʃɜˑk	ʃɜək
shirks	ʃɜˑks	ʃɜəks
shirked	ʃɜˑkt	ʃɜəkt
shirking	ˈʃɜˑkɪŋ	ˈʃɜəkɪŋ
shirker	ˈʃɜˑkə(r	ˈʃɜəkə
shirkers	ˈʃɜˑkəz	ˈʃɜəkəz
shirt	ʃɜˑt	ʃɜət
shirts	ʃɜˑts	ʃɜəts
shiver	ˈʃɪvə(r	ˈʃɪvə
shivers	ˈʃɪvəz	ˈʃɪvəz
shivered	ˈʃɪvəd	ˈʃɪvəd
shivering	ˈʃɪvərɪŋ	
shock	ʃɒk	ʃɑk
shocks	ʃɒks	ʃɑks
shocked	ʃɒkt	ʃɑkt
shocking	ˈʃɒkɪŋ	ˈʃɑkɪŋ
shockingly	ˈʃɒkɪŋlɪ	ˈʃɑkɪŋlɪ
shoe	ʃuˑ	
shoes	ʃuˑz	
SHONE *from* shine	ʃɒn	ʃoʊn
SHOOK *from* shake	ʃʊk	
shoot	ʃuˑt	
shoots	ʃuˑts	
shot	ʃɒt	ʃɑt
shooting	ˈʃuˑtɪŋ	
shop	ʃɒp	ʃɑp
shops	ʃɒps	ʃɑps
shopping	ˈʃɒpɪŋ	ˈʃɑpɪŋ
shore	ʃɔˑ(r, ʃɔə(r	ʃoə
shores	ʃɔˑz, ʃɔəz	ʃoəz

Traditional Spelling	Received Pronunciation	American Variants
short	ʃɔˑt	ʃɔət
shorter	ˈʃɔˑtə(r	ˈʃɔətə
shortest	ˈʃɔˑtɪst	ˈʃɔətɪst
shortcomings	ˈʃɔtˈkʌmɪŋz	ˈʃɔətˈkʌmɪŋz
shorten	ˈʃɔˑtn̩	ˈʃɔətn̩
shortens	ˈʃɔˑtn̩z	ˈʃɔətn̩z
shortened	ˈʃɔˑtn̩d	ˈʃɔətn̩d
shortening	ˈʃɔˑtnɪŋ	ˈʃɔətnɪŋ
shorthand	ˈʃɔˑthænd	ˈʃɔəthænd
shortly	ˈʃɔˑtlɪ	ˈʃɔətlɪ
shortness	ˈʃɔˑtnɪs	ˈʃɔətnɪs
short-sighted	ˈʃɔˑtˈsaɪtɪd	ˈʃɔətˈsaɪtɪd
shot	ʃɒt	ʃɑt
shots	ʃɒts	ʃɑts
SHOT *from* shoot	ʃɒt	ʃɑt
should	ʃʊd *s.f.*, ʃəd, ʃt *w.fs.*	
shoulder	ˈʃoʊldə(r	ˈʃoʊldə
shoulders	ˈʃoʊldəz	ˈʃoʊldəz
shouldered	ˈʃoʊldəd	ˈʃoʊldəd
shouldering	ˈʃoʊldərɪŋ	
shout	ʃaʊt	
shouts	ʃaʊts	
shouted	ˈʃaʊtɪd	
shouting	ˈʃaʊtɪŋ	
shovel	ˈʃʌvl̩	
shovels	ˈʃʌvl̩z	
show	ʃoʊ	
shows	ʃoʊz	
showed	ʃoʊd	
showing	ˈʃoʊɪŋ	
shower, ***noun***	ˈʃaʊə(r	ˈʃaʊə
showers	ˈʃaʊəz	ˈʃaʊəz
showy	ˈʃoʊɪ	
SHRANK *from* shrink	ʃræŋk	
shred	ʃrɛd	
shreds	ʃrɛdz	
shrewd	ʃruˑd	
shrewdly	ˈʃruˑdlɪ	
shrill	ʃrɪl	
shrink	ʃrɪŋk	
shrinks	ʃrɪŋks	
shrank	ʃræŋk	
shrunk	ʃrʌŋk	
shrinking	ˈʃrɪŋkɪŋ	
shrub	ʃrʌb	
shrubs	ʃrʌbz	
shrug	ʃrʌg	

Traditional Spelling	Received Pronunciation	American Variants
shrugs	ʃrʌgz	
shrugged	ʃrʌgd	
shrugging	ˈʃrʌgɪŋ	
SHRUNK *from* shrink	ʃrʌŋk	
shut	ʃʌt	
shuts	ʃʌts	
shutting	ˈʃʌtɪŋ	
shutter	ˈʃʌtə(r	ˈʃʌtə
shutters	ˈʃʌtəz	ˈʃʌtəz
shy	ʃaɪ	
shyer	ˈʃaɪə(r	ˈʃaɪə
shyest	ˈʃaɪɪst	
shyly	ˈʃaɪlɪ	
shyness	ˈʃaɪnɪs	
Siam	saɪˈæm, ˈsaɪæm	
Siamese	ˈsaɪəˈmiˑz	
Siberia	saɪˈbɪərɪə	saɪˈbɪˑrɪə
Siberian	saɪˈbɪərɪən	saɪˈbɪˑrɪən
Sicily	ˈsɪsɪlɪ	
sick	sɪk	
sickness	ˈsɪknɪs	
side	saɪd	
sides	saɪdz	
sided	ˈsaɪdɪd	
siding	ˈsaɪdɪŋ	
sideways	ˈsaɪdweɪz	
sidewise (*Amer.*)		ˈsaɪdwaɪz
siege	siˑdʒ	
sieges	ˈsiˑdʒɪz	
sift	sɪft	
sifts	sɪfts	
sifted	ˈsɪftɪd	
sifting	ˈsɪftɪŋ	
sigh	saɪ	
sighs	saɪz	
sighed	saɪd	
sighing	ˈsaɪɪŋ	
sight	saɪt	
sights	saɪts	
sighted	ˈsaɪtɪd	
sighting	ˈsaɪtɪŋ	
sign	saɪn	
signs	saɪnz	
signed	saɪnd	
signing	ˈsaɪnɪŋ	
signal	ˈsɪgnl̩	
signals	ˈsɪgnl̩z	

Traditional Spelling	Received Pronunciation	American Variants
signalled	'sɪgn̩d	
signalling	'sɪgnəlɪŋ	
signature	'sɪgnɪtʃə(r	'sɪgnɪtʃə
signatures	'sɪgnɪtʃəz	'sɪgnɪtʃəz
signboard	'saɪnbɔd, 'saɪnbɔəd	'saɪnboəd
signboards	'saɪnbɔdz, 'saɪnbɔədz	'saɪnboədz
significance	sɪg'nɪfɪkəns	
significant	sɪg'nɪfɪkənt	
significantly	sɪg'nɪfɪkəntlɪ	
signification	sɪgnɪfɪ'keɪʃən	
significative	sɪg'nɪfɪkətɪv	
signify	'sɪgnɪfaɪ	
signifies	'sɪgnɪfaɪz	
signified	'sɪgnɪfaɪd	
signifying	'sɪgnɪfaɪɪŋ	
silence	'saɪləns	
silences	'saɪlənsɪz	
silenced	'saɪlənst	
silencing	'saɪlənsɪŋ	
silent	'saɪlənt	
silently	'saɪləntlɪ	
silk	sɪlk	
silly	'sɪlɪ	
sillier	'sɪlɪə(r	'sɪlɪə
silliest	'sɪlɪɪst	
silliness	'sɪlɪnɪs	
silver	'sɪlvə(r	'sɪlvə
similar	'sɪmɪlə(r	'sɪmɪlə
similarity	sɪmɪ'lærɪtɪ	
similarities	sɪmɪ'lærɪtɪz	
similarly	'sɪmɪləlɪ	'sɪmɪləlɪ
simple	'sɪmpl̩	
simpler	'sɪmplə(r	'sɪmplə
simplest	'sɪmplɪst	
simplicity	sɪm'plɪsɪtɪ	
simplification	sɪmplɪfɪ'keɪʃən	
simplifications	sɪmplɪfɪ'keɪʃənz	
simplify	'sɪmplɪfaɪ	
simplifies	'sɪmplɪfaɪz	
simplified	'sɪmplɪfaɪd	
simplifying	'sɪmplɪfaɪɪŋ	
simply	'sɪmplɪ	
simultaneous	sɪməl'teɪnjəs sɪməl'teɪnɪəs	
simultaneously	sɪməl'teɪnjəslɪ sɪməl'teɪnɪəslɪ	
sin	sɪn	

Traditional Spelling	Received Pronunciation	American Variants
sins	sɪnz	
sinned	sɪnd	
sinning	′sɪnɪŋ	
since	sɪns	
sincere	sɪn′sɪə(r	sɪn′sɪə
sincerely	sɪn′sɪəlɪ	sɪn′sɪəlɪ
sincerity	sɪn′serɪtɪ	
sing	sɪŋ	
sings	sɪŋz	
sang	sæŋ	
sung	sʌŋ	
singing	′sɪŋɪŋ	
singer	′sɪŋə(r	′sɪŋə
singers	′sɪŋəz	′sɪŋəz
single	′sɪŋgl̩	
singly	′sɪŋglɪ	
singular	′sɪŋgjələ(r, ′sɪŋgjʊlə(r	′sɪŋgjələ, ′sɪŋgjʊlə
singularly	′sɪŋgjələlɪ, ′sɪŋgjʊləlɪ	′sɪŋgjələlɪ, ′sɪŋgjʊləlɪ
sink	sɪŋk	
sinks	sɪŋks	
sank	sæŋk	
sunk	sʌŋk	
sinking	′sɪŋkɪŋ	
sinner	′sɪnə(r	′sɪnə
sinners	′sɪnəz	′sɪnəz
sip	sɪp	
sips	sɪps	
sipped	sɪpt	
sipping	′sɪpɪŋ	
sir	sɜː(r *s.f.*, sə(r *w.f.*	sɜə *s.f.*, sə *w.f.*
sirs	sɜːz	sɜəz
sister	′sɪstə(r	′sɪstə
sisters	′sɪstəz	′sɪstəz
sit	sɪt	
sits	sɪts	
sat	sæt	
sitting	′sɪtɪŋ	
site	saɪt	
sites	saɪts	
situated	′sɪtjʊeɪtɪd	
situation	sɪtjʊ′eɪʃən	
situations	sɪtjʊ′eɪʃənz	
six	sɪks	
sixteen	′sɪks′tiːn	
sixteenth	′sɪks′tiːnθ	
sixteenths	′sɪks′tiːnθs	
sixth	sɪks*t*θ	

Traditional Spelling	Received Pronunciation	American Variants
sixths	sɪksɪθs	
sixtieth	ˈsɪkstɪɪθ	
sixtieths	ˈsɪkstɪɪθs	
sixty	ˈsɪkstɪ	
size	saɪz	
sizes	ˈsaɪzɪz	
sized	saɪzd	
skate	skeɪt	
skates	skeɪts	
skated	ˈskeɪtɪd	
skating	ˈskeɪtɪŋ	
skater	ˈskeɪtə(r	ˈskeɪtə
skaters	ˈskeɪtəz	ˈskeɪtəz
skeleton	ˈskɛlɪtn̩	
skeletons	ˈskɛlɪtn̩z	
sketch	skɛtʃ	
sketches	ˈskɛtʃɪz	
sketched	skɛtʃt	
sketching	ˈskɛtʃɪŋ	
skilful	ˈskɪlfʊl	
skilfully	ˈskɪlfʊlɪ, ˈskɪlfəlɪ	
skill	skɪl	
skilled	skɪld	
skillful (*Amer.*)	ˈskɪlfʊl	
skillfully (*Amer.*)	ˈskɪlfʊlɪ, ˈskɪlfəlɪ	
skin	skɪn	
skins	skɪnz	
skinned	skɪnd	
skinning	ˈskɪnɪŋ	
skip	skɪp	
skips	skɪps	
skipped	skɪpt	
skipping	ˈskɪpɪŋ	
skirt	skɜˑt	skɜət
skirts	skɜˑts	skɜəts
skull	skʌl	
skulls	skʌlz	
sky	skaɪ	
skies	skaɪz	
slab	slæb	
slabs	slæbs	
slack	slæk	
slacker	ˈslækə(r	ˈslækə
slackest	ˈslækɪst	
slacken	ˈslækən	
slackens	ˈslækənz	
slackened	ˈslækənd	

Traditional Spelling	Received Pronunciation	American Variants
slackening	ˈslæknɪŋ, ˈslækn̩ɪŋ	
slackly	ˈslæklɪ	
slackness	ˈslæknɪs	
slam	slæm	
slams	slæmz	
slammed	slæmd	
slamming	ˈslæmɪŋ	
slander	ˈslɑˑndə(r	ˈslaˑndə
slanders	ˈslɑˑndəz	ˈslaˑndəz
slandered	ˈslɑˑndəd	ˈslaˑndəd
slandering	ˈslɑˑndərɪŋ	ˈslaˑndərɪŋ
slanderous	ˈslɑˑndərəs	ˈslaˑndərəs
slang	slæŋ	
slant	slɑˑnt	slaˑnt
slants	slɑˑnts	slaˑnts
slanted	ˈslɑˑntɪd	ˈslaˑntɪd
slanting	ˈslɑˑntɪŋ	ˈslaˑntɪŋ
slap	slæp	
slaps	slæps	
slapped	slæpt	
slapping	ˈslæpɪŋ	
slate	sleɪt	
slates	sleɪts	
slaughter	ˈslɔˑtə(r	ˈslɔˑtə
slave	sleɪv	
slaves	sleɪvz	
slavery	ˈsleɪvərɪ	
slavish	ˈsleɪvɪʃ	
slavishly	ˈsleɪvɪʃlɪ	
Slavonic	sləˈvɒnɪk, slæˈvɒnɪk	sləˈvɑnɪk, slæˈvɑnɪk
sledge	slɛʤ	
sledges	ˈslɛʤɪz	
sleep	sliˑp	
sleeps	sliˑps	
slept	slɛpt	
sleeping	ˈsliˑpɪŋ	
sleeper	ˈsliˑpə(r	ˈsliˑpə
sleepers	ˈsliˑpəz	ˈsliˑpəz
sleepiness	ˈsliˑpɪnɪs	
sleepless	ˈsliˑplɪs	
sleeplessly	ˈsliˑplɪslɪ	
sleeplessness	ˈsliˑplɪsnɪs	
sleepy	ˈsliˑpɪ	
sleeve	sliˑv	
sleeves	sliˑvz	
sleigh	sleɪ	
sleighs	sleɪz	

Traditional Spelling	Received Pronunciation	American Variants
slender	'slɛndə(r	'slɛndə
slenderness	'slɛndənɪs	'slɛndənɪs
SLEPT *from* sleep	slɛpt	
slice	slaɪs	
slices	'slaɪsɪz	
sliced	slaɪst	
slicing	'slaɪsɪŋ	
slide	slaɪd	
slides	slaɪdz	
slid	slɪd	
sliding	'slaɪdɪŋ	
slight	slaɪt	
slighter	'slaɪtə(r	'slaɪtə
slightest	'slaɪtɪst	
slightly	'slaɪtlɪ	
slip	slɪp	
slips	slɪps	
slipped	slɪpt	
slipping	'slɪpɪŋ	
slipper	'slɪpə(r	'slɪpə
slippers	'slɪpəz	'slɪpəz
slippery	'slɪpərɪ	
slit	slɪt	
slits	slɪts	
slitting	'slɪtɪŋ	
slope	sloʊp	
slopes	sloʊps	
sloped	sloʊpt	
sloping	'sloʊpɪŋ	
slot	slɒt	slɑt
slots	slɒts	slɑts
sloven	'slʌvn̩	
slovenliness	'slʌvn̩lɪnɪs	
slovenly	'slʌvn̩lɪ	
slow	sloʊ	
slows	sloʊz	
slowed	sloʊd	
slowing	'sloʊɪŋ	
slower	'sloʊə(r	'sloʊə
slowest	'sloʊɪst	
slowly	'sloʊlɪ	
slowness	'sloʊnɪs	
slum	slʌm	
slums	slʌmz	
sly	slaɪ	
slyer	'slaɪə(r	'slaɪə
slyest	'slaɪɪst	

Traditional Spelling	Received Pronunciation	American Variants
slyly	ˈslaɪlɪ	
slyness	ˈslaɪnɪs	
smack	smæk	
smacks	smæks	
smacked	smækt	
smacking	ˈsmækɪŋ	
small	smɔˑl	
smaller	ˈsmɔˑlə(r	ˈsmɔˑlə
smallest	ˈsmɔˑlɪst	
smallish	ˈsmɔˑlɪʃ	
smallness	ˈsmɔˑlnɪs	
smart	smɑˑt	smɑət
smarts	smɑˑts	smɑəts
smarted	ˈsmɑˑtɪd	ˈsmɑətɪd
smarting	ˈsmɑˑtɪŋ	ˈsmɑətɪŋ
smarter	ˈsmɑˑtə(r	ˈsmɑətə
smartest	ˈsmɑˑtɪst	ˈsmɑətɪst
smartly	ˈsmɑˑtlɪ	ˈsmɑətlɪ
smartness	ˈsmɑˑtnɪs	ˈsmɑətnɪs
smash	smæʃ	
smashes	ˈsmæʃɪz	
smashed	smæʃt	
smashing	ˈsmæʃɪŋ	
smattering	ˈsmætərɪŋ	
smell	smɛl	
smells	smɛlz	
smelt	smɛlt	
smelling	ˈsmɛlɪŋ	
smelly	ˈsmɛlɪ	
smile	smaɪl	
smiles	smaɪlz	
smiled	smaɪld	
smiling	ˈsmaɪlɪŋ	
smoke	smoʊk	
smokes	smoʊks	
smoked	smoʊkt	
smoking	ˈsmoʊkɪŋ	
smoker	ˈsmoʊkə(r	ˈsmoʊkə
smokers	ˈsmoʊkəz	ˈsmoʊkəz
smoky	ˈsmoʊkɪ	
smooth	smuˑð	
smoother	ˈsmuˑðə(r	ˈsmuˑðə
smoothest	ˈsmuˑðɪst	
smooth(e)	smuˑð	
smoothes	smuˑðz	
smoothed	smuˑðd	
smoothing	ˈsmuˑðɪŋ	

Traditional Spelling	Received Pronunciation	American Variants
smoothly	ˈsmuˑðlɩ	
smoothness	ˈsmuˑðnɩs	
smother	ˈsmʌðə(r	ˈsmʌðə
smothers	ˈsmʌðəz	ˈsmʌðəz
smothered	ˈsmʌðəd	ˈsmʌðəd
smothering	ˈsmʌðərɩŋ	
smuggle	ˈsmʌgl̩	
smuggles	ˈsmʌgl̩z	
smuggled	ˈsmʌgl̩d	
smuggling	ˈsmʌglɩŋ, ˈsmʌgl̩ɩŋ	
smuggler	ˈsmʌglə(r	ˈsmʌglə
smugglers	ˈsmʌgləz	ˈsmʌgləz
snake	sneɩk	
snakes	sneɩks	
snap	snæp	
snaps	snæps	
snapped	snæpt	
snapping	ˈsnæpɩŋ	
snapshot	ˈsnæpˈʃɒt	ˈsnæpˈʃɑt
snapshots	ˈsnæpˈʃɒts	ˈsnæpˈʃɑts
snatch	snætʃ	
snatches	ˈsnætʃɩz	
snatched	snætʃt	
snatching	ˈsnætʃɩŋ	
sneer	snɩə(r	snɩə
sneers	snɩəz	snɩəz
sneered	snɩəd	snɩəd
sneering	ˈsnɩərɩŋ	ˈsnɪˑrɩŋ
sneeringly	ˈsnɩərɩŋlɩ	ˈsnɪˑrɩŋlɩ
sneeze	sniˑz	
sneezes	ˈsniˑzɩz	
sneezed	sniˑzd	
sneezing	ˈsniˑzɩŋ	
snow	snoʊ	
snows	snoʊz	
snowed	snoʊd	
snowing	ˈsnoʊɩŋ	
snowy	ˈsnoʊɩ	
snug	snʌg	
snugly	ˈsnʌglɩ	
so	soʊ *s.f.*, sə *w.f.*	
soak	soʊk	
soaks	soʊks	
soaked	soʊkt	
soaking	ˈsoʊkɩŋ	
so-and-so	ˈsoʊənsoʊ	
soap	soʊp	

Traditional Spelling	Received Pronunciation	American Variants
soaps	soups	
soaped	soupt	
soaping	'soupɪŋ	
soapy	'soupɪ	
sob	sɒb	sɑb
sobs	sɒbz	sɑbz
sobbed	sɒbd	sɑbd
sobbing	'sɒbɪŋ	'sɑbɪŋ
sober	'soubə(r	'soubə
soberly	'soubəlɪ	'soubəlɪ
soberness	'soubənɪs	'soubənɪs
so-called	'sou'kɔˑld	
sociable	'souʃəbl̩	
sociably	'souʃəblɪ	
social	'souʃəl	
socialism	'souʃəlɪzm̩	
socialist	'souʃəlɪst	
socialists	'souʃəlɪsts	
socialistic	souʃə'lɪstɪk	
socially	'souʃəlɪ	
society	†sə'saɪətɪ	
societies	†sə'saɪətɪz	
sociology	sousɪ'ɒlədʒɪ	sousɪ'ɑlədʒɪ
sock	sɒk	sɑk
socks	sɒks	sɑks
soda	'soudə	
sofa	'soufə	
sofas	'soufəz	
soft	sɔft, sɒft	
softer	'sɔftə(r, 'sɒftə(r	'sɔftə, 'sɒftə
softest	'sɔftɪst, 'sɒftɪst	
soften	'sɔfn̩, 'sɒfn̩	
softens	'sɔfn̩z, 'sɒfn̩z	
softened	'sɔfn̩d, 'sɒfn̩d	
softening	'sɔfnɪŋ, 'sɒfnɪŋ	
softly	'sɔftlɪ, 'sɒftlɪ	
softness	'sɔftnɪs, 'sɒftnɪs	
soil	sɔɪl	
soils	sɔɪlz	
soiled	sɔɪld	
soiling	'sɔɪlɪŋ	
solar	'soulə(r	'soulə
SOLD *from* sell	sould	
soldier	'souldʒə(r	'souldʒə
soldiers	'souldʒəz	'souldʒəz
sole	soul	
soles	soulz	

† See Note 30, p. xxxv. in Introduction.

Traditional Spelling	Received Pronunciation	American Variants
solely	'soulɪ	
solemn	'sɒləm	'sɑləm
solemnly	'sɒləmlɪ	'sɑləmlɪ
solicitor	†sə'lɪsɪtə(r	sə'lɪsɪtə
solicitors	†sə'lɪsɪtəz	sə'lɪsɪtəz
solid	'sɒlɪd	'sɑlɪd
solids	'sɒlɪdz	'sɑlɪdz
solidly	'sɒlɪdlɪ	'sɑlɪdlɪ
solidity	†sə'lɪdɪtɪ	
solitary	'sɒlɪtərɪ	'sɑlɪtɛrɪ
solo	'soulou	
solos	'soulouz	
soluble	'sɒljʊbl̩	'sɑljʊbl̩
solution	†sə'lu·ʃn̩, †sə'lju·ʃn̩	
solutions	†sə'lu·ʃn̩z, †sə'lju·ʃn̩z	
solve	sɒlv	sɑlv
solves	sɒlvz	sɑlvz
solved	sɒlvd	sɑlvd
solving	'sɒlvɪŋ	'sɑlvɪŋ
some	sʌm *s.f.*, səm *w.f.*	
somehow	'sʌmhaʊ	
something	'sʌmθɪŋ	
sometimes	'sʌmtaɪmz səm'taɪmz	
somewhat	'sʌm*h*wɒt	'sʌmhwɑt
somewhere	'sʌm*h*wɛə(r	'sʌmhwɛə
son	sʌn	
sons	sʌnz	
song	sɒŋ	sɑŋ
songs	sɒŋz	sɑŋz
soon	su·n	
soothe	su·ð	
soothes	su·ðz	
soothed	su·ðd	
soothing	'su·ðɪŋ	
soothingly	'su·ðɪŋlɪ	
sophomore	'sɒfəmɔ(r, 'sɒfəmɔə(r	'sɑfəmoə
sophomores	'sɒfəmɔz, 'sɒfəmɔəz	'sɑfəmoəz
soprano	†sə'prɑ·nou	sə'prɑ·nou
sore	sɔ·(r, sɔə(r	soə
sores	sɔ·z, sɔəz	soəz
sorely	'sɔ·lɪ, 'sɔəlɪ	'soəlɪ
soreness	'sɔ·nɪs, 'sɔənɪs	'soənɪs
sorrow	'sɒrou	'sɑrou
sorrows	'sɒrouz	'sɑrouz

† See Note 30, p. xxxv. in Introduction.

Traditional Spelling	Received Pronunciation	American Variants
sorrowful	†ˈsɒrəful	ˈsɑrəful
sorry	ˈsɒrɪ	ˈsɑrɪ
sort	sɔˑt	sɔət
sorts	sɔˑts	sɔəts
sorted	ˈsɔˑtɪd	ˈsɔətɪd
sorting	ˈsɔˑtɪŋ	ˈsɔətɪŋ
soul	soul	
souls	soulz	
sound	saʊnd	
sounds	saʊndz	
sounded	ˈsaʊndɪd	
sounding	ˈsaʊndɪŋ	
soundly	ˈsaʊndlɪ	
soundness	ˈsaʊndnɪs	
soup	suˑp	
sour	ˈsaʊə(r	ˈsaʊə
source	sɔˑs, sɔəs	soəs
sources	ˈsɔˑsɪz, ˈsɔəsɪz	ˈsoəsɪz
sourly	ˈsaʊəlɪ	ˈsaʊəlɪ
sourness	ˈsaʊənɪs	ˈsaʊənɪs
south	saʊθ	
southerly	ˈsʌðəlɪ	ˈsʌðəlɪ
southern	ˈsʌðən	ˈsʌðən
south-west	ˈsaʊθˈwɛst	
souvenir	ˈsuˑvənɪə(r	ˈsuˑvənɪə
souvenirs	ˈsuˑvənɪəz	ˈsuˑvənɪəz
sovereign	ˈsɒvrɪn	ˈsɑvrɪn
sovereigns	ˈsɒvrɪnz	ˈsɑvrɪnz
sow	sou	
sows	souz	
sowed	soud	
sown	soun	
sowing	ˈsouɪŋ	
space	speɪs	
spaces	ˈspeɪsɪz	
spaced	speɪst	
spacing	ˈspeɪsɪŋ	
spade	speɪd	
spades	speɪdz	
Spain	speɪn	
Spaniard	ˈspænjəd	ˈspænjəd
Spaniards	ˈspænjədz	ˈspænjədz
Spanish	ˈspænɪʃ	
spare	spɛə(r	spɛə
spares	spɛəz	spɛəz

† See Note 30, p. xxxv. in Introduction.

Traditional Spelling	Received Pronunciation	American Variants
spared	spɛəd	spɛəd
sparing	ˈspɛərɪŋ	ˈspɛ·rɪŋ
sparingly	ˈspɛərɪŋlɪ	ˈspɛ·rɪŋlɪ
spark	spɑ·k	spɑək
sparks	spɑ·ks	spɑəks
sparrow	ˈspærou	
sparrows	ˈspærouz	
SPAT *from* spit	spæt	
speak	spi·k	
speaks	spi·ks	
spoke	spouk	
spoken	ˈspoukən	
speaking	ˈspi·kɪŋ	
speaker	ˈspi·kə(r	ˈspi·kə
speakers	ˈspi·kəz	ˈspi·kəz
spear	ˈspɪə(r	ˈspɪə
spears	ˈspɪəz	ˈspɪəz
special	ˈspɛʃəl	
specialist	ˈspɛʃəlɪst	
specialists	ˈspɛʃəlɪsts	
speciality	spɛʃɪˈælɪtɪ	
specialities	spɛʃɪˈælɪtɪz	
specialize	ˈspɛʃəlaɪz	
specializes	ˈspɛʃəlaɪzɪz	
specialized	ˈspɛʃəlaɪzd	
specializing	ˈspɛʃəlaɪzɪŋ	
specially	ˈspɛʃəlɪ	
specialty	ˈspɛʃəltɪ	
specialties	ˈspɛʃəltɪz	
species	ˈspi·ʃiz, ˈspi·ʃɪz	
specific	spɪˈsɪfɪk	
specifically	spɪˈsɪfɪkəlɪ	
specify	ˈspɛsɪfaɪ	
specifies	ˈspɛsɪfaɪz	
specified	ˈspɛsɪfaɪd	
specifying	ˈspɛsɪfaɪɪŋ	
specimen	ˈspɛsɪmən, ˈspɛsɪmɪn	
specimens	ˈspɛsɪmənz ˈspɛsɪmɪnz	
speck	spɛk	
specks	spɛks	
spectacle	ˈspɛktəkl̩, ˈspɛktɪkl̩	
spectacles	ˈspɛktəkl̩z ˈspɛktɪkl̩z	
spectator	spɛkˈteɪtə(r	spɛkˈteɪtə
spectators	spɛkˈteɪtəz	spɛkˈteɪtəz
speculate	ˈspɛkjuleɪt	

Traditional Spelling	Received Pronunciation	American Variants
speculates	ˈspɛkjʊleɪts	
speculated	ˈspɛkjʊleɪtɪd	
speculating	ˈspɛkjʊleɪtɪŋ	
speculation	ˈspɛkjʊˈleɪʃən	
speculations	spɛkjʊˈleɪʃənz	
speculator	ˈspɛkjʊleɪtə(r	ˈspɛkjʊleɪtə
speculators	ˈspɛkjʊleɪtəz	ˈspɛkjʊleɪtəz
speech	spiˑtʃ	
speeches	ˈspiˑtʃɪz	
speechless	ˈspiˑtʃlɪs	
speed	spiˑd	
speeds	spiˑdz	
spell	spɛl	
spells	spɛlz	
spelled	spɛlt	
spelt	spɛlt	
spelling	ˈspɛlɪŋ	
spellings	ˈspɛlɪŋz	
spend	spɛnd	
spends	spɛndz	
spent	spɛnt	
spending	ˈspɛndɪŋ	
spendthrift	ˈspɛn*d*θrɪft	
spendthrifts	ˈspɛn*d*θrɪfts	
sphere	sfɪə(r	sfɪə
spheres	sfɪəz	sfɪəz
sphinx	sfɪŋks	
spice	spaɪs	
spices	ˈspaɪsɪz	
spider	ˈspaɪdə(r	ˈspaɪdə
spiders	ˈspaɪdəz	ˈspaɪdəz
spike	spaɪk	
spikes	spaɪks	
spill	spɪl	
spills	spɪlz	
spilled	spɪlt	
spilt	spɪlt	
spilling	ˈspɪlɪŋ	
spin	spɪn	
spins	spɪnz	
span	spæn	
spun	spʌn	
spinning	ˈspɪnɪŋ	
spine	spaɪn	
spiral	ˈspaɪərəl	
spirals	ˈspaɪərəlz	
spirally	ˈspaɪərəlɪ	

Traditional Spelling	Received Pronunciation	American Variants
spirit	ˈspɪrɪt	
spirits	ˈspɪrɪts	
spiritual	ˈspɪrɪtjuəl, ˈspɪrɪtʃuəl	
spiritually	ˈspɪrɪtjuəlɪ, ˈspɪrɪtʃuəlɪ	
spit	spɪt	
spits	spɪts	
spat	spæt	
spitting	ˈspɪtɪŋ	
spite	spaɪt	
spiteful	ˈspaɪtful	
spitefully	ˈspaɪtfulɪ, ˈspaɪtfəlɪ	
splash	splæʃ	
splashes	ˈsplæʃɪz	
splashed	splæʃt	
splashing	ˈsplæʃɪŋ	
splendid	ˈsplɛndɪd	
splendidly	ˈsplɛndɪdlɪ	
split	splɪt	
splits	splɪts	
splitting	ˈsplɪtɪŋ	
spoil	spɔɪl	
spoils	spɔɪlz	
spoiled	spɔɪlt, spɔɪld	
spoilt	spɔɪlt	
spoiling	ˈspɔɪlɪŋ	
SPOKE *from* speak	spouk	
SPOKEN *from* speak	ˈspoukən	
sponge	spʌnʤ	
sponges	ˈspʌnʤɪz	
spontaneous	spɒnˈteɪnjəs	spɑnˈteɪnjəs
spontaneously	spɒnˈteɪnjəslɪ	spɑnˈteɪnjəslɪ
spoon	spuˑn	
spoons	spuˑnz	
spoonful	ˈspuˑnful	
spoonfuls	ˈspuˑnfulz	
sport	spɔˑt	spoət
sports	spɔˑts	spoəts
sporting	ˈspɔˑtɪŋ	ˈspoətɪŋ
sportsman	ˈspɔˑtsmən	ˈspoətsmən
sportsmen	ˈspɔˑtsmən	ˈspoətsmən
spot	spɒt	spɑt
spots	spɒts	spɑts
spotted	ˈspɒtɪd	ˈspɑtɪd
spotting	ˈspɒtɪŋ	ˈspɑtɪŋ
spout	spaʊt	
spouts	spaʊts	
sprain	spreɪn	

Traditional Spelling	Received Pronunciation	American Variants
sprains	spreɪnz	
sprained	spreɪnd	
spraining	ˈspreɪnɪŋ	
SPRANG *from* spring	spræŋ	
spray	spreɪ	
sprays	spreɪz	
sprayed	spreɪd	
spraying	ˈspreɪɪŋ	
spread	sprɛd	
spreads	sprɛdz	
spreading	ˈsprɛdɪŋ	
spring	sprɪŋ	
springs	sprɪŋz	
sprang	spræŋ	
sprung	sprʌŋ	
springing	ˈsprɪŋɪŋ	
sprinkle	ˈsprɪŋkl̩	
sprinkles	ˈsprɪŋkl̩z	
sprinkled	ˈsprɪŋkl̩d	
sprinkling	ˈsprɪŋklɪŋ	
SPRUNG *from* spring	sprʌŋ	
SPUN *from* spin	spʌn	
spur	spɜˑ(r	spɜə
spurs	spɜˑz	spɜəz
spurred	spɜˑd	spɜəd
spurring	ˈspɜˑrɪŋ	
spurt	spɜˑt	spɜət
spurts	spɜˑts	spɜəts
spurted	ˈspɜˑtɪd	ˈspɜətɪd
spurting	ˈspɜˑtɪŋ	ˈspɜətɪŋ
spy	spaɪ	
spies	spaɪz	
spied	spaɪd	
spying	ˈspaɪɪŋ	
squadron	ˈskwɒdrən	ˈskwɑdrən
squadrons	ˈskwɒdrənz	ˈskwɑdrənz
squander	ˈskwɒndə(r	ˈskwɑndə
squanders	ˈskwɒndəz	ˈskwɑndəz
squandered	ˈskwɒndəd	ˈskwɑndəd
squandering	ˈskwɒndərɪŋ	
square	skwɛə(r	skwɛə
squares	skwɛəz	skwɛəz
squarely	ˈskwɛəlɪ	ˈskwɛəlɪ
squeeze	skwiˑz	
squeezes	ˈskwiˑzɪz	
squeezed	skwiˑzd	
squeezing	ˈskwiˑzɪŋ	

Traditional Spelling	Received Pronunciation	American Variants
squint	skwɪnt	
squints	skwɪnts	
squinted	′skwɪntɪd	
squinting	′skwɪntɪŋ	
St. (=Saint)	sən*t*	
stability	stə′bɪlɪtɪ	
stable	steɪbl̩	
stables	steɪbl̩z	
stack	stæk	
stacks	stæks	
stacked	stækt	
stacking	′stækɪŋ	
staff	stɑˑf	staˑf
staffs	stɑˑfs	staˑfs
stage	steɪʤ	
stages	′steɪʤɪz	
stain	steɪn	
stains	steɪnz	
stained	steɪnd	
staining	′steɪnɪŋ	
stair	stɛə(r	stɛə
stairs	stɛəz	stɛəz
staircase	′stɛəkeɪs	′stɛəkeɪs
staircases	′stɛəkeɪsɪz	′stɛəkeɪsɪz
stale	steɪl	
staleness	′steɪlnɪs	
stalk	stɔˑk	
stalks	stɔˑks	
stall	stɔˑl	
stalls	stɔˑlz	
stamp	stæmp	
stamps	stæmps	
stamped	stæm*p*t	
stamping	′stæmpɪŋ	
stand	stænd	
stands	stændz	
stood	stʊd	
standing	′stændɪŋ	
standard	′stændəd	′stændəd
standards	′stændədz	′stændədz
standstill	′stæn*d*stɪl	
STANK *from* stink	stæŋk	
star	stɑˑ(r	stɑə
stars	stɑˑz	stɑəz
starch	stɑˑʧ	stɑəʧ
stare	stɛə(r	stɛə
stares	stɛəz	stɛəz

Traditional Spelling	Received Pronunciation	American Variants
stared	stεəd	stεəd
staring	'stεərıŋ	'stε·rıŋ
starlight	'stɑ·laıt	'stɑəlaıt
start	stɑ·t	stɑət
starts	stɑ·ts	stɑəts
started	'stɑ·tıd	'stɑətıd
starting	'stɑ·tıŋ	'stɑətıŋ
startle	'stɑ·tl̩	'stɑətl̩
startles	'stɑ·tl̩z	'stɑətl̩z
startled	'stɑ·tl̩d	'stɑətl̩d
startling	'stɑ·tlıŋ	'stɑətlıŋ
starvation	stɑ'veıʃən	stɑə'veıʃən
starve	stɑ·v	stɑəv
starves	stɑ·vz	stɑəvz
starved	stɑ·vd	stɑəvd
starving	'stɑ·vıŋ	'stɑəvıŋ
state	steıt	
states	steıts	
stated	'steıtıd	
stating	'steıtıŋ	
statement	'steıtmənt	
statements	'steıtmənts	
stately	'steıtlı	
statesman	'steıtsmən	
statesmen	'steıtsmən	
station	'steıʃən	
stations	'steıʃənz	
stationed	'steıʃənd	
stationing	'steıʃənıŋ	
stationary	'steıʃənərı	'steıʃənεrı
stationer	'steıʃənə(r	'steıʃnə
stationers	'steıʃənəz	'steıʃnəz
stationery	'steıʃn̩ərı	'steıʃənεrı
statistics	stə'tıstıks, stæ'tıstıks	
statue	'stætju	
statues	'stætjuz	
stay	steı	
stays	steız	
stayed	steıd	
staying	'steııŋ	
steady	'stεdı	
steadies	'stεdız	
steadied	'stεdıd	
steadying	'stεdııŋ	
steadier	'stεdıə(r	'stεdıə
steadiest	'stεdııst	
steadily	'stεdılı	

Traditional Spelling	Received Pronunciation	American Variants
steadiness	ˈstɛdɪnɪs	
steak	steɪk	
steaks	steɪks	
steal	stiˑl	
steals	stiˑlz	
stole	stoʊl	
stolen	ˈstoʊlən	
stealing	ˈstiˑlɪŋ	
steam	stiˑm	
steams	stiˑmz	
steamed	stiˑmd	
steaming	ˈstiˑmɪŋ	
steel	stiˑl	
steep	stiˑp	
steeper	ˈstiˑpə(r	ˈstiˑpə
steepest	ˈstiˑpɪst	
steeply	ˈstiˑplɪ	
steepness	ˈstiˑpnɪs	
steer	stɪə(r	stɪə
steers	stɪəz	stɪəz
steered	stɪəd	stɪəd
steering	ˈstɪərɪŋ	ˈstɪˑrɪŋ
stem	stɛm	
stems	stɛmz	
step	stɛp	
steps	stɛps	
stepped	stɛpt	
stepping	ˈstɛpɪŋ	
step-, *prefix*	stɛp	
Stephen	ˈstiˑvn̩	
stern	stɜˑn	stɜən
sternly	ˈstɜˑnlɪ	ˈstɜənlɪ
sternness	ˈstɜˑnnɪs	ˈstɜənnɪs
steward	ˈstjuˑəd, stjʊəd	ˈstjuˑəd
stewards	ˈstjuˑədz, stjʊədz	ˈstjuˑədz
stick	stɪk	
sticks	stɪks	
stuck	stʌk	
sticking	ˈstɪkɪŋ	
sticky	ˈstɪkɪ	
stiff	stɪf	
stiffer	ˈstɪfə(r	ˈstɪfə
stiffest	ˈstɪfɪst	
stiffen	ˈstɪfn̩	
stiffens	ˈstɪfn̩z	
stiffened	ˈstɪfn̩d	
stiffening	ˈstɪfnɪŋ, ˈstɪfn̩ɪŋ	

Traditional Spelling	Received Pronunciation	American Variants
stiffly	ˈstɪflɪ	
stiffness	ˈstɪfnɪs	
stifle	ˈstaɪfl̩	
stifles	ˈstaɪfl̩z	
stifled	ˈstaɪfl̩d	
stifling	ˈstaɪflɪŋ	
still	stɪl	
stimulant	ˈstɪmjulənt	
stimulants	ˈstɪmjulənts	
stimulate	ˈstɪmjuleɪt	
stimulates	ˈstɪmjuleɪts	
stimulated	ˈstɪmjuleɪtɪd	
stimulating	ˈstɪmjuleɪtɪŋ	
stimulation	stɪmjuˈleɪʃən	
stimulus	ˈstɪmjʊləs	
stimuli	ˈstɪmjʊlaɪ	
sting	stɪŋ	
stings	stɪŋz	
stung	stʌŋ	
stinging	ˈstɪŋɪŋ	
stink	stɪŋk	
stinks	stɪŋks	
stank	ˈstæŋk	
stunk	stʌŋk	
stinking	ˈstɪŋkɪŋ	
stipulate	ˈstɪpjʊleɪt	
stipulates	ˈstɪpjʊleɪts	
stipulated	ˈstɪpjʊleɪtɪd	
stipulating	ˈstɪpjʊleɪtɪŋ	
stipulation	stɪpjʊˈleɪʃən	
stipulations	stɪpjʊˈleɪʃənz	
stir	stɜˑ(r	stɜə
stirs	stɜˑz	stɜəz
stirred	stɜˑd	stɜəd
stirring	ˈstɜˑrɪŋ	
stirrup	ˈstɪrəp	ˈstɜrəp
stirrups	ˈstɪrəps	ˈstɜrəp.
stitch	stɪtʃ	
stiches	ˈstɪtʃɪz	
stock	stɒk	stɑk
stocks	stɒks	stɑks
Stockholm	ˈstɒkhoum	ˈstɑkhoum
stocking	ˈstɒkɪŋ	ˈstɑkɪŋ
stockings	ˈstɒkɪŋz	ˈstɑkɪŋz
stoker	ˈstoʊkə(r	ˈstoʊkə
stokers	ˈstoukəz	ˈstoukəz
STOLE *from* steal	stoul	

Traditional Spelling	Received Pronunciation	American Variants
stomach	ˈstʌmək	
stomachs	ˈstʌməks	
stone	stoʊn	
stones	stoʊnz	
stony	ˈstoʊnɪ	
STOOD *from* stand	stʊd	
stool	stuˑl	
stools	stuˑlz	
stoop	stuˑp	
stoops	stuˑps	
stooped	stuˑpt	
stooping	ˈstuˑpɪŋ	
stop	stɒp	stɑp
stops	stɒps	stɑps
stopped	stɒpt	stɑpt
stopping	ˈstɒpɪŋ	ˈstɑpɪŋ
stoppage	ˈstɒpɪʤ	ˈstɑpɪʤ
stoppages	ˈstɒpɪʤɪz	ˈstɑpɪʤɪz
stopper	ˈstɒpə(r	ˈstɑpə
stoppers	ˈstɒpəz	ˈstɑpəz
store	stɔˑ(r, stɔə(r	stɔə
stores	stɔˑz, stɔəz	stɔəz
stored	stɔˑd, stɔəd	stɔəd
storing	ˈstɔˑrɪŋ, ˈstɔərɪŋ	ˈstɔˑrɪŋ
storm	stɔˑm	stɔəm
storms	stɔˑmz	stɔəmz
stormed	stɔˑmd	stɔəmd
storming	ˈstɔˑmɪŋ	ˈstɔəmɪŋ
stormy	ˈstɔˑmɪ	ˈstɔəmɪ
story	ˈstɔˑrɪ	
stories	ˈstɔˑrɪz	
stout	staʊt	
stouter	ˈstaʊtə(r	ˈstaʊtə
stoutest	ˈstaʊtɪst	
stoutly	ˈstaʊtlɪ	
stove	stoʊv	
stoves	stoʊvz	
straight	streɪt	
straighter	ˈstreɪtə(r	ˈstreɪtə
straightest	ˈstreɪtɪst	
straighten	ˈstreɪtn̩	
straightens	ˈstreɪtn̩z	
straightened	ˈstreɪtn̩d	
straightening	ˈstreɪtnɪŋ	
straightforward	ˈstreɪtˈfɔˑwəd	ˈstreɪtˈfɔəwəd
straightforwardly	ˈstreɪtˈfɔˑwədlɪ	ˈstreɪtˈfɔəwədlɪ
straightforwardness	ˈstreɪtˈfɔˑwədnɪs	ˈstreɪtˈfɔəwədnɪs

Traditional Spelling	Received Pronunciation	American Variants
straightness	ˈstreɪtnɪs	
strain	streɪn	
strains	streɪnz	
strained	streɪnd	
straining	ˈstreɪnɪŋ	
strait	streɪt	
straits	streɪts	
strand	strænd	
strands	strændz	
stranded	ˈstrændɪd	
stranding	ˈstrændɪŋ	
strange	streɪndʒ	
stranger	ˈstreɪndʒə(r	ˈstreɪndʒə
strangest	ˈstreɪndʒɪst	
stranger	ˈstreɪndʒə(r	
strangers	ˈstreɪndʒəz	
strangely	ˈstreɪndʒlɪ	
strangeness	ˈstreɪndʒnɪs	
strangle	ˈstræŋgḷ	
strangles	ˈstræŋgḷz	
strangled	ˈstræŋgḷd	
strangling	ˈstræŋglɪŋ	
strap	stræp	
straps	stræps	
strapped	stræpt	
strapping	ˈstræpɪŋ	
stratagem	ˈstrætɪdʒɪm ˈstrætədʒəm	
stratagems	ˈstrætɪdʒɪmz ˈstrætədʒəmz	
strategic	strəˈti·dʒɪk stræˈti·dʒɪk	
strategically	strəˈti·dʒɪkəlɪ stræˈti·dʒɪkəlɪ	
strategy	ˈstrætɪdʒɪ	
straw	strɔ·	
straws	strɔ·z	
strawberry	ˈstrɔ·bərɪ	ˈstrɔ·bɛrɪ
strawberries	ˈstrɔ·bərɪz	ˈstrɔ·bɛrɪz
stray	streɪ	
strays	streɪz	
strayed	streɪd	
straying	ˈstreɪɪŋ	
streak	stri·k	
streaks	stri·ks	
stream	stri·m	
streams	stri·mz	

Traditional Spelling	Received Pronunciation	American Variants
streamed	striːmd	
streaming	ˈstriːmɪŋ	
street	striːt	
streets	striːts	
strength	streŋkθ	
strengths	streŋkθs	
strengthen	ˈstreŋkθən	
strengthens	ˈstreŋkθənz	
strengthened	ˈstreŋkθənd	
strengthening	ˈstreŋkθənɪŋ	
strenuous	ˈstrenjuəs	
strenuously	ˈstrenjuəslɪ	
stress	stres	
stresses	ˈstresɪz	
stressed	strest	
stressing	ˈstresɪŋ	
stretch	stretʃ	
stretches	ˈstretʃɪz	
stretched	stretʃt	
stretching	ˈstretʃɪŋ	
strict	strɪkt	
stricter	ˈstrɪktə(r	ˈstrɪktə
strictest	ˈstrɪktɪst	
strictly	ˈstrɪktlɪ	
stride	straɪd	
strides	straɪdz	
strife	straɪf	
strike	straɪk	
strikes	straɪks	
struck	strʌk	
striking	ˈstraɪkɪŋ	
strikingly	ˈstraɪkɪŋlɪ	
string	strɪŋ	
strings	strɪŋz	
stringed	strɪŋd	
strung	strʌŋ	
stringing	ˈstrɪŋɪŋ	
strip	strɪp	
strips	strɪps	
stripped	strɪpt	
stripping	ˈstrɪpɪŋ	
stripe	straɪp	
stripes	straɪps	
striped	straɪpt	
striping	ˈstraɪpɪŋ	
strive	straɪv	
strives	straɪvz	

Traditional Spelling	Received Pronunciation	American Variants
strove	stroʊv	
striven	'strɪvn̩	
striving	'straɪvɪŋ	
stroke	stroʊk	
strokes	stroʊks	
stroked	stroʊkt	
stroking	'stroʊkɪŋ	
stroll	stroʊl	
strolls	stroʊlz	
strolled	stroʊld	
strolling	'stroʊlɪŋ	
strong	strɒŋ	
stronger	'strɒŋgə(r	'strɒŋgə
strongest	'strɒŋgɪst	
strongly	'strɒŋlɪ	
STROVE *from* strive	stroʊv	
STRUCK *from* strike	strʌk	
structure	'strʌkʧə(r	'strʌkʧə
structures	'strʌkʧəz	'strʌkʧəz
struggle	'strʌgl̩	
struggles	'strʌgl̩z	
struggled	'strʌgl̩d	
struggling	'strʌglɪŋ, 'strʌgl̩ɪŋ	
STRUNG *from* string	strʌŋ	
stubborn	'stʌbən	'stʌbən
stubbornly	'stʌbənlɪ	'stʌbənlɪ
stubbornness	'stʌbənnɪs	'stʌbənnɪs
STUCK *from* stick	stʌk	
student	'stjuˑdənt	
students	'stjuˑdənts	
studious	'stjuˑdjəs, 'stjuˑdɪəs	
study	'stʌdɪ	
studies	'stʌdɪz	
studied	'stʌdɪd	
studying	'stʌdɪɪŋ	
stuff	'stʌf	
stuffs	'stʌfs	
stuffed	'stʌft	
stuffing	'stʌfɪŋ	
stuffy	'stʌfɪ	
stumble	'stʌmbl̩	
stumbles	'stʌmbl̩z	
stumbled	'stʌmbl̩d	
stumbling	'stʌmblɪŋ	
stump	stʌmp	
stumps	stʌmps	
stun	stʌn	

Traditional Spelling	Received Pronunciation	American Variants
stuns	stʌnz	
stunned	stʌnd	
stunning	'stʌnɪŋ	
STUNG *from* sting	stʌŋ	
STUNK *from* stink	stʌŋk	
stupid	'stjupɪd, 'stju·pɪd	
stupidity	stju'pɪdɪtɪ, stju'pɪdɪtɪ	
stupidly	'stjupɪdlɪ, 'stju·pɪdlɪ	
stutter	'stʌtə(r	'stʌtə
stutters	'stʌtəz	'stʌtəz
stuttered	'stʌtəd	'stʌtəd
stuttering	'stʌtərɪŋ	
stutterer	'stʌtərə(r	'stʌtərə
stutterers	'stʌtərəz	'stʌtərəz
style	staɪl	
styles	staɪlz	
sub-, *prefix*	sʌb-, səb-	
subdivision	'sʌbdɪ'vɪʒən	
subdivisions	'sʌbdɪ'vɪʒənz	
subdued, *adj.*	səb'dju·d	
subject, *noun*	'sʌbʤɪkt	
subjects	'sʌbʤɪkts	
subject, *verb*	səb'ʤɛkt, 'sʌbʤɪkt	
subjects	səb'ʤɛkts 'sʌbʤɪkts	
subjected	səb'ʤɛktɪd 'sʌbʤɪktɪd	
subjecting	səb'ʤɛktɪŋ 'sʌbʤɪktɪŋ	
subjective	səb'ʤɛktɪv sʌb'ʤɛktɪv	
subjectively	səb'ʤɛktɪvlɪ svb'ʤɛktɪvlɪ	
sublime	sə'blaɪm	
sublimely	sə'blaɪmlɪ	
submarine	'sʌbmərin	
submarines	'sʌbmərinz	
submission	səb'mɪʃən	
submit	səb'mɪt	
submits	səb'mɪts	
submitted	səb'mɪtɪd	
submitting	səb'mɪtɪŋ	
subordinate, *noun*	sə'bɔ·dənɪt	sə'bɔədənɪt
subordinates	sə'bɔ·dənɪts	sə'bɔədənɪts
subordinate, *verb*	sə'bɔ·dɪneɪt	sə'bɔədɪneɪt
subordinates	sə'bɔ·dɪneɪts	sə'bɔədɪneɪts
subordinated	sə'bɔ·dɪneɪtɪd	sə'bɔədɪneɪtɪd

Traditional Spelling	Received Pronunciation	American Variants
subordinating	sə'bɔ·dɪneɪtɪŋ	sə'bɔədɪneɪtɪŋ
subscribe	səb'skraɪb	
subscribes	səb'skraɪbz	
subscribed	səb'skraɪbd	
subscribing	səb'skraɪbɪŋ	
subscriber	səb'skraɪbə(r	səb'skraɪbə
subscribers	səb'skraɪbəz	səb'skraɪbəz
subscription	səb'skrɪpʃən	
subscriptions	səb'skrɪpʃənz	
subsequent	'sʌbsɪkwənt	
subsequently	'sʌbsɪkwəntlɪ	
subsidy	'sʌbsɪdɪ	
subsidies	'sʌbsɪdɪz	
substance	'sʌbstəns	
substances	'sʌbstənsɪz	
substantial	səb'stænʃəl	
substantially	səb'stænʃəlɪ	
substitute	'sʌbstɪtjut	
substitutes	'sʌbstɪtjuts	
substituted	'sʌbstɪtjutɪd	
substituting	'sʌbstɪtjutɪŋ	
substitution	sʌbstɪ'tju·ʃən	
substitutions	sʌbstɪ'tju·ʃənz	
subtle	'sʌtl̩	
subtler	'sʌtlə(r	'sʌtlə
subtlest	'sʌtlɪst	
subtlety	'sʌtl̩tɪ	
subtleties	'sʌtl̩tɪz	
subtly	'sʌtlɪ	
subtract	səb'trækt	
subtracts	səb'trækts	
subtracted	səb'træktɪd	
subtracting	səb'træktɪŋ	
subtraction	səb'trækʃən	
subtractions	səb'trækʃənz	
suburb	'sʌbəb, 'sʌbəb	'sʌbəəb, 'sʌbəb
suburbs	'sʌbəbz, 'sʌbəbz	'sʌbəəbz, 'sʌbəbz
suburban	sə'bə·bən	sə'bəəbən
subway	'sʌbweɪ	
subways	'sʌbweɪz	
succeed	sək'si·d	
succeeds	sək'si·dz	
succeeded	sək'si·dɪd	
succeeding	sək'si·dɪŋ	aʊ
success	sək'sɛs	
successes	sək'sɛsɪz	
successful	sək'sɛsful	

Traditional Spelling	Received Pronunciation	American Variants
successfully	sək'sɛsfulɪ, sək'sɛsfəlɪ	
succession	sək'sɛʃən	
successive	sək'sɛsɪv	
successively	sək'sɛsɪvlɪ	
successor	sək'sɛsə(r	sək'sɛsə
successors	sək'sɛsəz	sək'sɛsəz
such	sʌtʃ, sətʃ	
such-and-such	'sʌtʃənsʌtʃ	
suck	sʌk	
sucks	sʌks	
sucked	sʌkt	
sucking	'sʌkɪŋ	
suction	'sʌkʃən	
sudden	'sʌdn̩	
suddenly	'sʌdn̩lɪ	
suddenness	'sʌdn̩nɪs	
Suez	'suːɪz, 'sjuːɪz	su'ɛz
suffer	'sʌfə(r	'sʌfə
suffers	'sʌfəz	'sʌfəz
suffered	'sʌfəd	'sʌfəd
suffering	'sʌfərɪŋ	
sufferer	'sʌfərə(r	'sʌfərə
sufferers	'sʌfərəz	'sʌfərəz
suffice	sə'faɪs	
suffices	sə'faɪsɪz	
sufficed	sə'faɪst	
sufficing	sə'faɪsɪŋ	
sufficient	sə'fɪʃənt	
sufficiently	sə'fɪʃəntlɪ	
suffix	'sʌfɪks	
suffixes	'sʌfɪksɪz	
suffocate	'sʌfəkeɪt	
suffocates	'sʌfəkeɪts	
suffocated	'sʌfəkeɪtɪd	
suffocating	'sʌfəkeɪtɪŋ	
suffocation	sʌfə'keɪʃən	
suffrage	'sʌfrɪdʒ	
sugar	'ʃugə(r	'ʃugə
suggest	sə'dʒɛst	While Krapp states that [səg'dʒɛst], etc., is a purist affectation, Kenyon maintains that the alternative form [sə'dʒɛst] is very rare in Northern Ohio and probably in the North generally. Martin agrees with Kenyon.
suggests	sə'dʒɛsts	
suggested	sə'dʒɛstɪd	
suggesting	sə'dʒɛstɪŋ	
suggestion	sə'dʒɛstʃən	
suggestions	sə'dʒɛstʃənz	
suggestive	sə'dʒɛstɪv	
suicidal	sjuɪ'saɪdl̩	
suicide	'sjuɪsaɪd	

Traditional Spelling	Received Pronunciation	American Variants
suicides	ˈsjuɪsaɪdz	
suit	sjuˑt	
suits	sjuˑts	
suited	ˈsjuˑtɪd	
suiting	ˈsjuˑtɪŋ	
suitability	sjutəˈbɪlɪtɪ	
suitable	ˈsjuˑtəbl̩	
suitably	ˈsjuˑtəblɪ	
sulk	sʌlk	
sulks	sʌlks	
sulked	sʌlkt	
sulking	ˈsʌlkɪŋ	
sulkily	ˈsʌlkɪlɪ	
sulky	ˈsʌlkɪ	
sulphur	ˈsʌlfə(r	ˈsʌlfɚ
sultry	ˈsʌltrɪ	
sum	sʌm	
sums	sʌmz	
summed	sʌmd	
summing	ˈsʌmɪŋ	
summarize	ˈsʌməraɪz	
summarizes	ˈsʌməraɪzɪz	
summarized	ˈsʌməraɪzd	
summarizing	ˈsʌməraɪzɪŋ	
summary	ˈsʌmərɪ	
summaries	ˈsʌmərɪz	
summer	ˈsʌmə(r	ˈsʌmɚ
summers	ˈsʌməz	ˈsʌmɚz
summon	ˈsʌmən	
summons	ˈsʌmənz	
summoned	ˈsʌmənd	
summoning	ˈsʌmənɪŋ	
summons	ˈsʌmənz	
sun	sʌn	
suns	sʌnz	
sunburn	ˈsʌnbɜn	ˈsʌnbɝn
sunburnt	ˈsʌnbɜnt	ˈsʌnbɝnt
Sunday	ˈsʌndɪ	
Sundays	ˈsʌndɪz	
sundry	ˈsʌndrɪ	
SUNG *from* sing	sʌŋ	
SUNK *from* sink	sʌŋk	
sunlight	ˈsʌnlaɪt	
sunny	ˈsʌnɪ	
sunrise	ˈsʌnraɪz	
sunset	ˈsʌnsɛt	
sunshine	ˈsʌnʃaɪn	

Traditional Spelling	Received Pronunciation	American Variants
super-, *prefix*	ˈsjuˑpə(r	ˈsjuˑpə
superb	sjuˈpəˑb	sjuˈpəəb
supercilious	sjupəˈsɪlɪəs	sjupəˈsɪlɪəs
superficial	sjupəˈfɪʃəl	sjupəˈfɪʃəl
superficially	sjupəˈfɪʃəlɪ	sjupəˈfɪʃəlɪ
superfluous	sjuˈpəˑfluəs	sjuˈpəəfluəs
superfluously	sjuˈpəˑfluəslɪ	sjuˈpəəfluəslɪ
superintend	sjupərɪnˈtɛnd	
superintends	sjupərɪnˈtɛndz	
superintended	sjupərɪnˈtɛndɪd	
superintending	sjupərɪnˈtɛndɪŋ	
superior	sjuˈpɪərɪə(r	sjuˈpɪˑrɪə
superiors	sjuˈpɪərɪəz	sjuˈpɪˑrɪəz
superiority	sjupɪərɪˈɒrɪtɪ	sjupɪˑrɪˈɒrɪtɪ
superlative	sjuˈpəˑlətɪv	sjuˈpəələtɪv
supersede	sjupəˈsiˑd	sjupəˈsiˑd
supersedes	sjupəˈsiˑdz	sjupəˈsiˑdz
superdeded	sjupəˈsiˑdɪd	sjupəˈsiˑdɪd
superseding	sjupəˈsiˑdɪŋ	sjupəˈsiˑdɪŋ
superstition	sjupəˈstɪʃən	sjupəˈstɪʃən
superstitions	sjupəˈstɪʃənz	sjupəˈstɪʃənz
superstitious	sjupəˈstɪʃəs	sjupəˈstɪʃəs
supervise	ˈsjuˑpəvaɪz sjupəˈvaɪz	ˈsjuˑpəvaɪz sjupəˈvaɪz
supervises	ˈsjuˑpəvaɪzɪz sjupəˈvaɪzɪz	ˈsjuˑpəvaɪzɪz sjupəˈvaɪzɪz
supervised	ˈsjuˑpəvaɪzd sjupəˈvaɪzd	ˈsjuˑpəvaɪzd sjupəˈvaɪzd
supervising	ˈsjuˑpəvaɪzɪŋ sjupəˈvaɪzɪŋ	ˈsjuˑpəvaɪzɪŋ sjupəˈvaɪzɪŋ
supper	ˈsʌpə(r	ˈsʌpə
suppers	ˈsʌpəz	ˈsʌpəz
supplement, *noun*	ˈsʌplɪmənt	
supplements	ˈsʌplɪmənts	
supplement, *verb*	ˈsʌplɪmɛnt	
supplements	ˈsʌplɪmɛnts	
supplemented	ˈsʌplɪmɛntɪd	
supplementing	ˈsʌplɪmɛntɪŋ	
supply	səˈplaɪ	
supplies	səˈplaɪz	
supplied	səˈplaɪd	
supplying	səˈplaɪɪŋ	
support	səˈpɔˑt	səˈpoət
supports	səˈpɔˑts	səˈpoəts
supported	səˈpɔˑtɪd	səˈpoətɪd
supporting	səˈpɔˑtɪŋ	səˈpoətɪŋ
supporter	səˈpɔˑtə(r	səˈpoətə

Traditional Spelling	Received Pronunciation	American Variants
supporters	sə'pɔ·təz	sə'poətəz
suppose	sə'pouz	
supposes	sə'pouzɪz	
supposed	sə'pouzd	
supposing	sə'pouzɪŋ	
supposition	sʌpə'zɪʃən	
suppositions	sʌpə'zɪʃənz	
suppress	sə'prɛs	
suppresses	sə'prɛsɪz	
suppressed	sə'prɛst	
suppressing	sə'prɛsɪŋ	
suppression	sə'prɛʃən	
suppressions	sə'prɛʃənz	
supremacy	sju'prɛməsɪ	
supremacies	sju'prɛməsɪz	
supreme	sju'pri·m	
supremely	sju'pri·mlɪ	
sure	ʃuə(r, ʃɔə(r	ʃuə
surer	'ʃuərə(r, 'ʃɔərə(r	'ʃu·rə
surest	'ʃuərɪst, 'ʃɔərɪst	'ʃu·rɪst
surely	'ʃuəlɪ, 'ʃɔəlɪ	'ʃuəlɪ
sureness	'ʃuənɪs, 'ʃɔənɪs	'ʃuənɪs
surf	sɜ·f	sɜəf
surface	'sɜ·fɪs	'sɜəfɪs
surfaces	'sɜ·fɪsɪz	'sɜəfɪsɪz
surgeon	'sɜ·ʤən	'sɜəʤən
surgeons	'sɜ·ʤənz	'sɜəʤənz
surgery	'sɜ·ʤərɪ	'sɜəʤərɪ
surgical	'sɜ·ʤɪkəl	'sɜəʤɪkəl
surgically	'sɜ·ʤɪkəlɪ	'sɜəʤɪkəlɪ
surly	'sɜ·lɪ	'sɜəlɪ
surmise	sɜ'maɪz, 'sɜ·maɪz	sɜə'maɪz, 'sɜəmaɪz
surmises	sɜ'maɪzɪz, 'sɜ·maɪzɪz	sɜə'maɪzɪz . . . .
surname	'sɜ·neɪm	'sɜəneɪm
surnames	'sɜ·neɪmz	'sɜəneɪmz
surpass	sɜ'pɑ·s, sə'pɑ·s	sɜə'p·as, sə'pa·s
surpasses	sɜ'pɑ·sɪz, sə'pɑ·sɪz	sɜə'pa·sɪz, sə'pa·sɪz
surpassed	sɜ'pɑ·st, sə'pɑ·st	sɜə'pa·st, sə'pa·st
surpassing	sɜ'pɑ·sɪŋ, sə'pɑ·sɪŋ	sɜə'pa·sɪŋ, sə'pa·sɪŋ
surplus	'sɜ·pləs	'sɜəpləs
surpluses	'sɜ·pləsɪz	'sɜəpləsɪz
surprise	sə'praɪz	sə'praɪz
surprises	sə'praɪzɪz	sə'praɪzɪz
surprised	sə'praɪzd	sə'praɪzd
surprising	sə'praɪzɪŋ	sə'praɪzɪŋ
surprisingly	sə'praɪzɪŋlɪ	sə'praɪzɪŋlɪ
surrender	sə'rɛndə(r	sə'rɛndə

Traditional Spelling	Received Pronunciation	American Variants
surrenders	sə'rɛndəz	sə'rɛndəz
surrendered	sə'rɛndəd	sə'rɛndəd
surrendering	sə'rɛndərɪŋ	
surround	sə'raʊnd	
surrounds	sə'raʊndz	
surrounded	sə'raʊndɪd	
surrounding	sə'raʊndɪŋ	
surroundings	sə'raʊndɪŋz	
survey, *noun*	'sɜːveɪ, sɜ'veɪ	'sɜəveɪ, sɜə'veɪ
surveys	'sɜːveɪz, sɜ'veɪz	'sɜəveɪz, sɜə'veɪz
survey, *verb*	sɜ'veɪ	sɜə'veɪ
surveys	sɜ'veɪz	sɜə'veɪz
surveyed	sɜ'veɪd	sɜə'veɪd
surveying	sɜ'veɪɪŋ	sɜə'veɪɪŋ
surveyor	sɜ'veɪə(r	sɜə'veɪə
surveyors	sɜ'veɪəz	sɜə'veɪəz
survive	sɜ'vaɪv, sə'vaɪv	sɜə'vaɪv, sə'vaɪv
survives	sɜ'vaɪvz, sə'vaɪvz	sɜə'vaɪvz, sə'vaɪvz
survived	sɜ'vaɪvd, sə'vaɪvd	sɜə'vaɪvd, sə'vaɪvd
surviving	sɜ'vaɪvɪŋ, sə'vaɪvɪŋ	sɜə'vaɪvɪŋ, sə'vaɪvɪŋ
survival	sɜ'vaɪvəl, sɜ'vaɪvəl	sɜə'vaɪvəl, sə'vaɪvəl
survivals	sɜ'vaɪvəlz	sɜə'vaɪvəlz
	sə'vaɪvəlz	sə'vaɪvəlz
survivor	sɜ'vaɪvə(r, sə'vaɪvə(r	sɜə'vaɪvə, sə'vaɪvə
survivors	sə'vaɪvəz, sə'vaɪvəz	sɜə'vaɪvəz, sə'vaɪvəz
Susan	'suːzn̩	
susceptibility	səsɛptɪ'bɪlɪtɪ	
susceptible	sə'sɛptɪbl̩	
suspect, *noun*	'sʌspɛkt	
suspects	'sʌspɛkts	
suspect, *verb*	səs'pɛkt	
suspects	səs'pɛkts	
suspected	səs'pɛktɪd	
suspecting	səs'pɛktɪŋ	
suspend	səs'pɛnd	
suspends	səs'pɛndz	
suspended	səs'pɛndɪd	
suspending	səs'pɛndɪŋ	
suspense	səs'pɛns	
suspension	səs'pɛnʃən	
suspicion	səs'pɪʃən	
suspicions	səs'pɪʃənz	
suspicious	səs'pɪʃəs	
suspiciously	səs'pɪʃəslɪ	
sustain	səs'teɪn	
sustains	səs'teɪnz	
• sustained	səs'teɪnd	

Traditional Spelling	Received Pronunciation	American Variants
sustaining	səs'teɪnɪŋ	
swallow	'swɒloʊ	'swɑloʊ
swallows	'swɒloʊz	'swɑloʊz
swallowed	'swɒloʊd	'swɑloʊd
swallowing	'swɒloʊɪŋ	'swɑloʊɪŋ
SWAM *from* swim	swæm	
swamp	swɒmp	swɑmp
swamps	swɒmps	swɑmps
swamped	swɒm*p*t	swɑm*p*t
swamping	'swɒmpɪŋ	'swɑmpɪŋ
swan	swɒn	swɑn
swans	swɒnz	swɑnz
swarm	swɔ·m	swɔəm
swarms	swɔ·mz	swɔəmz
swarmed	swɔ·md	swɔəmd
swarming	'swɔ·mɪŋ	'swɔəmɪŋ
sway	sweɪ	
sways	sweɪz	
swayed	sweɪd	
swaying	'sweɪɪŋ	
swear	swɛə(r	swɛə
swears	swɛəz	swɛəz
swore	swɔ·(r, swɔə(r	swoə
sworn	swɔ·n	swoən
swearing	'swɛərɪŋ	'swɛ·rɪŋ
sweat	swɛt	
sweats	swɛts	
sweated	'swɛtɪd	
sweating	'swɛtɪŋ	
Swede	swi·d	
Swedes	swi·dz	
Sweden	'swi·dn̩	
Swedish	'swi·dɪʃ	
sweep	swi·p	
sweeps	swi·ps	
swept	swɛpt	
sweeping	'swi·pɪŋ	
sweet	swi·t	
sweets	swi·ts	
sweeter	'swi·tə(r	'swi·tə
sweetest	'swi·tɪst	
sweeten	'swi·tn̩	
sweetens	'swi·tn̩z	
sweetened	'swi·tn̩d	
sweetening	'swi·tnɪŋ, 'swi·tn̩ɪŋ	
sweetly	'swi·tlɪ	
sweetness	'swi·tnɪs	

Traditional Spelling	Received Pronunciation	American Variants
swell	swɛl	
swells	swɛlz	
swelled	swɛld	
swollen	ˈswoulən	
swelling	ˈswɛlɪŋ	
swellings	ˈswɛlɪŋz	
SWEPT *from* sweep	swɛpt	
swerve	swɜːv	swɜəv
swerves	swɜːvz	swɜəvz
swerved	swɜːvd	swɜəvd
swerving	ˈswɜːvɪŋ	ˈswɜəvɪŋ
swift	swɪft	
swifter	ˈswɪftə(r	ˈswɪftə
swiftest	ˈswɪftɪst	
swiftly	ˈswɪftlɪ	
swiftness	ˈswɪftnɪs	
swim	swɪm	
swims	swɪmz	
swam	swæm	
swum	swʌm	
swimming	ˈswɪmɪŋ	
swimmer	ˈswɪmə(r	ˈswɪmə
swimmers	ˈswɪməz	ˈswɪməz
swindle	ˈswɪndḷ	
swindles	ˈswɪndḷz	
swindled	ˈswɪndḷd	
swindling	ˈswɪndlɪŋ	
swindler	ˈswɪndlə(r	ˈswɪndlə
swindlers	ˈswɪndləz	ˈswɪndləz
swing	swɪŋ	
swings	swɪŋz	
swang	swæŋ	
swung	swʌŋ	
swinging	ˈswɪŋɪŋ	
Swiss	swɪs	
switch	swɪʧ	
switches	ˈswɪʧɪz	
switched	swɪʧt	
switching	ˈswɪʧɪŋ	
Switzerland	ˈswɪtsələnd	
	ˈswɪtzələnd	ˈswɪtzələnd
SWOLLEN *from* swell	ˈswoulən	
sword	sɔːd, sɔəd	soəd
swords	sɔːdz, sɔədz	soədz
SWORE *from* swear	swɔː(r, swɔə(r	swoə
SWORN *from* swear	swɔːn	swoən
SWUM *from* swim	swʌm	

Traditional Spelling	Received Pronunciation	American Variants
SWUNG *from* swing	swʌŋ	
Sydney	'sɪdnɪ	
syllable	'sɪləbḷ	
syllables	'sɪləbḷz	
symbol	'sɪmbəl	
symbols	'sɪmbəlz	
symbolic	sɪm'bɒlɪk	sɪm'balɪk
symbolically	sɪm'bɒlɪkəlɪ	sɪm'balɪkəlɪ
symmetrical	sɪ'mɛtrɪkəl	
symmetrically	sɪ'mɛtrɪkəlɪ	
sympathetic	sɪmpə'θɛtɪk	
sympathetically	sɪmpə'θɛtɪkəlɪ	
sympathize	'sɪmpəθaɪz	
sympathizes	'sɪmpəθaɪzɪz	
sympathized	'sɪmpəθaɪzd	
sympathizing	'sɪmpəθaɪzɪŋ	
sympathy	'sɪmpəθɪ	
sympathies	'sɪmpəθɪz	
symptom	'sɪm*p*təm	
symptoms	'sɪm*p*təmz	
syndicate	'sɪndɪkɪt	
syndicates	'sɪndɪkɪts	
synonym	'sɪnənɪm	
synonyms	'sɪnənɪmz	
synopsis	sɪ'nɒpsɪs	sɪ'napsɪs
synopses	sɪ'nɒpsɪz	sɪ'napsɪz
synoptic	sɪ'nɒptɪk	sɪ'naptɪk
synoptically	sɪ'nɒptɪkəlɪ	sɪ'naptɪkəlɪ
syntax	'sɪntæks	
synthesis	'sɪnθɪsɪs	
syntheses	'sɪnθɪsɪz	
synthetic	sɪn'θɛtɪk	
syrup	'sɪrəp	
syrups	'sɪrəps	
system	'sɪstɪm	
systems	'sɪstɪmz	
systematic	sɪstɪ'mætɪk	
systematically	sɪstɪ'mætɪkəlɪ	
systematize	'sɪstɪmətaɪz	
systematizes	'sɪstɪmətaɪzɪz	
systematized	'sɪstɪmətaɪzd	
systematizing	'sɪstɪmətaɪzɪŋ	

Traditional Spelling	Received Pronunciation	American Variants

T

Traditional Spelling	Received Pronunciation	American Variants
T	tiˑ	
T's	tiˑz	
tab	tæb	
tabs	tæbz	
table	ˈteɪbl̩	
tables	ˈteɪbl̩z	
tablet	ˈtæblɪt	
tablets	ˈtæblɪts	
tabulate	ˈtæbjuleɪt	
tabulates	ˈtæbjuleɪts	
tabulated	ˈtæbjuleɪtɪd	
tabulating	ˈtæbjuleɪtɪŋ	
tack	tæk	
tacks	tæks	
tacked	tækt	
tacking	ˈtækɪŋ	
tackle	ˈtækl̩	
tackles	ˈtækl̩z	
tackled	ˈtækl̩d	
tackling	ˈtæklɪŋ	
tact	tækt	
tactful	ˈtæktful	
tactfully	ˈtæktfulɪ, ˈtæktfəlɪ	
tactics	ˈtæktɪks	
tactless	ˈtæktlɪs	
tactlessly	ˈtæktlɪslɪ	
tail	teɪl	
tails	teɪlz	
tailed	teɪld	
tailor	ˈteɪlə(r	ˈteɪlə
tailors	ˈteɪləz	ˈteɪləz
tailoring	ˈteɪlərɪŋ	
take	teɪk	
takes	teɪks	
took	tuk	
taken	ˈteɪkən	
taking	ˈteɪkɪŋ	
tale	teɪl	
tales	teɪlz	
talent	ˈtælənt	
talents	ˈtælənts	
talented	ˈtæləntɪd	
talk	tɔˑk	
talks	tɔˑks	
talked	tɔˑkt	

Traditional Spelling	Received Pronunciation	American Variants
talking	′tɔ·kɪŋ	
talker	′tɔ·kə(r	′tɔ·kə
talkers	′tɔ·kəz	′tɔ·kəz
talkative	′tɔ·kətɪv	
talking-to	′tɔ·kɪŋtu	
tall	tɔ·l	
taller	′tɔ·lə(r	′tɔ·lə
tallest	′tɔ·lɪst	
tallness	′tɔ·lnɪs	
tame	teɪm	
tames	teɪmz	
tamed	teɪmd	
taming	′teɪmɪŋ	
tamer	′teɪmə(r	′teɪmə
tamest	′teɪmɪst	
tamely	′teɪmlɪ	
tameness	′teɪmnɪs	
tamper	′tæmpə(r	′tæmpə
tampers	′tæmpəz	′tæmpəz
tampered	′tæmpəd	′tæmpəd
tampering	′tæmpərɪŋ	
tan	tæn	
tans	tænz	
tanned	tænd	
tanning	′tænɪŋ	
tangible	′tænʤɪbl̩	
tangle	′tæŋgl̩	
tangles	′tæŋgl̩z	
tangled	′tæŋgl̩d	
tangling	′tæŋglɪŋ	
tank	tæŋk	
tanks	tæŋks	
tantalize	′tæntəlaɪz	
tantalizes	′tæntəlaɪzɪz	
tantalized	′tæntəlaɪzd	
tantalizing	′tæntəlaɪzɪŋ	
tap	tæp	
taps	tæps	
tapped	tæpt	
tapping	′tæpɪŋ	
tape	teɪp	
tar	tɑ·(r	tɑə
tars	tɑ·z	tɑəz
tarred	tɑ·d	tɑəd
tarring	′tɑ·rɪŋ	
tardy	′tɑ·dɪ	′tɑədɪ
target	′tɑ·gɪt	′tɑəgɪt

Traditional Spelling	Received Pronunciation	American Variants
targets	ˈtɑˑgɪts	ˈtɑəgɪts
tariff	ˈtærɪf	
tariffs	ˈtærɪfs	
tart	tɑˑt	tɑət
tarts	tɑˑts	tɑəts
task	tɑˑsk	taˑsk
tasks	tɑˑsks	taˑsks
taste	teɪst	
tastes	teɪsts	
tasted	ˈteɪstɪd	
tasting	ˈteɪstɪŋ	
tasteful	ˈteɪstful	
tastefully	ˈteɪstfulɪ, ˈteɪstfəlɪ	
tasteless	ˈteɪstlɪs	
TAUGHT *from* teach	tɔˑt	
tawdry	ˈtɔˑdrɪ	
tax	tæks	
taxes	ˈtæksɪz	
taxed	tækst	
taxing	ˈtæksɪŋ	
taxation	tækˈseɪʃən, tækˈzeɪʃən	
taxi	ˈtæksɪ	
taxis	ˈtæksɪz	
tea	tɪˑ	
teas	tɪˑz	
teach	tɪˑtʃ	
teaches	ˈtɪˑtʃɪz	
taught	tɔˑt	
teaching	ˈtɪˑtʃɪŋ	
teachings	ˈtɪˑtʃɪŋz	
teacher	ˈtiˑtʃə(r	ˈtiˑtʃə
teachers	ˈtiˑtʃəz	ˈtiˑtʃəz
teacup	ˈtiˑkʌp	
teacups	ˈtɪˑkʌps	
teapot	ˈtɪˑpɒt	ˈtiˑpɑt
teapots	ˈtɪˑpɒts	ˈtiˑpɑts
tear, ***noun***	tɪə(r	tɪə
tears	tɪəz	tɪəz
tear, *verb*	tɛə(r	tɛə
tears	tɛəz	tɛəz
tore	tɔˑ(r, tɔə(r	toə
torn	tɔˑn	toən
tearing	ˈtɛərɪŋ	ˈtɛˑrɪŋ
tearful	ˈtɪəful	ˈtɪəful
tease	tɪˑz	
teases	ˈtiˑzɪz	
teased	tiˑzd	

Traditional Spelling	Received Pronunciation	American Variants
teasing	ˈtiˑzɪŋ	
teasingly	ˈtiˑzɪŋlɪ	
teaspoon	ˈtiˑspun	
teaspoons	ˈtiˑspunz	
teaspoonful	ˈtiˑspunful	
teaspoonfuls	ˈtiˑspunfulz	
tea-time	ˈtiˑtaɪm	
technical	ˈtɛknɪkəl	
technically	ˈtɛknɪkəlɪ	
technicality	tɛknɪˈkælɪtɪ	
technicalities	tɛknɪˈkælɪtɪz	
technique	tɛkˈniˑk	
tedious	ˈtiˑdɪəs, ˈtiˑdjəs	
TEETH *plur. of* tooth	tiˑθ	
telegram	ˈtɛlɪgræm	
telegrams	ˈtɛlɪgræmz	
telegraph	ˈtɛlɪgrɑf, ˈtɛlɪgræf	ˈtɛlɪgraf
telegraphs	ˈtɛlɪgrɑfs, ˈtɛlɪgræfs	ˈtɛlɪgrafs
telegraphed	ˈtɛlɪgrɑft, ˈtɛlɪgræft	ˈtɛlɪgraft
telegraphing	ˈtɛlɪgrɑfɪŋ ˈtɛlɪgræfɪŋ	ˈtɛlɪgrafɪŋ
telegraphic	tɛlɪˈgræfɪk	
telegraphically	tɛlɪˈgræfɪkəlɪ	
telegraphist	tɪˈlɛgrəfɪst	
telegraphists	tɪˈlɛgrəfɪsts	
telegraphy	tɪˈlɛgrəfɪ	
telephone	ˈtɛlɪfoun	
telephones	ˈtɛlɪfounz	
telephoned	ˈtɛlɪfound	
telephoning	ˈtɛlɪfounɪŋ	
telephonic	tɛlɪˈfɒnɪk	tɛlɪˈfanɪk
telescope	ˈtɛlɪskoup	
telescopes	ˈtɛlɪskoups	
telescoped	ˈtɛlɪskoupt	
telescoping	ˈtɛlɪskoupɪŋ	
telescopic	tɛlɪsˈkɒpɪk	tɛlɪsˈkapɪk
telescopically	tɛlɪsˈkɒpɪkəlɪ	tɛlɪsˈkapɪkəlɪ
tell	tɛl	
tells	tɛlz	
told	tould	
telling	ˈtɛlɪŋ	
temper	ˈtɛmpə(r	ˈtɛmpə
tempers	ˈtɛmpəz	ˈtɛmpəz
tempered	ˈtɛmpəd	ˈtɛmpəd
temperament	ˈtɛmpərəmənt	
temperaments	ˈtɛmpərəmənts	
temperance	ˈtɛmpərəns	

Traditional Spelling	Received Pronunciation	American Variants
temperate	'tɛmpərɪt	
temperately	'tɛmpərɪtlɪ	
temperature	'tɛmpərɪtʃə(r	'tɛmpərɪtʃə
	'tɛmpərətjə(r	
temperatures	'tɛmpərɪtʃəz	'tɛmprɪtʃəz
	'tɛmpərətjəz	
temple	'tɛmpl̩	
temples	'tɛmpl̩z	
temporarily	'tɛmpərərɪlɪ	'tɛmpərɛrɪlɪ
temporary	'tɛmpərərɪ	'tɛmpərɛrɪ
tempt	tɛm*p*t	
tempts	tɛm*p*ts	
tempted	'tɛm*p*tɪd	
tempting	'tɛm*p*tɪŋ	
temptation	tɛm*p*'teɪʃən	
temptations	tɛm*p*'teɪʃənz	
tempter	'tɛm*p*tə(r	'tɛm*p*tə
tempters	'tɛm*p*təz	'tɛm*p*təz
tempting	'tɛm*p*tɪŋ	
temptingly	'tɛm*p*tɪŋlɪ	
ten	tɛn	
tenant	'tɛnənt	
tenants	'tɛnənts	
tend	tɛnd	
tends	tɛndz	
tended	'tɛndɪd	
tending	'tɛndɪŋ	
tendency	'tɛndənsɪ	
tendencies	'tɛndənsɪz	
tender	'tɛndə(r	'tɛndə
tenderly	'tɛndəlɪ	'tɛndəlɪ
tenderness	'tɛndənɪs	'tɛndənɪs
tenfold	'tɛnfould	
tennis	'tɛnɪs	
tenor	'tɛnə(r	'tɛnə
tent	tɛnt	
tents	tɛnts	
tentative	'tɛntətɪv	
tenth	tɛnθ	
tenths	tɛnθs	
term	tɜˑm	tɜəm
terms	tɜˑmz	tɜəmz
terminate	'tɜˑmɪneɪt	'tɜəmɪneɪt
terminates	'tɜˑmɪneɪts	'tɜəmɪneɪts
terminated	'tɜˑmɪneɪtɪd	'tɜəmɪneɪtɪd
terminating	'tɜˑmɪneɪtɪŋ	'tɜəmɪneɪtɪŋ
termination	tɜmɪ'neɪʃən	tɜəmɪ'neɪʃən

Traditional Spelling	Received Pronunciation	American Variants
terminations	təmɪ'neɪʃənz	təəmɪ'neɪʃənz
terminology	təmɪ'nɒlədʒɪ	təəmɪ'nɑlədʒɪ
terminologies	təmɪ'nɒlədʒɪz	təəmɪ'nɑlədʒɪz
terminus	'tə·mɪnəs	'təəmɪnəs
termini	'tə·mɪnaɪ	'təəmɪnaɪ
terminuses	'tə·mɪnəsɪz	'təəmɪnəsɪz
terrace	'tɛrɪs	
terraces	'tɛrɪsɪz	
terrible	'tɛrɪbḷ	
terribly	'tɛrɪblɪ	
terrific	tɪ'rɪfɪk	
terrify	'tɛrɪfaɪ	
terrifies	'tɛrɪfaɪz	
terrified	'tɛrɪfaɪd	
terrifying	'tɛrɪfaɪɪŋ	
territory	'tɛrɪtərɪ	'tɛrɪtorɪ
territories	'tɛrɪtərɪz	'tɛrɪtorɪz
terror	'tɛrə(r	'tɛrə
terrors	'tɛrəz	'tɛrəz
test	tɛst	
tests	tɛsts	
tested	'tɛstɪd	
testing	'tɛstɪŋ	
testament	'tɛstəmənt	
testaments	'tɛstəmənts	
testimonial	tɛstɪ'mounjəl tɛstɪ'mounɪəl	
testimonials	tɛstɪ'mounjəlz tɛstɪ'mounɪəlz	
testimony	†'tɛstɪmənɪ	
testimonies	†'tɛstɪmənɪz	
text	tɛkst	
texts	tɛksts	
textile	'tɛkstaɪl	'tɛkstɪl
textual	'tɛkstjuəl	
textually	'tɛkstjuəlɪ	
Thames (*in England, Canada, New Zealand*)	tɛmz	
Thames (*in Connecticut*)	θeɪmz	
than	ðæn *s f*, ðən, ðn̩ *w.fs.*	
thank	θæŋk	
thanks	θæŋks	
thanked	θæŋ*k*t	

† See Note 30, p. xxxv in Introduction.

Traditional Spelling	Received Pronunciation	American Variants
thanking	'θæŋkɪŋ	
thankful	'θæŋkfʊl	
thankfully	'θæŋkfʊlɪ, 'θæŋkfəlɪ	
thankfulness	'θæŋkfʊlnɪs	
thankless	'θæŋklɪs	
thanksgiving	'θæŋks'gɪvɪŋ	
thanksgiving	'θæŋks'gɪvɪŋz	
that, *demonstr. pronoun*	ðæt	
that, *relative pronoun*	ðət	
that, *conj.*	ðæt *s f.*, ðət *w f.*	
the	ði·*s.f.*, ðɪ, ðə *w fs.*	
theatre	'θɪətə(r, θɪ'ɛtə(r	'θɪətə
theatres	'θɪətəz, θɪ'ɛtəz	'θɪətəz
theatrical	θɪ'ætrɪkəl	
theft	θɛft	
thefts	θɛfts	
their	ðɛə(r, *normal form* ðə(r. *occas weak form*	ðɛə ðə
theirs	ðɛəz	ðɛəz
them	ðɛm *s.f.*, ðəm *w.f.*	
themselves	ðəm'sɛlvz	
then	ðɛn	
theological	θɪə'lɒʤɪkəl θɪə'lɒʤɪkəl	θɪə'lɑʤɪkəl
theology	θɪ'ɒləʤɪ	θɪ'ɑləʤɪ
theorize	'θɪəraɪz	
theorizes	'θɪəraɪzɪz	
theorized	'θɪəraɪzd	
theorizing	'θɪəraɪzɪŋ	
theory	'θɪərɪ, 'θɪərɪ	
theories	'θɪərɪz, 'θɪərɪz	
there	ðɛə(r, *normal form* ðə(r, *w.f.*	ðɛə ðə
thereabouts	'ðɛərə'baʊts	'ðɛ·rə'baʊts
thereby	'ðɛə'baɪ	'ðɛə'baɪ
therefore	'ðɛəfɔ(r, 'ðɛəfɔə(r	'ðɛəfoə
thereupon	'ðɛərə'pɒn	'ðɛ·rə'pɑn
thermometer	θə'mɒmɪtə(r	θə'mɑmɪtə
thermometers	θə'mɒmɪtəz	θə'mɑmɪtəz
THESE, *plu. of* this	ði·z	
thesis	'θi·sɪs, 'θɛsɪs	
theses	'θi·sɪz, 'θɛsɪz	
they	ðeɪ, *normal form* ðɛ, *weak form*	
thick	θɪk	
thicker	'θɪkə(r	'θɪkə

Traditional Spelling	Received Pronunciation	American Variants
thickest	ˈθɪkɪst	
thicken	ˈθɪkən	
thickens	ˈθɪkənz	
thickened	ˈθɪkənd	
thickening	ˈθɪkənɪŋ	
thickish	ˈθɪkɪʃ	
thickly	ˈθɪklɪ	
thickness	ˈθɪknɪs	
thicknesses	ˈθɪknɪsɪz	
thief	θiˑf	
thieves	θiˑvz	
thimble	ˈθɪmbl̩	
thimbles	ˈθɪmbl̩z	
thin	θɪn	
thinner	ˈθɪnə(r	ˈθɪnə
thinnest	ˈθɪnɪst	
thing	θɪŋ	
things	θɪŋz	
think	θɪŋk	
thinks	θɪŋks	
thought	θɔˑt	
thinking	ˈθɪŋkɪŋ	
thinker	ˈθɪŋkə(r	ˈθɪŋkə
thinkers	ˈθɪŋkəz	ˈθɪŋkəz
thinly	ˈθɪnlɪ	
thinness	ˈθɪnnɪs	
thinnish	ˈθɪnɪʃ	
third	θɜˑd	θɜəd
thirds	θɜˑdz	θɜədz
thirst	θɜˑst	θɜəst
thirsty	ˈθɜˑstɪ	ˈθɜəstɪ
thirteen	ˈθɜˑˈtiˑn	ˈθɜəˈtiˑn
thirteenth	ˈθɜˑˈtiˑnθ	ˈθɜəˈtiˑnθ
thirteenths	ˈθɜˑˈtiˑnθs	ˈθɜəˈtiˑnθs
thirtieth	ˈθɜˑtɪɪθ	ˈθɜətɪɪθ
thirtieths	ˈθɜˑtɪɪθs	ˈθɜətɪɪθs
thirty	ˈθɜˑtɪ	ˈθɜətɪ
this	ðɪs	
tho' = though	ðoʊ	
Thomas	ˈtɒməs	ˈtɑməs
thorn	θɔˑn	θɔən
thorns	θɔˑnz	θɔənz
thorny	ˈθɔˑnɪ	ˈθɔənɪ
thorough	ˈθʌrə	ˈθɜrə
thoroughfare	ˈθʌrəfɛə(r	ˈθɜrəfɛə
thoroughfares	ˈθʌrəfɛəz	ˈθɜrəfɛəz
thoroughly	ˈθʌrəlɪ	ˈθɜrəlɪ

Traditional Spelling	Received Pronunciation	American Variants
thoroughness	'θʌrənɪs	'θɜrənɪs
THOSE, *plur of* that	ðouz	
though, *Amer* **tho**	ðou	
thought, *noun*	θɔˑt	
thoughts	θɔˑts	
THOUGHT *from* think	θɔˑt	
thoughtful	'θɔˑtful	
thoughtfully	'θɔˑtfulɪ, 'θɔˑtfəlɪ	
thoughtfulness	'θɔˑtfulnɪs	
thoughtless	'θɔˑtlɪs	
thoughtlessly	'θɔˑtlɪslɪ	
thoughtlessness	'θɔˑtlɪsnɪs	
thousand	'θauzənd	
thousands	'θauzəndz	
thousandth	'θauzəndθ	
thousandths	'θauzəndθs	
thrash	θræʃ	
thrashes	'θræʃɪz	
thrashed	θræʃt	
thrashing	'θræʃɪŋ	
thread	θrɛd	
threads	θrɛdz	
threaded	'θrɛdɪd	
threading	'θrɛdɪŋ	
threat	θrɛt	
threats	θrɛts	
threaten	'θrɛtn̩	
threatens	'θrɛtn̩z	
threatened	'θrɛtn̩d	
threatening	'θrɛtnɪŋ, 'θrɛtn̩ɪŋ	
threateningly	'θrɛtnɪŋlɪ, 'θrɛtn̩ɪŋlɪ	
three	θrɪˑ	
threepence	'θrɛpəns, 'θrʌpn̩s 'θrɪpəns, 'θrupn̩s	
threepenny	'θrɛpənɪ, 'θrɪpənɪ 'θrupənɪ, 'θrʌpənɪ	
thresh	θrɛʃ	
threshes	'θrɛʃɪz	
threshed	θrɛʃt	
threshing	'θrɛʃɪŋ	
THREW *from* throw	θruˑ	
thrift	θrɪft	
thrifty	'θrɪftɪ	
thrill	θrɪl	
thrills	θrɪlz	
thrilled	θrɪld	
thrilling	'θrɪlɪŋ	

Traditional Spelling	Received Pronunciation	American Variants
thrillingly	ˈθrɪlɪŋlɪ	
thrive	θraɪv	
thrives	θraɪvz	
thrived	θraɪvd	
throve	θroʊv	
thriven	ˈθrɪvn̩	
thriving	ˈθraɪvɪŋ	
thro' = through	θruˑ	
throat	θroʊt	
throats	θroʊts	
throb	θrɒb	θrɑb
throbs	θrɒbz	θrɑbz
throbbed	θrɒbd	θrɑbd
throbbing	ˈθrɒbɪŋ	ˈθrɑbɪŋ
throne	θroʊn	
thrones	θroʊnz	
through, *Amer* **thru**	θruˑ	
throughout	θruˈaʊt	
THROVE *from* thrive	θroʊv	
throw	θroʊ	
throws	θroʊz	
threw	θruˑ	
thrown	θroʊn	
throwing	ˈθroʊɪŋ	
thrust	θrʌst	
thrusts	θrʌsts	
thrusting	ˈθrʌstɪŋ	
thumb	θʌm	
thumbs	θʌmz	
thunder	ˈθʌndə(r	ˈθʌndɚ
Thursday	ˈθɜˑzdɪ	ˈθɝzdɪ
Thursdays	ˈθɜˑzdɪz	ˈθɝzdɪz
thus	ðʌs	
tick	tɪk	
ticks	tɪks	
ticked	tɪkt	
ticking	ˈtɪkɪŋ	
ticket	ˈtɪkɪt	
tickets	ˈtɪkɪts	
tickle	ˈtɪkl̩	
tickles	ˈtɪkl̩z	
tickled	ˈtɪkl̩d	
tickling	ˈtɪklɪŋ, ˈtɪkl̩ɪŋ	
ticklish	ˈtɪklɪʃ, ˈtɪkl̩ɪʃ	
tide	taɪd	
tides	taɪdz	
tidily	ˈtaɪdɪlɪ	

Traditional Spelling	Received Pronunciation	American Variants
tidy, *verb*	'taɪdɪ	
tidies	'taɪdɪz	
tidied	'taɪdɪd	
tidying	'taɪdɪɪŋ	
tidy, *adj.*	'taɪdɪ	
tidier	'taɪdɪə(r	'taɪdɪə
tidiest	'taɪdɪɪst	
tie	taɪ	
ties	taɪz	
tied	taɪd	
tying	'taɪɪŋ	
tiger	'taɪgə(r	'taɪgə
tigers	'taɪgəz	'taɪgəz
tight	taɪt	
tighter	'taɪtə(r	
tightest	'taɪtɪst	
tighten	'taɪtn̩	
tightens	'taɪtn̩z	
tightened	'taɪtn̩d	
tightening	'taɪtnɪŋ, 'taɪtn̩ɪŋ	
tightly	'taɪtlɪ	
tightness	'taɪtnɪs	
tile	taɪl	
tiles	taɪlz	
till	tɪl	
tilt	tɪlt	
tilts	tɪlts	
tilted	'tɪltɪd	
tilting	'tɪltɪŋ	
timber	'tɪmbə(r	'tɪmbə
time	taɪm	
times	taɪmz	
timed	taɪmd	
timing	'taɪmɪŋ	
timely	'taɪmlɪ	
timid	'tɪmɪd	
timidity	tɪ'mɪdɪtɪ	
timidly	'tɪmɪdlɪ	
tin	tɪn	
tint	tɪnt	
tints	tɪnts	
tinted	'tɪntɪd	
tinting	'tɪntɪŋ	
tiny	'taɪnɪ	
tinier	'taɪnɪə(r	'taɪnɪə
tiniest	'taɪnɪɪst	
tip	tɪp	

Traditional Spelling	Received Pronunciation	American Variants
tips	tɪps	
tipped	tɪpt	
tipping	ˈtɪpɪŋ	
tiptoe	ˈtɪpˈtoʊ	
tire, *noun* (*Amer.*)	ˈtaɪə(r	ˈtaɪə
tires (*Amer.*)	ˈtaɪəz	ˈtaɪəz
tired	ˈtaɪəd	ˈtaɪəd
tiresome	ˈtaɪəsəm	ˈtaɪəsəm
tiring	ˈtaɪərɪŋ	ˈtaɪrɪŋ
tissue	ˈtɪsju, ˈtɪʃu, ˈtɪʃju	
title	ˈtaɪtl̩	
titles	ˈtaɪtl̩z	
to	tuˑ *s f*, tʊ, tə *w.fs.*	
toad	toʊd	
toads	toʊdz	
to-and-fro	ˈtuˑənˈfroʊ	
toast	toʊst	
tobacco	təˈbækoʊ	
to-day	təˈdeɪ, tʊˈdeɪ	
toe	toʊ	
toes	toʊz	
together	təˈgɛðə(r, tʊˈgɛðə(r	təˈgɛðə, tʊˈgɛðə
toilet	ˈtɔɪlɪt	
token	ˈtoʊkən	
tokens	ˈtoʊkənz	
Tokio	ˈtoʊkjoʊ	
Tokyo	ˈtoʊkjoʊ	
tolerable	ˈtɒlərəbl̩	ˈtɑlərəbl̩
tolerably	ˈtɒlərəblɪ	ˈtɑlərəblɪ
tolerance	ˈtɒlərəns	ˈtɑlərəns
tolerant	ˈtɒlərənt	ˈtɑlərənt
tolerantly	ˈtɒlərəntlɪ	ˈtɑlərəntlɪ
tolerate	ˈtɒləreɪt	ˈtɑləreɪt
tolerates	ˈtɒləreɪts	ˈtɑləreɪts
tolerated	ˈtɒləreɪtɪd	ˈtɑləreɪtɪd
tolerating	ˈtɒləreɪtɪŋ	ˈtɑləreɪtɪŋ
toleration	tɒləˈreɪʃən	tɑləˈreɪʃən
tomato	təˈmɑˑtoʊ	təˈmaˑtoʊ, təˈmeɪtoʊ
tomatoes	təˈmɑˑtoʊz	təˈmaˑtoʊz təˈmeɪtoʊz
tomb	tuˑm	
tombs	tuˑmz	
to-morrow	təˈmɒroʊ, tʊˈmɒroʊ	təˈmɑroʊ, tʊˈmɑroʊ
ton	tʌn	
tons	tʌnz	
tone	toʊn	
tones	toʊnz	

Traditional Spelling	Received Pronunciation	American Variants
tongs	tɒŋz	tɑŋz
tongue	tʌŋ	
tongues	tʌŋz	
to-night	tə'naɪt, tʊ'naɪt	
too	tu·	
TOOK *from* take	tʊk	
tool	tu·l	
tools	tu·lz	
tooth	tu·θ	
teeth	ti·θ	
toothache	'tu·θeɪk	
toothbrush	'tu·θbrʌʃ	
toothbrushes	'tu·θbrʌʃɪz	
toothpick	'tu·θpɪk	
toothpicks	'tu·θpɪks	
top	tɒp	tɑp
tops	tɒps	tɑps
top-heavy	'tɒp'hɛvɪ	'tɑp'hɛvɪ
topic	'tɒpɪk	'tɑpɪk
topics	'tɒpɪks	'tɑpɪks
topical	'tɒpɪkəl	'tɑpɪkəl
topmost	'tɒpmoʊst, 'tɑpməst	'tɑpmoʊst
torch	tɔ·tʃ	tɔətʃ
torches	'tɔ·tʃɪz	'tɔətʃɪz
TORE *from* tear	tɔ·(r, tɔə(r	tɔə
torment, ***noun***	'tɔ·mɛnt, 'tɔ·mənt	'tɔəmɛnt, 'tɔəmənt
torments	'tɔ·mɛnts	'tɔəmɛnts
	'tɔ·mənts	'tɔəmənts
torment, ***verb***	tɔ'mɛnt	tɔə'mɛnt
torments	tɔ'mɛnts	tɔə'mɛnts
tormented	tɔ'mɛntɪd	tɔə'mɛntɪd
tormenting	tɔ'mɛntɪŋ	tɔə'mɛntɪŋ
TORN *from* tear	tɔ·n	tɔən
Toronto	tə'rɒntoʊ	tə'rɑntoʊ
torpedo	tɔ'pi·doʊ	tɔə'pɪ·doʊ
torpedoes	tɔ'pɪ·doʊz	tɔə'pɪ·doʊz
torrent	'tɒrənt	
torrents	'tɒrənts	
tortoise	'tɔ·təs	'tɔətəs
tortoises	'tɔ·təsɪz	'tɔətəsɪz
torture	'tɔ·tʃə(r	'tɔətʃə
tortures	'tɔ·tʃəz	'tɔətʃəz
tortured	'tɔ·tʃəd	'tɔətʃəd
torturing	'tɔ·tʃərɪŋ	'tɔətʃərɪŋ
toss	tɒs	
tosses	'tɒsɪz	
tossed	tɒst	

Traditional Spelling	Received Pronunciation	American Variants
tossing	ˈtɒsɪŋ	
total	ˈtoʊtl̩	
totals	ˈtoʊtl̩z	
totalled	ˈtoʊtl̩d	
totalling	ˈtoʊtəlɪŋ	
totality	toʊˈtælɪtɪ	
totally	ˈtoʊtəlɪ	
touch	tʌtʃ	
touches	ˈtʌtʃɪz	
touched	tʌtʃt	
touching	ˈtʌtʃɪŋ	
tough	tʌf	
tougher	ˈtʌfə(r	ˈtʌfə
toughest	ˈtʌfɪst	
toughen	ˈtʌfn̩	
toughens	ˈtʌfn̩z	
toughened	ˈtʌfn̩d	
toughening	ˈtʌfnɪŋ, ˈtʌfn̩ɪŋ	
toughly	ˈtʌflɪ	
toughness	ˈtʌfnɪs	
tour	tʊə(r	tʊə
tours	tʊəz	tʊəz
toured	tʊəd	tʊəd
touring	ˈtʊərɪŋ	ˈtʊˑrɪŋ
tourist	ˈtʊərɪst	ˈtʊˑrɪst
tourists	ˈtʊərɪsts	ˈtʊˑrɪst
tow	toʊ	
tows	toʊz	
towed	toʊd	
towing	ˈtoʊɪŋ	
toward	tɔˑd, toəd, təˈwɔˑd	toəd
towards	tɔˑdz, toədz, təˈwɔˑdz	toədz
towel	ˈtaʊɪl	
towels	ˈtaʊɪlz	
tower	ˈtaʊə(r	ˈtaʊə
towers	ˈtaʊəz	ˈtaʊəz
town	taʊn	
towns	taʊnz	
toy	tɔɪ	
toys	tɔɪz	
trace	treɪs	
traces	ˈtreɪsɪz	
traced	treɪst	
tracing	ˈtreɪsɪŋ	
tracings	ˈtreɪsɪŋz	
track	træk	

Traditional Spelling	Received Pronunciation	American Variants
tracks	træks	
tracked	trækt	
tracking	'trækıŋ	
tract	trækt	
tracts	trækts	
trade	treıd	
trades	treıdz	
traded	'treıdıd	
trading	'treıdıŋ	
trader	'treıdə(r	'treıdə
traders	'treıdəz	'treıdəz
tradesman	'treıdzmən	
tradesmen	'treıdzmən	
tradition	trə'dıʃən	
traditions	trə'dıʃənz	
traditional	trə'dıʃənl̩	
traditionally	trə'dıʃənəlı	
traffic	'træfık	
tragedy	'trædʒədı	
tragedies	'trædʒədız	
tragic	'trædʒık	
trail	treıl	
trails	treılz	
train	treın	
trains	treınz	
trained	treınd	
training	'treınıŋ	
trainer	'treınə(r	'treınə
trainers	'treınəz	'treınəz
traitor	'treıtə(r	'treıtə
traitors	'treıtəz	'treıtəz
tram	træm	
trams	træmz	
tramcar	'træmkɑ(r	'træmkɑə
tramcars	'træmkɑz	'træmkɑəz
tramp	træmp	
tramps	træmps	
tramped	træm*p*t	
tramping	'træmpıŋ	
trample	'træmpl̩	
tramples	'træmpl̩z	
trampled	'træmpl̩d	
trampling	'træmplıŋ	
trans-, *prefix*	‡træns, trɑ·ns ‡trænz, trɑ·nz	
transact	træn'zækt, træn'sækt	

‡ This variant [træns—trɑ·ns] applies to all words beginning with this prefix.

Traditional Spelling	Received Pronunciation	American Variants
transacts	træn'zækts	
	træn'sækts	
transacted	træn'zæktɪd	
	træn'sæktɪd	
transacting	træn'sæktɪŋ	
	træn'zæktɪŋ	
transaction	træn'zækʃən	
	træn'sækʃən	
transactions	træn'zækʃənz	
	træn'sækʃənz	
transcribe	træns'kraɪb	
transcribes	træns'kraɪbz	
transcribed	træns'kraɪbd	
transcribing	træns'kraɪbɪŋ	
transcription	træns'krɪpʃən	
transcriptions	træns'krɪpʃənz	
transfer, *noun*	'trænsfɜ(r	'trænsfɜə
transfers	'trænsfɜz	'trænsfɜəz
transfer, *verb*	træns'fɜ·(r	træns'fɜə
transfers	træns'fɜ·z	træns'fɜəz
transferred	træns'fɜ·d	træns'fɜəd
transferring	træns'fɜ·rɪŋ	
transform	træns'fɔ·m	træns'fɔəm
transforms	træns'fɔ·mz	træns'fɔəmz
transformed	træns'fɔ·md	træns'fɔəmd
transforming	træns'fɔ·mɪŋ	træns'fɔəmɪŋ
transformation	†trænsfə'meɪʃən	trænsfə'meɪʃən
transformations	†trænsfə'meɪʃənz	trænsfə'meɪʃənz
transgress	træns'grɛs	
transgresses	træns'grɛsɪz	
transgressed	træns'grɛst	
transgressing	træns'grɛsɪŋ	
transgression	træns'grɛʃən	
transgressions	træns'grɛʃənz	
transit	'trænsɪt	
transits	'trænsɪts	
transition	træn'sɪʒən, træn'zɪʃən	
transitions	træn'sɪʒənz	
	træn'zɪʃənz	
transitional	træn'sɪʒənl̩	
	træn'zɪʃənl̩	
translate	trɑns'leɪt	træns'leɪt
translates	trɑns'leɪts	træns'leɪts
translated	trɑns'leɪtɪd	træns'leɪtɪd
translating	trɑns'leɪtɪŋ	træns'leɪtɪŋ
translation	trɑns'leɪʃən	træns'leɪʃən

† See Note 30, p. xxxv in Introduction.

Traditional Spelling	Received Pronunciation	American Variants
translations	trɑns'leɪʃənz	træns'leɪʃənz
translator	trɑns'leɪtə(r	træns'leɪtə
translators	trɑns'leɪtəz	træns'leɪtəz
transmission	trænz'mɪʃən træns'mɪʃən	
transmissions	trænz'mɪʃənz træns'mɪʃənz	
transmit	trænz'mɪt, træns'mɪt	
transmits	trænz'mɪts træns'mɪts	
transmitted	trænz'mɪtɪd træns'mɪtɪd	
transmitting	trænz'mɪtɪŋ træns'mɪtɪŋ	
transparent	træns'pεərənt træns'pærənt	træns'pε·rənt
transparently	træns'pεərəntlɪ træns'pærəntlɪ	træns'pε·rəntlɪ
transplant	træns'plɑ·nt	træns'pla·nt
transplants	træns'plɑ·nts	træns'pla·nts
transplanted	træns'plɑ·ntɪd	træns'pla·ntɪd
transplanting	træns'plɑ·ntɪŋ	træns'pla·ntɪŋ
transport, *noun*	'trænspɔt	'trænspoət
transports	'trænspɔts	'trænspoəts
transport, *verb*	træns'pɔ·t	træns'poət
transports	træns'pɔ·ts	træns'poəts
transported	træns'pɔ·tɪd	træns'poətɪd
transporting	træns'pɔ·tɪŋ	træns'poətɪŋ
transpose	træns'pouz	
transposes	træns'pouzɪz	
transposed	træns'pouzd	
transposing	træns'pouzɪŋ	
Transvaal	'trænsvɑl	
trap	træp	
traps	træps	
trapped	træpt	
trapping	'træpɪŋ	
trash	træʃ	
trashy	'træʃɪ	
travel	'trævl̩	
travels	'trævl̩z	
traveled (*Amer.*) travelled	'trævl̩d	
traveling (*Amer.*) travelling	'trævl̩ɪŋ, 'trævlɪŋ	
traveler (*Amer.*) **traveller**	'trævl̩ə(r, 'trævlə(r	'trævlə
travelers (*Amer.*)		

Traditional Spelling	Received Pronunciation	American Variants
travellers	ˈtrævl̩əz, ˈtrævləz	ˈtrævləz
tray	treɪ	
trays	treɪz	
treacherous	ˈtretʃərəs	
treacherously	ˈtretʃərəslɪ	
treachery	ˈtretʃərɪ	
tread	tred	
treads	tredz	
trod	trɒd	trɑd
trodden	ˈtrɒdn̩	ˈtrɑdn̩
treading	ˈtredɪŋ	
treason	ˈtriˑzn̩	
treasure	ˈtreʒə(r	ˈtreʒə
treasures	ˈtreʒəz	ˈtreʒəz
treasured	ˈtreʒəd	ˈtreʒəd
treasuring	ˈtreʒərɪŋ	
treasurer	ˈtreʒərə(r	ˈtreʒərə
treasurers	ˈtreʒərəz	ˈtreʒərəz
treasury	ˈtreʒərɪ	
treat	triˑt	
treats	triˑts	
treated	ˈtriˑtɪd	
treating	ˈtriˑtɪŋ	
treatment	ˈtriˑtmənt	
treatments	ˈtriˑtmənts	
treaty	ˈtriˑtɪ	
treaties	ˈtriˑtɪz	
treble	ˈtrebl̩	
tree	triˑ	
trees	triˑz	
tremble	ˈtrembl̩	
trembles	ˈtrembl̩z	
trembled	ˈtrembl̩d	
trembling	ˈtremblɪŋ	
tremendous	trɪˈmendəs	
tremendously	trɪmendəslɪ	
trench	trentʃ	
trenches	ˈtrentʃɪz	
trend	trend	
trends	trendz	
trespass	ˈtrespəs	
trespasses	ˈtrespəsɪz	
trespassed	ˈtrespəst	
trespassing	ˈtrespəsɪŋ	
trespasser	ˈtrespəsə(r	ˈtrespəsə
trespassers	ˈtrespəsəz	ˈtrespəsəz
rial	ˈtraɪəl	
trials	ˈtraɪəlz	

Traditional Spelling	Received Pronunciation	American Variants
triangle	'traıæŋgḷ	
triangles	'traıæŋgḷz	
triangular	traı'æŋgjulə(r	traı'æŋgjulə
tribe	traıb	
tribes	traıbz	
tributary	'trıbjutərı	'trıbjuterı
tributaries	'trıbjutərız	'trıbjuterız
trick	trık	
tricks	trıks	
tricked	trıkt	
tricking	'trıkıŋ	
trickle	'trıkḷ	
trickles	'trıkḷz	
trickled	'trıkḷd	
trickling	'trıklıŋ, 'trıkḷıŋ	
trifle	'traıfḷ	
trifles	'traıfḷz	
trifled	'traıfḷd	
trifling	'traıflıŋ, 'traıfḷıŋ	
trim	trım	
trims	trımz	
trimmed	trımd	
trimmer	'trımə(r	'trımə
trimmest	'trımıst	
trimming	'trımıŋ	
trimmings	'trımıŋz	
trio	'triou	
trios	'triouz	
trip	trıp	
trips	trıps	
tripped	trıpt	
tripping	'trıpıŋ	
triple	'trıpḷ	
triply	'trıplı	
triumph	'traıəmf	
triumphs	'traıəmfs	
triumphed	'traıəmft	
triumphing	'traıəmfıŋ	
triumphal	traı'ʌmfəl	
trivial	'trıvıəl, 'trıvjəl	
TROD *from* tread	trɒd	trɑd
TRODDEN *from* tread	'trɒdṇ	'trɑdṇ
trolley	'trɒlı	'trɑlı
trolleys	'trɒlız	'trɑlız
troop	tru·p	
troops	tru·ps	
trooped	tru·pt	

Traditional Spelling	Received Pronunciation	American Variants
trooping	ˈtruˑpɪŋ	
trophy	ˈtroʊfɪ	
trophies	ˈtroʊfɪz	
tropical	ˈtrɒpɪkəl	ˈtrɑpɪkəl
tropically	ˈtrɒpɪkəlɪ	ˈtrɑpɪkəlɪ
tropics	ˈtrɒpɪks	ˈtrɑpɪks
trot	trɒt	trɑt
trots	trɒts	trɑts
trotted	ˈtrɒtɪd	ˈtrɑtɪd
trotting	ˈtrɒtɪŋ	ˈtrɑtɪŋ
trouble	ˈtrʌbl̩	
troubles	ˈtrʌbl̩z	
troubled	ˈtrʌbl̩d	
troubling	ˈtrʌblɪŋ	
troublesome	ˈtrʌbl̩səm	
troupe	truˑp	
troupes	truˑps	
trousers	ˈtraʊzəz	ˈtraʊzɚz
trout	traʊt	
truck	trʌk	
trucks	trʌks	
true	truˑ	
truer	ˈtruə(r	ˈtruɚ
truest	ˈtruˑɪst	
trueness	ˈtruˑnɪs	
truly	ˈtruˑlɪ	
trumpet	ˈtrʌmpɪt	
trumpets	ˈtrʌmpɪts	
trunk	trʌŋk	
trunks	trʌŋks	
trust	trʌst	
trusts	trʌsts	
trusted	ˈtrʌstɪd	
trusting	ˈtrʌstɪŋ	
trustful	ˈtrʌstful	
trustworthiness	ˈtrʌstwɜðɪnɪs	ˈtrʌstwɜəðɪnɪs
trustworthy	ˈtrʌstwɜðɪ	ˈtrʌstwɜəðɪ
truth	truˑθ	
truths	truˑðz, truˑθs	
truthful	ˈtruˑθful	
truthfully	ˈtruˑθfulɪ, ˈtruˑθfəlɪ	
try	traɪ	
tries	traɪz	
tried	traɪd	
trying	ˈtraɪɪŋ	
tub	tʌb	
tubs	tʌbz	

Traditional Spelling	Received Pronunciation	American Variants
tube	tjuˑb	
tubes	tjuˑbz	
tuck	tʌk	
tucks	tʌks	
tucked	tʌkt	
tucking	ˈtʌkɪŋ	
Tuesday	ˈtjuˑzdɪ	
Tuesdays	ˈtjuˑzdɪz	
tug	tʌg	
tugs	tʌgz	
tugged	tʌgd	
tugging	ˈtʌgɪŋ	
tuition	tjuˈɪʃən	
tulip	ˈtjuˑlɪp	
tulips	ˈtjuˑlɪps	
tumble	ˈtʌmbl̩	
tumbles	ˈtʌmbl̩z	
tumbled	ˈtʌmbl̩d	
tumbling	ˈtʌmblɪŋ, ˈtʌmbl̩ɪŋ	
tumbler	ˈtʌmblə(r	ˈtʌmblə
tumblers	ˈtʌmbləz	ˈtʌmbləz
tune	tjuˑn	
tunes	tjuˑnz	
tuned	tjuˑnd	
tuning	ˈtjuˑnɪŋ	
tunnel	tʌnl̩	
tunnels	tʌnl̩z	
tunnelled	tʌnl̩d	
tunnelling	ˈtʌnl̩ɪŋ	
Turk	tɜˑk	tɜək
Turks	tɜˑks	tɜəks
Turkey	ˈtɜˑkɪ	ˈtɜəkɪ
turkey	ˈtɜˑkɪ	ˈtɜəkɪ
turkeys	ˈtɜˑkɪz	ˈtɜəkɪz
Turkish	ˈtɜˑkɪʃ	ˈtɜəkɪʃ
turn	tɜˑn	tɜən
turns	tɜˑnz	tɜənz
turned	tɜˑnd	tɜənd
turning	ˈtɜˑnɪŋ	ˈtɜənɪŋ
turnings	ˈtɜˑnɪŋz	ˈtɜənɪŋz
turtle	ˈtɜˑtl̩	ˈtɜətl̩
turtles	ˈtɜˑtl̩z	ˈtɜətl̩z
tutor	ˈtjuˑtə(r	ˈtjuˑtə
tutors	ˈtjuˑtəz	ˈtjuˑtəz
twelfth	twɛlfθ	
twelfths	twɛlfθs	
twelve	twɛlv	

Traditional Spelling	Received Pronunciation	American Variants
twentieth	ˈtwɛntɪɪθ	
twentieths	ˈtwɛntɪɪθs	
twenty	ˈtwɛntɪ	
twice	twaɪs	
twilight	ˈtwaɪlaɪt	
twin	twɪn	
twins	twɪnz	
twinkle	ˈtwɪŋkl̩	
twinkles	ˈtwɪŋkl̩z	
twinkled	ˈtwɪŋkl̩d	
twinkling	ˈtwɪŋklɪŋ	
twist	twɪst	
twists	twɪsts	
twisted	ˈtwɪstɪd	
twisting	ˈtwɪstɪŋ	
two	tuˑ	
twopence	ˈtʌpəns	
type	taɪp	
types	taɪps	
typed	taɪpt	
typing	ˈtaɪpɪŋ	
typewriter	ˈtaɪpraɪtə(r	ˈtaɪpraɪtə
typewriters	ˈtaɪpraɪtəz	ˈtaɪpraɪtəz
typical	ˈtɪpɪkəl	
typically	ˈtɪpɪkəlɪ	
typist	ˈtaɪpɪst	
typists	ˈtaɪpɪsts	
tyrannical	tɪˈrænɪkəl, taɪˈrænɪkəl	
tyrannically	tɪˈrænɪkəlɪ taɪˈrænɪkəlɪ	
tyrant	ˈtaɪərənt	ˈtaɪrənt
tyrants	ˈtaɪərənts	ˈtaɪrənts
tyre	ˈtaɪə(r	ˈtaɪə
tyres	ˈtaɪəz	ˈtaɪəz

U

U	juˑ	
U's	juˑz	
ugliness	ˈʌglɪnɪs	
ugly	ˈʌglɪ	
uglier	ˈʌglɪə(r	ˈʌglɪə
ugliest	ˈʌglɪɪst	
ultimate	ˈʌltɪmɪt	
ultimately	ˈʌltɪmɪtlɪ	
ultra-, *prefix*	ˈʌltrə	

Traditional Spelling	Received Pronunciation	American Variants
umbrella	ʌm'brɛlə	
umbrellas	ʌm'brɛləz	
umpire	'ʌmpaɪə(r	'ʌmpaɪə
umpires	'ʌmpaɪəz	'ʌmpaɪəz
un-, *prefix*	ʌn-	
unable	'ʌn'eɪbḷ	
unacceptable	'ʌnək'sɛptəbḷ 'ʌnæk'sɛptəbḷ	
unaccompanied	'ʌnə'kʌmpənɪd	
unaccustomed	'ʌnə'kʌstəmd	
unadvisable	'ʌnəd'vaɪzəbḷ	
unaided	'ʌn'eɪdɪd	
unalterable	'ʌn'ɔ·ltərəbḷ 'ʌn'ɒltərəbḷ	
unalterably	'ʌn'ɔ·ltərəblɪ 'ʌn'ɒltərəblɪ	
unaltered	'ʌn'ɔ·ltəd, 'ʌn'ɒltəd	'ʌn'ɔ·ltəd
unanimous	jun'ænɪməs	
unanimously	jun'ænɪməslɪ	
unanswerable	'ʌn'ɑ·nsərəbḷ	'ʌn'a·nsərəbḷ
unasked	'ʌn'ɑ·skt	'ʌn'a·skt
unassisted	'ʌnə'sɪstɪd	
unassuming	'ʌnə'sju·mɪŋ	
unattractive	'ʌnə'træktɪv	
unauthorized	'ʌn'ɔ·θəraɪzd	
unavailing	'ʌnə'veɪlɪŋ	
unavoidable	'ʌnə'vɔɪdəbḷ	
unavoidably	'ʌnə'vɔɪdəblɪ	
unaware	'ʌnə'wɛə(r	'ʌnə'wɛə
unbalance	'ʌn'bæləns	
unbalanced	'ʌn'bælənst	
unbearable	ʌn'bɛərəbḷ	ʌn'bɛ·rəbḷ
unbearably	ʌn'bɛərəblɪ	ʌn'bɛ·rəblɪ
unbeaten	'ʌn'bi·tṇ	
unbecoming	'ʌnbɪ'kʌmɪŋ	
unbelievable	'ʌnbɪ'li·vəbḷ	
unbiassed	'ʌn'baɪəst	
unbolt	'ʌn'boʊlt	
unbolts	'ʌn'boʊlts	
unbolted	'ʌn'boʊltɪd	
unbolting	'ʌn'boʊltɪŋ	
unbound	'ʌn'baʊnd	
unbroken	'ʌn'broʊkən	
unbusiness-like	'ʌn'bɪznɪslaɪk	
unbutton	'ʌn'bʌtṇ	
unbuttons	'ʌn'bʌtṇz	
unbuttoned	'ʌn'bʌtṇd	

Traditional Spelling	Received Pronunciation	American Variants
unbuttoning	ˈʌnˈbʌtnɪŋ	
	ˈʌnˈbʌtn̩ɪŋ	
uncalled (*for*)	ʌnˈkɔˑld	
uncertain	ʌnˈsɜˑtən	ʌnˈsɜətən
uncertainty	ʌnˈsɜˑtəntɪ	ʌnˈsɜətəntɪ
unchallenged	ˈʌnˈtʃælɪndʒd	
unchangeable	ˈʌnˈtʃeɪndʒəbl̩	
uncharitable	ˈʌnˈtʃærɪtəbl̩	
uncharitably	ˈʌnˈtʃærɪtəblɪ	
uncivilized	ˈʌnˈsɪvɪlaɪzd	
uncle	ˈʌŋkl̩	
uncles	ˈʌŋkl̩z	
uncomfortable	ˈʌnˈkʌmfətəbl̩	ˈʌnˈkʌmfətəbl̩
uncomfortably	ˈʌnˈkʌmfətəblɪ	ˈʌnˈkʌmfətəblɪ
uncommon	ʌnˈkɒmən	ʌnˈkɑmən
uncommonly	ʌnˈkɒmənlɪ	ʌnˈkɑmənlɪ
uncommunicative	ˈʌnkəˈmjuˑnɪkətɪv	
	ˈʌnkəˈmjuˑnɪkeɪtɪv	
uncomplaining	ˈʌnkəmˈpleɪnɪŋ	
uncomplainingly	ˈʌnkəmˈpleɪnɪŋlɪ	
uncomplimentary	ˈʌnkɒmplɪˈmɛntərɪ	ˈʌnkɑmplɪˈmɛntərɪ
uncompromising	ʌnˈkɒmprəmaɪzɪŋ	ʌnˈkɑmprəmaɪzɪŋ
unconcern	ˈʌnkənˈsɜˑn	ˈʌnkənˈsɜən
unconcerned	ˈʌnkənˈsɜˑnd	ˈʌnkənˈsɜənd
unconditional	ˈʌnkənˈdɪʃənl̩	
unconditionally	ˈʌnkənˈdɪʃənəlɪ	
unconnected	ˈʌnkəˈnɛktɪd	
unconscious	ˈʌnˈkɒnʃəs	ˈʌnˈkɑnʃəs
unconsciously	ˈʌnˈkɒnʃəslɪ	ˈʌnˈkɑnʃəslɪ
unconsciousness	ˈʌnˈkɒnʃəsnɪs	ˈʌnˈkɑnʃəsnɪs
uncooked	ˈʌnˈkʊkt	
uncorrected	ˈʌnkəˈrɛktɪd	
uncover	ˈʌnˈkʌvə(r	ˈʌnˈkʌvə
uncovers	ˈʌnˈkʌvəz	ˈʌnˈkʌvəz
uncovered	ˈʌnˈkʌvəd	ˈʌnˈkʌvəd
uncovering	ˈʌnˈkʌvərɪŋ	
undamaged	ˈʌnˈdæmɪdʒd	
undeceive	ˈʌndɪˈsiˑv	
undeceives	ˈʌndɪˈsiˑvz	
undeceived	ˈʌndɪˈsiˑvd	
undeceiving	ˈʌndɪˈsiˑvɪŋ	
undecided	ˈʌndɪˈsaɪdɪd	
undefinable	ˈʌndɪˈfaɪnəbl̩	
under	ˈʌndə(r	ˈʌndə
underclothing	ˈʌndəklouðɪŋ	ˈʌndəklouðɪŋ
underestimate, *verb*	ˈʌndəˈrɛstɪmeɪt	
underestimates	ˈʌndəˈrɛstɪmeɪts	

Traditional Spelling	Received Pronunciation	American Variants
underestimated	ˈʌndəˈrɛstɪmeɪtɪd	
underestimating	ˈʌndəˈrɛstɪmeɪtɪŋ	
undergo	ʌndəˈgoʊ	ʌndəˈgoʊ
undergoes	ʌndəˈgoʊz	ʌndəˈgoʊz
underwent	ʌndəˈwɛnt	ʌndəˈwɛnt
undergone	ʌndəˈgɒn	ʌndəˈgɒn
	ʌndəˈgɔˑn	ʌndəˈgɔˑn
undergoing	ʌndəˈgoʊɪŋ	ʌndəˈgoʊɪŋ
underground, *noun*	ˈʌndəgraʊnd	ˈʌndəgraʊnd
underground, *adv.*	ˈʌndəˈgraʊnd	ˈʌndəˈgraʊnd
underlie	ˈʌndəˈlaɪ	ˈʌndəˈlaɪ
underlies	ˈʌndəˈlaɪz	ˈʌndəˈlaɪz
underlay	ˈʌndəˈleɪ	ˈʌndəˈleɪ
underlain	ˈʌndəˈleɪn	ˈʌndəˈleɪn
underlying	ˈʌndəˈlaɪɪŋ	ˈʌndəˈlaɪɪŋ
underline, *noun*	ˈʌndəlaɪn	ˈʌndəlaɪn
underlines	ˈʌndəlaɪnz	ˈʌndəlaɪnz
underline, *verb*	ˈʌndəˈlaɪn	ˈʌndəˈlaɪn
underlines	ˈʌndəˈlaɪnz	ˈʌndəˈlaɪnz
underlined	ˈʌndəˈlaɪnd	ˈʌndəˈlaɪnd
underlining	ˈʌndəˈlaɪnɪŋ	ˈʌndəˈlaɪnɪŋ
undermentioned	ˈʌndəˈmɛnʃənd	ˈʌndəˈmɛnʃənd
underneath	ˈʌndəˈniˑθ	ˈʌndəˈniˑθ
understand	ʌndəˈstænd	ʌndəˈstænd
understands	ʌndəˈstændz	ʌndəˈstændz
understood	ʌndəˈstʊd	ʌndəˈstʊd
understanding	ʌndəˈstændɪŋ	ʌndəˈstændɪŋ
understandable	ʌndəˈstændəbl̩	ʌndəˈstændəbl̩
undertake	ʌndəˈteɪk	ʌndəˈteɪk
undertakes	ʌndəˈteɪks	ʌndəˈteɪks
undertook	ʌndəˈtʊk	ʌndəˈtʊk
undertaken	ʌndəˈteɪkən	ʌndəˈteɪkən
undertaking	ʌndəˈteɪkɪŋ	ʌndəˈteɪkɪŋ
undertaking	ʌndəˈteɪkɪŋ	ʌndəˈteɪkɪŋ
undertakings	ʌndəˈteɪkɪŋz	ʌndəˈteɪkɪŋz
UNDERWENT *from* undergo	ˈʌndəˈwɛnt	ˈʌndəˈwɛnt
undeserved	ˈʌndɪˈzɜˑvd	ˈʌndɪˈzɜəvd
undeserving	ˈʌndɪˈzɜˑvɪŋ	ˈʌndɪˈzɜəvɪŋ
undesirability	ˈʌndɪzaɪərəˈbɪlɪtɪ	ˈʌndɪzaɪrəˈbɪlɪtɪ
undesirable	ˈʌndɪˈzaɪərəbl̩	ˈʌndɪˈzaɪrəbl̩
undeveloped	ˈʌndɪˈvɛləpt	
UNDID *from* undo	ˈʌnˈdɪd	
undigested	ˈʌndɪˈdʒɛstɪd	
	ˈʌndaɪˈdʒɛstɪd	
undignified	ˈʌnˈdɪgnɪfaɪd	
undiscovered	ˈʌndɪsˈkʌvəd	ˈʌndɪsˈkʌvəd

Traditional Spelling	Received Pronunciation	American Variants
undisturbed	ˈʌndɪsˈtɜˑbd	ˈʌndɪsˈtɜəbd
undo	ˈʌnˈduˑ	
undoes	ˈʌnˈdʌz	
undid	ˈʌnˈdɪd	
undone	ˈʌnˈdʌn	
undoing	ˈʌnˈduˑɪŋ	
undoubted	ʌnˈdaʊtɪd	
undoubtedly	ʌnˈdaʊtɪdlɪ	
undress	ˈʌnˈdrɛs	
undresses	ˈʌnˈdrɛsɪz	
undressed	ˈʌnˈdrɛst	
undressing	ˈʌnˈdrɛsɪŋ	
undue	ˈʌnˈdjuˑ	
unduly	ˈʌnˈdjuˑlɪ	
uneasiness	ˈʌnˈiˑzɪnɪs	
uneasy	ˈʌnˈiˑzɪ	
uneaten	ˈʌnˈiˑtn̩	
uneducated	ˈʌnˈɛdjʊkeɪtɪd ˈʌnˈɛdʒʊkeɪtɪd	
unemployed	ˈʌnɪmˈplɔɪd	
unemployment	ˈʌnɪmˈplɔɪmənt	
unending	ˈʌnˈɛndɪŋ	
unendurable	ˈʌnɪnˈdjʊərəbl̩ ˈʌnɪnˈdjɔərəbl̩	ˈʌnɪnˈdjʊˑrəbl̩
unequal	ˈʌnˈiˑkwəl	
unequally	ˈʌnˈiˑkwəlɪ	
uneven	ˈʌnˈiˑvn̩	
unevenly	ˈʌnˈiˑvn̩lɪ	
uneventful	ˈʌnɪˈvɛntfʊl	
unexpected	ˈʌnɪksˈpɛktɪd	
unexpectedly	ˈʌnɪksˈpɛktɪdlɪ	
unexplained	ˈʌnɪksˈpleɪnd	
unexplored	ˈʌnɪksˈplɔˑd ˈʌnɪksˈplɔəd	ˈʌnɪksˈploəd
unfailing	ʌnˈfeɪlɪŋ	
unfair	ˈʌnˈfɛə(r	ˈʌnˈfɛə
unfairly	ˈʌnˈfɛəlɪ	ˈʌnˈfɛəlɪ
unfairness	ˈʌnˈfɛənɪs	ˈʌnˈfɛənɪs
unfaithful	ˈʌnˈfeɪθfʊl	
unfaithfully	ˈʌnˈfeɪθfʊlɪ ˈʌnˈfeɪθfəlɪ	
unfamiliar	ˈʌnfəˈmɪljə(r	ˈʌnfəˈmɪljə
unfashionable	ˈʌnˈfæʃənəbl̩	
unfasten	ˈʌnˈfɑˑsn̩	ˈʌnˈfaˑsn̩
unfastens	ˈʌnˈfɑˑsn̩z	ˈʌnˈfaˑsn̩z
unfastened	ˈʌnˈfɑˑsn̩d	ˈʌnˈfaˑsn̩d
unfastening	ˈʌnˈfɑˑsnɪŋ	ˈʌnˈfaˑsnɪŋ

Traditional Spelling	Received Pronunciation	American Varian
unfinished	ˈʌnˈfɪnɪʃt	
unfit	ˈʌnˈfɪt	
unfix	ˈʌnˈfɪks	
unfixes	ˈʌnˈfɪksɪz	
unfixed	ˈʌnˈfɪkst	
unfixing	ˈʌnˈfɪksɪŋ	
unforeseen	ˈʌnfɔˈsi·n	ˈʌnfoəˈsi·n
unfortunate	ʌnˈfɔ·tʃənɪt	ʌnˈfɔətʃənɪt
unfortunately	ʌnˈfɔ·tʃənɪtlɪ	ʌnˈfɔətʃənɪtlɪ
unfriendly	ˈʌnˈfrɛndlɪ	
unfurnished	ˈʌnˈfɜ·nɪʃt	ˈʌnˈfɜənɪʃt
ungraceful	ˈʌnˈgreɪsful	
ungracefully	ˈʌnˈgreɪsfulɪ	
	ˈʌnˈgreɪsfəlɪ	
ungracious	ˈʌnˈgreɪʃəs	
ungraciously	ˈʌnˈgreɪʃəslɪ	
ungrammatical	ˈʌngrəˈmætɪkəl	
ungrammatically	ˈʌngrəˈmætɪkəlɪ	
ungrateful	ˈʌnˈgreɪtful	
ungratefully	ʌnˈgreɪtfulɪ	
	ʌnˈgreɪtfəlɪ	
unguarded	ˈʌnˈgɑ·dɪd	ˈʌnˈgɑədɪd
unhappily	ˈʌnˈhæpɪlɪ	
unhappiness	ˈʌnˈhæpɪnɪs	
unhappy	ˈʌnˈhæpɪ	
unhappier	ˈʌnˈhæpɪə(r	ˈʌnˈhæpɪə
unhappiest	ˈʌnˈhæpɪɪst	
unhealthy	ˈʌnˈhɛlθɪ	
unheard-of	ʌnˈhɜ·dɒv	ʌnˈhɜədɑv
unhesitating	ʌnˈhɛzɪteɪtɪŋ	
unhesitatingly	ʌnˈhɛzɪteɪtɪŋlɪ	
unhoped (*for*)	ʌnˈhoupt	
unhurt	ˈʌnˈhɜ·t	ˈʌnˈhɜət
unification	junɪfɪˈkeɪʃən	
unifications	junɪfɪˈkeɪʃənz	
uniform	ˈju·nɪfɔm	ˈju·nɪfɔəm
uniforms	ˈju·nɪfɔmz	ˈju·nɪfɔəmz
uniformly	ˈju·nɪfɔmlɪ	ˈju·nɪfɔəmlɪ
uniformity	junɪˈfɔ·mɪtɪ	junɪˈfɔəmɪtɪ
unify	ˈju·nɪfaɪ	
unifies	ˈju·nɪfaɪz	
unified	ˈju·nɪfaɪd	
unifying	ˈju·nɪfaɪɪŋ	
unimaginable	ˈʌnɪˈmæʤɪnəbl̩	
unimaginative	ˈʌnɪˈmæʤɪnətɪv	
uninfluenced	ˈʌnˈɪnfluənst	
uninhabitable	ˈʌnɪnˈhæbɪtəbl̩	

Traditional Spelling	Received Pronunciation	American Variants
uninhabited	ˈʌnɪnˈhæbɪtɪd	
uninjured	ˈʌnˈɪnʤəd	ˈʌnˈɪnʤəd
unintelligible	ˈʌnɪnˈtɛlɪʤɪbl̩	
unintentional	ˈʌnɪnˈtɛnʃənl̩	
unintentionally	ˈʌnɪnˈtɛnʃənəlɪ	
uninterested	ˈʌnˈɪntrɪstɪd	
uninteresting	ˈʌnˈɪntrɪstɪŋ	
uninterrupted	ˈʌnɪntəˈrʌptɪd	
uninvited	ˈʌnɪnˈvaɪtɪd	
union	ˈjuˑnjən	
unions	ˈjuˑnjənz	
unique	juˈniˑk	
uniquely	juˈniˑklɪ	
uniqueness	juˈniˑknɪs	
unit	ˈjuˑnɪt	
units	ˈjuˑnɪts	
unite	juˈnaɪt	
unites	juˈnaɪts	
united	juˈnaɪtɪd	
uniting	juˈnaɪtɪŋ	
unity	ˈjuˑnɪtɪ	
universal	junɪˈvɜˑsəl	junɪˈvɜəsəl
universally	junɪˈvɜˑsəlɪ	junɪˈvɜəsəlɪ
universe	ˈjuˑnɪvɜs	ˈjuˑnɪvɜəs
university	junɪˈvɜˑsɪtɪ	junɪˈvɜəsɪtɪ
universities	junɪˈvɜˑsɪtɪz	junɪˈvɜəsɪtɪz
unjust	ˈʌnˈʤʌst	
unjustifiable	ˈʌnˈʤʌstɪfaɪəbl̩ ˈʌnʤʌstɪˈfaɪəbl̩	
unjustly	ˈʌnˈʤʌstlɪ	
unjustness	ˈʌnˈʤʌstnɪs	
unkind	ˈʌnˈkaɪnd	
unkindly	ˈʌnˈkaɪndlɪ	
unkindness	ˈʌnˈkaɪndnɪs	
unknowingly	ˈʌnˈnoʊɪŋlɪ	
unknown	ˈʌnˈnoʊn	
unlawful	ˈʌnˈlɔˑful	
unlawfully	ˈʌnˈlɔˑfulɪ, ˈʌnˈlɔˑfəlɪ	
unless	ənˈlɛs, ʌnˈlɛs	
unlike	ˈʌnˈlaɪk	
unlikely	ˈʌnˈlaɪklɪ	
unlimited	ˈʌnˈlɪmɪtɪd	
unload	ˈʌnˈloʊd	
unloads	ˈʌnˈloʊdz	
unloaded	ˈʌnˈloʊdɪd	
unloading	ˈʌnˈloʊdɪŋ	
unlock	ˈʌnˈlɒk	ˈʌnˈlɑk

Traditional Spelling	Received Pronunciation	American Variants
unlocks	ʹʌnʹlɒks	ʹʌnʹlɑks
unlocked	ʹʌnʹlɒkt	ʹʌnʹlɑkt
unlocking	ʹʌnʹlɒkɪŋ	ʹʌnʹlɑkɪŋ
unlucky	ʹʌnʹlʌkɪ	
unluckier	ʹʌnʹlʌkɪə(r	ʹʌnʹlʌkɪə
unluckiest	ʹʌnʹlʌkɪɪst	
unluckily	ʹʌnʹlʌkɪlɪ	
unmanageable	ʹʌnʹmænɪʤəbl̩	
unmarried	ʹʌnʹmærɪd	
unmerciful	ʌnʹmɜːsɪfʊl	ʌnʹmɜəsɪfʊl
unmercifully	ʌnʹmɜːsɪfʊlɪ ʌnʹmɜːsɪfəlɪ	ʌnʹmɜəsɪfʊlɪ ʌnʹmɜəsɪfəlɪ
unmethodical	ʹʌnmɪʹθɒdɪkəl	ʹʌnmɪʹθɑdɪkəl
unmindful	ʌnʹmaɪndfʊl	
unmistakable	ʹʌnmɪsʹteɪkəbl̩	
unmistakably	ʹʌnmɪsʹteɪkəblɪ	
unmixed	ʹʌnʹmɪkst	
unmodified	ʹʌnʹmɒdɪfaɪd	ʹʌnʹmɑdɪfaɪd
unmov(e)able	ʹʌnʹmuːvəbl̩	
unmusical	ʹʌnʹmjuːzɪkəl	
unnatural	ʹʌnʹnætʃərəl ʹʌnʹnætʃʊrəl	
unnaturally	ʹʌnʹnætʃərəlɪ ʹʌnʹnætʃʊrəlɪ	
unnecessarily	ʹʌnʹnɛsɪsərɪlɪ	ʹʌnʹnɛsɪsɛrɪlɪ
unnecessary	ʹʌnʹnɛsɪsərɪ	ʹʌnʹnɛsɪsɛrɪ
unnoticed	ʹʌnʹnoʊtɪst	
unobjectionable	ʹʌnəbʹʤɛkʃnəbl̩	
unobserved	ʹʌnəbʹzɜːvd	ʹʌnəbʹzɜəvd
unoccupied	ʹʌnʹɒkjʊpaɪd	ʹʌnʹɑkjʊpaɪd
unofficial	ʹʌnəʹfɪʃəl	
unopened	ʹʌnʹoʊpənd	
unopposed	ʹʌnəʹpoʊzd	
unorganized	ʹʌnʹɔːgənaɪzd	ʹʌnʹɔəgənaɪzd
unpack	ʹʌnʹpæk	
unpacks	ʹʌnʹpæks	
unpacked	ʹʌnʹpækt	
unpacking	ʹʌnʹpækɪŋ	
unpaid	ʹʌnʹpeɪd	
unpardonable	ʹʌnʹpɑːdnəbl̩	ʹʌnʹpɑədnəbl̩
unpatriotic	ʹʌnpætrɪʹɒtɪk ʹʌnpeɪtrɪʹɒtɪk	ʹʌnpætrɪʹɑtɪk ʹʌnpeɪtrɪʹɑtɪk
unpleasant	ʹʌnʹplɛzn̩t	
unpleasantly	ʌnʹplɛzn̩tlɪ	
unpleasantness	ʌnʹplɛzn̩tnɪs	
unpopular	ʹʌnʹpɒpjʊlə(r	ʹʌnʹpɑpjʊlə
unpopularity	ʹʌnpɒpjʊʹlærɪtɪ	ʹʌnpɑpjʊʹlærɪtɪ

Traditional Spelling	Received Pronunciation	American Variants
unpractical	ˈʌnˈpræktɪkəl	
unprejudiced	ˈʌnˈprɛʤʊdɪst	
unprepared	ˈʌnprɪˈpɛəd	ˈʌnprɪˈpɛəd
unproductive	†ˈʌnprəˈdʌktɪv	
unprofitable	ˈʌnˈprɒfɪtəbl̩	ˈʌnˈprɑfɪtəbl̩
unprovided (*for*)	†ˈʌnprəˈvaɪdɪd	
unpublished	ˈʌnˈpʌblɪʃt	
unpunctual	ˈʌnˈpʌŋktjʊəl	
unpunished	ˈʌnˈpʌnɪʃt	
unqualified	ʌnˈkwɒlɪfaɪd	ʌnˈkwɑlɪfaɪd
unreadable	ˈʌnˈriˑdəbl̩	
unreal	ˈʌnˈriˑəl, ˈʌnˈrɪəl	
unreasonable	ˈʌnˈriˑznəbl̩ ˈʌnˈriˑzn̩əbl̩	
unreasoning	ˈʌnˈriˑzn̩ɪŋ ˈʌnˈriˑznɪŋ	
unrecognizable	ˈʌnˈrɛkəgnaɪzəbl̩	
unrecorded	ˈʌnrɪˈkɔˑdɪd	ˈʌnrɪˈkɔədɪd
unrelated	ˈʌnrɪˈleɪtɪd	
unreliable	ˈʌnrɪˈlaɪəbl̩	
unresisting	ˈʌnrɪˈzɪstɪŋ	
unrestricted	ˈʌnrɪˈstrɪktɪd	
unrewarded	ˈʌnrɪˈwɔˑdɪd	ˈʌnrɪˈwɔədɪd
unripe	ˈʌnˈraɪp	
unroll	ˈʌnˈroʊl	
unrolls	ˈʌnˈroʊlz	
unrolled	ˈʌnˈroʊld	
unrolling	ˈʌnˈroʊlɪŋ	
unsafe	ˈʌnˈseɪf	
unsaid	ˈʌnˈsɛd	
unsanitary	ˈʌnˈsænɪtərɪ	ˈʌnˈsænɪtɛrɪ
unsatisfactorily	ˈʌnsætɪsˈfæktərɪlɪ	
unsatisfactory	ˈʌnsætɪsˈfæktərɪ	
unsatisfied	ˈʌnˈsætɪsfaɪd	
unscrew	ˈʌnˈskruˑ	
unscrews	ˈʌnˈskruˑz	
unscrewed	ˈʌnˈskruˑd	
unscrewing	ˈʌnˈskruˑɪŋ	
unscrupulous	ˈʌnˈskruˑpjʊləs ˈʌnˈskruˑpjələs	
unseasonable	ˈʌnˈsiˑznəbl̩ ˈʌnˈsiˑzn̩əbl̩	
unseaworthy	ˈʌnˈsiˑwɜðɪ	ˈʌnˈsiˑwɜəðɪ
unsecured	ˈʌnsɪˈkjʊəd ˈʌnsɪˈkjɔəd	ˈʌnsɪˈkjʊəd

† See Note 30, p. xxxv in Introduction.

Traditional Spelling	Received Pronunciation	American Variants
unseen	'ʌn'siˑn	
unselfish	'ʌn'sɛlfɪʃ	
unselfishly	'ʌn'sɛlfɪʃlɪ	
unselfishness	'ʌn'sɛlfɪʃnɪs	
unsettle	'ʌn'sɛtl̩	
unsettles	'ʌn'sɛtl̩z	
unsettled	'ʌn'sɛtl̩d	
unsettling	'ʌn'sɛtl̩ɪŋ 'ʌn'sɛtlɪŋ	
unshaken	'ʌn'ʃeɪkən	
unsightly	ʌn'saɪtlɪ	
unskilful	'ʌn'skɪlfʊl	
unskilfully	'ʌn'skɪlfʊlɪ 'ʌn'skɪlfəlɪ	
unskilled	'ʌn'skɪld	
unsold	'ʌn'soʊld	
unsolicited	†'ʌnsə'lɪsɪtɪd	
unsound	'ʌn'saʊnd	
unspecified	'ʌn'spɛsɪfaɪd	
unspoiled	'ʌn'spɔɪld, 'ʌn'spɔɪlt	
unspoilt	'ʌn'spɔɪlt	
unspoken	'ʌn'spoʊkən	
unstable	'ʌn'steɪbl̩	
unstamped	'ʌn'stæm*p*t	
unsteadily	'ʌn'stɛdɪlɪ	
unsteadiness	'ʌn'stɛdɪnɪs	
unsteady	'ʌn'stɛdɪ	
unstressed	'ʌn'strɛst	
unsubstantial	'ʌnsəb'stænʃəl	
unsuccessful	'ʌnsək'sɛsfʊl	
unsuccessfully	'ʌnsək'sɛsfʊlɪ 'ʌnsək'sɛsfəlɪ	
unsuitable	'ʌn'sjuˑtəbl̩	
unsuitably	'ʌn'sjuˑtəblɪ	
unsuited	'ʌn'sjuˑtɪd	
unsupported	'ʌnsə'pɔˑtɪd	'ʌnsə'poətɪd
unsuspected	'ʌnsəs'pɛktɪd	
unsuspecting	'ʌnsəs'pɛktɪŋ	
unsuspicious	'ʌnsəs'pɪʃəs	
unsympathetic	'ʌnsɪmpə'θɛtɪk	
unsympathetically	'ʌnsɪmpə'θɛtɪkəlɪ	
unsystematic	'ʌnsɪstɪ'mætɪk	
unsystematically	'ʌnsɪstɪ'mætɪkəlɪ	
untasted	'ʌn'teɪstɪd	
untaught	'ʌn'tɔˑt	

† See Note 30, p. xxxv in Introduction.

Traditional Spelling	Received Pronunciation	American Variants
unthankful	ˈʌnˈθæŋkful	
unthinkable	ʌnˈθɪŋkəbl̩	
unthinking	ˈʌnˈθɪŋkɪŋ	
unthinkingly	ˈʌnˈθɪŋkɪŋlɪ	
untidily	ˈʌnˈtaɪdɪlɪ	
untidy	ˈʌnˈtaɪdɪ	
untidier	ˈʌnˈtaɪdɪə(r	ˈʌnˈtaɪdɪə
untidiest	ˈʌnˈtaɪdɪɪst	
untie	ʌnˈtaɪ	
unties	ʌnˈtaɪz	
untied	ʌnˈtaɪd	
untying	ʌnˈtaɪɪŋ	
until	ənˈtɪl, ʌnˈtɪl	
untouched	ˈʌnˈtʌtʃt	
untrained	ˈʌnˈtreɪnd	
untried	ˈʌnˈtraɪd	
untrodden	ˈʌnˈtrɒdn̩	ˈʌnˈtrɑdn̩
untrue	ˈʌnˈtru·	
untrustworthiness	ˈʌnˈtrʌstwɜðɪnɪs	ˈʌnˈtrʌstwɜəðɪnɪs
untrustworthy	ˈʌnˈtrʌstwɜðɪ	ˈʌnˈtrʌstwɜəðɪ
untruth	ˈʌnˈtru·θ	
untruths	ˈʌnˈtru·ðz ˈʌnˈtru·θs	
untruthful	ˈʌnˈtru·θful	
untruthfully	ˈʌnˈtru·θfulɪ ˈʌnˈtru·θfəlɪ	
unused, *not made use of*	ˈʌnˈju·zd	
unused, *not accustomed*	ˈʌnˈju·st	
unusual	ˈʌnˈju·ʒuəl ˈʌnˈju·ʒəl	
unusually	ˈʌnˈju·ʒuəlɪ ˈʌnˈju·ʒəlɪ	
unwanted	ˈʌnˈwɒntɪd	
unwarranted	ʌnˈwɒrəntɪd	
unwelcome	ˈʌnˈwɛlkəm	
unwholesome	ˈʌnˈhoulsəm	
unwilling	ˈʌnˈwɪlɪŋ	
unwillingly	ˈʌnˈwɪlɪŋlɪ	
unwillingness	ˈʌnˈwɪlɪŋnɪs	
unwise	ˈʌnˈwaɪz	
unwisely	ˈʌnˈwaɪzlɪ	
unworkable	ˈʌnˈwɜ·kəbl̩	ˈʌnˈwɜəkəbl̩
unworthily	ˈʌnˈwɜ·ðɪlɪ	ˈʌnˈwɜəðɪlɪ
unworthy	ˈʌnˈwɜ·ðɪ	ˈʌnˈwɜəðɪ
unwrap	ˈʌnˈræp	
unwraps	ˈʌnˈræps	

Traditional Spelling	Received Pronunciation	American Variants
unwrapped	ˈʌnˈræpt	
unwrapping	ˈʌnˈræpɪŋ	
unwritten	ˈʌnˈrɪtn̩	
up	ʌp	
upbringing	ˈʌpbrɪŋɪŋ	
upheaval	ʌpˈhiˑvəl	
uphill	ˈʌpˈhɪl	
uphold	ʌpˈhoʊld	
upholds	ʌpˈhoʊldz	
upheld	ʌpˈhɛld	
upholding	ʌpˈhoʊldɪŋ	
upon	əˈpɒn	əˈpɑn
upper	ˈʌpə(r	ˈʌpə
uppermost	ˈʌpəmoʊst, ˈʌpəməst	ˈʌpəmoʊst
upright, *noun*	ˈʌpraɪt	
uprights	ˈʌpraɪts	
upright, *adj.*	ˈʌpraɪt, ˈʌpˈraɪt	
uproar	ˈʌprɔ(r, ˈʌprɔə(r	ˈʌproə
upset	ʌpˈsɛt	
upsets	ʌpˈsɛts	
upsetting	ʌpˈsɛtɪŋ	
upstairs	ˈʌpˈstɛəz	ˈʌpˈstɛəz
upward	ˈʌpwəd	ˈʌpwəd
upwards	ˈʌpwədz	ˈʌpwədz
urge	ɜˑʤ	ɜəʤ
urges	ˈɜˑʤɪz	ˈɜəʤɪz
urged	ɜˑʤd	ɜəʤd
urging	ˈɜˑʤɪŋ	ˈɜəʤɪŋ
urgent	ˈɜˑʤənt	ˈɜəʤənt
urgently	ˈɜˑʤəntlɪ	ˈɜəʤəntlɪ
Uruguay	ˈjuˑrugweɪ, ˈjuˑrəgweɪ juˑrugwaɪ, juˑrəgwaɪ	
us	ʌs *s.f.*, əs *w.f.*	
usable	ˈjuˑzəbl̩	
usage	ˈjuˑzɪʤ	
usages	ˈjuˑzɪʤɪz	
use, *noun*	juˑs	
use, *verb*	juˑz	
uses	ˈjuˑzɪz	
used	juˑzd	
using	ˈjuˑzɪŋ	
used, *adj. made use of*	juˑzd	
used, *adj. accustomed*	juˑst	
use(d)n't	ˈjuˑsn*t*	
useful	ˈjuˑsful	
usefully	ˈjuˑsfulɪ, ˈjuˑsfəlɪ	
usefulness	ˈjuˑsfulnɪs	

Traditional Spelling	Received Pronunciation	American Variants
useless	'ju·slɪs	
uselessly	'ju·slɪslɪ	
uselessness	'ju·slɪsnɪs	
USEN'T	'ju·sn*t*	
user	'ju·zə(r	'ju·zə
users	'ju·zəz	'ju·zəz
USES, *plur. of* use	'ju·sɪz	
USES *from verb* use	'ju·zɪz	
usual	'ju·ʒʊəl, 'ju·ʒəl	
usually	'ju·ʒʊəlɪ, 'ju·ʒəlɪ	
usurp	ju'zɜ·p	ju'sɜəp
usurps	ju'zɜ·ps	ju'zɜəps
usurped	ju'zɜ·pt	ju'zɜəpt
usurping	ju'zɜ·pɪŋ	ju'zɜəpɪŋ
usurper	ju'zɜ·pə(r	ju'zɜəpə
usurpers	ju'zɜ·pəz	ju'zɜəpəz
utensil	ju'tɛnsɪl, ju'tɛnsɪl	
utensils	ju'tɛnsɪlz ju'tɛnsɪlz	
utilitarian	jutɪlɪ'tɛərɪən	jutɪlɪ'tɛ·rɪən
utility	ju'tɪlɪtɪ, ju'tɪlɪtɪ	
utilization	jutɪlaɪ'zeɪʃən	
utilize	'ju·tɪlaɪz	
utilizes	'ju·tɪlaɪzɪz	
utilized	'ju·tɪlaɪzd	
utilizing	'ju·tɪlaɪzɪŋ	
utmost	'ʌtmoust, 'ʌtməst	
utter	'ʌtə(r	'ʌtə
utters	'ʌtəz	'ʌtəz
uttered	'ʌtəd	'ʌtəd
uttering	'ʌtərɪŋ	
utterly	'ʌtəlɪ	'ʌtəlɪ
uttermost	'ʌtəmoust, 'ʌtəməst	'ʌtəmoust, 'ʌtəməst

V

Traditional Spelling	Received Pronunciation	American Variants
V	vi·	
V's	vi·z	
vacancy	'veɪkənsɪ	
vacancies	'veɪkənsɪz	
vacant	'veɪkənt	
vacation	və'keɪʃən	veɪ'keɪʃən
vaccinate	'væksɪneɪt	
vaccinates	'væksɪneɪts	
vaccinated	'væksɪneɪtɪd	
vaccinating	'væksɪneɪtɪŋ	

Traditional Spelling	Received Pronunciation	American Variants
vaccination	væksɪ'neɪʃən	
vacuum	'vækjʊəm	
vacua	'vækjʊə	
vacuums	'vækjʊəmz	
vague	veɪg	
vaguer	'veɪgə(r	'veɪgə
vaguest	'veɪgɪst	
vaguely	'veɪglɪ	
vagueness	'veɪgnɪs	
vain	veɪn	
vainer	'veɪnə(r	'veɪnə
vainest	'veɪnɪst	
vainly	'veɪnlɪ	
valid	'vælɪd	
validity	və'lɪdɪtɪ, væ'lɪdɪtɪ	
valley	'vælɪ	
valleys	'vælɪz	
valour	'vælə(r	'vælə
valuable	'væljʊəbl̩	
valuables	'væljʊəbl̩z	
value	'vælju, 'væljʊ	
values	'væljuz, 'væljʊz	
valued	'væljud, 'væljʊd	
valuing	'væljʊɪŋ	
valve	vælv	
valves	vælvz	
van	væn	
vans	vænz	
Vancouver	væn'kuˑvə(r	væn'kuˑvə
vanish	'vænɪʃ	
vanishes	'vænɪʃɪz	
vanished	'vænɪʃt	
vanishing	'vænɪʃɪŋ	
vanity	'vænɪtɪ	
vapour	'veɪpə(r	'veɪpə
vapours	'veɪpəz	'veɪpəz
variable	'vɛərɪəbl̩	'vɛˑrɪəbl̩
variably	'vɛərɪəblɪ	'vɛˑrɪəblɪ
variation	vɛərɪ'eɪʃən	vɛˑrɪ'eɪʃən
variations	vɛərɪ'eɪʃənz	vɛˑrɪ'eɪʃənz
varied	'vɛərɪd	'vɛˑrɪd
variety	və'raɪətɪ	
varieties	və'raɪətɪz	
various	'vɛərɪəs	'vɛˑrɪəs
variously	'vɛərɪəslɪ	'vɛˑrɪəslɪ
varnish	'vɑˑnɪʃ	'vɑənɪʃ
vary	'vɛərɪ	'vɛˑrɪ

Traditional Spelling	Received Pronunciation	American Variants
varies	ˈvɛərɪz	ˈvɛ·rɪz
varied	ˈvɛərɪd	ˈvɛ·rɪd
varying	ˈvɛərɪɪŋ	ˈvɛ·rɪɪŋ
vase	vɑ·z	veɪs
vases	ˈvɑ·zɪz	ˈveɪsɪz
vast	vɑ·st	va·st
vastly	ˈvɑ·stlɪ	ˈva·stlɪ
vault	vɔ·lt, vɒlt	
vaults	vɔ·lts, vɒlts	
veal	vi·l	
vegetable	ˈvɛʤɪtəbl̩	
vegetables	ˈvɛʤɪtəbl̩z	
vehicle	ˈvi·ɪkl̩, ˈvi·əkl̩	
vehicles	ˈvi·ɪkl̩z, ˈvi·əkl̩z	
veil	veɪl	
veils	veɪlz	
vein	veɪn	
veins	veɪnz	
velvet	ˈvɛlvɪt	
Venezuela	vɛnɪˈzwi·lə vɛnɪzjuˈi·lə vɛnɛˈzweɪlə	
vengeance	ˈvɛnʤəns	
Venice	ˈvɛnɪs	
ventilate	ˈvɛntɪleɪt	
ventilates	ˈvɛntɪleɪts	
ventilated	ˈvɛntɪleɪtɪd	
ventilating	ˈvɛntɪleɪtɪŋ	
ventilation	vɛntɪˈleɪʃən	
ventilator	ˈvɛntɪleɪtə(r	ˈvɛntɪleɪtə
ventilators	ˈvɛntɪleɪtəz	ˈvɛntɪleɪtəz
venture	ˈvɛntʃə(r	ˈvɛntʃə
ventures	ˈvɛntʃəz	ˈvɛntʃəz
ventured	ˈvɛntʃəd	ˈvɛntʃəd
venturing	ˈvɛntʃərɪŋ	
verb	vɜ·b	vɜəb
verbs	vɜ·bz	vɜəbz
verbal	ˈvɜ·bəl	ˈvɜəbəl
verbally	ˈvɜ·bəlɪ	ˈvɜəbəlɪ
verdict	ˈvɜ·dɪkt	ˈvɜədɪkt
verdicts	ˈvɜ·dɪkts	ˈvɜədɪkts
verge	vɜ·ʤ	vɜəʤ
verify	ˈvɛrɪfaɪ	
varifies	ˈvɛrɪfaɪz	
verified	ˈvɛrɪfaɪd	
verifying	ˈvɛrɪfaɪɪŋ	
Versailles	vɛəˈsaɪ	vɛəˈsaɪ, vəˈseɪlz

Traditional Spelling	Received Pronunciation	American Variants
verse	vɜ·s	vɜəs
verses	′vɜ·sɪz	′vɜəsɪz
version	′vɜ·ʃən	′vɜəʃən
versions	′vɜ·ʃənz	′vɜəʃənz
versus	′vɜ·səs	′vɜəsəs
very	′verɪ	
vessel	′vesl̩	
vessels	′vesl̩z	
vex	veks	
vexes	′veksɪz	
vexed	vekst	
vexing	′veksɪŋ	
via	′vaɪə	
vibrate	vaɪ′breɪt	
vibrates	vaɪ′breɪts	
vibrated	vaɪ′breɪtɪd	
vibrating	vaɪ′breɪtɪŋ	
vibration	vaɪ′breɪʃən	
vibrations	vaɪ′breɪʃənz	
vicar	′vɪkə(r	′vɪkə
vicars	′vɪkəz	′vɪkəz
vice, *noun*	vaɪs	
vices	′vaɪsɪz	
vice-, *prefix*	′vaɪs-	
vice versa	′vaɪsɪ′vɜ·sə	′vaɪsɪ′vɜəsə
vicious	′vɪʃəs	
viciously	′vɪʃəslɪ	
victim	′vɪktɪm	
victims	′vɪktɪmz	
victorious	vɪk′tɔ·rɪəs	
victoriously	vɪk′tɔ·rɪəslɪ	
victory	′vɪktərɪ	
victories	′vɪktərɪz	
vie	vaɪ	
vies	vaɪz	
vied	vaɪd	
vying	′vaɪɪŋ	
Vienna	vɪ′enə	
Viennese	vɪə′ni·z, vɪe′ni·z	
view	vju·	
views	vju·z	
viewed	vju·d	
viewing	′vjuɪŋ	
vigor (*Amer.*)	′vɪgə(r	′vɪgə
vigorous	′vɪgərəs	
vigorously	′vɪgərəslɪ	
vigour	′vɪgə(r	′vɪgə

Traditional Spelling	Received Pronunciation	American Variants
vile	vaɪl	
village	ˈvɪlɪʤ	
villages	ˈvɪlɪʤɪz	
vindictive	vɪnˈdɪktɪv	
vindictively	vɪnˈdɪktɪvlɪ	
vinegar	ˈvɪnɪgə(r	ˈvɪnɪgə
vineyard	ˈvɪnjəd, ˈvɪnjɑd	ˈvɪnjəd, ˈvɪnjɑəd
vineyards	ˈvɪnjədz, ˈvɪnjɑdz	ˈvɪnjədz, ˈvɪnjɑədz
violate	†ˈvaɪəleɪt	
violates	†ˈvaɪəleɪts	
violated	†ˈvaɪəleɪtɪd	
violating	†ˈvaɪəleɪtɪŋ	
violation	†vaɪəˈleɪʃən	
violations	†vaɪəˈleɪʃənz	
violence	†ˈvaɪələns	
violent	†ˈvaɪələnt	
violently	†ˈvaɪələntlɪ	
violet	†ˈvaɪəlɪt	
violets	†ˈvaɪəlɪts	
violin	†vaɪəˈlɪn	
violins	†vaɪəˈlɪnz	
violinist	†vaɪəˈlɪnɪst	
violinists	†vaɪəˈlɪnɪsts	
virgin	ˈvɜ·ʤɪn	ˈvɜəʤɪn
virgins	ˈvɜ·ʤɪnz	ˈvɜəʤɪnz
virtue	ˈvɜ·tju	ˈvɜətju
virtues	ˈvɜ·tjuz	ˈvɜətjuz
virtuous	ˈvɜ·tjʊəs	ˈvɜətjʊəs
viscount	ˈvaɪkaʊnt	
viscounts	ˈvaɪkaʊnts	
visible	ˈvɪzɪbl̩	
visibly	ˈvɪzɪblɪ	
vision	ˈvɪʒən	
visions	ˈvɪʒənz	
visit	ˈvɪzɪt	
visits	ˈvɪzɪts	
visited	ˈvɪzɪtɪd	
visiting	ˈvɪzɪtɪŋ	
visitor	ˈvɪzɪtə(r	ˈvɪzɪtə
visitors	ˈvɪzɪtəz	ˈvɪzɪtəz
visual	ˈvɪʒjʊəl, ˈvɪzjʊəl	
visually	ˈvɪʒjʊəlɪ, ˈvɪzjʊəlɪ	
vital	ˈvaɪtl̩	
vitally	ˈvaɪtəlɪ	
vitality	vaɪˈtælɪtɪ	

† See Note 30, p. xxxv in Introduction.

Traditional Spelling	Received Pronunciation	American Variants
vivacious	vaɪ'veɪʃəs, vɪ'veɪʃəs	
vivacity	vaɪ'væsɪtɪ, vɪ'væsɪtɪ	
vivid	'vɪvɪd	
vividly	'vɪvɪdlɪ	
viz.‡	vɪ'diˑlɪsɛt, vaɪ'diˑlɪsɛt	
vocabulary	†və'kæbjulərɪ	†və'kæbjulɛrɪ
vocabularies	†və'kæbjulərɪz	†və'kæbjulɛrɪz
vocal	'voukəl	
vocation	vou'keɪʃən, və'keɪʃən	
vocations	vou'keɪʃənz və'keɪʃənz	
vogue	voug	
voice	vɔɪs	
voices	'vɔɪsɪz	
volcanic	vɒl'kænɪk	vɑl'kænɪk
volcano	vɒl'keɪnou	vɑl'keɪnou
volcano(e)s	vɒl'keɪnouz	vɑl'keɪnouz
volition	†vəu'lɪʃən	
volley	'vɒlɪ	'vɑlɪ
volleys	'vɒlɪz	'vɑlɪz
volleyed	'vɒlɪd	'vɑlɪd
volleying	'vɒlɪɪŋ	'vɑlɪɪŋ
volt	voult, vɒlt	
volts	voults, vɒlts	
volume	'vɒljum, 'vɒljəm	'vɑljum, 'vɑljəm
volumes	'vɒljumz, 'vɒljəmz	'vɑljumz, 'vɑljəmz
voluminous	və'ljuˑmɪnəs vɒ'ljuˑmɪnəs	 vɑ'ljuˑmɪnəs
voluntarily	'vɒləntərɪlɪ	'vɑləntɛrɪlɪ
voluntary	'vɒləntərɪ	'vɑləntɛrɪ
volunteer	vɒlən'tɪə(r	vɑlən'tɪə
volunteers	vɒlən'tɪəz	vɑlən'tɪəz
volunteered	vɒlən'tɪəd	vɑlən'tɪəd
volunteering	vɒlən'tɪərɪŋ	vɑlən'tɪˑrɪŋ
vote	vout	
votes	vouts	
voted	'voutɪd	
voting	'voutɪŋ	
voter	'voutə(r	'voutə
voters	'voutəz	'voutəz
vowel	'vauəl, 'vauɛl, 'vauɪl	
vowels	'vauəlz, 'vauɛlz 'vauɪlz	

† See Note 30, p. xxxv in Introduction.

‡ Most persons in reading substitute *namely* ['neɪmlɪ] for this word. It should never be read as [vɪz].

Traditional Spelling	Received Pronunciation	American Variants
voyage	ˈvɔɪɪʤ	
voyages	ˈvɔɪɪʤɪz	
vulgar	ˈvʌlgə(r	ˈvʌlgə
vulgarity	vʌlˈgærɪtɪ	
vulgarly	ˈvʌlgəlɪ	ˈvʌlgəlɪ
VYING *from* vie	ˈvaɪɪŋ	

W

Traditional Spelling	Received Pronunciation	American Variants
W	ˈdʌblju	
W's	ˈdʌbljuz	
wade	weɪd	
wades	weɪdz	
waded	ˈweɪdɪd	
wading	ˈweɪdɪŋ	
wag	wæg	
wags	wægz	
wagged	wægd	
wagging	ˈwægɪŋ	
wage	weɪʤ	
wages	ˈweɪʤɪz	
waged	weɪʤd	
waging	ˈweɪʤɪŋ	
wager	ˈweɪʤə(r	ˈweɪʤə
wagers	ˈweɪʤəz	ˈweɪʤəz
waggon	ˈwægən	
waggons	ˈwægənz	
wagon	ˈwægən	
wagons	ˈwægənz	
waist	weɪst	
waists	weɪsts	
waistcoat	ˈwɛskət, ˈweɪs*t*kout	
waistcoats	ˈwɛskəts ˈweɪs*t*kouts	
wait	weɪt	
waits	weɪts	
waited	ˈweɪtɪd	
waiting	ˈweɪtɪŋ	
waiter	ˈweɪtə(r	ˈweɪtə
waiters	ˈweɪtəz	ˈweɪtəz
waitress	ˈweɪtrɪs	
waitresses	ˈweɪtrɪsɪz	
wake	weɪk	
wakes	weɪks	
waked	weɪkt	
woke	wouk	

Traditional Spelling	Received Pronunciation	American Variants
waking	'weɪkɪŋ	
waken	'weɪkən	
wakens	'weɪkənz	
wakened	'weɪkənd	
wakening	'weɪkənɪŋ	
Wales	weɪlz	
walk	wɔ·k	
walks	wɔ·ks	
walked	wɔ·kt	
walking	'wɔ·kɪŋ	
walker	'wɔ·kə(r	'wɔ·kə
walkers	'wɔ·kəz	'wɔ·kəz
wall	wɔ·l	
walls	wɔ·lz	
walnut	'wɔ·lnʌt, 'wɔ·lnət	
walnuts	'wɔ·lnʌts	
	'wɔ·lnəts	
Walter	'wɔ·ltə(r, 'wɒltə(r	'wɔ·ltə, 'wɑltə
wander	'wɒndə(r	'wɑndə
wanders	'wɒndəz	'wɑndəz
wandered	'wɒndəd	'wɑndəd
wandering	'wɒndərɪŋ	'wɑndərɪŋ
wanderer	'wɒndərə(r	'wɑndərə
wanderers	'wɒndərəz	'wɑndərəz
want	wɒnt	wɑnt
wants	wɒnts	wɑnts
wanted	'wɒntɪd	'wɑntɪd
wanting	'wɒntɪŋ	'wɑntɪŋ
war	wɔ·(r, wɔə(r	wɔə
wars	wɔ·z, wɔəz	wɔəz
wardrobe	'wɔ·droʊb	'wɔədroʊb
wardrobes	'wɔ·droʊbz	'wɔədroʊbz
warehouse	'wɛəhaʊs	'wɛəhaʊs
warehouses	'wɛəhaʊzɪz	'wɛəhaʊzɪz
warm	wɔ·m	wɔəm
warmer	'wɔ·mə(r	'wɔəmə
warmest	'wɔ·mɪst	'wɔəmɪst
warmly	'wɔ·mlɪ	'wɔəmlɪ
warmness	'wɔ·mnɪs	'wɔəmnɪs
warmth	wɔ·m*p*θ	'wɔəm*p*θ
warn	wɔ·n	wɔən
warns	wɔ·nz	wɔənz
warned	wɔ·nd	wɔənd
warning	'wɔ·nɪŋ	'wɔənɪŋ
warnings	'wɔ·nɪŋz	'wɔənɪŋz
warningly	'wɔ·nɪŋlɪ	'wɔənɪŋlɪ
warrant	'wɒrənt	'wɑrənt

Traditional Spelling	Received Pronunciation	American Variants
warrants	'wɒrənts	'wɑrənts
warranted	'wɒrəntɪd	'wɑrəntɪd
warranting	'wɒrəntɪŋ	'wɑrəntɪŋ
Warsaw	'wɔˑsɔ	'wɔəsɔ
WAS *from* be	wɒz *s.f.*, wəz *w.f.*	wɑz
wash	wɒʃ	wɑʃ
washes	'wɒʃɪz	'wɑʃɪz
washed	wɒʃt	wɑʃt
washing	'wɒʃɪŋ	'wɑʃɪŋ
Washington	'wɒʃɪŋtən	'wɑʃɪŋtən
wasp	wɒsp	wɑsp
wasps	wɒsps	wɑsps
waste	weɪst	
wastes	weɪsts	
wasted	'weɪstɪd	
wasting	'weɪstɪŋ	
wasteful	'weɪstfʊl	
wastefully	'weɪstfʊlɪ, 'weɪstfəlɪ	
watch	wɒtʃ	wɑtʃ
watches	'wɒtʃɪz	'wɑtʃɪz
watched	wɒtʃt	wɑtʃt
watching	'wɒtʃɪŋ	'wɑtʃɪŋ
watchful	'wɒtʃfʊl	'wɑtʃfʊl
water	'wɔˑtə(r	'wɔˑtə
waters	'wɔˑtəz	'wɔˑtəz
watered	'wɔˑtəd	'wɔˑtəd
watering	'wɔˑtərɪŋ	
waterproof	'wɔˑtəpruf	'wɔˑtəpruf
waterproofs	'wɔˑtəprufs	'wɔˑtəprufs
wave	weɪv	
waves	weɪvz	
waved	weɪvd	
waving	'weɪvɪŋ	
wavy	'weɪvɪ	
wax	wæks	
way	weɪ	
ways	weɪz	
waylay	weɪ'leɪ	
waylays	weɪ'leɪz	
waylaid	weɪ'leɪd	
waylaying	weɪ'leɪɪŋ	
we	wiˑ, *normal form*	
	wi, wɪ *w.fs.*	
weak	wiˑk	
weaker	'wiˑkə(r	'wiˑkə
weakest	'wiˑkɪst	
weaken	'wiˑkən	

Traditional Spelling	Received Pronunciation	American Variants
weakens	ˈwiˑkənz	
weakened	ˈwiˑkənd	
weakening	ˈwiˑkənɪŋ	
weakly	ˈwiˑklɪ	
wealth	wɛlθ	
wealthy	ˈwɛlθɪ	
wealthier	ˈwɛlθɪə(r	ˈwɛlθɪə
wealthiest	ˈwɛlθɪɪst	
weapon	ˈwɛpən	
weapons	ˈwɛpənz	
wear	wɛə(r	wɛə
wears	wɛəz	wɛəz
wore	wɔˑ(r, wɔə(r	woə
worn	wɔˑn	woən
wearing	ˈwɛərɪŋ	ˈwɛˑrɪŋ
wearer	ˈwɛərə(r	ˈwɛˑrə
wearers	ˈwɛərəz	ˈwɛˑrəz
weather	ˈwɛðə(r	ˈwɛðə
weathers	ˈwɛðəz	ˈwɛðəz
weave	wiˑv	
weaves	wiˑvz	
wove	woʊv	
woven	ˈwoʊvən	
weaving	ˈwiˑvɪŋ	
weaver	ˈwiˑvə(r	ˈwiˑvə
weavers	ˈwiˑvəz	ˈwiˑvəz
wedding	ˈwɛdɪŋ	
weddings	ˈwɛdɪŋz	
wedge	wɛʤ	
wedges	ˈwɛʤɪz	
wedged	wɛʤd	
wedging	ˈwɛʤɪŋ	
Wednesday	ˈwɛnzdɪ	
Wednesdays	ˈwɛnzdɪz	
weed	wiˑd	
weeds	wiˑdz	
weeded	ˈwiˑdɪd	
weeding	ˈwiˑdɪŋ	
week	wiˑk	
weeks	wiˑks	
weekly	ˈwiˑklɪ	
weigh	weɪ	
weighs	weɪz	
weighed	weɪd	
weighing	ˈweɪɪŋ	
weight	weɪt	
weights	weɪts	

Traditional Spelling	Received Pronunciation	American Variants
weird	wɪəd	wɪəd
welcome	ˈwɛlkəm	
welcomes	ˈwɛlkəmz	
welcomed	ˈwɛlkəmd	
welcoming	ˈwɛlkəmɪŋ	
welfare	ˈwɛlfɛə(r	ˈwɛlfɛə
well	wɛl	
wells	wɛlz	
well-to-do	ˈwɛltəˈduˑ	
Welsh	wɛlʃ	
Welshman	ˈwɛlʃmən	
Welshmen	ˈwɛlʃmən	
WENT *from* go	wɛnt	
WERE *from* be	wɜˑ(r, wɛə(r *s.fs.*	wɜə *s.f.*
	wə(r *w.f.*	wə *w.f.*
WEREN'T = were not	wɜˑnt, wɛənt	wɜənt
west	wɛst	
westerly	ˈwɛstəlɪ	ˈwɛstəlɪ
western	ˈwɛstən	ˈwɛstən
westerner	ˈwɛstənə(r	ˈwɛstənə
westerners	ˈwɛstənəz	ˈwɛstənəz
westward	ˈwɛstwəd	ˈwɛstwəd
westwardly	ˈwɛstwədlɪ	ˈwɛstwədlɪ
westwards	ˈwɛstwədz	ˈwɛstwədz
wet	wɛt	
wetter	ˈwɛtə(r	ˈwɛtə
wettest	ˈwɛtɪst	
wetness	ˈwɛtnɪs	
whale	*h*weɪl	
whales	*h*weɪlz	
what	*h*wɒt	hwɑt
whatever	*h*wɒtˈɛvə(r	hwɑtˈɛvə
wheat	*h*wiˑt	
wheel	*h*wiˑl	
wheels	*h*wiˑlz	
wheeled	*h*wiˑld	
wheeling	ˈ*h*wiˑlɪŋ	
when	*h*wɛn	
whenever	*h*wɛˈnɛvə(r	hwɛˈnɛvə
where	*h*wɛə(r	hwɛə
whereabouts, *noun*	ˈ*h*wɛərəbaʊts	ˈhwɛˑrəbaʊts
whereabouts, *interr.*	ˈ*h*wɛərəˈbaʊts	ˈhwɛˑrəˈbaʊts
whereas	*h*wɛəˈræz	hwɛˑræz
whereupon	*h*wɛərəˈpɒn	hwɛˑrəˈpɑn
wherever	*h*wɛəˈrɛvə(r	hwɛˑrɛvə
whether	ˈ*h*wɛðə(r	ˈhwɛðə
which	*h*wɪtʃ	

Traditional Spelling	Received Pronunciation	American Variants
whichever	*h*wɪˈtʃɛvə(r	hwɪˈtʃɛvə
while	*h*waɪl	
whiles	*h*waɪlz	
whiled	*h*waɪld	
whiling	ˈ*h*waɪlɪŋ	
whip	*h*wɪp	
whips	*h*wɪps	
whipped	*h*wɪpt	
whipping	ˈ*h*wɪpɪŋ	
whisker	ˈ*h*wɪskə(r	ˈhwɪskə
whiskers	ˈ*h*wɪskəz	ˈhwɪskəz
whiskey	ˈ*h*wɪskɪ	
whisper	ˈ*h*wɪspə(r	ˈhwɪspə
whispers	ˈ*h*wɪspəz	ˈ*h*wɪspəz
whispered	ˈ*h*wɪspəd	ˈhwɪspəd
whispering	ˈ*h*wɪspərɪŋ	
whistle	ˈ*h*wɪsl̩	
whistles	ˈ*h*wɪsl̩z	
whistled	ˈ*h*wɪsl̩d	
whistling	ˈ*h*wɪslɪŋ	
whit	*h*wɪt	
white	*h*waɪt	
whiter	ˈ*h*waɪtə(r	ˈ*h*waɪtə
whitest	ˈ*h*waɪtɪst	
whiteness	ˈ*h*waɪtnɪs	
whiten	ˈ*h*waɪtn̩	
whitens	ˈ*h*waɪtn̩z	
whitened	ˈ*h*waɪtn̩d	
whitening	ˈ*h*waɪtnɪŋ, ˈ*h*waɪtn̩ɪŋ	
whitewash	ˈ*h*waɪtwɒʃ	ˈ*h*waɪtwɑʃ
Whitsun	ˈ*h*wɪtsn̩	
Whitsunday	ˈ*h*wɪtˈsʌndɪ	
	ˈ*h*wɪtsənˈdeɪ	
Whitsuntide	ˈ*h*wɪtsn̩taɪd	
who, ***interr.***	huː, hu	
who, ***relative***	huː, *h*u	
whoever	huˈɛvə(r	huˈɛvə
whole	hoʊl	
wholesale	ˈhoʊlˈseɪl	
wholesome	ˈhoʊlsəm	
wholly	ˈhoʊl*l*ɪ	
whom	huːm, hum	
whose	huːz	
why	*h*waɪ	
wick	wɪk	
wicks	wɪks	
wicked	ˈwɪkɪd	

Traditional Spelling	Received Pronunciation	American Variants
wickedly	ˈwɪkɪdlɪ	
wickedness	ˈwɪkɪdnɪs	
wide	waɪd	
wider	ˈwaɪdə(r	ˈwaɪdɚ
widest	ˈwaɪdɪst	
widely	ˈwaɪdlɪ	
widen	ˈwaɪdn̩	
widens	ˈwaɪdn̩z	
widened	ˈwaɪdn̩d	
widening	ˈwaɪdnɪŋ, ˈwaɪdn̩ɪŋ	
widow	ˈwɪdoʊ	
widows	ˈwɪdoʊz	
widowed	ˈwɪdoʊd	
wife	waɪf	
wives	waɪvz	
wild	waɪld	
wilds	waɪldz	
wilder	ˈwaɪldə(r	ˈwaɪldɚ
wildest	ˈwaɪldɪst	
wildly	ˈwaɪldlɪ	
wildness	ˈwaɪldnɪs	
wilful	ˈwɪlfʊl	
wilfully	ˈwɪlfʊlɪ, ˈwɪlfəlɪ	
will, ***noun***	wɪl	
wills	wɪlz	
will, ***verb***	wɪl	
wills	wɪlz	
willed	wɪld	
willing	ˈwɪlɪŋ	
will, ***auxil. verb***	wɪl *s.f.*, wəl, l̩, l *w.fs.*	
would	wʊd *s.f.*, wəd, əd, d *w.fs.*	
William	ˈwɪljəm	
willing	ˈwɪlɪŋ	
willingly	ˈwɪlɪŋlɪ	
willingness	ˈwɪlɪŋnɪs	
win	wɪn	
wins	wɪnz	
won	wʌn	
winning	ˈwɪnɪŋ	
wind, ***noun***	wɪnd	
winds	wɪndz	
wind, ***verb***	waɪnd	
winds	waɪndz	
wound	waʊnd	
winding	ˈwaɪndɪŋ	
windmill	ˈwɪn*d*mɪl	

Traditional Spelling	Received Pronunciation	American Variants
windmills	'wɪndmɪlz	
window	'wɪndoʊ	
windows	'wɪndoʊz	
windy	'wɪndɪ	
wine	waɪn	
wines	waɪnz	
wing	wɪŋ	
wings	wɪŋz	
wink	wɪŋk	
winks	wɪŋks	
winked	wɪŋkt	
winking	'wɪŋkɪŋ	
winner	'wɪnə(r	'wɪnə
winners	'wɪnəz	'wɪnəz
winter	'wɪntə(r	'wɪntə
winters	'wɪntəz	'wɪntəz
wipe	waɪp	
wipes	waɪps	
wiped	waɪpt	
wiping	'waɪpɪŋ	
wire	'waɪə(r	'waɪə
wires	'waɪəz	'waɪəz
wired	'waɪəd	'waɪəd
wiring	'waɪərɪŋ	'waɪrɪŋ
wisdom	'wɪzdəm	
wise	waɪz	
wiser	'waɪzə(r	'waɪzə
wisest	'waɪzɪst	
wisely	'waɪzlɪ	
wish	wɪʃ	
wishes	'wɪʃɪz	
wished	wɪʃt	
wishing	'wɪʃɪŋ	
wit	wɪt	
wits	wɪts	
with	wɪð, wɪθ	
withdraw	wɪð'drɔ·, wɪθ'drɔ·	
withdraws	wɪð'drɔ·z, wɪθ'drɔ·z	
withdrew	wɪð'dru·, wɪθ'dru·	
withdrawn	wɪð'drɔ·n wɪθ'drɔ·n	
withdrawing	wɪð'drɔ·ɪŋ wɪθ'drɔ·ɪŋ	
wither	'wɪðə(r	'wɪðə
withers	'wɪðəz	'wɪðəz
withered	'wɪðəd	'wɪðəd
withering	'wɪðərɪŋ	

Traditional Spelling	Received Pronunciation	American Variants
withhold	wɪð'hould wɪθ'hould	
withholds	wɪð'houldz wɪθ'houldz	
withheld	wɪð'hɛld wɪθ'hɛld	
withholding	wɪð'houldɪŋ wɪθ'houldɪŋ	
within	wɪ'ðɪn	
without	wɪ'ðaut	
witness	'wɪtnɪs	
witnesses	'wɪtnɪsɪz	
witnessed	'wɪtnɪst	
witnessing	'wɪtnɪsɪŋ	
witted	'wɪtɪd	
wittily	'wɪtɪlɪ	
witty	'wɪtɪ	
wittier	'wɪtɪə(r	'wɪtɪə
wittiest	'wɪtɪɪst	
WIVES *from* wife	waɪvz	
wolf	wulf	
wolves	wulvz	
woman	'wumən	
women	'wɪmɪn	
WON *from* win	wʌn	
wonder	'wʌndə(r	'wʌndə
wonders	'wʌndəz	'wʌndəz
wondered	'wʌndəd	'wʌndəd
wondering	'wʌndərɪŋ	
wonderful	'wʌndəful	'wʌndəful
wonderfully	'wʌndəfulɪ 'wʌndəfəlɪ	'wʌndəfulɪ 'wʌndəfəlɪ
WON'T = will not	wount	
wood	wud	
woods	wudz	
wooden	'wudn̩	
wool	wul	
woollen	'wulən	
woolen (*Amer.*)		
word	wɜ·d	wɜəd
words	wɜ·dz	wɜədz
worded	'wɜ·dɪd	'wɜədɪd
wording	'wɜ·dɪŋ	'wɜədɪŋ
wordings	'wɜ·dɪŋz	'wɜədɪŋz
WORE *from* wear	wɔ·(r, wɔə(r	wɔə
work	wɜ·k	wɜək
works	wɜ·ks	wɜəks

Traditional Spelling	Received Pronunciation	American Variants
worked	wɜˑkt	wɜəkt
working	ˈwɜˑkɪŋ	ˈwɜəkɪŋ
workings	ˈwɜˑkɪŋz	ˈwɜəkɪŋz
worker	ˈwɜˑkə(r	ˈwɜəkə
workers	ˈwɜˑkəz	ˈwɜəkəz
workman	ˈwɜˑkmən	ˈwɜəkmən
workmen	ˈwɜˑkmən	ˈwɜəkmən
world	wɜˑld	wɜəld
worlds	wɜˑldz	wɜəldz
worm	wɜˑm	wɜəm
worms	wɜˑmz	wɜəmz
WORN *from* wear	wɔˑn	woən
worn-out	ˈwɔˑˈnaʊt	ˈwoəˈnaʊt
worry	ˈwʌrɪ	ˈwɜrɪ
worries	ˈwʌrɪz	ˈwɜrɪz
worried	ˈwʌrɪd	ˈwɜrɪd
worrying	ˈwʌrɪɪŋ	ˈwɜrɪɪŋ
worse	wɜˑs	wɜəs
worship	ˈwɜˑʃɪp	ˈwɜəʃɪp
worships	ˈwɜˑʃɪps	ˈwɜəʃɪps
worshipped	ˈwɜˑʃɪpt	ˈwɜəʃɪpt
worshipping	ˈwɜˑʃɪpɪŋ	ˈwɜəʃɪpɪŋ
worshipper	ˈwɜˑʃɪpə(r	ˈwɜəʃɪpə
worshippers	ˈwɜˑʃɪpəz	ˈwɜəʃɪpəz
worst	ˈwɜˑst	ˈwɜəst
worth	wɜˑθ	wɜəθ
worthily	ˈwɜˑðɪlɪ	ˈwɜəðɪlɪ
worthless	ˈwɜˑθlɪs	ˈwɜəθlɪs
worthlessly	ˈwɜˑθlɪslɪ	ˈwɜəθlɪslɪ
worthlessness	ˈwɜˑθlɪsnɪs	ˈwɜəθlɪsnɪs
worthy	ˈwɜˑðɪ	ˈwɜəðɪ
WOULD *from* will	wʊd *s.f.* wəd, d *w.fs.*	
wound	wuˑnd	
wounds	wuˑndz	
wounded	ˈwuˑndɪd	
wounding	ˈwuˑndɪŋ	
WOUND *from* wind	waʊnd	
WOVE *from* weave	wouv	
WOVEN *from* weave	ˈwouvən	
wrap	ræp	
wraps	ræps	
wrapped	ræpt	
wrapping	ˈræpɪŋ	
wrapper	ˈræpə(r	ˈræpə
wrappers	ˈræpəz	ˈræpəz
wreath	riˑθ	

Traditional Spelling	Received Pronunciation	American Variants
wreaths	ri·ðz, ri·θs	
wreck	rɛk	
wrecks	rɛks	
wrecked	rɛkt	
wrecking	'rɛkɪŋ	
wrestle	'rɛsl̩	
wrestles	'rɛsl̩z	
wrestled	'rɛsl̩d	
wrestling	'rɛslɪŋ	
wrestler	'rɛslə(r	'rɛslə
wrestlers	'rɛsləz	'rɛsləz
wretch	rɛtʃ	
wretches	'rɛtʃɪz	
wretched	'rɛtʃɪd	
wretchedly	'rɛtʃɪdlɪ	
wriggle	'rɪgl̩	
wriggles	'rɪgl̩z	
wriggled	'rɪgl̩d	
wriggling	'rɪglɪŋ, 'rɪgl̩ɪŋ	
wrinkle	'rɪŋkl̩	
wrinkles	'rɪŋkl̩z	
wrinkled	'rɪŋkl̩d	
wrinkling	'rɪŋklɪŋ	
wrist	rɪst	
wrists	rɪsts	
write	raɪt	
writes	raɪts	
wrote	rout	
written	'rɪtn̩	
writing	'raɪtɪŋ	
writer	'raɪtə(r	raɪtə
writers	'raɪtəz	'raɪtəz
writhe	raɪð	
writhes	raɪðz	
writhed	raɪðd	
writhing	'raɪðɪŋ	
writing	'raɪtɪŋ	
writings	'raɪtɪŋz	
wrong	rɒŋ	
wrongs	rɒŋz	
wronged	rɒŋd	
wronging	'rɒŋɪŋ	
wrongful	'rɒŋful	
wrongfully	'rɒŋfulɪ, 'rɒŋfəlɪ	
wrongly	'rɒŋlɪ	
wrongness	'rɒŋnɪs	
WROTE *from* write	rout	

X

Traditional Spelling	Received Pronunciation	American Variants
X	ɛks	
X's	ˈɛksɪz	

Y

Traditional Spelling	Received Pronunciation	American Variants
Y	waɪ	
Y's	waɪz	
yacht	jɒt	jɑt
yachts	jɒts	jɑts
yachting	ˈjɒtɪŋ	ˈjɑtɪŋ
yard	jɑˑd	jɑəd
yards	jɑˑdz	jɑədz
yarn	jɑˑn	jɑən
yawn	jɔˑn	
yawns	jɔˑnz	
yawned	jɔˑnd	
yawning	ˈjɔˑnɪŋ	
year	jɜˑ(r, jɪə(r	jɪə
years	jɜˑz, jɪəz	jɪəz
yearly	ˈjɜˑlɪ, ˈjɪəlɪ	ˈjɪəlɪ
yell	jɛl	
yells	jɛlz	
yelled	jɛld	
yelling	ˈjɛlɪŋ	
yellow	ˈjɛloʊ	
yellowish	ˈjɛloʊɪʃ	
yellowness	ˈjɛloʊnɪs	
yes	jɛs	
yesterday	ˈjɛstədɪ, ˈjɛstədeɪ	ˈjɛstədɪ, ˈjɛstədeɪ
yet	jɛt	
yield	jiˑld	
yields	jiˑldz	
yielded	ˈjiˑldɪd	
yielding	ˈjiˑldɪŋ	
you	juˑ *s.f.*, ju *w.f.* jə (*occasional weak form*)	
young	jʌŋ	
younger	ˈjʌŋgə(r	ˈjʌŋgə
youngest	ˈjʌŋgɪst	
your	jɔˑ(r, jʊə(r jɔə(r *s.fs.*, jə(r *w.f.*	jʊə *s.f.* jə *w.f.*

Traditional Spelling	Received Pronunciation	American Variants
yours	jɔ·z, jɔəz, juəz	juəz
yourself	jɔ'sɛlf, juə'sɛlf	juə'sɛlf *s.f.*
	jɔə'sɛlf *s.fs.*	
	jə'sɛlf *w.f.*	jə'sɛlf *w.f.*
yourselves	jɔ'sɛlvz, juə'sɛlvz	juə'sɛlvz *s.f.*
	jɔə'sɛlvz *s.fs.*	
	jə'sɛlvz *w.f.*	jə'sɛlvz *w.f.*
youth	ju·θ	
youths	ju·ðz	

Z

Z	zɛd	
Z (*Amer.*)		zi·
Z's	zɛdz	
Z's (*Amer.*)		zi·z
zeal	zi·l	
zero	'zɪərou	'zɪ·rou
zeros	'zɪərouz	'zɪ'rouz
zest	zɛst	
zinc	zɪŋk	
zone	zoun	
zones	zounz	
zoological	zouə'lɒʤɪkəl	zouə'lɑʤɪkəl
	zuə'lɒʤɪkəl	zuə'lɑʤɪkəl
zoology	zou'ɒləʤɪ	zou'ɑləʤɪ